Constitutional Law

BY JESSE H. CHOPER

University of California, Berkeley

Twenty-Ninth Edition

EDITORIAL OFFICES: 111 W. Jackson Blvd., 7th Floor, Chicago, IL 60604
REGIONAL OFFICES: Chicago, Dallas, Los Angeles, New York, Washington, D.C.

PROJECT EDITOR
Steven J. Levin, B.A., J.D.
Attorney At Law

SERIES EDITOR
Elizabeth L. Snyder, B.A., J.D.
Attorney At Law

QUALITY CONTROL EDITOR
Sanetta M. Hister

Summary of Contents

Text Correlation Chart

Gilbert Law Summary CONSTITUTIONAL LAW	Brest, Levinson, Balkin, Amar Processes of Constitutional Decisionmaking 2000 (4th ed.)	Choper, Fallon, Kamisar, Shiffrin Constitutional Law 2001 (9th ed.)	Cohen, Varat Constitutional Law 2001 (11th ed.)	Rotunda Modern Constitutional Law 2000 (6th ed.)	Stone, Seidman, Sunstein, Tushnet Constitutional Law 2001 (4th ed.)	Sullivan, Gunther Constitutional Law 2001 (14th ed.)
I. POWERS OF THE FEDERAL GOVERNMENT						
A. Judicial Power	Page	Page	Page	Page	Page	Page
1. Source and Scope of Power	109-117	1-19	24-43	1-28	1-55	2-68
2. Jurisdiction of the Supreme Court			43-55	28-30	135-137	73-82
3. Limitations on Jurisdiction of Federal Courts				40-43		
a. "Case or controversy"		1533-1542	58-61, 88-92	37-45, 1416-1423	85-135	46-68
b. Standing	732-733	1507-1533	61-88	1423-1473	87-112	48-66
c. Additional conditions for review of state court decisions	77-79			14-28	45-51	68-73
d. Other policies of "strict necessity"	285-296	53-55				
e. Challenges to state action in federal courts						
f. Political questions	733-736	25-40	103-125	45-70	112-133	29-46
4. Effect of Declaration of Unconstitutionality						
B. Legislative Power	Page	Page	Page	Page	Page	Page
1. Power of Congress—In General	79-96	55-65	128-164		160-203, 364-402	85-106
2. Commerce Power	126-143, 355-378	65-108	162-191	165-200	143-151	119-205
3. Taxing and Spending Powers	369-374	108-121	191-194	200-217	207-220	205-224
4. War Power	704-724	187-193	407-411	285-286	206-207	224-226
5. Power Over External Affairs		121-124				
6. Power Over Naturalization and Citizenship	926-953		214-215	319-326	370-377	
7. Property Power	104-117	305-324	210-212	524-542		
8. Investigatory Power						
9. Congressional Immunity	50-51	128		326-337		
C. Executive Power	214-231, 621-730	146-156, 193-206	400-421, 440-451	337-368	352-364, 402-410	386-409, 351-386
D. Power Over Foreign Affairs		184-193	405-407	271-286	406, 410-419	226-233

Capsule Summary

I. POWERS OF THE FEDERAL GOVERNMENT

A. JUDICIAL POWER

1. Source and Scope of Power

a. Source §1

The Constitution provides for one Supreme Court and such inferior courts as Congress may establish.

b. Scope §2

Jurisdiction of federal courts is generally limited to *cases:*

(1) Involving the *Constitution, acts of Congress,* or *federal treaties;*

(2) In which the *United States is a party;*

(3) Between a *state and citizens of another state; or*

(4) Between *citizens of different states.*

c. Limitations on scope of federal judicial power

(1) Sovereign immunity doctrine §4

Under this doctrine, the United States may not be sued without its consent. Suits against federal officers acting in their official capacity may also be subject to sovereign immunity.

(2) Eleventh Amendment §6

The Eleventh Amendment bars a citizen of one state from suing another state (without its consent) in federal court. It has also been interpreted as prohibiting federal suits by citizens of the state being sued as well as prohibiting private parties from bringing federal administrative proceedings against states or state agencies. States may waive their immunity only through an *express and unequivocal waiver.*

(a) Limitations on Eleventh Amendment

The Eleventh Amendment does *not* bar suits by the federal government, Supreme Court review, suits against state subdivisions, or suits against state officials who allegedly have violated plaintiff's constitutional or federal rights.

(b) Suits against states in their own courts §20

The states' historical immunity from suits against them in

their own courts is a fundamental aspect of their present sovereignty except as altered by subsequent constitutional amendments.

2. **Jurisdiction of the Supreme Court**

    a. **Original jurisdiction** §21
The Supreme Court's original (trial) jurisdiction is derived from Article III, Section 2 and is limited mainly to **controversies between two or more states**.

    b. **Appellate jurisdiction** §25
Article III, Section 2 also gives the Supreme Court appellate jurisdiction over the cases listed *supra* in §2.

        (1) **Power of judicial review** §26
Judicial review has **evolved from Supreme Court decisions** and allows the Court to hold acts of other branches of government unconstitutional, to hold state statutes and executive action unconstitutional, and to review state court judgments.

        (2) **Methods for invoking appellate jurisdiction** §27
Supreme Court review may be had either by **appeal** (mandatory) or **certiorari** (discretionary). However, mandatory appeal jurisdiction is very limited and so the Court's appellate jurisdiction is almost entirely by **certiorari**.

        (3) **Limitations on statutory regulation** §31
Ex parte McCardle has been interpreted as allowing Congress full power, subject to the language of Article III, to limit the Supreme Court's appellate jurisdiction.

3. **Limitations on Jurisdiction of Federal Courts**

    a. **"Case or controversy"** §33
Article III, Section 2 limits federal court jurisdiction to "cases and controversies." There must be a **real dispute affecting rights of parties with adverse interests.** The action must also be **ripe** and pose a **real and immediate danger** to complainants' interests. Thus, the Court will **not** render any **advisory opinions** (or review state court advisory opinions), nor opinions in **moot cases** (issue resolved) or **collusive suits**.

    b. **Standing** §49
To have standing to raise a constitutional issue, a claimant must show the following:

        (1) **Direct and immediate injury** §50
The claimant must show a direct and immediate **personal** injury due to the challenged action. The injury may be aesthetic, conservational, or recreational, as well as economic.

        (2) **Causation** §52
The injury must be traced to the challenged action and one that will be redressed by the remedy sought.

(3) Congressional conferral of standing   §53

Standing may be conferred by federal statutes that create new interests if an injury to those interests can be shown.

(4) Citizens' standing   §54

Persons have *no standing* as citizens to claim that federal statutes are unconstitutional. Their injury is too indirect, and Congress cannot change this by statute.

(5) Taxpayers' standing   §58

Although generally *federal taxpayers* have no standing to attack federal expenditures, a taxpayer can challenge spending or appropriation measures if there is a specific injury to the taxpayer from the expenditure in question (*i.e.,* a taxpayer may challenge the validity of a tax assessed against her). Standing may also exist where the taxpayer alleges that a *specific constitutional limitation* on the taxing and spending power (so far only Establishment Clause) has been *exceeded*. State taxpayer standing in federal courts is governed by these same rules.

(6) Legislators' standing   §66

Legislators may have standing to challenge the constitutionality of government action if they have a sufficient "personal stake" in the dispute and suffer a "concrete injury."

(7) Assertion of third party rights   §67

Absent a federal statute conferring standing, an injured party can assert *only his own* constitutional rights.

(a) Exceptions   §68

In certain special circumstances, *a person with his own claim* may also assert the rights of a third party: (i) where it is *difficult for the third party to assert rights* or (ii) where a *special relationship* exists between the claimant and third party.

(b) Standing of an association   §71

An association *may* have standing to represent its members if: (i) the *members have standing;* (ii) the interest asserted is *germane to the association's purpose*; and (iii) *neither* the claim nor relief requested *requires that members participate* in the suit.

(8) Standing of a state   §72

A state may attack the validity of federal action affecting the state's own *property* interest. However, absent authorization by Congress, the state *cannot* attack federal statutes on the ground that Congress exceeded its delegated powers, nor can a state assert as *parens patriae* the claims of its citizens against the federal government, although it *can* assert such claims against another state.

c. Additional conditions for review of state court decisions   §76

Additional conditions for review of state court decisions include the requirements that claimant have **exhausted all available state remedies** and that the **state judgment be final.** The state decision also must have **turned on a substantial federal question.** Finally, the Court will not review the case if there is an **adequate and independent state ground** for the ruling.

d. **Other policies of "strict necessity"** §90

In adhering to its policy of **judicial self-restraint,** the Court decides only those constitutional issues **raised in a case.** Furthermore, the Court attempts to interpret federal statutes so as to **avoid** constitutional questions and may **decline** to decide a case if the record is sketchy concerning the constitutional issue.

e. **Challenges to state action in federal courts** §93

In appropriate circumstances, a person may bring an action in federal court against a state officer seeking damages, an injunction, or a declaratory judgment to vindicate her rights.

(1) **Restrictions on injunctions** §94

Usually, federal statutes **bar** the issuance of federal injunctions against enforcement of state tax laws, pending state criminal proceedings, against state criminal statutes or prosecutions (absent irreparable injury or exceptional circumstances), pending state civil proceedings, or requiring the ongoing supervision of state executive activities.

(2) **Exhaustion of state remedies** §112

Exhaustion of state remedies is **not** required when seeking a federal injunction against state administrative actions.

(3) **Abstention** §113

A federal court may **abstain** from granting an injunction or declaratory judgment and remand the parties to the state court for interpretation of the state statute. However, where a statute is ambiguous or an **overbroad or vague regulation of speech or association,** or where the court finds **further delay unjustifiable,** it may grant the relief.

f. **Political questions** §118

The Court will **not** decide a case that presents a political question rather than a justiciable controversy.

4. **Effect of Declaration of Unconstitutionality** §129

Theoretically, a decision declaring an act unconstitutional is binding only on the parties to the suit. Practically, the decision establishes a principle of law applicable to all persons.

a. **Retroactive effect** §130

A declaration of unconstitutionality has full retroactive effect in all cases still open on appeal and as to all events, regardless of when they occur.

b. **Partial invalidity** §132

Where part of a statute is invalid, the Court looks to legislative intent (*i.e., severability*) in deciding whether the entire statute should be ruled invalid.

B. LEGISLATIVE POWER

1. Power of Congress—In General   §136
Legislative power is basically the power of Congress to make laws, but also includes the power to do other things necessary and proper to enactment of legislation.

a. Scope of federal powers   §137
Powers that are not delegated to the federal government and that are not prohibited are *reserved to the states* by the Tenth Amendment. *Enumerated powers* are those expressly delegated by the Constitution. Additionally, **McCulloch v. Maryland** held that certain broad federal powers may be *implied* from the Necessary and Proper Clause.

(1) Appropriate means   §140
Congress may use *any* appropriate means to achieve the ends expressed in the enumerated powers. Moreover, the Necessary and Proper Clause applies to *all* powers delegated to *any* federal branch.

(2) Inherent powers   §143
The theory that the government has inherent powers, independent of the Constitution, has been given some effect, but *only over external or foreign affairs*.

b. Delegation of legislative power   §144
To delegate its power, Congress must *possess* the particular power, that power must be *delegable,* and *intelligible standards* must be established to govern the exercise of the delegated power.

(1) Judicial branch   §148
Note that nonadjudicatory functions (*e.g.,* rulemaking) may be delegated to the judicial branch as long as the task does not encroach upon another branch's power and is an appropriate judicial duty.

2. Commerce Power   §149
This extensive congressional power is discussed *infra*.

3. Taxing and Spending Powers

a. Constitutional provision   §150
Congress has the power to tax, pay debts, and provide for the common defense and general welfare (Article I, Section 8).

b. Independent powers   §151
The powers to tax and to spend for the general welfare are independent powers, *i.e.,* Congress has the power to tax and spend in a manner not specified under any of Congress's enumerated regulatory powers.

c. Taxation with purpose or effect of regulation   §152
Where Congress has the power to regulate, a tax is valid as a necessary

and proper exercise of its regulatory power. Where there is **no** regulatory power, the tax will be upheld if its **dominant intent** is to raise revenue (*i.e.,* fiscal rather than penal).

(1) Application   §156

The **objective approach** will uphold a tax with an apparent regulatory purpose if it does **in fact** raise revenue. Under a **subjective standard** the Court looks to the statute's language and operative effect to determine its dominant intent. Both approaches have been used to examine tax statutes.

d. Spending with purpose or effect of regulation   §158

Many federal spending programs are expressly conditioned on regulating the recipient's activities. If Congress may **directly regulate** the target activity, the spending program is valid as a necessary and proper exercise of the regulatory powers.

(1) No power to regulate   §160

Congress rarely lacks the power to regulate activities related to federal spending programs. Federal funds have been used to "entice" states to conform to federal standards under the theory that Congress can spend for the general welfare, *e.g.,* conditioning receipt of certain highway funds on a recipient state's adoption of a minimum drinking age.

(2) Limitations   §161

Congress's power to spend **must be exercised for the general welfare** and it may **not violate an independent constitutional right.**

4. War Power   §163

Congress has the power to declare war, raise and support armed forces, and promulgate rules for regulation of the military (Article I, Section 8). Congressional power during war is quite broad and may continue **after** war ends so as to remedy resultant problems (*e.g.,* rent controls).

5. Power Over External Affairs   §167

This is discussed *infra.*

6. Power Over Naturalization and Citizenship   §168

Congress has **plenary** power over aliens (Article I, Section 8, Clause 4) and can prescribe the conditions upon which they may come to or remain in the country.

a. Plenary power over aliens

(1) Exclusion of aliens seeking entry   §169

An alien seeking entry must follow whatever procedure is required by Congress, and Congress may exclude aliens altogether **without** a hearing.

(2) Deportation of resident aliens   §171

Once an alien is physically present—legally or illegally—in the United States, he is entitled to certain **due process** rights before deportation (*i.e.,* notice and a hearing).

b. Removal power   §194

Although the Constitution is silent on the President's power to remove most of his appointees (*exception:* he cannot remove federal judges), the Court has held that he can remove some **purely executive appointees** even though the appointment required congressional approval (*e.g.,* postmaster).

(1) Appointed pursuant to act of Congress   §198

Officers of administrative bodies created by Congress may be removed by the President only for causes specified in the statute.

c. Pardon power   §199

The President can grant reprieves and pardons for "offenses against the United States," except for impeachment (Article II, Section 2). *But note:* Civil contempt is **not** subject to presidential pardon, although criminal contempt is.

d. "Legislative" power of President   §202

In certain areas, the President has *limited* legislative powers. Congress may *delegate* legislative power subject to the separation of powers doctrine.

(1) Veto power   §205

The President's veto power applies to *all* legislative action unless expressly excepted by the Constitution. An act must be vetoed in its entirety (*i.e.,* there is no line item veto). If vetoed, Congress can repass legislation by a two-thirds vote of each House. Decisions of the executive branch and its agencies may *not* be vetoed by Congress.

(2) Military powers   §208

The President has *no power* to declare war, but as Commander-in-Chief, he has extensive legislative power in "theaters of war." As such, he can deploy military forces against insurrection or invasion (foreign or domestic) without congressional action.

(3) Inherent "emergency" power   §210

It is *probable* that the President has inherent power to act, without congressional authorization, in cases of great national emergency. In any case, assuming such power exists, it does not extend to the power to do a specific act already prohibited to the President by Congress (*e.g.,* President had no power to seize steel mills where statutes denied such power).

e. Impoundment   §212

The President has *no power* to refuse to spend appropriated funds *expressly mandated* by Congress to be spent. It has yet to be decided when the President otherwise has this power.

f. Executing laws   §213

Presidential action may also be upheld as an exercise of the President's power to execute the laws.

3. Executive Privilege §214

The executive privilege is intended to protect against disclosure of presidential communications made in the exercise of executive power. It derives from both the separation of powers doctrine and the need for confidentiality.

a. Scope §215

The claim of executive privilege for military, diplomatic, or national security secrets is given great *deference* by the courts. However, other presidential communications are only *presumptively* privileged.

b. Civil damages §219

Damages are *not allowed* for private suits based on any presidential acts within the outer perimeters of presidential constitutional authority. This blanket immunity, however, does *not* extend to presidential aides. Note also that the immunity does not extend to private, as opposed to official, acts.

D. POWER OVER FOREIGN AFFAIRS

1. Constitutional Provisions §223

Article I, Section 8 grants *Congress* the power to regulate commerce with foreign nations, to declare war, to raise and support armies, and to provide and maintain a navy. Article II, Sections 2 and 3 provide that the *President* is Commander-in-Chief of the armed forces, has certain treaty-making powers, shall receive foreign ambassadors, and shall nominate and appoint U.S. ambassadors and ministers, subject to Senate confirmation.

2. Comparison with Domestic Powers §224

Federal power as to domestic affairs is shared with the powers of the states. In *foreign affairs,* the federal power is *exclusive.* Congress may delegate greater powers concerning foreign affairs to the President than is permissible in domestic affairs.

3. Treaty Power §229

The President can make treaties with the advice and consent of *two-thirds of the Senate*.

a. Status of treaties §230

A treaty is "the *supreme law* of the land" and supersedes state law. The Supremacy Clause places self-executing treaties on *an equal footing* with acts of Congress. Where there is a conflict between a treaty and an act of Congress, the *last expression* of the sovereign will stand.

b. Types of treaties §233

A treaty may be *self-executing* (no further congressional action necessary) or it may expressly or impliedly require that Congress pass *effectuating legislation*.

c. Independent source of power §234

The treaty power is an independent source of federal power, thus permitting federal action over subjects outside the other constitutionally enumerated federal powers.

(2) **Limitations**   §297

In the past, nearly all activities that in the aggregate had an effect on other states could be regulated by Congress. However, beginning in 1995, the Court made clear that Congress's power under the "affectation doctrine" cannot be used to obliterate the distinction between what is national and what is local. The Court will be slow to approve congressional regulation of what the Court considers to be noneconomic (or noncommercial) activity or activity that has traditionally been regulated by the states (*e.g.*, family law). Commerce Clause regulations are also impermissible if they would violate other constitutionally guaranteed rights.

3. **State Regulation of Interstate Commerce**   §300

The federal power over interstate commerce is potentially all pervasive, but it is not exclusive. Whether a state may regulate interstate commerce turns significantly on whether there is relevant federal legislation or, if there is no relevant federal legislation, whether the state law unduly burdens or discriminates against interstate commerce; this latter principle is known as the "Dormant Commerce Clause" or "Negative Commerce Clause."

a. **Federal legislation on point**

(1) **Where Congress expressly authorizes or prohibits state regulation** §301

The Commerce Clause gives Congress **complete** power to permit or prohibit state regulation of commerce that is within Congress's regulatory power, but Congress **cannot** authorize states to violate the **Equal Protection Clause**.

(2) **Where no express congressional authorization or prohibition of state law** §306

If there is relevant federal legislation, but no express authorization or prohibition of state law, the Court determines whether Congress **intended** to authorize or prohibit it. If the state regulation is found to be **superseded** or **preempted** by federal law, it will be held invalid under the Supremacy Clause. In determining congressional intent, the Court will look to: (i) whether there is an interest in uniform, national regulation, (ii) historical or traditional classifications of the subject matter as federal or local, (iii) completeness of the federal regulatory scheme, and (iv) the coincidence between federal and state statutes.

b. **Power of states to regulate where Congress has not acted**   §314

If Congress has not enacted legislation regarding the subject matter, states may regulate local transactions even though they affect interstate commerce—subject to certain limitations.

(1) **Discrimination**   §315

State regulations that discriminate against interstate commerce are **almost always invalid** (*e.g.*, statutes excluding incoming or restricting outgoing trade in order to protect economic interests of local industry) as an invasion of the federal commerce power.

However, even discriminatory regulations may be upheld to protect health and safety interests if there are no reasonable alternatives (*e.g.,* a state may prohibit importation of live baitfish from other states where they pose a health threat to the state's fragile fisheries).

(a) Market participant exception §323

When a state acts as a market participant, it may limit its purchases (or sales) to local residents or businesses. However, when a state funds public construction projects, regulations or expenditures that discriminate against out-of-staters are subject to review under the ***Interstate Privileges and Immunities Clause*** (*supra*, §257).

(2) Nondiscriminatory regulation §328

State regulations that do not discriminate against interstate commerce are given greater deference by the Court.

(a) "Subject matter" test (older approach) §329

If the subject matter involved does not require a uniform, national rule, but is of local concern and permits diverse regulation, the state regulation has usually been upheld if it has some ***rational basis***.

(b) "Balancing" test (modern approach) §331

The current (modern) approach employs a balancing test: the ***burden on interstate commerce*** imposed by the regulation is weighed against the ***strength of the state interest*** in the regulation, with the Court deciding whether the regulation imposes an ***unreasonable burden*** on interstate commerce. The Court gives greater weight to statutes that further local health, safety, or social welfare interests than to statutes that seek to protect local economic interests.

1) Judicial role §333

The Court makes its own determination as to the ***purposes*** of the state regulation and is not bound by recitals of purpose by the enacting legislature. However, the Court generally will defer to state legislative determinations of ***disputed factual questions*** on whether the state's purpose is served by the regulation or on the cost of compliance.

2) Economic regulations §339

The fact that a nondiscriminatory state regulation is designed to protect local economic interests does not automatically invalidate it under the Commerce Clause.

3) Reciprocity agreements §341

Reciprocity agreements between states respecting sale of products do not automatically violate the Commerce Clause; but a ***mandatory*** reciprocity requirement forbidding sale of products from another state unless that state reciprocates is invalid absent a substantial state interest that cannot be obtained by alternative means.

(3) Permits or licenses for interstate business §342
The traditional rule is that a state cannot require a permit or license for the privilege of engaging in interstate transportation, or of engaging in business that is *exclusively* interstate commerce, but the state may require a permit to promote safety rather than to prevent competition.

(4) Broader state power over liquor regulation §344
The Twenty-First Amendment has been held to give the states broader regulatory power over regulation of liquor than over any other type of interstate commerce. A state is unconfined by traditional Commerce Clause limitations when deciding whether to *permit importation or sale* of liquor *destined for local use or consumption.*

(a) Limitation—noncentral state interests §346
Even state liquor regulations concerning local sale and use may be subject to Congress's commerce power when the federal policies are particularly strong and the state's central interests in regulating the time, place, and manner of liquor importation and sale are not directly implicated (*e.g.,* a state ban on advertising was held to be preempted by a federal regulation of cable television).

(b) Discrimination §347
The Twenty-First Amendment does not permit state regulations or taxes on the local sale or use of liquor to discriminate against commerce.

(c) Extraterritorial effect §348
The Twenty-First Amendment does not permit state regulation or taxes on the local sale or use of liquor if the practical effect is to regulate liquor sales or prices in other states, such as a statute requiring beer sellers to sell at prices no higher than the prices in bordering states.

C. POWER OF STATES TO TAX INTERSTATE COMMERCE

1. General Considerations §350
Congress has complete power to authorize or forbid state taxation of interstate commerce. Where Congress has not acted, state taxes that *discriminate* against interstate commerce violate the Commerce Clause (and possibly the Interstate Privileges and Immunities Clause or Equal Protection Clause). *Nondiscriminatory* taxes may be valid under the Commerce Clause and Due Process Clause.

2. Ad Valorem Property Taxes §360
Ad valorem property taxes are taxes based on the value of property.

a. Tax on property used to transport goods interstate §361
The validity of taxes on property used to transport goods interstate (*e.g.,*

a tax on a semi-tractor) depends on (i) whether the property has a *nexus* with the taxing state (*i.e.*, receives benefits or protection from that state), and (ii) whether its value has been *properly apportioned* according to its contacts with each taxing state. An unfair apportionment may violate both the Due Process and Commerce Clauses.

b. Tax on cargo in transit §370
States *cannot* levy an ad valorem tax on property being shipped interstate that happens to be in the taxing state on tax day. However, a break in transit intended to end or suspend a shipment renders the property subject to state taxation.

3. "Doing Business" Taxes §373
"Doing business" taxes are taxes imposed for engaging in business within the state. States may impose such taxes if they meet a four-part test:

a. The activity taxed must have a *substantial nexus* to the taxing state;

b. The tax must be *fairly apportioned;*

c. The tax must *not discriminate* against interstate commerce; and

d. The tax must *fairly relate to services provided* by the taxing state.

4. Severance Taxes §381
A nondiscriminatory state tax on extraction of minerals from the state is valid, based on the four-part test (above).

5. Taxes on Solicitors §382
Flat license fees may not be levied on solicitors ("drummers") of local orders to be filled from goods shipped interstate.

6. Highway Use Taxes §384
License and similar taxes on interstate carriers will be upheld if they are nondiscriminatory and are imposed to compensate states for costs of maintaining roads.

7. Airport Use Fees §387
Similarly, a state or municipal tax imposed on emplaning commercial airline passengers is valid if the tax is not excessive when compared to governmental benefits and it does not discriminate against interstate commerce.

8. Sales and Use Taxes §388
A sales tax is a tax on sales consummated *within the state;* a use tax is imposed on the user of goods purchased *outside the state*.

a. Use tax by "consumer" state §389
A use tax imposed by the consumer's state is valid as long as the rate is *not higher* than the sales tax rate.

b. Sales tax by "seller" state §394
Such tax is valid when imposed on sales consummated *within* the state.

c. Sales tax by "consumer" state §398
A sales tax imposed by the seller's state is valid if the interstate seller has *substantial contacts* in the consumer state. Solicitation of orders

subject to acceptance at the seller's out-of-state office ("drummers") is **not** sufficient contact.

d. Collection of use tax §401

A requirement by the "consumer" state that the interstate seller collect the tax **is** permissible if the seller has the "minimum contacts" necessary to satisfy the Due Process Clause **and** the substantial nexus required by the Commerce Clause. **"Drummers" are** sufficient bases, as is maintenance of an **office** in the state. However, solicitation of sales by mail is insufficient.

9. Taxes on Foreign Corporations §406

A state is not required to admit foreign corporations to do business locally. However, under the Equal Protection Clause, a state cannot impose more burdensome taxes on foreign corporations than on domestic ones unless such discrimination is **rationally related** to a **legitimate** state purpose. Promoting domestic business is **not** "legitimate."

D. POWER OF STATES TO TAX FOREIGN COMMERCE

1. Import-Export Clause

a. Imports §408

No state may impose a tax on imports or related activity as such without congressional consent (Article 1, Section 10, Clause 2). However, a nondiscriminatory property tax on all goods in the state is valid.

b. Exports §412

State taxation of exports is prohibited only **after** the goods enter the "export stream."

2. Commerce Clause §414

The Commerce Clause gives Congress plenary power to regulate foreign commerce, and thus inherently limits a state's power to tax such commerce.

IV. PROTECTION OF INDIVIDUAL RIGHTS

A. INTRODUCTION—BILL OF RIGHTS

1. Bill of Rights—Limitation on Federal Power §416

The Bill of Rights as originally applied limits the actions of the **federal** government.

2. Fourteenth Amendment—Limitation on State Power §417

The Fourteenth Amendment incorporates many of the rights protected by the first 10 Amendments as restrictions on **state** action.

a. Privileges and Immunities Clause §418

The Fourteenth Amendment Privileges and Immunities Clause does **not** make the Bill of Rights applicable to the states.

b. Fourteenth Amendment Due Process Clause §419

Most provisions of the Bill of Rights have been held to be so fundamental as to be applicable to the states by incorporation through the Fourteenth Amendment Due Process Clause ("selective incorporation").

subsequent evidentiary hearing are sufficient for termination of disability benefits because disability benefits are *not* based on financial need and thus are not deemed vital.

d. **Termination of public employment** §445

An employee subject to removal only "for cause" generally must be given a *pretermination notice and opportunity to respond* followed by a *subsequent* full *evidentiary* hearing. If, however, there is a *significant* reason for not keeping the employee on the job, he may be suspended without a presuspension hearing and without pay, as long as there is a prompt post-suspension hearing.

e. **Public education—disciplinary suspension** §447

Although *no* prior hearing is required for *temporary* suspensions (10 days or less), *some notice* of charges and *some opportunity to explain* is usually required.

f. **Public education—academic dismissal** §449

Due process is satisfied in the case of an academic dismissal if the student is *adequately informed* of the deficiency and given an *opportunity to respond*.

g. **License suspension** §450

If there is *probable cause* that a license-related violation has occurred, the state's interest may *sometimes* be important enough to suspend a license *without a prior hearing,* provided there is a *prompt* post-suspension hearing.

h. **Creditor remedies** §452

Prior notice and hearing are required for a prejudgment *garnishment* of wages. Exceptions are allowed for certain prejudgment seizure procedures and in *extraordinary circumstances* (e.g., when the debtor is preparing to flee with his assets).

i. **Attachment of real property** §453

Prejudgment attachment of real property is not permitted without prior notice and hearing unless the facts show that the plaintiff is likely to recover.

j. **Commitment to a mental institution** §454

The standard of proof used at an *adult's* precommitment adversarial hearing must be at least that of *"clear and convincing"* evidence. Parents or a governmental agency can institutionalize a child without a prior hearing if a *prior neutral inquiry* and *subsequent periodic reviews* are made.

k. **Antipsychotic drugs for prisoners** §456

A trial-type hearing and right to counsel are *not* required to administer drugs against a prisoner's will, as long as the decisionmakers are not biased.

l. **Termination of parental status** §457

Parental unfitness must be shown by at least *"clear and convincing"* evidence. Counsel must be appointed for indigent parents in termination hearings *only* where fundamental fairness demands it.

C. SUBSTANTIVE DUE PROCESS

1. Introduction

In addition to procedural limitations, due process may limit government action involving economic or social interests and fundamental personal rights. Such laws must not be vague.

2. Economic and Social Regulations
§461

Until the mid-1930s, the Court reviewed the *substance* of legislation and used the Due Process Clause to invalidate economic and social regulations if the Justices felt that the *means* used were not *reasonably related* to a *legitimate* end. Today, the Court defers to legislative judgments in this area unless the regulations are demonstrably *arbitrary or irrational.* The effect has been the upholding of nearly all social and economic regulations.

3. Government Officers Depriving Persons of Life, Liberty, or Property
§471

Substantive due process provides some protection—in the form of money damages—against government behavior. If another explicit constitutional provision is applicable (*e.g.,* the Eighth Amendment prohibition against cruel and unusual punishment), that provision controls. A government officer's conduct violates substantive due process only if it is so arbitrary, egregious, and outrageous as to "*shock the contemporary conscience.*" *Intent* to harm is usually required.

4. Restrictions on Power of Eminent Domain
§473

The Fifth and Fourteenth Amendments prohibit *taking* of private property (for public use) without just compensation.

a. Substantive requirements

(1) Property
§476

Property interests include tangible and intangible interests, such as trade secrets.

(2) Public use
§479

If the "taking" is not for public use (which is very broadly defined), the government may not appropriate the property—even if "just compensation" is paid.

(3) "Taking" vs. "regulation"
§481

A *taking* requires just compensation, while a *regulation* under the police power does not. In determining whether a taking occurs, the Court asks whether *justice and fairness require government compensation.* A taking will almost always be found if there is an *actual appropriation* or a *permanent physical invasion* of private property.

(4) "Just" compensation
§498

The term "just compensation" usually is defined to mean the *fair market value* of the property taken.

b.	**Procedural requirements**	**§500**

Requirements of reasonable notice and opportunity to be heard must be met. However, due process does **not** require that the condemnation occur in advance of occupying the property.

5. Fundamental Personal Rights   **§501**

Due process is used to protect certain fundamental rights not enumerated in the Constitution. Infringement of such rights usually is subject to **strict scrutiny** (the infringement must be necessary to achieve a **compelling** government interest).

a. Right of privacy   **§502**

Although not mentioned in the Constitution, the right of privacy is one of those **basic human rights** that are of fundamental importance. It cannot be impaired except where the law is narrowly drawn and serves a **compelling state interest**. The right to privacy includes familial rights such as marriage, procreation, contraception, abortion, and a right to educate children as one chooses.

(1) Abortion   **§506**

Prior to viability, the state may not place undue burdens on (or substantial obstacles before) a woman's right of privacy to have an abortion. **After viability**, the state's interest in the woman's health and the fetus's life allow the state to prohibit abortion unless necessary to preserve the woman's life or health.

(2) Intimate sexual conduct   **§525**

The state has **no legitimate interest** in making it a crime for **consenting adults** to engage in **private** intimate sexual conduct that is not commercial (overruling sodomy legislation).

b. Right to interstate travel   **§527**

The right to travel from state to state is **virtually unqualified.** However, the right to travel abroad **may** be regulated within the traditional limitations of due process.

c. Right to vote   **§532**

The right to vote on an equal basis is a fundamental right and is constitutionally protected.

d. Rights of mentally ill   **§533**

Involuntary commitment to a mental hospital is subject to due process protection. A person must be found to be (i) **mentally ill** and (ii) **dangerous** (to himself or others) or **incapable of surviving** safely outside an institution. The rights of involuntarily committed persons **also** include adequate food, shelter, clothing, and medical care.

e. Right to reject medical treatment   **§539**

A competent person has the right to refuse unwanted medical treatment, but there is no general right to commit suicide or to have assistance in doing so.

6. Vagueness Doctrine   **§542**

A law will be void for vagueness under the Due Process Clauses if persons must guess at its meaning or it fails to provide minimal guidelines so as to prevent arbitrary and discriminatory enforcement.

D. IMPAIRMENT OF CONTRACTUAL OBLIGATIONS

1. State Government
§543

State legislatures (but not courts) are prohibited from impairing public or private contracts by the Contract Clause (Article I, Section 10); not all impairments are considered unconstitutional.

a. Private contracts
§548

Private contracts can be *modified* if the legislation is a reasonable, narrowly tailored means of promoting an *important public interest*.

b. Public contracts
§553

Modifications of public contracts must satisfy the same requirements necessary for modification of private contracts, but the courts give *less deference* to the legislative judgment of public contracts.

2. Federal Government
§556

The Contract Clause does *not apply* to the federal government. Congress can adjust economic interests retroactively if there is a rational purpose.

E. PROHIBITION AGAINST EX POST FACTO LAWS
§557

The prohibition against ex post facto laws is based on Article I, Sections 9 and 10, and applies to both federal and state governments. A law is unconstitutional if it involves a *retroactive alteration* of the law in a *substantially prejudicial* manner. A statute retroactively alters the law in a substantially prejudicial manner if it: (i) makes criminal an act that was *innocent when done* and punishes the act; (ii) prescribes *greater punishment* for an act than the law provided when it was committed; or (iii) *alters the rules of evidence* to require less evidence to convict.

V. FREEDOM OF SPEECH, PRESS, AND ASSOCIATION

A. INTRODUCTION

1. Constitutional Provision
§561

The rights of free speech, press, and association are based on the First Amendment, which is applicable to the states through the Fourteenth Amendment. The First Amendment encompasses the right to hold beliefs, the rights to speak and to remain silent, the right to associate and refrain from associating, and the rights to communicate and to receive information. The First Amendment also affords some protection to symbolic conduct.

2. Rights Not Absolute
§576

There is *no* absolute right to speak or publish whatever one chooses. Restrictions regarding defamation, obscenity, or incitement to violence may be valid. Similarly, because of a compelling interest in preventing race and sex discrimination, a state may prohibit certain large organizations from denying membership to women and minorities.

3. Validity of Restrictions
§579

The Court must *balance* First Amendment rights against the interest served by the imposed restraint. There usually exists a presumption against the validity of restraints on First Amendment rights. **Content-based** speech regulations are unconstitutional absent a showing that the regulation is **necessary** to serve a **compelling** interest and is **narrowly drawn** to achieve that end. **Content-neutral** regulations, on the other hand, are ordinarily subject to intermediate scrutiny: They must advance **important** interests unrelated to suppression of speech and they must not burden **substantially more** speech than is necessary to further those interests.

4. **"Overbreadth" and "Vagueness"** §584

The Court may permit regulations to be challenged **on their face** if they are overbroad or vague because such regulations may **chill** the exercise of free speech. If a law is **vague on its face,** it is totally **invalid.** Thus persons are immune from regulation under the law, even if their conduct is not constitutionally protected.

a. **Overbreadth** §586

An overbroad law is one that regulates a **substantial amount** of constitutionally protected expression or association along with unprotected expression or association.

b. **Overbreadth due to vagueness** §590

When vagueness in a regulation may be **interpreted** as proscribing protected as well as unprotected conduct, it may be overbroad.

c. **Vagueness alone** §591

A law may be impermissibly vague even though not overbroad (*e.g.,* a law making unlawful "speech not protected by the Constitution").

B. ADVOCACY OF UNLAWFUL ACTION

1. **Speech that Is Abusive of Government or Officials** §595

Unpatriotic or disrespectful speech is generally protected.

2. **Criminal Penalties for Advocacy of Illegal Action**

a. **Background** §596

In the past, speech that advocated forceful overthrow of the government could be penalized.

(1) **Holmes-Brandeis test** §597

However, Holmes and Brandeis dissented in these early cases by contending that government may punish speech only if it **produces (or is intended to produce) a clear and imminent danger of a serious substantive evil**.

b. **Dennis-Yates test** §600

There must be a **substantial governmental interest** (determined by the courts) and a **call to illegal action** (rather than a mere belief in such action) before speech may be punished.

c. **Brandenburg test** §606

More recently, the Court has held that speech advocating illegal actions may be penalized only when directed to **inciting or producing** *imminent lawless action* and the speech is *likely to result* in such action. Note that *imminence* and *evil intent* appear to be independent requirements for this test.

C. DEFAMATION

1. Introduction §607
Defamatory speech or writing is *generally* not protected and may be punished by civil or criminal libel laws. Defamation of a *group* might give rise to criminal charges, although doctrinal developments may have created significant doubt on this.

2. Matters of Public Interest §609
A constitutional privilege exists for *certain* public interest matters. Statements concerning the official conduct of *public officials* or candidates are privileged unless made with *actual malice* (*i.e.,* statement was *known to be false* or was published with *reckless disregard* as to its truth or falsity—*New York Times* rule).

a. Public figures §621
The *New York Times* rule also applies to those who, for *"all purposes and in all contexts,"* have achieved general fame or notoriety, or to those who voluntarily involve themselves in a *particular* public controversy.

b. Private individuals §623
The *New York Times* rule does *not* apply to defamation of private individuals. States may define standards for private person suits involving matters of public concern as long as (i) they do not impose *liability without fault*, and (ii) the factual misstatement *warns a reasonably prudent* publisher of its defamatory potential. Actual damages are permitted, but presumed or punitive damages are permitted only if the statement was known to be false or made with reckless disregard of truth or falsity.

c. "Fact" vs. "opinion" §629
Only statements that may be reasonably interpreted as stating *facts* about an individual may be actionable under the *New York Times* rule.

d. Intentional infliction of emotional distress §630
The *New York Times* rule applies to damage actions by public figures for intentional infliction of emotional distress.

e. Invasion of privacy suits §631
After the *Gertz* case in 1974, there is serious doubt as to whether the *New York Times* rule applies to damage actions by private individuals for invasion of privacy—even where the matter reported was of *substantial public interest*.

D. OBSCENITY

1. Introduction §632
Obscene expression is *not* protected by the First Amendment.

2.   **Definition**   §633
Obscene material is a description or depiction of sexual conduct which, taken *as a whole,* by the *average person:*

(i)   *Appeals to the prurient interest* in sex, using a *community standard*;

(ii) Is *patently offensive* and an affront to contemporary *community standards*; and

(iii) *Lacks serious value*, using a *national, reasonable person standard.*

   a.   **Contemporary community standards**   §640
These may be determined on a *statewide* (or even more local) basis; a nationwide standard is *not* required. A *distributor* whose audience includes different communities must abide by *each* community's standards.

3.   **"Obscenity" as Question of Fact and Law**   §645
What is obscene is a question of *fact* for the *jury*. However, *appellate courts* will *independently review* constitutional claims to assure that the proscribed materials are obscene.

   a.   **Scienter requirement**   §647
Greater proof (*i.e.,* a showing of *knowledge* of the contents of the materials) is required for prosecution of *book dealers*.

4.   **Special Rules for Minors**   §649
A state may restrict *minors'* access to obscene materials more so than that of adults. And a state may prohibit distribution of child pornography even though not "obscene." However, visual material that appears to depict minors engaging in sexually explicit conduct but which in fact uses young-looking adults or computer-generated images may *not* be prohibited (unless obscene).

5.   **Private Possession of Obscenity at Home**   §653
Except for child pornography, a state may *not* prohibit obscene materials in a person's own home, but the sale or distribution of such materials may be punishable.

6.   **Regulation of Sites of "Near" Obscene Material**   §655
A state (or municipality) may adopt land-use or zoning regulations regarding the size or location of adult entertainment businesses (*e.g.,* "strip clubs") if: (i) the predominant purpose is to reduce secondary effects of such places; and (ii) the ordinance does not suppress or substantially reduce speech.

E.   **"FIGHTING WORDS" AND "HOSTILE AUDIENCES"**

1.   **Introduction**   §659
Certain expressions may be prohibited under "breach of the peace" or "disorderly conduct" statutes *if* the regulations are *narrowly drawn* or *construed.*

2.   **"Fighting Words"**   §660
Words that by their utterance inflict injury or tend to incite an *immediate* breach of the peace are *not* protected by the First Amendment. However, fighting words statutes generally cannot be designed to punish only certain viewpoints except in certain special situations (*e.g.,* cross-burning).

on constitutional grounds. Instead, the person must seek judicial relief from the injunction.

H. SYMBOLIC CONDUCT

1. Some Protection Available §726
Conduct used to communicate an idea (*e.g.,* draft card burning, nude dancing) may be regulated *if* there is an important state interest *independent* of the speech aspects of the conduct, *especially* if the state has no less restrictive means of regulation.

a. But note §731
A symbolic *conduct conviction* must be *reversed* if protected *speech* is made part of the offense or may have been relied upon to convict.

I. FIRST AMENDMENT RIGHTS IN PUBLIC PLACES

1. Public Forum §734
Some places are so historically associated with the exercise of First Amendment rights that they cannot be totally closed to protected expression (*e.g.,* streets, sidewalks, parks, public schools). Other public property, although not a traditional public forum, may become one for such time as the state opens it for public use as a place for expressive activity (*e.g.,* schoolrooms for after-school meetings).

2. Time, Place, and Manner Regulations §736
Time, place, and manner regulations are permissible on both types of public forums if (i) they are *content-neutral*; (ii) they are *narrowly tailored* to serve (iii) a significant *government interest;* and (iv) if banned, an *alternative forum* is available for the protected expression.

3. Total Ban §757
A total ban is permissible if it meets the above criteria. Thus, the justification of a state interest in *protecting privacy* allows bans on unwanted mail, billboards, etc.

4. Not a Public Forum §761
Certain public property that is traditionally or by government designation *not open to the general public* may be closed to the exercise of First Amendment rights if the prohibition is nondiscriminatory and *reasonable* (*e.g.,* jailhouse grounds, military bases). Generally, *private property* owners may prohibit protected activities, although where the property is held to be the constitutional equivalent of a public place, no prohibition of the reasonable exercise of rights is allowed (*e.g.,* "company town").

5. Licensing §766
Licensing is a valid means of regulating speech in public areas when the requirements contain *clearly defined standards* as to time, place, manner, and duration. Furthermore, denial of a license may *not* be based on speech *content.* A *reasonable nondiscriminatory fee* for the license may be charged. A statute giving officials *unlimited discretion* is *void on its face* and one need not even apply for a permit.

6. Injunction §774

Injunctions that impose "time, place, and manner" restrictions on exercise of First Amendment rights in *public* forums must burden no more speech than *necessary* to serve a *significant* government interest.

J. FIRST AMENDMENT FREEDOMS AND SPECIAL GOVERNMENT INTERESTS

1. Administration of Justice §775

Restrictions on First Amendment rights during the judicial process will be sustained to the extent necessary to assure the orderly administration of justice.

a. In court §776

Disruptive or disrespectful statements directed to the judge during court proceedings are punishable by contempt.

b. Out of court §777

Utterances out of court are not punishable unless they pose a *clear and present danger of serious interference* with the administration of justice. Note that freedom of the press in these circumstances is broadly allowed. The permissible amount of freedom of speech or press depends substantially on the *type* of judicial proceeding involved. *Lawyers*, however, may be sanctioned for speech having a *substantial* likelihood of *materially prejudicing* the proceedings.

2. Electoral Process §787

The degree of scrutiny the Court applies to election regulation depends on how great a restriction the regulation imposes on the right to vote (*e.g.*, ballot qualifications, restrictions on political parties may be subject to the *compelling state interest* test). *Campaign financing laws* are generally permitted, but are subject to limitations. Note that the amount that individuals or political action committees *spend* on campaigns may *not* be limited.

a. Corporations §804

Laws prohibiting corporate expenditures to influence *referenda* issues are invalid, but contributions to *candidates* may be subject to limitations (excepting *nonprofit advocacy* organizations, subject to certain requirements).

b. Disclosure requirements §807

Political parties (but *not minor* parties) may be required to disclose information concerning campaign *contributions* and *expenditures*, but laws requiring disclosure of authors of *campaign literature* are subject to "exacting scrutiny."

3. Judicial Elections §810

Rules prohibiting judicial candidates from expressing views on disputed legal and political issues *violate* the First Amendment and are subject to strict scrutiny.

4. Subsidies §811

The government need not subsidize speech; thus, it can deny tax benefits to lobbying groups. And the government may fund programs conveying certain messages but not others (*e.g.,* government may fund family counseling but refuse to fund abortion counseling). Guidelines for grants may be more ***vague*** than is permitted for criminal statutes or regulatory schemes.

K. FREEDOM OF ASSOCIATION—SPECIAL RULES

1. **Association with Groups Engaging in Unprotected Advocacy or Activities** §842
An individual may be punished for membership in certain types of groups, but **only if** (i) the group itself engages in activities not constitutionally protected (*see supra*, §§659-663), **and** (ii) the individual has **knowledge** of the group's illegal advocacy and the **specific intent** that the illegal aims be accomplished.

2. **Compulsory Disclosure of Membership or Association** §846
Compulsory disclosure is permissible only where it **directly** serves a **substantial** government interest that **outweighs** the individual's need for privacy or anonymity.

   a. **Privilege against self-incrimination** §847
   Even though the government interest in disclosure prevails under the First Amendment, if the membership admission is used to prosecute the registrant under criminal statutes, registration of membership may violate the individual's Fifth Amendment privilege against self-incrimination.

3. **Disclosures Required in Legislative Investigations** §848
The legislative power to compel disclosure of one's political beliefs or associations is limited by the privilege against self-incrimination, **due process** ("pertinency" requirement), and the First Amendment. The last requires an **overriding** legislative interest, a **nexus** between the disclosure and the investigation, and current **relevancy**.

4. **Civil Penalties for Unprotected Association (or Advocacy)** §854
The government may impose civil penalties, such as denial of government benefits (*e.g.,* tax exemptions), on those who engage in unprotected association (or speech).

   a. **Burden of proof** §855
   If the civil disability is imposed to **penalize** the actions rather than to serve an important, independent government interest, the government has the burden of showing the person engaged in unprotected association (or advocacy).

   b. **Liability of organization** §857
   Organizations may be liable for damages only if the acts of their representatives were performed within the scope of actual or apparent authority, or if specifically ratified.

5. **Restrictions on Public Employment, Licensed Professions, and Other Public Benefits**

   a. **Standards of conduct and loyalty oaths** §858
   The government **may** require employees to take an **oath to support the Constitution.** As a **general rule**, the government may not base restrictions on specific speech or association unless it is **not** constitutionally protected and **could be made criminal.** Compulsory disclosure of memberships, as an employment prerequisite, is **limited** to associations in which the government has a **legitimate interest,** and even then, an

individual may be excluded from employment only if the **knowledge and intent test** (*supra,* §842) has been met. Neither standards of conduct concerning past or future conduct nor loyalty oaths may be **vague;** precision is required because of the potential "chilling effect."

(1) Compulsory unionism §863

A government employee cannot be compelled to pay union dues that are used to **support political or ideological ideas** with which the employee disagrees, although a nonunion employee may be required to pay a union a service fee for expenses connected to labor-management issues.

(2) Patronage §866

A public employee may **not** be hired, promoted, transferred, fired, or recalled because of political party affiliation unless that affiliation is necessary for the effective performance of the work. Similar rules apply to independent contractors working on government projects.

(3) Expression of views §867

A government employer may restrict speech of public employees (and independent contractors) on a "matter of public concern" only when, **on balance**, the employee's rights as a citizen are outweighed by the government's significant interest as an employer in efficient performance of public service.

(4) Political activities §871

Some limits are permissible on a public employee's right to engage in political activities (*e.g.,* the Hatch act). Such conditions of employment are allowed because of the overriding government interest in efficient, nonpartisan employees and to protect employees from being forced to work for the election of their superiors.

(5) Ban on honoraria §872

The government may not forbid **all** government employees from receiving compensation for speeches, appearances, or articles— even when these expressive activities have no nexus to their employment and thus could not pose the danger of improper influence or improper use of knowledge acquired as an employee.

(6) Mandatory advertising §874

The government may require businesses to pay a fee for generic advertising that is part of a comprehensive regulatory scheme with respect to a business or industry. However, if the **main purpose** of the scheme is to fund advertising, it may be invalid.

(7) State university students §875

Indecent speech is permissible if not obscene or otherwise constitutionally unprotected. Student **fees** may be **mandatory** even if used to support speech by student groups whose beliefs are offensive to a student as long as the program is **viewpoint-neutral**.

b. Disclosure §879

Requirements of disclosure of **certain** past or present organizational affiliations that are relevant to loyalty, fitness, and suitability are permissible for public employees, lawyers, and recipients of other public benefits. The requirements must **not** be **overbroad** so as to have a "chilling effect."

(1) Privilege against self-incrimination §885

An individual may not be denied public employment, bar membership, or other public benefits simply because she refuses to answer on a claim of the privilege.

L. FREEDOM OF PRESS—SPECIAL PROBLEMS

1. In General §886

Generally, the press is afforded no greater First Amendment rights than a private citizen. There is **no** privilege to refuse to answer good faith grand jury questions and **no guaranteed access** to prisons, prisoners, or **government information**. However, the public **and** the press have a **right to attend criminal (and probably civil) trials** and elaborate preliminary hearings unless the judge finds that right outweighed by a compelling and narrowly tailored interest. **Publication of truthful information lawfully obtained** (and sometimes, if unlawfully obtained) concerning a matter of public significance may be prohibited only if narrowly tailored to further a state interest of the highest order.

2. Broadcasting §899

Radio and television broadcasting may be more closely regulated than the press because the number of broadcasting licenses is limited. Thus, the paramount right is the right of the **viewers and listeners** to receive information of public concern rather than a broadcaster's right to broadcast what she pleases.

a. Note §900

The FCC can order a **right to reply,** forbid **common ownership,** or censor **indecent speech**. However, broadcasters need **not** accept political advertisements. Also, Congress may **not** ban editorials by noncommercial broadcasters or by broadcasters who receive government subsidies.

3. Taxation §907

The press is subject to general taxes and regulations, but a tax that applies only to the press is invalid unless necessary to a compelling interest.

4. Cable Television §910

While, generally, regulations of newspapers are subject to strict scrutiny and regulations of the broadcast media are subject to less critical review, regulations of cable television transmissions are subject to review by a standard somewhere between these two.

a. "Must carry" provision §911

A law requiring cable operators to carry local stations is subject to **intermediate scrutiny**: the law must not burden more speech than necessary to advance important government interests. However, **content-based regulations** are subject to strict scrutiny.

VI. FREEDOM OF RELIGION

The First Amendment prohibits Congress from making a law respecting an *establishment* of religion or prohibiting the *free exercise* of religion. The First Amendment's protection of religion is applied to the states through the Fourteenth Amendment.

B. ESTABLISHMENT CLAUSE

The Establishment Clause insures government *neutrality* in religious matters. It bars government *sponsorship or endorsement* of religion, government *financial support* of religion, active government *involvement* in religious activities, and *official preference* of one religious denomination over another.

To be valid under the Establishment Clause, a statute (or other government action) that does not involve government preference for one religious denomination must:

(i) Have a *secular purpose;*

(ii) Have a *principal or primary effect* that *neither advances nor inhibits* religion; and

(iii) Not foster *excessive government entanglement* with religion.

Some government aid that provides assistance to *all* students (public and private, including parochial) satisfies the test (*e.g.,* transportation; textbooks and certain other instructional materials; health services; guidance counseling, job counseling, or other auxiliary services *within* or outside the parochial school).

The Court has upheld a *state income tax deduction* to *all* taxpayers for public and private, including parochial, school expenses because the purpose and primary effect is secular. Similarly, *vouchers* that provide tuition for all students, with a preference for low income families, to attend a public or private school (including parochial) of the parent's choice are valid because the program itself was neutral and assists a broad class of citizens.

Direct aid to church-related institutions has usually been held valid in cases involving hospitals, colleges, and counseling agencies where the aid was used only for *secular* purposes. However, direct aid to elementary and secondary schools has often been held invalid, usually on the basis of *excessive government entanglement* with religion.

C. FREE EXERCISE CLAUSE

1. In General   §980
If the purpose of a statute (or government action) is to treat adversely or discriminate against a specific religion, it violates the Free Exercise Clause unless it is *narrowly tailored to advance a compelling interest*.

2. "Beliefs" vs. "Action" or "Conduct"

a. Beliefs   §982
The freedom to hold religious beliefs, which need not be theistic, is *absolute*. Courts may not examine the "***truth***" of one's asserted beliefs even if they appear to be illogical, inconsistent, or incomprehensible.

b. Conduct   §987
Conduct is *not absolutely* protected. Under *prior law*, the Court balanced the severity of the burden against the importance of the state interest in regulation and considered the availability of alternative means. More recently, the Court has held that there is *no right* to a religious exemption from a *neutral* law that happens to impose a substantial burden on religious practice.

(1) Application   §990
Thus, the Court has *upheld laws* prohibiting polygamy, requiring the closing of businesses on Sundays, limiting conscientious objectors to the draft, requiring military service or training for certain benefits, and taxing activities even though such laws burdened the exercise of religious practices.

(2) Decisions upholding "free exercise" claims   §999
For a few special reasons, the Court has required religious exemptions from neutral laws, including exemptions from: compelled secondary school attendance (for the Amish); and accepting any suitable work under workers' compensation statutes (for Sabbatarians who refuse to accept jobs requiring work on the Sabbath).

c. "Accommodations" that benefit only some religions   §1006
Government action effecting de facto discrimination (*e.g.,* draft exemption only for those religious objectors to all wars) is *not* violative of either religion clause if there is a neutral, secular basis for the government delineations.

3. Standing   §1007
A person claiming a violation of the *Free Exercise Clause* must show *direct personal injury* and *interference* with her own religious beliefs.

4. Judicial Resolution of Disputes Involving Church Doctrine   §1008
Courts are prohibited (on entanglement grounds) from determining *ecclesiastical* questions. However, civil courts may use neutral principles of property law to resolve church property disputes.

VII. EQUAL PROTECTION

A. INTRODUCTION

1. Constitutional Provisions §1010

Equal protection is applied to the states by the Fourteenth Amendment Equal Protection Clause and to the federal government through the Due Process Clause of the Fifth Amendment.

2. Three Major Tests §1012

Discriminatory treatment is not necessarily prohibited, as long as the statutory classification meets the relevant test: (i) the **traditional** (or rational basis) test, (ii) the **strict scrutiny** (or compelling interest) test, or (iii) the **intermediate level of scrutiny** (or quasi-suspect class) test.

B. ECONOMIC AND SOCIAL REGULATIONS—TRADITIONAL RATIONAL BASIS TEST

1. Extreme Judicial Deference §1013

Because most economic and social regulations are not based on suspect or quasi-suspect criteria, nearly all such regulations are reviewed by the Court under the **traditional** equal protection test. The test is **usually** stated as follows: The classification is valid if it is **rationally related** to a **proper** (or **constitutionally permissible** or **legitimate**) **state interest**. The **challenger** must prove that it is invidious, wholly arbitrary, or capricious in order to prevail. The enacting body need **not** show a justification for the legislation, and government action or regulation that is over- and under-inclusive in achieving its goal may still be valid.

2. Less Deferential Formulation §1016

Sometimes the Court states the traditional test in a slightly less deferential way: The classification must have a **fair and substantial relation** to the object of the legislation. However, even using this formulation, the Court almost always **sustains** the classification.

C. SUSPECT CLASSIFICATIONS—"STRICT SCRUTINY"

1. Test §1017

Government action that **intentionally** discriminates against racial or ethnic minorities is suspect and subject to strict scrutiny. Equal protection is violated unless the suspect classification is **necessary to promote a compelling state interest**.

    a. "Necessary" to promote compelling state interest §1018

    This may be found when there is **no less burdensome, alternative means** to accomplish the state interest.

    b. Requirement of intentional discrimination §1021

    Intentional or "de jure" discrimination may be found in three ways:

        1) **On its face;**

        2) **By unequal administration** of the law (claimant bears the burden); or

        3) **By impermissible motive** in enacting the law.

requirements for welfare and medical benefits, and for certain voting registrations. However, residence requirements for reduced tuition and divorce have been upheld because they neither are *necessities of life* nor serve *momentous government purposes.*

4. Right of Privacy §1140

The right of privacy has been recognized as implicit in the "liberty" protected by the Due Process Clause, and *burdensome* classifications are subject to *strict scrutiny.* The rights to *marry, procreate,* and have an *abortion* are classified as fundamental rights.

5. Freedom of Speech §1145

Any governmental restrictions on the freedom of speech must be *finely tailored* to serve *substantial* state interests. *Strict scrutiny* applies.

6. Right to Vote §1146

Several amendments prohibit specific restrictions on the right to vote. Apart from these, there is no general right to vote in the Constitution. However, the Court has held that government discrimination regarding voting is subject to *strict scrutiny* under the Equal Protection Clause.

    a. Denial of the vote §1147

    Denial of the voting right to some residents who meet the age and citizenship requirements, while granting the right to other citizens, has usually been held to violate equal protection because the classification failed to meet the *strict scrutiny* standard (*e.g.,* poll taxes).

        (1) Exceptions §1154

        The Court has upheld laws denying certain persons the right to vote:

            (a) *Denying felons* the right to vote is sanctioned by constitutional language (Fourteenth Amendment, Section 2) and is *not* subject to strict scrutiny;

            (b) *"Special purpose" elections* that apply to a limited group are judged by the *traditional* test; and

            (c) *Laws denying voting rights to nonresidents* are subject only to the *traditional* test.

        (2) Limiting "effectiveness" of the vote §1159

        Laws that *substantially* impair the effectiveness of the right to vote are subject to *fairly* strict scrutiny (*e.g.,* counting and recounting votes, primary election registration, absentee ballot restrictions, ballot qualification restrictions).

    b. "Dilution" of the vote—apportionment §1164

    In the past, the Court considered apportionment a political question, but now it will hear such cases to assure equal protection to each voter.

        (1) Congressional districts §1165

        Under the Constitution, *"precise mathematical equality"* (one person-one vote) is the goal in determining congressional districts *within a state*. The preservation of *political boundaries* (*i.e.,* city or county lines) does *not* justify deviations from the *equal population* requirement. However, Congress's apportionment of districts *among the states* is not subject to the same mathematical standard.

(2) State legislative districts §1171

In *state* legislative districts, mathematical exactness is not required, and so a *10% deviation* between any two districts is permissible. However, larger deviations *cannot* be upheld unless explained by some acceptable state policy. Existing political boundaries *may* be given consideration.

(a) Multi-member districts §1177

Multi-member districts do *not* violate the "one person-one vote" rule, but are violative of equal protection if they effectively minimize the voting power of a particular racial or political group.

(b) Gerrymandering §1179

State districting plans that disadvantage an identifiable racial or political group on a statewide basis *may* violate equal protection.

(c) Relevant population §1180

Districting need not be based on *total* population (*e.g.,* aliens, transients, and convicts may be excluded).

(d) Relevant officials §1181

The "one person-one vote" rule applies to the *election* of *all* officials who perform normal governmental functions. The rule also applies to the *nomination* of officials, but not to appointed officials.

(3) Supermajority requirements §1186

Provisions requiring approval (by the legislature or referendum) by more than a majority are *valid* as long as they do not discriminate against any identifiable class.

(4) Remedies for malapportionment §1187

The federal courts usually defer to state remedies (by courts or the legislature). If the state fails to act, the federal court will draw up a plan. Federal courts have less flexibility than the states and thus their plans are subject to stricter review.

7. Right to Be a Candidate §1189

The right to be a candidate for elective office has *not* been recognized as a fundamental right, but laws that impose burdensome requirements on candidates are subject to *fairly strict* review.

G. "NONFUNDAMENTAL" RIGHTS

1. Introduction §1192

Rights that are not implicitly or explicitly guaranteed by the Constitution are reviewable under the traditional **"rational basis"** test. Rights to welfare, disability benefits, housing, or a particular quality of education, although ***important,*** have not been held to be fundamental rights.

H. "IRREBUTTABLE PRESUMPTIONS" AND THE RIGHT TO A HEARING

1. Introduction §1204
In several "important interests" cases, the Court invalidated **over-inclusive** state classifications because they created improper irrebuttable presumptions. In such cases **procedural due process** requires some opportunity for persons to show that they should be treated differently.

2. Parental Custody §1205
An unwed father must be given a hearing to determine his fitness as a parent.

3. Residency Status §1206
A state law may require higher fees for nonresident students but applicants are entitled to a hearing to present evidence of their bona fide residency.

4. Pregnancy and Employee Fitness §1207
Due process requires a case-by-case determination of when a pregnant teacher is physically incapable of continuing her duties.

5. Food Stamps §1208
Similarly, a household must have an opportunity to present evidence as to whether it is needy for food stamp purposes.

6. Disability Benefits for Nonmarital Children §1209
Social Security benefits may not be denied some nonmarital children born after the parent's disability without giving them the opportunity to establish their dependency.

7. Decline of Doctrine §1210
The last of these "important interests" cases (in 1975) recognized that limiting Social Security benefits to wives and stepchildren who were such for more than nine months prior to the wage earner's death may be over- or under-inclusive in some cases. However, it was **upheld** on the basis of government efficiency.

VIII. THE "STATE ACTION" REQUIREMENT

A. THIRTEENTH AMENDMENT

1. Constitutional Text §1211
Unlike the Fourteenth and Fifteenth Amendments, the Thirteenth Amendment is not limited to "state action"; rather it prohibits involuntary servitude anywhere in the United States, whether by a state, the federal government, or a private individual.

2. What Is Involuntary Servitude? §1212
Peonage (impressing one into personal service of a creditor) is prohibited, as is imprisonment for nonpayment of a debt. However, certain **exceptional circumstances** permit enforcement of the performance of a personal obligation (*e.g.,* military conscription).

B. FOURTEENTH AND FIFTEENTH AMENDMENTS

1. Introduction §1214
The Fourteenth and Fifteenth Amendments restrict only **governmental** action, not the acts of private individuals. But "state action" includes **more** than acts by the legislative, executive, judicial, and administrative branches of government.

2. Acts of Government "Agents" §1215
State action includes conduct of government officials acting in their official capacity (*i.e.,* under color of law) even if they act illegally.

3. "Public" or "Government" Functions §1217
Occasionally, activities undertaken by private individuals or organizations are ones that are "traditionally the **exclusive** prerogative of the State," and are then treated as state action. These actions include **elections** (and primaries and preprimaries) and the operation of **company towns**.

a. Limits of doctrine §1222
In most cases, the Court has **not** found privately conducted activity to be a government function. *Examples:*

(1) Shopping centers §1223
A shopping center is **not** the functional equivalent of a municipality (as is a company town), because it does not possess **all** the attributes of a town.

(2) Monopoly businesses §1224
A heavily regulated utility granted a monopoly by the state did **not** engage in state action when it terminated a user's service without notice or hearing, because utility service is not traditionally the exclusive province of the state.

(3) Regulated businesses §1225
The same is true of businesses such as nursing homes or specialized private schools.

(4) Creditor's remedies §1226
A warehouseman authorized by state statute to sell stored goods for unpaid charges is **not** engaged in state action.

4. Significant State "Involvement" §1227
More frequently, state action by private individuals (usually racial discrimination violating equal protection) is found because the government has **required** or **significantly encouraged** the acts of discrimination. But merely allowing the conduct to occur is not sufficient for "state action"; the state must **compel** or **significantly participate** in the private conduct. State action has been found in:

a. **Government compulsion** of private discrimination (ordinance requiring segregation in restaurants);

b. **Government administration** of private discrimination (state as trustee of segregated park);

c. ***Joint action*** by government officials and private persons concerning creditors' remedies (*e.g.,* attachment laws);

d. ***Judicial enforcement*** of private discrimination **through restrictive covenants;**

e. ***Peremptory challenges*** based on race in civil and criminal trials;

f. ***Government encouragement*** of private conduct, but mere licensing by the state is **not** equivalent to state action;

g. ***"Symbiotic" relationships*** between government and individual; and

h. ***Great entwinement*** of state and private entities.

IX. CONGRESSIONAL POWER TO ENFORCE CONSTITUTIONAL RIGHTS

A. BASES OF POWER

1. In General §1239

The ***Necessary and Proper Clause*** and the ***Enabling Clauses*** of the Thirteenth, Fourteenth, and Fifteenth Amendments empower Congress to fashion remedies for and prevent violations of constitutional rights. Sometimes, Congress even has the power to legislate against practices that the Court would not find unconstitutional.

2. Government Action §1240

Congress may impose ***criminal or civil*** remedies for a violation of constitutional rights by government action ("acting under color of law").

3. Private Action §1241

If the constitutional right operates against private individuals as well as government action, Congress may legislate remedies against ***anyone*** who interferes.

B. NECESSARY AND PROPER CLAUSE §1242

Several rights "arise from the relationship of the individual and the federal government" and are protected from interference by both private and government actions under the Necessary and Proper Clause (*e.g.,* the right to travel interstate, the right to vote in federal elections and primaries, and the right to petition Congress for redress of wrongs).

C. THIRTEENTH AMENDMENT §1249

Under the Thirteenth Amendment's Enabling Clause, Congress may prohibit ***virtually all*** racial discrimination against ***blacks,*** and ***some*** discrimination against whites.

D. FOURTEENTH AMENDMENT

1. Power Over Equal Protection and Due Process Violations §1251

Under the Enabling Clause, Congress has the power to ***remedy and prevent*** equal protection and due process violations, and the Court will uphold such legislation as long as it perceives a ***basis*** for the congressional determination.

2. Scope of Power §1252

To remedy Fourteenth Amendment violations, Congress may sometimes prohibit conduct that is not itself unconstitutional. Remedies may be legislated for *prior violations* or to *prevent future violations* (*e.g.,* congressional ban on English literacy tests for voting upheld even though the Court would not have held such tests unconstitutional).

a. **Limitations**   §1255

Although Congress's power under the Fourteenth Amendment Enabling Clause is extensive, it is not absolute. Congress has *no power* to *expand substantive constitutional rights*; it can only fashion a remedy for an already-existing right, and the remedy must be *congruent and proportionate* to the injury (narrowly tailored). Congressional legislation cannot *conflict with other constitutional provisions,* nor can it *restrict, abrogate, or dilute* Fourteenth Amendment rights.

3. **Government vs. Private Action**   §1263

Although state action is required for violation of the Fourteenth Amendment, certain *private actions* (*e.g.,* by state or local officials, private citizens collaborating with officials, and perhaps private individuals alone) *may* be remedied by Congress's broad powers under the Fourteenth Amendment Enabling Clause.

a. **Distinguish—federal officials**   §1265

Although no federal statute provides redress for violation of an individual's constitutional rights by *federal* officials, the Court has held that the *Constitution itself* empowers courts to recognize such a cause of action.

E. FIFTEENTH AMENDMENT   §1267

Where Congress has a *rational basis* for finding government racial discrimination in voting, it has broad remedial powers under the Enabling Clause.

F. OTHER SOURCES OF POWER   §1269

Provisions of the Civil Rights Act of 1964 prohibiting racial discrimination have been upheld under the *Commerce Clause.* Similarly, the federal government may indirectly, through its *taxing and spending powers,* compel recognition of the constitutional rights of others.

X. SAFEGUARDS IN THE ADMINISTRATION OF CRIMINAL JUSTICE

A. EVIDENTIARY MATTERS

1. **Use of Involuntary Confessions**   §1272

The Fifth (federal) and Fourteenth (state) Amendments prohibit the use of *involuntary* confessions. *Voluntary* confessions may also be inadmissible if an accused's *Miranda* rights were violated.

2. **Privilege Against Self-Incrimination**   §1277

This right is guaranteed by the Fifth and Fourteenth Amendments. An accused cannot be compelled to give *testimony* that might subject him to a criminal prosecution.

a. **No comment on failure to testify**   §1280

A defendant's failure to take the witness stand in his own defense is assumed to be a claim of the privilege and *no adverse inference* of guilt may be drawn from such an action.

3. **Exclusion of Evidence Obtained by Illegal Searches and Seizures** §1281
    The Fourth Amendment exclusionary rule (applicable to states through the Fourteenth Amendment) makes inadmissible illegally obtained evidence. A *good faith exception* exists for evidence obtained with an invalid search warrant if issued by a *neutral magistrate*, and the officer was *neither dishonest nor reckless* in preparing the affidavit and had an objectively reasonable belief in the warrant's validity.

    a. **Enforcement** §1287
        The Fourth Amendment, implemented by the Fifth Amendment Self-Incrimination Clause, forbids federal criminal convictions obtained with use of testimony or papers obtained by unreasonable searches or seizures. Illegally seized evidence is *inadmissible* in federal and state courts whether seized by state or federal officers.

B. **TRIAL ISSUES**

1. **Right to Trial by Jury**

    a. **Petit jury**

        (1) **Constitutional provision** §1288
            Under the Sixth Amendment (and by incorporation, the Due Process Clause of the Fourteenth Amendment), a defendant charged with any *serious* offense is entitled to a jury trial in both federal and state courts.

        (2) **What constitutes "trial by jury"** §1290
            Federal *statute* requires 12 jurors in federal criminal trials. The Constitution requires a *sufficient number* to provide adequate deliberation and a *representative cross section* of the community. Thus, some states have a minimum of six jurors. *Unanimous verdicts* are required in *federal court*, but generally not in state courts (unless it is a six-member jury).

        (3) **"Serious" vs. "petty" offenses** §1294
            Any offense that carries a potential sentence of *more than six months* is a serious offense, and a jury trial *must* be given on demand.

    b. **Selection of jurors** §1296
        The Sixth Amendment guarantees the right to *trial* before an *impartial* jury drawn from a *fair cross section of the community*. Thus, systematic exclusions of an identifiable segment of the community violates this right. *But note:* Proportionate representation on the petit jury is *not* required.

        (1) **Impartial jury** §1303
            Factors used to consider whether a jury was impartial include pretrial publicity, possible influence of prejudicial associations

with jury during trial, and in *death penalty cases*, the composition of the jury. A defendant has *standing* to challenge a verdict based on unfair jury selection on this ground alone.

2. **Right to Public Trial** §1310

The right to a public trial is guaranteed by the Sixth and Fourteenth Amendments and belongs only to the *accused*. Thus the press (or public) has no *Sixth Amendment* ground to complain of exclusion.

3. **Right to a Fair Trial** §1314

Certain types of conduct may be so unfair as to violate due process, and actual prejudice need *not* be shown. *Inflammatory publicity* may be unfair, although media coverage (including television) of the trial, when properly controlled, does not necessarily violate due process. A conviction must be reversed when it is found that a jury was not impartial.

4. **Right to Counsel** §1318

The right to counsel is guaranteed by the Sixth and Fourteenth Amendments in *criminal prosecutions that result in imprisonment*. Indigents have a right to appointed counsel in such cases.

5. **Burden of Proof** §1324

Due process requires proof *beyond a reasonable doubt* of every element of the crime with which the defendant is charged and applies in every proceeding involving a criminal charge or in which criminal sanctions may be imposed.

6. **Requirement of Certainty in Criminal Statutes** §1328

Vagueness in criminal statutes renders them invalid. This requirement provides fair notice and *prevents arbitrary and discriminatory enforcement*.

C. RIGHTS REGARDING PUNISHMENT

1. **Cruel and Unusual Punishment** §1331

Cruel and unusual punishment is prohibited by the Eighth and Fourteenth Amendments and imposes substantive limits on *what can be made "criminal"* (e.g., drug addiction), limits the *kinds of punishment* (i.e., barbaric), and proscribes punishments that are *excessive or grossly disproportionate* to the crime (e.g., for rape of an adult).

   a. **Capital punishment** §1343

The death penalty is *not* cruel and unusual punishment under all circumstances. If the sentencing body is allowed to consider *aggravating and mitigating factors* and if there is a *review procedure,* the death penalty is permissible. However, the death penalty cannot be imposed on one who is *insane* at the *time of punishment* nor on a *mentally retarded* person.

2. **Excessive Fines** §1354

The Eighth Amendment forbids the imposition of excessive fines, including *punitive forfeitures*.

D. POST-TRIAL ISSUES

1. **Rights on Appeal** §1359

A state is *not required* to provide appellate review, but if it does so, it cannot discriminate on the basis of poverty. An indigent has the ***right to counsel*** and the right to a ***free transcript*** to prepare his ***first appeal***.

2. Habeas Corpus Review §1363

By federal statute, a state prisoner may seek review of her conviction in federal court on the basis of violation of her federal constitutional rights, after ***exhaustion*** of all state remedies. The writ is subject to certain other limitations.

3. Retroactive Application of Determinations Regarding Constitutional Rights of Accused §1368

Whether a Supreme Court decision is to be applied retroactively depends on the ***purpose*** of the new standards, the ***extent of reliance*** on the old standards by the police, and the ***effect*** of retroactivity on administration of justice.

a. Rules applied retroactively §1373

The Court has given retroactive effect to a decision only when the decision affects the ***very integrity of the fact-finding process*** (e.g., right to counsel).

b. Cases on appeal §1375

Even if the new rule is not applied retroactively, it will still be applied to cases ***pending*** on direct appeal at the time of the decision (unless the rule is an unanticipated new principle of law).

Approach to Exams

Constitutional law problems almost always involve action by an arm of federal or state government (*e.g.*, a statute, an executive order, an administrative or judicial decision, a legislative or administrative investigation, conduct of government officers) that affects an individual or group of persons (including artificial persons such as corporations). But the range of constitutional issues that may arise concerning action by the federal government is greater than those that may arise from action by state (or local) governments.

As an initial matter, any exercise of power by any branch of the federal government must find its source in the Constitution. In addition, action by the federal government sometimes may abridge constitutional limitations that protect individual rights.

State governments, on the other hand, possess inherent, sovereign powers that have their source outside the Constitution. Furthermore, although state constitutions and statutes may designate the powers of the different branches and levels of state government, the Constitution does not ordinarily require any particular separation of powers within the states. [**Sweezy v. New Hampshire,** 354 U.S. 234 (1957)] Thus, the only federal constitutional issues that arise from the actions of state (or local) governments are whether those actions conflict with constitutional limitations on state power.

A.   ACTION BY THE FEDERAL GOVERNMENT

For exam questions concerning action by the federal government, first determine what type of action is involved (*e.g.*, statute, executive order, etc.), and then use the specific analytical approach below.

1.   Statutes

If a federal statute is under consideration, two general issues may arise:

(i)   *Whether Congress has the delegated power* to enact such a statute (*e.g.*, under the commerce, taxing, or spending power), because Congress generally may legislate only by virtue of its powers enumerated in the Constitution; and

(ii)   *Whether the statute*, either on its *face or as applied* in the particular case, *violates a limitation of the Constitution* that protects individual rights (*e.g.*, a provision in the Bill of Rights).

Furthermore, your question may require you to determine whether a federal statute *preempts* certain state action (by virtue of the Supremacy Clause). Finally, remember that the federal statute may be *interpreted so as to avoid a constitutional question*—thus requiring discussion of constitutional problems to demonstrate how they may be avoided.

2. Executive Orders

Executive orders usually present the same general problems as congressional statutes:

(i) *Whether the executive* (usually the President) has been *specifically delegated* by the Constitution the power exercised or whether the executive has *"inherent" constitutional power* to undertake the action; and

(ii) *Whether the order violated a constitutional limitation* that protects individual rights.

Similar issues of *preemption* or *interpretation* may also arise. Also, watch for the presence of a federal statute that is relevant to an executive order. This may present an issue of whether (or to what extent) Congress may *delegate or limit* executive authority in this area and, if so, whether it has done so.

3. Administrative Actions

Two general issues may arise concerning administrative actions:

(i) *Whether Congress has granted the general power* exercised by the administrative agency (not itself a constitutional matter, but possibly requiring a discussion of constitutional problems in the context of avoiding constitutional questions); and

(ii) *Whether the action—on its face*, or more frequently, *as applied* in the particular instance—*violates a constitutional limitation* that protects individual rights.

Besides these main issues, you may need to consider the *scope of congressional delegation* to the administrative agency (a constitutional issue), and *preemption* of state action by the administrative action or interpretation thereof, depending on your question.

4. Legislative and Administrative Investigations

The usual issues that arise concerning legislative or administrative investigations are:

(i) *What specific authority*, both substantive and procedural, has been *granted by Congress* to the investigative body (again, not itself a constitutional matter, but possibly requiring a discussion of constitutional problems in the context of interpreting the authorization to avoid a constitutional question); and

(ii) *Whether the specific action* taken against the person investigated *violates any constitutional limitation* that protects individual rights (*e.g.*, privilege against self-incrimination, freedom of expression or association).

Other possible issues may concern problems of *delegation*, and there may be a question of whether the investigation authorized is in pursuit of a *valid legislative purpose*—*i.e.*, whether Congress's authorization is within the scope of its constitutionally delegated powers.

5. Conduct of Government Officers

Exam questions concerning conduct of government officers involve action taken by law enforcement officers (*e.g.*, searches and seizures), prosecutors (*e.g.*, obtaining confessions), judges (*e.g.*, appointment of counsel), and executive officials (*e.g.*, condemnation of property). The usual issue is whether the action taken against a person *violates any constitutional limitation* that protects individual rights.

B. ACTION BY STATE (OR LOCAL) GOVERNMENT

For exam questions raising issues of state action, use the following approaches:

1. Statutes (or Ordinances)

As indicated above, the only federal constitutional issues that arise regarding a state statute or municipal ordinance are whether the statute or ordinance, on its face or as applied in the particular case:

(i) *Violates a constitutional limitation* that protects individual rights against state action (*e.g.*, bill of attainder, due process, equal protection, right of privacy);

(ii) *Is contrary to an implied constitutional limitation* on state power (*e.g.*, the grant of the "commerce power" to the federal government operates as an implied limitation on state regulation of interstate commerce); or

(iii) *Has been preempted* by federal treaty, statute, or an administrative rule.

Note: The interpretation of state statutes and municipal ordinances is a matter of state law for state courts and generally presents no federal constitutional issues.

2. State Executive, Judicial, or Administrative Orders or Rules

The issues here are generally the same as for state statutes (above).

3. Conduct of Government Officers

The issues here are generally the same as for conduct of federal officers (*supra*).

C. JURISDICTION OF THE FEDERAL COURTS AND REQUIREMENTS FOR SUPREME COURT REVIEW

For questions that ask for a federal court decision or for review by the Supreme Court, consider:

1. The Constitution and Acts of Congress

Remember that the Constitution and federal statutes (i) designate the *jurisdiction* of the federal courts (*e.g.,* federal courts may decide only "cases or controversies"); and (ii) specify *procedural requirements* that must be met to obtain Supreme Court review (*e.g.,* a decision from a state court is reviewable only by certiorari).

2. **Judicial Self-Restraint**

And even though a case may clearly fall within the constitutional and statutory jurisdiction of the federal courts, the Supreme Court has adopted certain "prudential" principles of "judicial self-restraint" to *limit the occasions on which it will decide constitutional questions* (*e.g.,* the Court will ordinarily not decide a constitutional issue before the time that it is necessary to do so, or when the record presents some other ground upon which the case may be decided).

Chapter One: Powers of the Federal Government

CONTENTS

Chapter Approach

This chapter examines the sources and scope of federal judicial, legislative, and executive power. Under our system of federalism, the general power to govern is reserved to the individual states, and the federal government is granted only certain enumerated powers. Thus, whenever an exam question deals with any act by the federal government, you must *first determine whether the federal government has been granted the power to so act*. To make this determination, look first to the Constitution. However, keep in mind that certain indisputably federal powers are not explicitly granted in the Constitution. Moreover, judicial interpretation has often expanded federal power well beyond what is obvious from the explicit language of the Constitution.

1. **Judicial Power**

    The federal courts generally have power to hear most cases where federal law is in issue, where the United States is a party, or where the suit is between a state and a citizen of another state or between citizens of different states. But there are a number of limitations that you must remember for exam purposes: (i) The doctrine of *sovereign immunity* prevents suits against the United States and its officers without its consent. (ii) The *Eleventh Amendment* provides some limitation on suits against states in federal courts, although states can be sued on causes of action passed by Congress pursuant to delegated powers, and state officials can be sued for violating complainants' constitutional rights. (iii) The federal courts can hear only *cases or controversies*, meaning that there must be a genuine, present dispute. (iv) The harm complained of must be *real* (although not necessarily economic) and the litigants must have a *personal stake* in the outcome. (v) The injury must be *remediable* by the judicial relief sought. (vi) The Supreme Court will not review a state court decision unless *all state procedures have been exhausted*, judgment is *final*, and a *federal issue is conclusive*. (vii) The Supreme Court will also refrain from deciding *political questions*.

2. **Legislative Power**

    The Constitution grants Congress the power to legislate in many specific areas. Recall that Congress also has power to enact any law that is *necessary and proper* to effectuate any specifically enumerated power of any branch of the federal government. ("Necessary" includes any *appropriate* means.) In addition to its enumerated powers, Congress has the *inherent power* to regulate external or foreign affairs.

    Regarding Congress's specifically enumerated powers, the most important for exam purposes is the commerce power, discussed in Chapter III. Some important things to know about other enumerated powers are: Congress's specifically enumerated power to tax allows it to regulate through taxation where it otherwise lacks power to regulate, provided that the tax has a revenue raising purpose. Similar results are possible under Congress's spending power. The war power gives Congress broad authority to declare war and to enact necessary legislation in times of war. Congress also has plenary power over naturalization and citizenship.

3. Executive Power

The executive power is vested in the President. Some key things to remember concerning executive power are: The President has *broad appointment powers* for federal judges, ambassadors, and federal officers, with the advice and consent of the Senate. However, Congress may vest the power to appoint inferior officers in the heads of departments or the courts instead of the President. The President's *veto power* allows him to veto acts of the legislature, which then must be repassed by a two-thirds vote of each House to be effective. Although the President *cannot declare war*, he does have power to commit armed forces in the event of insurrection or invasion without waiting for Congress to declare war. The President also has an extensive *privilege against disclosure* of presidential communications.

4. Power Over Foreign Affairs

Unlike the power over domestic affairs, the power over foreign affairs is *exclusively vested in the federal government*. Congress has the power to regulate foreign commerce. The President has the power to make treaties with foreign nations with the consent of two-thirds of the Senate, and such treaties are the supreme law of the land—of equal weight with acts of Congress. The President also has power to enter into agreements or compacts with other countries without the consent of the Senate, but the scope of this power is uncertain.

A. Judicial Power

1. Source and Scope of Power

a. Source of federal judicial power [§1]

Article III, Section 1 of the United States Constitution provides that the federal judicial power "shall be vested in one Supreme Court, and in such inferior Courts as the Congress may from time to time ordain and establish." Thus, the Constitution actually creates only one court—the Supreme Court—and leaves it up to Congress to establish other courts.

(1) Lower courts

Article III *does not require* Congress to establish any lower federal courts nor grant them full jurisdiction to decide all matters within the federal judicial power. [**Sheldon v. Sill,** 49 U.S. 441 (1850)] Of course, Congress has, in fact, created lower federal courts (*e.g.,* district courts and circuit courts of appeal).

(a) Limitation

In any case, congressional power over lower federal courts may be limited by other constitutional provisions (*e.g.*, a federal statute withholding jurisdiction of lower federal courts to decide cases in which one party is a Methodist would probably violate the First Amendment).

b. Scope of federal judicial power [§2]

Article III does not grant the federal courts power to hear every type of case; rather it specifies the types of cases over which the federal courts have jurisdiction. Specifically, Article III, Section 2 limits the jurisdiction of federal courts to *cases* (among others):

(1) *Arising under the Constitution, an act of Congress, or a federal treaty* (*i.e.*, cases whose disposition depends on construction of one of these);

(2) *In which the United States is a party*;

(3) *Between a state and citizens of another state*; and

(4) *Between citizens of different states ("diversity" cases).*

c. Limitations on scope of federal judicial power [§3]

Just because a case is one of the types of cases listed in Article III does not mean that the federal courts will have jurisdiction to hear the case. Certain other doctrines and constitutional provisions, such as the doctrine of sovereign immunity and the Eleventh Amendment, place limitations on the power of the federal courts.

(1) Sovereign immunity doctrine [§4]

Although the Constitution gives federal courts the power to hear suits in which the United States is a party, the United States may not be sued without its consent. Consent is generally afforded by a federal statute. [**United States v. McLemore**, 45 U.S. 286 (1846)]

(a) Suits against federal officers acting in their official capacity [§5]

Suits against federal officers acting in their official capacity are deemed actions against the United States itself and may be subject to sovereign immunity. If the relief sought would expend the public treasury, interfere with public administration, or restrain the government from acting or compel it to act, the suit is subject to sovereign immunity. [**Larson v. Domestic & Foreign Commerce Corp.**, 337 U.S. 682 (1949)]

1) Exceptions

Suits against federal officers are *not* subject to sovereign immunity if the officer's action was plainly beyond the officer's delegated statutory powers, *or* if the powers themselves (or the manner in which they are exercised) are constitutionally void. [**Malone v. Bowdoin**, 369 U.S. 643 (1962)]

(2) Eleventh Amendment [§6]

The Eleventh Amendment provides:

> The judicial power of the United States shall not be construed to extend to any suit in law or equity, commenced or prosecuted against one of the United States by citizens of another state, or by citizens or subjects of any foreign state.

While on its face the Eleventh Amendment appears to provide only that a citizen of one state may not sue another state in federal court without the state's consent, it has also been interpreted to prevent federal court suits by citizens of the state being sued. [**Hans v. Louisiana**, 134 U.S. 1 (1890)]

(a) Suits against state officials [§7]

The Eleventh Amendment has been held to bar not only private suits against the states, but also private suits against state officials that require a federal court to award money damages for *past conduct* that must be paid from the state treasury. [**Edelman v. Jordan**, 415 U.S. 651 (1974)—suit against state official for retroactive payment of wrongfully withheld welfare benefits]

(b) Suits against states before federal administrative agencies [§8]

The Eleventh Amendment also bars private parties from bringing federal administrative adjudicative proceedings against states or state agencies. *Rationale:* The preeminent purpose of state sovereign immunity—protecting state dignity—and the strong similarity between federal administrative actions and federal court actions lead to the conclusion that the framers of the Constitution would have found such administrative actions unacceptable. [**Federal Maritime Commission v. South Carolina State Ports Authority**, 535 U.S. 743 (2002)]

(c) Waiver of immunity [§9]

The states may waive their immunity under the Eleventh Amendment, but a waiver must be *express and unequivocal* (or by voluntarily invoking a federal court's jurisdiction, such as when a state moves for removal of a case from a state court to a federal court [*see, e.g.,* **Lapides v. Board of Regents**, 535 U.S. 613 (2002)]). A state will not be held to have impliedly or constructively waived its immunity.

---

e.g. **Example:** Plaintiff marketed and sold specialized annuity contracts to help people fund future college education expenses. The state of Florida created an agency to administer a tuition prepayment program for Florida residents that provided similar benefits. Plaintiff brought suit against the agency in federal court, alleging that the agency made false representations in its sales brochures and annual reports in violation of the Lanham Act, which created a federal private right of action against "any person" who makes false representations in interstate commerce. An amendment to the Lanham Act specifically provided that the term "any person" included states and their instrumentalities and officials. The state moved to dismiss the federal action, arguing that it was barred by the doctrine of sovereign immunity. Plaintiff argued that by voluntarily engaging in interstate marketing of its products, the state had impliedly waived its immunity from Lanham Act suits. The Supreme Court ruled that a state will not be held to have *impliedly or constructively* waived its immunity simply because Congress provides that a state will be subject to private suit if it engages in certain conduct and the state chooses to engage in that conduct. [**College Savings Bank v. Florida Prepaid Postsecondary Education Expense Board,** 527 U.S. 666 (1999)—*overruling* **Parden v. Terminal Railway,** 377 U.S. 184 (1964)]

(d) Limitations on scope of Eleventh Amendment [§10]

It is important to note that the following cases are *not* within the Eleventh Amendment's proscriptions:

1) Suits by federal government [§11]

The Eleventh Amendment does not bar federal court suits by the *federal government* against the states. [**United States v. Texas,** 143 U.S. 621 (1892)]

2) Supreme Court review [§12]

The Eleventh Amendment also does not block *appellate review* in the Supreme Court of a civil or criminal action from a state court that would (because a state is a party) have been barred if it had been brought originally in a federal court. [**McKesson Corp. v. Florida Division of Alcoholic Beverages & Tobacco,** 496 U.S. 18 (1990)]

3) State subdivisions [§13]

The Eleventh Amendment also does not prevent suits against state *subdivisions* (*e.g.*, counties, municipalities) or state governmental corporations. [**Lincoln County v. Luning,** 133 U.S. 529 (1890)]

4) Suits against state officials [§14]

As noted above (§7), the Eleventh Amendment bars a suit against a state official if the suit will result in the state paying damages for past conduct. The scope of this prohibition is actually very narrow, as illustrated by the discussion below.

a) Suit for violation of federal rights [§15]

If a suit alleges that a state official violated the plaintiff's rights under the Constitution or federal law and seeks an *injunction* against future violations or *damages from the official personally*, the suit is not barred by the Eleventh Amendment. *Rationale:* A suit against a state official for injunctive relief or damages to be paid by the official is not one against the state. The official is allegedly enforcing an unconstitutional enactment (which is void) and is therefore held to be "stripped of his official or representative character." [*Ex parte* **Young,** 209 U.S. 123 (1908); **Scheuer v. Rhodes,** 416 U.S. 232 (1974)]

1/ Distinguish—violations of state law

The Eleventh Amendment does, however, bar federal court suits against state officials for alleged violations of *state* law. Unlike claimed violations of a plaintiff's constitutional rights, the federal court suit in this instance is not needed to "vindicate the supreme authority of federal law." [**Pennhurst State School & Hospital v. Halderman,** 465 U.S. 89 (1984)]

b) Retroactive vs. prospective relief from state funds [§16]

The Eleventh Amendment does not forbid suits against state officials that have a financial impact on the state treasury by requiring *prospective* payment of state funds. Unlike retroactive payments from the state treasury, such prospective relief will not affect already defined allocations of state funds. [**Edelman v. Jordan,** *supra*, §7]

5) Congressional enforcement of Fourteenth Amendment [§17]

The broadest exception to state immunity from private suits in federal court concerns statutory causes of action passed by Congress pursuant to section 5 of the Fourteenth Amendment (giving Congress power to enforce provisions of the amendment). *Rationale:* The Fourteenth Amendment embodies significant limitations on state authority, thus allowing Congress (in enforcing its provisions) to provide for private suits against the states that are otherwise impermissible under the Eleventh Amendment. [**Fitzpatrick v. Bizter,** 427 U.S. 445 (1976)]

a) No exception for Article I powers [§18]

However, Congress has no authority under the powers delegated to it by Article I of the Constitution to abrogate state immunity under the Eleventh Amendment. [**Seminole Tribe of Florida v. Florida,** 517 U.S. 114 (1996)—*overruling* **Pennsylvania v. Union Gas Co.,** 491 U.S. 1 (1989)—Commerce Clause; **Florida Prepaid Postsecondary Education**

Expense Board v. College Savings Bank, 527 U.S. 627 (1999)—Congress has no power to abrogate state immunity under the Patent Clause]

6) Courts of other states [§19]
Neither the Eleventh Amendment nor any other provision of the Constitution affords a state immunity from being sued in the courts of another state. [**Nevada v. Hall,** 440 U.S. 410 (1979)]

(3) Suits against states in their own courts [§20]
The Constitution's structure and original understanding make clear that the states' historical immunity from suits against them in their own courts is a fundamental aspect of their present sovereignty except as altered by subsequent constitutional amendments (*supra*, §17). [**Alden v. Maine,** 527 U.S. 706 (1999)—state may refuse to entertain federal statutory private party cause of action against state arising under the overtime provisions of the federal Fair Labor Standards Act]

IMPACT OF ELEVENTH AMENDMENT — gilbert

WHAT IS BARRED?	WHAT IS NOT BARRED?
• Actions against state government for past *damages* • Actions against state government for *violating state laws*	• Actions in which state has **expressly and unequivocally waived its immunity** • **Appellate review** in the Supreme Court of a civil or criminal action from state court that would have been barred if originally brought in federal court • Actions against **local governments** (e.g., cities or counties) • Actions against state officers **to enjoin future action** • Actions against state officers for **monetary damages from the officer personally** • Actions against state officers for **prospective payments from the state** • Actions where Congress has **removed the immunity under** its power to enforce constitutional rights in the **Fourteenth Amendment**

2. Jurisdiction of the Supreme Court

a. Original (trial) jurisdiction [§21]

Under Article III, Section 2, the Supreme Court has original jurisdiction "in all Cases affecting Ambassadors, other public Ministers and Consuls and those in which a State shall be a Party."

(1) Provision is self-executing [§22]

Congress may neither restrict nor enlarge the Supreme Court's original jurisdiction. [**Marbury v. Madison,** 5 U.S. 137 (1803)]

(2) Concurrent jurisdiction [§23]

However, Congress may give concurrent jurisdiction to lower federal courts.

(3) "Controversies between two or more States" [§24]

At present, the Supreme Court's original jurisdiction is mainly occupied by "controversies between two or more States." [28 U.S.C. §1251]

b. Appellate jurisdiction [§25]

Article III, Section 2 further provides that "in all other Cases before mentioned [*see supra,* §2], the Supreme Court shall have appellate Jurisdiction, both as to Law and Fact, with such Exceptions, and under such Regulations as the Congress shall make."

(1) Power of judicial review [§26]

Although the Constitution does not expressly so provide, the Court early held that its appellate jurisdiction includes the power to hear appeals regarding the constitutionality of: (i) acts of other *branches of the federal government* (Congress and Executive) [**Marbury v. Madison,** *supra*]; (ii) *state statutes* [**Fletcher v. Peck,** 10 U.S. 87 (1810)]; and (iii) *judgments of state courts* in cases that fall within the federal "judicial power" (*see supra,* §12) [**Martin v. Hunter's Lessee,** 14 U.S. 304 (1816)].

Example: Before leaving office, President Adams signed a number of commissions appointing justices of the peace for the District of Columbia, but the commissions were not delivered before Adams left office. Upon taking office, President Jefferson's administration refused to honor the undelivered commissions (for political reasons—Jefferson was a republican and Adams and his appointees were federalists). Marbury and several other would-be justices brought suit directly in the Supreme Court seeking a writ of mandamus compelling Jefferson's secretary of state (James Madison) to deliver the commissions. At the time, the federal Judiciary Act provided that the Supreme Court had original jurisdiction to issue writs of mandamus against federal officials. This arguably exceeded the scope of the Constitution's grant of Supreme Court original jurisdiction. The Supreme Court held that: (i) it (rather than the legislature) had the power to interpret federal laws ("[i]t is emphatically the province and duty of the judicial department to say what the law is") and determine whether they conflict with the Constitution; (ii) the Judiciary Act did indeed conflict with the Constitution; and (iii) therefore the Court did not have jurisdiction to issue the requested writ. [**Marbury v. Madison,** *supra*]

Example: In 1798 Virginia confiscated land owned by Martin, a British subject, and granted it to Hunter, who brought an ejectment action against Martin. A Virginia district court ruled for Martin pursuant to anti-confiscation clauses included in treaties between Great Britain and the United States, but the Virginia Court of Appeals reversed. Martin appealed to the United States Supreme Court, which remanded the case to Virginia's Court of Appeals with instructions to enter judgment in favor of Martin. However, the Virginia Court of Appeals refused to obey the Supreme Court's mandate, claiming that the Judiciary Act was unconstitutional insofar as it allowed the Supreme Court to hear appeals regarding the constitutionality of state court decisions. The case came again to the Supreme Court, which unanimously held that the Constitution gives the Supreme Court power to review the constitutionality of decisions by a state's highest court. [**Martin v. Hunter's Lessee,** *supra*]

(2) **Statutory regulation of appellate jurisdiction [§27]**

Congress has provided two methods for invoking Supreme Court appellate jurisdiction: (i) *appeal* (where jurisdiction is mandatory) and (ii) *certiorari* (where it is within the Court's discretion). However, mandatory appeal is very limited; therefore, the Court's appellate jurisdiction is almost entirely by certiorari.

(a) **Review of state court judgments [§28]**

A party may file a *petition for certiorari* for review of final judgments or decrees rendered by the highest court of a state in which a decision could be had where:

1/ The *constitutionality of a United States statute or treaty* is in question; or

2/ A *state statute* is drawn into question on the ground that it is *repugnant to the Constitution, treaties, or other federal law.*

(b) **Review of federal court judgments [§29]**

A party may file a *petition for certiorari* from a federal court of appeals in *any* civil or criminal case, whether or not constitutional issues are involved. [28 U.S.C. §1254] Mandatory appellate jurisdiction (by *appeal*) is available only as to decisions of three-judge federal district court panels that grant or deny injunctive relief. [28 U.S.C. §1253]

(3) Denials of certiorari [§30]

Certiorari will be granted "only when there are special and important reasons"—*e.g.*, conflict of decisions in lower courts or an important federal question not yet decided by the Supreme Court. [U.S. Sup. Ct. R. 17] Denial of certiorari carries no implication of the Court's view on the merits of the case. It simply means that fewer than four members of the Court believed it desirable to review the decision in question. [**Maryland v. Baltimore Radio Show, Inc.,** 338 U.S. 912 (1950)]

(4) Limitations on statutory regulation [§31]

Under the "exceptions and regulations" language of Article III (*supra,* §25) Congress may limit the Supreme Court's appellate jurisdiction. [***Ex parte* McCardle,** 74 U.S. 506 (1868)]

---

e.g. **Example:** After the Civil War, Congress passed Reconstruction Acts that allowed former Confederate states to be ruled by a military government. McCardle, a racist editor of a Mississippi newspaper, was imprisoned by the military government for publishing articles that the military government held would tend to incite violence and impede Reconstruction. McCardle brought a habeas corpus action in federal court, claiming that his imprisonment was unconstitutional. The federal circuit court rejected his claim, and McCardle appealed to the Supreme Court. After the Supreme Court heard oral arguments in McCardle's case but before it handed down a decision, Congress repealed the portion of the Reconstruction Act that gave the Supreme Court jurisdiction to hear McCardle's appeal (out of fear that the Supreme Court's decision in *McCardle* would hold the entire Reconstruction Act unconstitutional). The Supreme Court upheld the repeal and found that it did not have jurisdiction to hear McCardle's appeal. [***Ex parte* McCardle,** *supra*]

(a) Possible limitations [§32]

Possible limitations on such congressional power have been suggested:

1) *Congress may eliminate certain avenues* for Supreme Court review, *but not all* avenues—since this would destroy the Court's essential role in the constitutional plan.

2) *Although Congress may eliminate Supreme Court review of certain cases* within the federal judicial power, it must permit jurisdiction to remain in *some lower federal court.*

3) *If Congress were to deny all Supreme Court review of an alleged violation* of constitutional rights—or go even further and deny

a hearing before any federal judge on such a claim—this would *violate due process* of law.

3. Limitations on Jurisdiction of Federal Courts

a. "Case or controversy" [§33]

Article III, Section 2 limits the jurisdiction of federal courts to "cases" and "controversies." The terms are interchangeable and refer to a matter "appropriate for judicial determination," as distinguished from disputes that are hypothetical, academic, or moot. The matter must be *"definite and concrete*, touching the legal relations of parties having *adverse legal interests*. It must be a *real and substantial controversy* admitting of specific relief through a decree of a conclusive character." [**Aetna Life Insurance Co. v. Haworth**, 300 U.S. 227 (1937)]

(1) Advisory opinions [§34]

The Court will not render an advisory opinion to Congress or the President on the constitutionality of some contemplated action or legislation because such an opinion does not involve a "case or controversy."

(a) Review of advisory opinions also foreclosed [§35]

Under the laws of some states, a state court may be allowed to give advisory opinions. The Supreme Court will refuse to review such opinions, even if they decide constitutional issues, because they do not constitute cases or controversies.

(b) Distinguish—declaratory judgments [§36]

Advisory opinions must be distinguished from declaratory judgments. A federal court may issue a final judgment declaring the rights and liabilities of parties even though no affirmative relief is sought.

1) Genuine controversy required [§37]

In an action seeking a declaratory judgment, even though no affirmative relief is sought, there still must be an actual controversy. A "case or controversy" will be present if there is an *actual dispute*—a definite threat of interference with defined rights—between parties having *adverse legal interests*. [**United Public Workers v. Mitchell**, 330 U.S. 75 (1947)—civil service plaintiffs who claimed they desired to engage in political campaigning in violation of statute but had not yet done so did not meet the case or controversy requirement]

2) "Ripeness" [§38]

Both under the "case or controversy" requirement and pursuant to "prudential principles of *judicial self-restraint*," the Court will ordinarily not decide constitutional questions before it is necessary to do so. [**Rescue Army v. Municipal Court**, 331 U.S. 549 (1947)]

3) Real threat of harm required [§39]

Complainants must demonstrate that they have engaged (or wish to engage) in specific (not hypothetical) conduct *and* that the challenged action poses a *real and immediate danger* to their interests. [**Boyle v. Landry,** 401 U.S. 77 (1971)]

a) No enforcement by state [§40]

The Court will not determine the constitutionality of a statute when it has never been enforced and there is no real fear that it ever will be—even though the state prosecutor says that it will be enforced. [**Poe v. Ullman,** 367 U.S. 497 (1961)—anticontraceptive law not enforced for 80 years despite "ubiquitous, open, public sales"]

b) No specific conduct by complainants [§41]

Neither will the Court afford equitable relief in respect to the constitutionality of bail and sentencing practices when complainants fail to show that they are in imminent danger of being prosecuted (or even that they expect to violate any laws) and thus will become subject to the allegedly invalid practices. [**O'Shea v. Littleton,** 414 U.S. 488 (1974)] This is true even if complainants have suffered injury from such practices in the past, and thus, have standing to sue for damages. [**City of Los Angeles v. Lyons,** 461 U.S. 95 (1983)]

c) No claim of harm [§42]

If there is no claim of present harm, there is no case or controversy.

---

e.g. **Example:** During the Vietnam War era, a time of great civil unrest in the United States, the military established a data-gathering system, which involved watching persons who, in the opinion of the military, had a potential for causing civil disorder. Justification for the system rested on the fact that the President could call on the military to quell insurrection and domestic violence. Plaintiffs claimed that the existence of this system chilled their First Amendment rights to speech and assembly (*i.e.*, plaintiffs would avoid speaking out at and attending public meetings for fear that the military would gather data on them and use it to plaintiffs' detriment in future). The Supreme Court found that there was no justiciable controversy because there was no claim of a specific present harm or threat of specific future harm, but only the fear that the military "might" take some additional action "detrimental" to complainants. [**Laird v. Tatum,** 408 U.S. 1 (1972)]

---

(2) **Moot cases [§43]**

The Court will not review moot cases. Since the matter has been resolved, there is no "case or controversy." [**Liner v. Jafco, Inc.,** 375 U.S. 301 (1964)]

(a) **Collateral legal consequences [§44]**

Even if a jail sentence has been fully served, a criminal conviction is not moot for purposes of Supreme Court review (or postconviction attack such as habeas corpus) unless there is no possibility that any collateral legal consequences (*e.g.*, loss of civil rights, impeachment as a witness) will be imposed because of the challenged conviction. [**Sibron v. New York,** 392 U.S. 40 (1968)]

(b) **Recurring issue [§45]**

An attack on a periodic event (*e.g.*, alleged denial of the right to vote) is not moot even if the event occurs before the case is decided (election already held). The claim is "capable of repetition, yet evading review" because it will apply equally to the next election, and the judicial machinery may again be too slow for determination before the election. [**Moore v. Ogilvie,** 394 U.S. 814 (1969)]

(c) **Voluntary cessation [§46]**

If defendant voluntarily stops allegedly unlawful practices when a suit is threatened or filed, the case need not be held moot because "otherwise, the defendant is free to return to his old ways." [**United States v. W. T. Grant Co.,** 345 U.S. 629 (1953)]

(d) **Class actions [§47]**

In a class action, the class representative may continue to pursue the class action even though the representative's controversy has become moot, as long as the claims of others in the class are still viable. [**United States Parole Commission v. Geraghty,** 445 U.S. 388 (1980)]

(3) **Collusive or friendly suits [§48]**

The Court will not hear a claim where there is no antagonistic assertion of conflicting claims. Generally, in collusive suits, one side finances and controls the whole litigation; there is no real "case or controversy," and the Court will not decide such a case—particularly on a constitutional issue. [**Chicago & Grand Trunk Railway v. Wellman,** 143 U.S. 339 (1892)]

(a) **Distinguish—"test" cases**

Collusive suits may be distinguished from "test" cases, which are true controversies but planned by the parties in order to expedite a decision on certain issues.

b. **Standing [§49]**

The doctrine of standing concerns both the "case or controversy" requirement of Article III and "prudential principles of judicial self-restraint." The second concern, which is a judicially self-imposed "policy limitation," is "not always clearly distinguished from the constitutional limitation." [**Flast v. Cohen,** 392 U.S. 83 (1968)]

EXAM TIP | **gilbert**

Remember that standing merely allows the plaintiff to get into court. Thus, a successful ruling on the standing issue does not mean that the plaintiff wins his suit; it merely means that he *gets an opportunity to try* his case on the merits.

---

(1) Direct and immediate injury [§50]

Article III requires that a person asserting the violation of a constitutional (or statutory) right show *a direct and immediate personal injury* due to the challenged action. Otherwise, he has no standing, and the Court will not decide the issue. [**Sierra Club v. Morton,** 405 U.S. 727 (1972)] *Rationale:* The person must allege "such a personal stake in the outcome of the controversy as to assure that concrete adverseness which sharpens the presentation of issues." [**Baker v. Carr,** 369 U.S. 186 (1962)]

Example: A statute making it a crime to be a member of the Communist Party may be attacked by a Communist Party member as denying freedom of association, because a member suffers direct and immediate personal injury due to the statute. In contrast, a non-Party member would have no standing to attack the statute on these grounds.

Example: Congress adopted a statute authorizing anyone to bring a civil damages action against a person who has defrauded the government and providing that the person bringing suit shall receive a share of any proceeds of the action paid to the government. The Supreme Court found that the statute is sufficient under Article III to confer standing. *Rationale:* The plaintiff suffers direct and immediate personal injury ("injury in fact") *not* simply because he stands to gain if the suit succeeds; if that were true, "someone who has placed a wager upon the outcome" would have standing. Rather, the plaintiff has standing as a *partial assignee* of the government's claim to redress for its injury. [**Vermont Agency of Natural Resources v. United States** *ex rel.* **Stevens,** 529 U.S. 765 (2000)]

Example: An undergraduate affirmative action program that granted benefits to underrepresented racial and ethnic minorities may be challenged by a nonminority applicant, even though that applicant may not have been ultimately admitted, because the injury suffered by the applicant under the Equal Protectin Clause is the denial of equal treatment in the application process. [**Gratz v. Bollinger,** 123 S. Ct. 2411 (2003)]

(a) Nature of injury [§51]

Neither criminal sanctions nor economic harm is necessary—the injury "may reflect aesthetic, conservational, and recreational as well as economic values." [**Association of Data Processing Service Organizations, Inc. v. Camp,** 397 U.S. 150 (1970)] And the fact that the injury is widely shared and relatively insubstantial to any particular litigant will not defeat a showing of "injury in fact." [**United States v. SCRAP,** 412 U.S. 669 (1973)]

Example: A law student group was allowed to challenge an Interstate Commerce Commission rate-setting policy on the ground that the policy discouraged recycling and thereby diminished the quality of each student's physical environment. [**United States v. SCRAP,** *supra*]

---

(2) Causation [§52]

Besides requiring an assertion of injury, Article III requires that a person asserting the violation of a constitutional (or statutory) right show that the injury suffered (i) "can fairly be *traced to the challenged action*" and (ii) will be *redressed by the judicial relief* sought.

Example: Parents of black public school students brought a class action against the Internal Revenue Service ("IRS") alleging that the IRS had not adopted sufficient standards and procedures to fulfill its obligation to deny tax-exempt status to racially discriminatory private schools. The parents argued that by granting tax exempt status to private schools that discriminate, the IRS effectively lowered tuition costs at these schools, which enabled more parents of white students to send their children to discriminatory private schools and in turn deprived the black students of the opportunity to attend integrated public schools. The Supreme Court held that the *link* between lax IRS policies and the continued segregation of public schools was too tenuous to provide standing. No proof was offered to show that if the IRS denied tax-exempt status to any particular school that the school would *change* its discriminatory policies or that parents would stop sending their children to the school. [**Allen v. Wright,** 468 U.S. 737 (1984)]

Example: Zoning policies of Penfield, New York, ensured that only expensive houses would be built in the city. Several groups sought to challenge the city's exclusionary zoning policies, including low-income individuals who said they would move to Penfield if lower-cost housing were available there. The Supreme Court held that such individuals lacked standing. One who seeks to challenge exclusionary zoning practices must show more than that the challenged zoning makes housing too expensive for him to buy. He must allege specific facts showing that, absent the zoning, there is a "substantial probability" that he would be able to buy—

i.e., that he would benefit in a tangible way from judicial intervention. [**Warth v. Seldin,** 422 U.S. 490 (1975)]

CHECKLIST OF STANDING ELEMENTS　　gilbert

THE FOLLOWING ELEMENTS MUST BE PRESENT TO ESTABLISH STANDING:

☑ *Injury*—plaintiff must show that she has been or will be directly and personally injured by the allegedly unlawful government action; the injury need not be economic

☑ *Causation*—there must be a causal connection between the injury and the conduct complained of

☑ *Redressability*—a decision in the plaintiff's favor must be capable of eliminating her grievance

---

(3) Congressional conferral of standing [§53]

A federal statute may create new interests, injury to which may be sufficient for standing. But Congress may not go beyond Article III's requirement of "injury in fact." [**Trafficante v. Metropolitan Life Insurance Co.,** 409 U.S. 205 (1972)—federal statute may give standing to tenants of an apartment complex who allege loss of important benefits from lack of interracial association by claiming rental discrimination by the owner in violation of the Civil Rights Act; *but see* **Sierra Club v. Morton,** *supra*—club had no standing to challenge construction of recreation area in a national forest as violating a federal statute since club failed to allege that it or its members used the site or would be significantly affected by the proposed construction]

(4) Citizens' standing [§54]

Persons have *no standing* as citizens to claim that federal statutes violate the Constitution. Any interest in constitutional governance is only a "generalized interest of all citizens," resulting in an "abstract injury," which is no substitute for the actual injury needed to focus litigation efforts and judicial decisionmaking. The fact that *no one* may have sufficient injury to establish standing is not a reason to find standing when no injury exists. [**Schlesinger v. Reservists Committee,** 418 U.S. 208 (1974)—citizens have no standing to contend that a senator's or representative's membership in the Armed Forces Reserve violates Art. I, §6, cl. 2 forbidding senators and representatives from "holding any office under the United States"]

(a) Application—federal statutes [§55]

The citizen standing limitation prevents Congress from creating an individual right in "any citizen" (even though such person has not suffered any distinctive concrete injury) to bring suit to enforce government observance of the Constitution or federal laws. [**Lujan v. Defenders of Wildlife,** 504 U.S. 555 (1992)—no "citizen" standing to challenge regulation under the Endangered Species Act, despite statutory language allowing "any person [to] commence a civil suit on his own behalf . . . to enjoin any person . . . who is alleged to be in violation of" the Act]

(b) Distinguish—voters' standing [§56]

A federal statute that provides voters with information about campaign activities of certain groups *does* afford voters standing to challenge a federal agency's refusal to require a particular group's disclosure. *Rationale:* Although the harm is "widely shared," the injury is *not* "abstract or indefinite"—such as "harm to the common concern for obedience to law." [**Federal Election Commission v. Akins**, 524 U.S. 11 (1998)]

(5) Taxpayers' standing

(a) Municipal taxpayers [§57]

Taxpayers have standing to challenge municipal actions involving *measurable expenditures.*

Example: Municipal taxpayers have standing to challenge school district expenditures for busing children to parochial schools. [**Everson v. Board of Education**, 330 U.S. 1 (1947)]

Compare: A taxpayer has *no* standing as such to challenge Bible reading in public schools since there is no measurable expenditure and hence no "good-faith pocketbook action." [**Doremus v. Board of Education**, 342 U.S. 429 (1952)]

(b) Federal taxpayers [§58]

Taxpayers generally have *no standing* to attack allegedly unconstitutional federal expenditures; the theory is that their interest in such expenditures is too remote, indeterminate, and minute, and that any injury is suffered in common with people generally. [**Frothingham v. Mellon**, 262 U.S. 447 (1923)] However, this is merely self-imposed judicial restraint, to which there are *exceptions.*

1) Personal liability exception [§59]

A taxpayer may attack the validity of a federal tax *assessed against her.* If the taxpayer prevails, she will have reduced her tax liability—and her interest is therefore substantial, definite, and personal. [**United States v. Butler**, 297 U.S. 1 (1936)]

2) Unconstitutional spending program exception [§60]

The Supreme Court has held that a taxpayer may challenge a federal expenditure if (i) she alleges that it "*exceeds a specific constitutional limitation* on the taxing and spending power," and (ii) it is part of a *federal spending program* (as opposed to an incidental expenditure under a regulatory statute).

a) Establishment Clause [§61]

The Establishment Clause of the First Amendment—designed to bar taxation and spending for support of religion—is such a "specific constitutional limitation." Thus, a federal taxpayer has standing to challenge federal *expenditures* to aid parochial schools on the ground that they violate the Establishment Clause. [**Flast v. Cohen**, *supra*, §49]

1/ Inapplicable to Property Clause [§62]

In **Valley Forge Christian College v. Americans United,** 454 U.S. 464 (1982), a federal taxpayer was *denied* standing to challenge a gift of federal surplus property to a church college as violating the Establishment Clause. *Rationale:* The challenge was not to a federal expenditure under Congress's taxing and spending power, but rather it was to an exercise of Congress's power under Article IV, Section 3, Clause 2, to "dispose of . . . property belonging to the United States."

b) Necessary allegations [§63]

The taxpayer must allege that the expenditure exceeds a specific constitutional provision. In *Frothingham, supra,* the taxpayer did not argue that the federal expenditure (for maternity care programs) exceeded "specific constitutional limitations," but only that it was "generally beyond the powers delegated to Congress" and was reserved to the states by the Tenth Amendment.

c) Violation of statute insufficient [§64]

In **United States v. Richardson,** 418 U.S. 166 (1974), a federal taxpayer was denied standing to contend that a federal statute permitting summary C.I.A. reports on expenditure of its funds violated Article I, Section 9, Clause 7 (which requires a "regular statement and account" of how all public money is expended). *Rationale:* The challenge was not addressed to "a specific constitutional limitation upon the taxing and spending power" but only to statutes regulating the C.I.A.

EXAM TIP	gilbert

Unless the validity of the federal tax assessed against the taxpayer is at stake, remember that a federal *taxpayer generally does not have standing* as such unless the claim involves a *specific constitutional limitation on the spending power*. Thus, for example, there is no standing to challenge federal grants of surplus property to religious groups because such action involves the property power rather than the spending power.

(c) State taxpayers [§65]

The standing rules for state taxpayers to attack allegedly unconstitutional state expenditures in a federal court are the *same* as for federal taxpayers challenging federal expenditures. [**Asarco, Inc. v. Kadish,** 490 U.S. 605 (1989)]

(6) Legislators' standing [§66]

Legislators may have standing to challenge the constitutionality of government action if they have a sufficient "personal stake" in the dispute and suffer sufficient "concrete injury." [**Raines v. Byrd,** 521 U.S. 811 (1997)]

e.g. Example: A state's lieutenant governor cast the deciding vote to break a tie in the state senate. *Held:* Legislators who had voted against the prevailing position had standing to challenge the right of the lieutenant governor to vote because that vote completely nullified the legislators' vote and caused a specific legislative enactment to go into effect. [**Coleman v. Miller,** 307 U.S. 433 (1939)]

cf. Compare: Members of Congress had *no* standing to challenge the Line Item Veto Act authorizing the President to cancel (veto) certain spending and tax measures that are part of a bill that he signs into law. *Rationale:* Rather than causing a "personal" and "concrete" injury, the challenged statute caused only a type of "institutional" injury to all members of Congress equally; *i.e.,* rather than losing something to which they are "personally" entitled, the legislators' claim was based on a loss of "political" power. [**Raines v. Byrd,** *supra*]

(7) Assertion of third party rights [§67]

Absent a federal statute conferring standing, the Court—pursuant to principles of judicial self-restraint—will permit only the injured person to claim a violation of his constitutional (or statutory) rights—generally, third parties cannot assert violations of another person's rights. [**Tileston v. Ullman,** 318 U.S. 44 (1943)—doctor bringing a declaratory judgment action had no standing to contend that anticontraceptive law violated his patients' constitutional rights]

(a) Exceptions [§68]

In certain special circumstances, a claimant may assert the rights of third parties *(provided he himself has also suffered injury)*.

1) Where difficult for third party to assert rights [§69]

A claimant may assert the rights of a third party where the third party would find it difficult or impossible to vindicate his own rights.

Example: A state statute required the NAACP to disclose its membership lists. The Court held that the NAACP—which was *injured* because disclosure would result in its losing members—could assert the freedom-of-association rights of its members. If members had to assert their own rights, the rights would be nullified in the process of assertion (since they depended on anonymity). [**NAACP v. Alabama,** 357 U.S. 449 (1958)]

Example: Defendant, a white homeowner, sold her home to a black buyer. Another white homeowner sued for damages for breach of a racially restrictive covenant. Defendant—who would be *injured* by an award for damages—had standing to assert equal protection rights of blacks. If defendant could not assert such rights, they would be lost—since whites would not sell to blacks and the latter would find it very difficult to bring their grievance before any court. [**Barrows v. Jackson,** 346 U.S. 249 (1953)]

2) Where special relationship exists between claimant and third party [§70]

Several cases have permitted assertion of the rights of third parties when the injury suffered by the claimant deters his relationship with the third party, thereby indirectly resulting in a violation of the third party's rights.

Example: The seller of beer had standing to assert constitutional rights of males under 21 years of age against a law prohibiting sale of beer to them. [**Craig v. Boren,** 429 U.S. 190 (1976)]

Example: The seller of contraceptives had standing to assert the constitutional rights of potential purchasers against a law regulating distribution to them. [**Carey v. Population Services International,** 431 U.S. 678 (1977)]

(b) Standing of an association [§71]

Even if an association has itself suffered no injury, it may have standing to assert the rights of its members in a representative capacity *if* (i) the *members themselves have standing*, (ii) the interest asserted is *germane to the association's purpose*, and (iii) *neither the claim asserted nor the relief requested requires that the members participate* in the suit. [**Hunt v. Washington State Apple Advertising Commission,** 432 U.S. 333 (1977)]

e.g. **Example:** A North Carolina statute prohibited closed containers of apples sold in the state from being labeled with any grade other than the applicable U.S. grade. Washington had a thriving apple industry. It established its own apple grading system and an agency—the Washington State Apple Advertising Commission—made up of certain local apple growers to promote the sale of Washington apples. Washington growers complained that the North Carolina statute was causing them injury because they were forced to the bear the expense of obliterating the Washington grade on packages of apples shipped to North Carolina and the statute diminished the effectiveness of their advertising. The Commission was allowed to represent the interests of the injured growers because: (i) the members of the Commission themselves had an injury because they were growers affected by the statute as well; (ii) the interest they asserted—promotion of Washington apples—was the main purpose of the Commission; and (iii) neither the claim asserted (that the North Carolina statute violated the Commerce Clause; *see infra*) nor the relief requested (enjoin application of the statute) required participation of individual growers in the suit. [**Hunt v. Washington State Apple Advertising Commission,** *supra*]

(8) Standing of a state

(a) Property interests [§72]

A state may attack the validity of federal action affecting the state's own property interests. [**Missouri v. Holland,** 252 U.S. 416 (1920)—a treaty prohibited killing birds that migrated between Canada and the United States; Missouri had standing to challenge the treaty because it has a property interest in wild birds found within the state]

(b) Tenth Amendment claims [§73]

Absent congressional authorization of such a suit, however, a state has no standing to attack a federal statute on the ground that Congress has exceeded its delegated powers. The state has suffered no injury as such, and the matter is merely a "political question." [**Massachusetts v. Mellon,** 262 U.S. 447 (1923)]

(c) *Parens patriae* [§74]

Similarly, a state has no standing, as *parens patriae*, to assert the claims of its citizens *against the federal government*—at least with respect to a federal spending program. Where citizens' rights respecting their relations with the federal government are concerned, "it is the United States, and not the state, which represents them as *parens patriae*." [*Compare* **Massachusetts v. Mellon,** *supra, with* **South Carolina v. Katzenbach,** 383 U.S. 301 (1966)]

1) **Distinguish**

A state has standing, as *parens patriae* of the general welfare of its citizens, to challenge the constitutionality of *another state's law* that causes substantial injury to the complaining state's population. [**Maryland v. Louisiana**, 451 U.S. 725 (1981)—Maryland successfully challenged a Louisiana use tax that discriminated against interstate commerce]

(9) Freedoms of expression and religion [§75]

Special applications of the "standing" doctrine related to freedom of expression and freedom of religion are discussed *infra*, §§584 *et seq.; and see infra*, §§979, 1007.

c. **Additional conditions for review of state court decisions [§76]**

Apart from the matters discussed above, several other requirements must be satisfied before the Supreme Court will review a state court decision.

(1) Exhaustion of state procedures [§77]

The Supreme Court will not review a state court judgment unless the claimant has exhausted all available state remedies (*e.g.*, has appealed to the highest court in the state in which a decision could be had).

(2) Final judgments [§78]

The Court will review only final judgments of state courts; *i.e.*, no further proceedings can be pending that could alter or modify the judgment. The Supreme Court decides for itself whether a judgment is final, but in at least the following four categories of cases, a judgment may be considered "final" even when further proceedings may be had in the state courts. [**Cox Broadcasting Corp. v. Cohn**, 420 U.S. 469 (1975)]

(a) Federal issue is conclusive [§79]

If the federal issue involved in the case has been conclusively decided by the state courts, it is final. For example, if a criminal defendant admits the facts charged but moves to dismiss the indictment on the ground that his action is constitutionally protected, and a denial of this motion is affirmed on appeal, the judgment may be treated as "final" even though a trial on the facts could still be had. [**Mills v. Alabama**, 384 U.S. 214 (1966)]

(b) Federal issue will survive [§80]

If a state appellate court decides a federal issue and remands for retrial on damages, the judgment may be treated as "final" because the issue will require federal review regardless of the outcome of the retrial. [**Radio Station WOW, Inc. v. Johnson**, 326 U.S. 120 (1945)]

(c) Later federal review impossible [§81]

If a state appellate court reverses a criminal conviction (on the ground that the defendant was denied a constitutional right) and orders a new trial, the judgment may be treated as "final" because the prosecution could not appeal the reversal if the defendant is acquitted on retrial. [**California v. Stewart,** 384 U.S. 436 (1966)]

(d) Delayed review would seriously erode federal policy [§82]

If a state appellate court holds that a state law does not violate a newspaper's First Amendment freedom of the press and remands for trial, the judgment may be treated as "final" because the newspaper might win at trial on nonfederal grounds and the unreviewed state court decision would leave the law on the books—thus possibly chilling First Amendment rights on other newspapers. [**Cox Broadcasting Corp. v. Cohn,** *supra*]

(3) "Federal question" [§83]

The Supreme Court will review state court judgments or the validity of state statutes only if they involve a *"substantial federal question"*—*i.e.*, a purported violation of the Constitution, a federal statute, or treaty. The Court will *not* review a state act challenged solely on the ground that it violates state law or the state constitution.

(a) Review of state statute [§84]

When reviewing a *state* statute or municipal ordinance, the Court is ordinarily bound by the final interpretation of the state courts.

(b) State procedure [§85]

The federal question must be *properly and timely raised* in the state proceedings, in a reasonably clear fashion and in accordance with *reasonable* state rules of procedure.

1) But note

The state procedure may not be used to *evade* decision of the federal question. It must afford the claimant a fair opportunity to present the question. Thus, the state court may not prescribe a novel procedure and then claim that failure to comply with the procedure precludes review. [**NAACP v. Alabama,** *supra*, §69—state court found that constitutional issue should have been raised through mandamus proceeding, which was inconsistent with its prior holdings]

(4) "Adequate and independent state ground" [§86]

It must appear that the state court decision *turned* on the federal question. If the state court judgment can be *supported entirely on a state ground* (*e.g.,* state court refuses to decide the federal issue because of the claimant's failure to comply with a reasonable state rule of procedure in asserting the federal claim), the Supreme Court will *not* review. To do so would be to

TO DETERMINE WHETHER THE SUPREME COURT WILL REVIEW A STATE LAW DECISION INVOLVING A FEDERAL ISSUE ASK:

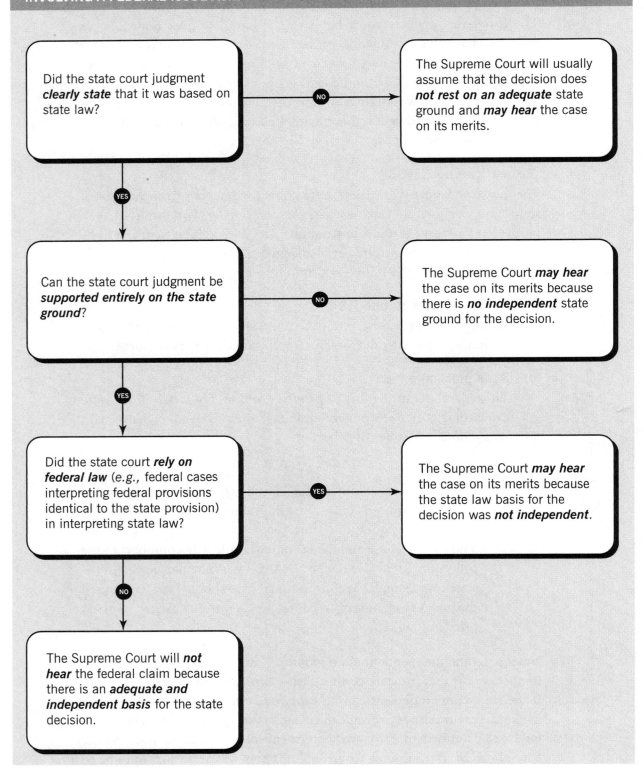

Did the state court judgment *clearly state* that it was based on state law?

NO → The Supreme Court will usually assume that the decision does *not rest on an adequate* state ground and *may hear* the case on its merits.

YES ↓

Can the state court judgment be *supported entirely on the state ground*?

NO → The Supreme Court *may hear* the case on its merits because there is *no independent* state ground for the decision.

YES ↓

Did the state court *rely on federal law* (e.g., federal cases interpreting federal provisions identical to the state provision) in interpreting state law?

YES → The Supreme Court *may hear* the case on its merits because the state law basis for the decision was *not independent*.

NO ↓

The Supreme Court will *not hear* the federal claim because there is an *adequate and independent basis* for the state decision.

render an "advisory opinion" on the federal question, since the state judgment would not be changed. [**Herb v. Pitcairn**, 324 U.S. 117 (1945)]

(a) Adequacy of state ground [§87]

The state ground must be "adequate"; *i.e.*, it must be capable of supporting entirely the court's decision in the case. Moreover, it may not be unreasonable or unfair, and it must serve a legitimate state interest. [**Henry v. Mississippi**, 379 U.S. 443 (1965)]

(b) Independent state ground [§88]

Even if the state court decides a federal question in the case, the Supreme Court will not review if the state court *also* grounded its decision on a matter of state law *and* the state law matter was decided independently of the federal law matter (*e.g.*, the state court did not rely on federal cases interpreting a federal law identical to the state law).

(c) Unclear whether state or federal ground [§89]

If it is unclear as to whether the state court decision turned on state or federal law, the Supreme Court may:

(i) *Dismiss* because its jurisdiction is ambiguous; or

(ii) *Remand* to the state court for clarification.

However, the Court disfavors these alternatives and has adopted a rule that requires a clear and express statement by the state court that its decision actually rests on state law. Thus, if the state court decision appears to rest primarily on federal law or is interwoven with federal law, absent a clear statement to the contrary, the Court will assume that there is *no* adequate state ground. [**Michigan v. Long**, 463 U.S. 1032 (1983)]

EXAM TIP | **gilbert**

Be sure to remember that the Supreme Court will not exercise jurisdiction if the state court judgment is based on adequate and independent state law grounds—even if federal issues are involved. State law grounds are adequate if they are *fully dispositive* of the case. They are independent if the decision is *not based on federal case interpretations of identical federal provisions*. If the state court has not clearly indicated that its decision rests on state law, the Supreme Court may hear the case.

---

d. Other policies of "strict necessity" [§90]

The Court has developed additional prudential principles of judicial self-restraint pursuant to its practice of "strict necessity in disposing of constitutional issues"—"the most important and the most delicate of the Court's functions." [**Rescue Army v. Municipal Court**, *supra*, §38] Ordinarily, the Court will decide only those constitutional issues that are actually raised in the case before it, and will not decide them in broader terms than are required by the precise facts to which the ruling is to be applied.

(1) Construction of federal statutes [§91]

Where serious doubts are raised as to the constitutionality of an act of Congress, the Court will first ascertain "whether a construction of the statute is fairly possible by which the questions may be avoided." [**Ashwander v. Tennessee Valley Authority,** 297 U.S. 288 (1936)]

(2) Sketchiness of record [§92]

Even when the Court clearly has jurisdiction over an appeal from a state or federal court, and even when there is no nonconstitutional ground for decision, the Court may decline to decide a case raising a constitutional issue if the facts in the record concerning the precise reach or meaning of the law being challenged, or its consequences for the litigants, are not sufficiently in a "clean cut and concrete form." [**Socialist Labor Party v. Gilligan,** 406 U.S. 583 (1972)]

e. Challenges to state action in federal courts [§93]

In appropriate circumstances, a person may bring an action in federal court—for damages, an injunction, or a declaratory judgment—against a state officer (but not against the state itself) to remedy or to prevent a violation of rights under the Constitution, federal law, or treaty. *Rationale:* Such an action is not one against the state itself (and thus barred by the Eleventh Amendment, *supra,* §7) because, by attempting to enforce a state law that violates a federal right, the state officer is "stripped of his official capacity"—and hence is personally accountable for his actions. [***Ex parte* Young,** *supra,* §16]

(1) Statutory restrictions on federal injunctions [§94]

Statutes restrict the use of federal injunctions regarding state action.

(a) Tax laws and rate orders [§95]

Federal statutes bar the issuance of a federal injunction against certain types of state action (*e.g.,* enforcement of state tax laws [28 U.S.C. §1341], rate orders of a state administrative agency [28 U.S.C. §1342]), as long as there are "plain, speedy and efficient" remedies available in the state courts.

(b) Pending proceedings [§96]

A federal statute [28 U.S.C. §2283] provides that federal courts may *not* enjoin state court proceedings *already instituted* "except as expressly authorized by Act of Congress." An express congressional exception [42 U.S.C. §1983] *authorizes* federal injunctions to correct the deprivation of constitutional rights. However, section 1983 injunctions against pending state court proceedings may be issued only if consistent with "announced principles of equity, comity, and federalism"—amplified and illustrated in the discussion that follows. [**Mitchum v. Foster,** 407 U.S. 225 (1972)]

(2) Enjoining state criminal statutes or prosecutions [§97]

Because of principles of "equity, comity, and federalism," a federal court will *not* enjoin state criminal statutes or prosecutions absent *"irreparable injury"* or *"exceptional circumstances"*—*i.e.*, a showing of significant harm that could not be avoided by state adjudication and appellate review of the proceedings. [**Douglas v. City of Jeannette**, 319 U.S. 157 (1943); **Wooley v. Maynard**, 430 U.S. 705 (1977)—injunction may issue against further prosecutions that would seriously burden one already convicted of violating state law, where such prosecutions violate his constitutional rights]

(a) Distinguish—declaratory judgment [§98]

However, no special circumstances or "irreparable injury" need be shown for a federal court to issue a declaratory judgment that a state criminal statute (under which a prosecution is genuinely threatened) is unconstitutional—either on its face or as applied. [**Steffel v. Thompson**, 415 U.S. 452 (1974)] *Rationale:* A declaratory judgment is "a less harsh and abrasive remedy than the injunction." Furthermore, denying all federal relief would place a citizen in the dilemma of either intentionally flouting state law (and risking imprisonment) or forgoing what she believes to be a constitutionally protected activity.

1) Preliminary injunction permitted [§99]

If a proper federal declaratory judgment proceeding has been initiated by the plaintiff, the federal judge may grant a preliminary injunction against threatened prosecution by state officials pending final resolution of the federal declaratory judgment action. [**Doran v. Salem Inn, Inc.**, 422 U.S. 922 (1975)]

(b) Free speech [§100]

A federal injunction may be issued if a state criminal statute or regulation is alleged to be invalid on its face as an "overbroad" or "vague" regulation of freedom of expression or association (discussed *infra*, §§584-594). [**Dombrowski v. Pfister**, 380 U.S. 479 (1965)]

1) Limitation for pending prosecution [§101]

But principles of "equity, comity, and federalism" forbid *injunctions*—or *declaratory judgments*—against pending state criminal proceedings even when the state statute affects freedom of expression or association, except perhaps where the statute is "flagrantly and patently" unconstitutional in every way. [**Younger v. Harris**, 401 U.S. 37 (1971)]

(3) Pending civil proceedings [§102]

The prohibition against federal injunctions or declaratory judgments against pending state criminal proceedings also extends to pending state-initiated civil proceedings that are "akin to a criminal prosecution"—*e.g.*, a civil suit by a state prosecutor to close a theater exhibiting obscene films [**Huffman v. Pursue, Ltd.**, 420 U.S. 592 (1975)], or a civil action to remove a child from his parents for child abuse [**Moore v. Sims**, 442 U.S. 415 (1979)].

(a) **Applications [§103]**
The prohibition against federal injunctions also applies in the following situations.

1) **Contempt proceedings [§104]**
The prohibition applies to pending state contempt proceedings—even where the contempt is civil in nature (*e.g.*, to enforce a court subpoena). [**Juidice v. Vail**, 430 U.S. 327 (1977)—contempt power is at the core of state judicial system]

2) **Execution of judgments [§105]**
It also applies to state laws that seek to ensure compliance with court judgments. [**Pennzoil Co. v. Texaco, Inc.**, 481 U.S. 1 (1987)—law permitting judgment creditor to execute lien on debtor's property unless debtor posts bond in amount of judgment]

3) **Proceedings to recover state funds [§106]**
It applies to a pending civil action by the state to recover state funds fraudulently obtained, since this vindicates the important state policy of safeguarding its treasury. [**Trainor v. Hernandez**, 431 U.S. 434 (1977)]

4) **Bar disciplinary proceedings [§107]**
It also applies to state bar disciplinary proceedings. [**Middlesex County Ethics Committee v. Garden State Bar Association**, 457 U.S. 423 (1982)]

5) **Administrative proceedings [§108]**
It applies to state administrative proceedings involving *important* state interests. [**Ohio Civil Rights Commission v. Dayton Christian Schools, Inc.**, 477 U.S. 619 (1986)—sex discrimination charge]

(b) **Definition of "pending" [§109]**
If the relevant state proceeding (criminal or civil) is begun after an action for a federal injunction (or declaratory judgment) is filed, but before any substantial proceedings on the merits in federal court, the federal action ordinarily must be dismissed. [**Hicks v. Miranda**, 422 U.S. 332 (1975)]

(c) **"Bad faith" exception [§110]**
A federal injunction (or declaratory judgment) may issue against a pending state criminal prosecution (or state-initiated civil action) if the claimant shows that state officials are acting in bad faith—*i.e.*, with no hope of prevailing, to harass claimants and deter them from engaging in constitutionally protected activities—and will continue to do so regardless of what the state courts do. [**Dombrowski v. Pfister**, *supra*; **Younger v. Harris**, *supra*, §101]

(4) Ongoing supervision of state executive activities [§111]

Principles of "equity, comity, and federalism" also impose significant restrictions on federal court supervision of the practices of state executive or administrative agencies—*e.g.*, disciplining of police [**Rizzo v. Goode,** 423 U.S. 362 (1976)], and bail, sentencing, and jury fee policies [**O'Shea v. Littleton,** *supra*, §41].

(a) Note

Such federal equitable relief will not be granted unless the plaintiff shows "the likelihood of substantial and immediate irreparable injury, and the inadequacy of remedies at law." [**O'Shea v. Littleton,** *supra*]

(5) Exhaustion of state remedies [§112]

Although the rule had been that a person seeking a federal injunction against state administrative action must have exhausted all adequate state administrative remedies, federal law [28 U.S.C. §1983] has been interpreted to excuse this requirement. [**Damico v. California,** 389 U.S. 416 (1967)] Thus, as to federal injunctions there is *no* requirement of exhausting state judicial remedies.

(6) "Abstention" doctrine [§113]

In "narrowly limited special circumstances" [**Zwickler v. Koota,** 389 U.S. 241 (1967); *and see* below], a federal court may abstain from granting an injunction or declaratory judgment and remand the parties to state court for an interpretation of the statute [**Railroad Commission v. Pullman Co.,** 312 U.S. 496 (1941)]. *Rationale:* This promotes harmonious federal-state relations, since the state court may interpret the statute so as to make a decision of the constitutional question unnecessary.

(a) Ambiguity [§114]

The federal court may abstain if the state statute or regulation is unclear, giving state courts the opportunity to avoid the constitutional issue. [**Harris County Commissioners' Court v. Moore,** 420 U.S. 77 (1975)]

1) "Free speech" exception [§115]

When a state statute is attacked on the ground that it is an "overbroad" or "vague" regulation of expression or association (*infra*, §§584-594), a federal court generally will *not abstain*, even if the statute might be given a limiting interpretation.

a) Rationale

The right of free speech is fundamental in a democratic society, and the mere existence of a vague or overbroad regulation might deter people from exercising that right. If the statute is invalid on its face, the federal court should generally so hold unless the statute can be clarified in a single state proceeding. [**Dombrowski v. Pfister,** *supra*]

b) Note

If the state official wishes to avoid federal adjudication, she may promptly seek a declaratory judgment in the state courts, clarifying the scope of the statute.

2) "Unjustifiable delay" exception [§116]

The federal court may decline to abstain if it finds further delays unjustifiable—especially in civil rights cases. [**Griffin v. County School Board**, 377 U.S. 218 (1964)—further delay in integration of school system unjustified]

(b) Procedure to be followed [§117]

If the parties are remanded to state court, the claimant may expressly reserve the right to litigate the federal question ultimately in federal court and still present constitutional arguments in the state court. [**England v. Louisiana State Board of Medical Examiners**, 375 U.S. 411 (1963)]

f. Political questions [§118]

If a case presents a "political question" rather than a justiciable controversy, the Court will not decide the question (on the basis of separation of powers). Final determination of such questions is left to the political branches—*i.e.*, Congress and/or the executive branch.

(1) Criteria [§119]

The basic criteria for determining whether a question is "political" are [**Baker v. Carr**, *supra*, §50]:

(i) A *"textually demonstrable" constitutional commitment* of the issue *to the political branches*;

> **Example:** Nixon, a federal judge, was impeached on allegations of bribery. Hearings on the charges were held by a Senate committee, which then presented its findings to the full Senate. The full Senate then voted to impeach Nixon by a more than two-thirds vote. Nixon appealed this conviction to the Supreme Court, arguing that the Constitution requires impeachments to be tried by the Senate, and that this requirement was not satisfied because hearings against him were held by a committee rather than by the full Senate. The Supreme Court held that Nixon's claim presented a nonjusticiable issue because the Impeachment Clause [Art. I, §3, cl. 6] states that "the Senate shall have *sole* power to try all impeachments." [**Nixon v. United States**, 506 U.S. 224 (1993)]

(ii) *Lack of manageable standards* for judicial resolution;

(iii) *A need for finality* in the action of the political branches; and

(iv) *Difficulty or impossibility* of devising effective judicial remedies.

(a) Note—interrelationship

The lack of judicially manageable standards may strengthen the conclusion that there is a textually demonstrable commitment to a coordinate branch. [**Nixon v. United States,** *supra*]

(2) Case-by-case determination [§120]

Beyond these criteria, the Court decides each claim of a nonjusticiable issue on a case-by-case basis.

(3) Application

(a) Foreign relations [§121]

Certain basic issues of foreign relations (*e.g.*, what the recognized government of a foreign country is; on what date hostilities ceased against a foreign government) may be "political questions." [**Martin v. Mott,** 25 U.S. 19 (1827)] *Rationale:* Resolution of such issues frequently turns on standards that defy judicial application, involves the exercise of discretion demonstrably committed to Congress or the President, or uniquely demands a single-voiced statement of the government's views.

Example: A plurality of the Court has stated that the issue of whether the President has unilateral power to terminate a treaty (*i.e.*, without the consent of Congress) is a "political question"; there are no judicially manageable standards. [**Goldwater v. Carter,** 444 U.S. 996 (1979)]

(b) Military organization [§122]

Detailed issues concerning the composition, training, equipping, and disciplining of U.S. military forces are "political questions" committed to Congress by Article I, Section 8, Clause 16. [**Gilligan v. Morgan,** 413 U.S. 1 (1973)]

(c) Constitutional amendments [§123]

Details respecting proposed constitutional amendments (*e.g.*, how long they remain open to ratification, or what effect a prior rejection by the state legislature may have on subsequent ratification) have been held to involve "political questions." They are committed to Congress by Article V, and there are no manageable judicial standards. [**Coleman v. Miller,** 307 U.S. 433 (1939)]

(d) Impeachment [§124]

As noted above, Article I, Section 3, Clause 6 states that the "Senate shall have the sole power to try all impeachments." This provision commits to the Senate the determination of procedures for trying an impeached official, which are unreviewable by the courts. [**Nixon v. United States,** *supra*]

(e)   Republican form of government [§125]

Questions under Article IV, Section 4, providing that the United States shall guarantee every state a republican form of government, have been held "political," because there are no judicially manageable standards to determine whether the form of government is "republican." [**Pacific States Telegraph & Telephone Co. v. Oregon,** 223 U.S. 118 (1912)]

(f)   Internal political party disputes [§126]

The Court has indicated "grave doubts" whether the federal judiciary should intervene in certain disputes at political party conventions. [**O'Brien v. Brown,** 409 U.S. 1 (1972)—"the convention itself is the proper forum for determining intraparty disputes to which delegates shall be seated"]

(g)   Political rights [§127]

Constitutional issues concerning political rights or the allocation of political power within a state (such as deprivation of the right to vote, or legislative apportionment) are *not* necessarily "political questions." They may involve claims under the Fifteenth Amendment or the Equal Protection Clause of the Fourteenth Amendment, which have well-developed and familiar judicial standards. [**Baker v. Carr,** *supra*, §119; **Gomillion v. Lightfoot,** 364 U.S. 339 (1960)]

(h)   Congressional membership [§128]

The Constitution prescribes certain minimum requirements for membership in each House [Art. I, §2] and provides that "each House shall be the judge of the elections, returns and qualifications of its members" [Art. I, §5].

---

e.g.   **Example:** Since Article I, Section 5 commits to the House of Congress the final decision of which candidate "received more lawful votes," the issue is a "political question." [**Roudebush v. Hartke,** 405 U.S. 15 (1972)]

---

cf.   **Compare:** But Article I, Section 5 does not constitute a demonstrable commitment of nonreviewable power to Congress to set and evaluate qualifications of members beyond the age, citizenship, and residence requirements of Article I, Section 2, Clause 2. Thus, such issues are *not* "political questions." [**Powell v. McCormack,** 395 U.S. 486 (1969)—House could not refuse to seat delegate on committee finding of wrongdoing]

---

4. **Effect of Declaration of Unconstitutionality [§129]**

    In legal theory, a decision declaring an act unconstitutional is binding on no one but the parties to the suit. In fact, of course, such a decision establishes a principle of law applicable to all persons. However, certain problems may arise in applying the declaration to litigation involving other parties:

    a. **Retroactive effect**

        (1) **General rule [§130]**

            The Court's declaration of unconstitutionality is the controlling interpretation of federal law. It has full retroactive effect in all cases still open on appeal, and as to all events, regardless of when they occur. [**Harper v. Virginia Department of Taxation,** 509 U.S. 86 (1993)]

        (2) **Application—criminal cases [§131]**

            The issue of retroactivity has been encountered repeatedly in recent years in connection with rulings by the Court that declare unconstitutional some statute or procedure affecting those charged with a crime. Are persons imprisoned under the invalid statute or procedure whose convictions have been affirmed on appeal entitled to be freed, or at least given a new trial? (*See infra,* §§1368-1375.)

    b. **Partial invalidity [§132]**

        When part of a statute has been declared invalid, whether the remaining portion shall also be declared unconstitutional, or enforced as valid, depends on the intention of the legislature.

        (1) **Statute severable [§133]**

            If the parts are so *distinctly severable* that each can stand alone, and it was the apparent intention of the legislature that the valid part should be enforceable even though another part should fail, then one part of the statute may be enforced even if another is declared unconstitutional. [**Carter v. Carter Coal Co.,** 298 U.S. 238 (1936)]

        (2) **Statute not severable [§134]**

            On the other hand, if the different parts of a statute are so mutually *connected and interdependent* that the legislature must have intended them to be effective only as a whole, then all provisions dependent on or connected with the unconstitutional portion must also fall. [**Pollock v. Farmers' Loan & Trust Co.,** 158 U.S. 601 (1895)]

        (3) **"Severability clause" [§135]**

            A statute may provide that "if any section or provision of this act shall be held to be invalid, this shall not affect the validity of other sections or provisions hereof." A legislative declaration of this type ("severability clause") provides a *rebuttable* presumption as to the intent of the legislature, but it is not conclusive. [**Williams v. Standard Oil,** 278 U.S. 235 (1929)]

B. Legislative Power

1. Power of Congress—In General [§136]

Legislative power is basically the power to make laws, but it also includes the power to investigate, hear, and consider matters upon which legislation may be enacted, and do all other things necessary or proper to the enactment of legislation. Article I, Section 1 of the Constitution provides: "All legislative powers herein granted shall be vested in a Congress of the United States . . . ."

a. Scope of federal powers

(1) Doctrine of enumerated powers [§137]

The Tenth Amendment provides: "The powers not delegated to the United States by the Constitution, nor prohibited by it to the States, are *reserved to the States* respectively, or to the people." Thus, the doctrine early developed that the federal government was one of "enumerated" or "delegated" powers, and that the powers not expressly delegated were "reserved" to the states. [**Kansas v. Colorado,** 206 U.S. 46 (1907)]

(2) Doctrine of implied powers [§138]

Nevertheless, the Court (per Chief Justice Marshall) in **McCulloch v. Maryland,** 17 U.S. (4 Wheat.) 316 (1819), held that in addition to those powers specifically enumerated in the Constitution, certain broad federal powers are to be implied from the *Necessary and Proper Clause.* [Art. I, §8, cl. 18]

(a) Necessary and Proper Clause [§139]

Article I, Section 8, Clause 18 provides that Congress has the power "[t]o make all laws which shall be *necessary and proper* for carrying into execution the foregoing powers, and all other powers vested by this Constitution in the Government of the United States, or in any Department or Officer thereof."

(b) Congress may use any appropriate means [§140]

Congress is not limited to only those means that are absolutely necessary. Rather, it may use *any appropriate means* to achieve the ends specified in the enumerated powers—*i.e.*, any means not prohibited by the Constitution. The need for a particular means is for Congress—not the Supreme Court—to determine.

> **Example:** The enumerated powers do not include the power to incorporate a national bank, but Congress may do so as a "necessary and proper" means of carrying out its delegated powers to lay and collect taxes [Art. I, §8, cl. 1], borrow money [Art. I, §8, cl. 2], regulate commerce among the several states [Art. I, §8, cl. 3], declare and conduct war [Art. I, §8, cl. 11], and raise and support armies and navies [Art. I, §8, cls. 12, 13]. [**McCulloch v. Maryland,** *supra*]

(c) Powers traceable to grants of power to other branches [§141]

The provisions of the Necessary and Proper Clause apply to *all* powers delegated to *any* branch of the federal government.

1) Admiralty and maritime power [§142]

Thus, Congress has the power to legislate concerning admiralty and maritime matters even though the Constitution contains no express grant of such power to Congress. Article III, Section 2 extends the federal *judicial* power to "all cases of admiralty and maritime jurisdiction"; and the Court has held that the framers intended to place the entire subject—substantive as well as procedural aspects—under national control. [*Ex parte* **Garnett**, 141 U.S. 1 (1891)]

EXAM TIP **gilbert**

Remember that the Necessary and Proper Clause, standing alone, cannot support federal law. It *must work in conjunction with another federal power*. Thus, if an exam question involves the source of power for particular congressional action, be sure to discuss one of Congress's enumerated powers before discussing the Necessary and Proper Clause.

---

(3) Inherent powers [§143]

There is one broad exception to the doctrine that Congress's authority is limited to the enumerated powers. *International powers* (*i.e.*, powers over *external or foreign affairs*) are considered inherent federal powers even though not expressly recited in the Constitution. [**United States v. Curtiss-Wright Export Corp.**, 299 U.S. 304 (1936)]

Example: A joint resolution of Congress authorized the President to ban arms sales to Bolivia and Paraguay if the President decided that such a prohibition would contribute to reestablishing peace between the two warring countries. The President proclaimed an embargo under the resolution. Subsequently, Curtiss-Wright was indicted for violating the terms of the embargo. Curtiss-Wright argued that the joint resolution was an unconstitutional delegation of legislative power to the President. The Supreme Court upheld the delegation and stressed that the federal government is one of enumerated power only in the arena of internal affairs. The federal government's power over foreign affairs is much broader. [**United States v. Curtiss-Wright Export Corp.**, *supra*]

---

b. Delegation of legislative power [§144]

Several decisions in the 1930s held that congressional delegations of lawmaking power to the executive branch or administrative agencies were impermissible because they were unduly broad. [**Panama Refining Co. v. Ryan**, 293 U.S. 388 (1935); **Schechter Poultry Co. v. United States**, 295 U.S. 495 (1935)]

e.g. Example: The National Industrial Recovery Act was part of President Roosevelt's "New Deal" economic stimulus package, which was intended to help pull the United States out of the Depression in the early 1930s. The Act authorized the President to adopt fair competition codes by regulating, among other things, wages, hours, prices, etc. Schecter Poultry was convicted of violating a number of provisions of the Live Poultry Code, adopted pursuant to the Act. The Supreme Court held that the Act was unconstitutional, in part because Congress delegated its power without sufficient standards—it did not sufficiently define what constitutes "fair competition." [**Schecter Poultry Co. v. United States,** *supra*]

(1) Requirement of standards [§145]

To avoid "delegation running riot," and to ensure that the fundamental purposes of the separation of powers are observed, the Court required that delegations of legislative power contain "intelligible standards" to confine the discretion of the delegate. [**Yakus v. United States,** 321 U.S. 414 (1944)]

(2) Effective demise of the nondelegation doctrine [§146]

But no decision since 1935 has invalidated a congressional delegation of power, and the Court has been extremely liberal on the sufficiency of "standards," no matter how broadly phrased (*e.g.*, upholding "public interest, convenience, or necessity").

(a) Note

In recent years, some justices have invoked the nondelegation doctrine in arguing that a delegation of legislative power was invalid because Congress had not made the critical policy decisions. [*See, e.g.*, **American Textile Manufacturers Institute v. Donovan,** 452 U.S. 490 (1981)]

(b) Independent constitutional authority [§147]

Whatever the required specificity of standards may be for congressional delegations of power, they are more flexible when the entity exercising the delegated authority has independent power over the subject matter. [**Loving v. United States,** 517 U.S. 748 (1996)—congressional delegation to President in respect to military court martials]

EXAM TIP   **gilbert**

Although you should mention in your answer that a valid delegation of legislative power technically requires *"intelligible standards"* for the delegate to follow (*see* above), remember that when the Court applies that rule, *almost anything* will pass for an intelligible standard (*e.g.,* "upholding public interest, convenience, or necessity"); thus, no legislative delegation has been invalidated since 1935.

(3) Delegation to judicial branch [§148]

Congress may delegate rulemaking authority (and other nonadjudicatory functions) to the judicial branch (as well as to the executive branch or administrative agencies) as long as the task delegated does not invade the prerogatives of some other branch and is appropriate to the duties of the judicial branch. [**Mistretta v. United States,** 488 U.S. 361 (1989)—upholding placement in judicial branch of commission to promulgate sentencing guidelines]

2. Commerce Power [§149]

Congress's all important powers under Article I, Section 8, Clause 3, "to regulate commerce with foreign nations, and among the several states . . ." are discussed in a separate section (*see infra,* §§283 *et seq.*).

3. Taxing and Spending Powers

a. Constitutional provision [§150]

Article I, Section 8, Clause 1 provides that "Congress shall have the power to lay and collect taxes . . . to pay the debts and provide for the common defense and general welfare of the United States."

b. Independent powers [§151]

The powers (i) to tax to raise revenue; and (ii) to spend for the general welfare are *independent* powers. That is, Congress may (i) tax subjects and (ii) spend money on activities that it could not regulate directly under any of its enumerated regulatory powers (such as the commerce power).

EXAM TIP   **gilbert**

Be sure to remember that Article I, Section 8, Clause 1 does **not** give Congress the power to legislate for the general welfare. The "general welfare power" **belongs to the states**. The phrase "general welfare" in Article I, Section 8, Clause 1 is actually a *limitation* on the federal taxing and spending power. Congress may tax and spend **only** to provide for the common defense and general welfare of the United States. But the Court has left virtually complete authority with Congress to determine what constitutes spending for the general welfare.

---

c. Taxation with purpose or effect of regulation [§152]

Virtually all taxes have some ancillary regulatory effect, in that they tend to encourage or discourage various types of activity.

(1) Where Congress has power to regulate [§153]

If Congress has the power to regulate the subject or activity taxed, the tax—even though enacted for a regulatory rather than a revenue-raising purpose—can be upheld as a "necessary and proper" exercise of one of Congress's regulatory powers.

 Example: A tax levied on banknotes issued by state banks was upheld (even though it drove the banknotes out of existence), because

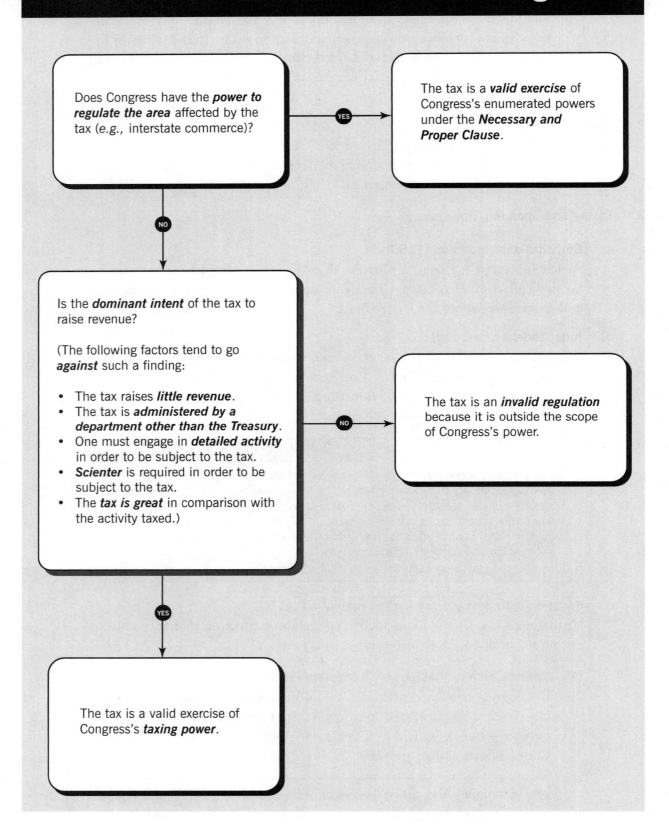

Does Congress have the **power to regulate the area** affected by the tax (*e.g.,* interstate commerce)?

YES → The tax is a **valid exercise** of Congress's enumerated powers under the **Necessary and Proper Clause**.

NO ↓

Is the **dominant intent** of the tax to raise revenue?

(The following factors tend to go **against** such a finding:

- The tax raises **little revenue**.
- The tax is **administered by a department other than the Treasury**.
- One must engage in **detailed activity** in order to be subject to the tax.
- **Scienter** is required in order to be subject to the tax.
- The **tax is great** in comparison with the activity taxed.)

NO → The tax is an **invalid regulation** because it is outside the scope of Congress's power.

YES ↓

The tax is a valid exercise of Congress's **taxing power**.

Congress has the power to regulate the national currency. [Art. I, §8, cl. 5] Its validity as a revenue-raising measure was immaterial. [**Veazie Bank v. Fenno,** 75 U.S. (8 Wall.) 533 (1869)]

(a) Effect

Because Congress has almost limitless regulatory power under the Commerce Clause (discussed *infra*), virtually *all* federal taxes may be upheld as "necessary and proper" exercises of the commerce power, without reliance on the taxing power at all.

(2) Where Congress has no power to regulate [§154]

In those rare instances where Congress has no power to regulate the subject or activity taxed, the tax must be justified under the taxing power. But even here, the tax is not necessarily invalid merely because it regulates the activity taxed to some extent—since virtually every tax has this effect.

(a) Test [§155]

The tax will be upheld under the taxing power if its *dominant intent* is revenue-raising (rather than prohibition or regulation). Phrased another way, the tax will be invalid only if its dominant intent is penal (rather than fiscal).

(b) Objective approach [§156]

The Court has sometimes applied this test very objectively. If the tax *in fact* raises revenue, it will be upheld: *i.e.,* its dominant intent will be considered fiscal, despite the apparent regulatory purpose.

Examples: The following taxes that obviously had substantial regulatory effects were nonetheless upheld as revenue-raising measures:

1) *Tax of 10¢ per pound on yellow oleomargarine,* as compared to one-fourth of a cent per pound on white oleo [**McCray v. United States,** 195 U.S. 27 (1904)—the tax was intended to protect the sale of butter; white margarine apparently looked less appetizing than yellow margarine];

2) *Special excise tax on dealers in narcotics* [**United States v. Doremus,** 249 U.S. 86 (1919)];

3) *Tax on dealers in firearms* [**Sonzinsky v. United States,** 300 U.S. 506 (1937)]; and

4) *Tax on bookmaking activities* [**United States v. Kahriger,** 345 U.S. 22 (1953)].

(c) Subjective approach [§157]

On other occasions, the Court has examined the statute more care-fully, looking to the *language* and *operative effect* to determine its dominant intent. The following factors may be important:

1) *Who enforces* the tax statute. (If the Treasury Department en-forces, this evidences fiscal intent; if the Labor Department, regulatory intent.)

2) *How much detailed activity* one must engage in to be subject to, or to avoid, the tax. (The more detailed the activity, the greater the evidence of a penal or regulatory intent.)

3) *Whether scienter* (*i.e.,* intent) *is required*. (A scienter require-ment usually indicates a penal or regulatory intent.)

4) *Amount* of the tax. (If the amount is so great that virtually all activity is structured to avoid liability—resulting in almost no revenue—this evidences a penal or regulatory intent.)

---

e.g. **Examples—penal or regulatory taxes:** A special tax on those who employ child labor was held invalid; several of the above factors were present. [**Bailey v. Drexel Furniture Co.,** 259 U.S. 20 (1922)] A special tax on liquor businesses conducted contrary to state law was also held invalid; the purpose was held to be imposi-tion of a federal penalty for commission of a state crime. [**United States v. Constantine,** 296 U.S. 287 (1935)]

---

cf. **Compare:** A special tax on those engaged in gambling has been upheld, since the tax produced revenue despite its regulatory effect. Although the tax statute requires the filing of much detailed information, this *aids in collection of the tax*. Since gambling is not illegal everywhere, this is *not* an added federal penalty for state law violation. [**United States v. Kahriger,** *supra*] (*Note:* This doctrine concerning the taxing power is still "good law," although the gam-bling tax statute was subsequently held to violate the Fifth Amend-ment privilege against self-incrimination. [**Marchetti v. United States,** 390 U.S. 39 (1968)])

---

d. Spending with purpose or effect of regulation [§158]

Almost all spending programs likewise produce an ancillary regulatory effect, because they tend to encourage or discourage various activities by individuals. Indeed, many federal spending programs ("grants-in-aid") are specifically con-ditioned on the recipient states using the funds pursuant to federally designated standards.

(1) Where Congress has power to regulate [§159]

As in the case of the taxing power, if Congress may *directly regulate* the activity or conduct in which persons must engage to receive funds under a federal spending program, the spending program is valid as a "necessary and proper" exercise of the regulatory powers.

(2) Where Congress has no power to regulate [§160]

As in the case of the taxing power, Congress rarely lacks the power to regulate activities related to federal spending programs.

Example: A congressional program has been upheld solely under the spending power (the Court assuming no regulatory power available) where federal funds were granted to all states enacting unemployment compensation schemes conforming to federal requirements. [**Steward Machine Co. v. Davis**, 301 U.S. 548 (1937)] The Court found that the federal program did not "coerce" state adoption of unemployment plans, but merely served as a "temptation." The Court also noted that the federal program satisfied a *federal fiscal purpose*, because if the states did not provide unemployment compensation, Congress could clearly do so for the general welfare. This theory could sustain broad exercises of the spending power that have substantial regulatory effects.

Example: Assuming (but *not* deciding) that the Twenty-First Amendment (*see infra*, §§344-349) would bar Congress from enacting a national minimum drinking age, the Court has held that Congress may condition some percentage of federal highway funds on a recipient state's adopting a minimum drinking age. [**South Dakota v. Dole**, 483 U.S. 203 (1987)]

(a) Limitations on the spending power

1) "General welfare" [§161]

Congress's power to spend must be exercised for the "general welfare"; *i.e.*, the expenditure must be "for the common benefit as distinguished from some mere local purpose." [**United States v. Gerlach Live Stock Co.**, 339 U.S. 725 (1950)] However, the determination of what is in the nation's "general welfare" is left to Congress. [**Helvering v. Davis**, 301 U.S. 619 (1937)]

2) Individual rights [§162]

Congress may not use the spending power to violate an independent constitutional limitation, *e.g.*, by inducing states to engage in activities that would themselves be unconstitutional (such as to inflict cruel and unusual punishment).

4. **War Power**

a. **Constitutional provisions [§163]**
Article I, Section 8 grants Congress the power to declare war, to raise and support armies, to provide and maintain a navy, to make rules for the government and regulation of the land and naval forces, and to provide for organizing, arming, disciplining, and calling forth the militia.

    (1) **Broad scope of powers [§164]**
These powers give Congress a wide scope of authority *during war* to wage war effectively. For example, Congress may take action affecting domestic matters, such as the national economy, independent of its authority to regulate such matters under any other enumerated power.

        (a) **After war [§165]**
Congressional authority under the war power may also continue after cessation of hostilities to remedy evils created by the war. [**Woods v. Cloyd W. Miller Co.**, 333 U.S. 138 (1948)—post-World War II rent controls held valid because housing shortage was attributable to the war]

            1) **Limits on power [§166]**
This *post-war* power is probably not so unlimited as to "swallow up" the limits on congressional power; although, absent a constitutionally protected personal liberty, the Court would probably give very limited judicial review to an exercise of such power.

5. **Power Over External Affairs [§167]**
The scope of Congress's power over external affairs is discussed elsewhere (*see infra*, §§223 *et seq.*).

6. **Power Over Naturalization and Citizenship**

a. **Constitutional provision [§168]**
Article I, Section 8, Clause 4 provides that Congress shall have power "to establish a uniform rule of naturalization . . . ."

b. **Plenary power over aliens [§169]**
The authority of Congress over admission, exclusion, and deportation of aliens is plenary. Congress may exclude aliens altogether, or prescribe the conditions upon which they may come into or remain in the country. [**Kleindienst v. Mandel**, 408 U.S. 753 (1972)]

    (1) **Exclusion of aliens seeking entry [§170]**
An alien who seeks admission to the country does so only on such terms as Congress shall prescribe. Whatever procedure Congress authorizes is "due process," as far as the alien is concerned. [**United States *ex rel.* Knauff v. Shaughnessy**, 338 U.S. 537 (1950)]

Example: Congress may authorize the Attorney General to determine (on the basis of confidential information the disclosure of which, in the Attorney General's judgment, would endanger the public security) that the admission of an alien would be prejudicial to the interests of the United States; and *without a hearing*, the government may constitutionally order an alien *excluded* from the United States. [**United States *ex rel*. Knauff v. Shaughnessy,** *supra*; **Shaughnessy v. United States *ex rel*. Mezei,** 345 U.S. 206 (1953)]

(2) Deportation of resident aliens [§171]

While Congress may prescribe conditions for expulsion and deportation of resident aliens, such aliens in a deportation proceeding do have constitutional protections not available to nonresident aliens seeking entry into the country; *i.e.*, an alien physically present in the United States (legally or illegally) is a "person" within the provisions of the Fifth Amendment and is entitled to *certain procedural due process rights*.

Example: Before a resident alien may be expelled and deported, he is at least entitled to notice of the nature of the charges against him and a hearing before an executive or administrative tribunal. [**Kwong Hai Chew v. Colding,** 344 U.S. 590 (1953)]

(a) Substantive rights [§172]

The Court has *suggested* that resident aliens may also have certain *substantive* constitutional rights, such as freedom from "arbitrary or capricious" restraint, but both the existence and scope of such rights are unclear. [*See* **Zadvydas v. Davis,** 533 U.S. 678 (2001)]

(b) Comment

Note that the Alien Registration Act of 1940, which authorized the deportation of resident aliens because of membership in the Communist Party (even though such membership terminated before the enactment of the Act), was held *not* to be an ex post facto law (*see infra*, §558) since deportation was not deemed to constitute "punishment." [**Harisiades v. Shaughnessy,** 342 U.S. 580 (1952)]

(3) State regulation of aliens [§173]

This subject is discussed elsewhere (*see infra*, §§1081 *et seq.*).

c. Naturalization [§174]

The constitutional basis for federal and state citizenship is found in Section 1 of the Fourteenth Amendment, which states that "all persons born or *naturalized* in the United States, and subject to the jurisdiction thereof, are citizens of the United States and the State wherein they reside."

(1) Congressional power [§175]

The power of naturalization is vested *exclusively* in Congress. [**Holmgren v. United States,** 217 U.S. 509 (1910)]

(2) Rights of naturalized citizens [§176]

The rights of native-born and naturalized citizens are of the *same dignity* and are *coextensive* (except that only a native-born citizen can be elected President). Hence, a statute that attempts to discriminate between the two classes of citizenship is unconstitutional. [**Schneider v. Rusk,** 377 U.S. 163 (1964)—statute that deprived naturalized citizens of their citizenship if they resumed foreign residence held to violate equal protection]

d. Loss of citizenship [§177]

Under Section 1 of the Fourteenth Amendment, Congress does *not* have the power to take away the citizenship of a citizen born or naturalized in the United States unless the government establishes, by a preponderance of evidence, that the citizen *intended to relinquish citizenship*. Such intent can be expressed in words or found as a fair inference from proven conduct. [**Afroyim v. Rusk,** 387 U.S. 253 (1967)—holding unconstitutional statute that provided for loss of citizenship for voting in a foreign election; **Vance v. Terrazas,** 444 U.S. 252 (1980)—upholding a rebuttable presumption that, when a statutory expatriating act is proven, there was intent to relinquish citizenship; but the government must still prove that the act was performed with the necessary intent to relinquish citizenship]

(1) Distinguish

Congress does have power to revoke the citizenship of persons who are not "born or naturalized in the United States"—*e.g.*, by being born abroad to an American parent. [**Rogers v. Bellei,** 401 U.S. 815 (1971)]

(2) And note

Statutes that provide for revocation of naturalization obtained unlawfully or by fraud have also been upheld. [**Schneiderman v. United States,** 320 U.S. 118 (1945)]

7. Property Power

a. Power over property of the United States [§178]

Article IV, Section 3, Clause 2 provides that Congress shall have power "to dispose of and make all needful rules and regulations respecting the territory or other property belonging to the United States."

b. Scope of power [§179]

The power over United States property—including the power to determine what are "needful" rules "respecting" the public lands—is vested in Congress *without limitation*. [**Kleppe v. New Mexico,** 426 U.S. 529 (1976)]

8. Investigatory Power

a. Implied from power to legislate [§180]

While there is no constitutional provision expressly conferring upon Congress the power to make investigations and exact testimony, it has long been recognized as a necessary incident of the power to legislate. [**McGrain v. Daugherty,** 273 U.S. 135 (1927)]

(1) Application

Pursuant to this implied power, either House of Congress may compel the attendance of witnesses before that House (or any duly constituted committee thereof), and order that the witnesses answer questions. [**McGrain v. Daugherty,** *supra*; **Sinclair v. United States,** 279 U.S. 263 (1929)]

b. Scope of investigatory power [§181]

The power to investigate is limited to inquiries of which the particular House has *jurisdiction*—*i.e.*, in respect to which it rightfully may take legislative action. Neither House of Congress possesses a general power to inquire into the private affairs of citizens. [**Kilbourn v. Thompson,** 103 U.S. 168 (1880)]

(1) Application

For the purpose of determining the essential character of a congressional inquiry, recourse is usually had to the statute or resolution under which the investigation is authorized. However, the information need *not* be pertinent to any pending legislation. The investigatory power extends to *all matters upon which Congress could choose to act.*

c. Enforcement of investigatory power [§182]

The principal method for enforcing the congressional investigative power is punishment by *contempt*. Congress has the power to punish a person, other than a member, for contempt in order to assure the integrity of its authority. [**Anderson v. Dunn,** 19 U.S. (6 Wheat.) 204 (1821)] Either House of Congress may convene as a court to try, convict, and direct a fine against, and/or imprisonment of, the contemnor, but any imprisonment is limited to the duration of the current term of Congress.

d. Limits on investigatory power [§183]

The principal grounds upon which witnesses may refuse to answer questions before congressional committees are discussed elsewhere; *e.g.*, privilege against self-incrimination (*infra*, §§1277-1280); interference with First Amendment rights (*infra*, §§851-853); and lack of due process safeguards in hearing procedures (*infra*, §850).

9. Congressional Immunity [§184]

Article I, Section 6, Clause 1 provides that "Senators and Representatives . . . shall not be questioned in any other Place . . . for any Speech or Debate in either House." The Speech or Debate Clause forbids criminal or civil proceedings against members of Congress for "legislative acts." [**United States v. Johnson,** 383 U.S. 169 (1966)] *Rationale:* Defending criminal or civil actions of all kinds (including suits for injunctions or damages) diverts the time, energy, and attention of members of Congress from their legislative tasks. [**Eastland v. United States Servicemen's Fund,** 421 U.S. 491 (1975)]

a. Persons covered [§185]

Besides Senators and Representatives, the immunity also covers aides who engage in acts that would be immune if performed by the legislator. [**Gravel v. United States,** 408 U.S. 606 (1972)]

(1) Distinguish

The Speech or Debate Clause does *not* extend to state legislators who are prosecuted for violation of federal law. [**United States v. Gillock,** 445 U.S. 360 (1980)—state officials could be prosecuted under federal statutes prohibiting bribe-taking and racketeering by officials]

b. Scope of immunity [§186]

Neither "acts that occur in the *regular course of the legislative process*" nor "the *motivation* for those acts" may be used against the legislator in a judicial proceeding.

(1) Distinguish

Note that *promises* by a legislator to perform a *future* legislative act are not immune and may be introduced into evidence. [**United States v. Brewster,** 408 U.S. 501 (1972)—permitting prosecution for bribery to influence legislation]

c. "Legislative acts" [§187]

In addition to statements or acts on the floor of Congress, the term "legislative acts" includes such matters as how a legislator voted or decided to vote, and extends to conducting committee hearings, introducing material at such hearings, and preparing committee reports.

(1) But note

The protection does *not* extend to *public distribution* of committee reports, even when authorized by statute [**Doe v. McMillan,** 412 U.S. 306 (1973)], nor to *republication* (*e.g.,* in press releases or newsletters) of defamatory statements originally made in Congress [**Hutchinson v. Proxmire,** 443 U.S. 111 (1979)].

d. "Political acts" [§188]

Political acts are *not* subject to the protection of the Speech or Debate Clause. They include communications with and services for constituents, and speeches and publications outside of Congress. [**United States v. Brewster,** *supra*]

SOURCES OF CONGRESSIONAL POWER—EXAMPLES gilbert

GOVERNMENT ACTION	SOURCE OF POWER
1. Congress pays for highways.	Spending Power and Commerce Clause.
2. Federal tax on airline tickets.	Taxing Power and Commerce Clause.
3. Congress conditions aid to states for medical programs on state funding of AIDS research.	Spending Power.
4. Congress adopts a tax to regulate banknotes rather than to raise revenue.	Power to coin money.
5. Congress prohibits hunting on federal lands.	Property Power.
6. Congress bars racial discrimination at places of public accommodation.	Commerce Clause.

C. Executive Power

1. **Source of Presidential Powers [§189]**

    Article I, Section 1 confers the *whole* executive power to the President. The President is given broad authority to delegate and to appoint members of the executive branch, but all executive power ultimately rests in the hands of the President.

2. **Scope of Powers**

    a. **Appointment power [§190]**

        Article II, Section 2 specifies that the President shall nominate and appoint "with the advice and consent of the Senate" all "Ambassadors, other public Ministers and Consuls, Judges of the Supreme Court, and all other Officers of the United States, whose appointments are not herein otherwise provided for . . . but Congress may vest the appointment of inferior officers as they think proper in the President alone, in the Courts of Law, or in the Heads of Departments."

        (1) **Congressional appointees [§191]**

             Although Congress may appoint officials to exercise such investigative power as it might delegate to one of its own committees, it may *not* appoint members of an agency or commission with administrative powers (*e.g.*, promulgating rules or issuing advisory opinions) or law enforcement powers (*e.g.*, conducting litigation in the courts). Such persons are "officers of the United States" and must be appointed pursuant to Article II, Section 2. [**Buckley v. Valeo**, 424 U.S. 1 (1976)]

Example: Congress adopted the Federal Election Campaign Act, which gave the President Pro Tem of the Senate and the Speaker of the House the power to appoint the majority of the members of the Federal Election Commission. The Act gave the Commission power to bring civil actions against violators and to adopt rules regulating elections. The Supreme Court held that these tasks were executive in nature and so Congress could not constitutionally appoint officers to the Commission. [**Buckley v. Valeo**, *supra*]

(2) "Principal" vs. "inferior" officers [§192]

"Principal" officers may be appointed only by the President with the advice and consent of the Senate. Appointment of "inferior" officers may be vested in other departments. [**Morrison v. Olson**, 487 U.S. 654 (1988)]

Example: Independent prosecutors—who are appointed with limited tenure and authority, and are subject to removal by executive officials—have been held to be "inferior" officers and thus may be appointed by the "courts of law." [**Morrison v. Olson**, *supra*]

(a) Limits on power [§193]

Congress may not vest courts with appointment power if it is "incongruous" with the functions normally performed by courts; *e.g.*, if the courts were given undue discretion over the appointees' jurisdiction. [**Morrison v. Olson**, *supra*]

b. Removal power [§194]

The Constitution is silent on the President's power to remove most presidential appointees.

(1) Federal judges [§195]

The President has *no power* to remove Supreme Court justices or lower court judges appointed by him, as the Constitution provides that they are to remain in office "during good behavior." [Art. III, §1]

(2) Executive appointees [§196]

However, in order that the President may accomplish his constitutional role, there are *some* "purely executive" officials who must be removable by the President at will, even though the appointment may have originally required the "advice and consent" of the Senate and even though Congress may have forbidden such removal. [*Compare* **Myers v. United States**, 272 U.S. 52 (1926)—Congress may *not* forbid removal of a postmaster; *with* **Morrison v. Olson**, *supra*—Congress *may* condition removal of independent prosecutor on "good cause"]

(a) Attempted removal by Congress [§197]

Congress may not vest executive functions (*e.g.*, exercising discretion in interpreting and implementing the legislative mandate) in an officer who is ***removable only*** by Congress (by means other than impeachment). *Rationale:* If Congress could do so, it would give Congress control over execution of the laws and violate the constitutional separation of powers. [**Bowsher v. Synar,** 478 U.S. 714 (1986)—Congress cannot give comptroller general power to establish amount of budget reductions that would be required if Congress failed to make budget reductions, because by law comptroller general may be removed by joint resolution of Congress]

(3) Officers appointed pursuant to act of Congress [§198]

On the other hand, officers of administrative bodies created by acts of Congress—where the act specifies the term of office and causes for removal—may be removed by the President only for causes specified in the statute. [**Humphrey's Executor v. United States,** 295 U.S. 602 (1935)—removal of Federal Trade Commission officer; **Weiner v. United States,** 357 U.S. 349 (1958)—removal of War Claims Commission officer]

c. Pardon power [§199]

Article II, Section 2 grants the President power "to grant reprieves and pardons for offenses ***against the United States***, except in cases of impeachment."

(1) Scope of power [§200]

The President's power to pardon is not subject to control by Congress. It includes the power to ***commute a sentence*** on conditions not authorized in the statute (as long as the conditions do not offend some other provision in the Constitution). [**Schick v. Reed,** 419 U.S. 256 (1974)]

(2) Contempt [§201]

A *criminal* contempt is deemed an "offense against the United States," and thus can be pardoned by the President. [***Ex parte* Grossman,** 267 U.S. 87 (1925)]

d. "Legislative" power of President [§202]

Article I, Section 1 vests all legislative powers in the Congress. The President thus has ***no*** general power to enact legislation. In respect to certain matters, however, the President does have limited legislative powers.

(1) By delegation [§203]

Congress may, of course, delegate legislative power to the President and other executive agencies, subject to the limits of the separation of powers doctrine (*see supra*, §§144-148). [*See* **National Cable Television Association v. United States,** 415 U.S. 336 (1974)]

(a) Exceeding statutory delegation [§204]

If the President claims a general power to legislate (*i.e.*, to engage in general lawmaking without a congressional delegation of such authority), then the President acts unconstitutionally. But if the Court finds that the President simply has exceeded the statutory authority granted by Congress, this does not ordinarily violate the Constitution. Thus, the President's decision to close a certain shipyard under the Defense Base Closure and Realignment Act of 1990 was not reviewable on constitutional grounds merely because it may have been based on a recommendation using criteria improper under the Closure Act. [**Dalton v. Specter,** 511 U.S. 462 (1994)]

(2) Veto power [§205]

Article I, Section 7 specifies that every act of Congress shall be approved by the President before it can take effect, or being disapproved, must be repassed by a two-thirds vote of each House.

(a) Congressional veto [§206]

The President's veto power applies to all legislative action unless explicitly excepted by the Constitution (*e.g.*, Senate ratification of treaties). Thus, acts of Congress that authorize one or both Houses (or a congressional committee) to change decisions or rules delegated by Congress to executive departments or administrative agencies are invalid—such changes are "legislative actions" and must therefore be presented to the President and subject to his veto. [**Immigration & Naturalization Service v. Chadha,** 462 U.S. 919 (1983)]

> **e.g.** **Example:** Congress granted the Immigration & Naturalization Service ("INS") the power to deport or suspend from deportation illegal aliens, but the law required INS decisions to be submitted to Congress and allowed either House to override the INS decision by resolution. This is an unconstitutional legislative veto. [**Immigration & Naturalization Service v. Chadha,** *supra*]

(b) No line item veto [§207]

The veto power allows the President only to approve or reject a bill in toto; he cannot cancel part (through a line item veto) and approve other parts. *Rationale:* The President's veto power does not authorize him to amend or repeal laws passed by Congress. [**Clinton v. City of New York,** 524 U.S. 417 (1998)]

(3) Military powers [§208]

Although the President has **no power** to declare war (*see supra*, §163), Article II, Section 2 makes the President Commander-in-Chief of the military. This affords the President extensive legislative power in "theaters of war," *e.g.*, to establish military governments in occupied territories. Such actions generally are not subject to judicial review.

(a) Commitment of armed forces [§209]

In the event of insurrection or invasion, the President may deploy military forces against any enemy, foreign or domestic, without waiting for a congressional declaration of war. [**Prize Cases,** 67 U.S. (2 Black) 635 (1863)—upholding seizure of vessels and cargoes belonging to foreign neutrals and residents of southern states pursuant to presidential directive blockading southern ports during Civil War]

(4) Inherent "emergency" power [§210]

Even without congressional authorization, the President *probably* has some "inherent" power to act in cases of great national emergency. It has been suggested that this derives from the aggregate of the President's constitutional powers and the need created by emergencies. [**Youngstown Sheet & Tube Co. v. Sawyer,** 343 U.S. 579 (1952)]

(a) Limitation—congressional denial of authority [§211]

In the *Youngstown* case, President Truman's executive order seizing the steel mills to keep them operating during the Korean War was held to be a *legislative* act and thus beyond his power. Whether he had "inherent emergency power" in this situation was not at issue because some Justices read congressional statutes as *denying* the President the power of seizure.

e. Impoundment [§212]

The President has *no power* to refuse to spend appropriated funds when Congress has *expressly mandated* that they be spent. [**Kendall v. United States ex rel. Stokes,** 37 U.S. (12 Pet.) 524 (1838)] The Court has avoided deciding other issues concerning the extent, if any, to which the President has "inherent" power to impound funds authorized by Congress. [**Train v. New York,** 420 U.S. 35 (1970)—interpreting federal statute as mandating expenditure]

f. Executing laws [§213]

Presidential action may also be upheld as an exercise of the President's power to execute the laws—on the theory that it is not unilateral action on the President's part, but action *implicitly authorized* by Congress. (Here, the Court simply engages in statutory interpretation.)

3. Executive Privilege [§214]

Although not expressly mentioned in the Constitution, a privilege is recognized to protect against the disclosure of presidential communications made in the exercise of executive power. This privilege derives from the doctrine of separation of powers. [**United States v. Nixon,** 418 U.S. 683 (1974)]

a. Scope [§215]

Where the presidential communications relate to military, diplomatic, or sensitive national security secrets, the claim of privilege is given the utmost deference by the courts. However, other presidential communications are only *presumptively* privileged. [**United States v. Nixon,** *supra*]

(1) Use in criminal trial [§216]

Thus, although a generalized claim of presidential privilege is accorded considerable respect, it must yield to a demonstrated specific need for essential evidence in a criminal trial. [**United States v. Nixon,** *supra*] In such cases, the trial court must make an *in camera* inspection of the communications, and "scrupulously protect" against disclosure of materials not found to be relevant and admissible in the criminal case. [**United States v. Nixon,** *supra*]

(2) Governmental and historical purposes [§217]

Similarly, the need to preserve presidential material for legitimate governmental and historical purposes has been held to justify legislation requiring that such materials be reviewed and classified by federal archivists—as long as the statute provides safeguards to insure minimal intrusion into executive confidentiality. [**Nixon v. Administrator of General Services,** 433 U.S. 425 (1977)]

(3) Other uses [§218]

It is an open question whether the same considerations would require disclosure of presidential communications in a civil trial, or in response to congressional demands for information.

b. Civil damages [§219]

At least absent an expressly created congressional cause of action against him, our "constitutional heritage and structure" affords the President an *absolute immunity* from private suits for damages based on any acts within the "outer perimeter" of his constitutional authority. [**Nixon v. Fitzgerald,** 457 U.S. 731 (1982)]

(1) Distinguish—aides [§220]

This blanket immunity does *not* extend to cabinet officers or other presidential aides. They *may* be entitled to *absolute* immunity in respect to discretionary authority in such sensitive areas as foreign policy, but ordinarily, they have only a *qualified* immunity—being shielded from civil damages if their conduct does not violate clearly established statutory or constitutional rights of which a reasonable person would have known. [**Harlow v. Fitzgerald,** 457 U.S. 800 (1982); **Mitchell v. Forsyth,** 472 U.S. 511 (1985)]

(2) Unofficial acts [§221]

The President has *no* immunity from private suits for damages in *federal* court based on unofficial acts. The immunity for "official" conduct—in contrast to personal, private acts—is to enable the President to perform his designated functions without fear of personal liability. [**Clinton v. Jones,** 520 U.S. 681 (1997)]

(a) **Stay of proceedings [§222]**

The separation of powers doctrine does not require federal courts to stay *all* private actions against the President until he leaves office. However, pursuant to the broad discretion of a federal judge to schedule the timing of proceedings, the judge may weigh the potential burdens imposed on the President by the particular litigation. [**Clinton v. Jones**, *supra*]

D. Power Over Foreign Affairs

1. Constitutional Provisions [§223]

Article I, Section 8 grants *Congress* the power to regulate commerce with foreign nations (*see infra*, §226), to declare war, to raise and support armies, and to provide and maintain a navy. Article II, Sections 2 and 3 provide that the *President* shall be Commander in Chief of the Army and Navy, that he has certain powers in regard to treaty-making (*see* below), that he shall receive foreign ambassadors and ministers, and that he shall nominate and appoint U.S. ambassadors and other public ministers, subject to Senate confirmation.

2. Comparison with Domestic Powers [§224]

The powers of the federal government concerning foreign or external affairs are different in origin and nature from those involving domestic or internal affairs. [**United States v. Curtiss-Wright Export Corp.**, *supra*, §143]

a. Domestic affairs—federal power shared with states [§225]

In regard to internal affairs, the power of the federal government was carved from the general legislative powers originally possessed by the states. Thus, the federal government has only those powers *specifically granted* to it by the Constitution and those *"necessary and proper"* to exercising those enumerated powers (*see supra*, §§137-139).

b. Foreign affairs—exclusive federal power [§226]

However, powers over foreign affairs—such as the power to declare war, conclude peace, make treaties, and maintain diplomatic relations with other nations—were never possessed by the individual states, but passed directly to the federal government from the sovereign nation of Great Britain. Thus, these powers are held *exclusively* by the federal government. [**United States v. Curtiss-Wright Export Corp.**, *supra*]

(1) State regulation [§227]

Because the federal power over foreign affairs is exclusive, no state regulation is permitted to intrude into the area. [**Zschernig v. Miller**, 389 U.S. 429 (1968)—invalidating state law that sought to prevent aliens from inheriting local property, where their country confiscated property therein inherited by United States citizens]

> **e.g.** **Example:** California adopted a statute to assist Holocaust survivors that required all insurance companies doing business in California to disclose data about their sale of policies in Europe between 1920 and 1945. The Supreme Court invalidated the statute because it conflicts both with executive agreements (*see infra*, §238) that reflect presidential foreign policy to accomplish the same goals and diplomatic objectives stated by high-level Executive Branch officials. [**American Insurance Association v. Garamendi,** 123 S. Ct. 2374 (2003)]

c. **Greater delegation permitted regarding external affairs [§228]**

Congress may delegate greater powers in respect to foreign affairs to the President—who represents the nation in that realm—than would be permissible in regard to internal affairs. [**United States v. Curtiss-Wright Export Corp.,** *supra*]

3. **Treaty Power [§229]**

As indicated above, the President is empowered to make treaties with foreign nations "with the advice and consent of [two-thirds of] the Senate."

a. **Status of treaties [§230]**

Under the Supremacy Clause (Article VI, Section 2), treaties confirmed by the Senate are *"the supreme law of the land."*

(1) **Effect on state laws [§231]**

Thus, any state statute or constitutional provision that conflicts with a treaty provision is *invalid*. [**Hauenstein v. Lynham,** 100 U.S. 483 (1880)—treaty providing inheritance rights for aliens prevailed over state law disqualifying aliens from inheriting]

(2) **Conflict with act of Congress [§232]**

Where there is conflict between a treaty and an act of Congress, they are of equal weight; thus, the *last expression* of the sovereign will control. [**Chae Chan Ping v. United States,** 130 U.S. 581 (1889)]

(a) **Effect**

Congress can by subsequent statute alter or repeal United States treaty rights and obligations. [**Head Money Cases,** 112 U.S. 580 (1884)]

(b) **But note**

Although an act of Congress repealing a treaty would preclude enforcement of any rights under the treaty in the courts, the nation might still remain accountable to the other parties to the treaty under the "law of nations." [*See* **Clark v. Allen,** 331 U.S. 503 (1947)]

b. **Types of treaties [§233]**

A treaty may be *"self-executing"*; *i.e.*, rights and liabilities are created under the treaty without the necessity of further action by Congress. Or a treaty may expressly or impliedly require that Congress pass *effectuating legislation* to create rights and liabilities thereunder.

c. **Independent source of power [§234]**

Because the Supremacy Clause places treaties on an equal footing with the Constitution and acts of Congress, the treaty power is an *independent* source of federal power, and Congress may legislate pursuant to a treaty under the Necessary and Proper Clause. The treaty power thereby permits federal action over subjects outside the other enumerated federal powers in the Constitution. (The Tenth Amendment reserves to the states only nondelegated powers, and the treaty power is a delegated power.)

(1) **Limitations on treaty power [§235]**

In **Missouri v. Holland,** *supra,* §72, the Court noted that while an act of Congress must be made "in pursuance of the Constitution," a treaty need only be made "under the authority of the United States." This *suggests* that the *only* limitations on the federal treaty power and congressional legislation pursuant to a treaty are the formal requirements of presidential proposal and Senate ratification.

(a) **Individual rights [§236]**

But the Court has made clear that treaties may not contravene constitutional prohibitions (*e.g.*, the Bill of Rights) that protect individual rights. [**Reid v. Covert,** 454 U.S. 1 (1957)]

EXAM TIP   **gilbert**

If a question involves a treaty, be sure to remember that treaties are *subject to constitutional limitations* on the government's power to interfere with individual rights. Thus, no treaty may confer on Congress authority to take property without due process of law, deny freedom of speech or religion, etc.

(b) **"Proper subject of negotiation" [§237]**

The Court has also *suggested* a further limitation: that the treaty must concern a "proper subject of negotiation between our government and the governments of other nations." [**Geofroy v. Riggs,** 133 U.S. 258 (1890)] It seems clear that treaties dealing with matters such as control of wildlife that moves between our country and another [**Missouri v. Holland,** *supra*] concern "proper subjects of negotiation." And the Court has stated that the cession of a portion of a state without its consent is *not* a "proper subject of negotiation" with a foreign power. [**Geofroy v. Riggs,** *supra*] However, it is unclear what scope of review the Court would give to a determination by the political branches that a treaty involved a "proper subject of negotiation."

4. **Executive Agreements [§238]**

The President has power to enter into agreements or compacts with other countries. This authority is independent of the treaty power and thus may be exercised without the consent of the Senate.

a. **Scope of power uncertain [§239]**

The full scope of the President's power to bypass the Senate, by entering into executive agreements that cover the same subjects as treaties, is uncertain. However, the Court has recognized certain bases of the President's authority to do so:

(1) **Executive power over foreign affairs [§240]**

The constitutional powers granted to the President in Article II include the power to make executive agreements. [**United States v. Belmont,** 301 U.S. 324 (1937)—President's power of "diplomatic recognition" supports executive agreement with Soviet Union concerning its claims against Americans]

(2) **Implied power from Congress [§241]**

The President, with the implicit approval of Congress, has power to settle claims of United States citizens against foreign governments through an executive agreement. [**Dames & Moore v. Regan,** 453 U.S. 654 (1981)]

Example: In 1979 Americans were seized and held hostage at the American Embassy in Tehran, Iran. In response, Congress adopted the International Emergency Economic Powers Act ("IEEPA"), which gave the President broad power to deal with the crisis. Pursuant to the Act, President Carter declared a national state of emergency and issued an executive order blocking the removal or transfer of all Iranian property over which the United States had jurisdiction. The Treasury Department issued regulations pursuant to the order, that provided, among other things, that the property interests affected by the order included judicial liens, attachments, and the like. In 1981, the hostages were released pursuant to an executive agreement. The agreement provided, in part, that the United States would terminate all legal proceedings in United States courts involving United States nationals against Iran and would nullify all attachments and judgments obtained from such suits (claims were to be brought before an international arbitration committee instead). The President issued an executive order implementing the agreement, and Dames & Moore, which obtained judgments against Iranian interests, filed suit against the United States claiming that the executive agreement was unconstitutional. The Supreme Court upheld the agreement. Although the IEEPA did not specifically authorize the President's action, the President was acting within the power implicitly granted by the IEEPA, as evidenced by a long history of Congress acquiescing to similar presidential conduct (*e.g.,* a 1949 Act allowed the President to settle claims with Yugoslavia). [**Dames & Moore v. Regan,** *supra*]

---

b. **Status [§242]**

Executive agreements have a status and dignity "similar" to treaties in that they prevail over any *state law* inconsistent with the agreements. [**United States v. Pink,** 315 U.S. 203 (1942)] However, it is unclear whether, like treaties, they also prevail over inconsistent acts of Congress.

United States Constitution

prevails over

Treaties and Federal Statutes
(if a conflict between these
two, last in time prevails)

prevail over

Executive Agreements

prevail over

State Law

Chapter Two:
The Federal System—
Intergovernmental
Relations

CONTENTS

Chapter Approach

Chapter Approach

This chapter concerns the interrelationship of state and federal powers in our federal system of government. While this topic is not usually a major source of exam questions, you may see a question raising one or more of the following issues:

1. **Nature of Federal and State Powers**

   Although the Tenth Amendment states that all powers not delegated by the Constitution to the federal government are reserved to the states, today federal powers are given an expansive interpretation. Thus, if an examination question involves state legislation, to determine whether the legislation is valid you must examine whether the area regulated is *exclusively federal*. A power may be made exclusively federal by explicit *constitutional limitations* on state power (*e.g.*, states are prohibited from coining money), by the *nature* of the power (*e.g.*, only the federal government can borrow money on the credit of the United States), or by *explicit language* in the Constitution making the power exclusively federal (*e.g.*, legislation over the District of Columbia). Also note that even where the states have *concurrent power* to regulate, because of the *Supremacy Clause* a state may not enact legislation that interferes with federal legislation.

2. **Intergovernmental Privileges and Immunities**

   Under the Fourteenth Amendment Privileges and Immunities Clause, states are prohibited from making or enforcing laws that abridge the privileges or immunities of citizens of the United States. These "privileges and immunities" are rights that arise out of the *relationship of the individual and the national government* (*e.g.*, the right to petition Congress for redress). Perhaps more importantly, for exam purposes, the Interstate Privileges and Immunities Clause of Article IV, Section 2 prohibits states from *discriminating against noncitizens or nonresidents* in respect to *essential activities* (*e.g.*, pursuing a livelihood) or *basic rights* (*e.g.*, obtaining an abortion), unless the discrimination is closely or substantially related to a substantial state purpose.

3. **Intergovernmental Immunity**

   If an examination question involves *federal regulation or taxation of state governments,* be sure to note that the Tenth Amendment limits the federal government's power to interfere with state and local functions, but here again, the Tenth Amendment is a fairly weak argument; the Court generally will not hold an otherwise permissible exercise of congressional power invalid just because it regulates or taxes the states as well as private persons. If a question involves *state taxation of the federal government* or state regulation of federal property or activities, be aware that Congress may permit such taxation or regulation; otherwise, it is forbidden. However, be sure to distinguish between a tax on persons dealing with the federal government and a tax on the government itself. A tax on those who deal with the government is permissible as long as the legal incidence of the tax does *not fall on the United States.*

A. Nature and Scope of Federal and State Powers

1. In General [§243]

The powers of government under the federal system may be classified as follows: (i) those given *exclusively to the federal* government, (ii) those *exclusively reserved to the states,* and (iii) those that can be *exercised concurrently* by both the federal and state governments. Difficult questions arise in determining whether a particular federal power is "exclusive" or "concurrent."

2. Exclusive vs. Concurrent Powers

a. Exclusive state powers [§244]

The Tenth Amendment reserves to the states all powers not delegated by the Constitution to the federal government. However, federal powers are now given an expansive interpretation.

b. Exclusive federal powers [§245]

A particular federal power may be considered "exclusive" based on: (i) a *constitutional limitation on state power* in the area, (ii) the *nature of the power* itself, or (iii) the *words granting the power.*

(1) State action prohibited [§246]

Certain federal powers are "exclusive" by virtue of express provisions in the Constitution prohibiting any state action.

> **Example:** Article I, Section 10 expressly prohibits various state actions: "No State shall enter into any treaty . . . coin money . . . lay any Imposts or Duties on Imports or Exports . . . lay any duty on Tonnage, keep Troops or Ships of War in time of Peace . . . ."

(2) Nature of power [§247]

Other federal powers are held to be "exclusive" because the nature of the power itself is such that it can be exercised only by the federal government, and any exercise of power by the state government would be inconsistent with the federal power.

> **Example:** The federal government has the power "[t]o borrow Money on the credit of the United States." [Art. I, §8, cl. 2] While there is no express prohibition in the Constitution on state power to do likewise, such action would obviously be inconsistent with the powers of the national government, and thus federal power in this area is held to be "exclusive." Similar reasoning applies to federal powers concerning naturalization and citizenship, to declare war, provide for national defense, etc.

(3) Exclusive grant of power [§248]

Finally, a few federal powers are considered "exclusive" because the Constitution grants the power in such terms. For example, Congress has the power "[t]o exercise exclusive Legislation in all Cases whatsoever, over the District of Columbia." [Art. I, §8, cl. 17]

c. Concurrent federal and state power—effect of Supremacy Clause [§249]

Article VI, Section 2 (the "Supremacy Clause") provides: "The Constitution and the Laws of the United States which shall be made in pursuance thereof . . . shall be the supreme Law of the Land . . . ." The effect of this clause is that to whatever extent Congress has exercised its powers, any "inconsistent" state laws are prohibited.

(1) "Inconsistency" of state law [§250]

A state law will be held void under the Supremacy Clause if it would retard, impede, burden, or otherwise stand as an obstacle to the accomplishment and execution of the full purposes and objectives of Congress in enacting the federal law. [**McCulloch v. Maryland,** *supra,* §140—state law that sought to impose tax on Bank of United States, created by Congress, held void as burden on federal power to regulate currency under Art. I, §8, cl. 5]

(a) Note

This is true even where the state law was enacted for some *valid purpose—i.e.,* where it was not intended to frustrate federal law. [**Perez v. Campbell,** 402 U.S. 637 (1971)]

Example: A state law provided for suspension of the driver's license of any person who failed to pay off a judgment against him arising out of an auto accident, regardless of that person's discharge in bankruptcy. The state law had a valid purpose (keeping irresponsible drivers off the roads), but impeded the purpose of the Federal Bankruptcy Act (giving discharged debtors a new start) by forcing persons to pay off discharged judgments if they wanted to drive a car. [**Perez v. Campbell,** *supra*]

(2) Where Congress has not yet acted [§251]

Normally, the Supremacy Clause applies only where Congress has exercised its power; until then, the states are free to regulate subject matter that is clearly within the federal power. [**Sturges v. Crowninshield,** 17 U.S. (4 Wheat.) 122 (1819)—upholding state bankruptcy laws, because no federal bankruptcy law had yet been enacted]

(a) But note

As to certain federal powers (*e.g.,* the commerce power), the mere existence of the federal power is held to inhibit state power to some degree (*see infra*, §§314-315).

d. Absence of federal and state power—Qualifications Clauses [§252]

The provisions of Article I, Section 2, Clause 2 and Article I, Section 3, Clause 3—enumerating the age, citizenship, and residence requirements for members of Congress—are exclusive. Neither Congress nor the states may alter or add to these qualifications, because this would be contrary to the Framers' intent of a uniform national legislature elected by the people voting for whom they wish. [**United States Term Limits, Inc. v. Thornton**, 514 U.S. 779 (1995)]

(e.g.) **Example:** The Arkansas Constitution was amended to prohibit the name of an otherwise eligible candidate for Congress from appearing on the general election ballot if the candidate has already served three terms in the United States House of Representatives or two terms in the United States Senate. An Arkansas citizen sued for declaratory relief claiming the amendment was unconstitutional and void. The Supreme Court agreed. The sole purpose of the amendment is to impose an additional qualification for office, which violates the Qualifications Clauses. [**United States Term Limits, Inc. v. Thornton**, *supra; and see* **Cook v. Gralike**, 531 U.S. 510 (2001)—state law instructing each member of its congressional delegation to support a constitutional amendment for term limits, and providing that failure to do so be noted on the ballot, was held to violate the Qualifications Clauses because it imposes a substantive qualification rather than regulating the "manner" in which elections are held]

B. Intergovernmental Privileges and Immunities

1. National Citizenship [§253]

The Fourteenth Amendment provides in part: "No State shall make or enforce any law which shall abridge the *privileges or immunities of citizens* of the United States."

a. What constitutes "privileges and immunities" of national citizenship [§254]

These privileges and immunities have been limited to those rights that *arise out of the relationship of the individual and the national government.* [**Twining v. New Jersey**, 211 U.S. 78 (1908)]

(e.g.) **Examples:** Among the rights and privileges of national citizenship that may not be infringed by state action are the right to pass freely from state to state; the right to petition Congress for redress of grievances; the right to vote for national officers; the right to assemble peaceably; and the right to discuss matters growing out of valid national legislation and to communicate with respect to them. [**Twining v. New Jersey,** *supra*] Note that the right to travel freely from state to state has also been grounded on other sections of the Constitution; *see* below.

Example: California had relatively generous welfare benefits when compared to other states. To discourage out-of-state welfare recipients from moving to California in order to receive better welfare benefits, California adopted a statute providing that California citizens who lived within the state for less than one year could receive welfare benefits only in an amount equal to the benefits that they would have received in their prior state of residence. The Supreme Court found that the right to travel protected under the Fourteenth Amendment includes the right of new citizens to be treated the same as other state citizens. Therefore, the Court held that the statute here violates the Fourteenth Amendment Privileges and Immunities Clause. [**Saenz v. Roe,** 526 U.S. 489 (1999)]

---

b. Bill of Rights not included [§255]

In the **Slaughterhouse Cases,** 83 U.S. (16 Wall.) 36 (1873), the Court held that the fundamental rights protected against federal action by the first eight amendments to the Constitution were *not* "privileges and immunities of national citizenship" so as to be protected from state action under the Fourteenth Amendment Privileges and Immunities Clause.

(1) Effect

The decision rendered the Fourteenth Amendment Privileges and Immunities Clause largely a dead letter in protecting individual rights from state abridgment. Subsequently, the Court has relied on the Fourteenth Amendment Due Process and Equal Protection Clauses to provide basic protection of individual rights against state action. (*See infra,* §§427 *et seq.; and see* §§1010 *et seq.*)

(2) Right to travel "exception"

As noted above, a recent case holds that the Fourteenth Amendment Privileges and Immunities Clause protects an aspect of the "right to travel from one state to another," a right that already has long been protected under both the Due Process Clause (*see infra,* §§527-529) and the Equal Protection Clause (*see infra,* §§1129 *et seq.*). [**Saenz v. Roe,** *supra*]

c. Distinguish—Enabling Clause [§256]

While the Privileges and Immunities Clause of the Fourteenth Amendment has not in itself proved to be a significant limitation on state power, the same amendment contains an *Enabling Clause* (section 5), which authorizes *Congress* "to enforce, by appropriate legislation, the provisions of this article." As discussed below, this Enabling Clause is an important *source of federal power—i.e.,* to protect the "privileges and immunities" of the citizenry from violation by the states, or even from the acts of other citizens (*see infra,* §§1239 *et seq.*).

2. **State Citizenship [§257]**

Article IV, Section 2 (interstate privileges and immunities) provides: "The Citizens of each State shall be entitled to all Privileges and Immunities of Citizens in the several States."

a. **General rule [§258]**

This clause prohibits state discrimination against noncitizens (or nonresidents) of the state in respect to "essential activities" or "basic rights" (such as access to courts), unless the discrimination is *closely* or *substantially related* to a *substantial* state purpose. [**Hicklin v. Orbeck,** 437 U.S. 518 (1978)] In deciding whether the discrimination is closely related to a state purpose, the Court will consider whether the state could have avoided some of the discrimination by using *less restrictive means* than the means employed by the state to achieve its purpose. [**Supreme Court of New Hampshire v. Piper,** 470 U.S. 274 (1985)]

(1) **Municipal residency [§259]**

State action that discriminates against noncitizens (or nonresidents) of a particular municipality within the state is subject to the strictures of this clause. [**United Building & Construction Trades Council v. Mayor & Council of Camden,** 465 U.S. 208 (1984)]

> **e.g.** **Example:** The Court held that a city ordinance requiring that 40% of the employees of contractors and subcontractors working on city construction projects be city residents was an apparent violation of the Article IV Privileges and Immunities Clause. *Rationale:* The requirement gave a preference in private employment to city residents. However, the Court did not make a final determination on the issue because the Court could not determine whether the preference was justified—the record from the lower courts did not address whether the preference was necessary to counteract grave economic and social ills in urban environments caused by spiraling employment and declines in the population base of such cities. [**United Building & Construction Trades Council v. Mayor of Camden,** *supra*]

(2) **Corporations and aliens [§260]**

Corporations and aliens are not "citizens of a state" within the meaning of Article IV's Privileges and Immunities Clause and thus are *not* entitled to its protection. [**Bank of Augusta v. Earle,** 38 U.S. 519 (1839)]

b. **Illustrations—invalid discrimination [§261]**

The following have been held invalid by the Court.

(1) *A statute requiring a $2,500 license fee from nonresident* commercial fishermen seeking shrimp offshore, while residents paid $25; this statute burdened the essential activity of "pursuing a livelihood" without a substantial justification related to state costs or enforcement. [**Toomer v. Witsell,** 334 U.S. 385 (1948)]

(2) *A statute giving resident creditors priority* over nonresident creditors to assets of foreign corporations in receivership proceedings was found to unconstitutionally infringe on nonresident creditors' rights of "ownership and disposition of property." [**Blake v. McClung,** 172 U.S. 239 (1898)]

(3) *A statute imposing a residency requirement for abortions* imposed unconstitutional discrimination against nonresidents by interfering with the basic right to seek medical care. [**Doe v. Bolton,** 410 U.S. 179 (1973)]

(4) *A state law requiring employers to give hiring preferences* to residents was held unconstitutional because it involved the essential activity of "pursuing a livelihood" and the law was not closely related to solving peculiar state unemployment problems. [**Hicklin v. Orbeck,** *supra*]

(5) *A rule limiting bar admission* to state residents was held unconstitutional because it involved the basic right to pursue an occupation. [**Supreme Court of Virginia v. Friedman,** 487 U.S. 59 (1988); **Supreme Court of New Hampshire v. Piper,** *supra*, §258]

c. **Illustration—discrimination upheld [§262]**

A statute requiring nonresidents to pay a $225 license fee (as opposed to $30 resident fee) for *recreational* hunting was upheld. [**Baldwin v. Fish & Game Commission,** 436 U.S. 371 (1978)—no "essential activity" or "basic right" was involved]

(1) **State ownership [§263]**

The Court has *stated* that a discrimination against nonresidents will be given special—but not conclusive—weight if its purpose is conservation of *state-owned* natural resources. [**Hicklin v. Orbeck,** *supra; and see* **Sporhase v. Nebraska,** 458 U.S. 941 (1982)—scarce water resources]

ARTICLE IV PRIVILEGES AND IMMUNITIES CLAUSE—EXAMPLES   gilbert

INVALID DISCRIMINATION

1. Statute requiring $2,500 license fee from nonresident *commercial fishermen*, while residents paid $25.

2. Statute giving resident *creditors priority* over nonresident creditors to assets of foreign corporations in receivership proceedings.

3. Statute imposing a *residency requirement for abortion*.

4. Statute requiring *private sector* employers to give hiring preference to residents.

5. Rule *limiting bar admission* to state residents.

DISCRIMINATION UPHELD

Statute requiring nonresidents to pay $225 license fee, as opposed to $30 residents' fee, for *recreational* hunting.

d. Relationship to Commerce Clause [§264]

Although the Interstate Privileges and Immunities Clause and the Commerce Clause may apply different standards and may produce different results (*see infra*, §325), they do tend to "mutually reinforce" each other. [**Hicklin v. Orbeck**, *supra*] Consequently, issues arising under Article IV, Section 2 may be decided on the basis of the Commerce Clause limitation on state regulation of interstate commerce. (*See infra*, §§284 *et seq.*)

C. Intergovernmental Immunity

1. In General [§265]

The Supremacy Clause places certain implied limitations on state power to regulate and tax the property and activities of the federal government, and the Tenth Amendment places such limitations on federal power to regulate and tax the property and activities of state governments.

a. Intergovernmental differences [§266]

Under modern doctrine, federal property and activities enjoy a greater immunity from state regulation and taxation than the states are afforded from federal regulation and taxation. *Rationale:* The states are represented in Congress and have political voices in Congress—but the federal government has no similar political representation in state government. Thus, the Court infers a greater immunity for the federal government.

2. Federal Regulation of State Governments [§267]

The Tenth Amendment preserves "a significant measure of sovereign authority" for the states and limits the federal government's regulatory power to interfere with state and local functions. However the Court has held that ordinarily these state interests are more properly protected by the inherent restraints of state participation that are built into the structure of the federal system (*e.g.*, state representation in Congress) than by judicial review. Thus—at least absent a showing of "some extraordinary defects" in the procedural safeguards for the states in the national political process—the *Court* will *not* find that an otherwise permissible exercise of congressional power violates the Tenth Amendment merely because it *regulates the states as well as private persons.* [**Garcia v. San Antonio Metropolitan Transit Authority**, 469 U.S. 528 (1985)—*overruling* **National League of Cities v. Usery**, 426 U.S. 833 (1976) In other words, *a general regulation* that happens to *affect the states as well as others* who engage in a certain activity *does not violate the Tenth Amendment*.

Example: In 1974, Congress extended the minimum wage and overtime provisions of the Fair Labor Standards Act ("FLSA") to most state employees. In 1976, the Supreme Court struck down the amendments as they applied to municipal employees, fearing that the amendments would impair state integrity and interfere with the ability of states to carry out government functions (*e.g.*, they might not be

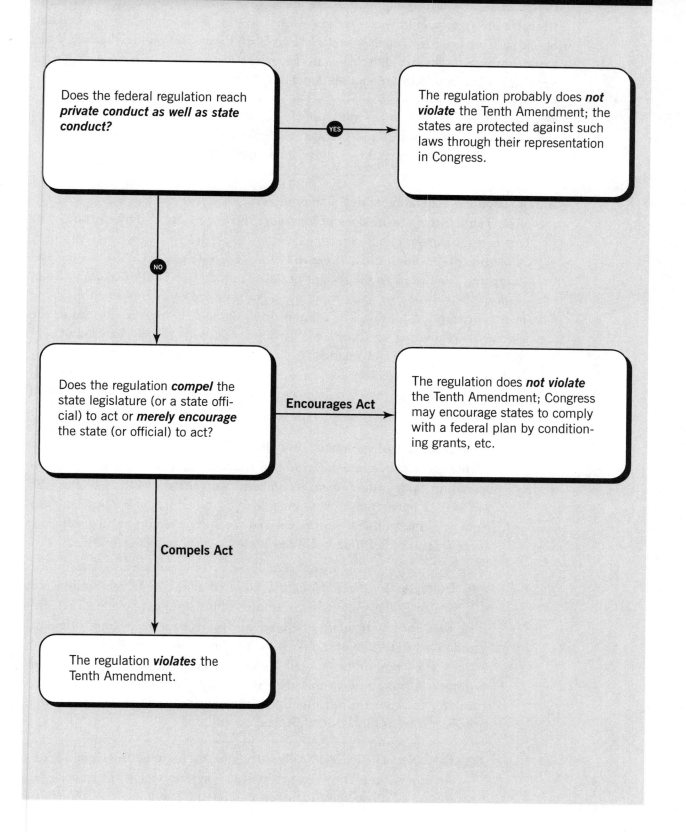

Does the federal regulation reach *private conduct as well as state conduct?*

YES →

The regulation probably does *not violate* the Tenth Amendment; the states are protected against such laws through their representation in Congress.

NO ↓

Does the regulation *compel* the state legislature (or a state official) to act or *merely encourage* the state (or official) to act?

Encourages Act →

The regulation does *not violate* the Tenth Amendment; Congress may encourage states to comply with a federal plan by conditioning grants, etc.

Compels Act ↓

The regulation *violates* the Tenth Amendment.

able to afford to pay for police and firefighters if they have to follow the FLSA). [**National League of Cities v. Usery,** *supra*] Subsequently, the San Antonio Metropolitan Transit Authority, a state mass-transit company, informed its employees that after *National League of Cities*, the FLSA no longer applied to them. Garcia, a transit employee, brought suit seeking overtime pay. When the case reached the Supreme Court, it overruled *National League of Cities*, upholding the FLSA because nothing in the act destroys state sovereignty or violates any constitutional provision. [**Garcia v. San Antonio Metropolitan Transit Authority,** *supra*]

Example: The Supreme Court upheld the federal Driver's Privacy Protection Act, which bars states and private resellers from disclosing personal information required for obtaining a driver's license. [**Reno v. Condon,** 528 U.S. 41 (2000)]

a.   **Exception—regulating states alone [§268]**
The Tenth Amendment *does place limits*, however, on Congress's power to regulate the *states alone* by directing the states to act in a particular way. Although Congress may hold out *incentives* to influence a state's policy choices—*e.g.,* by attaching conditions to the receipt of federal funds [*see* **South Dakota v. Dole,** *supra,* §160—Congress may condition a grant for highway construction on the recipient state's adopting a minimum drinking age], or by offering states the choice of regulating in accord with federal standards rather than being preempted by federal law, Congress may not compel states to *enact* or *enforce* a federal regulatory program. *Rationale:* Federal direction of state regulation will insulate the federal government from political accountability. [**New York v. United States,** 505 U.S. 144 (1992)]

(1)   **Legislative/executive/judicial branches [§269]**
Although historical practice and constitutional structure permit Congress to require state *judges* to enforce federal law [**Testa v. Katt,** 330 U.S. 386 (1947)], Congress may not commandeer the states' *legislative* process [**New York v. United States,** *supra*] nor require state *executive* officials to enforce federal law [**Printz v. United States,** 521 U.S. 898 (1997)].

Example: In 1985, Congress adopted the Low-Level Radioactive Waste Policy Act, which, among other things, provided that any state that did not regulate low level nuclear wastes according to federal standards by 1996, must take title to the waste generated within the state and become liable for all damages incurred by the state's failure promptly to take title to the property. *Held:* The Act compels states to regulate, thus unconstitutionally commandeering the states' legislative process. [**New York v. United States,** *supra*]

Example: The federal Brady Handgun Act required the United States Attorney General to create a national system to instantly check the background of prospective handgun purchasers. Pending establishment of the national system, the Act required the chief law enforcement officer of each local jurisdiction to collect from gun dealers reports regarding prospective handgun purchasers and to conduct background checks on them. *Held:* The Act's commandeering of state executive officials is unconstitutional. The structure of the Constitution gives Congress the power to regulate individuals but not states. Congress cannot get around the prohibition against regulating states by conscripting the states' officers directly. [**Printz v. United States,** *supra*]

3. Federal Taxation of State Governments [§270]

Although the Court has not specifically so held, the same general rule seemingly applies to federal taxation of the property and activities of state and local governments—the Court will not find that an otherwise permissible exercise of Congress's taxing power violates the Tenth Amendment merely because it taxes states as well as private persons. [*See* **New York v. United States,** 326 U.S. 572 (1946)—sale of mineral waters by state is subject to a general federal excise tax; *and see* **South Carolina v. Baker,** 485 U.S. 505 (1988)—state bond interest may be subject to nondiscriminatory federal tax]

4. State Taxation of Federal Government

a. When Congress has spoken [§271]

Pursuant to its delegated powers (and the Necessary and Proper Clause), Congress has complete power to regulate state taxation of federal property and activities. Congress may permit (or consent to) state taxes that, absent federal legislation, would be impliedly forbidden by the Constitution. Or, Congress may immunize federal activities as to which, absent such legislation, state taxes would not be forbidden.

b. When Congress has not spoken [§272]

Absent federal legislation, the Court assumes that Congress intended all implied constitutional limitations on state taxation to apply. Thus, in general, the Supremacy Clause impliedly forbids (i) state taxes that *discriminate* against federal property or activities, and (ii) nondiscriminatory state taxes that *"unduly interfere"* with or place a *"substantial burden"* on the federal government. Pursuant to this general policy, the following rules apply:

(1) No tax on federal property or activity [§273]

States may not tax the property or activities of the federal government itself—or of federal agencies. [**McCulloch v. Maryland,** *supra*, §250]

(2) Tax on those dealing with federal government [§274]

States may tax persons who merely contract or deal with the federal government as long as the tax does not discriminate against such persons by taxing them and not other persons similarly situated. [**United States v. Fresno County,** 429 U.S. 452 (1977)] *Examples:*

(a) State income tax [§275]

The state income tax may be applied to the salaries of federal employees within the state. [**Graves v. New York** *ex rel.* **O'Keefe,** 306 U.S. 466 (1939)—tax did not unduly interfere with federal functions; and although there is economic burden on United States because it will have to pay higher salaries, burden is not substantial]

(b) State sales tax [§276]

The state sales tax may be applied to purchases made by a person who has a "cost-plus" contract (*i.e.,* a contract under which a contractor is paid on the basis of the cost of the materials and labor plus an agreed percentage as profit) with the United States. [**Alabama v. King & Boozer,** 314 U.S. 1 (1941)—tax upheld even though cost is passed on to the United States, and it is thus economically burdened]

1) Legal incidence determinative [§277]

As long as the legal incidence of the tax does not fall on the United States, the fact that it results in an economic burden on a United States function will not invalidate it.

a) Note

If the *United States* itself actually purchases the goods to be used by the "cost-plus" contractor, a state sales tax may not be applied to the purchase—because the legal incidence of the tax would fall on the federal government itself. [**Kern-Limerick, Inc. v. Scurlock,** 347 U.S. 110 (1954)] The rule against taxes on the United States applies even though the economic effect is the same whether the purchase is made by the United States or a "cost-plus" contractor.

b) And note

If state law requires that a sales tax be passed on to the purchaser and collected by the seller, the legal incidence of the tax is on the purchaser. Thus, the tax may not be applied when the United States or its instrumentality is the purchaser. [**United States v. Mississippi Tax Commission,** 421 U.S. 599 (1975)]

(c) State property tax [§278]

Federal property may be used to measure a nondiscriminatory state tax on persons who deal with the United States. [**Detroit v. Murray Corp.,** 355 U.S. 489 (1958)—state property tax measured by value of property upheld as applied to contractor who used property owned by the United States] The Court will consider all relevant circumstances in determining whether the state tax is on United States property (invalid) or on a person dealing with the United States and merely measured by United States property (valid).

> **e.g. Example:** A state tax on all private persons using real property whose owners are tax-exempt is valid as applied to the lessee of federal property. It does not discriminate against those who deal with the United States if it also applies to those who used the property of other tax-exempt owners—*i.e.,* the state and its political subdivisions, churches, charitable organizations, etc. Also, those who use property that is not tax-exempt pay higher rent (because the owner passes on the property tax she pays). [**United States v. Detroit,** 355 U.S. 466 (1958)]

1) Distinguish—tax on United States property [§279]

If the property is subject to a lien for unpaid taxes, the tax may be construed as being one on United States property itself—and thus invalid—even if the state does not seek to hold the United States liable, but attempts to collect from a person who uses or possesses it. [**United States v. Detroit,** *supra*]

(3) Discrimination [§280]

In determining whether a state tax discriminates against those who deal with the federal government, the state's whole tax structure is examined. Thus, a special tax may be imposed on contractors who deal with the federal government as long as the economic burdens that result do not discriminate against the United States. [**Washington v. United States,** 460 U.S. 536 (1983)—special tax valid; general tax on purchasers from contractors was not imposed on federal government because of its immunity]

5. State Regulation of Federal Government [§281]

Congress has complete power to forbid or permit state regulation of federal property or activities. However, absent consent by Congress, the Supremacy Clause impliedly immunizes the instrumentalities and agents of the federal government from state regulations that interfere with the performance of federal functions. [**Hancock v. Train,** 426 U.S. 167 (1976)] State regulation is also invalid if inconsistent with the policy of a federal statute.

> **e.g. Examples:** A post office employee need not obtain a state driver's license to perform his official duty of driving a mail truck. [**Johnson v. Maryland,** 254 U.S. 51 (1920)] And a federal contractor need not obtain a state license to construct facilities at an Air Force base pursuant to government contract. [**Leslie Miller, Inc. v. Arkansas,** 352 U.S. 187 (1956)]

a. Federal lands [§282]

Article IV, Section 3, Clause 2 gives Congress power "to dispose of and make all needful rules and regulations respecting" lands of the United States. Thus, federal enclaves (*e.g.,* federal Indian reservations, military bases, post offices) are subject to state regulation only to the extent that the state, when ceding the land to the federal government, reserved jurisdiction, or to the extent that Congress has enacted legislation granting jurisdiction to the state. [**United States v. Sharpnack,** 355 U.S. 286 (1958)—federal legislation authorizing application of state criminal laws to federal enclaves upheld against challenge of excessive delegation]

Chapter Three: Regulation and Taxation of Commerce

CONTENTS

Chapter Approach

This chapter focuses on the concurrent power of the states and the federal government to regulate and tax interstate commerce and the power of the states to regulate and tax interstate and foreign commerce.

1. **Regulation of Foreign Commerce**

   All you need to know here is that *only the federal government* can regulate foreign commerce.

2. **Regulation of Interstate Commerce**

   a. **By federal government**

   If your examination question involves federal government regulation of interstate commerce, the exercise is *most likely valid*. The Commerce Clause grants Congress power to regulate commerce among the states, and this power has been broadly held to extend to regulation of the *channels or instrumentalities* of interstate commerce and to any commercial or economic *activity affecting more than one state* (which includes seemingly local concerns, such as a farmer's production of wheat for home consumption, which affects what he will buy from interstate commerce). Of course, this power is limited by the specific limitations imposed elsewhere in the Constitution (*e.g.,* in the Bill of Rights).

   b. **By state**

   On the other hand, if your examination question involves state regulation of interstate commerce, use the following approach:

   (1) **Where Congress has acted**

   First you must review federal legislation in the area, because Congress's acts are controlling. Recall that Congress *may authorize* state regulations that otherwise would violate the Commerce Clause (because the regulations discriminate against interstate commerce) or *may prohibit* state regulation that would otherwise be valid. However, on an exam, there usually will be no express congressional authorization or prohibition. Thus, if there is federal legislation concerning an area, but Congress was silent as to states' rights to act, look to Congress's intent. A *conflicting* state law will be held invalid, and *any* state law (whether or not conflicting) will be invalid if Congress is found to have *preempted* the field.

   (2) **Where Congress has not acted**

   If there is no federal legislation at all in an area, states may regulate local transactions even though the transactions affect interstate commerce. However, watch for state laws that *discriminate* against interstate commerce. These are almost always invalid unless (i) they are necessary to protect noneconomic interests (*e.g.*, health and safety) *and* there are no reasonable alternative ways to protect those interests or (ii) the state is a market participant. If state regulation does *not discriminate* against interstate commerce, but does burden it, the Court will *balance the burden* against the strength of the state's interest to determine whether it is reasonable.

3. **State Taxation of Interstate Commerce**
Your approach to state taxation of interstate commerce is basically the same as for state regulation of interstate commerce: First see whether Congress has acted; recall that Congress has complete power to authorize or forbid state taxation that affects interstate commerce. If there is no federal legislation, watch for *discriminatory* state action. Unless authorized by Congress, a state tax that discriminates against interstate commerce is *invalid*. If the tax is *nondiscriminatory*, the Court will *balance* the state's need for revenue against the burden on interstate commerce. Remember that the Commerce Clause prohibits multiple burdens and the Due Process Clause requires a nexus to the taxing state. Be sure to identify the type of tax levied (*e.g.*, property tax, sales tax, etc.).

4. **State Taxation of Foreign Commerce**
Again, the federal government has the ultimate power over foreign commerce. Thus, a state tax on imported goods, as such, is *invalid* without congressional consent, as is a tax on exports that have entered into the stream of exportation.

A. Regulation of Foreign Commerce— Exclusive Federal Power

1. **General Rule [§283]**
Regulation of foreign commerce is exclusively a federal power. *Rationale:* The federal government must speak with one voice when regulating commercial relations with foreign governments. [**Michelin Tire Corp. v. Wages,** 423 U.S. 276 (1976)]

B. Regulation of Interstate Commerce

1. **Concurrent Power [§284]**
The federal power to regulate interstate commerce is concurrent with state power over transactions within the state. Thus, the Court has frequently been called on to determine the respective scope of federal power and state power in regulating interstate commerce.

2. Scope of Federal Power [§285]

The Commerce Clause [Art. I, §8, cl. 3] grants Congress the power "to regulate commerce . . . among the several states." Early on, the Court held that the term "commerce" is not limited to traffic and the purchase and sale of commodities, but rather "describes the commercial intercourse between nations, and parts of nations, in all its branches, and is regulated by prescribing rules for carrying on that intercourse." [**Gibbons v. Ogden**, 22 U.S. 1 (1824)] More recently, the Court has explained that the commerce power allows Congress to adopt legislation that either:

(i) *Regulates the channels* of interstate commerce;

(ii) *Regulates the instrumentalities* of interstate commerce and persons and things in interstate commerce; or

(iii) *Regulates activities that have a substantial effect* on interstate commerce.

[**United States v. Lopez**, 514 U.S. 549 (1995); **United States v. Morrison**, 529 U.S. 598 (2000)] This power to regulate includes the power to prohibit as well as the power to encourage activity, as will be illustrated below.

a. Regulation of channels and instrumentalities of interstate commerce [§286]

Although an early 20th century decision held that "the grant of power to Congress over the subject of interstate commerce was to enable it to regulate such commerce, and not to give it authority to control the states in their exercise of the police power over local trade and manufacture" [**Hammer v. Dagenhart**, 247 U.S. 251 (1918)], the modern rule is that Congress has *plenary* power to regulate the "channels" of interstate commerce. This includes power over interstate roads, waterways, airways, and transmission facilities (among other things). Congress also has plenary power to regulate "instrumentalities" of interstate commerce, which include the people, machines, and other things that carry things in commerce.

 Example: The state of New York granted Robert Fulton and Robert Livingston a monopoly to operate a steamboat to ferry passengers in New York waters. They granted a license to Aaron Ogden to operate a ferry between New York City and New Jersey. Thomas Gibbons operated a competing ferry boat in the same waters pursuant to a federal license that he had obtained. Ogden sued Gibbons in New York court and obtained an injunction prohibiting Gibbons from operating his ferry. Gibbons appealed to the Supreme Court, which held that the Commerce Clause includes the power to grant licenses in navigable waterways; thus, the New York monopoly was preempted by federal law (*see infra*, §300). [**Gibbons v. Ogden**, *supra*]

Example: A railroad company in Texas charged substantially lower rates on its intrastate lines than on its interstate lines, making it difficult for merchants in Shreveport, Louisiana (near the Texas border) to compete with Texas merchants in Texas markets. The Interstate Commerce Commission ("ICC") found the interstate rates to be unreasonable and ordered the railroad to desist from charging higher rates on its interstate lines than on its intrastate lines. The railroad challenged the ICC order, claiming that the federal government did not have the power to control the railroad's intrastate pricing. The Supreme Court upheld the ICC's ruling, finding that Congress's power over interstate commerce necessarily extends to all other operations having a close and substantial relation to interstate traffic. [**Houston, East & West Texas Railway v. United States ("the Shreveport Case")**, 234 U.S. 342 (1914)]

---

(1) Federal "police power" [§287]

Congress's plenary power over the channels and instrumentalities of interstate commerce includes the authority to *exclude* from shipment or travel in the channels of interstate commerce any goods, persons, or activities found by Congress to be harmful to the public health, safety, welfare, or morals.

(a) Motive irrelevant [§288]

Congress's motive in enacting the regulation is irrelevant. Thus, Congress may exclude from interstate commerce:

1) *Goods harmful* to interstate commerce itself—*e.g.,* diseased animals that might infect other animals in interstate transit.

2) *Commercial items* generally—*e.g.,* lottery tickets [**Champion v. Ames ("the Lottery Case")**, 188 U.S. 321 (1903)], or goods produced under substandard conditions [**United States v. Darby Lumber**, 312 U.S. 100 (1941)—discussed *infra,* §295].

3) *Noncommercial items*—*e.g.,* persons fleeing prosecution or persons kidnapping others. [**Gooch v. United States**, 297 U.S. 124 (1936)]

(b) Furthering state law [§289]

The federal "police power" includes congressional power to further state laws or policies—*e.g.,* a federal statute banning interstate transportation of convict-made goods into a state where their receipt, sale, or possession is unlawful. [**Kentucky Whip & Collar Co. v. Illinois Central Railroad**, 299 U.S. 334 (1937)]

(2) Regulation after interstate commerce "ends" [§290]

The federal commerce power is broad enough to allow regulation even after interstate commerce has ended. For example, a congressional requirement that labels on bottles that have been in interstate commerce be retained *after* the shipment ends has been upheld. [**McDermott v. Wisconsin,**

228 U.S. 115 (1913)] *Rationale:* This made inspection convenient; *i.e.,* it assured that the bottles were so labeled while they were *in* interstate commerce.

(a) Extension [§291]

This "convenience of inspection" rationale has been extended to a requirement that labels be placed on *different* containers into which contents were transferred after interstate shipment—even as to persons who had not directly received the interstate shipment, but had obtained the contents from a local merchant who had received them from interstate commerce. [**United States v. Sullivan**, 332 U.S. 689 (1948)]

(b) Power not unlimited [§292]

The decisions above concern federal statutes governing the *condition* of goods. They do not hold that Congress may regulate the *use* of such goods after they come to rest within a state (*e.g.,* a statute fixing the price at which such goods may be sold locally).

1) Activities of persons in interstate commerce [§293]

Nor do the cases hold that Congress may regulate the activities of persons who have been in interstate commerce once their interstate travel has ended—although Congress may prohibit persons from using the facilities of interstate commerce to accomplish certain ends (and may seek to prove the user's purpose by pointing to acts engaged in shortly after interstate commerce ended).

2) "Intrastate" commerce [§294]

There *may* be a limit to this basis of congressional power on the theory that, at some point, the subject of regulation has become local or "intrastate"—although a congressional power to regulate might still be found under the "substantial economic effect" theory (below).

b. Activities that have a substantial economic effect on interstate commerce [§295]

In addition to giving Congress the power to regulate channels and instrumentalities of interstate commerce, the Commerce Clause gives Congress the power to regulate activities that have a *substantial economic effect* on interstate commerce. [**United States v. Morrison**, *supra,* §285] This includes intrastate activities that "have such a close and substantial relationship to interstate commerce that their control is essential or appropriate to protect that commerce from burdens and obstructions . . . ." [**NLRB v. Jones & Laughlin Steel Corp.**, 301 U.S. 1 (1937)—upholding Congress's power to adopt legislation to prevent unfair labor practices] This prong of Commerce Clause power is sometimes referred to as the "affectation doctrine." As with the other prongs of Commerce Clause power, this prong allows Congress to prohibit activity as well as to encourage activity. Illustrations of these principles include the following cases:

(i) *A factory that produces goods within the state* may have working conditions regulated by Congress if the goods compete with goods produced in other states, because substandard working conditions may destroy competition, thus having an effect in other states. [**United States v. Darby Lumber,** *supra,* §288]

(ii) *A factory that produces goods to be sold both locally and interstate* may have *all* of its working conditions regulated by Congress, because labor strife among employees producing local goods may affect employees producing interstate goods, thus having an effect in other states. [**Maryland v. Wirtz,** 392 U.S. 183 (1968)]

(iii) *A motel that serves interstate travelers* may be barred from engaging in racial discrimination, because such discrimination may deter persons from traveling, thus having an effect in other states. [**Heart of Atlanta Motel, Inc. v. United States,** 379 U.S. 241 (1964)]

(iv) *A restaurant that purchases supplies from other states* may be barred from racial discrimination under the commerce power, because such discrimination may affect the quantity of the restaurant's business, thus having an effect in other states. [**Katzenbach v. McClung,** 379 U.S. 294 (1964)] *Note:* The Court has observed that racial unrest has a generally depressant effect on business. This indicates a broad power in Congress, under the Commerce Clause, to regulate all forms of racial discrimination, because locally depressed business will affect those in other states who deal with the local business.

(v) *Coal companies that strip-mine land previously used for farming* may be required to reclaim land and comply with other extensive regulations, because strip-mining, rather than farming, may create environmental problems and affect agricultural production in other states. [**Hodel v. Virginia Surface Mining & Reclamation Association,** 452 U.S. 264 (1981); **Hodel v. Indiana,** 452 U.S. 314 (1981)]

(1) Volume of commerce affected [§296]
The fact that any single business or individual regulated by Congress has only a small impact on interstate commerce is immaterial. The crucial question is whether there is an *aggregate* effect on other states by the *class of activities* regulated. [**NLRB v. Fainblatt,** 306 U.S. 601 (1939)]

Example: Filburn, a farmer, was penalized for growing wheat in excess of his allotment under the federal Agricultural Adjustment Act of 1934. He sued to enjoin the penalty, claiming that the crop quota could not be applied to his wheat because he grew it for use on his farm rather than for sale. The Supreme Court found that the purpose of the act was to restrict the supply of wheat in order to maintain wheat prices, and that although the amount of wheat grown by Filburn for consumption on his farm was trivial, when taken together with many other farmers similarly situated, it could have an effect on interstate prices. [**Wickard v. Filburn**, 317 U.S. 111 (1942)]

---

e.g. **Example:** The intrastate activity of "loan sharking" may affect interstate commerce and thus may be made criminal by Congress—and the courts have no power "to excise, as trivial, individual instances of the class." [**Perez v. United States**, 402 U.S. 146 (1971)]

EXAM TIP	gilbert

Note that because **almost any** commercial activity, taken in aggregate, might have a **substantial economic effect on interstate commerce**, the Commerce Clause is an important basis for civil rights laws.

---

(2) Interstate commerce limitation [§297]

Between 1937 and 1995, the Supreme Court generally upheld Congress's power to regulate virtually every aspect of business under the Commerce Clause, as long as the activity regulated in aggregate could have an effect on other states. Congressional findings of this effect were given great deference. However, in 1995 and again in 2000, the Court made clear that the power of Congress to regulate commerce under the "affectation doctrine," although very broad, does have limits so as not to obliterate the distinction between what is national and what is local. [**United States v. Lopez**, *supra,* §285; **United States v. Morrison**, *supra,* §295] It appears that the Court will be slow to approve congressional regulation of what the Court considers to be noneconomic activity, or activity that has traditionally been regulated by the states (*e.g.*, family law, criminal law enforcement, and education). However, the exact parameters of "noneconomic activity" and "activity that has traditionally been regulated by the states" are as yet unclear.

---

e.g. **Example:** After finding that gender-motivated violence had a serious impact on victims and their families and cost the nation billions of dollars in health costs and lost productivity, Congress adopted the Violence Against Women Act ("VAWA"). Among other things, the VAWA authorized victims of gender-motivated violence to sue their attackers for damages. After Morrison allegedly raped Brzonkala, she sued him for damages under the VAWA. Morrison argued that Congress lacked the power to enact the VAWA's civil remedy because violence against women does not involve interstate commerce. The Court noted that the Constitution distinguishes between national and local issues, and that the police power (the general power to regulate for health, safety, welfare, and morals) belongs to the states. Congress has no authority to regulate noneconomic, criminal conduct based solely on the conduct's aggregate effect on interstate commerce. [**United States v. Morrison**, *supra;* and see **United States v. Lopez**, *supra*—federal statute barring possession of a gun in a school zone is invalid because possessing a gun is a criminal act, not an economic one] Otherwise, the Court observed, it would be "hard pressed to posit any activity by an individual that Congress is without power to regulate."

(3) Individual rights limitations [§298]

The commerce power also is subject to the specific limits imposed elsewhere in the Constitution (*e.g.*, in the Bill of Rights). For example, if Congress forbade wheat production by Catholics only, the act would violate the First Amendment and would be invalid even though regulation of wheat would generally be valid under the Commerce Clause.

(4) Interpretation function [§299]

Because Congress's power under the Commerce Clause is extremely broad, one of the Court's major functions respecting federal statutes enacted under the Commerce Clause is *statutory interpretation*: Did Congress *intend* its regulation to apply to the particular activity involved in the case?

EXAM TIP   gilbert

If you run into a question on your exam involving a federal statute that regulates criminal activity and the statute is based on the Commerce Clause, be sure to keep in mind the Court's current stance on the issue: The federal government may regulate (i) channels of interstate commerce; (ii) instrumentalities of interstate commerce; or (iii) economic or commercial activities that have a substantial effect on interstate commerce. Thus, if the criminal activity involves use of the roads, airways, waterways, etc., it probably can be sustained under the Commerce Clause. Similarly, the statute could be upheld if it involves the use of trains, trucks, or the like. But if the statute regulates a *wholly intrastate activity*, assess how closely related the activity is to commercial activity. If *economic activity is directly involved*, the statute can probably be upheld. But if the activity is noneconomic, it is unlikely that the court will uphold the statute unless it includes a jurisdictional hook (*i.e.*, it connects the noneconomic activity to the channels of interstate commerce or to an instrumentality of interstate commerce).

---

3. State Regulation of Interstate Commerce [§300]

Although the federal power over interstate commerce is potentially "all pervasive," it is *not* exclusive. The states have power to regulate local aspects of interstate commerce. However, the states' power is limited by both the Supremacy Clause and the Commerce Clause. Because the Constitution grants Congress plenary power to regulate interstate commerce and provides that valid federal laws are supreme over state laws, if Congress has adopted a statute regulating the same area as a state statute, the state statute may be held invalid under the Supremacy Clause. Moreover, even where Congress has not exercised its commerce power, the Supreme Court has held that a state law that unduly burdens or discriminates against interstate commerce can violate the Commerce Clause. This principle is sometimes referred to as the "Dormant Commerce Clause" or the "negative implications of the Commerce Clause." Thus, the first issue to address when determining whether a state regulation of commerce is valid is whether there is any federal legislation on point.

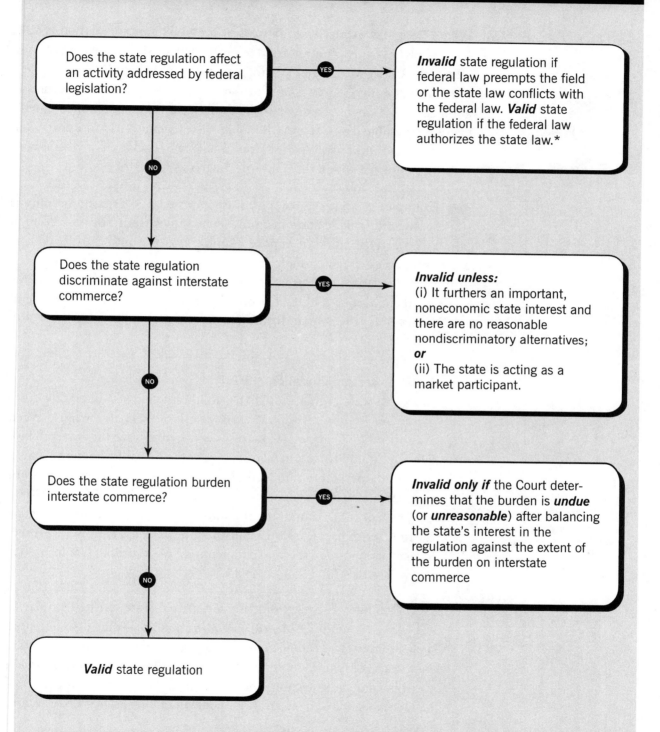

Does the state regulation affect an activity addressed by federal legislation?

YES → *Invalid* state regulation if federal law preempts the field or the state law conflicts with the federal law. *Valid* state regulation if the federal law authorizes the state law.*

NO ↓

Does the state regulation discriminate against interstate commerce?

YES → *Invalid unless:*
(i) It furthers an important, noneconomic state interest and there are no reasonable nondiscriminatory alternatives; *or*
(ii) The state is acting as a market participant.

NO ↓

Does the state regulation burden interstate commerce?

YES → *Invalid only if* the Court determines that the burden is *undue* (or *unreasonable*) after balancing the state's interest in the regulation against the extent of the burden on interstate commerce

NO ↓

Valid state regulation

*Of course, Congress has no power to authorize legislation that would violate other constitutional provisions, such as the Privileges and Immunities Clause of Article IV.

a. **If there is federal legislation on point [§301]**

If there is federal legislation on point, the Court will look to the legislation to see whether or not it expressly authorizes or prohibits the state regulation in question.

(1) Where Congress expressly authorizes or prohibits state regulation [§302]

If Congress has expressly authorized or prohibited the state regulation of commerce, the Court will judge the state regulation according to Congress's express intent; *i.e.,* the Court will uphold a state regulation of commerce expressly authorized by Congress and will strike down a state regulation of commerce expressly prohibited by Congress. *Rationale:* The Commerce Clause gives Congress **complete** authority to permit or prohibit state regulation of what is concededly commerce within the scope of Congress's regulatory power.

> **Example:** A South Carolina statute imposed a 3% tax on premiums received by out of state insurance companies from business done in South Carolina, but did not impose a similar tax on South Carolina insurance companies. Even though states generally are prohibited from discriminating against interstate commerce under the "Dormant Commerce Clause," the Court upheld the tax because it was authorized by the federal McCarran Act. [**Prudential Insurance Co. v. Benjamin,** 328 U.S. 408 (1946)]

(a) Equal protection limitation [§303]

Although state regulations that discriminate against interstate commerce are immune from attack under the Commerce Clause when authorized by Congress, Congress cannot authorize the states to violate the Equal Protection Clause. Under the Equal Protection Clause, discriminatory economic legislation will be struck down if it is not rationally related to a legitimate state interest (*see infra,* §§1013-1016), and the Court has found that the states do not have a legitimate interest in discriminating against out-of-state business simply to protect local economic interests from competition. [**Metropolitan Life Insurance Co. v. Ward,** 470 U.S. 869 (1985)]

> **Example:** A congressionally authorized state statute—similar to the statute in *Prudential Insurance, supra*—that discriminated against interstate commerce by imposing a higher tax on out-of-state insurance companies than on domestic insurance companies was held to violate equal protection where the state's only purpose was to protect local economic interests. [**Metropolitan Life Insurance Co. v. Ward,** *supra*]

> **Compare—"legitimate" state purpose:** A California statute, authorized by Congress, discriminated against interstate insurance companies whose home states discriminated against California

insurance companies. The Court found no equal protection violation; California had a "legitimate" purpose—*i.e.,* to deter other states from discriminating against interstate commerce. [**Western & Southern Life Insurance Co. v. California Board of Equalization**, 451 U.S. 648 (1981)]

1) Scope uncertain [§304]

The reach of the *Metropolitan Life Insurance* case, *supra,* is uncertain. In **Northeast Bancorp, Inc. v. Board of Governors**, 472 U.S. 159 (1985), a Connecticut statute, authorized by Congress, permitted only local companies and out-of-state companies from New England to acquire local banks. Although the statute's purpose seemed no different than that in *Metropolitan Life Insurance*, the Court found no equal protection violation, stressing that banking is "of profound local concern."

(b) Note—Congress may reverse Court result [§305]

Note that because Congress may authorize states to adopt regulations that would otherwise violate the Commerce Clause, or may prohibit states from adopting commerce regulations that they otherwise could adopt, congressional legislation can have the effect of changing the result of a prior court decision (*e.g.,* if the Court rules that a state's discriminatory tax violates the Commerce Clause, Congress can subsequently adopt legislation authorizing the state to impose the tax. [*See* **Clark Distilling Co. v. Western Maryland Railroad**, 242 U.S. 311 (1917)—upholding federal statutes authorizing state regulation of liquor shipped into state from interstate commerce, enacted after such state regulations were held invalid in **Leisy v. Hardin**, 135 U.S. 100 (1890)]

(2) Where no express congressional authorization or prohibition of state law—"supersession" or "preemption" doctrine [§306]

If there is relevant federal legislation, but the legislation does not expressly authorize or prohibit the state law in question, the Court must decide whether Congress *intended* to authorize the state legislation or prohibit it. The Court will hold state laws invalid under the *Supremacy Clause* [Art. VI, §2] if they are found to be superseded by *conflicting federal law* or if federal law is held to *preempt* (or occupy) the entire field.

(a) Issue of statutory construction [§307]

The issue is one of statutory construction, based on the federal law's *language* and *legislative history*: Does the state regulation conflict with the federal statute? Or if there is no "direct" conflict, did Congress intend to provide complete national regulation of the subject matter, thereby excluding *any* state regulation, even one that reinforces or complements the federal regulation? [**Campbell v. Hussey**, 368 U.S. 297 (1961)]

(b) **Applicability of doctrine beyond interstate commerce area [§308]**
When Congress properly enacts legislation pursuant to *any* of its delegated powers, state regulations that conflict are invalid because of the *Supremacy Clause*. Similarly, if congressional legislation is found by the Court to be intended to occupy the entire field, state laws are preempted. Thus, the Court has periodically avoided constitutional challenges to a state regulation by finding that a federal statute either conflicts with it or preempts the field.

> **Example:** A state sedition law was challenged as violating freedom of speech and due process. The court was able to avoid ruling on these constitutional issues by holding the law invalid because a series of federal "anti-communist" statutes "evince a congressional plan . . . as to make reasonable the inference that Congress left no room for the States to supplement it." [**Pennsylvania v. Nelson**, 350 U.S. 497 (1956)]

(c) **Factors in determining congressional intent [§309]**
The Court examines the entire text of the federal statute(s), legislative history, and administrative interpretations to determine whether Congress intended to occupy the entire field. Significant factors are:

1) **Interest in uniform, national regulation [§310]**
The Court usually holds that Congress intended to occupy the field completely and to supersede state regulation whenever it finds that the subject matter requires uniform national regulation or is of "inherent national interest."

> **Example:** The Alien Registration Act, a federal statute that simply required aliens to register with the government, was held to preempt a state law requiring that aliens register annually and carry a registration card to show to state officials. The Court stressed that the field of aliens and immigration "affects international relations, the one aspect of our government that from the first has been most generally conceded imperatively to demand broad national authority." [**Hines v. Davidowitz**, 312 U.S. 52 (1941)]

2) **Historical or traditional classification of subject matter as federal or local [§311]**
If the subject matter has traditionally been the subject of local regulation, the Court is less likely to find federal preemption. [**Rice v. Santa Fe Elevator Co.**, 331 U.S. 218 (1947)—regulation of public warehouses] This is particularly true with respect to state laws designed to protect the public health or safety of

local citizens. Congress is not deemed to have intended to supersede such state laws unless the intent is clearly manifested (or the state law actually conflicts with federal law). [**Maurer v. Hamilton,** 309 U.S. 598 (1940)—safety on highways]

3) Completeness of federal regulatory scheme [§312]

The more complete the federal regulation, the more likely it is that Congress will be held to have intended to occupy the entire field and supersede state regulation. [**Pennsylvania v. Nelson,** *supra*]

4) Coincidence between federal and state statutes [§313]

A similarity or identity between federal and state regulations suggests a congressional intent to supersede. However, such similarity is not a controlling factor [**California v. Zook,** 366 U.S. 725 (1949)], and may be given little weight if the purpose of the federal statute is not frustrated by the identical state statute [**Colorado Anti-Discrimination Commission v. Continental Airlines, Inc.,** 372 U.S. 714 (1963)], or if it is possible to comply with both regulations [**Florida Lime & Avocado Growers, Inc. v. Paul,** 373 U.S. 132 (1963)].

b. Power of states to regulate where Congress has not acted [§314]

Where Congress has *not* enacted legislation regarding the subject matter, states may regulate local transactions even though the transactions affect interstate commerce. However, as will be discussed below, such regulations generally may *not discriminate against* or *unduly burden* interstate commerce. If it does, the state or local regulation will violate the Commerce Clause.

EXAM TIP   **gilbert**

Your professor may use the term "Dormant Commerce Clause" or "Negative Commerce Clause." These are merely descriptive terms that reflect the above idea—even where Congress has not acted, the Commerce Clause restricts state and local regulation of interstate commerce; states may **not favor local economic interests or unduly burden interstate commerce**.

---

(1) Discrimination [§315]

State regulations that discriminate against interstate commerce—*i.e.,* single out such commerce for regulation or impose more burdensome regulations on interstate commerce than on comparable local commerce—are *almost always invalid* as an invasion of the federal commerce power. *Rationale:* A primary concern of the Framers was to combat economic protectionism by the states that had led to retaliatory economic warfare among the states. There are only two exceptions: (i) where the state regulation concerns *health or safety* and there are *no reasonable alternatives*; and (ii) where the state is acting as a *market participant* (*see infra,* §§322-323).

(a) Illustrations

1) Excluding incoming trade [§316]

A state statute that excludes entry of products from another state in order to further the economic interests of a local industry violates the Commerce Clause. [*See* **Edwards v. California**, 314 U.S. 160 (1941)—holding invalid a state statute prohibiting bringing nonresident indigents into state, because transporting indigents across state lines is commerce and seeking to exclude indigents to protect the state economy violates Commerce Clause]

Example: Under the Milk Control Act, New York set minimum prices for milk sales by producers and prohibited the sale in New York of milk purchased at a lower rate. Seelig, Inc., a New York milk dealer, purchased milk in Vermont below the minimum statutory price (enabling to sell the milk in New York for less than the prevailing market price). The state revoked Seelig, Inc.'s license to sell milk and Seelig, Inc. sued, claiming that the Act violated the Commerce Clause. New York argued that the Act was necessary to: (i) stabilize the milk supply; (ii) keep small, local farmers profitable, and (iii) ensure the quality of milk. *Held*: The Act is unconstitutional. The state may impose regulations to assure the health of its citizens, but not by protecting against competition from outside the state. [**Baldwin v. G.A.F. Seelig, Inc.**, 294 U.S. 511 (1935)]

---

a) Protection of environment [§317]

A state statute that excludes entry of products from another state in order to further the state's environmental goals also violates the Commerce Clause. [**Philadelphia v. New Jersey**, 437 U.S. 617 (1978)—statute that excluded wastes from outside state to conserve state's remaining landfill space and to reduce pollution held insufficient to justify discrimination against interstate commerce]

2) Requiring higher price for incoming trade [§318]

A state statute that requires that a higher price be paid for goods coming from interstate commerce violates the Commerce Clause. [**Welton v. Missouri**, 91 U.S. 275 (1876)—special license tax on those who sold goods produced outside the state]

3) Restricting outgoing trade [§319]

A state statute restricting export of goods or resources from within the state in order to benefit local industries and consumers violates the Commerce Clause. [**H.P. Hood & Sons v. DuMond**, 336 U.S. 525 (1949)—to protect local supply of milk, state refused to permit company to open a milk receiving depot from which it would ship milk out of state; **C & A Carbone, Inc. v. Clarkstown,** 511 U.S. 383 (1994)—to insure income for waste control facility, city required that all solid waste generated within city be processed at it]

a) Conservation of natural resources [§320]

A state statute restricting export of fish taken from the state's waters violates the Commerce Clause. [**Hughes v. Oklahoma,** 441 U.S. 322 (1979)—legitimate state interest not enough to justify state discrimination against interstate commerce; *and see* **Sporhase v. Nebraska,** 458 U.S. 941 (1982)—although public ownership of ground water is "not without significance," state restriction on export of ground water is invalid because it "does not survive the 'strictest scrutiny' reserved for facially discriminatory legislation"]

4) Requiring performance of business operations locally [§321]

A state statute requiring that state products be processed within the state before being shipped in interstate commerce violates the Commerce Clause. [**Pike v. Bruce Church, Inc.,** 397 U.S. 137 (1970)—striking requirement that home-grown cantaloupes be packaged within the state before shipment]

---

e.g. **Example:** A state statute prohibiting the sale of meat not inspected within the state violates the Commerce Clause because it discriminates against out-of-state slaughterhouses (*i.e.,* it prevents importation of sound meat from animals slaughtered in other states). [**Minnesota v. Barber,** 136 U.S. 313 (1890)]

(b) Exception—absence of alternatives [§322]

Although state regulations that discriminate against interstate commerce *almost always* violate the Commerce Clause (unless there is congressional authorization, *see supra,* §302), they are *not automatically* invalid. Rather, the Court has said that they may be upheld to protect *health and safety* (*i.e., noneconomic*) interests if there are *no reasonable and adequate nondiscriminatory alternatives* available. [**Dean Milk Co. v. City of Madison,** 340 U.S. 349 (1951)]

---

e.g. **Example:** A Maine statute that discriminated against interstate commerce by prohibiting the importation of live baitfish was upheld. The statute served a "legitimate local purpose" (live baitfish from other states posed health threats to Maine's unique and fragile fisheries and there was no developed means of inspection to detect parasites, etc.) and that purpose could not "be served as well by available nondiscriminatory means." [**Maine v. Taylor,** 476 U.S. 1138 (1986)]

> **cf. Compare:** A city ordinance made it unlawful to sell milk in the city unless it was pasteurized within five miles of the city. The ordinance purportedly was to enable city health inspectors to inspect pasteurization plants to assure the wholesomeness of the city's milk supply. The ordinance was held *invalid* as it discriminated in favor of local pasteurizing businesses and there were nondiscriminatory alternatives available to assure milk's quality (*e.g.,* the city could rely on the United States Public Health Service inspections or use other out-of-town ratings and inspections). [**Dean Milk Co. v. City of Madison,** *supra*]

(c) Exception—state as market participant [§323]

The Commerce Clause does not prevent a state, when acting as a purchaser (or seller) of goods, from buying only from (or selling only to) local business or from giving subsidies only to its residents. Such discrimination merely affects a market created by a state's own purchase (or subsidies), and the state is thus a market participant, rather than a market regulator.

> **e.g. Example:** Maryland paid a bounty to Maryland in-state scrap processors that destroyed old automobiles if the processors signed an agreement to indemnify the state from claims arising from destruction of the automobiles. The state would pay out-of-state processors a similar bounty only if they provided more extensive documentation showing that they had title to the automobile hulks that they destroyed. *Held:* The more onerous documentation requirements for out-of-state scrap processors do not violate the Commerce Clause because the state is not seeking to restrict the interstate flow of automobile hulks; rather, it has entered the market to bid up the price of hulks (in an effort to rid the state of inoperable automobiles), and nothing in the Commerce Clause forbids a state that enters into a market from restricting its trade to its own citizens. [**Hughes v. Alexandria Scrap Corp.,** 426 U.S. 794 (1976); *and see* **Reeves, Inc. v. Stake,** 447 U.S. 429 (1980)—no Commerce Clause violation where state that operated a cement factory sold to in-state customers rather than out-of-state customers when supplies ran low]

1) "Downstream" restrictions [§324]

It is *doubtful* whether a state may impose restrictions on the subsequent use of goods purchased from the state—*e.g.,* that timber from the state must be processed in the state. [**South-Central Timber Development, Inc. v. Wunnicke**, 467 U.S. 82 (1984)—no holding by a majority of the Court]

2) **Interstate Privileges and Immunities Clause [§325]**

Although a state may act as a market participant when it funds public construction projects and thus avoid Commerce Clause restrictions [**White v. Massachusetts Council of Construction Employers**, 460 U.S. 204 (1983)], state regulations or expenditures that discriminate against out-of-staters *are subject* to the standard of judicial review applied under Article IV, Section 2 (*see supra*, §§257 *et seq.*). [**United Building & Construction Trades Council v. Mayor & Council of Camden**, *supra*, §259—city ordinance requiring contractors who work on city or state funded projects to give a hiring preference to local residents may be valid under the Commerce Clause, nonetheless may be invalid under Interstate Privileges and Immunities Clause because "the two clauses have different aims and set different standards for state conduct"]

(d) **Discriminatory impact also improper [§326]**

A state regulation that affects interstate commerce may be neutral on its face but still be discriminatory due to its *impact*. [**Hunt v. Washington State Apple Advertising Commission**, *supra*, §71—statute requiring all apple producers to use uniform grading system (or none at all) was discriminatory because local producers (unlike interstate competitors) already used the statutory system]

(e) **Discrimination also against in-state counties [§327]**

A state regulation that discriminates against interstate commerce is *not* viewed differently merely because it *also* discriminates against certain counties within the state. [**Fort Gratiot Sanitary Landfill, Inc. v. Michigan Department of Natural Resources**, 504 U.S. 353 (1992)—state law prohibiting landfill of solid waste generated from outside the county invalid]

(2) **Nondiscriminatory regulation [§328]**

State regulations that do not discriminate against interstate commerce are given greater deference by the Court. *Rationale:* If the burden of the state regulation falls *proportionally* on local interests as well as those outside the state, *political restraints* within the state legislature protect against the abuse of interstate commerce (*i.e.*, residents of the state can pressure the legislature to change the law). [**South Carolina State Highway Department v. Barnwell Bros.**, 303 U.S. 177 (1938)]

---

e.g. **Example:** South Carolina prohibited trucks wider than 90 inches or heavier than 20,000 pounds from using state highways. This measure burdened interstate commerce because most interstate trucks exceeded

	COMMERCE CLAUSE	PRIVILEGES AND IMMUNITIES CLAUSE OF ARTICLE IV
STATE/LOCAL ACTION *DISCRIMINATES* AGAINST OUT-OF-STATE ENTITIES	If the discrimination unduly burdens interstate commerce and there is no applicable federal legislation, the action is *invalid unless*: (i) It furthers an ***important, noneconomic state interest*** and there are no reasonable nondiscriminatory alternatives; or (ii) The state is a ***market participant*** (*i.e.,* purchaser, seller, subsidizer).	If the action denies the out-of-state person important economic interests (*e.g.,* livelihood) or civil liberties, the law is ***invalid unless*** the state has a ***substantial*** justification and there are no less restrictive means.
STATE/LOCAL ACTION DOES *NOT DISCRIMINATE*	If the law burdens interstate commerce and the burden outweighs the state's interest in the action, the law is ***invalid***.	Privileges and Immunities Clause ***does not apply*** where there is no discrimination.
IS THERE A MARKET PARTICIPANT EXCEPTION?	Yes	No

the state limits. Nevertheless, the limits were upheld. The fact that the limitations here affect a large number of intrastate shippers as well as interstate shippers serves as a safeguard against abuse. The Court also noted that state highways are peculiarly local, as their nature varies from state to state (or at least they did in 1938). [**South Carolina State Highway Department v. Barnwell Bros.**, *supra; compare* **Kassell v. Consolidated Freightways Corp.**, 450 U.S. 662 (1981)—Iowa statute that generally prohibited the use of 65-foot double trailers on Iowa highways struck down; Court doubted state's claimed safety interests because the limitation had exemptions, and it is less likely that local political restraints will serve as a check against abuse because the limitation placed a disproportionate burden on interstate commerce]

(a) "Subject matter" test (older approach) [§329]

Under an older approach used by the Court, if the subject matter involved does not require a uniform national rule, but is of local concern and permits diverse regulation, the state regulation usually was *upheld* if the state regulation had some *rational basis*. [**Cooley v. Board of Wardens of Philadelphia**, 53 U.S. (12 How.) 299 (1851)—requirement that ships receive a local pilot while entering or leaving the Port of Philadelphia upheld because piloting a ship within a harbor is a local concern; *and see* **South Carolina Highway Department v. Barnwell Bros.**, *supra*—upholding maximum weight and width limitations for trucks on state highways because state highways (the subject matter of the regulation) are "peculiarly of local concern"]

1) Limited use of test [§330]

The "subject matter" test has not been employed often in modern decisions, although its language has been used occasionally with respect to regulation of interstate transportation facilities on state highways. Even here, however, the Court uses the "balancing" test, below.

(b) "Balancing" test (modern approach) [§331]

Under the current approach, the fact that the state regulation has some "rational basis" is not enough. Rather, the *burden on interstate commerce* imposed by the regulation (*i.e.,* difficulty and cost of compliance, inefficiency involved, etc.) is weighed against the *strength of the state interest* in the regulation, with the Court deciding whether the regulation imposes an *unreasonable burden* on interstate commerce. [**Southern Pacific Co. v. Arizona**, 325 U.S. 761 (1945)]

e.g. **Example:** The Arizona Train Limit Law restricted the length of passenger trains traveling through Arizona to 14 cars and restricted the length of freight trains to 70 cars. Because most other states allow longer trains, the Arizona statute would necessitate breaking trains down before they enter Arizona, which would cause great expense and delay. On the other hand, most gains in safety arising from the shorter trains will be offset by the fact that there will be more trains. Thus, the law violates the Commerce Clause because its burden on interstate commerce outweighs its public safety purpose. [**Southern Pacific Co. v. Arizona,** *supra*]

EXAM TIP	gilbert

When a bar exam question involves a state regulation that affects the free flow of interstate commerce, you should ask:

- Do the facts refer to any *federal legislation* that might (i) *authorize* state regulation that is otherwise impermissible; or (ii) *supersede* the state regulation or *preempt* the field?

- If neither of these possibilities is dispositive, does the state regulation either *discriminate* against interstate (or out-of-state) commerce or place an *undue burden* on the free flow of interstate commerce? If the regulation is discriminatory, it will be *invalid unless* (i) it furthers an important, noneconomic state interest *and* there are no reasonable nondiscriminatory alternatives, or (ii) the state is a market participant. Remember that discriminatory regulations almost always are invalid. If the regulation does not discriminate but burdens interstate commerce, it will be invalid if the burden on commerce outweighs the state's interest.

(c) Application of "balancing" test [§332]

In balancing the burden imposed on interstate commerce against the state interest served, the Court gives greater weight to statutes that further local *health, safety,* or *social welfare* interests than to statutes that seek to protect local *economic* interests. [**H.P. Hood & Sons v. DuMond,** *supra*, §319]

1) Judicial role [§333]

The Court makes its own determination as to the *purposes* of the state regulation. It is not bound by recitals by the state legislature in enacting the statute, or by state court determinations as to such objectives. However, the Court generally will defer to a state legislative determination of *disputed factual questions on whether the state's purpose is served* by the regulation or on the cost of compliance. [**Minnesota v. Clover Leaf Creamery Co.,** 449 U.S. 456 (1981)]

Example: A Minnesota statute prohibited the sale of milk in nonreturnable plastic containers but allowed milk to be sold in other nonreturnable containers (such as cardboard). Despite the fact that no Minnesota firm made plastic milk containers, while pulpwood used to make cardboard milk containers is a major Minnesota product, the Court upheld the statute, finding that its purpose was indeed to the environment as opposed to the state economy. [**Minnesota v. Clover Leaf Creamery Co.,** *supra*]

---

2) **Statutes furthering social welfare, health, and safety**

   a) **Social welfare [§334]**
   A statute forbidding solicitation by door-to-door sellers without invitation by the homeowner, applied to interstate magazine salespeople, has been upheld. Although the statute burdened interstate commerce by making solicitation much more difficult, this was outweighed by the state interest in protecting privacy. [**Breard v. City of Alexandria,** 341 U.S. 622 (1951)]

   b) **Health [§335]**
   A statute requiring that cattle or meat imported from other states be certified as free from disease by the state of origin has been upheld. The burden on interstate commerce involved in supplying such certificate was outweighed by the "public health" objectives of the state law. [**Mintz v. Baldwin,** 289 U.S. 346 (1933); *but see* **Minnesota v. Barber,** *supra*, §321—*discriminatory* statute seeking to protect same state interest held *invalid*]

   c) **Safety [§336]**
   A statute requiring that all trains operated within the state carry "full crews" has been upheld. The burden on interstate commerce was outweighed by the "public safety" objective of the regulation. [**Brotherhood of Locomotive Firemen v. Chicago, Rock Island & Pacific Railroad,** 393 U.S. 129 (1968)]

   d) **Unreasonable burden may still be found [§337]**
   The fact that a nondiscriminatory state regulation has the purpose of protecting local health, safety, or social welfare interests does not automatically immunize it. Although such a regulation carries a "strong presumption of validity," it is *invalid* if, on balance, it furthers the state's interest only *speculatively or marginally* and imposes a *substantial* burden on interstate commerce. [**Kassel v. Consolidated Freightways Corp.,** *supra*, §328; **Raymond Motor Transportation, Inc. v. Rice,** 434 U.S. 429 (1978)—state laws limiting length of trucks on local highways]

e.g. **Example:** An Illinois statute required all trucks to be equipped with contour mudguards, instead of the flat mudguards permitted in all other states (contour mudguards actually being illegal in one state). The safety benefit of the contour mudguards was found to be minimal at best and was held *outweighed* by the costs and inconvenience to interstate carriers in complying (*i.e.*, requiring truckers to change mudguards before entering Illinois). [**Bibb v. Navajo Freight Lines, Inc.**, 359 U.S. 520 (1959)]

e) Alternative means [§338]

In determining whether a state interest outweighs the burden on interstate commerce, the Court periodically considers whether there are any alternatives available to the state that could achieve the same objective without imposing as great a burden. [**Pike v. Bruce Church, Inc.**, *supra*, §321]

3) Economic regulations [§339]

The fact that a nondiscriminatory state regulation is designed to protect local economic interests does *not automatically* invalidate it under the Commerce Clause. The Court has upheld a number of state laws requiring that minimum prices be paid to local producers, thus enhancing local industry, despite the fact that a large amount of the product was sold in interstate commerce. [**Milk Control Board v. Eisenberg Farm Products Co.**, 306 U.S. 346 (1939)—*most* of the milk subject to minimum price law was sold within state]

a) Relevance of national policy [§340]

Several of these cases stressed that the regulation was consistent with certain national policies, even though Congress had not specifically acted in this area. [*See* **Parker v. Brown**, 317 U.S. 431 (1943)—state marketing program regulating sale of locally grown raisin crop in interstate commerce upheld because state program coincided with congressional policies regulating agriculture]

4) "Reciprocity agreements" [§341]

Reciprocity agreements between states respecting the sale of products do *not automatically* violate the Commerce Clause. *But note:* A *mandatory* reciprocity requirement forbidding sale of products from another state unless that state reciprocates is invalid unless there is a substantial state interest (health or welfare, etc.) which cannot be attained by alternative means. [**Great Atlantic & Pacific Tea Co. v. Cottrell**, 424 U.S. 366 (1976)]

(3) Permits or licenses for interstate business [§342]

The traditional rule is that a state cannot require a permit or license for the privilege of engaging in interstate transportation [**Buck v. Kuykendall,** 267 U.S. 307 (1925)], or of engaging in trade or business that is *exclusively* interstate commerce (*e.g.*, an interstate company that *only* sends "drummers" into the state who take orders that are accepted and filled outside the state, and the goods for which are sent in from out of state). [*But see* **Eli Lilly & Co. v. Sav-On-Drugs, Inc.,** 366 U.S. 276 (1961)—interstate seller was not engaged *exclusively* in interstate commerce because it provided local customers with various services and sales aids]

(a) Note

This rule has been qualified by **Complete Auto Transit, Inc. v. Brady,** *see infra,* §374.

(b) Exception for permissible noneconomic interests [§343]

But a state may require and deny a permit to promote safety rather than simply to prevent competition. [**Bradley v. Public Utilities Commission,** 280 U.S. 92 (1933)]

(4) Broader state power over liquor regulation [§344]

The Twenty-First Amendment prohibits "the transportation or importation into any State for delivery or use therein of intoxicating liquors in violation of local laws." This amendment has been held to give the states broader regulatory power over regulation of liquor than over any other type of interstate commerce. By virtue of the Twenty-First Amendment, a state is "unconfined by traditional Commerce Clause limitations" in deciding whether to *permit importation or sale* of liquor *destined for local use* or consumption and in structuring the liquor distribution system. [**Hostetter v. Idlewild Bon Voyage Liquor Corp.,** 377 U.S. 324 (1964)]

(a) Power limited to local sale or use [§345]

The Twenty-First Amendment does not give the states power to regulate or tax liquor shipments intended for delivery *overseas, outside the state*, or to federal enclaves (*e.g.*, military posts) within the state. As to such shipments, the federal commerce power is exclusive and supreme. [**Hostetter v. Idlewild Bon Voyage Liquor Corp.,** *supra*; **United States v. Mississippi Tax Commission,** 412 U.S. 363 (1973)]

1) Further limitation—noncentral state interests [§346]

Even those state liquor regulations that concern local sale and use may be subject to Congress's commerce power when the federal policies are particularly strong and the state's central interests in regulating the time, place, and manner of liquor importation and sale are not directly implicated. [**California Retail Liquor Dealers Association v. Midcal Aluminum, Inc.,** 445 U.S.

97 (1980)—state's fair trade law allowing wine wholesalers to set minimum prices violates Sherman Antitrust Act; **Capital Cities Cable, Inc. v. Crisp**, 467 U.S. 691 (1984)—state ban on alcoholic beverage advertising preempted by federal regulation of cable television]

2) **Discrimination [§347]**
Furthermore, the Twenty-First Amendment does not permit state regulations or taxes on the local sale or use of liquor to discriminate against interstate commerce. A central tenet of the Commerce Clause is to forbid economic protectionism. [**Bacchus Imports, Ltd. v. Dias**, 468 U.S. 263 (1984)]

3) **Extraterritorial effect [§348]**
Neither does the Twenty-First Amendment permit state regulations or taxes on the local sale or use of liquor if the practical effect is to regulate liquor sales or prices in other states. [**Healy v. The Beer Institute, Inc.**, 491 U.S. 324 (1989)—*overruling* **Joseph E. Seagram & Sons, Inc. v. Hostetter**, 384 U.S. 35 (1966)—state statute requiring sellers of beer to sell at prices no higher than prices in bordering states violates Commerce Clause, because it operates to force sellers to account for this state's price in evaluating market conditions in other states]

(b) **Import-Export Clause [§349]**
Note that the Twenty-First Amendment does not repeal the explicit limitation of the Import-Export Clause (*see infra*, §408). [**Department of Revenue v. James B. Beam Distilling Co.**, 377 U.S. 341 (1964)—state license tax on importers of liquor from abroad invalid]

C. Power of States to Tax Interstate Commerce

1. **General Considerations**

a. **Congressional supremacy [§350]**
Pursuant to the Commerce Clause, Congress has complete power to authorize or forbid state taxation that affects interstate commerce. [**Prudential Insurance Co. v. Benjamin**, 328 U.S. 408 (1946)—upholding Congress's power to authorize state taxes that discriminate against interstate commerce]

b. **When Congress has not spoken**

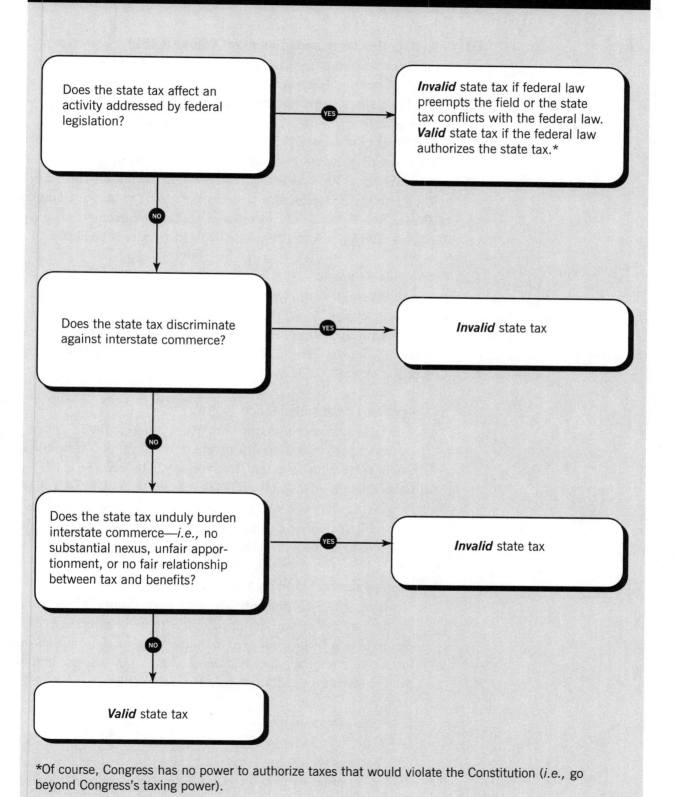

Does the state tax affect an activity addressed by federal legislation?

YES → *Invalid* state tax if federal law preempts the field or the state tax conflicts with the federal law. *Valid* state tax if the federal law authorizes the state tax.*

NO ↓

Does the state tax discriminate against interstate commerce?

YES → *Invalid* state tax

NO ↓

Does the state tax unduly burden interstate commerce—*i.e.,* no substantial nexus, unfair apportionment, or no fair relationship between tax and benefits?

YES → *Invalid* state tax

NO ↓

Valid state tax

*Of course, Congress has no power to authorize taxes that would violate the Constitution (*i.e.,* go beyond Congress's taxing power).

(1) Discriminatory taxes [§351]

Unless authorized by Congress, state taxes that discriminate against interstate commerce violate the *Commerce Clause*. [**Boston Stock Exchange v. State Tax Commission,** 429 U.S. 318 (1977)]

(a) Interstate Privileges and Immunities Clause [§352]

Taxes that discriminate against nonresidents of the state may also be held to violate the Interstate Privileges and Immunities Clause [Art. IV, §2]. [**Austin v. New Hampshire,** 420 U.S. 656 (1975)]

(b) Equal Protection Clause [§353]

State taxes that discriminate against interstate commerce may also violate the Equal Protection Clause if the discrimination is not *rationally* related to a *legitimate* state purpose. [**WHYY, Inc. v. Borough of Glassboro,** 393 U.S. 117 (1968)—denial of tax exemption solely because taxpayer was incorporated in another state is invalid]

(c) Finding discrimination [§354]

If a state tax singles out interstate commerce for taxation, the Court ordinarily will not "save" the tax by finding other state taxes imposed only on local commerce (which might arguably eliminate the "apparent" discrimination against interstate commerce). [**Nippert v. City of Richmond,** 327 U.S. 416 (1946)]

1) Apparent nondiscrimination [§355]

A facially nondiscriminatory tax may be coupled with another statutory provision that effectively renders the tax discriminatory. [**West Lynn Creamery, Inc. v. Healy,** 512 U.S. 186 (1994)—tax on all sales of milk by wholesalers to local retailers, regardless of whether the milk was produced in or out of state, becomes discriminatory when tax proceeds are used to make subsidy payments to local milk producers]

2) "Compensatory" tax exception [§356]

However, a facially discriminatory tax *may* be upheld if the state shows that the tax was designed simply to make interstate commerce bear a burden *no greater* than that already imposed on intrastate commerce by an *identified tax*. [**Associated Industries of Missouri v. Lohman,** 511 U.S. 641 (1994)]

a) Equivalent events

The "compensatory" (or "complementary") taxes must tax persons who are in essentially the same class, *i.e.*, engaged in essentially the same transaction. (*See, e.g.,* sales and use taxes, discussed below.)

(2) Nondiscriminatory taxes [§357]

In the absence of relevant federal legislation, the Court reviews nondiscriminatory state taxes affecting interstate commerce—under both the Commerce Clause and the Due Process Clause—and *balances* the state's need to obtain revenue against the burden such taxes impose on the free flow of commerce. Interstate commerce is *not immune* from such taxation; it must pay its fair share.

(a) Commerce Clause [§358]

The Commerce Clause is principally used to prevent state taxes that impose multiple burdens on interstate commerce.

(b) Due Process Clause [§359]

The principal focus of the Due Process Clause is "jurisdiction." It is mainly used to require that the benefits and protection afforded by the taxing state have a sufficient relationship to the subject matter taxed ("minimum or adequate contacts") so that the subject matter has a "tax situs" in the taxing state.

(c) Comment

The use of these two constitutional provisions is often not sharply delineated and may overlap in many instances.

2. Ad Valorem Property Taxes [§360]

Ad valorem property taxes are taxes based on the value of the property being taxed.

a. Tax on property used to transport goods interstate [§361]

The validity of ad valorem property taxes on "instrumentalities of commerce" (airplanes, railroad cars, etc.) depends on: (i) whether the property has acquired a *"taxable situs"* in or *"nexus"* to the taxing state—*i.e.,* whether there are sufficient "contacts" with the taxing state to justify the tax, and (ii) because the property may move from state to state during the year, whether its value has been *properly apportioned* according to the amount of "contacts" with each taxing state. (The taxable situs ("nexus") is required by the Due Process Clause to establish the state's power to tax at all, and apportionment is required by the Commerce Clause to prevent an undue or multiple burden on interstate commerce.)

(1) Taxable situs ("nexus") [§362]

In general, property has a taxable situs in a state if it receives *benefits or protection* from the state. [**Braniff Airways v. Nebraska Board of Equalization**, 347 U.S. 590 (1954)—airplanes have taxable situs in state where airline company owned no property but made 18 regularly scheduled flights per day from rented depot space, even though same aircraft did not land every day]

(a) **More than one taxable situs possible [§363]**

An "instrumentality of commerce" may have more than one taxable situs, each of which can impose a tax subject to the required apportionment (below).

(2) **Apportionment [§364]**

If an "instrumentality of commerce" has more than one taxable situs, a fair apportionment of its value to the taxing state is required—*i.e.*, one that fairly approximates the average physical presence of the property within the taxing state. [**Union Tank Line Co. v. Wright**, 249 U.S. 275 (1919)]

(a) **Fair apportionment [§365]**

The following methods of apportionment have been upheld by the Court:

(i) Using the *proportion of miles* traveled within the taxing state to the total number of miles traveled by the instrumentalities in the entire operation. [**Ott v. Mississippi Valley Barge Line Co.**, 336 U.S. 169 (1949)]

(ii) Computing the *average number of instrumentalities (e.g., tank cars) physically present* in the taxing state on any one day during the tax year and taxing that portion at full value—*i.e.*, as if in the state all year. [**Johnson Oil Refining Co. v. Oklahoma**, 290 U.S. 158 (1933)]

1) **Note**

Because different states may use different apportionment formulas to tax the same property, there may still be some multiple taxation of the same property. However, this should be minimal if fair apportionment formulas have been used.

(b) **Unfair apportionment [§366]**

The apportionment formula used must be *rational*, both on its face and as applied, to property values connected with the taxing state. A state is not permitted to use imprecise formulas resulting in totally unrealistic assessments; this would violate both the Due Process and Commerce Clauses. [**Norfolk & Western Railway v. Missouri Tax Commission**, 390 U.S. 317 (1968)—apportionment based on track mileage within state, as compared to total track mileage, resulted in apportioning over twice the value of railroad cars actually present in taxing state because railroad had unusually high amount of track in taxing state]

1) **Burden of proof [§367]**

The taxpayer has a heavy burden of showing "gross overreaching." [**Norfolk & Western Railway v. Missouri Tax Commission**, *supra*]

(c) Domiciliary state need not automatically apportion [§368]

The taxpayer's domiciliary state need not apportion the value of "instrumentalities of commerce" and may tax the **full value** of the property—unless the taxpayer can prove that the property has acquired a taxable situs elsewhere.

1) Proving situs elsewhere [§369]

Mere proof that the property was absent from the domiciliary state for part of the tax year is not enough. The taxpayer must prove that the property is either: (i) **permanently located** or (ii) **habitually employed** in some other state, thus acquiring a taxable situs outside the domiciliary state. *But note:* The taxpayer need not prove that the property was actually taxed by a nondomiciliary state. [**Central Railroad v. Pennsylvania,** 370 U.S. 607 (1962)]

b. Tax on cargo in transit [§370]

States cannot levy an ad valorem tax on property being shipped interstate that happens to be in the taxing state on the tax day; otherwise, each state could tax as the property passed through, thus imposing multiple taxation on interstate commerce. [**Standard Oil Co. v. Peck,** 342 U.S. 382 (1952)]

(1) When does interstate transit begin? [§371]

Interstate transit begins when (i) the cargo is **delivered to an interstate carrier** (the shipper thereby relinquishing further control) *or* (ii) the cargo actually **starts its interstate journey**. Goods merely being prepared for transit are not immune from state taxation. [**Coe v. Errol,** 116 U.S. 517 (1886)]

(2) Effect of a "break" in transit [§372]

Once started, a shipment remains in interstate transit unless actually diverted. Temporary interruptions for the convenience of transportation do **not** destroy the interstate nature of the shipment. [**Hughes Bros. Timber Co. v. Minnesota,** 272 U.S. 469 (1926)] However, a break intended to end or suspend the shipment (*e.g.,* for possible sale of the property) renders the property subject to state taxation. [**Minnesota v. Blasius,** 290 U.S. 1 (1933)]

3. "Doing Business" Taxes [§373]

"Doing business" taxes are taxes imposed for engaging in business within the state. They may be labeled "privilege," "occupation," "license," or "franchise" taxes—or simply "gross receipts" or "net income" taxes—and may be measured either by a flat annual fee or by a proportional rate based on revenue derived from the taxing state.

a. Four-part test [§374]

States may generally impose such taxes·on persons doing business in the state—both on companies engaged exclusively in interstate commerce as well as on interstate companies engaged in local commerce—if four criteria are met:

(i)   The activity taxed must have a *"substantial nexus"* to the taxing state;

(ii)   The tax must be *"fairly apportioned"*;

(iii) The tax must *not "discriminate"* against interstate commerce; and

(iv)   The tax must *"fairly relate to services provided"* by the taxing state.

[**Complete Auto Transit, Inc. v. Brady,** 430 U.S. 274 (1977)—*overruling* **Spector Motor Service, Inc. v. O'Connor,** 340 U.S. 602 (1951)]

(e.g.) **Example:** A privilege tax for doing business, based on the gross income derived from transporting goods within the state, can be applied to a trucking company that delivers goods coming from outside the state. [**Complete Auto Transit, Inc. v. Brady,** *supra*]

(e.g.) **Example:** An occupation tax on all business, based on gross income derived within the state, can be applied to a stevedoring company operating within the state that loads and unloads ships carrying goods in interstate commerce. [**Washington Revenue Department v. Association of Washington Stevedoring Companies,** 435 U.S. 734 (1978)—*overruling* **Joseph v. Carter & Weekes Stevedoring Companies,** 330 U.S. 422 (1947)]

(e.g.) **Example:** A gross receipts tax on all railroads doing business within the state, apportioned on the basis of track mileage in the taxing state, may be applied to a railroad that operates totally within the state hauling goods in interstate commerce. [**Canton Railroad v. Rogan,** 340 U.S. 511 (1951)]

---

(1) Burden of proof [§375]
A taxpayer challenging a state's tax apportionment has the burden of showing that the apportionment formula is unfair. [**General Motors Corp. v. Washington,** 377 U.S. 436 (1964)]

b. Net income taxes [§376]
As indicated above, a net income tax is another type of "doing business" tax that has been upheld as applied to an interstate company engaged in business within the taxing state. [**Northwestern States Portland Cement Co. v. Minnesota,** 358 U.S. 450 (1959)]

(1) Adequate contacts [§377]
In *Portland Cement*, the taxpayer had several salespeople and a rented office in the taxing state, and the Court found this a sufficient "nexus" for the tax. (*Note:* Congress subsequently enacted a statute [15 U.S.C. §§381-384] prohibiting state net income taxes, irrespective of fair apportionment, on out-of-state businesses whose only contacts with the taxing state are salespeople.)

(2) Fair apportionment [§378]

In *Portland Cement*, the state used the approved "three-factor" apportionment formula (ratio of property, payroll, and sales within state to taxpayer's total property, payroll, and sales). The taxpayer could not show that this was unfair given state protection and services for the taxpayer's local activities, and there was no showing of "multiple burden."

(a) A "single-factor" formula [§379]

Note that a "single-factor" formula (ratio of sales within state to taxpayer's total sales) has also been upheld as "presumptively valid"—the taxpayer being unable to prove by "clear and cogent evidence" that it "led to a grossly distorted result." The fact that some income may be subject to overlapping taxes because other states (even a majority) use a different formula (the "three-factor" formula) does not prove that the single-factor formula is arbitrary. [**Moorman Manufacturing Co. v. Bair,** 437 U.S. 267 (1978)]

(b) Income includible [§380]

Income from separate corporate divisions, or from subsidiary corporations operating in other states or foreign countries, may be included in the tax base—unless the taxpayer proves that the divisions or subsidiaries were not part of its "single unitary business" [**Mobil Oil Corp. v. Vermont Commissioner of Taxes,** 445 U.S. 425 (1980)], but rather were conducted as "discrete business enterprises" [**Asarco, Inc. v. Idaho Tax Commission,** 458 U.S. 307 (1982)]. Substantial deference will be given to the judgment of state courts on this issue. [**Container Corp. of America v. Franchise Tax Board,** 463 U.S. 159 (1983)]

4. Severance Taxes [§381]

A nondiscriminatory state tax on extraction of minerals from the state, measured by a percentage of the value of such minerals, is valid even though most of the minerals are sold in interstate commerce. The tax satisfies the "four-part test" of **Complete Auto Transit, Inc. v. Brady** (*supra*, §374): (i) since the minerals are taken from the taxing state, there is a "substantial nexus"; (ii) since extraction can occur in no other state, there is "fair apportionment"; (iii) if the rate is the same for in-state and out-of-state consumers, there is no "discrimination against interstate commerce"; and (iv) as long as the tax is imposed on activity within the taxing state, the Court will *not* inquire into the *amount* of the tax or the *value* of benefits received by the taxpayer. [**Commonwealth Edison Co. v. Montana,** 453 U.S. 609 (1981)]

5. Taxes on Solicitors [§382]

Flat license fees may not be levied on solicitors ("drummers") who seek local orders to be filled from goods shipped interstate—even if the same fee is levied on those selling intrastate goods. [**Nippert v. City of Richmond,** *supra,* §354] Otherwise each municipality visited by the drummer could impose such a tax (resulting in a tremendous cumulative burden), while the local retail merchant would be subject to only one local tax—thus, in *practical effect*, discriminating against interstate commerce.

a. Distinguish—peddlers [§383]

However, the state *may* impose a license tax on a peddler who actually sells and delivers wares within a state (even though the goods are shipped into the state from interstate commerce), provided the tax rates are nondiscriminatory. [**Dunbar Stanley Studios, Inc. v. Alabama,** 393 U.S. 537 (1969)—transient photographers took the delivered pictures locally but had them developed outside the state]

(1) Comment

As a practical matter, however, such a tax may affect peddlers as severely as it does drummers, thus placing an undue burden on interstate commerce.

6. Highway Use Taxes [§384]

License and similar taxes on interstate carriers will be upheld if they are nondiscriminatory and are imposed to compensate states for the costs of maintaining and administering their roads.

a. Burden of proof [§385]

The taxpayer bears the burden of proving that the tax requires more than "fair compensation" for road use. [**Capitol Greyhound Lines v. Brice,** 339 U.S. 542 (1950)]

b. Formula to determine amount of tax [§386]

The Court has, of course, approved formulas that are reasonably related to road use (*e.g.*, mileage within the state, number and capacity of vehicles), but it has also upheld *flat fees*, even though not directly related to use, as long as they were not shown to be "unreasonable in amount." [**Capitol Greyhound Lines v. Brice,** *supra*—flat fee upheld when imposed in addition to mileage tax]

7. Airport Use Fees [§387]

Similarly, a one-dollar state or municipal tax, imposed on emplaning commercial airline passengers to help defray airport construction costs, does not violate the Commerce Clause (or the Equal Protection Clause, or the "right to travel"). As long as: (i) the amount of the tax is based on some fair approximation of use and is not excessive in comparison with the government benefit conferred, and (ii) the tax does not discriminate against interstate commerce by taxing all passengers, it is valid even though some other formula might better reflect the relative use of airports by individual users. [**Evansville-Vanderburgh Airport Authority District v. Delta Airlines, Inc.,** 405 U.S. 707 (1972)]

8. Sales and Use Taxes [§388]

A sales tax is one imposed on sales consummated *within the state*. A use tax is imposed on the user of goods purchased *outside the state*. (Use taxes are designed to prevent residents from purchasing goods outside the state in order to avoid a state sales tax.)

a. Compensatory use tax by "consumer" state [§389]

Although use taxes single out interstate commerce for taxation (*i.e.*, they are imposed only on goods purchased outside the state), they do not violate the Commerce Clause. [**Henneford v. Silas Mason Co.**, 300 U.S. 577 (1937)] *Rationale:* As long as the use tax rate is *not higher* than the sales tax rate, the purpose is to equalize the tax on goods purchased outside the state with the tax on goods purchased within the state (and subject to the state sales tax).

(1) Defining "not higher" [§390]

Where sales taxes vary within a state because of differing local tax rates, the Supreme Court will look to the effect of the use tax in each locality rather than compare the use tax rate to the average sales tax rate. The use tax will be held invalid as to those localities where the use tax rate exceeds the sales tax rate. [**Associated Industries of Missouri v. Lohman**, *supra*, §356]

(2) Credit for sales tax paid in "seller" state [§391]

It has been argued that: (i) if the sale is consummated outside the state and is subjected there to a sales tax, (ii) if the goods are then brought into the consumer state to be used there, and (iii) if the consumer state imposes a use tax, then the consumer state must give credit for the sales tax already paid in the seller state; *i.e.*, if no credit is given, the transaction is subjected to two taxes (a multiple burden) simply because the transaction involved interstate commerce. However, the Court has not decided whether such a credit must be given. [**Southern Pacific Co. v. Gallagher**, 306 U.S. 167 (1939)]

(a) Discrimination against nonresidents [§392]

In the absence of *some* "legitimate" purpose, if a consumer state gives such a credit *only to its own residents* who pay a sales tax in the seller state, it violates the Equal Protection Clause. [**Williams v. Vermont**, 472 U.S. 14 (1985)]

b. Use tax by "seller" state [§393]

Use taxes by the "seller" state do not exist, since use taxes are not imposed by the state where the sale is made. In any case, since the "seller" state has no contact with the use or consumption of the goods, an attempt to impose a use tax would probably violate due process.

c. Sales tax by "seller" state [§394]

The issue here concerns sales by local sellers to buyers from outside the state.

(1) Sale within state [§395]

If the sale is consummated *within* the state (*i.e.*, buyer takes possession within the state), the Commerce Clause does not prohibit a sales tax by the seller state—even though the buyer takes the goods outside the state for use. [**International Harvester Co. v. Department of Treasury**, 322 U.S. 340 (1944)—tax is one on a "local sale"]

(2) Sale outside state [§396]

If the sale is made to a buyer *outside* the state (*i.e.*, goods delivered there by the seller or a common carrier), the Commerce Clause *prohibits* a sales tax by the seller state—at least if the tax is *unapportioned*. [**Adams Manufacturing Co. v. Storen**, 304 U.S. 307 (1938)—tax is one on "interstate sale"]

(a) Comment

The Court has not passed on a *fairly apportioned* sales tax sought to be imposed by a "seller" state on goods sold to a buyer outside the state. But such a tax might well be valid if it satisfied the "four-part test" of **Complete Auto Transit, Inc. v. Brady**, *supra*, §374.

(b) Sales tax on services performed outside state [§397]

If the *sale* of a service is consummated within the state (*e.g.*, the sale of a bus ticket), the seller state may impose a sales tax on the full amount of the sale—even though this covers some service (*e.g.*, bus transportation) that takes place outside the state. No other state can claim to be the site of the sale. [**Oklahoma Tax Commission v. Jefferson Lines, Inc.**, 514 U.S. 175 (1995)]

d. Sales tax by "consumer" state [§398]

Here, the sales are to local buyers by sellers engaged in interstate commerce.

(1) Sufficient contacts [§399]

If the interstate seller has substantial contacts in the consumer state (*e.g.*, office, salesroom, property, etc.), the Commerce Clause does not prohibit a sales tax by the consumer state—even though the goods are delivered from outside the state. [**McGoldrick v. Berwind-White Coal Mining Co.**, 309 U.S. 33 (1940)—tax is on a "local sale," and no multiple burden because no other state may impose sales or use tax]

(2) "Drummers" insufficient [§400]

But if the only contact between the interstate seller and the consumer state consists of "drummers" (*i.e.*, solicitation of orders subject to acceptance at seller's out-of-state office, and goods shipped by carrier with payment by mail), both the Commerce Clause and the Due Process Clause prohibit any sales tax by the consumer state. [**McLeod v. J. E. Dilworth Co.**, 322 U.S. 327 (1944)—tax is on an "interstate sale" taking place beyond state jurisdiction]

e. "Consumer" state's ability to require interstate seller to collect use tax [§401]

The consumer state may require collection of a use tax if the interstate seller has the "minimum contacts" with the consumer state required by the Due Process Clause *and* the "substantial nexus" required by the Commerce Clause. [**Quill Corp. v. North Dakota**, 504 U.S. 298 (1992)—"substantial nexus" may require more than "minimum contacts"]

(1) "Drummers" sufficient [§402]

In the situation described in *McLeod, supra* (interstate seller with drummers in consumer state), the consumer state could impose a use tax on the purchaser. [*See* **Henneford v. Silas Mason Co.**, *supra*, §389] Furthermore, although the consumer state may not impose a sales tax on the interstate seller [*see* **McLeod v. J. E. Dilworth Co.**, *supra*], it may force the interstate seller to collect the use tax from the local purchaser and remit it to the consumer state [**General Trading Co. v. Iowa Tax Commission**, 322 U.S. 335 (1944)].

(a) "Independent contractors" [§403]

The same result applies where the seller uses "independent contractors" instead of the seller's own salespeople. [**Scripto v. Carson**, 362 U.S. 207 (1960)]

(2) Offices sufficient [§404]

Where the interstate seller has offices in the consumer state, there is sufficient nexus even though the use tax was imposed on interstate mail order sales of merchandise not solicited by the local offices. [**National Geographic Society v. California Board of Equalization**, 430 U.S. 551 (1977)]

(3) Mail solicitation insufficient [§405]

If the interstate seller solicits sales by mail, with orders shipped by mail or common carrier, the interstate seller gains the benefit of an economic market in the forum state that constitutes adequate "contacts" to satisfy the Due Process Clause. However, the seller lacks the "substantial nexus" required by the Commerce Clause, and thus the consumer state may *not* impose a duty on the interstate seller to collect a use tax on sales to local residents. [**Quill Corp. v. North Dakota**, *supra*—*modifying* **National Bellas Hess, Inc. v. Illinois Department of Revenue**, 386 U.S. 753 (1967)]

(a) And note

Nor is there sufficient nexus if the interstate seller occasionally advertises and makes truck deliveries in the consumer state. [**Miller Bros. v. Maryland**, 347 U.S. 340 (1954)]

9. Taxes on Foreign Corporations [§406]

A state is not required to admit foreign corporations (those incorporated in other states) to do business locally since a corporation is not a "citizen" within the Interstate Privileges and Immunities Clause [Art. IV, §2]. The extent to which the *Commerce Clause* bars burdensome state taxes or regulations on such corporations is uncertain. But, under the *Equal Protection Clause*, a state may *not* impose more onerous taxes or other burdens on foreign corporations than on domestic corporations unless the discrimination is *rationally related* to a *legitimate state purpose*. [**Western & Southern Life Insurance Co. v. California Board of Equalization**, *supra*, §303]

a. Illegitimate purpose [§407]

A state may *not* impose a more onerous tax on foreign corporations simply for the purpose of promoting the business of domestic competitors. [**Metropolitan Life Insurance Co. v. Ward**, *supra*, §303]

EXAM TIP	gilbert

When a question involves state taxation that affects interstate commerce, you should ask:

1. Does the question refer to any federal legislation that might (i) *forbid* the state tax or *preempt* the field or (ii) *authorize* state taxation?

2. If neither of these possibilities is dispositive, does the state tax *discriminate* against or *unduly burden* the free flow of interstate commerce? If the state tax discriminates or is unduly burdensome (no substantial nexus, unfair apportionment, or no fair relationship), it is invalid.

D. Power of States to Tax Foreign Commerce

1. Import-Export Clause [§408]

Article I, Section 10, Clause 2 provides: "No state shall, without the Consent of the Congress, lay any Imposts or Duties on Imports or Exports, except what may be absolutely necessary for executing its inspection Laws . . . ."

a. State taxation of "imports" [§409]

The Import-Export Clause prohibits the states from imposing any tax on imported goods *as such* or on commercial activity connected with imported goods *as such* (*i.e.*, taxes discriminating against imports), except with congressional consent. [**Brown v. Maryland**, 25 U.S. (12 Wheat.) 419 (1827)—license tax on importer invalid because it would increase price of his commodities]

(1) Nondiscriminatory taxes [§410]

A nondiscriminatory ad valorem property tax on all goods located in the state (including imported goods) is *not* prohibited. [**Michelin Tire Corp. v. Wages**, *supra*, §283] *Rationale:* Such taxes merely apportion the cost of state services among all beneficiaries, and imports must bear their fair share.

(a) **Goods in transit [§411]**

The Court has left as an *open question* whether a nondiscriminatory *property tax* may be imposed on imported goods that are still in transit. But a nondiscriminatory *occupation tax* on all businesses operating within the state may be applied to a company that services imported (or exported) goods even when the goods are still in transit. [**Washington Revenue Department v. Association of Washington Stevedoring Companies**, *supra*, §374]

b. **State taxation of "exports" [§412]**

The Import-Export Clause only prohibits the states from taxing exports after they have begun their "*physical entry* into the stream of exportation." [**Kosydar v. National Cash Register Co.**, 417 U.S. 62 (1974)—goods in warehouse *pending shipment* abroad pursuant to completed sale may still be taxed]

2. Commerce Clause [§413]

The Commerce Clause gives Congress plenary power to regulate foreign commerce, and thus inherently limits a state's power to tax that commerce.

a. **In general [§414]**

As a *first step*, the Commerce Clause imposes the same limits on state taxation of foreign commerce as it does on state taxation of interstate commerce (*see supra*, §§350 *et seq.*). [**Barclays Bank PLC v. Franchise Tax Board**, 512 U.S. 298 (1994)—sustaining same apportionment formula for corporate franchise tax on foreign businesses as has been upheld for interstate businesses]

b. **Additional considerations [§415]**

In the absence of congressional authorization, there are stricter limits on state taxation of foreign commerce than of interstate commerce because of (i) the enhanced risk of multiple taxation and (ii) the greater need for federal uniformity. [**Container Corp. of America v. Franchise Tax Board**, *supra*, §380]

(1) **Illustration—instrumentalities of foreign commerce**

A state may not impose an ad valorem property tax on instrumentalities that are *foreign owned* and used *exclusively in international commerce*. This is true even if the property has a situs in the taxing state and the tax is nondiscriminatory and fairly apportioned (*compare supra*, §361, regarding state taxation of instrumentalities of *interstate* commerce). [**Japan Line, Ltd. v. County of Los Angeles**, 441 U.S. 434 (1979)]

(2) **Distinguish**

But a state *may* impose a fairly apportioned sales tax on a lease within its borders of instrumentalities that are *domestically owned*, even though used exclusively in international commerce. [**Itel Containers International Corp. v. Huddleston**, 507 U.S. 60 (1993)]

(a) Government's position

Although not dispositive, the views expressed by the United States in the litigation on whether the state tax interferes with the need for federal uniformity may help reconcile the results in the *Japan Line* and *Itel* cases, which are otherwise very difficult to distinguish. [*See* **Itel Containers International Corp. v. Huddleston,** *supra*]

Chapter Four: Protection of Individual Rights

CONTENTS

Chapter Approach

Chapter Approach

This chapter focuses on some of the limitations on the exercise of governmental power over individuals. The Constitution explicitly provides protections for individuals against certain actions by the federal government and certain actions by state governments. Other limitations have been read into other constitutional provisions; most significantly, most of the Bill of Rights has been held applicable to the states through the Fourteenth Amendment Due Process Clause. You will almost certainly see an exam question concerning one or more of the following topics:

1. **Due Process Clauses**

   The Due Process Clauses (in the Fifth and Fourteenth Amendments) provide two types of protection: substantive and procedural.

   a. **Procedural Due Process**

   Procedurally, the Due Process Clauses guarantee that liberty and property interests shall not be impaired without some form of *notice and hearing* by an unbiased decisionmaker. Whether a *prior* evidentiary hearing is required is determined by weighing the importance of the interest involved, the value of the safeguards to the interest, and the government interest in fiscal and administrative efficiency.

   b. **Substantive Due Process**

   Your approach to determining whether a law violates substantive due process should start with an analysis of whether the law is an economic or social regulation or whether a fundamental right is involved.

   (i) *If economic or social regulations* are involved, the court will ordinarily use the traditional test: The regulations are *presumed valid,* and thus will be upheld if they bear a *rational relationship* to the end sought. Note, however, that the Court uses a different approach to interpret several *specific* constitutional provisions (*e.g.,* the Just Compensation Clause (*infra,* §473), and the Contract Clause (*infra,* §543)) that also deal with economic matters.

   (ii) *If fundamental rights* are affected by the regulation, the strict scrutiny test is used: The regulation will be held *invalid unless* it is *necessary* to achieve a *compelling* governmental interest, a much more difficult test.

2. **Other Constitutional Protections of Individual Rights**

   Although somewhat less likely to be an exam question, you should be aware of other constitutional protections of individual rights. For example, the Ex Post Facto Clause (*see infra,* §557) prohibit the states and the federal government from adopting retroactive legislation aimed at punishment.

A. Introduction—Bill of Rights

1. **Bill of Rights—Limitation on Federal Power [§416]**

   The first eight amendments to the Constitution (known as the Bill of Rights) as originally enacted protected only against actions of the *federal* government; these provisions were not limitations on the states. [**Barron v. Baltimore**, 32 U.S. (7 Pet.) 243 (1833)]

2. **Fourteenth Amendment—Limitation on State Power [§417]**

   Section I of the Fourteenth Amendment, adopted in 1868, provides: "No State shall make or enforce any law which shall abridge the *privileges or immunities* of citizens of the United States; nor shall any State deprive any person of life, liberty, or property without *due process* of law; nor deny to any person within its jurisdiction the *equal protection* of the laws."

   a. **Fourteenth Amendment Privileges and Immunities Clause [§418]**

      As already discussed (*see supra*, §255), it was early held that the guarantees in the Bill of Rights were *not* privileges and immunities of national citizenship protected from state abridgment through the Fourteenth Amendment Privileges and Immunities Clause. [**Slaughterhouse Cases**, *supra*, §255]

   b. **Fourteenth Amendment Due Process Clause [§419]**

      After the **Slaughterhouse Cases**, the Court held that provisions of the Bill of Rights may be sufficiently "fundamental" as to be protected against state abridgment through the Fourteenth Amendment Due Process Clause.

      (1) **"Selective incorporation" [§420]**

          Although the Court was willing to accept that the Fourteenth Amendment Due Process Clause could protect the rights provided in the Bill of Rights, it rejected the view that the Clause incorporates the Bill of Rights *in toto*. [**Adamson v. California**, 332 U.S. 46 (1947)] Instead, the Court has decided whether each right is included on a case-by-case basis, in a process called "selective incorporation." Through this process, the Court has held that *most* of the rights provided in the Bill of Rights are protected by the Fourteenth Amendment Due Process Clause.

EXAM TIP   **gilbert**

The lexicon of lawyers is quite precise. A lawyer's choice of words often can greatly affect an argument. To this end, you should note that it would be quite imprecise simply to write that a state has violated a person's First, Fourth, Fifth, etc., Amendment rights, because those amendments, on their face, do not prevent the states from doing anything. A better answer will acknowledge the *doctrine of selective incorporation*; e.g., "Plaintiff will argue that the state has violated his First Amendment right to freedom of speech, applicable to the states through the Due Process Clause of the Fourteenth Amendment."

(a) Standard for incorporation [§421]

In determining which provisions of the Bill of Rights are protected from *both* federal and state action, the Court has used various criteria, *e.g.*, stating that the Fourteenth Amendment incorporates those principles "implicit in the concept of ordered liberty" [**Palko v. Connecticut,** 302 U.S. 319 (1947)], or *"fundamental to the American scheme of justice"* [**Duncan v. Louisiana,** 391 U.S. 145 (1968)].

(b) Extent of incorporation [§422]

A majority of the Court has concluded that if a right is incorporated by the Fourteenth Amendment, then *all aspects and elements* of the right must be deemed incorporated, so that the right receives the same protection against state action (via the Fourteenth Amendment) that it receives against federal action (under the Bill of Rights).

1) Dissent

However, some Justices take the position that there may be some aspects of a provision of the Bill of Rights that are not so "fundamental" that they must be held binding on the states as a matter of due process. Following this view, a right—although incorporated by the Fourteenth Amendment—may not be protected to the same extent against state action as it is against federal action. [*See* **Crist v. Bretz,** 437 U.S. 28 (1978)—Burger, C.J., Powell and Rehnquist, JJ.]

---

e.g. **Example:** In **Apodaca v. Oregon,** 406 U.S. 404 (1972), four Justices concluded that the Sixth Amendment right to a jury trial included the right to a unanimous verdict; and, because the right to a jury trial had been incorporated by the Fourteenth Amendment Due Process Clause, the requirement of a unanimous verdict was binding on the state courts. Four other Justices concluded to the contrary. The deciding vote was cast by the ninth Justice (Powell), who reasoned that even though the right to jury trial was incorporated by the Fourteenth Amendment, the unanimous verdict aspect of this right was not so fundamental as to be required by due process, and hence, although the states must afford a jury trial, they do not have to afford a unanimous verdict. The net result is that the Sixth Amendment right to jury trial receives *lesser* protection in state than in federal courts (*see infra,* §§1292-1293).

(c) Provisions of Bill of Rights incorporated [§423]

Most provisions of the Bill of Rights have been held to be so fundamental as to be applicable to the states. They are:

1) The First Amendment protections for *religion, speech, assembly,* and *petition for grievances.* (*See infra,* §§561 *et seq.*)

2) The Fourth Amendment provisions regarding *arrest,* and *search and seizure.* [**Ker v. California,** 374 U.S. 23 (1963)]

3) The Fifth Amendment protection against *double jeopardy* [**Benton v. Maryland,** 395 U.S. 784 (1969)], the privilege against *self-incrimination* [**Malloy v. Hogan,** 378 U.S. 1 (1964)], and the bar on taking of property *without just compensation.*

4) The Sixth Amendment rights in criminal prosecutions to *counsel* [**Gideon v. Wainwright,** 372 U.S. 335 (1963)]; *confrontation* and *cross-examination* of witnesses [**Pointer v. Texas,** 380 U.S. 400 (1965)]; *speedy trial* [**Klopfer v. North Carolina,** 386 U.S. 213 (1967)]; *public trial* [**In re Oliver,** 333 U.S. 257 (1948)]; *jury trial* [**Duncan v. Louisiana,** *supra,* §421]; and *compulsory process* for obtaining witnesses [**Washington v. Texas,** 388 U.S. 14 (1967)].

5) The Eighth Amendment prohibition against *cruel and unusual punishment* (*see infra,* §§1331 *et seq.*). *But note:* The Court has *not* ruled on the applicability to the states of the Eighth Amendment's bar on "excessive bail." [*See* **Schilb v. Kuebel,** 404 U.S. 357 (1971)]

(d) Provisions of Bill of Rights not incorporated [§424]
The following have been held not to be so fundamental as to be applicable to the states:

1) The *grand jury indictment* guarantee of the Fifth Amendment. [**Hurtado v. California,** 110 U.S. 516 (1884)]

2) The *civil jury trial* guarantee of the Seventh Amendment for all suits at common law involving more than $20. [**Walker v. Sauvinet,** 92 U.S. 90 (1876)]

(e) "Due process" as protecting rights beyond those enumerated in Bill of Rights [§425]
Modern decisions by the Court indicate that the "due process" guaranteed by the Fourteenth Amendment goes *further* than merely incorporating various rights enumerated in the first eight amendments. Rather, it reaches various rights that are *not* expressed in the Bill of Rights (or anywhere else in the Constitution)—for example, that proof in a criminal prosecution must be "beyond a reasonable doubt." [*In re* **Winship,** 397 U.S. 358 (1970); *and see infra,* §§427-542, 1324 *et seq.*]

SELECTIVE INCORPORATION OF BILL OF RIGHTS INTO FOURTEENTH AMENDMENT DUE PROCESS CLAUSE   **gilbert**

RIGHTS SELECTED		RIGHTS REJECTED
• Freedom of religion • Freedom of speech • Freedom of assembly • Right to petition government • Protections against unreasonable arrest, search, and seizure • Right against double jeopardy • Right against self-incrimination	• Bar against taking property without just compensation • Rights in criminal cases to counsel, confront and cross-examine witnesses, speedy, public jury trial, and compulsory process for obtaining witnesses • Prohibition against cruel and unusual punishment	• Right to grand jury indictment • Right to civil jury trial for all suits at common law involving more than $20

c. Fourteenth Amendment Equal Protection Clause [§426]

The Fourteenth Amendment guarantee of "equal protection of the laws" by its terms limits only actions of the *states*. There is no similar provision in the Constitution applicable to the federal government. However, it has been held that most acts by the federal government that would deny equal protection constitute a "deprivation of liberty" within the *Fifth* Amendment Due Process Clause ("No person . . . shall be deprived of life, liberty, or property without due process of law"). [*See* **Bolling v. Sharpe**, 347 U.S. 497 (1954)—racial segregation in public schools in the District of Columbia held to deprive African-American children of their "liberty" in violation of Fifth Amendment Due Process Clause]

(1) But note

Fourteenth Amendment "equal protection" and Fifth Amendment "equality" are usually but not always coextensive. The Court has indicated that where the federal law has nationwide impact, there may be special national interests that justify discrimination by the federal government that would be unacceptable if imposed by a state. (However, federal discrimination with only local impact, and no special national interest involved, is judged by the same standard as state discrimination.)

Example: The federal Civil Service Commission adopted a regulation barring most resident aliens from employment in most positions of federal service. A number of resident aliens brought suit seeking to have the regulation declared unconstitutional. *Held:* While the federal government has broad power over immigration and naturalization, and Congress or the President could expressly impose this citizenship requirement, an agency such as the Commission cannot do so arbitrarily and without identifying an overriding national interest in respect to a matter so far removed from its normal responsibilities. [**Hampton v. Mow Sun Wong,** 426 U.S. 88 (1976)]

B. Procedural Due Process

1. Introduction [§427]

Both the Fifth and Fourteenth Amendments protect against the deprivation of "life, liberty, or property without due process of law." The Due Process Clause is most often used to provide procedural safeguards to persons accused of crime before they may be deprived of "life, liberty, or property" (*see supra,* §§423-425; *and see infra,* §§1272 *et seq.*). But the Due Process Clause of the Fifth and Fourteenth Amendments protects an additional range of *"liberty"* and *"property"* interests from being impaired without *some form* of *notice and hearing before an unbiased decisionmaker.* The Court uses a two-step analysis in determining whether this procedural due process has been denied: (i) it first determines whether a "liberty" or "property" interest has been impaired; and (ii) *if so,* it then determines what procedures are due.

2. Definition of "Liberty" and "Property" [§428]

The Court has not comprehensively defined what constitutes the "liberty" and "property" that may not be denied without procedural due process.

a. Liberty [§429]

"Liberty" plainly encompasses the right to be free of *physical restraints* imposed by government in the noncriminal context as well as by the criminal process. [**Addington v. Texas,** 441 U.S. 418 (1979)—involuntary commitment of an adult to a mental institution] It also includes the *right to contract* and to engage in *gainful employment.* [**Board of Regents v. Roth,** 408 U.S. 564 (1972)]

Example: A Nebraska law provided that if a designated physician finds that a prisoner suffers from a mental defect that cannot properly be treated in prison, the director of correctional services may transfer the prisoner to a mental hospital. Appellee was transferred under the statute and claimed that the transfer violated his procedural due process rights because he was not given sufficient notice of the proceedings against him or an opportunity to be heard. *Held:* Involuntary transfer of a prisoner to a mental hospital implicates a constitutionally protected liberty interest that cannot be taken away without the protections of due process. [**Vitek v. Jones,** 445 U.S. 480 (1980)]

cf. **Compare:** Roth was hired by the University of Wisconsin under a one-year contract and was given no tenure rights to continued employment. The University did not rehire Roth after his contract expired, and he sued, arguing that the University violated his due process rights because it did not give him a reason for its decision or an opportunity to challenge the decision at a hearing. The Court found that the University's decision not to rehire Roth did not impinge on any of his liberty interests—the state did not make any charges against Roth that might seriously damage his reputation in the community or impose upon him any stigma that foreclosed his freedom to take advantage of other employment activities. [**Board of Regents v. Roth,** *supra*]

(1) Defamation by government [§430]

"Liberty" also includes the right to be free of defamation by a government official, when such defamation is *made public* and occurs in connection with denial of some *significant tangible interest.* [**Goss v. Lopez,** 419 U.S. 565 (1975)—disciplinary suspension from public school implicates a liberty interest because a person's reputation is at stake; **Wisconsin v. Constantineau,** 400 U.S. 433 (1971)—police posting names of "excessive drinkers" in liquor stores, thereby forbidding sales to them for one year, implicates liberty interests]

(a) Distinguish—defamation alone

However, defamation resulting *only* in damage to one's reputation is not a denial of protected "liberty." [**Paul v. Davis,** 424 U.S. 693 (1976)—plaintiff suffered no deprivation of liberty when the police distributed a flyer to local merchants identifying plaintiff as an active shoplifter]

(b) Distinguish—loss of employment alone

Similarly, mere loss of public employment without publicity as to the defamatory reasons therefor is *not* a denial of "liberty." [**Bishop v. Wood,** 426 U.S. 341 (1976)]

e.g. **Example:** Petitioner was discharged as a city police officer without reason and without a hearing. He sued to be reinstated, claiming that he was terminated without due process. During pretrial discovery, petitioner was informed that he was discharged for insubordination, causing low morale, and conduct unsuited to an officer. Petitioner's dismissal did not implicate a liberty interest because before he sued for reinstatement, no defamatory reason was given for his dismissal. [**Bishop v. Wood,** *supra*]

(2) Parental interests [§431]

A parent has a "liberty" interest in a *developed* parent-child relationship—

e.g., when a father plays a substantial role in his illegitimate child's rearing. But the mere biological fact of parenthood does not merit equivalent constitutional protection. [**Lehr v. Robertson**, 463 U.S. 248 (1983)—putative father never had any significant relationship with his illegitimate child and therefore a liberty interest was not implicated when child was adopted without giving notice to putative father]

(3) Prison discipline [§432]

Disciplinary action by prison officials to punish a prisoner's misconduct does *not* encroach upon a "liberty" interest unless it results in a restraint that imposes "*atypical and significant hardship* in relation to the ordinary incidents of prison life." [**Sandin v. Conner**, 515 U.S. 472 (1995)—30-day segregated confinement was *not* outside range of hardship normally expected by prisoner serving 30 years to life]

b. Property [§433]

"Property" denotes more than ownership of realty, chattels, or money. It also includes "entitlements"—*i.e.*, "interests already acquired in specific benefits." This requires more than an abstract need or desire for (or unilateral expectation of) the benefit: there must be a *legitimate claim* to the benefit under applicable local, state, or federal law. [**Board of Regents v. Roth**, *supra*]

Examples: There is a constitutionally protected "property" interest in *public education* when school attendance is required [**Goss v. Lopez**, *supra*]; in *continued welfare benefits* if the applicant meets statutory criteria [**Goldberg v. Kelly**, 397 U.S. 254 (1970)]; in *retention of a driver's license* under prevailing statutory standards [**Bell v. Burson**, 402 U.S. 535 (1971)]; and in *continued utility service* if state law permits a municipal utility company to terminate service only "for cause" [**Memphis Light, Gas & Water Division v. Craft**, 436 U.S. 1 (1978)].

Compare: A lawyer licensed in one state has no property interest to appear in the courts of another state in the absence of a state rule or "mutually explicit understanding" to that effect. [**Leis v. Flynt**, 439 U.S. 438 (1979)]

(1) Public employment [§434]

Whether there is a "property" interest in continued public employment is determined by applicable local, state, or federal law. A statute (or ordinance), the employment contract, or some clear practice or understanding must provide that the employee can be terminated only for "cause." [**Arnett v. Kennedy**, 416 U.S. 134 (1974)] There is *no* "property" interest if the position is held "at the will of" the public employer. [**Bishop v. Wood**, *supra*]

(2) Causes of action [§435]

There may be a "property" interest in a legislatively or judicially created cause of action.

e.g. Example: Logan filed a charge with the Illinois Employment Practices Commission alleging that his employment had been unlawfully terminated because of his physical handicap. By statute, the Commission was required to convene a fact-finding conference within 120 days, but through apparent inadvertence, the conference was not held until five days after the 120-day period ended. A state court held that failure to hold the conference within the statutory period deprived the Commission of jurisdiction to consider Logan's claim. Logan appealed to the Supreme Court, which held that Logan had a property right in the state-created cause of action. The Court further held that the 120-day limitation was not a substantive element of Logan's claim, but instead was a procedural requirement, that once the state creates a property interest, the minimum procedures required to deprive a person of the property interest are determined by federal law, and that Logan's cause of action was taken away without due process of law. [**Logan v. Zimmerman Brush Co.,** 455 U.S. 422 (1982)]

cf. Compare: Plaintiff marketed and sold specialized annuity contracts to help people fund future college education expenses. The state of Florida created an agency to administer a tuition prepayment program for Florida residents that provided similar benefits. Plaintiff brought suit against the agency in federal court, alleging that the agency made false representations in its sales brochures and annual reports in violation of the Lanham Act. The Court held that there is no "property" interest in a common law or statutory right to be free from a competitor's false advertising. [**Florida Prepaid Postsecondary Education Expense Board v. College Savings Bank,** *supra,* §9—a "hallmark of a protected property interest is the right to exclude others"; no case has recognized "a property right in freedom from a competitor's false advertising about its own products"]

EXAM TIP **gilbert**

It is important to remember that the term "property" includes more than personal belongings and realty; however, an abstract need or desire for (or unilateral expectation of) a government benefit is not enough. On your exam, be sure to remember that to have a property interest in a government benefit, the claimant must have a *legitimate claim or entitlement* to the benefit as defined by the applicable state or federal substantive law.

3. **Definition of "Deprivation" [§436]**

A "deprivation" of life, liberty, or property without due process requires something more than *mere negligent conduct* by government officials, even though such conduct causes injury. It is an open question whether something less than intentional conduct—such as "recklessness" or "gross negligence"—may constitute a deprivation. [**Daniels v. Williams,** 474 U.S. 327 (1986)]

a. **Indirect effect [§437]**

Government action that affects a person only *indirectly or incidentally* is *not* deemed a deprivation of any interest in that person's "liberty" or "property." [**O'Bannon v. Town Court Nursing Center,** 447 U.S. 773 (1980)—patients of nursing home not entitled to a hearing solely because government revoked nursing home's certification to receive payments; patients had no statutory right to receive benefits at *that particular* nursing home]

(1) **"Deprivation" by private persons [§438]**

Failure of a government entity or its agents to adequately protect an individual against being harmed by others does not constitute a deprivation of life, liberty, or property without due process. The purpose of the Due Process Clause is to protect people from government, not to ensure that government protects people from each other.

---

e.g. **Example:** DeShaney, a two-year old, was repeatedly and severely beaten by his father. The incidents were reported to the Winnebago Department of Social Services ("DSS"), which investigated the incidents but took no action. One year later, DeShaney was hospitalized for further child abuse. The DSS required DeShaney's father to undergo counseling, but the father did not fully comply. During the course of the following year, a DSS caseworker recorded acts of further abuse by DeShaney's father, but no action was taken. Eventually, DeShaney's father beat him so badly that he suffered permanent brain damage. DeShaney then sued the DSS for depriving him of his liberty without due process of law. The Supreme Court held that the government's failure to protect a child from his parent's abuse does not constitute a deprivation of liberty without due process of law. [**DeShaney v. Winnebago County Department of Social Services,** 489 U.S. 189 (1989)]

---

b. **Limitations on remedies [§439]**

To amount to a "deprivation" of life, liberty, or property there must be more than a mere denial of certain kinds of remedies. Only when the government affords *no* remedy or *inadequate* remedies may a deprivation of life, liberty, or property result. [**Florida Prepaid Postsecondary Education Expense Board v. College Savings Bank,** 527 U.S. 627 (1999)]

4. **Timing and Scope of Required Hearing [§440]**

An *adversary, judicial-type* hearing—whether before or after deprivation of a protected liberty or property interest—is *not* required in all circumstances. Rather, whether a *prior* evidentiary hearing is required, and the *extent* of procedural requirements, is determined by weighing:

(i) The *importance of the individual interest* involved;

(ii) The *value of specific procedural safeguards* to that interest; and

(iii) The *government interest in fiscal and administrative efficiency.*

[**Mathews v. Eldridge,** 424 U.S. 319 (1976)]

a. Civil forfeiture of real property used in connection with crime [§441]

Due process requires notice and an adversary hearing *prior* to government seizure and forfeiture of *real property* allegedly used in connection with crime. The private interest in possession of a home (even when rented to others), for example, is of historic and continuing importance, and a subsequent hearing may not recompense losses caused by an erroneous seizure. In the absence of exigent circumstances—such as easy removal of personal property [*see* **Calero-Toledo v. Pearson Yacht Leasing Co.,** 416 U.S. 663 (1974)]—the government has no pressing need for an ex parte seizure [**United States v. James Daniel Good Real Property,** 510 U.S. 43 (1993)].

b. Termination of welfare benefits [§442]

Due process *requires an evidentiary* hearing *before* termination of welfare benefits. It need not be a judicial or quasi-judicial trial if there is adequate post-termination review; but the recipient must have timely and adequate *notice* of the reasons for the proposed termination, the right to *confront and cross-examine* adverse witnesses, and the right to *present his own arguments* and evidence orally. *Counsel* need *not* be provided, but must be permitted. Finally, the decision must be based *solely on evidence* adduced at the hearing and must be rendered by an *impartial decisionmaker.* [**Goldberg v. Kelly,** *supra*]

Example: New York City residents who were receiving financial aid from the state—under the aid to Families with Dependent Children program or the Home Relief program—brought suit against the state, claiming that their benefits had been, or were about to be, terminated without prior notice or hearing, in violation of the Due Process Clause. While the case was pending, New York adopted new benefits termination procedures. Before termination: (i) a caseworker had to interview a recipient and recommend termination to a supervisor; (ii) if the supervisor agreed, he had to send the recipient a letter stating the reasons for termination and giving the recipient seven days to request a review by a higher officer (the recipient could submit written statements supporting her claim); (iii) after review, the higher officer could immediately terminate the benefits but had to inform the recipient by letter of the termination and the right to a post-termination hearing. The plaintiffs claimed that the revised procedures also were unconstitutional because they did not provide the recipients with a pretermination opportunity to appear at a hearing or the right to confront and cross-examine witnesses. The Supreme Court found that the state's interest in conserving fiscal and administrative resources was significant. However, because the recipients need their benefits to pay for food, clothing, housing, and medical care, their need to avoid erroneous termination of benefits outweighs the state's interest, and their interests can be protected adequately only by a pretermination hearing that allows them to appear personally to present evidence and confront and cross-examine witnesses. [**Goldberg v. Kelly**, *supra*]

c. **Termination of disability benefits [§443]**

No prior evidentiary hearing is required for termination of disability benefits, provided there is prior *notice* to the recipient, an *opportunity to respond* in writing, and a *subsequent evidentiary hearing* (with retroactive payment of benefits if the recipient prevails). *Rationale:* Disability benefits (unlike welfare benefits) are not based on financial need, and thus are not deemed "vital." [**Mathews v. Eldridge**, *supra*]

(1) **Limit on attorneys' fees [§444]**

Because of Congress's desire that the proceedings be "as informal and nonadversarial as possible" and that claimants' benefits not be unnecessarily diverted to lawyers, a federal law limiting to $10 the fee that may be paid an attorney or agent who represents a veteran seeking service-connected disability benefits does *not* violate due process, absent a *strong* showing of likely errors under the existing system that would likely be cured by the presence of lawyers. [**Walters v. National Association of Radiation Survivors**, 468 U.S. 1323 (1985)]

d. **Termination of public employment [§445]**

A public employee subject to removal only for "cause" may be removed *without a prior evidentiary* hearing on "cause," at least if there is *some form of pretermination notice and opportunity to respond* (to determine whether there are reasonable grounds to believe the charge), and a *subsequent evidentiary* hearing (with reinstatement and back pay if the employee prevails). [**Arnett v. Kennedy**, *supra*, §434]

Example: When Loudermill was hired by the board of education as a security guard, he stated on his job application that he had never been convicted of a felony. Subsequently, the board discovered that Loudermill had been convicted of grand larceny and dismissed him for dishonesty in filling out the job application without giving him an opportunity to respond to the dishonesty charge or to challenge the dismissal. Under state law, Loudermill could be fired only "for cause." He filed an administrative appeal, but his dismissal was upheld. He then appealed in federal court, claiming that the dismissal process was unconstitutional because it did not provide an opportunity for a discharged employee to respond to charges against him prior to removal, thus depriving him of liberty and property without due process. The Supreme Court found that the employee's and government's interest in avoiding an erroneous firing outweighed the government's interests in quickly removing unsatisfactory employees enough to prevent the government from immediately terminating an employee—some form of pretermination notice and an opportunity to respond is required.

But requiring an elaborate pretermination hearing would unduly interfere with the government's interest in removing unsatisfactory employees; therefore such a procedure is not required when a post-termination evidentiary hearing is provided. [**Cleveland Board of Education v. Loudermill,** 470 U.S. 532 (1985)]

(1) Suspension [§446]

If there is a *significant reason* for not keeping the employee on the job, he may be suspended without a limited presuspension hearing and without pay—as long as there is an adequately prompt post-suspension hearing (with reinstatement and back pay if the employee prevails). [**Gilbert v. Homer,** 520 U.S. 994—police officer arrested and formally charged with a felony]

e. Public education—disciplinary suspension [§447]

Although *no formal evidentiary* hearing is required before a student may be *temporarily* suspended (for 10 days or less), due process usually requires *some notice of* the charges and *some opportunity to explain*. But if the student's presence poses a danger to persons or property or threatens to disrupt the academic process, notice and hearing may *follow* removal as soon as practicable. [**Goss v. Lopez,** *supra,* §430]

(1) Corporal punishment in public school [§448]

Corporal punishment in public school may involve a constitutionally protected liberty. However, the traditional common law remedies for excessive punishment satisfy procedural due process and *no prior hearing* is required. [**Ingraham v. Wright,** 430 U.S. 651 (1977)]

f. Public education—academic dismissal [§449]

No prior *evidentiary* hearing is required when a student is dismissed for "academic" deficiencies rather than for "disciplinary" reasons. Due process is satisfied if the student is *adequately informed* of the deficiency and given an *opportunity to respond*. [**Board of Curators v. Horowitz,** 435 U.S. 78 (1978)]

g. License suspension [§450]

If there is *probable cause* to believe that the conditions of a license have been violated, the state's interest may *sometimes* be important enough to permit suspension of the license *without* any *prior* hearing—but there must be a *prompt* post-suspension hearing and decision on any disputed issues. [**Barry v. Barchi,** 443 U.S. 55 (1979)—horse trainer's license suspended without prior hearing regarding drugging of horse; **Mackey v. Montrym,** 443 U.S. 1 (1979)—driver's license suspended without prior hearing for refusing to submit to breathalyzer test]

(1) "Promptness" [§451]

The permissible length of time between suspension and a decision after a hearing is determined by weighing: (i) the importance of the interest and the harm occasioned by delay; (ii) the government's justification for delay; and (iii) the likelihood that the interim decision may have been mistaken. [**Federal Deposit Insurance Corp. v. Mallen**, 486 U.S. 232 (1988)—upholding procedure for decision within 90 days of suspension of bank official who is indicted]

h. Creditor remedies [§452]

Due process *requires* notice and a hearing *prior* to any prejudgment *garnishment of wages*. [**Sniadach v. Family Finance Corp.**, 395 U.S. 337 (1969)] However, in other commercial settings, creditors can cause prejudgment seizures of their debtors' property (or a conditional seller can seize or sequester the asset sold), *without* prior notice and hearing to the debtor *if* the following requirements are met:

(i) *Application for the prejudgment seizure is made to a judge* (rather than a court clerk or other ministerial official);

(ii) *The application contains an affidavit based on personal knowledge* setting forth *"specific facts"* (not mere conclusions) establishing the creditor's right to issuance of the writ ("narrowly confined facts susceptible of a summary disposition");

(iii) *The creditor posts an adequate surety bond* prior to issuance of the writ; and

(iv) *Provision is made for an early hearing*, at which the creditor must prove "probable cause for the seizure."

[*See* **Mitchell v. W. T. Grant Co.**, 416 U.S. 600 (1974); **Fuentes v. Shevin**, 407 U.S. 67 (1972); **North Georgia Finishing, Inc. v. Di-Chem, Inc.**, 419 U.S. 601 (1975)]

i. Attachment of real property [§453]

Prejudgment attachment of real property without prior notice and hearing is not permitted unless the plaintiff's factual allegations demonstrate a likelihood of recovery. This is more easily shown in uncomplicated matters that lend themselves to documentary proof (*e.g.*, the existence of a debt or delinquent payments) than cases of a factually valid complaint that is subject to dispute (*e.g.*, for assault and battery). The risk of erroneous deprivation of significant property interests (*e.g.*, cloud on title) is too great in the latter instances. [**Connecticut v. Doehr**, 501 U.S. 1 (1991)]

j. Commitment to a mental institution [§454]

The Court has not detailed the procedural safeguards required by due process prior to the involuntary commitment of an adult to a mental institution. But it has held that, although the standard of proof of the criteria for such commitment need *not* be "beyond a reasonable doubt," it must at least require *"clear and convincing"* evidence. [**Addington v. Texas**, *supra*, §429]

(1) Children [§455]

Parents, or a governmental agency acting on behalf of a child, can institutionalize a child for mental treatment *without* a *prior* adversary hearing if:

(i) *Prior to admission, an inquiry is made by a neutral fact finder* (who may be a physician) to determine whether the statutory requirements for admission are satisfied;

(ii) *The inquiry carefully probes the child's background*; and

(iii) *The child's continued need for institutionalization is subject to periodic review* by a similarly independent procedure.

[**Parham v. J.R.**, 442 U.S. 584 (1979)]

(a) Note

The Court has left open the question of whether the periodic review required when a governmental agency commits a ward should differ from the review required when parents commit their child.

k. Antipsychotic drugs for prison inmates [§456]

Due process does not require a trial-type hearing before a judicial officer or outside psychiatrist prior to a state's treating a mentally ill prisoner with antipsychotic drugs against his will. Nor does the mentally ill prisoner have a right to counsel with respect to such treatment. [**Washington v. Harper**, 494 U.S. 210 (1990)—pretreatment notice and hearing before staff medical professionals who are not institutionally biased is sufficient]

l. Termination of parental status [§457]

Procedural due process does *not* require appointment of counsel for indigent parents in *every* hearing to terminate parental status, but only when "fundamental fairness" demands it. [**Lassiter v. Department of Social Services**, 452 U.S. 18 (1981)]

(1) Burden of proof [§458]

Procedural due process requires that the state establish its allegations of parental unfitness by at least *"clear and convincing evidence."* [**Santosky v. Kramer**, 455 U.S. 745 (1982)]

(a) Distinguish—paternity [§459]

However, due process does *not* require "clear and convincing evidence" in a civil action to establish paternity. The "preponderance of the evidence" standard is constitutional. [**Rivera v. Minnich**, 483 U.S. 574 (1987)]

TYPE OF PROCESS REQUIRED—A SUMMARY

gilbert

INTEREST INVOLVED	PROCESS REQUIRED
• Civil forfeiture of **real property**	**Prior notice** and **prior adversary hearing**
• Termination of **welfare benefits**	**Prior notice** and **prior adversary hearing**
• Termination of **disability benefits**	**Prior notice and opportunity to respond in writing** but **subsequent evidentiary hearing**
• Termination of **public employment** (when employee is tenured or terminable only for cause)	**Prior notice and opportunity to respond** but **subsequent evidentiary hearing**
• **Disciplinary suspension** from public school	**Prior notice and opportunity to respond** but **subsequent evidentiary hearing;** if student poses a danger, **notice and hearing may be subsequent**
• **Academic dismissal** from public school	**Subsequent notice and opportunity to respond**
• Suspension of **license**	If there is probable cause to believe that conditions of the license have been violated, **subsequent notice and opportunity to respond**
• Prejudgment **garnishment of wages**	**Prior notice** and **prior hearing**
• Prejudgment **seizures in a commercial setting**	**Subsequent notice and hearing if:** (i) application is made to a judge; (ii) the application includes an affidavit based on personal knowledge setting forth facts establishing the creditor's rights; (iii) the creditor posts a bond; and (iv) an early hearing is set
• Commitment to **mental institution**	**Children:** On application of parents or government agency responsible for the child, **no prior notice or hearing is required if:** (i) prior to admission, a neutral fact finder inquires into the matter and carefully assesses the child's background; and (ii) the child's need for institutionalization is subject to periodic review **Adults:** The Court has not detailed the procedural safeguards, but need must be shown by "clear and convincing evidence"
• Forced use of **antipsychotic drugs for prisoners**	**Prior notice and hearing** (but hearing does not have to be trial-type and can be by medical staff)

EXAM TIP   **gilbert**

If an exam question involves a person whose rights have been terminated (or otherwise adversely affected) without a hearing, be sure to remember that a procedural due process claim involves a multi-step analysis:

❶ First, you must determine whether the person had a *legitimate claim to the interest at stake*.

❷ You must then determine whether the government's action has *directly deprived the person of his interest*.

If so, the person is entitled to notice and a decision before an unbiased decisionmaker.

❸ To determine the timing and scope of the hearing (*e.g.*, whether notice is required before termination of the interest or whether post-termination notice is sufficient; whether a hearing must be pre-termination or whether a post-termination hearing is sufficient; whether there is a right to present oral testimony, have counsel, cross-examine witnesses etc.), you must then *balance:*

 • The *importance of the individual interest;* and

 • The *value of the procedural safeguard sought;* against

 • The *government's interest in fiscal and administrative efficiency*.

If the individual interest is very strong (*e.g.*, welfare benefits without which a person will be unable to buy food, clothing, and shelter) and the specific safeguards sought are likely to prevent an erroneous termination of the interest, a pre-termination hearing will be required with the sought-after procedural safeguards.

C. Substantive Due Process

1. Introduction [§460]

In addition to providing procedural limitations on the government when it deprives a person of life, liberty, or property, the Due Process Clauses place substantive limitations on government action. As will be seen, what will be deemed constitutional under the Due Process Clauses generally depends on the nature of the interest involved: (i) economic or social interests; or (ii) fundamental personal rights. However, in any case, a law that is too vague to give people or law enforcement officers notice of what is prohibited will be held void for vagueness (*see infra,* §542).

2. Economic and Social Regulations [§461]

In the first third of the twentieth century, the Court often reviewed the *substance* of legislation and used the Due Process Clause to invalidate economic and social regulations. The basic rationale was that the legislation *unreasonably* interfered with "liberty" and "property" interests protected by the Due Process Clause. The Justices made their own *personal judgments* as to whether the *means* used by the regulation were *reasonably related* to a *legitimate* end. [*See, e.g.,* **Allgeyer v. Louisiana,** 165

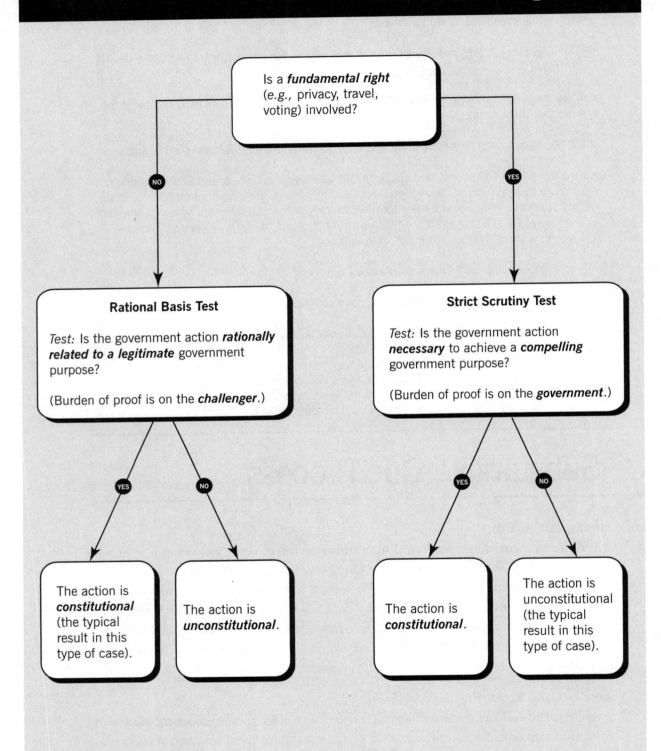

Is a *fundamental right* (*e.g.,* privacy, travel, voting) involved?

NO

YES

Rational Basis Test

Test: Is the government action *rationally related to a legitimate* government purpose?

(Burden of proof is on the *challenger*.)

Strict Scrutiny Test

Test: Is the government action *necessary* to achieve a *compelling* government purpose?

(Burden of proof is on the *government*.)

YES

NO

YES

NO

The action is *constitutional* (the typical result in this type of case).

The action is *unconstitutional*.

The action is *constitutional*.

The action is unconstitutional (the typical result in this type of case).

U.S. 578 (1897)—"liberty" protected by Due Process Clause includes *right to contract*, which was abridged by state insurance regulation]

a. *Lochner* case [§462]

The most famous decision of this era was ***Lochner v. New York***, 198 U.S. 45 (1905), which held that a law limiting the number of hours that bakers could work unreasonably interfered with "the freedom of master and employee to contract in relation to their employment." *Rationale:* The freedom to contract may be restricted through the state's police power to protect public health, safety, welfare, or morals, but the *means* used by this statute (limiting baker's hours) were *not reasonably related* to such ends. Rather, this was "purely a labor law," and government had *no legitimate purpose* in this type of regulation ("We do not believe in the soundness of the views which uphold this law").

b. Modern approach [§463]

Since the mid-1930s, the Court has adopted a different approach; it defers to legislative judgments in respect to economic and social regulations unless they are "demonstrably *arbitrary* or *irrational*." [**Duke Power Co. v. Carolina Environmental Study Group, Inc.**, 438 U.S. 59 (1978)] Such laws are *presumed* valid and will be upheld unless no reasonable state of facts can be conceived to support them, or unless they bear no rational relationship to the end sought—the burden of proof being on the person challenging the law. [**United States v. Carolene Products Co.**, 304 U.S. 144 (1938)] The Court will *not* "weigh the wisdom" of such legislation or substitute its own judgment for that of the legislative body. [**Ferguson v. Skrupa**, 372 U.S. 726 (1963)]

Example: Congress adopted a statute (the "Filled Milk Act") prohibiting the interstate shipment of skimmed milk that has been combined with any fat or oil other than milk fat so as to resemble milk or cream. The Carolene Products Company was indicted for shipping its imitation condensed milk product—Milnut—which was a combination of milk and coconut oil, in violation of the statute. In upholding the indictment, the Supreme Court noted that the results of a congressional investigation supported the law, but even absent the investigation, "the existence of facts supporting the legislation is to be presumed, for regulatory legislation affecting ordinary commercial transactions is not to be pronounced unconstitutional unless [facts are shown that] preclude the assumption that it rests on some rational basis . . . . " [**United States v. Carolene Products Co.**, *supra*]

Example: A Kansas statute made it a misdemeanor for any person to engage in the business of "debt adjusting" (defined as making a contract whereby the debtor agrees to pay a certain amount of money periodically to the person engaged in the debt adjusting business, who, for consideration, distributes the money among creditors in accordance with an agreed-upon plan). Skrupa was charged with violating the statute. He argued that his business was useful and desirable and not inherently immoral, dangerous or contrary to public welfare, and therefore it could not be completely prohibited. In upholding the legislation, the Supreme Court found that "it is up to the legislatures, not the courts, to decide on the wisdom and utility of legislation." [**Ferguson v. Skrupa,** *supra*]

---

(1) Effect [§464]

Under this approach, public health and safety measures—as well as various regulations of business, such as the following—are effectively *immune* from a general Due Process Clause attack:

(a) *Price controls* [*see* **Nebbia v. New York,** 291 U.S. 502 (1934)];

(b) *Trade practices* [*see* **North Dakota Board of Pharmacy v. Snyder's Drug Stores,** 414 U.S. 156 (1973)];

(c) *Wage and hour laws* [*see* **West Coast Hotel Co. v. Parrish,** 300 U.S. 379 (1937)];

(d) *Bans on discrimination against union or nonunion employees* [*see* **Lincoln Federal Labor Union v. Northwestern Iron & Metal Co.,** 335 U.S. 525 (1949)]; and

(e) *Limitations on engaging in certain occupations* [*see* **Williamson v. Lee Optical Co.,** 348 U.S. 483 (1955)].

Example: New York passes a law establishing minimum and maximum retail prices for milk. The purpose of the statute was to aid the dairy industry, which was in a desperate situation because the prices received by farmers for milk were below the cost of production. Nebbia, a retail grocer, sold milk below the minimum price and was convicted of violating the statute. He appealed his conviction, claiming the New York statute violated due process. The Court upheld the conviction. As long as the law has a reasonable relationship to a proper legislative purpose, is not arbitrary or discriminatory, and is reasonably related to achieving its purpose, it does not offend due process. [**Nebbia v. New York,** *supra*]

Example: Lee Optical Co. challenged an Oklahoma law that, among other things, forbade opticians from fitting or duplicating lenses without a prescription from an ophthalmologist or optometrist. This had the effect of prohibiting opticians from replacing lost or broken lenses in old frames without a prescription. The district court held this provision to arbitrarily interfere with an optician's right to do business and violate the Due Process Clause because it was unrelated to the health and welfare of the people. The district court explained that an optician can, through mechanical means, determine the power of a broken lens and accurately reproduce it, making the statute neither reasonably necessary nor reasonably related to the end of ensuring the health and safety of eyewear. However, the Supreme Court upheld the statute. "The Oklahoma law may exact a needless, wasteful requirement in many cases. But it is for the legislature, not the courts, to balance the advantages and disadvantages of" their laws. The Court then went on to suggest rationalizations that the Oklahoma legislature might have used to support the law (*e.g.*, eye examinations are so important for health that whenever a lens is replaced, the patient should get a prescription). [**Williamson v. Lee Optical Co.**, *supra*]

(2) Application to punitive damage awards [§465]

The Supreme Court has held that the Eighth Amendment's prohibition of "excessive fines" places limits only on *government* and does not apply to punitive damage awards in civil litigation. [**Browning Ferris Industries of Vermont, Inc. v. Kelso Disposal, Inc.**, 492 U.S. 257 (1989)] Nevertheless, the Court has held that punitive damages in such cases are limited by the Due Process Clause. Awards that are grossly excessive—unreasonably high to vindicate the state's interests in retribution and deterrence—are invalid. [**TXO Production Corp. v. Alliance Resources Corps.**, 509 U.S. 443 (1993)] The Due Process Clause requires that a person receive *fair notice of the possible magnitude* of punitive damages in order for them to be constitutional.

(a) Factors [§466]

The Court has indicated that it will look to the following factors in determining whether the defendant had adequate notice that a severe penalty might be imposed: (i) the degree of *reprehensibility* of the defendant's conduct, (ii) the disparity between the actual or potential *harm suffered* by the plaintiff and the *amount of punitive damages* awarded, and (iii) the difference between the punitive *damages awarded* and the *criminal and civil penalties authorized* for comparable misconduct. [**BMW of North America, Inc. v. Gore**, 517 U.S. 559 (1996)]

> **Example:** The paint on a new, $40,000 BMW was damaged during shipment. BMW repaired the damage for $601 and sold the car as new without giving any notice of the damage. When the purchaser discovered the repair nine months later, he sued for fraud in Alabama state court. The jury awarded him $4,000 in compensatory damages (for the decrease in the value of the car as a result of its having been damaged and repaired) and $4 million in punitive damages, which the trial judge reduced to $2 million. BMW eventually appealed

to the Supreme Court, claiming that the award violated due process. The Supreme Court found the award excessive under the Due Process Clause because BMW's actions were not terribly reprehensible (the damage to the car was purely economic and did not involve performance, safety, or appearance), there was a large disparity between the punitive damages awarded and the harm suffered (a ratio of 500 to 1), and there was a large difference between the damages awarded ($2 million) and the civil or criminal sanctions available (Alabama's maximum fine for deceptive trade practices here was $2,000). [**BMW of North America, Inc. v. Gore,** *supra*]

---

1) **"Reprehensibility" [§467]**

In determining this most important element, a court considers whether (i) the harm was physical rather than economic, (ii) the defendant's conduct was indifferent or with reckless disregard, (iii) the conduct was repeated rather than an isolated incident, and (iv) the harm resulted from intentional malice or deceit rather than mere accident.

2) **Defendant's conduct [§468]**

The defendant's action cannot be punished if it was lawful where it occurred. Nor, as a general rule, may it be punished even if unlawful when committed outside the state's jurisdiction. And if punitive damages are based on prior transgressions, they must bear a relationship to the plaintiff's harm—*i.e.*, they must be similar to that which harmed plaintiff.

3) **Ratio of punitive to compensatory damages [§469]**

Except for particularly egregious conduct—especially if it has resulted in only a small amount of compensatory damages—punitive damages should not exceed **10 *times*** compensatory damages. [**State Farm Mutual Auto Insurance Co. v. Campbell,** 123 S. Ct. 1513 (2003)—punitive damages of 145 times compensatory damages violate due process]

(b) **Standard of review [§470]**

A jury award of punitive damages is not a finding of fact. Thus, when determining whether a jury award constitutes "grossly excessive" punishment, appellate courts should review the awards de novo rather than under an "abuse of discretion" standard. [**Cooper Industries, Inc. v. Leatherman Tool Group, Inc.,** 532 U.S. 424 (2001)]

3. **Government Officers Depriving Persons of Life, Liberty, or Property [§471]**

Substantive due process not only protects against arbitrary regulation, but also provides some protection against government *behavior* that deprives persons of life, liberty, or property. However, the Supreme Court is reluctant to rely on substantive due process, so if there is another constitutional provision that applies to the government behavior in question (*e.g.*, the Eighth Amendment's prohibition against cruel and unusual punishment), that provision will be controlling. If other explicit textual provisions of the Constitution are not implicated, action by government executive officers (*e.g.*, the police) that deprive persons of life, liberty, or property may be held to violate the more generalized notion of substantive due process, but only if the officer's conduct is so arbitrary, egregious, and outrageous as to "*shock the contemporary conscience.*" [**County of Sacramento v. Lewis**, 523 U.S. 833 (1998)]

Example: Police officers chased a motorcycle that sped by them for no apparent reason. A passenger on the motorcycle fell off and was killed when struck by the patrol car driven by one of the officers. The victim's parents sued the officer and county for depriving the victim of his constitutional right to due process under color of law (commonly called a section 1983 action, from its statutory source, 42 U.S.C. section 1983). The Court held that because the chase was not undertaken with an intent to physically harm the victim, there was no due process violation. [**County of Sacramento v. Lewis,** *supra*]

a.   **Intent [§472]**

Deliberate indifference by a government official may *sometimes* rise to a constitutionally shocking level. [**Estelle v. Gamble**, 429 U.S. 97 (1976)—prison officials, with time for unhurried judgments, violate due process when they are deliberately indifferent to prisoner's medical needs] But ordinarily, *intent* to harm is required. [**County of Sacramento v. Lewis,** *supra*]

4.   **Restrictions on Power of Eminent Domain**

a.   **Fifth Amendment [§473]**

The Fifth Amendment provides in part: ". . . nor shall private property be taken for public use without just compensation."

(1)   **Federal government [§474]**

The Fifth Amendment is *not* an implied grant to the federal government of a general power to take property, provided it pays. Rather, it is a restriction. If some *other* constitutional provision gives the federal government the power to take private property, the Fifth Amendment requires the government to pay just compensation for the property taken.

(2)   **State government [§475]**

The Fifth Amendment restraint on the power to take private property applies to the states through the Fourteenth Amendment Due Process Clause. [**Chicago, Burlington & Quincy Railroad v. Chicago**, 166 U.S. 226 (1897)]

b.   **Substantive requirements**

(1) Property [§476]

"Property" interests are not created by the Constitution, rather, they are derived from independent sources, such as state or federal law. They may include intangible (as well as tangible) interests, such as trade secrets. [**Ruckelshaus v. Monsanto Co.,** 467 U.S. 986 (1984)]

(a) Nature of property [§477]

It is clear that the Takings Clause applies where a *specific* interest in physical or intellectual property (*e.g.*, a certain part of a tract of land) is involved. No opinion for the Court, however, has decided whether the Takings Clause is triggered by a *general obligation* to pay money to the government or to a third party (*e.g.*, where a federal law requires a company to pay money into an employee retirement fund). [*See* **Eastern Enterprises v. Apfel,** 524 U.S. 498 (1998)—in the Court's plurality opinion, four Justices found that a general obligation could be the subject of a taking, but five Justices in concurring and dissenting opinions found it could not]

1) Interest [§478]

Interest earned on deposited funds is the "property" of the owner of the funds even though circumstances may be such that the interest has *no economically realizable value* to the owner. *Rationale*: There are other valuable rights that inhere in this property, such as possession, control, and disposition. [**Phillips v. Washington Legal Foundation,** 524 U.S. 156 (1998)]

---

e.g. **Example:** Under Texas law, an attorney who receives client funds must place them in a special interest-bearing account if the attorney determines that the funds will not earn sufficient interest to offset the costs of maintaining the account, accounting for the interest, and reporting for tax purposes. All interest from such special accounts is paid to a foundation that finances legal services for low income persons. The Court found that such interest was the property of the client or attorney entitled to the funds earning the interest, despite the fact that the interest had no economic value to the owners. [**Phillips v. Washington Legal Foundation,** *supra*] However, a subsequent case [**Brown v. Legal Foundation of Washington,** 123 S. Ct. 1406 (2003)] held that it is possible that no compensation is due for taking such property. (*See infra,* §498.)

---

(2) Public use [§479]

Note that the government may take property only for a "public use." The government may not forcibly take private property at all if it will not be used for public use, even if "just compensation" is paid.

(a) Broadly defined [§480]

The Court's role in determining whether a taking is for a "public use" is *extremely narrow*. A use is held to be "public" if it is *rationally related* to a *conceivable* public purpose—*e.g.*, if it furthers health, welfare, safety, moral, social, economic, political, or even aesthetic ends. The Court will *not* consider the desirability of a particular taking, or the extent to which the property must be taken in order to satisfy the public purposes. [**Berman v. Parker,** 348 U.S. 26 (1954)]

> **e.g.** **Example:** Congress created an agency to acquire and assemble real property for redevelopment of blighted areas in the District of Columbia. Berman owned a well-maintained department store that was in an area targeted for redevelopment and objected to the taking of his property for the purposes of the project. The Court held that the concept of public welfare is broad and includes aesthetic values. Thus, the legislature may deem it in the public interest to promote beautiful and balanced communities. Moreover, the fact that the property might be turned over to a private redeveloper after it is taken does not negate the public objective. [**Berman v. Parker,** *supra*]

1) And note

Uses may be "public" if there is public advantage or benefit, even though the property is not *used* by the general public. Thus, the state may authorize takings and use by private persons or companies if thought to be in the public interest. [**Hawaii Housing Authority v. Midkiff,** 467 U.S. 229 (1984)]

> **e.g.** **Example:** In Hawaii land ownership was concentrated in a few owners who leased the land to tenants. To reduce the concentration of land ownership, the state adopted a statute providing that when a certain percentage of the tenants with single-family residential homes on leased tracts requested, the state could condemn and take title to the leased tracts (with compensation to the owners) and transfer ownership to the tenants. A number of owners objected, claiming that the takings did not serve a public purpose. The court held that any conceivable public purpose could justify the takings, and the transfers of ownership here were rationally related to reducing the perceived evils of a land oligopoly that interfered with the normal functioning of the residential land market. [**Hawaii Housing Authority v. Midkiff,** *supra*]

(3) "Taking" vs. "regulation" [§481]

The crucial issue is whether the government action is a *taking*, requiring just compensation, or merely a *regulation* under the police power (not requiring compensation).

(a) No clear formula [§482]

The Court has been unable to develop any "set formula" for determining when a "taking" occurs. Rather, the Court asks whether *"justice and fairness" require* that economic loss caused by public action must be *compensated by the government* and thus borne by the public as a whole, or whether the loss should remain concentrated on those few persons subject to the public action. [**Penn Central Transportation Co. v. New York City,** 438 U.S. 104 (1978)]

(b) Appropriation or permanent invasion [§483]

A "taking" will almost always be found if there is an *actual appropriation* or a *permanent physical invasion* of private property by the government or by authorization of state law. This is true regardless of the state's interest or the economic impact on the owner. [**Loretto v. Teleprompter Manhattan CATV Corp.,** 455 U.S. 904 (1982)—statute that required landlords to allow television cables to be installed in their buildings constituted a taking] Illustrations of such government action held to constitute a "taking" include the following:

1) Formal condemnation [§484]

Formal condemnation of property for some public use constitutes a taking.

2) Descent of property [§485]

Although the government has broad authority to *regulate* the descent and devise of property, *abolishing* these rights is a taking. [**Hodel v. Irving,** 481 U.S. 704 (1987)] It is also a taking if the government *severely restricts* a person's right to devise property by drastically shrinking the universe of possible devisees. [**Babbit v. Youpee,** 519 U.S. 234 (1997)—law prohibiting or greatly limiting the descent or devise of certain interests in land and providing for such interests to escheat to Indian tribes in order to consolidate ownership of tribal lands]

3) Exactions [§486]

Municipalities often attempt to condition building or development permits on a landowner's (i) conveying title to part or all of the property to the government, or (ii) granting the public access to the property (*e.g.,* an easement across the property). Such a condition is commonly referred to as an exaction and constitutes an uncompensated taking unless (i) the government

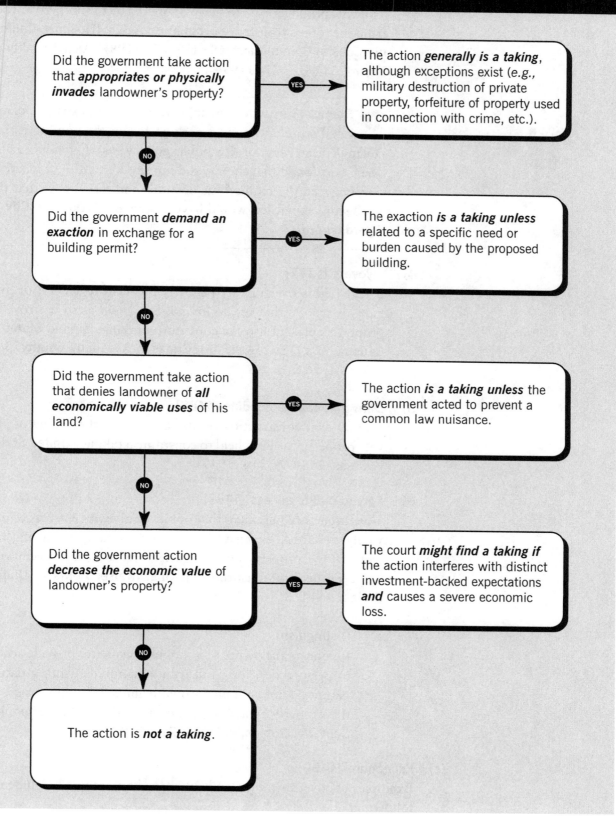

Did the government take action that **appropriates or physically invades** landowner's property?

YES → The action **generally is a taking**, although exceptions exist (*e.g.,* military destruction of private property, forfeiture of property used in connection with crime, etc.).

NO ↓

Did the government **demand an exaction** in exchange for a building permit?

YES → The exaction **is a taking unless** related to a specific need or burden caused by the proposed building.

NO ↓

Did the government take action that denies landowner of **all economically viable uses** of his land?

YES → The action **is a taking unless** the government acted to prevent a common law nuisance.

NO ↓

Did the government action **decrease the economic value** of landowner's property?

YES → The court **might find a taking if** the action interferes with distinct investment-backed expectations **and** causes a severe economic loss.

NO ↓

The action is **not a taking**.

can show that an "essential nexus" exists between the condition and a "legitimate government interest" and (ii) the adverse impact of the proposed building/development on the area is "roughly proportional" to the loss suffered by the property owner from the forced transfer of occupation rights. [**Nollan v. California Coastal Commission,** 483 U.S. 825 (1987); **Dolan v. City of Tigard,** 512 U.S. 374 (1994)]

> **Example:** City agreed to approve a permit to expand Dolan's retail store and pave a parking lot on the condition that Dolan dedicate land for (i) a public greenway and (ii) a bike path. The Court found that the city did not show a sufficient relationship between the required dedications and the impact that the retail store expansion would have on the area. [**Dolan v. City of Tigard,** *supra*]

4) **Flyovers [§487]**

Direct flights over private property adjacent to federal or municipal airports that are *so low and frequent* as to destroy the property's present use can constitute a taking. [**United States v. Causby,** 328 U.S. 256 (1946); **Griggs v. Allegheny County,** 369 U.S. 84 (1962)]

5) **Dam that causes flooding [§488]**

Federal dam construction resulting in repeated flooding of private property has been held to constitute a taking. [**United States v. Cress,** 243 U.S. 316 (1917)]

6) **Forced public access [§489]**

Government requirement that public be given free access to privately developed waterway, thus unreasonably impairing the value of the property and its owners' reasonable expectations has been held to constitute a taking. [**Kaiser Aetna v. United States,** 444 U.S. 164 (1979)]

a) **Distinguish**

Requiring the owner of a shopping center to provide access to persons desiring to distribute handbills is not a taking because it does not unreasonably impair the value or use of the property as a shopping center. [**Prune Yard Shopping Center v. Robins,** 447 U.S. 74 (1980)]

(c) **Exceptions [§490]**

Examples of government action held *not* to be a "taking" include the following:

1) *Military destruction of strategic private property* simply to avoid its falling into enemy hands, and the destruction of private property to stop the spread of a fire have been held *not* to be "takings" because the public need outweighed the private injury. [**United States v. Caltex, Inc.**, 344 U.S. 149 (1952)]

2) *Forfeiture of property used in connection with crimes* was held not a "taking" even though the property owner (*e.g.*, lessor or co-owner) did not know that the property was to be put to such use—at least where (i) the "innocent" owner *voluntarily entrusted* the property to the wrongdoer and (ii) the forfeiture law affords the judge some discretion to prevent inequitable application. [**Calero-Toledo v. Pearson Yacht Leasing Co.**, 416 U.S. 663 (1974); **Bennis v. Michigan**, 516 U.S. 442 (1996)]

3) *A temporary, unplanned occupation of private property by the military during a riot* was not a "taking" when done primarily to defend the property rather than the general public interest. [**National Board of Y.M.C.A. v. United States**, 395 U.S. 85 (1969)]

(d) Severe economic impact [§491]

Government action that amounts to only a *temporary* physical invasion of property, that adversely affects property value, or that prohibits the most beneficial use of the property does *not necessarily* result in a "taking," since reduction in economic value is an inevitable effect of much government regulation. The Court has stated that it is a *matter of degree.* [**Pennsylvania Coal Co. v. Mahon**, 260 U.S. 393 (1922)]

1) No economically valuable use [§492]

A regulation that permanently denies *all* economically beneficial or productive use of land is, from the owner's point of view, equivalent to a physical appropriation. It thus is a "taking" unless principles of nuisance or property law that existed when the owner acquired the land make the use prohibitable. [**Lucas v. South Carolina Coastal Council**, 505 U.S. 1003 (1992)]

Example: Lucas purchased two residential lots near the seashore, intending to build single-family homes. Two years later, South Carolina passed an anti-erosion law that barred making "occupiable improvements" near the shoreline. This effectively barred Lucas from building homes on his land: *Held:* The regulation leaves Lucas's land valueless and constitutes a taking. [**Lucas v. South Carolina Coastal Council**, *supra*]

---

a) **Temporary land development moratorium [§493]**

Temporarily denying an owner of all use of property does not constitute a per se taking. Instead, the Court will carefully examine and weigh all of the circumstances—the planners' good faith, the reasonable expectation of the owners, the length of the delay, the delay's actual effect on the value of the property, etc.—in order to determine whether "fairness and justice" require just compensation. [**Tahoe-Sierra Preservation Council, Inc. v. Tahoe Regional Planning Agency,** 535 U.S. 302 (2002)—finding no taking where there was a 32-month moratorium on land development in the Lake Tahoe Basin while a comprehensive land-use plan was being developed for the area]

b) **Jury question [§494]**

The issue of whether a landowner has been deprived of all economically viable use of his property is predominantly a fact question, and therefore it is a matter for the jury. [**City of Monterey v. Del Monte Dunes at Monterey, Ltd.,** 526 U.S. 687 (1999)]

2) **Other significant factors [§495]**

A restriction on use of property may constitute a "taking" if not "*reasonably necessary*" to the effectuation of a *substantial* public purpose," or if it has an "*unduly harsh* impact" on the "distinct *investment-backed expectations*" of the owner. But the Court balances the *public need* against the *private cost*, and no compensation is required for burdens imposed on "*all similarly situated property*" in order to produce "*widespread* public benefit." [**Penn Central Transportation Co. v. New York City,** *supra,* §482]

Example: The *state-ordered destruction* of cedar trees that were spreading disease to apple orchards was *not* a "taking," despite great reduction of value—because the cedar trees were causing harm to an important state industry. [**Miller v. Schoene,** 276 U.S. 272 (1928)]

Example: The Penn Central Transportation Company owned the Grand Central Terminal in New York City. The terminal was designated a "landmark" under New York City's landmark preservation law. The law prohibited destruction of the building. Penn Central applied for and was denied permission to build offices over the terminal solely because of the landmark law and challenged the law as an unconstitutional taking. *Held*: Because Penn Central could continue to obtain a "reasonable return" on its investment in the building without the additional office space and the restriction here is reasonably related to the public policy of historic preservation, there was *no* taking. [**Penn Central Transportation Co. v. New York City,** *supra*]

e.g. **Example:** Members of the Keystone Bituminous Coal Association purchased the mineral rights from landowners but not the surface rights. A Pennsylvania statute intended to prevent subsidence of surface land caused by coal mining required that 50% of the coal beneath existing public buildings and dwellings be left in place for surface support. The Association brought suit claiming that the statute amounted to a taking of their property. The Supreme Court found that the statute here has a clear public purpose (to protect health, the environment, and fiscal integrity to support the tax base) and the Association failed to show that the statute made it commercially impracticable for its members to continue mining coal. Indeed, when looking at the general effect of the statute, it prevented the mining of only 2% of the available coal. Therefore, there was *no* taking. [**Keystone Bituminous Coal Association v. DeBenedictis,** 480 U.S. 470 (1987)]

cf. **Compare:** Mahon owned the surface rights to a tract of land under which the Pennsylvania Coal Company owned the mineral rights. After the coal company purchased the mineral rights, the state enacted a statute prohibiting mining under buildings that would cause the buildings to sink. Mahon sued under the statute to prevent the coal company from mining all of the coal under his house. The Supreme Court found that the statute made it commercially impracticable to mine coal under Mahon's house and therefore found that the statute constituted a taking. [**Pennsylvania Coal Co. v. Mahon,** 260 U.S. 393 (1922)] *Note:* It is difficult to reconcile the results of *Keystone, supra,* with *Pennsylvania Coal* and it seems doubtful that *Pennsylvania Coal* would be decided the same way today. Nevertheless, it was one of the first cases to use the principle that the more drastic the reduction in value of the owner's property, the more likely that a taking will be found. (*See supra,* §491.)

3) **Who may sue [§496]**

The right to claim a "taking" is *not* limited to persons who held title to the property at the time a challenged use restriction was imposed. *Rationale:* Although the Court must consider the "reasonable investment-backed expectations" of the claimant, automatic denial of the right of subsequent purchasers to claim a taking, on the ground that they had notice of an earlier enacted restriction, would effectively strip the ability of the owner to transfer the property after a challenged restriction was enacted. [**Palazzolo v. Rhode Island,** 533 U.S. 606 (2001)]

4) **Taxes [§497]**

A tax is not deemed a "taking"—even when it is so excessive as to render continuation of a business unprofitable, so that the owner is forced to shut down. [**City of Pittsburgh v. Alco Parking Corp.,** 417 U.S. 369 (1974)]

"TAKING" VS. "REGULATION"—EXAMPLES	**gilbert**
GOVERNMENT ACTION	CHARACTERIZATION
1. Condemnation of land to build highway	Taking
2. Creating public access easement on private property	Taking
3. Abolishing inheritance rights	Taking
4. Zoning ordinances that merely prohibit the most beneficial use of property	Regulation
5. Ordering destruction of diseased trees	Regulation
6. Landmark ordinances	Regulation

5) **"Just" compensation [§498]**

If a "taking" is found, the property owner normally must be paid the "*fair market value*" of the property. Absent special circumstances, *neither* the value of the private owner's unique need for the property nor the value of the gain to the taker are compensable. [**United States v. 564.54 Acres of Land,** 441 U.S. 506 (1979)]

Example: Washington requires attorneys to place client funds into interest bearing accounts. If a client's funds will not earn enough interest to cover the costs of distributing the interest to the client, the state requires the funds to be placed into an interest on lawyers' trust account ("IOLTA"), and the attorney must direct the bank to pay interest from the IOLTA account over to a state charity that, among other things, funds legal services for the needy. The Court has already held that the interest that is earned in such accounts is the client's property under the Fifth Amendment (*see supra*, §478), and persons with funds deposited in Washington IOLTA accounts brought suit claiming that their property was being taken without just compensation. *Held:* Although a taking had occurred, no compensation need be paid here. Just compensation is measured by the owner's pecuniary loss, and here the owners have lost nothing. [**Brown v. Legal Foundation of Washington**, *supra*, §478]

(a) Note

If, after the taking, the owner has some property left whose value has been *enhanced* as a result thereof, the gain in value may be considered as an offset against the value of the property taken. [**Blanchette v. Connecticut General Insurance**, 419 U.S. 102 (1974)]

c. Remedy [§499]

If a "taking" occurs, just compensation must be paid for damages suffered during the *entire* time that the property was "taken." The government *cannot* disallow damages for the period of time between enactment of the challenged regulation and its ultimate invalidation. [**First English Evangelical Lutheran Church v. County of Los Angeles**, 482 U.S. 304 (1987)]

d. Procedural requirements [§500]

When the federal or state government exercises its power of eminent domain, due process requires that it give the property owner reasonable notice and a reasonable opportunity to be heard and offer evidence regarding the amount of compensation due her. [**Bragg v. Weaver**, 251 U.S. 57 (1919)]

(1) But note

Due process does *not* require that the condemnation of land occur in advance of its occupation by the condemning authority [**Bailey v. Anderson**, 326 U.S. 203 (1945)]; nor does it require a hearing on the necessity and expediency of the taking [**Bragg v. Weaver**, *supra*].

5. Fundamental Personal Rights [§501]

Since the mid-1960s, the Court has revived substantive due process review as a means of protecting certain *fundamental* personal rights not specifically enumerated in the Constitution if they are "so rooted in the traditions and conscience of our people as to be ranked as *fundamental*." [**Michael H. v. Gerald D.**, 491 U.S. 110 (1989)] If a government regulation impinges on such a fundamental right, it is subjected to essentially the same type of strict scrutiny applicable to "fundamental rights" issues under the Equal Protection Clause (*see infra*, §§1121 *et seq.*); *i.e.*, the regulation is invalid unless the government proves that the regulation is *necessary* (narrowly drawn) to achieve a *compelling* government interest.

EXAM TIP   **gilbert**

It is difficult for the government to overcome a due process challenge when strict scrutiny applies. Thus, if an exam question involves a regulation of any of the fundamental rights discussed below, your answer should set out the test (the *government* must show that the regulation is *necessary* to achieve a *compelling* state interest), and you should be wary of upholding the regulation. However, as will be discussed below, if the question involves abortion, be sure to remember that a different test applies.

---

a.   **Right of privacy [§502]**

The right of privacy is nowhere mentioned in the Constitution. Nevertheless, the Court has recognized that a right of personal privacy, or at least a guarantee of certain areas or zones of privacy, *is* constitutionally protected. Some Justices have found the right recognized by the *Ninth Amendment* ("The enumeration of certain rights shall not be construed to deny or disparage others retained by the people"), while other Justices felt it was within the *"penumbras"* or *"emanations"* of various provisions of the Bill of Rights. [**Griswold v. Connecticut,** 381 U.S. 479 (1965)] More recently, the Court has simply held that the right of personal privacy is implicit in the concept of "liberty" within the protection of the Due Process Clause; *i.e.*, it is one of those *basic human rights* which are of "fundamental" importance in our society. [**Roe v. Wade,** 410 U.S. 113 (1973)]

(1)   **Marriage [§503]**

The right to marry has been referred to as a "basic civil right." [**Loving v. Virginia,** 388 U.S. 1 (1967)—invalidating prohibition of racial intermarriage; *and see infra*, §1141]

(2)   **Procreation [§504]**

The right to procreate has been referred to as "one of the basic civil rights of man." [**Skinner v. Oklahoma,** 316 U.S. 535 (1942)—invalidating a law requiring sterilization of habitual criminals; *and see infra*, §1143]

(3)   **Contraception [§505]**

The right to purchase and use contraceptives has been found to be included within the right to privacy. In **Griswold v. Connecticut,** *supra*, the Court invalidated a state law that made it a crime for any person to use contraceptives, including married persons. The Court held that the statute infringed on a constitutionally protected "zone of *marital privacy*."

Example: In **Eisenstadt v. Baird,** 405 U.S. 438 (1972), the Court reasoned that the decision whether to use contraceptives was one of *individual* privacy, and thus the right belonged to *single* as well as married persons.

---

e.g. **Example:** In **Carey v. Population Services International,** *supra,* §70, the Court held that a state could not prohibit distribution of non-medical contraceptives to adults except through licensed pharmacists, nor prohibit sales of such contraceptives to persons under age 16 who did not have approval of a licensed physician.

---

(4) Abortion [§506]

In 1972, the Supreme Court held that the right of privacy includes the right of a woman to decide whether or not to have an abortion. [**Roe v. Wade,** *supra*] However, the Court also held that the states have a compelling interest in protecting the health of both the woman and the fetus that may become a child. Thus, it is difficult to apply the regular "strict scrutiny" analysis to abortion regulations (because these two compelling interests may conflict with each other and with the woman's privacy right). Moreover, abortion is a highly debated public issue, and the Justices have had a difficult time agreeing on applicable standards.

---

e.g. **Example:** A Texas statute made procuring an abortion a crime unless it was performed to save the mother's life. Roe was an unmarried, pregnant Texas resident. She wanted to obtain an abortion in Texas but was unable to do so because her life was not threatened. She brought suit against Wade, a county district attorney, seeking declaratory and injunctive relief to prevent enforcement of the Texas statute. The Supreme Court held that the right of privacy is broad enough to include a woman's decision whether to have an abortion. However, the state's interest in the health of the woman can override this right after the first trimester. After the first trimester, states can adopt *regulations* reasonably related to the woman's health. The Court reasoned that (at that time) mortality rates arising from abortion during the first trimester were lower than mortality rates arising from childbirth, but this was not so for second and third trimester abortions. The court then went on to hold that the state's interest in protecting the potential life of the fetus became compelling, and overrode the mother's interest in privacy, at the start of the third trimester, because (at the time) that is when the fetus presumably had the capacity to live outside the mother's womb (*i.e.*, the point of viability). Thus, during the third trimester, a state could *prohibit* abortions except when necessary to preserve the life or health of the mother. [**Roe v. Wade,** *supra*]

(a) *Roe* trimester approach abandoned [§507]

The decision in *Roe* has been challenged both in the political arena and in the courts many times since 1972. In 1992, a majority of the Court reaffirmed much of *Roe,* but abandoned *Roe's* trimester approach. Instead the Court adopted two rules to govern the constitutionality of abortion regulations: a pre-viability rule and a post-viability rule. Prior to viability, the state's interests in protecting the mother's health and the fetus that may become a child are outweighed by the woman's right to have an abortion without imposition of *"undue burdens"* (or *"substantial obstacles"*) by the state. After viability, the state may prohibit abortion except when necessary to preserve the mother's life or health. [**Planned Parenthood of Southeastern Pennsylvania v. Casey,** 505 U.S. 833 (1992)]

1) Determining viability [§508]

Viability itself is a medical question. A state cannot unduly interfere with the attending physician's judgment, on the particular facts of the case, as to whether there is a reasonable likelihood of the fetus's survival outside the womb, with or without artificial support. [**Colautti v. Franklin,** 439 U.S. 379 (1979)] However, the state's interest in protecting a viable fetus is sufficiently compelling to allow the state to require performance of tests that are *medically prudent and useful* in determining whether a fetus is viable. [**Webster v. Reproductive Health Services,** 492 U.S. 490 (1989)]

2) Determining what is an undue burden [§509]

The Court did not specifically define what will constitute an undue burden. However, the Court did state that a law that serves a valid purpose (*i.e.,* "is not a law designed to strike at the right itself") does *not* impose an undue burden simply because it has the incidental effect of making it more difficult or expensive to procure an abortion. Neither does a law designed to persuade a pregnant woman to choose childbirth over abortion impose an "undue burden" unless it has the effect of placing a "substantial obstacle" in her path. [**Planned Parenthood of Southeastern Pennsylvania v. Casey,** *supra*]

(b) Informed consent [§510]

Requiring informed consent to an abortion is not necessarily an undue burden. Thus, the state *may* require a woman to give written, informed consent to the abortion, and that she be of a certain age or maturity in order to consent. [**Planned Parenthood v. Danforth,** 428 U.S. 52 (1976)] Furthermore, the state may require that a physician provide the woman with truthful information about the nature of the abortion procedure, the health risks of abortion and childbirth, and the probable gestational age of the fetus. [**Planned Parenthood of Southeastern Pennsylvania v. Casey,** *supra*]

(c) Waiting period [§511]

A state-required 24-hour waiting period between the time the woman gives her informed consent and the time of the abortion does *not* amount to an undue burden. [**Planned Parenthood of Southeastern Pennsylvania v. Casey,** *supra*]

(d) "Physician-only requirement" [§512]

A law restricting the performance of abortions to licensed physicians does not pose a "substantial obstacle" to an abortion. [**Mazurek v. Armstrong,** 520 U.S. 968]

(e) Data collection [§513]

Recordkeeping and reporting provisions that are reasonably directed to preserving maternal health and that properly respect a patient's privacy do *not* impose an undue burden. [**Planned Parenthood v. Danforth,** *supra*]

(f) "Partial-birth abortion" ban [§514]

A state may *not* completely proscribe so-called partial-birth abortion procedures, because they are the *most commonly* used methods for pre-viability, second-trimester abortions. Such a ban would impose an undue burden on a woman's right to choose a pre-viability abortion. [**Stenberg v. Carhart,** 530 U.S. 914 (2000)]

1) Distinguish—limited restriction

A state may bar one type of partial-birth abortion if there are other adequate, safe methods of abortion available *and* the law provides an exception for those instances when the banned procedure is necessary to preserve the life or *health* of the mother. [**Stenberg v. Carhart,** *supra*—no majority opinion]

(g) Husband's consent [§515]

A state may not require the consent of the pregnant woman's husband to an abortion during the first trimester. Since the state itself cannot proscribe during this period, it cannot delegate such authority to some person other than the woman's physician. [**Planned Parenthood v. Danforth,** *supra*]

(h) Unmarried minors [§516]

For the same reasons, the state may not require parental consent for an abortion during the first trimester of an unmarried minor (who is old enough and mature enough to give effective consent). [**Planned Parenthood v. Danforth,** *supra*] Nor, where a mature minor is involved, may the state require the consent of a judge. [**Bellotti v. Baird,** 443 U.S. 622 (1979)]

PRE-VIABILITY ABORTION REGULATION—A SUMMARY gilbert

NOT AN UNDUE BURDEN	UNDUE BURDEN
• Requiring a woman to *give written, informed consent* to the abortion procedure	• Requiring a woman to *obtain her spouse's consent* before obtaining an abortion
• Requiring a *doctor to give a woman information* about the nature of the procedure, the health risks, and the probable gestational age of the fetus	• *Completely prohibiting* so-called *partial birth abortion procedures*
• Requiring a woman to *wait 24 hours* after giving consent before an abortion may be performed	• Requiring a *mature minor to obtain her parent's* consent before obtaining an abortion
• Requiring that abortions be performed by *licensed physicians*	
• Requiring that *records be kept and reports be made* relevant to the woman's health	
• Requiring an *immature minor to obtain parental or judicial consent* before obtaining an abortion	
• Requiring *any unemancipated minor to notify one or both parents* of her intention to obtain an abortion and requiring her to *wait 48 hours* before obtaining the abortion if there is a judicial bypass procedure available	

1) **Parental consent [§517]**

A state may require parental or judicial consent for an immature minor—as long as she has the opportunity to demonstrate that she is mature or that, despite her immaturity, an abortion would be in her best interests. [**Planned Parenthood v. Ashcroft**, 462 U.S. 476 (1983)]

2) **Parental notification [§518]**

A state may require that notice be given to *one or both* parents of an unemancipated minor, and that she wait up to 48 hours thereafter before an abortion if the minor has an opportunity to obtain a court order permitting the abortion to proceed by showing that abortion *without notification* is in her best interest. [**Ohio v. Akron Center for Reproductive Health**, 497 U.S. 502 (1990); **Lambert v. Wicklund**, 520 U.S. 292 (1997)]

(i) **Funding and facilitating abortion [§519]**

The right to terminate a pregnancy does not carry with it the right to receive public funds for such termination. [**Harris v. McRae**, 448 U.S. 297 (1980)] Nor must the state permit public employees or the use of public facilities to perform abortions. [**Webster v. Reproductive Health Services**, *supra*]

(j) **Other regulations uncertain [§520]**

Prior to **Planned Parenthood of Southeastern Pennsylvania v. Casey**, the Court had invalidated requirements that abortions be performed only in specially accredited hospitals or health facilities, or that they be approved by more than one physician or a hospital committee. [**Doe v. Bolton**, 410 U.S. 179 (1973)] It is unclear whether these types of regulations will now be held to impose an "undue burden."

(5) **Rights of parents [§521]**

Parents have a fundamental right to make decisions concerning the care, custody, and control of their children. [**Troxel v. Granville**, 530 U.S. 914 (2000)]

(a) **Education [§522]**

Although the state may prescribe reasonable educational standards, it may *not* require that all children be educated in public schools. [**Pierce v. Society of Sisters**, 268 U.S. 510 (1925)] Neither may the state forbid education in a language other than English. [**Meyer v. Nebraska**, 262 U.S. 390 (1923)]

(b) **Visitation [§523]**

A state law was found to be overbroad and in violation of parents' rights where it authorized the courts to grant "any person" (including grandparents) a right to visit a child if the court finds that this would be in the child's best interests—without the judge giving significant weight to: (i) the traditional presumption that a fit parent will act in the child's best interests; and (ii) the parent's offer of meaningful visitation opportunity. [**Troxel v. Granville,** *supra*]

(6) Familial rights [§524]

The Court has recognized the right of *related persons* to live together in a single household. [**Moore v. City of East Cleveland,** 431 U.S. 494 (1977)]

(7) Intimate sexual conduct [§525]

The state has *no legitimate interest* in making it a crime for fully *consenting adults* to engage in *private* intimate sexual conduct that is not commercial. [**Lawrence v. Texas,** 123 S. Ct. 2472 (2003)—state law making it a crime for members of the same sex to engage in sodomy invalid; *overruling* **Bowers v. Hardwick,** 478 U.S. 573 (1986)]

(8) Interests not protected by right of privacy [§526]

The right of privacy does *not* protect:

(a) *The right not to have the state publicize a record* of an official act, such as an arrest. [**Paul v. Davis,** 424 U.S. 693 (1976)]

(b) *The right of parents to send their children to private schools that refuse to admit blacks.* [**Runyon v. McCrary,** 427 U.S. 160 (1976)]

(c) *The right of a large and basically unselective organization to exclude women from full membership.* [**Roberts v. United States Jaycees,** 468 U.S. 609 (1984)]

(d) *The right of the father of an illegitimate child to veto the child's adoption*—at least where the father has never sought custody and adoption is found to be in the child's "best interests" because the child would continue to live in the same family unit (with its mother and her husband). [**Quilloin v. Walcott,** 434 U.S. 246 (1978)]

(e) *The right of police officers to have their hair length unregulated.* Assuming that the general public has some Fourteenth Amendment "liberty" with respect to personal appearance, the state interest in public safety requires only that regulations concerning the organization of a police force be "rational." [**Kelley v. Johnson,** 425 U.S. 238 (1976)]

(f) *The right not to have the state accumulate and computerize the names and addresses of patients for whom dangerous drugs are prescribed* (at least where there are appropriate precautions against indiscriminate public disclosures). [**Whalen v. Roe,** 429 U.S. 589 (1977)—leaving open the questions of *unwarranted* disclosures, or the accumulation of such data *without* security measures]

(g) *The right of a United States President to protect personal communications from review and screening* by federal archivists, when such communications are commingled with other materials of important public interest and cannot be segregated from the private communications without comprehensive screening. [**Nixon v. Administrator of General Services,** 433 U.S. 425 (1977)]

SCOPE OF PRIVACY INTERESTS—EXAMPLES	gilbert
INTERESTS PROTECTED UNDER RIGHT OF PRIVACY	**INTERESTS NOT PROTECTED UNDER RIGHT OF PRIVACY**
• Marriage • Procreation • Contraception • Abortion • Homosexual sodomy	• Public records of an official act (*e.g.,* arrest) • Education of children at schools that discriminate based on race • Exclusion of women from large unselective organizations • Hair length of police officers • Accumulating data on patients to whom dangerous drugs are prescribed

b. **Right to interstate travel [§527]**

The right to travel freely from state to state is constitutionally protected and is *virtually unqualified.* [**United States v. Guest,** 383 U.S. 745 (1966)] The right to travel encompasses the right of citizens (i) to enter and leave another state, (ii) to be treated as welcome visitors, and (iii) to be treated equally if they become permanent residents of that state. [**Saenz v. Roe,** 526 U.S. 489 (1999)]

Example: California has more generous welfare benefits compared to other states. Consequently, some people move to California just to obtain the better benefits. To stanch the flow of California welfare money, the state adopted a law limiting welfare benefits for the first 12 months of a person's residency in the state to what the person would have received in their prior state of residence. *Held:* The California law is unconstitutional. The right to travel includes the right of new citizens to be treated the same as old citizens. A state cannot create degrees of citizenship based on length of residence. [**Saenz v. Roe,** *supra*]

(1) Source of right [§528]

Although the right to travel is not specifically mentioned in the Constitution, the third aspect above—to be treated equally when becoming a permanent resident—is a right of national citizenship, protected under the Fourteenth Amendment Privileges and Immunities Clause. [**Saenz v. Roe,** *supra*]

(2) Limits [§529]

The right to travel interstate is **not** violated by a law that forbids a person who has committed a crime within the state from leaving that state—at least if such departure would aggravate the consequences of the original crime. [**Jones v. Helms,** 452 U.S. 280 (1981)—law increased penalty of those who leave state after abandoning their children]

c. Right to international travel [§530]

The right to travel abroad has been held to be part of the "liberty" guaranteed by due process. [**Kent v. Dulles,** 357 U.S. 116 (1958)]

(1) Scope of right [§531]

The right of international travel is not as unqualified as the right to travel interstate and **may be regulated** within the bounds of due process; *i.e.*, a regulation will be upheld if it is rationally related to a legitimate government interest. Note that in reviewing federal restrictions on international travel, the Court defers to the judgment of the political branches on matters of foreign policy. [**Regan v. Wald,** 468 U.S. 222 (1984)]

Examples—valid restrictions

- *Denial of Social Security benefits* when recipients are outside the country has been upheld as being "rationally based." [**Califano v. Aznavorian,** 439 U.S. 170 (1978)]

- It is "reasonable" to revoke the passport of a person whose conduct in foreign countries presents a *serious danger to national security* and foreign policy. [**Haig v. Agee,** 453 U.S. 280 (1981)—secretary of state revoked passport of ex-CIA employee who was exposing undercover CIA agents in foreign countries]

- Reasonable "area restrictions" for passports (*prohibiting travel to certain countries or danger zones*) have also been upheld because of a substantial justification of national security and foreign policy. [**Zemel v. Rusk,** 381 U.S. 1 (1965)—Cuban passport denied]

> **cf.** **Compare—"overbroad" restriction:** A provision of the Subversive Activities Control Act that authorized the denial of passports to *all* members of the Communist Party or front groups was held invalid as too broad in scope. It applied to persons who were not aware that they were members of an organization requiring them to register; it was independent of the degree of activity in the organizations; and it authorized the Secretary of State to prohibit *all* travel by such persons, even for legitimate purposes (*e.g.,* to receive medical treatment). [**Aptheker v. Secretary of State**, 378 U.S. 500 (1964)]

d. Right to vote [§532]

The Constitution generally empowers the states to set the requirements for voting in both state and federal elections. [*See* Art. I, §2—House of Representatives; Seventeenth Amendment—Senate] However, even beyond several amendments to the Constitution that forbid government denial of the right to vote on specified grounds (*see infra*, §1146), the Court has held that voting is a "fundamental" right at the heart of our constitutional system, and thus there is a constitutionally protected right to participate in elections on an equal basis. (*See infra*, §§1146 *et seq.*)

e. Rights of mentally ill [§533]

The Court has held that commitment to a mental hospital is a deprivation of liberty subject to protection by the Due Process Clause. [**O'Connor v. Donaldson,** 422 U.S. 563 (1975)]

(1) Standards for commitment [§534]

A finding that an adult is "mentally ill" is not enough to justify involuntary deprivation of his right to liberty. No legitimate state interest is served by involuntarily confining a mentally ill adult unless it appears that the person is *dangerous* to himself or others, or *incapable of surviving* safely outside an institution either through his own efforts or through the help of willing friends and relatives. [**O'Connor v. Donaldson,** *supra*]

(a) Two conditions required [§535]

Even though an adult may be found to be dangerous to himself or others, he may not be involuntarily confined unless he is also found to be "mentally ill." [**Foucha v. Louisiana,** 504 U.S. 71 (1992)—defendant who is found not guilty by reason of insanity may not be held in a psychiatric hospital after it is determined that he is no longer mentally ill]

1) "Mentally ill" [§536]

States have discretion to define terms for describing "mental illness." [**Kansas v. Hendricks,** 521 U.S. 346 (1997)—upholding commitment requirement of "mental abnormality" or "personality disorder" for person likely to engage in "predatory acts of sexual violence"]

(b) Prisoners [§537]

A prison inmate who has a serious mental illness may be treated with antipsychotic drugs against his will, *if* the inmate is dangerous to himself or others and the treatment is in the inmate's medical interest. [**Washington v. Harper,** *supra,* §456]

(2) Conditions of confinement [§538]

The constitutional right to liberty of involuntarily committed, mentally retarded persons includes rights of adequate food, shelter, clothing, and medical care. It also requires reasonably safe conditions, freedom from bodily restraint, and minimally adequate training to ensure these rights, but an appropriate professional's judgment that these obligations have been satisfied (given all relevant circumstances) is entitled to a presumption of correctness. [**Youngberg v. Romeo,** 457 U.S. 307 (1982)]

f. Right to reject medical treatment [§539]

The liberty protected by the Due Process Clause guarantees a competent person the right to refuse unwanted medical treatment—at least with respect to a terminally ill person directing the withdrawal of life sustaining treatment. [**Cruzan v. Director, Missouri Department of Health,** 497 U.S. 261 (1990)]

(1) Standard of proof [§540]

A state may apply a clear and convincing evidence standard to determine an individual's actual wishes in the matter and need not accept the "substituted judgment" of others (including close family). [**Cruzan v. Director, Missouri Department of Health,** *supra*]

Example: Cruzan was in a hospital and in a vegetative state as a result of injuries she suffered in an automobile accident. She was being kept alive through artificial nutrition and hydration. Cruzan's parents asked the hospital to terminate the artificial procedures and allow her to die. The hospital refused to honor the parents' request absent a court order. Cruzan's parents brought an action on behalf of their daughter. At trial, one of Cruzan's friends testified that before the accident, Cruzan had told her that she would not want to live if she ever became a vegetable. The trial court granted the relief sought, but the Missouri Supreme Court reversed, reasoning that Missouri requires clear and convincing evidence of a person's intent on whether to reject medical treatment, and the evidence at trial was not clear and convincing. The parents appealed to the Supreme Court, which affirmed the Missouri Supreme Court decision. *Rationale:* A competent individual has the right to refuse medical treatment, but the state has a strong interest in preserving a person's life. The choice between life and death is a deeply personal decision, and the state may safeguard the decision by requiring a high standard of proof when the person herself cannot speak. [**Cruzan v. Director, Missouri Department of Health,** *supra*]

(2) Distinguish—no right to assisted suicide [§541]

The Due Process Clause does *not* include a *general* right to commit suicide or to assistance in doing so. [**Washington v. Glucksberg,** 521 U.S. 702 (1997)] But the Court has left open the situation of a *competent* person facing *imminent* death who *voluntarily* seeks to hasten it because of great *pain* that *cannot be relieved.*

Example: Washington enacted a statute that prohibited assisting in a suicide. Glucksberg and a number of terminally ill patients and other physicians who occasionally assisted in patients' suicides brought suit seeking to have the law declared unconstitutional, claiming that patients have a liberty interest—protected by the Fourteenth Amendment Due Process Clause—to have a physician-assisted suicide. The Supreme Court held that the law did not violate the Fourteenth Amendment. There is no fundamental constitutional right to assistance in committing suicide; there is no history of such a right, and it is a crime in almost every western democracy. Thus, the statute here can be upheld as long as it is rationally related to a legitimate state interest. The state has an interest in preserving life. [**Washington v. Glucksburg,** *supra*] The Court distinguished *Cruzan, supra,* because the right to refuse medical care, involved in *Cruzan,* is based on the common law concept of battery (*i.e.,* an unauthorized touching), and no such similar right is involved here.

6. Vagueness Doctrine [§542]

Under the Due Process Clauses, a law will be held "void for vagueness" if it forbids conduct that is so unclearly defined that: (i) persons "of common intelligence must necessarily guess at its meaning and differ as to its application" [**Connally v. General Construction Co.,** 269 U.S. 385 (1926)]; or (ii) it fails to provide minimal guidelines to govern law enforcement officers so as to prevent arbitrary and discriminatory enforcement [**Kolender v. Lawson,** 461 U.S. 352 (1983)]. Vagueness issues also arise in cases where the government has sought to restrict First Amendment rights (*e.g.,* speech assembly, etc.), and will be discussed more fully later in this book.

Example: A city ordinance made it illegal "to remain in any one place with no *apparent purpose.*" The ordinance could be invoked only if a police officer reasonably believed at least one of the loitering persons to be a member of a criminal street gang. Nevertheless, the ordinance was held unconstitutional because it was too vague to give officers sufficient guidelines, which could result in arbitrary police enforcement. [**City of Chicago v. Morales,** 527 U.S. 41 (1999)]

D. Impairment of Contractual Obligations

1. State Government

a. Constitutional provision [§543]

Article I, Section 10 (Contract Clause) provides: "No State shall . . . pass any . . . Law impairing the Obligation of Contracts . . . ."

(1) Applicable to state legislation [§544]

Because only a legislature can *"pass"* a law, the Contract Clause applies only to state legislation; it does not apply to decisions by state courts. Thus, the overruling of a prior decision by a state court is not prohibited by this clause, even though the reversal may affect contracts. [**Tidal Oil Co. v. Flanagan,** 263 U.S. 444 (1924)]

(2) "Impairs" [§545]

A law that *"impairs"* is one that *substantially* invalidates, releases, or extinguishes the obligations of a contract, or that derogates substantial contractual rights. [**Home Building & Loan Association v. Blaisdell,** 290 U.S. 398 (1923)] The more substantial the impairment, the greater the justification that must be shown by the state.

Example: During the depression, Minnesota passed a law that permitted extensions of the period after a foreclosure sale during which a mortgagor could redeem his property by paying off his debt. The Blaisdells obtained such an extension, and their mortgagee—Home Building & Loan Association—claimed that the statute unconstitutionally interfered with the parties' contract in violation of the Contract Clause. The Supreme Court held that the statute did indeed constitute an impairment, but found the impairment justified (*see infra,* §548). [**Home Building & Loan Association v. Blaisdell,** *supra*]

(3) "Obligation" [§546]

"Obligation" connotes not only the terms of the contract but also the *legal rules in force when the contract was made* and which enter into and comprise a part of the agreement; *i.e.,* it is presumed that the contracting parties adopted the terms of their bargain in reliance on the law in effect at the time the agreement was reached. However, the law is not required to remain static, since only the legitimate expectations of the parties regarding the law are deemed obligations to the government. [**United States Trust Co. v. New Jersey,** 431 U.S. 1 (1977)]

e.g. **Example:** New York and New Jersey created the Port Authority by interstate compact. In 1962, both states passed statutes prohibiting using port authority funds to finance passenger railroads unless the railroads were self-supporting. United Trust Company subsequently purchased a number of bonds sold by the port authority. In 1974, New York and New Jersey repealed their 1962 statutes in order to permit greater subsidizing of mass transit. The trust company challenged the repeal based on Contract Clause grounds. The Supreme Court held the repealing acts void under the Contracts Clause. [**United States Trust Co. v. New Jersey,** *supra*]

(4) "Contracts" [§547]

"Contracts" includes both public agreements (*i.e.*, those entered into by a state either as a sovereign or in its proprietary capacity) and private bargains (*i.e.*, those entered into between persons). It includes both executed agreements and executory agreements. [**Fletcher v. Peck,** 10 U.S. (6 Cranch) 87 (1810)—land grant case; **Dartmouth College v. Woodward,** 17 U.S. (4 Wheat.) 518 (1819)—college charter case]

b. Limitations on protection afforded to private contracts

(1) Modification reasonable and necessary for public purpose [§548]

Not all substantial "impairments" of contracts are deemed unconstitutional. Thus, although the Contract Clause prevents state destruction of *all* rights or *all* enforcement of existing contracts, rights and responsibilities in a private contract can be *modified* by legislation that: (i) serves an *important and legitimate* public interest, and (ii) is a *reasonable and narrowly tailored means* of promoting that interest.

(a) Factors considered [§549]

In determining these issues, the Court will consider, among other things, the *severity* of the impairment, the *reasonable reliance* and expectations of the contracting parties, the *strength and breadth* of the social-economic problem involved, whether the law serves the *general* public welfare or benefits only *special interests*, whether the law operates in an area *already regulated* by the state, and whether the impact of the law is *permanent* (rather than temporary) or *immediate* (as opposed to gradual). [**Allied Structural Steel Co. v. Spannaus,** 438 U.S. 234 (1978); **Energy Reserves Group Inc. v. Kansas Power & Light Co.,** 459 U.S. 400 (1983)]

e.g. **Example:** Allied Structural Steel Co. established a pension plan pursuant to IRS regulations. After the pension plan was established, Minnesota adopted a law imposing a pension funding charge on companies that terminated their pension plans in Minnesota or closed their Minnesota offices. The charge had the effect of requiring Allied to fund pensions for some employees that were not contractually entitled to a pension and resulted in a charge of $185,000. Allied sued for relief, claiming that the Minnesota law violated the Contract Clause. The Supreme Court held that the law here impairs the private contract because it greatly increases Allied's liabilities. Moreover, the law here is permanent rather than temporary, is directed at a narrow class (those employers with voluntary private pensions plans who either terminate the plan or close their office in Minnesota) rather than at a large class, and was not adopted to deal with a broad and desperate economic emergency. Therefore, the law violates the Contracts Clause. [**Allied Structural Steel Co. v. Spannaus,** *supra*]

1) **General applicability [§550]**

The Court will more likely uphold a law that imposes a general rule of conduct on all persons within the purpose of the regulation than a law that is limited to altering the contractual duties of persons who are parties to existing contracts. Otherwise, people could obtain immunity from state regulation by private contractual arrangements. [**Exxon Corp. v. Eagerton,** 462 U.S. 176 (1983)]

(b) **Modification of contract remedy [§551]**

Without "impairing the obligation" of a contract, the *remedy* provided by the legislature to enforce that obligation may be modified, as long as the modification is reasonable and does not impair substantial contractual rights. [**Von Hoffman v. City of Quincy,** 71 U.S. (4 Wall.) 535 (1867)]

Example: A state could not retroactively impair the obligation of a debtor to pay interest after the maturity of the debt, where the contract is silent, but it could shorten the statute of limitations applicable to suit on the contract, as long as a reasonable time is given in which the contract can be enforced.

(2) **Deference to legislative judgment [§552]**

Courts generally give substantial deference to a legislature's judgment regarding the reasonableness of, and necessity for, laws that impair the obligations of private contracts. [**East New York Savings Bank v. Hahn,** 326 U.S. 230 (1945)] Ultimately, however, the Court makes its own judgment regarding these requirements.

c. Limitations on protection afforded to public contracts

(1) Subsequent impairments [§553]

Subsequent impairments of public contracts are subject to basically similar limitations as private contracts; they are allowed if: (i) there is an important public interest; and (ii) there is a reasonable and narrowly tailored means of promoting that interest (*see supra*, §548).

(2) Less deference to legislative judgment [§554]

Where a public contract is involved, the legislature's own self-interest is at stake (*i.e.*, the legislature is modifying its own obligation). Therefore, its judgment as to whether the modification is both (i) *reasonable* under the circumstances, *and* (ii) *narrowly tailored* to an *important* state purpose is given less deference. [**United States Trust Co. v. New Jersey,** *supra*, §546—state repeal of financial covenant in state bonds held invalid because not essential to meet public need for mass transit and not reasonable in that importance of public mass transit was foreseeable at time state sold bonds with covenant]

(a) But note

The protection of the Contract Clause is limited by a rule of construction that requires that public contracts be construed narrowly against the grantee. [**Charles River Bridge v. Warren Bridge,** 36 U.S. (11 Pet.) 420 (1837)]

 Example: Although a state may contract irrevocably to exempt property from taxation, whenever in doubt, such contracts are usually construed as revocable and as providing only an exemption from some, but not all, types of taxation. [*See, e.g.,* **Hale v. Iowa State Board of Assessment and Review,** 302 U.S. 95 (1937)—income from state and municipal bonds, which by statute was "exempt from taxation," was held subject to the state income tax, because the exemption was construed as only providing a property tax exemption]

(b) *Ab initio* impairments of reserved powers [§555]

The Contract Clause does not require a state to adhere to a contract by which the state surrenders, *ab initio*, an essential attribute of its sovereignty. Thus, a state cannot bargain away its power of eminent domain or its police powers, or enter into a contract prohibiting the exercise of such powers.

Example: A state's grant of an exclusive privilege to maintain a toll bridge does not prevent the state from later taking and paying for the bridge under its power of eminent domain. [**West River Bridge Co. v. Dix**, 47 U.S. 507 (1848)]

Example: Similarly, a lottery company chartered by the state for 25 years could be put out of business three years later by legislation prohibiting lotteries adopted under the exercise of the state's police powers. [**Stone v. Mississippi**, 101 U.S. 814 (1879)]

Compare: However, a state can enter into contracts that are binding as to the exercise of its *taxing and spending powers*. [**New Jersey v. Wilson**, 11 U.S. (7 Cranch) 164 (1812)—Contract Clause prohibits impairment of permanent tax exemption granted by state]

---

2. **Federal Government [§556]**

The Contract Clause does *not apply* to the national government. Federal legislation adjusting economic interests may be applied retroactively as long as Congress has a "rational" purpose. [**Usery v. Turner Elkhorn Mining Co.**, 428 U.S. 1 (1976)]

E. Prohibition Against Ex Post Facto Laws

1. **Constitutional Provisions [§557]**

Article I, Section 9, Clause 3 provides: "No . . . ex post facto law shall be passed"; and Article I, Section 10, Clause 1 provides: "No state shall . . . pass any ex post facto law." These clauses prohibit *both federal and state legislatures* from passing ex post facto laws.

2. **Definition [§558]**

An ex post facto law is one that retroactively alters the law in a *substantially prejudicial* manner, so as to deprive a person of any right (civil, criminal, or political) previously enjoyed, for the purpose of *punishing* the person *for some past activity*. [**Cummings v. Missouri**, 71 U.S. (4 Wall.) 277 (1867)]

a. **Definition of "punishment" [§559]**

If a law's *purpose* is civil rather than punitive, it is not an ex post facto law unless its *effect* is so *clearly* punitive as to negate the legislature's intention.

Example: In 1994, Alaska adopted a statute—known as Megan's Law—requiring any sex offender within the state to register and provide his name, address, place of employment, vehicle information, etc. to law enforcement authorities. The act provided that some of this information could be made public, and this provision was carried out through publication over the Internet. Failure to comply with the registration requirements could result in a criminal penalty. John Doe I and John Doe II pleaded *nolo contendere* to child abuse charges and were released from prison in 1990. They brought an action seeking to have Megan's Law declared void as to them under the Ex Post Facto Clause. Looking at the structure and text of the law, the Supreme Court found that the goal of the law is **not to punish or stigmatize**. Rather, the legislature had found that sex offenders pose a high risk of reoffending and that the release of the information here was intended to protect the public from sex offenders. That some of the law's provisions were found in the Code of Criminal Procedure was not dispositive in deciding whether the law was punitive because location and labels do not themselves transform a civil remedy into a criminal remedy. Moreover, the regulatory means were reasonable in light of the act's nonpunitive purpose; its stigma resulted from dissemination of accurate information that was mostly public already; and the act did not impose any physical restraints. [**Smith v. Doe,** 123 S. Ct. 1140 (2003)]

Example: Also, a statute is **not** ex post facto if its principal purpose is regulation of some **present** status or activity, as opposed to punishment for past acts. Thus, the Court upheld a statute prohibiting the future practice of medicine by any person previously convicted of a felony, because the principal purpose was deemed to be the protection of the health and safety of citizens, rather than an additional punishment for convicted doctors. [**Hawker v. New York,** 170 U.S. 189 (1898)]

EXAM TIP   gilbert

Be sure to remember that the Ex Post Facto Clauses apply *only to criminal cases*. Be wary of exam questions that attempt to apply the prohibitions in a *civil* case (*e.g.,* regarding the denial of a professional license).

---

3. Retroactive Effects [§560]

A statute retroactively *alters* the law in a substantially prejudicial manner if it: (i) *makes criminal an act innocent* when done, and punishes the act, (ii) *prescribes greater punishment* for an act than the law provided when it was committed, or (iii) *alters the rules of evidence* as to require *less evidence to convict*.

Example—punishing past acts: A statute enacted after the Civil War required all officeholders, teachers, and preachers to execute an oath, swearing they had not participated in the rebellion. This requirement was held *invalid* as an attempt to punish for past acts, since the oath had no relationship to fitness to practice. [**Cummings v. Missouri,** *supra*]

---

e.g. **Example—requiring less evidence:** A law that raises the age of a sexual abuse victim whose testimony need not be corroborated in order to convict is an ex post facto law. [**Carmell v. Texas,** 529 U.S. 513 (2000)]

e.g. **Example—statute of limitations:** A law that revives the possibility of a criminal prosecution after the previously applicable statute of limitations has expired is an ex post facto law because it inflicts punishment on a person who was no longer liable for that punishment. [**Stogner v. California,** 123 S. Ct. 2446 (2003)]

cf. **Compare:** But because deportation of aliens is not deemed to be "punishment," a statute authorizing deportation for conduct that took place prior to enactment of the statute (and which was not grounds for deportation at that time) is *not* an ex post facto law. [**Harisiades v. Shaughnessy,** *supra*, §171]

EXAM TIP	gilbert

If an exam question raises an ex post facto issue, remember the basics: The law is prohibited if it: (i) punishes as a crime an act that was *legal when committed*; (ii) *increases the punishment* for a crime after its commission; or (iii) *deprives a defendant of a defense* that was available when the act was committed. Note that the motivation for the change is irrelevant.

Chapter Five:
Freedom of Speech, Press, and Association

CONTENTS

Chapter Approach

The First Amendment provides protection against abridgment of the freedoms of speech, association, and press. These rights are protected from state abridgment by the Fourteenth Amendment. The freedoms of speech and association are quite broad. They include not only the freedom to speak and associate, but also the freedom to refrain from speaking and associating. And the freedoms extend not only to speaking and associating; they also may extend to conduct related to speech and association. But none of these freedoms is absolute—all may be regulated to some extent.

1. **Content-Based Speech Regulations**

    If an examination question includes a regulation of speech, the first issue that you should address is whether the regulation is based on the content of the speech. Content regulations are *presumptively unconstitutional*. They will be upheld only if they are *necessary to serve a compelling purpose*. Moreover, the Court has *never* upheld a regulation of speech that favors one viewpoint over another. Note that the Supreme Court has found that the government has a compelling interest in eliminating speech in certain types of cases, *e.g.*, speech that presents a *clear and present danger of imminent lawless action*. Finally, note that the Court has ruled that some categories of speech fall outside the First Amendment's protection: (i) many kinds of *defamatory speech*; (ii) *obscenity*; (iii) *fighting words*; and (iv) *false or deceptive commercial speech. Caution:* The mere fact that the speech regulated falls into one of the above categories does not mean that the regulation is valid. The regulation still must not be *overbroad* (*i.e.*, regulate speech that is constitutionally protected in addition to the speech that can be proscribed) or *vague* (*i.e.*, leave a person of common intelligence uncertain of what is and is not proscribed).

    a. **Truthful commercial speech**

        While the government does not have a compelling interest in eliminating truthful commercial speech, the Supreme Court does allow government more leeway in regulating the content of commercial speech. Regulations of commercial speech will be upheld if they: (i) *directly advance* a *substantial government interest* and (ii) the restriction is *no more extensive than necessary* to serve that interest.

2. **Content-Neutral Speech Regulations**

    If the regulation in question is not based on the content of the speech involved, it generally will be subject to intermediate scrutiny and will be upheld only if the regulation advances an *important interest* unrelated to the suppression of speech and does not burden *substantially more speech than necessary*. Here too, the regulation may not be overbroad or vague.

3. **Censorship and Prior Restraints**

    If an exam question involves trying to stop speech before it happens (*e.g.*, by an injunction, censorship, or a system of licensing), be sure to note that a prior restraint may not be imposed merely because the speech involved is within a category of speech that can constitutionally be punished (*e.g.*, defamation, obscenity, fighting words). Our system of government prefers to allow people to air their ideas and punish speech that goes outside the boundaries of protected speech rather than proscribe speech in advance and risk accidentally proscribing speech that is constitutionally protected. Nevertheless, prior restraints will be allowed where the unprotected speech is so detrimental to the public welfare that normal remedies are inadequate (*e.g.*, preserving national security or a fair trial; preventing obscenity). However, even here, unless time is of the essence, a prior restraint may not be imposed absent notice and a judicial hearing.

4. **Symbolic Conduct**

If a question involves a regulation of conduct undertaken to convey a message, the conduct might or might not be protected. Government may proscribe such conduct to serve an *important interest unrelated to the speech involved* (*e.g.*, during the Vietnam War era, the Court ruled that the government could ban draft-card burning—done in protest of the war—because the government had a strong interest in maintaining an efficient draft system, but it could not ban public school students from wearing black arm bands in protest of the war, because such a ban served no government purpose other than the suppression of speech).

5. **First Amendment Rights in Public Places**

The right to speak and associate includes the right to do these activities on some public property. Of course, the rights do not extend to all public property at any time.

a. **Public forums and designated public forums**

Certain public property, such as streets, sidewalks, and parks, is so historically associated with the exercise of First Amendment activities that it cannot be totally closed to protected speech activities. Such property is called a *public forum*. Other public property, while not a traditional public forum, may become a *designated public forum* when the government, by policy or practice, opens the property up to expressive activities (*e.g.*, a public school auditorium that is open for use by civic groups when school is not in session). Speech and association in public forums and designated public forums may be subject to time, place, and manner regulations that: (i) are *content-neutral;* (ii) are *narrowly tailored;* (iii) serve a *significant government interest;* and (iv) leave open *ample alternative forums* or channels of communication for protected expression.

b. **Nonpublic forums**

Speech activities at forums that are neither public forums nor designated public forums (*i.e.*, nonpublic forums) may be regulated by reasonable, *viewpoint-neutral* regulations not meant to suppress expression merely because officials oppose it.

6. **Licensing**

The government may require people to obtain a license to use a public area for speech-related activities. However, the licensing law must contain clearly defined standards, and while fees may be charged, the fee cannot be based on the actual expense of maintaining public order (*i.e.,* it is unconstitutional to charge speakers more just because they hold unpopular views). Neither may licensing officials have unlimited discretion whether to grant a license. If the law gives an official unlimited discretion, it will be *void on its face* and people wishing to speak may do so without even applying for a license.

7. Special Governmental Interests

There are also a number of areas in which the government has special interests at stake that merit special considerations when assessing regulations on the freedom of speech, press, and association (*e.g.,* election laws invariably impose some burden on First Amendment freedoms, but some regulation is necessary in order to run smooth and fair elections; the government may subsidize some speech while choosing not to subsidize other speech; First Amendment rights can be curtailed in schools in order to avoid "material and substantial interference with school work, discipline, or the rights of others"; prisoners' First Amendment rights may be impinged by regulations "reasonably related to legitimate penological interests"; etc.). Be sure to keep these special interests in mind when writing exam answers.

8. Freedom of Association

A number of different issues can arise in a question involving the freedom of association. Perhaps the two most important are when one may be punished for group membership and when membership must be disclosed.

a. Punishment

The basic rule to remember here is that association can be punished only if the *group or organization engages in unprotected activities or advocacy* and the *member knows* of the group's illegal activities and has the *specific intent* to further those illegal aims.

b. Disclosure

Groups cannot be forced to disclose the names of members, and members cannot be forced to disclose their membership in groups, unless the required disclosure *directly serves substantial government interests.*

9. Freedom of Press

If a question involves the freedom of the press, you should remember the general rule that the press has no greater First Amendment freedoms than others.

a. Broadcast media

If a question involves regulation of radio or television stations, note that the general rule against content-regulation does not apply. Because of the limited number of frequencies available, the Supreme Court puts the interests of the viewers and listeners above that of the broadcaster and allows more restrictive content regulation than it allows in other areas.

A. Introduction

1. **Constitutional Provision [§561]**

   The First Amendment provides: "Congress shall make no law . . . abridging the freedom of *speech*, or of the *press*; or the right of people peaceably to *assemble*, and to petition the government for a redress of grievances." This provision has been held applicable to the states through the Due Process Clause of the Fourteenth Amendment. [**Gitlow v. New York,** 268 U.S. 652 (1925)]

   a. **Includes freedom to believe [§562]**

      The First Amendment freedom of speech goes beyond mere speech; it plainly protects the freedom to hold beliefs. [**Dawson v. Delaware,** 503 U.S. 159 (1992)—admitting evidence that convicted defendant was a member of a racist group in order to enhance his punishment violated First Amendment because it penalized him for his abstract beliefs]

   b. **Includes freedom not to speak [§563]**

      The First Amendment protects not only the right to speak freely, but also the right to *refrain* from speaking at all. [*See, e.g.,* **Pacific Gas & Electric Co. v. Public Utilities Commission,** 475 U.S. 1 (1986)—privately owned utilities may not be required to insert into their billing envelopes material from third parties that contains speech with which the utilities disagree] These are complementary components of the broader concept of "individual freedom of mind."

      (e.g.) **Example:** The New Hampshire automobile license plate included the state motto, "Live Free or Die." Maynard and his wife were of the Jehovah's Witnesses faith and found the motto repugnant to their religious beliefs. They therefore covered the motto on their automobile license plates and were prosecuted and convicted on misdemeanor charges for doing so. They appealed their conviction on constitutional grounds. The Supreme Court held that as applied to the Maynards, the misdemeanor statute violates the First Amendment because it forces them to adhere to an ideological viewpoint with which they disagree. [**Wooley v. Maynard,** 430 U.S. 705 (1977)]

      ---

      (1) **Distinguish—private property open to public [§564]**

         If private property is open to the public, a state may force the owner to allow third parties to use the property for speech activities even if the owner disagrees with the message conveyed, at least where the state does not dictate the message and the owner is free to disclaim association with the speaker. [**PruneYard Shopping Center v. Robins,** *supra,* §489]

         (e.g.) **Example:** PruneYard Shopping Center prohibited persons within the center from distributing pamphlets and collecting signatures unless they related to the center's commercial activities. Robins entered the center, set up a table, and started soliciting signatures for a petition opposing a United Nations resolution against "Zionism." Robins was asked to leave by shopping center employees and did so. Robins then filed a suit in California court to enjoin the shopping center from prohibiting the solicitation. The California Supreme Court held that the *California Constitution* gave Robins a right to collect signatures in the shopping center. On appeal, the United States Supreme Court held that while the United States Constitution does not grant Robins the right to solicit signatures on private property, the states are free to provide more extensive rights. Moreover, the state constitutional policy does not violate the shopping center owner's freedom not to speak—at least as long as the particular message is not dictated by the state and is not likely to be identified with the owner of the shopping center. [**PruneYard Shopping Center v. Robins,** *supra*]

---

(2) Required disclosures as a condition of speech [§565]

Mandating speech that a speaker would not otherwise make necessarily alters the content of the speech. Therefore, it is subject to the same close scrutiny as a law that forbids speech. [**Riley v. National Federation of the Blind of North Carolina,** 487 U.S. 781 (1988)—state may not require that professional fundraisers disclose their fees to potential donors before an appeal for funds]

c. Includes freedom to associate and not to associate [§566]

The First Amendment protects the "freedom to associate and privacy in one's associations." [**NAACP v. Alabama,** *supra*, §69—state cannot compel NAACP to disclose its membership list] This extends to some right to *refuse* to associate. [**Abood v. Detroit Board of Education,** 431 U.S. 209 (1977)—state cannot require employees to contribute money for support of ideological causes with which they disagree; *see infra*, §864]

(1) Illustration—parades [§567]

The state may not require private citizens who organize a parade to express their collective views to include among the marchers a group imparting a message that the organizers oppose. The First Amendment gives the organizers the right to choose the content of what may be expressed or not expressed through the parade. [**Hurley v. Irish-American Gay, Lesbian & Bisexual Group of Boston,** 515 U.S. 557 (1995)—organizers of St. Patrick's Day parade could not be forced to allow a group of gay, lesbian, and bisexual descendants of Irish immigrants to march in the parade as a group]

(2) "Expressive association" and "intimate association" [§568]

The freedom of association includes the right to associate for the purpose of engaging in First Amendment activities—speech, assembly, and religious exercise. It also includes the right to enter into and maintain certain intimate human relationships—to share ideals and beliefs. [**Roberts v. United States Jaycees**, *supra*, §526] These freedoms of "expressive association" and "intimate association," however, do not include a general right of "societal association." [**City of Dallas v. Stanglin**, 409 U.S. 19 (1989)—no right of association in coming to dance hall for recreational dancing]

---

e.g. **Example:** The Boy Scouts of America ("BSA") have a rule prohibiting gay people from being members. Upon discovering that Dale, an eagle scout and assistant scoutmaster, was a gay activist, the BSA revoked Dale's membership. Dale sued the BSA under a New Jersey state law that, among other things, prohibits discrimination in public accommodations based on sexual preference. The state supreme court ordered Dale reinstated under the statute, but the United States Supreme Court reversed the state decision. The Court held that a state antidiscrimination law may not bar the BSA from excluding Dale. Forced inclusion would *significantly burden* the right of expressive association of the BSA, because one of the *sincerely held* purposes of the BSA is to instill certain moral values in young people, including the value that "homosexual conduct is not morally straight." [**Boy Scouts of America v. Dale**, 530 U.S. 640 (2000)]

---

d. Includes freedom to receive information [§569]

The First Amendment protects both the right to communicate and the right to receive information. [**Lamont v. Postmaster General**, 381 U.S. 301 (1965)—government may not require that addressee specifically request post office to deliver "communist political propaganda"]

e. Includes solicitation of funds [§570]

The First Amendment protections can extend to the right to seek financial support for particular causes and views because this is often necessary to the flow of information and advocacy. [**Village of Schaumburg v. Citizens for a Better Environment**, 444 U.S. 620 (1980)]

f. Includes some conduct [§571]

Freedom of expression and association encompasses certain *action* or *conduct* in addition to purely verbal or visual expression. For example, distributing membership applications, setting up facilities for a meeting, hanging signs announcing a point of view, and similar conduct are among the numerous actions incidental to the freedoms protected by the First Amendment—and thus these activities are not subject to the ordinary state power to regulate conduct.

(1) Distinguish—action to acquire information [§572]

The First Amendment does *not* protect conduct simply because it is undertaken to acquire information to be used in connection with the freedoms of speech, press, or association. [**Zemel v. Rusk,** *supra,* §531—travel to Cuba not within ambit of First Amendment]

(2) Distinguish—action motivated by beliefs [§573]

The First Amendment does not protect conduct simply because it happens to be motivated by a person's point of view or beliefs. [**Wisconsin v. Mitchell,** 508 U.S. 476 (1993)—upholding law enhancing punishment for crime of aggravated battery when defendant selects victim because of race]

(3) "Symbolic" conduct [§574]

The First Amendment affords *some* protection to action undertaken to communicate an idea. (*See infra,* §926.)

g. But note—does not include right to be heard [§575]

The First Amendment right of free speech does not include the right to have public decisionmaking bodies listen or respond to the views communicated. [**Minnesota State Board for Community Colleges v. Knight,** 465 U.S. 271 (1984)]

2. Rights Not Absolute [§576]

First Amendment rights do not unqualifiedly protect all verbal or visual expression. The government may punish utterances that impose such undesirable results on society as to outweigh the value of free speech. For example, disclosure of U.S. intelligence operations and names of intelligence personnel for the purpose of obstructing intelligence operations is "clearly not protected" speech. [**Haig v. Agee,** *supra,* §431] It is often repeated that "the most stringent protection of free speech would not protect a person in falsely shouting 'Fire!' in a crowded theater." Other examples of verbal and visual expression held to be outside the protection of the First Amendment include "obscenity" (*see infra,* §§632 *et seq.*) and "fighting words" (*see infra,* §659).

a. Threats [§577]

The First Amendment does not protect "true threats"—statements meant to communicate an intent to place an individual or group in fear of bodily harm. [**Virginia v. Black,** 123 S. Ct. 1536 (2002)—upholding ban on cross burning *carried out with the intent to intimidate* even though *some forms* of cross burning may be core political speech]

b. Freedom not to associate [§578]

States have a compelling interest in eradicating race and sex discrimination. Based on this interest, a state may prohibit large and basically unselective organizations and organizations that are often used for business contacts from denying membership to women and minorities, at least when it is not shown that this would impede the individuals' ability to engage in First Amendment activities. [**Board of Directors of Rotary International v. Rotary Club of Duarte,** 481 U.S. 537 (1987); **Roberts v. United States Jaycees,** *supra,* §568]

3. General Approach to Validity of Restrictions [§579]

When the government acts to limit speech, press, or association, the Court will usually **weigh** (i) the great **importance of these rights** in a democratic society, (ii) the **nature and scope of the restraint** imposed on the individual, (iii) the **type and strength of the government interest** sought to be served, and (iv) whether the restraint is a **narrowly tailored means** to achieving that interest.

a. Content-based regulations [§580]

It is presumptively unconstitutional for government to place burdens on speech because of its content, and such government action is subject to strict scrutiny. To justify such differential treatment of speech, the government must show that the regulation (or tax) is **necessary** to serve a **compelling** state interest and is narrowly drawn to achieve that end. [**Simon & Schuster, Inc. v. Members of the New York State Crime Victims Board,** 502 U.S. 105 (1991)—striking a law requiring that proceeds of criminals from books and other productions describing their crime be placed in escrow for five years to pay claims of victims of the crime]

(1) Expressive association [§581]

Likewise, the freedom of expressive association (*see supra,* §568) may be overridden "by regulations adopted to serve compelling state interests, unrelated to the suppression of ideas, that cannot be achieved through means significantly less restrictive of associational freedoms." [**Roberts v. United States Jaycees,** *supra; and see* **Boy Scouts of America v. Dale,** *supra,* §568]

(2) Viewpoint discrimination [§582]

Regulations are **not** content-neutral if—either by their **terms** or their **manifest purpose**—they distinguish favored speech from disfavored speech on the basis of the ideas or views expressed. [**Turner Broadcasting System v. FCC,** 512 U.S. 622 (1994)]

Example: A school district allowed its classrooms to be used for holding social, civic, and recreational meetings as long as the meetings were nonexclusive and open to the general public. The district specifically provided that school premises could not be used by any group for religious purposes. Lamb's Chapel, an evangelical church within the school district, asked for permission to use a classroom to show a film series on family planning. The district denied the request, finding the film series to be religion-related. The church sued for access under the First Amendment. The school district argued that its rule was viewpoint neutral because it prohibited all religious groups from presenting their views on family planning. The Supreme Court, however, found viewpoint discrimination because the rule prohibited only presenting religious views on family planning; nonreligious groups were free to use the classrooms to present their views on the matter. [**Lamb's Chapel v. Center Moriches Union Free School District**, 508 U.S. 384 (1993)]

(a) Note

It appears that the Court has *never* upheld what it has recognized as "viewpoint discrimination." Indeed, even though the Court has stated that a government interest in avoiding an Establishment Clause violation (*see infra*, §§917 *et seq.*) may be "compelling" so as to justify a content-based regulation [**Widmar v. Vincent**, 454 U.S. 263 (1981)], in *Lamb's Chapel* the Court suggested that such an interest might not justify viewpoint discrimination.

b. Content-neutral speech regulations [§583]

Content-neutral regulations of speech are ordinarily subject to "intermediate scrutiny" and will be upheld only if they: (i) advance *important* interests unrelated to the suppression of speech and (ii) do not burden *substantially more* speech than necessary to further those interests. (For amplification, *see infra*, §§753, 726.) [**Turner Broadcasting System, Inc. v. FCC**, 520 U.S. 180 (1997)]

SUMMARY OF GENERAL SPEECH REGULATION STANDARDS	gilbert
CONTENT-BASED REGULATION	Upheld only if *necessary* to serve a *compelling interest*
REGULATION OF EXPRESSIVE ASSOCIATION	Upheld only if adopted to serve a *compelling interest unrelated to the suppression of speech* that cannot be achieved through *significantly less restrictive means*
VIEWPOINT DISCRIMINATION	Probably *cannot* be upheld
CONTENT-NEUTRAL REGULATION	Upheld if it *advances an important* interest unrelated to the suppression of speech and *does not burden substantially* more speech than necessary

4. "Overbreadth" and "Vagueness" [§584]

In the free speech area, the Court sometimes permits regulations to be challenged "on their face" if they are "overbroad" or "vague." *Rationale:* The very existence of such regulations may "chill" the exercise of First Amendment rights—*i.e.*, may cause others not before the Court to refrain from constitutionally protected expression. [**Broadrick v. Oklahoma**, 413 U.S. 601 (1973)]

a. Consequences of facial invalidity [§585]

A law held to be "void on its face" is *totally invalid*; *i.e.*, it is held incapable of any valid application. Thus, persons are immune from regulation under the law even though their speech or association is *not* constitutionally protected—

i.e., even if they could be regulated by a statute drawn with the requisite specificity. In effect, the Court (i) permits litigants to raise the First Amendment rights of third parties not before the Court, (ii) penalizes the government for permitting such statutes to remain on the books (because of their chilling effect), and (iii) forces enactment of a new statute—or an interpretation of the existing one (*see infra*, §593)—to eliminate the overbreadth or vagueness.

b. Overbreadth [§586]

An overbroad law is one that regulates "a substantial amount of constitutionally protected" expression or association (as well as speech or conduct that is not constitutionally protected). [**Village of Hoffman Estates v. Flipside, Hoffman Estates, Inc.,** 455 U.S. 489 (1982)] Overbreadth may be more readily found if the law is "directed at speech as such"; *i.e.*, it covers *only* verbal and visual expression rather than *any* conduct. [**Broadrick v. Oklahoma,** *supra*]

---

e.g. **Example:** A city ordinance provided: "It shall be unlawful and a breach of the peace for any person wantonly to curse or revile or to use obscene or opprobrious language toward or with reference to any member of the city police while in the actual performance of his duty." The statute is unconstitutionally overbroad. While a state can regulate "fighting words" (*i.e.*, words that, by their very nature, inflict injury or tend to incite an immediate breach of the peace; *see infra*, §§659-664), the regulation here goes beyond fighting words. For example, the limitation on opprobious words, according to the common dictionary definition of the word, would prohibit words that convey or intend to convey disgrace. Under the First Amendment, people have a right to convey such words toward the police. Therefore, the ordinance is overbroad and unconstitutional. [**Lewis v. City of New Orleans,** 415 U.S. 130 (1974)]

---

(1) Limitation—substantial overbreadth [§587]

A "facial challenge" will not be permitted if only *marginal applications* of the statute would infringe on First Amendment rights—*i.e.*, if the statute mainly covers a wide range of easily identifiable and constitutionally proscribable conduct. [**United States Civil Service Commission v. National Association of Letter Carriers,** 413 U.S. 548 (1973)—upholding prohibition of government employees from acts of political management and campaigning, such as holding party office, working the polls, campaigning for office, etc.]

(2) Limitation—proper party before court [§588]

If those challenging the law actually desire to engage in protected speech that the overbroad law proscribes, only that part of the law that reaches too far will be declared invalid. *Rationale:* Since the proper parties are before the court, there is no concern that an attack on the law will be unduly delayed or that protected speech will be chilled. [**Brockett v. Spokane Arcades, Inc.,** 472 U.S. 491 (1985)]

Example: A Washington statute provided that any place "where lewd films are publicly exhibited as a regular course of business" is a moral nuisance. The statute defined "lewd matter" to include something that incites lust. Purveyors of sexually oriented books and movies challenged the statute on First Amendment grounds. A lower court held the statute facially invalid *in toto* because the inclusion of the word "lust" made the statute overbroad (*i.e.,* it would outlaw material that provoked normal sexual reactions, and such material is protected under the First Amendment; *see infra,* §636). However, the Supreme Court held that because the plaintiffs before the Court were seeking to engage in protected speech that the statute proscribed (*i.e.,* they desired to show films that were lustful), it was improper to strike the entire statute on its face; rather, it was proper only to strike the part of the statute that prohibited showing lustful films. [**Brockett v. Spokane Arcades, Inc.,** *supra*]

Compare: In **Lewis v. City of New Orleans,** *supra,* the lower courts found that the speech in which Lewis engaged was not protected speech (*i.e.,* she went beyond speech that was merely "opprobious"). Because the defendant was not making a claim that the speech she engaged in was protected, it was proper to strike the whole statute because of its chilling effect.

c. **Explicit overbreadth [§589]**

Regulations may be explicitly overbroad—*e.g.,* a statute prohibiting *"all"* membership in groups that engage in unprotected advocacy. Some such membership is protected by the First Amendment (*i.e.,* membership without specific intent to achieve the association's illegal aims—*see infra,* §§842-844), while other membership may not be constitutionally protected.

d. **Overbreadth due to vagueness [§590]**

Alternatively, a regulation may contain imprecise language that, because of vagueness or uncertainty, may be read by persons "of common intelligence" as proscribing or regulating speech or association that is protected by the First Amendment. Such "standardless" statutes likewise permit arbitrary and discriminatory law enforcement by police, prosecutors, and juries. Because of their "chilling effect," *special precision* is required of statutes that proscribe or regulate speech or association.

Example: A state law requiring teachers to take the oath, "That I have not and will not lend aid, support, advice, counsel, or influence to the

Communist Party," was held impermissibly vague; the language might embrace anyone who ever supported a candidate supported by the Communist Party, who supported any cause that the Party had supported, or who (as a journalist or otherwise) had supported the constitutional rights of the Communist Party. [**Cramp v. Board of Public Instruction,** 368 U.S. 278 (1961)]

---

e.g **Example:** An ordinance making it a crime for "three or more persons to assemble on any of the sidewalks and there conduct themselves in a manner annoying to persons passing by" was held to violate the general due process standard of vagueness, because people of "common intelligence must necessarily guess at its meaning." It also violated the First Amendment "right of free assembly and association" because "mere public intolerance or animosity" cannot be the basis for its abridgment, and because the ordinance "contains an obvious invitation to discriminatory enforcement" against those whose association is "annoying" due to their ideas or physical appearance. [**Coates v. Cincinnati,** 402 U.S. 611 (1971); *and see* **City of Chicago v. Morales,** *supra,* §542]

EXAM TIP	gilbert

If an exam question includes statutory language prohibiting certain speech or limiting the right of association, be sure to analyze the language for *overbreadth and vagueness*. If the statute can be read to prohibit speech that is constitutionally protected, it is probably overbroad. If you, as a person "of common intelligence," cannot tell what speech or conduct is prohibited, it is probably unconstitutionally vague. As a practical matter, overbreadth and vagueness almost always go together—*i.e.,* the same regulation will usually *violate both concepts*—so you should usually discuss both concepts in an essay question involving this area.

e. **Vagueness alone [§591]**

A statute regulating expression or association may also be impermissibly vague even though not overbroad—*e.g.,* "It shall be unlawful to make any speech not protected by the First and Fourteenth Amendments."

f. **Exceptions to facial challenges**

(1) **"Hard core" violator [§592]**

Sometimes (but not always) the Court will refuse to permit a person to attack a statute on its face—if the person's conduct is not even arguably constitutionally protected but is "the sort of hard-core conduct that would be prohibited under any construction of the statute," *e.g.,* burning down a person's home because you disagree with his political views. [**NAACP v. Button,** 371 U.S. 415 (1963)]

(2) **Saving judicial interpretation [§593]**

If an overbroad or vague statute is authoritatively construed (*i.e.,* a state statute by the state courts, a federal statute by the federal courts) to cure the overbreadth or vagueness—so that it proscribes or regulates *only* expression or association *not* protected by the First Amendment—it may be applied to unprotected conduct occurring *prior* to the limiting construction as long as the person had *fair warning* that the conduct was covered. [**Osborne v. Ohio**, 495 U.S. 103 (1990)—statute making it a crime to possess *any* nude photo of a minor except for proper purpose was construed by state supreme court to require scienter and to be limited only to nudity involving lewd exhibitions]

(a) Legislative repeal or amendment [§594]

However, an overbreadth defense continues to be available even if the overbroad statute under which a person is charged is subsequently repealed or amended to cure its overbreadth. *Rationale:* Legislators who can cure their mistakes by amendment or repeal without significant cost might not be careful to avoid passing overbroad laws. [**Massachusetts v. Oakes**, 491 U.S. 576 (1989)]

B. Advocacy of Unlawful Action

1. Speech That Is Vituperative, Abusive, or Contemptuous of Government or Public Officials [§595]

As long as this type of expression does not incite others to perform unlawful acts or involve breach of the peace (*see infra*, §§659 *et seq.*), it is protected by the First Amendment—even though "unpatriotic," "disrespectful," "defiant," or "patently offensive to the community." [**Watts v. United States**, 394 U.S. 705 (1969)—"If they ever make me carry a rifle the first man I want to get in my sights is [the President]"; **Street v. New York**, 394 U.S. 576 (1969)—"We don't need no damn American flag"] *Rationale:* The right of uninhibited debate on public issues is an essential ingredient of our political system.

Example: A federal statute making it a crime to engage in a theatrical production while wearing an army uniform if the portrayal "tends to discredit" the armed forces violates the First Amendment. [**Schacht v. United States**, 398 U.S. 58 (1970)]

2. Criminal Penalties for Advocacy of Illegal Action

a. Background [§596]

In the first three decades of the 20th century, the Court held that speech (or writing) advocating *forceful overthrow* of the government may be penalized; that a legislative finding that such speech was inherently dangerous—even though the speech might not succeed in stimulating the action advocated—was presumptively valid; that it was reasonable for the legislature to punish such speech before the conduct being advocated was imminent; and that the Court would not make an independent determination as to whether the speech posed a danger of the advocated conduct's taking place. [**Gitlow v. New York,** 268 U.S. 652 (1925)—upholding defendants' convictions for publishing a radical manifesto urging the use of militant strikes to bring about a socialist state]

(1) Holmes-Brandeis view [§597]

In the earliest of the cases during this period, affirming convictions for speech to obstruct military recruitment, Justice Holmes, writing for unanimous Courts, adopted a substantially different position: The question "is whether the words used are in such circumstances and are of such a nature as to create a *clear and present danger* that they will bring about the substantive evils that Congress has a right to prevent. It is a question of proximity and degree." [**Schenck v. United States,** 249 U.S. 47 (1919)] Holmes also suggested that the defendant's *intent* to produce this set of circumstances was necessary for the speech to lose its constitutional protection. [**Debs v. United States,** 249 U.S. 211 (1919)] But in subsequent separate opinions, Justices Holmes and Brandeis slightly altered their view. They contended that government may punish only speech that *produces, or is intended to produce, a clear and imminent danger of a serious substantive evil*; *i.e.*, speech advocating illegal action may be punished only when the advocated action is serious and there is no time for further discussion before the advocated action will take place. Furthermore, whether these elements exist in a given case must be determined according to federal constitutional standards, and ultimately, by the Supreme Court—not by a legislature, jury, or trial court. [**Abrams v. United States,** 250 U.S. 616 (1919)—Holmes, J. dissenting; **Whitney v. California,** 274 U.S. 357 (1927)—Brandeis, J. concurring]

(a) Learned Hand view [§598]

Judge Learned Hand articulated a similar approach, narrowly construing a provision of the Espionage Act to bar only "direct advocacy of resistance to the recruiting and enlistment service," rather than prohibiting speech that expressed only sympathy, admiration, and approval of draft resistance. [**Masses Publishing Co. v. Patten,** 244 Fed. 535 (S.D.N.Y. 1917)] In reversing, the Second Circuit adopted the position of the *Gitlow* decision, *supra*.

(b) Contemporary influence [§599]

The Holmes-Brandeis "clear and present danger" test has great influence today, even though (as noted below) it has not been adopted in every respect by the modern Court.

b. *Dennis-Yates* "test" [§600]

In **Dennis v. United States,** 341 U.S. 494 (1951), and **Yates v. United States,**

354 U.S. 298 (1957), leaders of the American Communist Party were charged with conspiring to advocate forceful overthrow of the government and were prosecuted under the Smith Act. In *Dennis*, the Court affirmed the convictions, rejecting the argument that defendants' activities were protected by the First Amendment. In *Yates*, the Court reversed the convictions, interpreting the Smith Act as not making unlawful the particular activities in which the defendants had engaged. Thus, *Yates* did not involve a *constitutional* interpretation.

(1) Significance of *Yates* [§601]

Since the Smith Act was a federal statute, the Court had final judicial authority to construe it. In doing so, the Court used the common technique of interpreting the federal statute so as to *avoid the constitutional question* of whether the statute violated the First Amendment. Nevertheless, the Court's discussion had constitutional significance, and the *Yates* interpretation on the limits of the Smith Act has since been referred to in defining the limits of the First Amendment. [*See, e.g.,* **Communist Party of Indiana v. Whitcomb,** 414 U.S. 441 (1974)]

(2) Rationale of *Dennis* and *Yates* [§602]

The rationale of *Dennis* and *Yates* is as follows:

(a) Must be substantial governmental interest [§603]

Government must have a *substantial* interest before it may punish speech—and this must be independently determined by the courts, not by the legislature or a jury.

(b) Call to action punishable [§604]

Advocacy aimed at promoting the forceful overthrow of government—*i.e.*, a *call to action*, urging that people *act* (rather than *merely believe*)—can be punished without violating the First Amendment. [**Dennis v. United States,** *supra*]

1) But note

Advocating or justifying the forceful overthrow of government as an *abstract principle*—*i.e.*, urging that people *believe* this *ought* to be done (rather than that they do it)—is *not* punishable. [**Yates v. United States,** *supra*] And this is true even when such advocacy is urged as a moral necessity, and/or when the advocate has evil intent.

(c) Gravity and imminence weighed [§605]

Government need not wait until the last moment before it punishes advocacy of illegal action: The *graver* the evil being advocated, the *less imminent* its actually happening need be before the speaker can be punished. Thus, imminence is *not* an independent factor, but one to be *weighed* with the *gravity* of the evil.

c. **Brandenburg "test" [§606]**

More recently, the Court has held that a state may not penalize advocacy of the use of force or of law violation except where such advocacy is *"directed to inciting or producing imminent lawless action and is likely to incite or produce such action."* [**Brandenburg v. Ohio**, 395 U.S. 444 (1969)]

Example: Brandenburg, a Ku Klux Klan leader, was convicted under an Ohio statute for advocating criminal terrorism and criminal syndicalism. His activities consisted of inviting television reporters to a secluded gathering where weapons were presented and speeches were made threatening that revenge would be taken against the government if it "continues to suppress the white, Caucasian race." The Supreme Court overturned the conviction. The First Amendment does not permit states to forbid mere advocacy of the use of force except when such advocacy is directed to inciting or producing imminent lawless action and is likely to produce such action. [**Brandenburg v. Ohio,** *supra*]

---

(1) **Note**

This test makes *imminence* an independent requirement, and appears to make *evil intent* on the part of the speaker ("directed to . . . ") an independent requirement as well.

(2) **But note**

Brandenburg cites *Dennis* and *Yates* (in which imminence was *not* an independent factor) with approval. The cases may perhaps be squared on the ground that when the evil advocated is *very* grave or serious (*e.g.*, forceful overthrow of government, as in *Dennis*, or widespread riot), imminence is only one factor to be weighed; but when the evil advocated is a mere legal violation (*e.g.*, peaceful civil disobedience) or the *use* of *some* force (minor property damage), imminence is an independent requirement.

EXAM TIP   gilbert

Analysis of exam questions testing on this branch of First Amendment law—advocacy of illegal conduct—is really a *three-step process* under *Brandenburg*. You should first assess whether the speech involved was *directed at inciting lawless action*. If it was, assess whether it sought to incite lawlessness *now* as opposed to at some future time. If it was intended to incite immediate lawlessness, assess *how likely it was that the speaker would succeed* given the circumstances. For example, suppose a group of peaceful anti-war protesters was marching down a sidewalk as permitted. A few protesters stray into the street and are shoved back onto the sidewalk by the police. One of the protesters yells, "We'll take the fucking street back later." Can the protester be convicted for advocating illegal conduct? No. First, it is not clear that the statement was directed at inciting lawlessness (it could be taken as counsel for present moderation). Second, even if it did advocate lawless action, it seems to be contemplating action at some indefinite future time. If these first two hurdles were met, we would still have to assess whether the statement was loud enough, fiery enough, and directed to enough people to make lawless action likely.

C. Defamation

1. Introduction [§607]

Speech or writing that is defamatory is *generally* not protected by the First Amendment and may therefore be subject to criminal libel laws or civil laws awarding damages. [**Beauharnais v. Illinois**, 343 U.S. 250 (1952)]

FAULT AND DAMAGES RULES IN CONSTITUTIONAL DEFAMATION ACTIONS		gilbert
TYPE OF PLAINTIFF/ DEFAMATION	**FAULT REQUIRED**	**DAMAGES RECOVERABLE**
PUBLIC OFFICIAL OR PUBLIC FIGURE	*Actual malice* (knowledge of falsity or reckless disregard as to truth or falsity)	Presumed damages under common law rules (and punitive damages where appropriate) if other state law damage requirements are met
PRIVATE PERSON • **MATTER OF PUBLIC CONCERN**	*At least negligence* as to statement's truth or falsity	Damages only for proved "actual injury" (if plaintiff proves actual malice, presumed and punitive damages may be available) if other state law damage requirements are met
• **MATTER OF PRIVATE CONCERN**	*No fault* as to truth or falsity need be proved	Presumed damages under common law rules (and punitive damages where appropriate) if other state law damage requirements are met

2. Group Libel Laws [§608]

Group libel laws punish false statements or vilification of a group—if likely to cause violence or disorder. *Note:* Truth here may not be a defense if the utterance is made with bad motive or for unjustifiable ends. In the 1950s, the Court upheld a group libel law as applied to circulation of anti-black literature [**Beauharnais v. Illinois**, *supra*], but doctrinal developments under the First Amendment have cast significant doubt on the continued validity of the decision.

e.g. **Example:** Beauharnais published a leaflet calling on Chicago officials to halt the encroachment of African Americans on whites' property, warning of the "rapes, robberies, knives, guns, and marijuana of the Negro." He was convicted under a statute prohibiting exhibition of any publication portraying "depravity, criminality, unchastity," etc., of any "race, color, creed, or religion" which exposes such citizens to "contempt, derision, or obloquy or which is productive of breach of the peace or riots." The Supreme Court upheld the conviction despite the lack of showing a clear and present danger because libel was not then protected by the First Amendment. [**Beauharnais v. Illinois**, *supra*]

3. **Matters of Public Interest [§609]**

There is an inherent conflict between the need for full disclosure and debate on matters of public interest (protected by the First Amendment), and the need to protect personal reputations against injurious falsehoods (through state laws against libel). The Court has resolved this conflict by creating a constitutional privilege protecting freedom of expression as to *certain kinds* of defamations.

a. **Defamation of "public officials" [§610]**

Freedom of speech and press bars a civil libel judgment for criticism of "*public officials*" in respect to their "*official conduct*," unless the plaintiff shows "*malice*" by clear and convincing evidence. [**New York Times v. Sullivan,** 376 U.S. 254 (1964)—reversing a large civil libel judgment awarded in Alabama courts based on a newspaper's publishing a paid advertisement critical of conduct of Alabama officials in handling of racial matters]

(1) **Rationale [§611]**

To allow recovery in such cases could lead to self-censorship on matters of public concern; *i.e.*, persons might well avoid expressing justified criticisms of official conduct for fear of being held liable for "erroneous statements honestly made" or because of the costs of defending legal actions arising from such criticism. Furthermore, public officials may protect their reputations through their opportunity for public rebuttal and thus are not greatly in need of legal remedies. [**New York Times v. Sullivan,** *supra*]

(2) **"Malice" defined [§612]**

"Malice" requires a showing that the publication was *known to be false or* was published with *reckless disregard* as to its truth or falsity. Mere negligence is not enough—even if the publication was made with ill will or the intent to injure. Since there is no public interest in protecting calculated falsehoods, First Amendment protection does not extend to speech made with "malice." [**New York Times v. Sullivan,** *supra*; **Garrison v. Louisiana,** 379 U.S. 64 (1964)]

EXAM TIP — **gilbert**

Although the Supreme Court has talked in terms of "actual malice," this is really a term of art referring to the requirement of *deliberate falsity or reckless disregard for the truth* of the information published. As such, it is quite different from the "malice" usually required under state tort law to support an award of *punitive damages*—which requires a showing of hatred, spite, or ill will toward a plaintiff.

(a) Inaccurate quotations [§613]

Even if an author deliberately misquotes a person, there is no "malice" unless the false quotation results in a material change in the meaning of the actual statement. [**Masson v. New Yorker Magazine, Inc.,** 501 U.S. 496 (1991)]

(b) Reference to individual required [§614]

Even if "malice" is shown, no damages will be awarded to an individual member of a group *if only a large group is defamed*. To recover, the individual must prove particular reference to himself—or that a relatively small group was defamed and that he is a *clearly identifiable* member thereof. [**Rosenblatt v. Baer,** 383 U.S. 75 (1966)] Thus, a criticism of "the police" does not give the commissioner of police a cause of action. [**New York Times v. Sullivan,** *supra*]

1) Distinguish—criminal group libel laws

Although a private cause of action might not lie for defamation of a group, recall that defamation of a group might give rise to charges for criminal group libel. (*See supra,* §608.)

(c) Discovery [§615]

In attempting to prove knowing or reckless falsehood, the plaintiff may inquire (i) into the state of mind of those who edited, produced, or published the allegedly defamatory material (*i.e.*, about their thoughts, opinions, and conclusions concerning the accuracy of the material gathered), and (ii) as to what took place in the editorial process (*i.e.*, conversations with editorial colleagues). [**Herbert v. Lando,** 441 U.S. 153 (1979)]

(d) Summary judgment [§616]

If the defendant moves for summary judgment on the ground that there is no "genuine issue as to any material fact," the plaintiff must show that the quality or quantity of the documentary evidence would allow the fact finder to find "malice" by "clear and convincing evidence." [**Anderson v. Liberty Lobby, Inc.,** 477 U.S. 242 (1986)]

(e) Appellate review [§617]

Ordinarily, when an appellate court reviews questions of fact, it will uphold the trial court's findings unless they are "clearly erroneous." However, this is not so in cases involving defamation of public officials. In such cases, "malice" must be shown by clear and convincing evidence, and appellate courts must exercise independent judgment when reviewing a finding of "malice"; they are *not* restricted by the usual "clearly erroneous" standard of review for questions of fact. [**Bose Corp. v. Consumers Union,** 467 U.S. 1267 (1984)]

(3) "Official conduct" [§618]

The *New York Times* rule applies only to criticism of "official conduct"—although, of course, such criticism may also damage private reputation. "Official conduct" extends to anything touching on an official's fitness for office. [**Monitor Patriot Co. v. Roy**, 401 U.S. 265 (1971)—criticism that candidate was a "former small-time bootlegger" is relevant to candidate's fitness for office and is subject to the *New York Times* rule]

(4) "Public officials" [§619]

"Public officials" include both elected officials and candidates for public office. The rule also applies to those public employees who have substantial responsibility for the conduct of government affairs—*i.e.*, those who hold *positions of public interest*, not merely employees who happen to do something of public interest. [**Rosenblatt v. Baer**, *supra*]

(5) Criminal libel [§620]

The *New York Times* rule applies to prosecutions for criminal libel as well as to civil defamation suits. [**Garrison v. Louisiana**, *supra*]

b. Defamation of "public figures" [§621]

The *New York Times* rule likewise applies to defamation actions by persons who are "public figures," although not "public officials." *Rationale*: Like public officials, such persons have significant access to channels of communication in order to counteract false statements, and they invite the attention and comment to which they have usually exposed themselves. [**Gertz v. Robert Welch, Inc.**, 418 U.S. 323 (1974)]

(1) Definition [§622]

A citizen may become a "public figure" in two ways: (i) he may be such for *"all purposes and in all contexts"* if he achieves "general fame or notoriety in the community and pervasive involvement in the affairs of society"; or (ii) he may "voluntarily inject himself or be drawn into a *particular* controversy, thus becoming a public figure for a limited range of issues." [**Gertz v. Robert Welch, Inc.**, *supra*]

(e.g.) **Examples—"public figures":** "Public figures" has been held to include the following persons: a *former football coach* reported to have "thrown" a football game [**Curtis Publishing Co. v. Butts**, 388 U.S. 130 (1967)] and a *retired army general and political commentator* reported to have participated in race riots [**Associated Press v. Walker**, 388 U.S. 130 (1967)].

(cf.) **Compare—not "public figures":** A person is not a "public figure" simply because she is extremely wealthy and engaged in divorce proceedings of interest to the reading public. The fact that she files for divorce (and even holds press conferences during the proceedings) does not mean she voluntarily chooses to publicize her married life—since going to court is the only way she can legally dissolve her marriage. [**Time, Inc. v. Firestone,** 424 U.S. 448 (1976)] Nor is a person a "public figure" simply because he is charged with a crime [**Wolston v. Reader's Digest Association,** 443 U.S. 157 (1979)]; or applies for federal grants and publishes in professional journals [**Hutchinson v. Proxmire,** *supra*, §181]; or is counsel in a case that receives extensive media exposure [**Gertz v. Robert Welch, Inc.,** *supra*].

(a) Note

In *Gertz,* the Court indicated that it might be possible for a person to become a public figure through no purposeful action of his own, but considered such instances to be "exceedingly rare." It also underlined the fact that when a citizen participates in *some* community and professional affairs, that does *not* make him a public figure for *all* purposes.

c. Defamation of "private individuals" [§623]

The *New York Times* rule does *not* apply to private individuals who, unlike "public officials" or "public figures," have no significant access to the media to counteract false statements and have not voluntarily exposed themselves to an increased risk of defamation. [**Gertz v. Robert Welch, Inc.,** *supra*] Even so, there are still constitutional limitations in defamation actions by private individuals:

(1) Standard of liability [§624]

To protect the freedoms of speech and press guaranteed by the First Amendment, the states may define liability standards in defamation actions by private individuals *involving matters of public concern* only as long as (i) they *do not impose liability without fault* (*i.e.,* the defendant must at least be negligent); (ii) the factual misstatement *warns a reasonably prudent* editor or broadcaster of its defamatory potential; and (iii) damages are limited to compensation for *actual* injury—including impairment of reputation, personal humiliation, and mental suffering. The Court stated that *presumed or punitive* damages may not be imposed unless the plaintiff proves that the defendant acted with knowledge of the falsity or with reckless disregard for truth.

(a) "Matters of public concern" [§625]

If defamation of a private individual does *not* involve *matters of public concern,* presumed or punitive damages, as well as actual damages, may be granted. This approach accommodates "the strong and legitimate state interest in compensating private individuals for injury to reputation" with "the danger of media self-censorship." [**Dun & Bradstreet, Inc. v. Greenmoss Builders, Inc.,** 472 U.S. 749 (1985)]

1) **Factors considered [§626]**

Whether a statement is a matter of public concern is determined by the statement's *content, form,* and *context*—considering all the relevant circumstances.

---

e.g. **Example:** Dun & Bradstreet ("D&B"), a credit reporting agency, reported that Greenmoss Builders had filed for bankruptcy. The statement was false and based on a negligently prepared report. Greenmoss Builders sued D&B for defamation, and the state court awarded compensatory and punitive damages. D&B appealed, arguing that the state could not impose punitive damages without proof of malice. The Supreme Court found that D&B's report was intended only for the benefit of D&B and its business audience of five subscribers. Therefore, the report did not involve a matter of public concern and punitive damages could be imposed. [**Dun & Bradstreet, Inc. v. Greenmoss Builders, Inc.**, *supra*]

---

2) **Nonmedia defendants [§627]**

A majority of the Justices have stated that the *New York Times* and *Gertz* protections for media defendants apply as well to defamation suits against nonmedia defendants. [**Dun & Bradstreet, Inc. v. Greenmoss Builders, Inc.**, *supra*]

3) **Falsity [§628]**

In a suit for *damages* by a private individual for a defamation involving a "matter of public concern," the plaintiff must bear the burden of proving that the defamatory statements are false—at least against a media defendant. [**Philadelphia Newspapers, Inc. v. Hepps**, 475 U.S. 767 (1986)]

d. **"Fact" vs. "opinion" [§629]**

There is no separate "opinion" privilege. Any statement (including a statement of "opinion") that may be reasonably interpreted as stating actual facts about an individual may be actionable under the *New York Times* rule. [**Milkovich v. Lorain Journal Co.**, 497 U.S. 1 (1990)]

e. **Intentional infliction of emotional distress [§630]**

The *New York Times* requirement of a "false statement of fact" made with "malice" applies to damage actions by public figures for the tort of intentional infliction of emotional distress for publications that are parodies of the plaintiff, even if the publication is "patently offensive" or "outrageous." [**Hustler Magazine v. Falwell**, 485 U.S. 46 (1988)]

f. **Invasion of privacy suits [§631]**

Prior to the *Gertz* decision, the Court held that the *New York Times* rule *applies* to damage actions for invasion of privacy (for false reporting) if the matter reported was of **substantial public interest**—even though the plaintiff is neither a "public official" nor a "public figure." [**Time, Inc. v. Hill**, 385 U.S. 374 (1967)] There is serious question whether this principle in **right of privacy** (false reporting) suits by private individuals survives after *Gertz* (which held that the *New York Times* rule does **not** apply to **defamation** suits by private individuals).

D. Obscenity

1. Introduction [§632]

Obscene expression is **not** protected by the First Amendment. It is "not an essential part of the exposition of ideas, is of slight social value, and the benefits therefrom are outweighed by the social interest in morality." [**Chaplinsky v. New Hampshire**, 315 U.S. 568 (1942)] Obscenity is "not communication and is, by definition, utterly without social value." [**Roth v. United States**, 354 U.S. 476 (1957)] Obscenity is "assumed to be harmful to society and is, by definition, without serious literary, artistic, political, or scientific value." [**Miller v. California**, 413 U.S. 15 (1973); **Paris Adult Theatre I v. Slaton**, 413 U.S. 49 (1973)]

2. Definition [§633]

Sex and obscenity are not synonymous. The discussion of "sex" may be of public concern and is thus entitled to First Amendment protection. "Obscenity" is a description or depiction of sexual conduct which, taken as a *whole*, by the *average person*:

(i) *Appeals to the prurient interest* in sex, using a *community standard*;

(ii) Is *patently offensive* and an affront to contemporary *community standards*; and

(iii) *Lacks serious value* (literary, artistic, political, or scientific), using a *national reasonable person standard*.

[**Roth v. United States**, *supra*—*as modified by* **Miller v. California**, *supra*]

EXAM TIP   gilbert

Your professor isn't very likely to show you a movie clip or include a juicy written passage in your final exam and ask you to determine whether it is obscene! Instead, exam questions will often ask about the **standards** a judge or jury should use to determine whether material is obscene. Be sure to learn the above three-part *Miller* test for obscenity, and note that while whether the material appeals to the prurient interest in sex and whether the material is patently offensive can be judged by a (local) **community standard**, whether the material lacks serious value must be judged using a **national standard**.

a. **Elements of "obscenity" [§634]**

Several separate elements must be found before matter can be held to be "obscene":

(1) Prurient interest [§635]

The *dominant* theme of the material—considered as a *whole*—must appeal to prurient interest in sex to the *average (normal) person*. If speech does not appeal to the prurient interest in sex, it is not obscene.

---

e.g. **Example:** To protest the Vietnam war, Cohen wore a jacket into a Los Angeles courthouse emblazoned with the words "Fuck the Draft." He was charged with violating a California law against disturbing the peace. A state court found him guilty, finding Cohen's conduct offensive. On appeal, the United States Supreme Court found Cohen's jacket constitutionally protected. *Rationale:* Cohen's only conduct was wearing his jacket, and therefore his conviction could only be based on his speech. The state has no power to stifle the message that Cohen was trying to convey (*i.e.,* the state has no power to prevent people from stating their views opposing war). Neither can Cohen's words be banned as obscenity, as they are in no way erotic. "It cannot plausibly be maintained that this vulgar allusion to the Selective Service System would conjure up . . . stimulation in anyone . . . ." [**Cohen v. California,** 403 U.S. 15 (1971)]

(a) Prurience [§636]

"Prurience" identifies speech that appeals to a *shameful* or *morbid*—rather than *normal*—interest in sex. [**Brockett v. Spokane Arcades, Inc.,** *supra,* §588]

(b) Average person [§637]

Both "sensitive" and "insensitive" adults may be included in determining contemporary community standards, but children may not be considered part of the relevant community. [**Pinkus v. United States,** 436 U.S. 293 (1978)]

---

e.g. **Example:** A statute prohibiting the sale of any book "tending to the corruption of the morals of youth" is invalid. *Rationale:* The effect of the statute was to reduce the adult population to reading only what was fit for children. [**Butler v. Michigan,** 352 U.S. 380 (1959)]

---

e.g. **Example:** Similarly, government cannot impose a *total ban* on "indecent" commercial telephone messages ("dial-a-porn") in order to prevent children from gaining access to such messages. [**Sable Communications of California, Inc. v. FCC,** 492 U.S. 115 (1989)]

> **e.g.** **Example:** Because of the present lack of "gateway" technology that would permit speakers on the Internet to block their communications, a federal statute's bar on transmitting "indecent" or "patently offensive" messages to minors effectively amounted to a total ban and thus violated the First Amendment right of adults to receive such materials. [**Reno v. American Civil Liberties Union,** 521 U.S. 844 (1997)]

(c) Material designed for deviant group [§638]

If the allegedly obscene material is designed for and primarily disseminated to a clearly defined deviant sexual group (*e.g.*, sadists), rather than to the public at large, the "prurient appeal" requirement will be present only if the dominant theme of the material, taken as a whole, appeals to the prurient interest of *that group*. That is, the material will not be considered obscene unless it appeals to what the deviant group would consider to be a shameful or morbid interest in sex. [**Mishkin v. New York,** 383 U.S. 509 (1966)]

(2) Patently offensive [§639]

The material must be "patently offensive" in affronting contemporary community standards regarding the description or portrayal of sexual matters.

(3) Contemporary community standards [§640]

In assessing whether material is patently offensive, a "national" standard is *not* required. A statewide standard is permissible, but not mandatory. A juror may draw on knowledge of the vicinity from which she comes; and the court may either direct the jury to apply "community standards" without specifying what "community," or to define the standard in more precise geographic terms. [**Hamling v. United States,** 418 U.S. 87 (1974); **Jenkins v. Georgia,** 418 U.S. 153 (1974)]

(a) Note

The "community standards" criterion applies only to the "prurient interest" and "patently offensive" parts of the *Miller* definition. A "reasonable person" standard applies to the third part (*supra*, §633). [**Pope v. Illinois,** 481 U.S. 497 (1987)]

(b) Burden on distributors [§641]

A distributor whose audience is comprised of different communities with different local standards has the burden to abide by *each* community's standards. [*See e.g.,* **Hamling v. United States,** *supra*—applying rule to mailed advertising containing sexually explicit pictures; *and see* **Sable Communications of California, Inc. v. FCC,** *supra*—applying rule to operator of sexually explicit commercial telephone service *(i.e.,* "dial-a-porn")] However, a majority of the Court could not agree on whether the national variation in community standards imposes a special burden on Internet speech that would justify applying a different standard (*e.g.,* a national community standard) to Internet speech. [*See* **Ashcroft v. American Civil Liberties Union,** 535 U.S. 564 (2002)— involving statute prohibiting "material harmful to minors" on the World Wide Web]

(4) Lacking in serious social value [§642]

The fact that the material may have *some* redeeming social value will *not* necessarily immunize it from a finding of obscenity. [**Miller v. California,** *supra*] For example, interspersing a public service announcement on dental hygiene in what would otherwise would be an obscene movie will not immunize the movie from regulation as obscenity.

(5) "Pandering" [§643]

In *close cases*, evidence of "pandering" on the part of the defendant (commercial exploitation for the sake of prurient appeal) may be probative on whether the material is obscene. Such evidence may be found in the defendant's advertising, his instructions to authors and illustrators of the material, or his intended audience. In effect, this simply accepts the purveyor's own estimation of the material as relevant. [**Ginzburg v. United States,** 383 U.S. 643 (1966)]

(a) Profit purpose irrelevant [§644]

But the mere fact that a publisher may have profited from the sale of particular publications is entitled no weight in determining whether his publication is "obscene." [**Ginzburg v. United States,** *supra*]

3. "Obscenity" as Question of Fact and Law [§645]

What is "obscene" is a question of *fact* for the *jury*, "accompanied by the safeguards that judges, rules of evidence, presumption of innocence, and other protective features provide." [**Miller v. California,** *supra*] But juries do not have unbridled discretion in determining what is "patently offensive," even if they are properly charged. Appellate *courts* will conduct an *independent review* of constitutional claims, when necessary, to assure that the proscribed materials "depict or describe patently offensive 'hard core' sexual conduct." [**Jenkins v. Georgia,** *supra*]

a. Evidence [§646]

The prosecution need not produce "expert" testimony. And evidence that similar materials are available on community newsstands, or that the publication has acquired a second-class mailing privilege, does not necessarily show that the material is not obscene and hence, that evidence is not automatically admissible. Nor is there any automatic right to have other materials held not to be obscene admitted into evidence. [**Hamling v. United States,** *supra*]

b. **Scienter requirement for booksellers [§647]**

A bookseller may be convicted of selling obscenity only if the bookseller had *knowledge* that the contents of the material were obscene. *Rationale:* Strict or absolute criminal responsibility might well cause booksellers to be exceedingly careful as to what materials they would sell; the resulting *self-censorship* might deprive the public of access to constitutionally protected materials. [**Smith v. California**, 361 U.S. 147 (1959)]

(1) **Proof of "knowledge" [§648]**

Scienter need not be shown by direct proof. It is probably enough that a *reasonable* seller or distributor should have shown the contents of the materials and their nature and character. [**Smith v. California**, *supra*; **Hamling v. United States**, *supra*]

4. **Special Rules for Minors [§649]**

States may apply more restrictive rules for materials involving minors. A state can adopt a *specific* definition of "obscenity" in terms of the sexual interests of minors, since it is rational to conclude that minors' exposure to such material might be harmful. [**Ginsberg v. New York**, 390 U.S. 629 (1968)]

a. **Child pornography [§650]**

Because of the strong interest in preventing child abuse, a state may prohibit distribution of pictures, even though not "obscene," that depict children engaging in sexual acts or lewdly displaying genitalia. However, serious educational or scientific use of such pictures as in medical textbooks or *National Geographic* is probably constitutionally protected. [**New York v. Ferber**, 456 U.S. 942 (1982)]

(1) **Distinguish—simulated pictures of minors [§651]**

The government may not bar visual material that "appears to" depict, or "conveys the impression" that it depicts, minors engaged in sexually explicit conduct, but that in fact uses young-looking adults or computer-generated images. [**Ashcroft v. Free Speech Coalition**, 535 U.S. 234 (2002)] *Rationale:* A holding otherwise would bar speech that is not obscene under the *Miller* definition and that does not involve children who were exploited by the production process as in *Ferber*. Finally, the argument that such material might encourage pedophiles to engage in illegal conduct fails because the mere tendency of speech to encourage unlawful acts is not a sufficient reason for banning it.

(2) **Private possession [§652]**

In contrast to **Stanley v. Georgia** (below), the strong interest in protecting the victims of child pornography permits the state to make its possession a crime, *even within the privacy of the home*. [**Osborne v. Ohio**, *supra*, §593]

EXAM TIP

Be sure to remember that while obscenity is not protected under the First Amendment, under **Stanley v. Georgia,** the home is nearly sacrosanct. Thus, the states cannot make mere possession of even obscene material in one's home a crime. However, the state's strong interest in *protecting children* from exploitation is even stronger than an individual's privacy interest in his home. Thus, states *can prohibit the mere possession of child pornography*—even in the privacy of one's home.

5. **Private Possession of Obscenity at Home [§653]**

A person's possession of obscene materials in his home *cannot* be made a crime because of the "constitutional right of personal privacy." [**Stanley v. Georgia,** 394 U.S. 557 (1969)] But the zone of privacy does not extend beyond the home. Thus, *distribution* of obscene material may be made a crime even as to willing recipients who state that they are adults [**United States v. Reidel,** 402 U.S. 351 (1971)], as may *exhibition* of obscene materials in places of public accommodation, including theaters for consenting adults only [**Paris Adult Theatre I v. Slaton,** *supra*, §632].

a. **Transportation and importation [§654]**

Transportation and importation of obscene material for either *public* or *private* use may be prohibited. [**United States v. Orito,** 413 U.S. 139 (1973); **United States v. 12 200-Ft. Reels,** 413 U.S. 123 (1973)]

(1) **Note—procedures**

Any such seizure is a form of prior restraint, and therefore adequate procedural safeguards must be afforded (*see infra,* §§709 *et seq.*).

6. **Regulation of Sites of "Near" Obscene Material [§655]**

A state or municipality may adopt a land-use (or zoning) ordinance that regulates the location or size of adult entertainment establishments (*e.g.,* strip clubs, adult movie theaters, etc.), as long as (i) the predominant purpose of the ordinance is to reduce the secondary effects of such businesses (*e.g.,* rise in crime rates, drop in property values and neighborhood quality); and (ii) the ordinance does not suppress or substantially reduce speech. This rule is applicable even if the establishments regulated are presenting material that is not obscene under *Miller.* [**Young v. American Mini Theatres, Inc.,** 427 U.S. 50 (1976); **City of Los Angeles v. Alameda Books, Inc.,** 535 U.S. 425 (2002)]

Example: A city ordinance limiting adult entertainment establishments to one corner of the city occupying less than 5% of the city's area was deemed constitutional. [**City of Renton v. Playtime Theatres, Inc.,** 475 U.S. 41 (1986)]

a. **Factual basis needed [§656]**

A municipality must be given a reasonable opportunity to experiment with solutions, and may rely on evidence that it "reasonably believes to be relevant" to fairly support its rationale. But if challengers cast doubt on this, the burden shifts back to the municipality to supplement the record. [**City of Los Angeles v. Alameda Books, Inc.,** *supra*]

b. Limits on zoning [§657]

A municipality that permits a *broad range* of commercial establishments may *not* prohibit all live entertainment (including nonobscene, nude dancing) from its commercial district—at least if such entertainment is not available in reasonably nearby areas. [**Schad v. Borough of Mount Ephraim,** 452 U.S. 61 (1981)]

c. Display [§658]

The display of nonobscene (but sexually related) material may be regulated to prevent it from being so obtrusive that the unwilling viewer cannot avoid exposure to it. [**Redrup v. New York,** 386 U.S. 767 (1967)]

E. "Fighting Words" and "Hostile Audiences"

1. Introduction [§659]

Certain types of expression used in connection with public speeches, parades, meetings, demonstrations, and the like may be prohibited under "breach of the peace" or "disorderly conduct" statutes—provided such statutes are *narrowly drafted* or *narrowly construed* (*i.e.*, are neither "overbroad" nor "vague").

2. "Fighting Words" [§660]

"Fighting words" are words, usually intended as a personal insult to the person addressed, which by their very utterance inflict injury or tend to incite an *immediate* breach of the peace. "Fighting words" are *not* protected by the First Amendment, their slight social value being outweighed by the public interest in order. [**Chaplinsky v. New Hampshire,** 315 U.S. 568 (1942)—the words "You are a God damned racketeer" and "a damned Fascist," when aimed at a city marshal are fighting words unprotected by the First Amendment]

a. Distinguish—offensive language [§661]

The fact that certain words are generally offensive does *not* make them "fighting words." Thus, the First Amendment forbade a conviction of "disturbing the peace by offensive conduct" of a peace demonstrator for wearing a jacket bearing the words "Fuck the Draft" in a courthouse corridor. *Rationale:* The underlying content of the message was clearly protected, it did not incite immediate violence, and it was not directed as a personal insult to any person. [**Cohen v. California,** *supra,* §635]

b. Statutes generally cannot be content-based [§662]

Although the general class of "fighting words" is proscribable under the First

Amendment, the Supreme Court generally will not tolerate in fighting words statutes restrictions that are designed to punish only certain viewpoints (*i.e.,* proscribing fighting words only if they convey a particular message). [**R.A.V. v. City of St. Paul,** 505 U.S. 377 (1992)—ordinance that applies only to those "fighting words" that insult or provoke violence on the basis of race, religion, or gender is invalid]

(1) Exception—cross burning

Despite the Court's general rule against fighting word statutes that are content-based, it will uphold a content-based fighting words statute if the reason for the prohibition is the very reason that the entire class of speech is unprotected, just as a state may specially regulate a form of obscenity because of its specially prurient content. [**Virginia v. Black,** *supra,* §577—because of cross burning's long history as a signal of impending violence, the state may specially regulate this form of threat, which is most likely to inspire fear of bodily harm]

c. "Hostile audience" [§663]

If the speaker does not use "fighting words" but is nonetheless convicted for "breach of the peace" or "disorderly conduct," the Court will independently examine the record to determine whether the speaker's activities produced *imminent danger* of *uncontrolled violence* by the onlookers or addressees of the speaker. If so, the exercise of First Amendment rights is outweighed by the public interest in order.

---

e.g. **Example:** A speaker on a city street used very inflammatory language about public officials; the crowd was angry and pushing—one member threatened violence—and two police officers arrived. Believing a fight was imminent, the police twice asked the speaker to leave. He refused and was arrested for disorderly conduct. His conviction was *upheld.* [**Feiner v. New York,** 340 U.S. 315 (1951)]

---

cf. **Compare:** A civil rights leader led an orderly protest of black students, who urged store boycotts and sang songs. The leader urged nonviolence and sit-ins at segregated lunch counters. Although onlookers grumbled, ample police were present. The leader's conviction for "disturbing the peace" was *reversed.* The Court found no imminent danger of uncontrollable violence. "Mere expression of unpopular views cannot be held to be a breach of the peace." [**Cox v. Louisiana,** 377 U.S. 288 (1965)]

---

d. Overbreadth or vagueness [§664]

Breach of the peace and disorderly conduct statutes are frequently drafted or interpreted in an overbroad or vague manner, and are thereby subject to attack "on their face" (*see supra,* §§584 *et seq.*). [**Gooding v. Wilson,** 405 U.S. 518 (1972)—statute prohibiting "abusive language . . . tending to cause a breach of the peace" is overbroad; *i.e.*, not limited to "fighting words"; **Lewis v. City of New Orleans,** *supra,* §586—statute prohibited "opprobrious language"]

F. Commercial Speech

1.   Introduction [§665]

Commercial speech is protected by the First Amendment but is subject to *greater regulation* than other forms of protected speech. [**Bigelow v. Virginia,** 421 U.S. 809 (1975)]

2.   Definition [§666]

Commercial speech is speech whose *dominant theme* simply *proposes a commercial transaction.* [**Bolger v. Youngs Drug Products Corp.,** 463 U.S. 60 (1983)]

a.   Advertisements [§667]

The fact that a communication appears as an advertisement does *not* automatically make it commercial speech. [**New York Times v. Sullivan,** *supra,* §610—paid advertisement critical of official conduct was not merely commercial speech]

b.   Economic motivation [§668]

The fact that a communication is economically motivated or refers to a specific product does *not* automatically make it commercial speech. [**Bigelow v. Virginia,** *supra*—advertisement by abortion referral service contained substantial information of significant public interest, making it more than mere commercial speech]

c.   Dominant theme commercial [§669]

If a communication's dominant theme is to propose a commercial transaction, it is commercial speech despite *some discussion* of important public issues. Advertisers may not immunize themselves from public regulation "simply by including references to public issues." [**Bolger v. Youngs Drug Products Corp.,** *supra*—advertisement for contraceptives was commercial speech despite discussion of venereal disease and family planning]

3.   Regulation of Content Permissible [§670]

Because commercial advertising has greater potential for deception and confusion than noncommercial speech, the Supreme Court allows the content of commercial speech to be more heavily regulated than the content of other speech.

a.   False or misleading commercial speech [§671]

Commercial speech that is false or misleading may be prohibited.

APPROACH TO COMMERCIAL SPEECH

gilbert

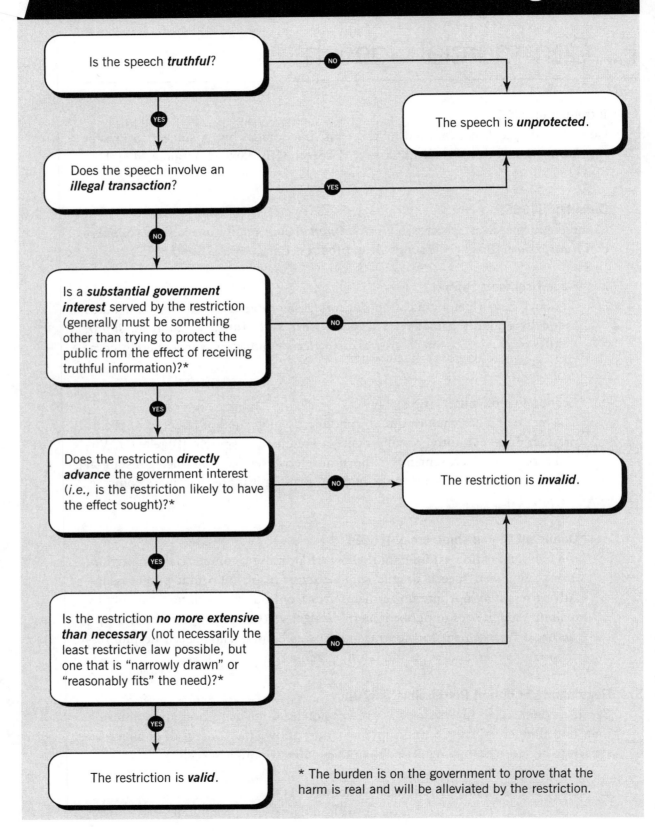

Is the speech **truthful**? — NO → The speech is **unprotected**.

YES ↓

Does the speech involve an **illegal transaction**? — YES → The speech is **unprotected**.

NO ↓

Is a **substantial government interest** served by the restriction (generally must be something other than trying to protect the public from the effect of receiving truthful information)?* — NO → The restriction is **invalid**.

YES ↓

Does the restriction **directly advance** the government interest (*i.e.*, is the restriction likely to have the effect sought)?* — NO → The restriction is **invalid**.

YES ↓

Is the restriction **no more extensive than necessary** (not necessarily the least restrictive law possible, but one that is "narrowly drawn" or "reasonably fits" the need)?* — NO → The restriction is **invalid**.

YES ↓

The restriction is **valid**.

* The burden is on the government to prove that the harm is real and will be alleviated by the restriction.

> **Example—trade names:** Since practicing optometry under a trade name has only an incidental effect on the content of commercial speech and may be used to mislead the public, it can be prohibited. [**Friedman v. Rogers,** 440 U.S. 1 (1979)]

b.   Speech proposing illegal transactions [§672]

Commercial speech that proposes illegal transactions may be prohibited (*e.g.*, advertisements of narcotics or prostitution, or help-wanted ads that foster discrimination in employment). [**Pittsburgh Press Co. v. Pittsburgh Human Relations Committee,** 413 U.S. 376 (1973)—newspaper enjoined from running help-wanted columns headed "male" or "female" because such classifications constituted illegal sex discrimination under local ordinance]

> **Example:** Speech that furthers illegal price-fixing may be prohibited if this "represents a reasonable method of eliminating the consequences of the illegal conduct." [**National Society of Professional Engineers v. United States,** 435 U.S. 679 (1978)]

4.   Overbreadth [§673]

The First Amendment "overbreadth" doctrine (*see supra*, §§584 *et seq.*) does *not* apply to commercial speech. Thus, the person seeking to use commercial speech must demonstrate that the speech actually used is protected by the First Amendment. [**Ohralik v. Ohio State Bar Association,** 436 U.S. 447 (1978)]

5.   Prior Restraint [§674]

The Court has suggested that the usual prohibition on prior restraints (*see infra*, §696) *may* not apply to commercial speech. [**Virginia State Board v. Virginia Citizens Consumer Council,** 425 U.S. 748 (1976); *and see* **Pittsburgh Press Co. v. Pittsburgh Human Relations Committee,** *supra*]

6.   Scope of Protection [§675]

Truthful commercial speech concerning a lawful activity has an informational function and cannot be prohibited unless (i) a *substantial* government interest is served by the restriction, (ii) the restriction *directly advances* that government interest, and (iii) the restriction is *no more extensive than necessary* to serve that interest. [**Central Hudson Gas & Electric Corp. v. Public Service Commission,** 447 U.S. 557 (1980)—ban on *all* promotional advertising by electric utility directly serves substantial state interest in energy conservation but is nonetheless invalid because it is not drawn sufficiently narrow]

EXAM TIP	gilbert

Central Hudson Gas is the key to most commercial speech questions. If you are faced with an exam question restricting truthful commercial speech, be sure to set out the above ***three-part test*** and ***apply it to the facts***. If the restriction fails any part of the test, it is unconstitutional.

a. **Burden on state [§676]**

The state must show that the harms attributable to the truthful commercial speech are real and will be alleviated by the state restriction imposed. [**Ibanez v. Florida Department of Business & Professional Regulation**, 512 U.S. 136 (1994)—ban on lawyer's use in advertising of CPA and CFA designations is invalid]

b. **"No more extensive than necessary" [§677]**

The part of the *Central Hudson Gas* test that requires regulations to be no more extensive than necessary does *not* require that the "least restrictive means" be used. Rather, the regulation must be "narrowly drawn" and there must be a "reasonable fit" between the legislature's ends and the means chosen. [**Board of Trustees v. Fox**, 492 U.S. 469 (1989)]

c. **Regulating consumer choice [§678]**

If the government's reason for banning truthful commercial speech is not to protect consumers from deception or overreaching, but rather is because the government believes that the public will respond irrationally to the advertising, the regulation will *almost never* be upheld. [**44 Liquormart, Inc. v. Rhode Island**, 517 U.S. 484 (1996)—view of five Justices in separate opinions striking regulation that prohibited *all* advertisements of liquor prices]

d. **"For sale" signs [§679]**

An ordinance prohibiting the posting of "for sale" signs on real estate has been held invalid even though deemed by the township to be in the best interests of the community (to prevent "white flight" from racially integrated neighborhoods). [**Linmark Associates, Inc. v. Township of Willingboro**, 431 U.S. 85 (1977)]

e. **Mailed contraceptive advertisements [§680]**

A law prohibiting the mailing of unsolicited advertisements for contraceptives has been held invalid. The government's interest in protecting recipients from mail they find "offensive" is *insubstantial*. And although the interest in aiding parents to discuss birth control with their children *is* substantial, the law serves that interest only marginally. [**Bolger v. Youngs Drug Products Corp.**, *supra*]

f. **Disclosing alcoholic strength of beer [§681]**

A law prohibiting beer bottle labels from displaying alcohol content has been held invalid. Although the government's interest in preventing "strength wars" is *substantial*, the government did not carry its burden of showing that the law advanced this interest in a *direct and material way*. [**Rubin v. Coors Brewing Co.**, 515 U.S. 618 (1995)]

g. **Liquor price advertising [§682]**

A law prohibiting advertising of retail prices of alcoholic beverages has been held invalid. It was *more extensive than necessary* to serve the state's interest in keeping prices high so as to keep consumption low. The state could directly accomplish its goal (for example, by establishing minimum prices) without any restriction on speech. [**44 Liquormart, Inc. v. Rhode Island,** *supra*]

(1) Twenty-First Amendment [§683]

The Twenty-First Amendment gives the states special power concerning the regulation of liquor, such as state power to regulate interstate commerce (*supra*, §§344-349). However, the Supreme Court has held that the Twenty-First Amendment does *not* qualify First Amendment rights. [**44 Liquormart, Inc. v. Rhode Island,** *supra*]

h. Tobacco advertising [§684]

Even though a law prohibiting advertising of smokeless tobacco and cigars within 1,000 feet of a school or playground *directly advances* the *substantial* government interest in preventing underage use of those products, its geographic reach—amounting to nearly a complete ban in many areas—demonstrates a "lack of tailoring," thus unduly affecting use of tobacco products by adults (which is a legal activity). [**Lorillard Tobacco Co. v. Reilly,** 533 U.S. 525 (2001)]

(1) Distinguish—access law [§685]

A law requiring retailers to place tobacco products behind counters and requiring customers to have contact with a salesperson before they are able to handle such a product is valid. It directly serves a substantial interest in preventing access to tobacco products by minors and does not significantly impede adult access to the products. [**Lorillard Tobacco Co. v. Reilly,** *supra*]

i. Advertising drug compounds [§686]

A law prohibiting advertisement of specially compounded drugs, which need not go through the FDA approval process, has been held invalid. There are a number of non-speech related alternatives to serve the government's important interest in striking a balance between the economic burdens of the drug approval process and the needs of small scale compounding of drugs by pharmacists to meet the unique needs of individual patients. [**Thompson v. Western States Medical Center,** 535 U.S. 357 (2002)]

j. Interstate advertising of state lottery [§687]

Congress may prohibit the broadcast of lottery advertising by stations licensed in nonlottery states—even as applied to a station that has most of its listeners in an adjoining lottery state, and even when broadcasters in the lottery state reach many listeners in the nonlottery state. *Rationale:* The forbidden advertising concerned an activity that was *illegal* in the state where the broadcaster was located. [**United States v. Edge Broadcasting Co.,** 509 U.S. 418 (1993)]

(1) Distinguish—legal in broadcaster's state [§688]

A federal statute that prohibited broadcasters from carrying advertising for casino gambling even though it was legal in the broadcaster's state was held to violate the First Amendment. The statute's exemption and inconsistencies failed the second and third parts of the *Central Hudson Gas* test (*supra*, §675). [**Greater New Orleans Broadcasting Association v. United States**, 527 U.S. 173 (1999)]

k. Differential treatment of commercial speech [§689]

A city could not prohibit the use of newsracks on sidewalks for the distribution of commercial publications (such as free publications advertising products or real estate for sale) while allowing sidewalk newsracks for the distribution of newspapers. This city law failed the *Central Hudson Gas* test because there was no reasonable fit between the category of commercial speech restricted and any substantial interest. Commercial newsracks did not cause any physical or aesthetic harm different from that caused by newspapers newsracks. [**City of Cincinnati v. Discovery Network, Inc.**, 507 U.S. 410 (1993)]

l. Billboards [§690]

To advance its interests in traffic safety and aesthetics, a state may prohibit all billboards carrying commercial advertising, except those advertising the business of the property's occupant. [**Metromedia, Inc. v. City of San Diego**, 453 U.S. 490 (1981)]

REGULATIONS ON COMMERCIAL SPEECH—EXAMPLES gilbert

ASSERTED INTEREST	STATUTE	VALIDITY
lowering alcohol consumption	prohibiting price advertising (in order to prevent comparison shopping to keep prices high)	invalid because it keeps truthful information away from public
preventing "white flight"	prohibiting "for sale" signs	invalid because it keeps truthful information away from public
protecting people from receiving unwanted mail	prohibiting the mailing of unsolicited ads for contraceptives	invalid because no substantial government interest here
preventing alcohol "strength wars"	prohibiting beer bottle labels from disclosing alcohol strength	invalid because restriction would not advance interest in a material way
traffic safety and aesthetics	prohibiting advertising billboards except those on the premises of the business advertised	valid

m. Legal services [§691]

Truthful advertising of the *availability* and *price* of *routine* legal services cannot be prohibited. [**Bates v. State Bar of Arizona**, 433 U.S. 350 (1977)] Furthermore, in the absence of evidence that it is misleading or potentially misleading, a lawyer cannot be prohibited from stating that a bona fide national organization has "certified" him as a specialist in a certain area [**Peel v. Illinois Attorney Registration & Disciplinary Commission**, 496 U.S. 91 (1990)]; nor from advertising specific areas of practice and the jurisdictions in which licensed; nor from mailing cards to the general public that announce the opening of a law office [***In re* R.M.J.**, 455 U.S. 191 (1982)]; nor from including illustrations in advertisements; nor from mailing letters to potential clients known to have particular legal problems [**Shapero v. Kentucky Bar Association**, 486 U.S. 466 (1988)], or including accurate information or advice regarding the legal rights of potential clients [**Zauderer v. Office of Disciplinary Counsel**, 471 U.S. 626 (1985)]. The Court has *left open* the issue of advertising the *quality* of legal services.

(1) Required disclosures [§692]

Since commercial speech is protected mainly because of its value to consumers, an advertiser's First Amendment interest in *not* providing information is minimal. Thus, states may require commercial advertisers to make disclosures if they are not unduly burdensome and are reasonably related to the state's interest in preventing deception. [**Zauderer v. Office of Disciplinary Counsel**, *supra*—lawyers who advertise representation for a contingent *fee* may be required to state that client may have to pay *costs*]

(2) In-person solicitation for pecuniary gain [§693]

A state may discipline lawyers for *in-person* solicitation of clients for *pecuniary* gain—at least under circumstances likely to present dangers such as misrepresentation, overreaching, invasion of privacy, or stirring up litigation. Unlike advertising legal services, such solicitation may pressure clients without providing time for reflection. [**Ohralik v. Ohio State Bar Association**, *supra*, §673]

(a) Distinguish—accountants [§694]

A state ban on in-person, uninvited solicitation of business clients by accountants does *not* directly and materially advance state interests. While a lawyer may be soliciting an unsophisticated, injured, or distressed lay person, a CPA's typical prospective client is a sophisticated and experienced business executive who has an existing professional relation with a CPA, who selects the time and place for their meeting, and for whom there is no expectation or pressure to retain the CPA on the spot. [**Edenfield v. Fane**, 507 U.S. 761 (1993)]

(3) Mail solicitation of personal injury victims [§695]

A state may prohibit personal injury lawyers from sending mail solicitations to victims and their relatives for 30 days following an accident. Studies demonstrated that such advertising intrudes on the privacy of victims (a "substantial" interest) and reflects poorly on lawyers. [**Florida Bar v. Went For It, Inc.,** 515 U.S. 618 (1995)]

G. Censorship and Prior Restraint

1. **Generally Prohibited [§696]**

   As seen above, some kinds of speech (obscenity, "fighting words," certain defamations, etc.) are not protected by the First Amendment. Thus, the government may impose various sanctions—including criminal punishment—on those who engage in such unprotected speech. But even in dealing with unprotected expression, the government generally may not establish a system of *censorship* to regulate *in advance* what may be uttered or published, or *enjoin* speech, or employ other "*prior restraints.*" [**Near v. Minnesota,** 283 U.S. 697 (1931); **New York Times Co. v. United States,** 403 U.S. 713 (1971)]

2. **"Informal" Government Action [§697]**

   The prohibition against prior restraints applies to acts of government that have the *effect* of preventing speech in advance. Thus, even "informal" sanctions taken by state agencies may be invalid.

   Example: A state juvenile delinquency commission was empowered to make "informal recommendations" to book distributors as to which publications were objectionable for sale to youths. The recommendations were followed up by threats of court action, visits from police, etc., and the distributors were given no notice or hearing (*see* below) before their publications were listed as objectionable. The Court held compliance with the commission's directives by distributors was not voluntary and represented unconstitutional censorship. [**Bantam Books, Inc. v. Sullivan,** 372 U.S. 58 (1963)]

   a. **Speech of foreign governments [§698]**

      Foreign governments may be required to label as "foreign propaganda" any expressive materials disseminated in this country that are intended to influence U.S. foreign policy. The Court found that the word "propaganda" (as defined in the statute) was a neutral (not a pejorative) term *and* that there was no evidence that public reaction had actually interfered with distribution of the foreign materials. [**Meese v. Keene,** 481 U.S. 465 (1987)]

3. **Exceptional Situations [§699]**

   Although prior restraints of speech bear a heavy presumption of unconstitutionality, in a few exceptional situations, injunctions or censorship may be allowed; basically, where the unprotected speech is so inimical to the public welfare that normal remedies (such as subsequent criminal punishment) are inadequate.

a. **National security [§700]**

For example, the First Amendment would not bar an injunction against publishing the date of sailing for troop ships in *time of war*. [**Near v. Minnesota,** *supra*]

---

e.g. **Example:** The First Amendment does not forbid agreements between the CIA and an employee that require *prepublication review* by the CIA of any writing related to his employment, even if it does not contain classified material. (A constructive trust on all profits from publishing is an appropriate remedy for violation of such agreement.) [**Snepp v. United States,** 444 U.S. 507 (1980)]

---

b. **Preserving a "fair trial" [§701]**

The strong presumption against prior restraints applies especially where an injunction against media reporting of criminal proceedings is sought to preserve a fair trial for the accused (*see infra*, §§775-786). Before such an injunction may issue, the court must find that (i) there is a clear and present danger that pretrial publicity *would* (not merely could) threaten a fair trial, (ii) alternative measures are inadequate, and (iii) an injunction would effectively protect the accused. [**Nebraska Press Association v. Stuart,** 427 U.S. 539 (1976)]

(1) **Public proceedings [§702]**

An injunction against media reporting is especially inappropriate if the proceedings are open to the public and press. [**Oklahoma Publishing Co. v. District Court,** 430 U.S. 308 (1977)]

c. **Pretrial discovery [§703]**

A court may issue a protective order against dissemination of information gained through the pretrial discovery process and not yet admitted at trial. There is a substantial government interest in preventing abuse of information that would not have been obtained from other sources. [**Seattle Times Co. v. Rhinehart,** 467 U.S. 20 (1984)]

d. **Obscenity [§704]**

Certain forms of censorship and prior restraint have also been upheld in the area of obscenity (*see* below).

e. **Regulation of public property [§705]**

A city may require a license for the use of its property for the exercise of First Amendment rights if certain requisites are satisfied (*see infra*, §§766-774).

4. **Procedural Safeguards Required [§706]**

Even in those exceptional situations where prior restraints are permissible, adequate procedural and judicial safeguards are constitutionally required.

EXAM TIP   **gilbert**

If you encounter a prior restraint in an exam question, be sure to remember that as a general rule, prior restraints are disfavored, on the theory that it is better to punish unprotected speech *after it occurs* than to restrain speech before it occurs, because the prior restraint might prevent some protected speech from occurring. Nevertheless, a prior restraint will be upheld *where the need is great* (e.g., national security, preserving a fair trial, preventing obscenity) and *procedural and judicial safeguards* are imposed to help insure that protected speech is not prohibited through the prior restraint.

---

a.   **General requirement of notice and hearing [§707]**

Unless time is of the essence, an adversary hearing, after notice to all interested parties, is normally essential to any procedure by which freedom of speech is burdened by prior restraints. [**Carroll v. Princess Anne County,** 393 U.S. 175 (1969)—invalidating ex parte injunctions restraining members of political party from holding rallies]

b.   **Injunctions [§708]**

A state procedure permitting an injunction against further distribution of a publication found to be "obscene" after a *full judicial hearing* may be upheld. Such an injunction, after the publication has had some distribution, may even be a lesser deterrent to free speech than "subsequent punishment" since it does not put the bookseller in the predicament of not knowing whether the sale of a book may subject him to criminal prosecution. The civil procedure assures him that such consequences will not follow unless he ignores a court order specifically directed to him and based on a *carefully circumscribed* determination of obscenity. [**Kingsley Books, Inc. v. Brown,** 354 U.S. 436 (1957)]

c.   **Seizure of books and films [§709]**

"Large scale" seizures of allegedly obscene books and films—"to destroy them or block their distribution or exhibition"—constitute a prior restraint and must be *preceded* by a *full adversary hearing* and a *judicial determination of obscenity.* [**Marcus v. Search Warrant,** 367 U.S. 717 (1961)] But the seizure of copies of a film (or book) to preserve them as evidence need only be made "pursuant to a warrant issued after a determination of probable cause by a neutral magistrate." Even here, however, a *prompt* judicial determination of obscenity in an adversary proceeding must be available *after* the seizure. [**Heller v. New York,** 413 U.S. 483 (1973)]

(1)   **Jury trial [§710]**

A jury trial is not required in a civil forfeiture proceeding for obscene materials. [**Alexander v. Virginia,** 413 U.S. 836 (1973)]

(2)   **Standard of proof [§711]**

The Court has not set the standard of proof in a civil proceeding involving obscene material. But it has held that the First Amendment does *not* require proof beyond a reasonable doubt. [**Cooper v. Mitchell Brothers' Santa Ana Theater,** 454 U.S. 90 (1981)]

(3) Forfeiture after criminal conviction [§712]

The First Amendment does not forbid forfeiture and destruction of an adult bookstore chain's entire inventory of films and books (including some held not to be obscene) after the owner's conviction for sale of obscene material and a finding that the chain's assets were related to violation of the federal racketeering act. This is permissible criminal punishment with only an "incidental effect" on First Amendment activities. [**Alexander v. United States,** 509 U.S. 544 (1993)]

d. Movie censorship [§713]

Although government may not establish licensing or censorship boards to examine written publications in advance for approval of content (*see* above), some such system of prior submission is permissible *for motion pictures if* it contains the following procedural safeguards: (i) the standards for denial of a license or permit must be "narrowly drawn, reasonable, and definite," so as to include only unprotected films; (ii) if the censor does not wish to issue a permit, the censor must *promptly* seek an injunction; (iii) in such judicial proceedings, the *censor* must bear the *burden of proof* that the film is unprotected; and (iv) there must be *prompt judicial* determination. [**Freedman v. Maryland,** 380 U.S. 51 (1965)]

(1) Rationale—movies are different [§714]

In upholding such censorship systems for movies, the Court has noted that "films differ from other forms of expression," and that the time delays incident to censorship are less burdensome for movies than for other forms of expression. [**Times Film Corp. v. City of Chicago,** 365 U.S. 43 (1961)]

EXAM TIP   **gilbert**

Be sure to remember that prior restraints are more readily tolerated when it comes to movies and that the standards for movie censorship are different from the standards for other kinds of censorship. Movies may be subjected to a licensing system if:

- The *standards* for denial of a license or permit are *narrowly drawn, reasonable, and definite*;

- The *censor promptly seeks an injunction* if a license or permit is to be denied;

- The *censor bears the burden of proof* at the hearing to show that the movie is unprotected; and

- There is a *prompt judicial determination* of the matter.

---

(2) Narrow and definite standards [§715]

A number of decisions involve the banning of movies by censor boards under standards that were vague or overbroad.

(a) **Vagueness [§716]**

A film may not be banned merely because the censor concludes it is "sacrilegious" [**Joseph Burstyn, Inc. v. Wilson,** 343 U.S. 495 (1952)] or "immoral" [**Commercial Pictures Corp. v. Regents,** 346 U.S. 587 (1954)].

(b) **Overbreadth [§717]**

A film may not be banned because it "portrays adultery alluringly and as proper behavior." The Court reasoned that protected speech "is not confined to the expression of ideas that are conventional or shared by a majority. [The First Amendment] protects advocacy of the opinion that adultery may sometimes be proper, no less than advocacy of socialism or the single tax." [**Kingsley International Pictures Corp. v. Regents,** 360 U.S. 684 (1959)]

e. **Use of municipal theaters [§718]**

A public agency's denial of the use of publicly owned theaters dedicated to expressive activities must conform to the procedural safeguards of **Freedman v. Maryland,** *supra.* [**Southeastern Promotions, Ltd. v. Conrad,** 420 U.S. 546 (1975)]

f. **Licensing businesses that deal in potentially obscene books and films [§719]**

An ordinance requiring that "sexually oriented businesses" obtain a license is subject to the **Freedman v. Maryland** procedural safeguards concerning a decision within a reasonable period of time, because undue delay results in suppression of constitutionally protected speech. However, the city need *not* bear the burden of going to court or the burden of proof once in court—the businesses affected have adequate incentive to assume this burden themselves. [**FW/PBS Inc. v. City of Dallas,** 493 U.S. 215 (1990)]

g. **Licensing charitable solicitors [§720]**

Raising money on behalf of charitable causes is protected by the First Amendment (*see supra,* §570), and therefore a law requiring that professional fundraisers obtain a license is subject to the **Freedman v. Maryland** procedural safeguards. [**Riley v. National Federation of the Blind of North Carolina,** *supra,* §565]

h. **Use of the mails [§721]**

Use of the mails is a part of freedom of expression, and consequently any restrictions on a citizen's use of the mails are subject to constitutional limitations.

(1) **"Obscene" mail [§722]**

The government is not permitted to deny a citizen the right to mail materials (or to detain incoming mail) on the ground they are "obscene," unless it affords adequate procedural safeguards. [**Blount v. Rizzi,** 400 U.S. 410 (1971)]

(a) Procedure [§723]

The procedural safeguards required are basically those stipulated in **Freedman v. Maryland,** *supra:* the government must promptly initiate proceedings to obtain a final *judicial* determination of "obscenity" (administrative hearings are invalid); it must bear the burden of proving the mail "obscene"; and any restraint in advance of a final judicial determination for preserving the status quo must be for "the shortest fixed period compatible with sound judicial resolution." [**Blount v. Rizzi,** *supra*]

i. Importation [§724]

The government may exclude "obscene" materials from import into this country, provided, again, that adequate procedural safeguards are afforded. [**United States v. Thirty-Seven Photographs,** 402 U.S. 363 (1971)—construing federal statute for seizure and confiscation of obscene imports requiring prompt proceedings, in accord with **Freedman v. Maryland,** *supra*]

5. Challenging Invalid Injunctions [§725]

If persons seeking to exercise First Amendment rights are enjoined from doing so, they usually may *not* violate the injunction and then defend a contempt prosecution on the ground that the injunction violated their constitutional rights. (*But note:* There is a possible exception where the court has no jurisdiction, or the injunction is "transparently invalid.") Instead, they must seek reasonably available judicial relief; *i.e.,* they must appeal the injunction unless the time is such that an appeal would effectively frustrate exercise of their rights. [**Walker v. City of Birmingham,** 388 U.S. 307 (1967)—contempt charge for violating an injunction against holding a civil rights march was upheld even though the injunction appeared to violate the First Amendment and was issued only two days before the march was scheduled because an expedited appellate review procedure was available]

H. Symbolic Conduct

1. Some Protection Available [§726]

The First Amendment does not automatically protect conduct simply because the person engaging in it shows that it is undertaken to communicate an idea. If there is an important state interest *independent* of the speech aspects of the conduct, it may be regulated despite the incidental limitation on speech—*especially* if the state does not have less restrictive means available to accomplish its regulatory purpose. [**United States v. O'Brien,** 391 U.S. 367 (1968)]

2. Draft Card Burning [§727]

A prohibition on draft card burning was upheld. The government's interest was not simply to suppress speech aspects of the conduct; it had an independent interest of facilitating the smooth functioning of the draft system. [**United States v. O'Brien,** *supra*; *and see* **Clark v. Community for Creative Non-Violence,** 468 U.S. 288 (1984)—upholding prohibition on sleeping in national parks, applied to demonstrators calling attention to plight of the homeless]

3. **Armbands to Protest War [§728]**

   But a prohibition on students wearing black armbands in schools (to protest the Vietnam War) was found to be invalid. The government had no independent regulatory interest; its interest was *only* in prohibiting the communication. Thus, the conduct was "akin to pure speech" within the First Amendment ambit. [**Tinker v. Des Moines Independent Community School District,** 393 U.S. 503 (1969)]

4. **Flag Desecration [§729]**

   A prohibition on burning the American flag is likewise invalid—at least as applied to a situation where the conduct was intended (and understood by those who viewed it) as expressive and there was no actual or imminent breach of the peace. Government may not prohibit expression of an idea merely because society finds it offensive or disagreeable, even when the government's interest is preserving the flag as a symbol of nationhood and national unity. [**United States v. Eichman,** 496 U.S. 310 (1990); **Texas v. Johnson,** 491 U.S. 397 (1989)] A prohibition on displaying the flag with the peace symbol attached similarly violates the First Amendment. A person may not be punished "for failing to show proper respect for our national emblem." [**Spence v. Washington,** 418 U.S. 405 (1974)]

5. **Nude Dancing [§730]**

   Although "totally nude" dancing as entertainment is expressive conduct "within the outer perimeter" of the First Amendment, it may be prohibited under a state law against public nudity. Government has a "substantial" interest in combating crime and other "secondary effects" caused by the presence of adult entertainment establishments that is unrelated to the suppression of free expression. [**Barnes v. Glen Theatre, Inc.,** 501 U.S. 560 (1991); **City of Erie v. Pap's A.M.,** 529 U.S. 277 (2000)—city council made findings regarding secondary effects]

6. **Conviction for Conduct and Protected Speech [§731]**

   Irrespective of whether the conduct engaged in is protected by the First Amendment, a conviction must be reversed if constitutionally protected *speech* is made *part of the offense* or *may have been relied upon* by the fact finder to convict.

   ---

   e.g. **Example:** Defendant was convicted of flag burning. The Court reversed, finding it unnecessary to determine whether flag burning was symbolic conduct akin to pure speech because defendant's statements while burning flag ("We don't need no damn flag") were introduced into evidence and may have been relied upon to convict. [**Street v. New York,** 394 U.S. 576 (1969)]

   ---

7. **Regulation of Nonexpressive Conduct [§732]**

   A general regulation of conduct which itself has no communicative element is *not* invalid simply because the regulation incidentally burdens First Amendment activities. [**Arcara v. Cloud Books, Inc.,** 478 U.S. 697 (1986)—upholding closure of adult bookstore because it was used for acts of prostitution]

SYMBOLIC CONDUCT COMPARISON CHART	gilbert
CONDUCT HELD PROTECTED	**CONDUCT HELD UNPROTECTED**
Wearing black armbands to school to protest war (school had no regulatory interest other than the suppression of speech) ***Burning the flag***	***Burning a draft card*** (government has a strong interest in a smooth functioning draft system) ***Camping overnight in park*** to highlight the plight of the homeless (government has an interest in protecting parks) ***Nude dancing*** (government has a substantial interest in preventing the secondary effects caused by the presence of nude dancing facilities) ***Closure of adult bookstore for hosting prostitutes*** (government has an interest in preventing prostitution)

I. First Amendment Rights in Public Places

1. Introduction [§733]

The right to express one's views in public places is fundamental to a free society; however, it is ***not absolute*** and is subject to valid regulation.

2. Public Forum [§734]

Certain public property is so historically associated with the exercise of First Amendment rights that it cannot be totally closed to protected expression—such as speeches, meetings, parades, and demonstrations.

e.g. **Examples:** Streets, sidewalks, and parks fall within this category [**Hague v. CIO,** 307 U.S. 496 (1939)], including the public sidewalks abutting the Supreme Court building and grounds [**United States v. Grace,** 461 U.S. 171 (1983)], as apparently do the grounds around a statehouse [**Edwards v. South Carolina,** 372 U.S. 229 (1963)].

a. Designated public forum [§735]

Other public property, although not a "traditional" public forum, may become a designated public forum for such time as the state "by policy or by practice" opens it for expressive activity by the general public or a particular class of people. [**Lamb's Chapel v. Center Moriches Union Free School District,** 508 U.S. 384 (1993), *supra*, §582—school rooms open for after-school meetings by social, civic, and recreational groups are designated public forums]

3. Time, Place, and Manner Regulations [§736]

Speech in public forums and designated public forums may be subject to reasonable time, place, and manner regulations. To be constitutional, such regulations must:

(i)   Be *content-neutral* (*see* below);

(ii) Be *narrowly tailored* (*see infra*, §§753-756);

(iii) Serve a *significant government interest* (*see infra*, §§742-752); and

(iv) Leave open *ample alternative* forums or channels of communication for protected expression.

[**Heffron v. International Society for Krishna Consciousness,** 452 U.S. 640 (1981)]

EXAM TIP   gilbert

Remember that even if a regulation meets the time, place, and manner requirements above, it could still be invalid *if it is overbroad or vague*.

---

a. Content-neutral [§737]

A time, place, and manner regulation may not be based on the content or subject matter of the speech unless the regulation is "necessary to serve a compelling state interest and narrowly drawn to achieve that end." [**Perry Education Association v. Perry Local Educators' Association,** 460 U.S. 37 (1983); *and see* **Chicago Police Department v. Mosley,** 408 U.S. 92 (1972)—ordinance permitting peaceful labor picketing near schools but forbidding all other peaceful picketing discriminated in respect to the content of the expression and was a denial of *equal protection*] *Examples:*

(1) Drive-in theaters [§738]

A law may *not* single out nudity in regulating films shown by drive-in theaters whose screens are visible from the highway. [**Erznoznik v. Jacksonville,** 422 U.S. 205 (1975)]

(2) Foreign embassies [§739]

A law may not forbid only those picket signs within 500 feet of a foreign embassy that are critical of the foreign government. [**Boos v. Barry,** 485 U.S. 312 (1988)]

Is the place a *public forum* (or designated public forum) or a *nonpublic forum*?

Public forum

Nonpublic forum

The regulation must:

(i)   Be *content-neutral*;

(ii) Be *narrowly tailored*;

(iii) *Serve a significant government interest*; and

(iv) *Leave open ample alternative opportunities for communication* of the expression.

The regulation must be:

(i)   Reasonable (*i.e., viewpoint-neutral*, but speaker's status may be considered); and

(ii) *Not meant to suppress expression* merely because officials oppose it.

(3) Billboards [§740]

A city may regulate billboards for purposes of traffic safety and aesthetics. But it may *not* permit billboards with commercial messages while prohibiting those with noncommercial messages; nor may it distinguish between different types of noncommercial messages. [**Metromedia, Inc. v. City of San Diego**, *supra*, §690—also upholding prohibition on commercial advertising]

(4) State university facilities [§741]

A state university that creates a forum open to students may not exclude a group that wants to use the facilities for religious discussion and worship unless the university shows that this is necessary to a compelling state interest. [**Widmar v. Vincent**, *supra*, §582]

b. Significant government interest

(1) Illustrations—insignificant interest [§742]

The state does *not* have an adequate interest in ascertaining the identity of *every* person who wishes to distribute handbills in public to justify requiring disclosure of the name and address of the author of all such handbills. [**Talley v. California**, 362 U.S. 60 (1960)]

(a) Permits [§743]

While the state *may* have the power to require a permit for door-to-door solicitation of funds and commercial transactions, its interest in preventing fraud does *not* justify requirement of a permit for *all* door-to-door religious proselytization, advocacy of anonymous political speech, and enlisting support for unpopular causes. Even if a permit is promptly issued to solicitors with no fee or exercise of administrative discretion, the permit requirement unduly interferes with this highly important and effective method of the dissemination of ideas. [**Watchtower Bible and Tract Society of New York, Inc. v. Village of Stratton**, 536 U.S. 150 (2002)]

(2) Illustrations—significant interests [§744]

The following have been found by the Court to be significant government interests.

(a) Orderly movement of crowds [§745]

A state's interest in orderly movement of crowds at a state fair justifies a regulation restricting organizations' distribution and sale of literature and solicitation of donations to assigned booths at fixed locations. [**Heffron v. International Society for Krishna Consciousness**, *supra*, §736—emphasizing that "alternative channels for communication of the information" had been left open]

(b) Privacy

1) Home [§746]

A state's interest in protecting residential privacy justifies a regulation that bans picketing that takes place solely in front of a particular residence. Usually in such instances, the information is not directed to the public but rather is narrowly directed only at the resident, who has no ready means of avoiding the unwanted speech. [**Frisby v. Schultz,** 487 U.S. 474 (1988)]

2) Access to health care facilities [§747]

The state interest in protecting peoples' access to health care facilities justifies prohibiting persons within 100 feet of a health care facility from "knowingly approaching" within eight feet of those seeking access to the health care facility to leaflet, handbill, protest, educate, or counsel. [**Hill v. Colorado,** 530 U.S. 703 (2000)—statute upheld against challenge by petitioners who wished to "counsel" women as they entered abortion clinics]

3) Door-to-door solicitation [§748]

A state's interest in protecting citizens from crime *may* justify requiring door-to-door solicitors or canvassers to identify themselves to local officials. [**Hynes v. Mayor of Oradell,** 425 U.S. 610 (1976)—ordinance *invalid* because of vagueness]

4) Sound trucks [§749]

A state's interest in protecting privacy justifies prohibiting the operation on public streets of sound trucks that emit messages amplified to a "loud and raucous volume." [**Kovacs v. Cooper,** 336 U.S. 77 (1949)—unwilling listener has no reasonable way of protecting himself]

a) But note

As will be discussed (*infra*, §§766-774), an ordinance that required that anyone seeking to use a sound truck or other amplifiers on public streets to first obtain a permit from the chief of police was held unconstitutional where *no standards* were established for the granting or denial of the permit. Vesting complete discretion in the chief made him a censor of what could be broadcast on the public streets. [**Saia v. New York,** 334 U.S. 558 (1948)]

5) Unwanted mail [§750]

The government interest in protecting privacy justifies the Post

Office, upon a householder's request, to order a mailer to stop *all future mailings* to that householder and to remove her name from the mailing list. [**Rowan v. United States Post Office**, 397 U.S. 728 (1970)—mailer's First Amendment right to communicate must give way to householder's "right to be let alone"]

6) **Distinguish—dissemination of information [§751]**

A person's interest in privacy does *not* justify the state's preventing public dissemination of information about that person, urging that pressure be put on him to cease certain business practices (real estate "blockbusting"). [**Organization for a Better Austin v. Keefe**, 402 U.S. 415 (1971)]

(c) **Zoning [§752]**

Zoning laws may properly be used to restrict the locations in which "adult" movies can be shown because a state's interest in regulating the secondary land use effects of commercial property outweighs the "less vital" First Amendment interest in uninhibited exhibition of material "on the borderline between pornography and artistic expression." [**Young v. American Mini Theatres, Inc.**, *supra*, §655; **City of Renton v. Playtime Theatres, Inc.**, *supra*, §655]

c. **Narrowly tailored [§753]**

A time, place, and manner regulation must be narrowly tailored; *i.e.*, it may not burden substantially more speech than is necessary to further the significant government interest involved. However, the regulation need *not* be the least restrictive or least intrusive means of achieving the government interest. Courts should respect the government's reasonable determination that the regulation best serves its interest. [**Ward v. Rock Against Racism**, 491 U.S. 781 (1989)—upholding a regulation requiring performers at an amphitheater in a city park use the city's sound-amplification equipment and sound technician]

(1) **Littering [§754]**

The significant state interest in keeping streets clean does *not* justify barring all distribution of handbills—because this would suppress a great quantity of speech that does not cause the evils sought to be prevented. [**Schneider v. State**, 308 U.S. 147 (1939)]

(2) **Door-to-door solicitation [§755]**

The significant state interest in protecting homeowner's privacy does *not* justify a *total* prohibition on knocking at door or ringing of bell to distribute handbills—because the city has other effective means, such as having unwilling homeowners post a "No Solicitors" sign. [**Martin v. Struthers**, 319 U.S. 141 (1943)]

(a) Fraud [§756]

The state has a significant interest in preventing fraudulent charitable solicitations. [**Illinois *ex rel.* Madigan v. Telemarketing Associates, Inc.,** 123 S. Ct. 1829 (2003)—telemarketing firm soliciting donations for a charity whose fee was 85% of gross receipts may be charged with intentional false or misleading representations for saying that it will pay "a significant amount of each donation" to the charity] However, this interest does *not* justify a *categorical ban* on solicitations by *all* organizations (including groups engaged in advocacy on matters of public concern) whose overhead exceeds either a specified or a "reasonable" percent of receipts—because the state has effective means beyond such a "broad prophylactic rule" for preventing fraud that will burden substantially less speech. [**Riley v. National Federation of the Blind of North Carolina,** *supra,* §720]

4. Total Ban [§757]

Laws that foreclose an entire medium of expression pose a danger of suppressing too much speech. The state may impose a "total ban" on a particular medium of communication only if it satisfies the criteria for a valid time, place, and manner regulation; *i.e.,* the ban must be *"content-neutral"*; it must further a *"significant government interest"*; it must be *"narrowly tailored"*; and there must be *alternative media* available for the protected expression. [**Metromedia, Inc. v. City of San Diego,** *supra,* §740] Illustrations follow.

a. Sound amplification [§758]

It is unclear whether the state interest in protecting privacy justifies an absolute prohibition on any kind of sound amplification in public places in connection with First Amendment activities. [*See* **Kovacs v. Cooper,** *supra,* §749]

b. Temporary signs [§759]

A state's interest in aesthetics and eliminating "visual blight" justifies a total ban on posting signs on *public* property such as sidewalks, utility poles, etc. [**Los Angeles City Council v. Taxpayers for Vincent,** 466 U.S. 789 (1984)]

c. Residential signs [§760]

Residential signs are an important, inexpensive, and convenient form of communication. The state's need to regulate all such speech from the home is not sufficiently strong to justify a near-total ban. [**City of Ladue v. Gilleo,** 512 U.S. 43 (1994)—municipality could not prohibit resident from placing sign in her window reading, "For peace in the Gulf"]

5. Not a Public Forum [§761]

Certain types of public property—that which is *not* traditionally or by government designation *open to the general public,* or where the state concludes that First Amendment activities would be *incompatible with the normal use to which the property is put*—may be closed to the exercise of First Amendment rights if the regulation is reasonable and not meant to suppress expression merely because officials oppose it.

a. Reasonableness [§762]

Although the prohibition may not discriminate on the basis of the speaker's *viewpoint* (by seeking to discourage one and advance another), it may draw distinctions on the basis of the *type of subject* or the *speaker's status*—as long as the distinction is reasonable in light of the purpose that the property serves. [**Perry Education Association v. Perry Local Educators' Association**, 460 U.S. 37 (1983)]

Example: An internal mail system among schools within a district is not a "public forum." Thus, the school district may provide access to the union that is the exclusive bargaining representative of the teachers and not to a rival union—because this is a reasonable distinction based on status. [**Perry Education Association v. Perry Local Educators' Association**, *supra*]

Example: A public television station debate for congressional candidates from major parties or who have strong popular support is not a "public forum." The program is not generally available to a certain class of speakers, but rather is available only to selected members of the class. The criteria for access are permissible because they are (i) reasonable in light of the logistics for an educationally valuable debate, and (ii) viewpoint neutral. [**Arkansas Educational Television Commission v. Forbes**, 523 U.S. 666 (1998)]

Example: A government-created charity drive for federal employees, which has not traditionally been open to all charitable organizations, is not a "public forum." Thus, it is permissible to limit participation to traditional health and welfare charities and to exclude groups that engage in political advocacy, lobbying, and litigation. This is reasonable in light of the government's purposes of minimizing disruption to the federal workplace, insuring the success of the fundraising, and avoiding the appearance of political favoritism. [**Cornelius v. NAACP Legal Defense & Education Fund**, 473 U.S. 788 (1985)]

Example: Airport terminals operated by a public authority have not historically been available for speech activities, nor have they been intentionally opened by their operators to such activities. Thus, they are not "public forums." It is reasonable to ban *solicitation* within the terminals that presents risks of fraud and duress to hurrying and vulnerable travelers and impedes the normal flow of traffic, and limit it to the outside sidewalk areas. [**International Society for Krishna Consciousness, Inc. v. Lee**, 505 U.S. 672 (1992)] However, it is *not* reasonable to ban *leafletting*, which does not pose these types of problems, in those terminals that are multipurpose facilities much like shopping malls. [**Lee v. International Society for Krishna Consciousness, Inc.**, 505 U.S. 830 (1992)—no majority rationale]

> **Example:** School property when not in use for school purposes is not a "public forum." But to permit it to be used for presentation of all views about family issues except those from a religious perspective does not satisfy the requirement of "viewpoint neutrality." [**Lamb's Chapel v. Center Moriches Union Free School District,** *supra,* §582]

b. **Illustrations of property that is not a "public forum" [§763]**
   The following public property has been held *not* to be a "public forum":

   (1) *Jailhouse* grounds [**Adderley v. Florida,** 385 U.S. 39 (1966)];

   (2) The *area immediately surrounding a courthouse while a trial is being held* [**Cox v. Louisiana,** *supra,* §663];

   (3) *Military bases* may be closed to political speeches and distribution of leaflets—if done even-handedly. And this is true even when the public is generally permitted to visit the base, because of the strong government interest in keeping the military free of partisan political entanglements [**Greer v. Spock,** 424 U.S. 828 (1976)];

   (a) *Note:* Even if a military base is temporarily opened to the public for expressive activities, persons who have been validly barred for prior misconduct may continue to be excluded—as long as this is done on a "content-neutral" basis. [**United States v. Albertini,** 472 U.S. 675 (1985)]

   (4) The *area immediately surrounding a school during school sessions* may be closed to expressive activity that disrupts (or is about to disrupt) normal school activities [**Grayned v. City of Rockford,** 408 U.S. 104 (1972)];

   (5) A *private letter box* approved by the Postal Service for receipt of mail is *not* a public forum. The deposit of unstamped communications in such boxes would interfere with the safe and efficient delivery of mail and may be prohibited [**United States Postal Service v. Council of Greenburgh Civic Associations,** 453 U.S. 114 (1981)];

   (6) A *city transit system* which sold advertising space for "car cards" did not constitute a "public forum." Thus the city's refusal to accept any political advertising by candidates did not violate the First Amendment—the city's policy was "reasonable" in order to minimize chances of abuse, the appearance of favoritism, and the risk of imposing upon a captive audience. Four Justices disagreed. [**Lehman v. City of Shaker Heights,** 418 U.S. 298 (1974)]; and

   (7) *The Court has split* on whether a *postal sidewalk leading from the parking area* to the post office door is a traditional "public forum," akin

to ordinary public sidewalks that facilitate the daily commerce and the life of the neighborhood or city [**United States v. Kokinda**, 497 U.S. 720 (1990)].

c. **Private property [§764]**
The First Amendment does not require the owner of private property to allow others to access the property for the purpose of picketing or distributing handbills. [**Hudgens v. NLRB**, 424 U.S. 507—shopping center] On the other hand, the First Amendment does not prohibit a state from requiring the owner of private property to permit others to access the property for the purpose of distributing handbills unrelated to the business conducted on the private property. [**PruneYard Shopping Center v. Robins**, *supra*, §564]

(1) **Distinguish—"equivalent to a public place" [§765]**
In some cases, privately owned property may be held to be the functional *equivalent of a public place*—in which event neither criminal nor civil trespass rules may be applied to limit the *reasonable* exercise of First Amendment rights on the property. [**Marsh v. Alabama**, 326 U.S. 501 (1946)—distribution of religious literature in privately owned "company town"]

6. **Licensing [§766]**
One method of reasonably regulating public areas for protected speeches, meetings, parades, demonstrations, etc., is to require a permit or license for such use, specifying the time, place, manner, and duration of the activity. The state may require a reasonable fee for the use in order to defray public expenses. [**Cox v. New Hampshire**, 312 U.S. 569 (1941)]

a. **Censorship forbidden [§767]**
In providing for the issuance of such permits, the state may *not* vest the licensing official (mayor, police chief, etc.) with *unlimited discretion* to determine who may receive permits [**Lovell v. City of Griffin**, 303 U.S. 444 (1938)] or how much to charge for police protection or administrative time [**Forsyth County, Georgia v. Nationalist Movement**, 505 U.S. 123 (1992)]. To do so would limit the exercise of First Amendment rights to what the official approved of, and would vest the official with censorship power over the content of what is said.

(1) **Requirement of defined standards [§768]**
The licensing authority must therefore contain *clearly defined standards* as to time, place, manner, and duration.

(2) **Denial based on content [§769]**
The Court has *suggested* that, in certain *special circumstances*, a permit may be denied because of the content of speech (*e.g.*, a speech that would present the clear and present danger of a riot)—but such a "prior

restraint" could take place only under narrowly and clearly defined standards. [**Kunz v. New York**, 340 U.S. 290 (1951)] Moreover, the Court has *never upheld* a licensing system based on the content of the speech.

(a) Licensing organizations [§770]

Before a state college may deny official recognition and use of college facilities to a student group, a "heavy burden" rests on the college to justify this form of "prior restraint." Neither the group's general affiliation with a national organization nor its philosophy (even if one of violence) will justify denial of recognition, but denial *may* be justified if the group poses a *substantial threat of material disruption* or refuses to affirm its willingness to adhere to reasonable campus rules respecting conduct. [**Healy v. James**, 408 U.S. 169 (1972)—denial to Students for a Democratic Society chapter of use of facilities is invalid]

(b) Fees [§771]

The amount of the fee charged to maintain public order may not be based on actual expense if this would result in greater costs because of the need to control those who might oppose the speech, parade, etc. Listeners' reaction to speech is not a content-neutral basis for regulation. [**Forsyth County, Georgia v. Nationalist Movement**, *supra*]

EXAM TIP   **gilbert**

Requiring people to obtain a license to hold a rally, parade, etc., is a common First Amendment issue. Be sure to look for evidence of the following two licensing scheme flaws: First, the licensing scheme *lacks clearly defined standards* (e.g., "Permits shall be granted to use Mainstreet Square for speeches and rallies on a first come, first served basis. Requests for permission to use the Square must be made in writing at least 10 days in advance. The Square may be reserved by a single speaker or group for no more than two consecutive days and may be used only between the hours of 10 a.m. and 4 p.m. . . . "). Second, while a municipality may charge a fee to offset its expenses, the *fee cannot vary depending on the speaker* (e.g., the municipality cannot charge Father John from the local church $25 to use the Square for his "Up With God Rally" and charge Adolph, the leader of a local Nazi Party, $500 to pay for the extra police protection that is needed whenever Adolph speaks). Also, note that a scheme that gives officials discretion (on who may speak, what they may talk about, the amount of the fee, etc.) will be held invalid on its face (see below).

---

b. Effect of unlimited discretion [§772]

If the statute gives licensing officials undue discretion, it is *"void on its face"*; *i.e.*, applicants need not even apply for a permit. (Note the similarity to facial invalidity because of "overbreadth" or "vagueness," *supra*, §585.) Thus, even if speakers could properly have been denied a permit under a narrowly drafted statute, they may exercise their First Amendment rights on the public property *without a permit* and may not be convicted for violating the licensing statute. [**Staub v. Baxley,** 355 U.S. 313 (1958)]

Example: A city ordinance that vested in local licensing officials the power to grant parade permits on the basis of their judgment as to the effect of such parade on the "welfare" or "morals" of the community was held unconstitutional *on its face*—for lack of adequate standards. [**Shuttlesworth v. City of Birmingham,** 394 U.S. 147 (1969)]

Example: A city ordinance that gave the mayor complete discretion to grant annual permits for placement of newsracks on public property was held unconstitutional *on its face.* [**Lakewood v. Plain Dealer Publishing Co.,** 486 U.S. 750 (1988)]

c. **Statutes valid on their face [§773]**
If the licensing statute is valid on its face—*i.e.,* if it contains clearly defined standards as to time, place, manner, and duration—it may not be ignored. The applicant *must seek a permit*, and if the permit is refused for any reason—even arbitrarily or unconstitutionally—the applicant must seek *reasonably available administrative or judicial relief.* The applicant may not speak without a permit and then defend prosecution for violating the statute on the ground that the permit was improperly denied or that his speech was constitutionally protected. [**Poulos v. New Hampshire,** 345 U.S. 395 (1953)]

(1) **Note**
In **Shuttlesworth v. City of Birmingham,** *supra,* the licensing statute was void on its face (due to inadequate standards)—but on appeal of the conviction for parading without a permit, the state courts gave the statute a narrow (and probably constitutional) construction. The Supreme Court reversed the conviction on the ground that the applicants had no reason to anticipate such a limiting construction and, in any case, were told by the officials that they would not get a permit under any circumstances. The Court *left open* the question of whether applicants must generally seek a narrowing construction if "expeditious judicial review" is available.

7. **Injunctions [§774]**
A slightly more rigorous degree of scrutiny governs content-neutral injunctions that impose "time, place, and manner" restrictions on the exercise of First Amendment rights in public forums: an injunction is valid if it burdens no more speech than *necessary* to serve a *significant* government interest. [**Madsen v. Women's Health Center, Inc.,** 512 U.S. 753 (1994)—upholding injunction against focused picketing near entrance to abortion clinic so as to ensure ingress and egress]

Example: An injunction providing for a "floating buffer zone" of 15 feet between protestors and persons entering and leaving an abortion clinic violates the First Amendment. *Rationale:* The floating zone barred *all* verbal and written communication from a normal conversational distance on public sidewalks and thus burdened more speech than necessary to ensure ingress and egress. [**Schenck v. Pro-Choice Network of Western New York,** 510 U.S. 357 (1997)]

J. First Amendment Freedoms and Special Government Interests

1. Administration of Justice [§775]

Statutes and rules of court restricting the freedoms of speech and press will be sustained to the extent necessary to ensure the orderly administration of justice.

a. In court [§776]

Disruptive or obviously disrespectful statements directed to the *judge* or an *officer of the court* during the course of a trial are punishable by contempt.

b. Out of court [§777]

Speech or publications by the news media about pending judicial proceedings are not punishable unless they pose a *clear and present danger of serious interference* with the administration of justice—and this issue is ultimately determined by the Supreme Court. [**Bridges v. California,** 315 U.S. 252 (1941)]

(1) Freedom of the press [§778]

The Court has noted that "freedom of the press must be allowed in the *broadest* scope compatible with the supremacy of order" [**Pennekamp v. Florida,** 328 U.S. 331 (1946)], and the strong presumption against prior restraints applies [**Nebraska Press Association v. Stuart,** *supra,* §701].

(2) Pending proceedings [§779]

If the judicial proceedings are *over*, there is no danger that the utterances or publications will interfere with the administration of justice. But close issues may arise as to whether the proceedings are really complete (*i.e.,* whether there can be an appeal, new trial, etc.).

(3) Distinguish—lawyers [§780]

Speech of lawyers representing clients in pending cases may be regulated under a less demanding standard than for the news media. These lawyers are "officers of the court" and may be sanctioned for speech having *"substantial likelihood of materially prejudicing"* the jury venire or the actual outcome of the proceedings. [**Gentile v. State Bar of Nevada,** 501 U.S. 1030 (1991)]

(4) Type of proceeding [§781]

The permissible amount of restriction on speech and press also depends substantially on the *type* of judicial proceeding involved.

(a) Trial by jury [§782]

The greatest restrictions are seemingly permitted to protect the impartiality of a petit jury. [**Sheppard v. Maxwell,** 384 U.S. 333 (1966)]

(b) Trials without a jury [§783]

Freedom of speech and press are given *more leeway* in trials without a jury, on the theory that judges are better trained than juries to withstand criticism and intimidation. [**Craig v. Harney,** 331 U.S. 367 (1947)]

(c) Grand jury proceedings [§784]

Still greater leeway is afforded speech and press in respect to grand jury proceedings, because of their nonfinal nature. And there is even more liberality where the grand jury is engaged in a general investigation. Commentary *criticizing this process* may be curtailed only if it is manifestly unjust and likely to impede the outcome of the investigation. This will be an extremely rare situation, since full and free discussion generally furthers, rather than impedes, a grand jury investigation. [**Wood v. Georgia,** 370 U.S. 375 (1962)]

(d) Confidential proceedings [§785]

A state may have a legitimate interest in maintaining confidentiality about some proceedings (*e.g.,* inquiries into the fitness of judges). The Court has *not decided* whether a state may punish disclosures about such proceedings by (i) participants or (ii) persons who secure the information by illegal means. But criminal sanctions may not be imposed on other persons (including the press) for divulging truthful information regarding such confidential proceedings, absent substantial interests that justify encroachment on freedom of speech and press. [**Landmark Communications, Inc. v. Virginia,** 435 U.S. 829 (1978)]

1) Grand jury testimony [§786]

The secrecy of what transpires in grand jury proceedings serves a number of important interests. However, on balance, these interests do not justify a *permanent ban* on disclosure by a witness of *any* of his *own* testimony, even after the grand jury has been *discharged.* [**Butterworth v. Smith,** 494 U.S. 624 (1990)]

2. Electoral Process [§787]

Election laws inevitably impose some burdens on individuals' right to vote and on political parties' rights to advance common goals, which have protection under the First Amendment freedoms of speech and association. The degree of scrutiny that the Court will apply to such laws depends on how great a restriction the regulation imposes on the right to vote. If the restriction on the electoral process is severe, strict scrutiny applies and the restriction will be upheld only if it is **narrowly** tailored to serve a **compelling** interest. If the restriction is less burdensome and nondiscriminatory, scrutiny is less strict and the restriction generally will be upheld as long as it is justified by some important regulatory purpose. [**Buckley v. American Constitutional Law Foundation,** 525 U.S. 182 (1999); **Burdick v. Takushi,** 504 U.S. 428 (1992); *see infra*, §791]

a. Campaign activity restrictions [§788]

A state law prohibiting any campaigning on election day has been held invalid as applied to a newspaper editorial urging voters to vote a certain way. There was no showing of any clear and present danger to conducting the election, and the right to comment on political issues is one of the most essential elements of free speech. [**Mills v. Alabama,** 384 U.S. 214 (1966)]

(1) Exception—campaigning near polling place [§789]

A state law forbidding campaign activity within 100 feet of a polling place is valid. Even though the law bars only political speech in a public forum (and is thus not content-neutral, *see supra*, §737), it is **necessary** to serve the **compelling** interest of preventing voter intimidation and election fraud in regard to the fundamental right to vote. [**Burson v. Freeman,** 504 U.S. 191 (1992)]

(2) Campaign promises [§790]

Some kinds of campaign promises may be illegal (*e.g.*, a promise to pay for a vote). But a **publicly made** promise to benefit the public fisc (*e.g.*, a promise to serve at reduced salary) is constitutionally protected political speech. [**Brown v. Hartladge,** 456 U.S. 45 (1982)—no compelling state interest to justify voiding election of candidate who makes a good faith promise to serve at reduced salary even when promise cannot be kept because state law forbids reduced salary]

b. Write-in voting [§791]

A state may prohibit write-in voting when the state's overall election scheme provides adequate ballot access. [**Burdick v. Takushi,** *supra*—"slight" burden on right to vote outweighed by states' "legitimate" interest in avoiding unrestrained party factionalism and related matters]

c. Restrictions on political parties [§792]

Laws that place a *severe* burden on the freedom of speech or freedom of association rights of political parties and their members must be *"narrowly tailored"* to serve a *"compelling state interest."* [**Eu v. San Francisco County Democratic Central Committee,** 489 U.S. 214 (1989)—state cannot prohibit a political party from endorsing candidates in its primary; *and see* **California Democratic Party v. Jones,** 530 U.S. 567 (2000)—state cannot require political parties to include candidates in their primary elections regardless of candidates' party affiliation]

(1) Internal party organization [§793]

A political party's freedom of association right includes discretion in how to organize itself, conduct its affairs, and select its leaders. [**Eu v. San Francisco County Democratic Central Committee,** *supra*—state cannot regulate composition and criteria of state central committee members, nor time and place of their meetings]

(2) Closed primaries [§794]

A state may not require that voters in a party's primary be registered in the party if the party itself wishes to permit independent voters to participate. [**Tashjian v. Republican Party of Connecticut,** 479 U.S. 208 (1986)]

(3) Distinguish—one-party limit [§795]

A state law that prohibits an individual from appearing on the ballot as the candidate of more than one party does ***not*** impose a severe burden on the association rights of political parties. The state's interest in ballot integrity and political stability are "sufficiently weighty" to justify the law. [**Timmons v. Twin Cities Area New Party,** 520 U.S. 35 (1997)]

d. Limits on contributions [§796]

Laws limiting the amount of money that a person or group may ***contribute*** to a political candidate are ***valid***, since the government has a sufficiently important interest in stopping the fact (or appearance) of corruption that may result from large contributions. Moreover, such laws do not substantially restrict freedom of expression or freedom of association (as long as the contributor may spend her money ***directly*** to discuss candidates and issues). [**Buckley v. Valeo,** 424 U.S. 1 (1976)] *Note:* Federal or state laws limiting amounts that persons may contribute to a political candidate need not be adjusted for inflation. [**Nixon v. Shrink Missouri Government PAC,** 528 U.S. 377 (2000)]

Example: North Carolina Right to Life, Inc. ("NCRL") is a nonprofit advocacy organization (*see infra,* §981) that solicits and spends funds urging alternatives to abortion. Under a Federal Election Commission ("FEC") rule, NCRL is allowed to freely spend funds advocating its views. However, it cannot contribute money directly to political candidates, although it can contribute funds to committees that themselves make contributions to candidates. NCRL wanted to contribute money directly to political candidates and sued to have the FEC's rule declared unconstitutional as it applied to NCRL. The Supreme Court upheld the rule. *Rationale:* Such contributions may be misused as conduits for ***circumventing*** the contribution limits imposed on individuals.

Moreover, the law is not a *complete ban* because it permits the organizations to contribute to committees that contribute to candidates. [**Federal Election Commission v. Beaumont**, 123 S. Ct. 2200 (2003)]

---

(1) Political action groups [§797]

Laws limiting the amount of money that an incorporated or unincorporated organization may contribute to a committee that itself makes contributions to political candidates are similarly valid. [**California Medical Association v. Federal Election Commission**, 453 U.S. 182 (1981)] So, too, are laws that forbid incorporated or unincorporated organizations from making campaign contributions with funds solicited from the public generally rather than from their members. [**Federal Election Commission v. National Right to Work Committee**, 456 U.S. 914 (1982)]

(2) Distinguish—ballot measures [§798]

But laws limiting the amount that persons may contribute to a committee that supports or opposes a ballot measure are invalid—at least absent a showing that the restriction is needed to preserve voter confidence in the ballot measure process. In this context, there is no state interest in stopping the fact (or appearance) of corruption of officials. [**Citizens Against Rent Control v. Berkeley**, 454 U.S. 290 (1981)]

e. Limits on expenditures [§799]

Laws limiting the amount that an individual (including a candidate) or group may *spend* on a political campaign are *invalid*. Such laws impose "direct and substantial restraints" on political speech and do not satisfy the "exacting scrutiny applicable to limitations on core First Amendment rights of political expression." Government may not restrict the speech of wealthy persons in order to enhance the voice of others. [**Buckley v. Valeo**, *supra*] However, such expenditures may not be prearranged or coordinated with the candidate (otherwise they would be "contributions").

(1) Political action groups [§800]

Laws that limit the amount that an organization of persons may spend on a political campaign are similarly invalid. [**Federal Election Commission v. National Conservative Political Action Committee**, 470 U.S. 480 (1985)]

(2) Political parties [§801]

A law that limits political parties from making expenditures that are independent of (*i.e.*, not actually coordinated with) the candidate is also invalid. [**Colorado Republican Federal Campaign Committee v. Federal Election Commission**, 518 U.S. 604 (1996)]

(a) "Coordinated" expenditures [§802]

If political parties, like others, make expenditures "in cooperation, consultation, or concert" with a candidate, the expenditures are treated like "contributions" and may be limited accordingly. *Rationale*: The opposite rule would induce individuals to circumvent contribution limits by simply giving money to the party with the understanding that it should go to the candidate, thus furthering corruption or its appearance. [**Federal Election Commission v. Colorado Republican Federal Campaign Committee,** 533 U.S. 431 (2001)]

(3) Petition circulators [§803]

A law that prohibits paying persons to obtain signatures for a ballot initiative is also invalid because its effect is to reduce the quantum of "core political speech." [**Meyer v. Grant,** 484 U.S. 414 (1988)]

(4) Corporations [§804]

Laws prohibiting corporate expenditures to influence the vote on a *referendum* violate the First Amendment. Such speech is "indispensable to decisionmaking in a democracy." [**First National Bank v. Bellotti,** 435 U.S 765 (1978)—law limiting corporate expenditures to referenda that "materially affect" corporate business or property are invalid] A law forbidding a corporation from using bill inserts to express its views on controversial issues of public policy also violates the First Amendment. [**Consolidated Edison Co. v. Public Service Commission,** 447 U.S. 530 (1980)]

(a) Candidate elections [§805]

While the Court has held that corporations may not be limited in the amount of money that they spend on referendum issues, it has been held that the amount of money that corporations can spend to influence partisan candidate elections can be limited. The rationale is that corporations can amass great wealth through state-conferred legal advantages, and government has a legitimate interest in assuring that that wealth is not used to gain unfair advantage in the political marketplace through the corruption of elected officials.

1) Exception—nonprofit advocacy organization [§806]

Although the amount of money that an ordinary corporation may spend to influence candidate elections may be limited, the Court carved out an exception for nonprofit advocacy organizations (*e.g.,* voluntary political associations formed to oppose abortion). To qualify for the exception, the organization must: (i) be formed exclusively (or mainly) to promote political ideas, (ii) have no shareholders with claims on its assets or members who wish to benefit from its nonpolitical programs, and (iii) not serve as a conduit for campaign spending by business corporations or labor unions. Voluntary political associations of this kind do not present the problem of actual or apparent corruption of the political process through concentrated corporate wealth. [**Federal Election Commission v. Massachusetts Citizens for Life, Inc.,** 479 U.S. 238 (1986); **Austin v. Michigan Chamber of Commerce,** 494 U.S. 328 (1990)]

a)   Limitation

More recently, the Court has held that contributions even by nonprofit advocacy organizations can be limited. [*See* **Federal Election Commission v. Beaumont,** *supra*, §796]

b)   Corporate treasury funds

State laws may prohibit corporate expenditures for state political candidates except from funds segregated to be used for political purposes. [**Austin v. Michigan Chamber of Commerce,** *supra*]

EXAM TIP   **gilbert**

There have been quite a few cases concerning campaign funding by certain groups or individuals and under certain circumstances. The cases can be summarized as follows:

- The government *may* limit the amount of money that anyone—whether an individual, corporation, or nonprofit political group—*may contribute to a candidate* (although the government may not limit the amount of a candidate's own money that may be spent).

- Generally, the government *may not* limit the amount of money that anyone—whether an individual, corporation, or nonprofit political group—*may spend to influence the vote in elections* as long as such expenditures are *not coordinated with a candidate. Exception:* While corporations are free to influence the vote on referenda issues, because of their great wealth, corporations can be prohibited from expending corporate funds to influence the vote in candidate elections.

- The government *may not* prohibit persons from *paying others to circulate petitions* for signatures.

---

f.   Disclosure requirements [§807]

Laws requiring political parties to disclose information concerning campaign *contributions* and *expenditures* may be justified by such substantial government interests as enhancement of voter knowledge, deterrence of corruption, and enforcement of contribution limitations. [**Buckley v. Valeo,** *supra*, §799]

(1)   Minor parties [§808]

But such laws are *invalid* when applied to a minor political party that shows a "reasonable probability" that the disclosure will subject those identified to "threats, harassment, or reprisals from either government

INVALID REGULATIONS	VALID REGULATIONS
• Prohibition against *all campaigning on election day*	• Prohibition against *campaigning within 100 feet of a polling place on election day*
• Prohibition against *paying people to circulate ballot petitions*	• Prohibition against *write-in voting where the state provides otherwise adequate ballot access*
• Limitation on the *amount of money a person or group may spend to support an election* (other than that of a candidate)	• Prohibition against *appearing on the ballot as the candidate of more than one party*
• Limitation on the *amount of money that an individual or group may spend on a political campaign*	• Prohibition against *political parties allowing nonmembers to vote in their primaries*
• Prohibition against *corporations spending money to influence a referendum vote*	• Requirement that *political parties allow nonmembers to vote in their primaries*
• Prohibition against *corporations using bill inserts to express their views on a controversial issue*	• Regulation setting the *criteria for party membership and time and place of meetings*
• Requirement that *minor political parties* (e.g., communist, Nazi) *disclose information on contributions and expenditures* where the party shows that disclosure may subject members to harassment	• Prohibition against *appearing on the ballot as the candidate of more than one party*
• Prohibition against *anonymous campaign literature*	• Limitation on *amount that any group or individual may contribute to a political candidate*
	• Requirement that *major political parties disclose information on contributions and expenditures*

officials or private parties." (For further discussion, *see infra*, §§845-846.) In these circumstances, the government interests described above are diminished and the threat to political and associational freedom is much greater. [**Brown v. Socialist Workers '74 Campaign Committee,** 454 U.S. 1122 (1982)]

(2) Campaign literature [§809]

Speech intended to influence the electoral process occupies the core of protection afforded by the First Amendment. Therefore, laws that require disclosure of the identity of those who author such documents are subject to "exacting scrutiny." [**McIntyre v. Ohio Elections Commission,** 514 U.S. 334 (1995)—state interests in providing information or in preventing fraud and libel are insufficient to justify ban on *all* anonymous campaign literature]

3. Judicial Elections [§810]

A rule prohibiting candidates for judicial election from announcing their views on disputed legal and political issues violates the First Amendment. This is both a content-based restriction and a restriction on core political speech. In ether case, it can be justified only if it is necessary to a compelling state interest. Two state interests were suggested to support the rule here: it is necessary to maintain an impartial judiciary and it is necessary to preserve the appearance of impartiality. The Court found that the rule is "woefully underinclusive" and so is not tailored at all toward achieving these goals. For example, it allows candidates to show bias toward political parties while it prohibits them from stating an opinion about political issues. The Court also found that finding judges without any preconceptions in favor of particular legal views is not a compelling interest because it would be both impossible to find such a person and undesirable. [**Republican Party of Minnesota v. White,** 536 U.S. 765 (2002)]

4. Subsidies [§811]

The First Amendment does *not* require government to subsidize the exercise of the right of speech. [**Regan v. Taxation with Representation of Washington,** 461 U.S. 540 (1983)—Congress may deny tax benefits (which amount to government subsidies) for lobbying activities of organizations] Moreover, the government may subsidize lobbying activities of some groups and not others as long as it does not do so on the basis of the *content* of their speech. [*Id.*—Congress may rationally decide to subsidize lobbying by veterans' groups]

a. Funded programs [§812]

The government may fund programs to encourage certain activities and not others. In doing so, it may prohibit employees within the funded programs from giving certain kinds of information to program beneficiaries. This is *not* considered to be government discrimination on the basis of content of speech (it would be if government restricted fund recipients from certain kinds of speech outside the scope of the funded programs). Rather, the government is just assuring that its funds are used only to further the purposes of its program. [**Rust v. Sullivan,** 500 U.S. 173 (1991)—upholding federal regulations prohibiting federally funded family planning programs from counseling or giving information about abortion] Similarly, Congress's refusal to give food stamps to persons who meet the low income test because they are on strike does not abridge the strikers' First Amendment right of expression. [**Lyng v. International Union,** 485 U.S. 360 (1988)]

b. **Vagueness [§813]**

If the government acts as a "patron," as when funding some speech activities, greater imprecision in criteria for grants is permitted than with criminal statutes or regulatory schemes. (*See supra*, §§584-591.) *Rationale*: Speakers are less likely to steer clear of forbidden areas when only a subsidy is at stake. [**National Endowment for the Arts v. Finley,** 524 U.S. 569 (1998)—requirement that the National Endowment for the Arts consider standards of "decency" and "respect for values of American people" when deciding whether to make grants is not invalid on its face]

c. **Funding political campaigns [§814]**

The government *may* provide funds for political campaigns subject to various restrictions (discussed *infra*, §1128).

d. **Government encouragement of private speech [§815]**

In contrast to government funding of speech for the purpose of promoting its own policies (such as the family planning program in **Rust v. Sullivan,** *supra*), viewpoint restrictions are ordinarily invalid when government funds *private* speech. [**Rosenberger v. Rector and Visitors of the University of Virginia,** 515 U.S. 819—state university exclusion of religious magazine from program for support of student publications violates First Amendment]

---

e.g. **Example:** A federal statute funding legal assistance to indigents, but forbidding assisting lawyers from challenging the validity of welfare regulations, violates the First Amendment. [**Legal Services Corp. v. Velazquez,** 531 U.S. 533 (2001)—federal program was designed to promote private (not government) speech, and prohibition would substantially distort traditional role of lawyers]

---

5. **Public Schools [§816]**

Students in public schools do not shed their First Amendment rights at the schoolhouse gate. Student speech that happens to occur on school premises may not be prohibited unless "necessary to avoid material and substantial interference with school work, discipline, or the rights of others." [**Tinker v. Des Moines Independent Community School District,** *supra*, §728]

a. **Classrooms [§817]**

The First Amendment rights of students in public classrooms or assemblies (where other students are a captive audience) are not coextensive with the rights of adults in other settings. Thus, schools may prohibit the use of lewd, indecent, vulgar, and offensive speech in this context when it would undermine the school's basic educational mission. [**Bethel School District v. Fraser,** 478 U.S. 675 (1986)—student suspended for using sexually explicit speech in a school assembly]

b. **Publications [§818]**

Similarly, as long as their actions are reasonably related to legitimate pedagogical concerns, school officials may regulate the style and content of school-sponsored publications, theatrical productions, and other expressive activities that are part of the educational curriculum (whether or not in a traditional classroom setting) or that are perceived to bear the school's imprimatur. Thus, schools may prohibit speech that is ungrammatical, poorly written, inadequately researched, biased or prejudiced, or unsuitable for immature audiences. [**Hazelwood School District v. Kuhlmeier,** 484 U.S. 260 (1988)]

c. **Libraries [§819]**

A school board has broad discretion in respect to school affairs. Pursuant to its authority to promote fundamental civic and cultural values, it may remove books from the school library that it finds to be "pervasively vulgar" or "educationally unsuitable."

(1) **Note [§820]**

The Court has not clearly decided the extent to which the First Amendment rights of students deny a school board the discretion to remove books because the board disapproves of their ideas on narrow partisan or political grounds. [**Board of Education v. Pico,** 457 U.S. 853 (1982)]

6. **Internet Access at Public Libraries [§821]**

To prevent minors from getting harmful material, government may condition its support of Internet access in public libraries on their installing software to block obscenity and child pornography—at least when the library will unblock filtered material on any adult user's request. [**United States v. American Library Association, Inc.,** 123 S. Ct. 2297 (2003)]

7. **Academic Freedom [§822]**

The First Amendment includes a right against government attempts to influence the content of academic speech. However, the right does not protect confidential peer review materials from disclosure in appropriate proceedings, because it is unlikely that such disclosure will deter candid evaluations. The Court has not, however, resolved whether certain information in the materials may be redacted. [**University of Pennsylvania v. Equal Employment Opportunity Commission,** 493 U.S. 182 (1990)— EEOC subpoena of tenure review file in connection with dismissed teacher's claim of discrimination]

8. **Prison Administration [§823]**

Prison inmates retain constitutional rights that are consistent with their status as prisoners. Prison regulations impinging on those rights are valid if *"reasonably related to legitimate penological interests,"* but should not represent an "exaggerated response" to those concerns. Courts must ordinarily give **broad deference** to the **reasonable** judgments of prison administrators. [**Turner v. Safley,** 482 U.S. 78 (1987)—upholding prison ban on most inmate-to-inmate mail correspondence, but invalidating a requirement that prisoners obtain the prison superintendent's permission to marry]

a. **Interviews by news media [§824]**

Prison inmates can be prohibited from being interviewed by the news media as long as alternative means of communication are still available (*e.g.,* inmates can communicate by mail or through visitors). [**Pell v. Procunier,** 417 U.S. 817 (1974)]

b. **Prison unions [§825]**

Prison inmates may be prohibited from soliciting other inmates to join a union, from holding union meetings, and from receiving bulk union mailings. [**Jones v. North Carolina Prisoners' Labor Union,** 433 U.S. 119 (1977)]

c. **Legal aid [§826]**

Inmates have no *special* First Amendment right to give legal assistance to other inmates. The general rule—allowing prison regulations to impinge on prisoner rights as long as the regulations are reasonably related to legitimate penological interests—governs this form of speech. [**Shaw v. Murphy,** 532 U.S. 223 (2001)]

d. **Mail searches [§827]**

Incoming mail to prisoners (even from their attorneys) may properly be opened in the presence of the prisoners, but not read, in order to insure that contraband is not smuggled into the prison. [**Wolff v. McDonnell,** 418 U.S. 539 (1974)]

e. **Incoming publications [§828]**

A regulation allowing prison officials to reject incoming publications reasonably found to be detrimental to prison security is valid on its face. [**Thornburgh v. Abbott,** 490 U.S. 401 (1989)]

f. **Outgoing correspondence [§829]**

Outgoing mail presents a lesser threat to prison security. Thus, the Court has invalidated prison regulations that authorized censorship of prisoner mail that "unduly complains" or "magnifies grievances," that expresses "inflammatory political, racial, religious or other views," or that is deemed "defamatory or otherwise inappropriate." Such regulations are *too broad* for First Amendment purposes. [**Procunier v. Martinez,** 416 U.S. 396 (1974)]

9. **Military Personnel [§830]**

Members of the military do have First Amendment protection, but speech on their part that "undermines the effectiveness of response to command" may be limited even if it could not be limited in a civilian setting. Thus, "facial invalidity" is found less readily in cases involving speech of military personnel because of "significant differences between military law and civilian law." [**Parker v. Levy**, 417 U.S. 733 (1974)]

e.g. **Example:** "Protest" expressions by military personnel have been held punishable as undermining the effectiveness of command, even though similar expressions by civilians are constitutionally protected. [**Parker v. Levy**, *supra*—upholding court-martial conviction of officer who urged soldiers to refuse to obey orders to go to Vietnam]

e.g. **Example:** Also, because of the military's interest in maintaining discipline and respect for duty, a requirement that members of the military obtain their commander's approval before circulating petitions on bases is not void on its face. [**Brown v. Glines**, 444 U.S. 348 (1980)]

10. **Practice of Law [§831]**

Statutes regulating the professional conduct of attorneys in soliciting cases, or in accepting employment or referrals from groups, cannot be applied in a manner that interferes with the group's "freedom of expression and association"—*e.g.*, freedom to band together to advise each other and use counsel in their common interest.

a. **Requirement of substantial state interest [§832]**

To overcome the group's exercise of First Amendment rights, the state must show a *substantial* interest—*i.e.*, evidence of objectionable practices actually occurring, or an actual or clearly threatened conflict of interest between lawyer and client. [**Brotherhood of Railroad Trainmen v. Virginia**, 377 U.S. 1 (1964)]

e.g. **Example:** The NAACP encouraged, instructed, and offered to represent parents of black children to litigate against school segregation. *Held:* Such litigation was a form of political expression and political association; and since the NAACP sought no monetary gain, there was no danger of conflict of interest, which was the purpose of the state ban on solicitation of legal business. [**NAACP v. Button**, *supra*, §592] *Note:* Even where politically motivated groups (such as the NAACP or ACLU) seek a court award of counsel fees in litigation, solicitation by their lawyers is protected as long as they have no personal pecuniary gain at stake. [*In re* **Primus**, 436 U.S. 412 (1978)] (Compare solicitation for personal gain, discussed *supra*, §693.)

Example: Likewise, a union has the right to hire an attorney on a salary basis to represent its members on their workers' compensation claims in state tribunals absent any evidence of abuse or conflict of interest. [**United Mine Workers v. Illinois Bar Association,** 389 U.S. 217 (1967)]

11. Labor Picketing [§833]

The dissemination of information regarding a labor or other economic dispute by means of *peaceful picketing* is a type of expression protected by the First Amendment and may not be *absolutely* prohibited. [**Thornhill v. Alabama,** 310 U.S. 88 (1940)]

a. Violence [§834]

Even peaceful picketing may be enjoined if it is enmeshed with violence or a justifiable fear that violence will ensue. [**Milk Wagon Drivers' Union v. Meadowmoor Dairies, Inc.,** 312 U.S. 287 (1941)]

b. Current doctrine [§835]

When peaceful economic picketing involves more than "publicity" and seeks to pressure the subject of the picketing to take action contrary to lawful state policy—*i.e.,* a state policy not barred by federal statute or the Constitution—it may be enjoined (or otherwise prohibited) without abridging the First Amendment. [**International Brotherhood of Teamsters v. Vogt, Inc.,** 354 U.S. 284 (1957)]

(1) Lawful state policy [§836]

State policy may be reflected in a statute making the action sought to be induced by the picketing a crime or civil wrong; or a state court may determine that the action sought is contrary to public policy.

Example: A state court enjoined peaceful picketing for the purpose of inducing the picketed wholesaler to refrain from selling to non-union peddlers; the state court found this to be a restraint of trade in violation of state antitrust laws. *Held:* Valid—the state statute reflected a lawful state policy not contrary to any federal statute or the Constitution. [**Giboney v. Empire Storage & Ice Co.,** 336 U.S. 490 (1949)]

Example: A state court enjoined peaceful picketing for the purpose of forcing the picketed business to hire employees in percentage of the race of its customers; the state court reasoned that employment on racial lines was contrary to public policy as determined by the state's courts. *Held:* Valid—the state policy is lawful and not contrary to any federal statute or the Constitution. [**Hughes v. Superior Court,** 339 U.S. 460 (1950)]

(2) Illustration of unlawful state policy [§837]

However, if peaceful picketing were used to induce the business picketed to cease racial discrimination in hiring, and a state court enjoined such picketing on the ground that state policy *favored* racial discrimination in hiring (and the picketing thus sought to induce the business to violate state policy), the picketing could not be enjoined since the state policy would be unlawful.

12. Boycotts [§838]

Nonviolent, politically motivated boycotts (including threats of social ostracism for nonparticipation) that seek to secure *constitutional rights* (in contrast to goals prohibited by valid state laws) are protected by the First Amendment and cannot be prohibited—at least absent a narrowly tailored statute prohibiting certain forms of anticompetitive conduct. [**NAACP v. Claiborne Hardware Co.,** 458 U.S. 886 (1982)]

a. Money damages limitation [§839]

A court may impose damages for consequences of a boycott only if the court makes specific *findings* showing that the damages were *proximately caused* by unlawful conduct (*e.g.*, violence). They may not be imposed merely because the defendant belonged to a group, some of whose members acted unlawfully. [**NAACP v. Claiborne Hardware Co.,** *supra*]

13. Trademarks [§840]

When a word acquires value through the special efforts of a person (or entity), Congress may, consistent with the First Amendment, grant that person (or entity) a "limited property right" in the word, thus enabling the person (or entity) to prevent others from using the word without authorization. [**San Francisco Arts & Athletics, Inc. v. United States Olympic Committee,** 483 U.S. 522 (1987)—U.S. Olympic Committee may prevent another group from calling its athletic competition "Gay Olympic Games"]

14. Copyright [§841]

Similarly, Congress may grant authors (including those who are important public figures) exclusive control over publication of their writing for a limited period. [**Harper & Row v. Nation Enterprises,** 471 U.S. 539 (1985)—magazine published article with 300 words from former President Ford's forthcoming memoirs; *and see infra*, §895] Although copyrights are not *categorically* beyond the First Amendment's protection, the Court has reasoned that the purpose of a copyright's limited monopoly is to *promote* the creation and publication of free expression. [**Eldred v. Ashcroft,** 123 S. Ct. 769 (2003)—Congress may extend the number of years set in original grant of copyright]

K. Freedom of Association—Special Rules

1. Association with Groups Engaging in Unprotected Advocacy or Activities [§842]

Even though an individual does not himself engage in unprotected advocacy or other constitutionally unprotected activities, he may be punished for being a member of a certain type of group—but only if *both* of the following criteria are met:

a. Culpability of group [§843]

The group or organization itself must engage in advocacy (as defined *supra*, §§600-606) or activities that are not constitutionally protected.

b. Culpability of individual member [§844]

In addition, the individual must have (i) *knowledge* of the group's illegal advocacy or activities, and (ii) the *specific intent* that its illegal aims be accomplished. [**Scales v. United States,** 367 U.S. 203 (1961)]

---

e.g. **Example:** Mere attendance at a meeting or assistance in the holding of a meeting may not be proscribed; the government's interest in penalizing such conduct is too weak, and the inhibition on freedom of association is too broad. [**DeJonge v. Oregon,** 299 U.S. 353 (1937)]

---

(1) Rationale

A prohibition against membership that is knowledgeable but without specific intent is *overbroad*; it would encompass persons (i) who might belong to the organization only to pursue certain of its lawful aims, or (ii) who might wish to change the organization's unlawful aims. Such persons pose no threat to any substantial government interest. [**Elfbrandt v. Russell,** 384 U.S. 11 (1966)]

EXAM TIP **gilbert**

It is important to remember that the First Amendment protects not only the freedom to speak, but also the freedom to associate, *i.e.,* to come together with people who hold similar views and ideologies. Because of this freedom of association, the government cannot punish a person *merely for belonging* to a group that advocates violence or the like. The government may punish a person for associating with a group that advocates violence only if the person *knows* of the group's illegal advocacy or activities and has the *specific intent to accomplish those illegal goals*.

---

2. Compulsory Disclosure of Membership or Association [§845]

Several cases have dealt with the power of government to require an individual to disclose her organizational memberships—or, conversely, to compel an organization to disclose the names of its members. The Court has recognized that disclosure of the fact that a person is a member of (or contributes to) a particular group or organization may *deter* the person from becoming a member or contributing—especially if the group espouses unpopular views—and therefore may deter freedom of association. [**NAACP v. Alabama,** *supra,* §566]

a. General standard [§846]

The Court will *closely scrutinize* compulsory disclosure (or compelled registration of membership) to determine whether it *"directly* serves **substantial** government interests," thus *outweighing* the individual's need for anonymity (or privacy) in exercising the First Amendment right of association. [**Buckley v. Valeo**, *supra*, §796]

---

e.g. **Example:** Alabama sought to compel disclosure of NAACP membership lists to determine whether the NAACP was engaged in intrastate activities and thus subject to a state registration statute for foreign corporations "doing business" in the state. *Held:* The state interest was insufficient to overcome the substantial deterrent effect on freedom of association that disclosure in Alabama would have (as demonstrated by threats, harassment, etc.). [**NAACP v. Alabama**, *supra*]

---

cf. **Compare:** A federal statute required registration of Communist Party membership. *Held:* The strong government interest in identifying membership of the Communist Party—which depended on secrecy for forceful overthrow of the government—outweighs individual interests in freedom of association. In upholding the registration requirement, the Court noted that the requirement became operative only after specific findings about the Communist Party following notice and hearing, which were subject to judicial review. [**Communist Party v. Subversive Activities Control Board**, 367 U.S. 1 (1967)]

---

b. **Privilege against self-incrimination [§847]**

Although the government interest in compelling disclosure of membership may be sufficient to outweigh the individual's First Amendment freedom of association, if—because of other criminal statutes—the admission of membership may be used to prosecute the registrant, the registration statute may violate the individual's Fifth Amendment privilege against self-incrimination. [**Albertson v. Subversive Activities Control Board**, 382 U.S. 70 (1965)]

3. **Disclosures Required in Legislative Investigations**

a. **Investigatory powers [§848]**

The power of Congress (or a state legislature) to conduct investigations in aid of proposed legislation is inherent in its legislative functions, and is implied under the Necessary and Proper Clause. (*See* discussion *supra*, §180.) Thus, a legislative body may compel the attendance of witnesses, order that they answer questions, and punish as a contempt any refusal by a witness to appear or testify (*see supra*, §182).

b. **Limitations [§849]**

There are important limitations on the power of a legislative investigating committee to compel a witness appearing before it to answer questions:

(1) Due process [§850]

If a witness is cited for contempt for refusing to answer a question, due process requires that the person be given fair notice of the prohibited conduct. Thus, the *nature of the legislative inquiry* and the *pertinency of the question* must be made clear to the witness, or the contempt conviction cannot stand. [**Watkins v. United States,** 354 U.S. 178 (1957)]

(2) First Amendment [§851]

Regardless of pertinency, a legislative investigating committee cannot abridge First Amendment rights that protect the privacy of one's views or associations.

(a) Requirement of overriding legislative interest [§852]

Therefore, a legislative committee may require disclosure of an individual's political beliefs or associations only upon the showing of a valid legislative interest in the information sought that is so *compelling* that it *outweighs* the individual's right to privacy in his associations. [**Gibson v. Florida Legislative Investigation Committee,** 372 U.S. 539 (1963)]

Example: In **Barenblatt v. United States,** 360 U.S. 109 (1960), the witness refused to answer questions about past or present Communist Party membership. His conviction was upheld because the strong government interest in Communist infiltration of education (the matter being investigated) outweighed the relatively slight deterrence on freedom of association resulting from disclosure.

---

1) Note

The First Amendment, unlike the Fifth Amendment privilege against self-incrimination, does not specifically protect the right of silence. Congress may inquire beyond the specific elements of what may be made criminal. And while exposure cannot be required simply for the sake of exposure, the Court will generally not question congressional motives in making the inquiry when it appears that Congress is pursuing a valid legislative goal.

(b) "Nexus" requirement [§853]

To establish an overriding legislative interest in the information sought, a *substantial connection* ("nexus") between the information sought and the subject matter of the legislative inquiry must be shown. Without this, disclosure cannot be compelled. [**Gibson v. Florida Legislative Investigation Committee,** *supra*]

> **Example:** In the *Gibson* case, the Court reversed a contempt conviction for a witness's refusal to disclose to a state legislative committee the names of members of local chapters of the NAACP. The committee was investigating local Communist activities (a valid legislative interest) and sought to determine whether certain named Communists were NAACP members. However, there was no "nexus" between the local NAACP and Communist activities where the evidence showed only that a few Communists were NAACP members. The *Barenblatt* case was distinguished: It involved inquiry about membership in an *unlawful* group (Communist Party), whereas the NAACP was a *lawful* group.

4. Civil Penalties for Unprotected Association (or Advocacy) [§854]

Government may also impose civil penalties (*e.g.*, denial of governmental benefits, such as tax exemptions) on those who engage in constitutionally unprotected association (or speech).

a. Burden of proof [§855]

If the civil disability is imposed to *penalize* (*i.e.*, to punish or deter) the association (or speech), rather than to serve some important government interest (below), the government has the burden of showing that the individual has engaged in unprotected association (or advocacy). [**Speiser v. Randall,** 357 U.S. 513 (1958)]

b. Overriding government interest [§856]

Some civil disabilities (*e.g.*, denial of certain kinds of public employment, or of licenses to practice certain professions) may not be "penalties." Rather, they may be imposed only to satisfy an independent state interest, such as assuring that public employees loyally and faithfully carry out their duties. The Court has not held that the government must bear the burden of persuasion in connection with imposition of these disabilities.

c. Liability of organization [§857]

Organizations may be held responsible (*e.g.*, for damages) for acts of their representatives only if undertaken within the scope of actual or apparent authority, or if specifically ratified. [**NAACP v. Claiborne Hardware Co.,** *supra*, §838]

5. Restrictions on Public Employment, Licensed Professions, and Other Public Benefits [§858]

Federal and state government may prohibit certain types of persons (*e.g.*, the disloyal or dishonest) from being public employees, lawyers, government contractors, or the like. To this end, it may (i) impose certain *standards* concerning past or future conduct; (ii) require *oaths* in respect to conduct; and (iii) require certain *disclosures* concerning past or present conduct.

a. **Standards of conduct and loyalty oaths**

(1) **Support of the Constitution [§859]**

The government *may* require an oath from public employees and lawyers to "support the Constitution of the United States" and the state constitution. This type of oath does not relate to political beliefs or protected First Amendment rights. [**Connell v. Higginbotham,** 403 U.S. 207 (1971); **Law Students Civil Rights Research Council v. Wadmond,** 401 U.S. 154 (1971)]

(2) **Vagueness [§860]**

Neither standards of conduct requirements, nor loyalty oaths with respect to conduct, may be vague. If First Amendment rights may be affected, precision is required because of the potential "chilling effect." (*See supra*, §584.)

Example: A loyalty oath for public employees that they "promote respect for the flag and . . . reverence for law and order" is void for vagueness, since a refusal to salute the flag on religious grounds might be found in breach of the oath and such a refusal is protected by the First Amendment. [**Baggett v. Bullitt,** 377 U.S. 360 (1964)]

Example: A statute providing for removal of public school teachers for "treasonable or seditious" utterances or acts is void for vagueness; "it would be a bold teacher who would not stay as far as possible from utterances or acts which might jeopardize his living." [**Keyishian v. Board of Regents,** 385 U.S. 589 (1967)]

Compare: An oath required of all state employees "to *oppose the overthrow* of the government . . . by *force, violence or* by an *illegal* or unconstitutional method" has been upheld. The Court read this oath as akin to those requiring the taker simply to "support" the Constitution, *i.e.,* "to commit themselves to live by the constitutional processes of our system." Moreover, the oath provided fair notice, because its violation could be punished only by a prosecution for perjury (which required proof of knowing falsity). [**Cole v. Richardson,** 405 U.S. 676 (1972)]

(3) **Substantive content [§861]**

As a *general rule*, the government may not restrict public employment, licensed professions, or other public benefits for specific speech or association unless the speech or association is *not* constitutionally protected and *could be made criminal.* [**Bond v. Floyd,** 385 U.S. 116 (1966)— state legislature could not exclude duly elected legislator for expressing unpopular political views] Nor may the government require loyalty oaths that public employees or licensees will not engage in such types of speech or association. [**Elfbrandt v. Russell,** *supra*, §844]

The validity of loyalty oaths has been litigated with some frequency and is often tested on law school exams. Be sure to remember the basic rule—the government may require a potential employee to *"uphold the Constitution"* or to *"oppose the overthrow of the government through illegal means."* But a loyalty oath that goes any further (*e.g.,* to "support democracy") will *not* be permitted.

(a) Government employees

1) Membership in groups [§862]

Public employment cannot be denied to persons who are simply *members* of the Communist Party, or who refuse to take an oath that they are not *members* of a "communist front or subversive organization." Such regulations are "overbroad" because only "knowing" membership with "specific intent to further unlawful aims" is not constitutionally protected. [**Keyishian v. Board of Regents**, *supra*; **Wieman v. Updegraff**, 344 U.S. 183 (1955)]

Example: A statute denying *all* employment in a defense facility to *any* member of a "communist-action organization" was held invalid. The Court held that the statute was "overbroad" in two ways: (i) it applied to members who might be *unaware* of the organization's aims or who were without *specific intent to* further those aims; and (ii) it applied even to *nonsensitive* positions in defense facilities. [**United States v. Robel**, 389 U.S. 258 (1967)] There is thus the *possible suggestion* that, if a *sensitive* position were involved, the government's strong interest in national security might permit denial of employment to a knowing member who had no specific intent— even though such membership could not be criminally punished.

Keep an eye out for exam questions testing on the government's right to fire a person based on the person's membership in an organization. The standard is the same as the standard the courts use to determine whether a person may be prosecuted for being a member of the organization—the organization must engage in advocacy or activities that are not constitutionally protected (*see supra*, §§600-606) and the person must *know* of the organization's aims and have the *specific intent to achieve those illegal aims*.

2) Compulsory unionism [§863]

A government employee cannot be compelled (*e.g.*, by threat of loss of employment) to pay union dues that go to *support political or ideological ideas and beliefs* with which the employee disagrees.

a) Exclusive bargaining agent [§864]

If a majority of government employees in an appropriate bargaining unit elect an exclusive representative, the public employer may negotiate exclusively with that representative on matters of collective bargaining, contract administration, and adjustment of grievances. And nonunion members of the bargaining unit may be required to pay the representative union a service fee for reasonable expenses connected with labor-management issues—*e.g.*, cost of union's national convention. *Rationale:* This is justified by the important contribution to peaceful labor relations made by exclusive bargaining agents. [**Abood v. Detroit Board of Education,** *supra*, §566; **Ellis v. Brotherhood of Railway, Airline & Steamship Clerks,** 466 U.S. 435 (1984)]

b) Procedural safeguards [§865]

Since nonunion employees' First Amendment rights of freedom of speech and association are at stake, procedural safeguards are necessary to assure that the service fee is not excessive—*i.e.*, that the employees' funds will not be used for political or ideological activities unrelated to collective bargaining. Thus, although the employee may have the burden of objecting, the union must provide an adequate explanation of the propriety of the fee and has the burden of proving that it was not excessive. Furthermore, the procedure must provide for a reasonably prompt decision by an impartial decisionmaker and an escrow for the amount reasonably in dispute while a challenge is pending. [**Chicago Teachers Union v. Hudson,** 475 U.S. 292 (1986)]

3) "Patronage" [§866]

The First Amendment forbids the hiring, promotion, transfer, firing, or recall of a public employee because of political party affiliation unless the hiring authority demonstrates that party affiliation is an appropriate requirement for the effective performance of the public office involved, *e.g.*, "policymaking" or "confidential" nature of work. [**Rutan v. Republican Party of Illinois,** 497 U.S. 62 (1990); **Branti v. Finkel,** 445 U.S. 507 (1980); **Elrod v. Burns,** 427 U.S. 347 (1976)]

Example: Supervision of a state's election laws may be based on party affiliation if the state requires such supervision by persons of different political parties.

Example: Appointees of a governor who are used to write speeches, explain views to the press, or communicate to the legislature may properly be required to share the political beliefs and party commitments of the governor.

Compare: Continued employment of an assistant public defender cannot be properly conditioned on allegiance to the political party in control of the county government, since whatever policymaking occurs in a public defender's office must relate to the needs of its clients, not to partisan political interests. [**Branti v. Finkel,** *supra*]

4) Expression of views [§867]

A government employer may restrict speech of public employees on a "matter of public concern" only when, *on balance,* the public employee's right *as a citizen* to comment on issues of public interest are outweighed by the government's significant interest as an employer in efficient performance of public service. [**Pickering v. Board of Education,** 391 U.S. 563 (1968)]

a) Job related speech [§868]

In contrast, a government employer has no special burden of justification in restricting speech of public employees that concerns nothing more than their employment conditions, their personal status in the workplace, or other "internal office affairs." [**Connick v. Myers,** 461 U.S. 138 (1983)—upholding firing of employee for distributing a questionnaire to fellow employees asking about confidence in superiors and similar matters]

b) Independent contractors [§869]

The principles in **Pickering v. Board of Education,** *supra,* with respect to speech on matters of public concern, and **Elrod v. Burns** and **Branti v. Finkel,** *supra,* with respect to political party affiliation—adjusted to weigh the government's interest as a contractor rather than as an employer—apply to retaliatory *termination* or *nonrenewal* of existing commercial relationships with independent contractors working on government projects. [**Board of County Commissioners v. Umbehr,** 518 U.S. 668 (1996); **O'Hare Truck Service Inc. v. City of Northlake,** 518 U.S. 712]

c) Procedural requirements [§870]

The public employer must conduct a *reasonable* investigation to determine whether the employee's speech was on a "matter of public concern" or, if it was, whether it was outweighed by the government's interest in accomplishing its mission as an employer. [**Waters v. Churchill,** 511 U.S. 661 (1994)]

5) Political activities [§871]

The government may place *some* limits on a public employee's right to engage in political activities. In contrast to the regulation of *specific* kinds of speech and association (*see infra,* §§879 *et seq.*), the Court has upheld the Hatch Act provision barring federal executive branch employees from all "partisan political activity" in respect to "political management" and "political campaigning," *irrespective of political party* (*i.e.,* "in an evenhanded and neutral manner"). [**Broadrick v. Oklahoma,** *supra,* §584] While such activity clearly could not be made criminal, it could be made a condition of federal employment because of the overriding government interest in *efficient, nonpartisan* employees and in protecting employees from being forced to work for the election of their superiors.

6) Ban on honoraria [§872]

The government may not forbid *all* government employees (specifically, lower echelon executive branch employees) from receiving compensation for speeches, appearances, or articles—even when these expressive actions have no nexus to their employment and thus could not pose the danger (or appearance) of (i) improper influence by the payor or (ii) improper use by the employee of knowledge or resources acquired in the course of the government employment. [**United States v. National Treasury Employees Union,** 513 U.S. 454 (1995)] This ban on honoraria was especially vulnerable under the First Amendment because it burdened only speech and not other off-duty activities that may pose the same dangers of misuse of public employment, and because it applied to a broad category of expression by a massive number of potential speakers.

(b) Integrated bar [§873]

Compulsory state bar membership presents issues similar to compulsory unionism (*supra,* §863). Lawyers may be required to pay state bar dues for reasonable costs connected with improving legal services and regulating the legal profession (*e.g.,* disciplining lawyers). However, mandatory dues may not be used for political or ideological activities (*e.g.*, endorsing a gun control or nuclear freeze initiative). [**Keller v. State Bar of California**, 496 U.S. 1 (1990)]

(c) Mandatory advertising fees [§874]

If the government adopts a comprehensive regulatory scheme with respect to a business or industry, and as part of the scheme members of the business or industry are forced to pay a fee to pay for advertising of the business or industry, the Court will treat the regulation as a regular business regulation and the fee will be upheld as long as it is rationally related to a legitimate government purpose. No special First Amendment scrutiny is warranted if the subsidized speech neither conflicts with the businesses' political or ideological views nor promotes any specific message with which they disagree. [**Glickman v. Wileman Brothers & Elliott, Inc.**, 521 U.S. 2130 (1997)—upholding law that, among other things, required California peach, plum, and nectarine growers to share in costs of generic advertising for those fruits; *and see supra*, §463] However, if the *main purpose* of the government's program is to fund advertising, more exacting First Amendment standards will apply and industry members who object to paying the fee generally must be exempted. [**United States v. United Foods, Inc.**, 533 U.S. 405 (2001)—requiring mushroom handlers to pay assessments for advertising *violate* the First Amendment when the government's only purpose is to require individuals to pay subsidies for speech to which they object]

(d) State university students [§875]

A student may not be expelled from a public university for "indecent" speech, as long as it was not constitutionally obscene (*see supra*, §§632 *et seq.*) or otherwise unprotected. [**Papish v. Board of Curators**, 410 U.S. 667 (1973)]

1) Mandatory student fees [§876]

A student may be required to pay a student fee to attend a public university even if the fee is used to support political and ideological speech by student groups whose beliefs are offensive to the student, as long as the program is *viewpoint neutral*. Such a program facilitates free and open exchange of ideas by students. [**Board of Regents v. Southworth**, 529 U.S. 217 (2000)]

(e) Ballot position [§877]

A political party may not be denied a place on the ballot for refusing to take a loyalty oath that it does not advocate violent overthrow of the government as an *abstract doctrine* (*see supra*, §852). [**Communist Party of Indiana v. Whitcomb**, *supra*, §601]

(f) Procedural rules [§878]

When the complainant shows that her speech or association was constitutionally protected and that it was a "substantial factor" in her being denied the benefit in question, the denial may still be upheld if the government shows by a preponderance of the evidence that it would have taken the same action regardless of the protected conduct. [**Mount Healthy Board of Education v. Doyle,** 429 U.S. 274 (1977)]

b. Disclosure [§879]

As mentioned previously (*see supra*, §§845, 847), government requirements that disclosure be made of beliefs or associational memberships present issues under both the First Amendment freedom of association and the Fifth Amendment privilege against self-incrimination.

(1) Freedom of association [§880]

The government may require disclosure of *certain* past or present organizational affiliations that are relevant to loyalty, fitness, and suitability for the position of public employees, lawyers, and recipients of other public benefits. [**Garner v. Los Angeles Board of Public Works,** 341 U.S. 716 (1951)]

(a) Overbroad inquiries [§881]

Requiring disclosure of First Amendment activities may have a "chilling effect" (*see supra*, §584). Persons may be deterred from engaging in constitutionally protected activity for fear of displeasing those who control their professional livelihood, or for fear of public disclosure and consequent social obloquy. Thus, such inquiries—even though relevant to a proper state interest—may not be "overbroad." [**Shelton v. Tucker,** 364 U.S. 479 (1960)—state cannot force every teacher to disclose *every* organizational membership; state has "less drastic means" available to achieve its purpose]

(b) Obstructing investigation [§882]

The government may deny public employment, bar membership, or other public benefits for obstructing a proper investigation by *refusing to answer relevant inquiries*—even though the required disclosures touch on First Amendment activities. [**Konigsberg v. State Bar,** 366 U.S. 36 (1961); *In re* **Anastaplo,** 366 U.S. 82 (1961)—bar admission denied for refusal to answer questions on First Amendment grounds regarding Communist Party membership, even though such membership (absent knowledge and specific intent) could not be made a substantive ground for denial of bar admission]

1) Impermissible questions [§883]

More recent decisions appear to have qualified *Konigsberg*

and *Anastaplo* (at least as to their facts). The Court has held that the First Amendment forbids a state to require bar applicants (or public employees) to disclose (i) whether they were *merely members* in organizations that advocate violent or forceful overthrow of the government, or (ii) whether they *merely believe* in such action. Although there was no majority opinion, the decisions appear to hold that such inquiry must be confined to *knowing* membership, and that a state may not act against any person "merely because of his beliefs." (In these cases, the record was "wholly barren" of evidence that the applicants were not "morally and professionally fit" to become members of the bar.) [**Baird v. State Bar,** 401 U.S. 1 (1971); *In re* **Stolar,** 401 U.S. 23 (1971)]

2) Permissible questions [§884]

At the same time, the Court has made clear that a state may require bar applicants (and public employees) to disclose (i) whether they had ever organized or become a member of a group with *knowledge* that the group advocated or taught violent or unlawful overthrow of the government, *and* (ii) whether they had the *specific intent* to further such aims of the group. *Rationale:* Dividing the questions in this way is permissible because it "narrows the class of applicants as to whom the Committee is likely to find further investigation appropriate." [**Law Students Civil Rights Research Council v. Wadmond,** *supra*, §859]

a) Effect

While *both* knowledge and specific intent are clearly necessary to deny bar admission (or public employment), *refusal to disclose either* may be proper grounds for denial.

(2) Privilege against self-incrimination [§885]

Denial of public employment, bar membership, or other public benefits simply because an individual refuses to answer questions on a claim of the privilege against self-incrimination violates the Fifth Amendment. [**Spevack v. Klein,** 385 U.S. 511 (1967)] For further discussion, *see* the Evidence Summary.

L. Freedom of Press—Special Problems

1. In General [§886]

As a general matter, the press's First Amendment rights are no greater than the First Amendment freedom of speech afforded to other members of the public.

There is a common misconception (especially among members of the media) that the press has greater First Amendment protection than the general public. On your exam, if a member of the press claims that some action or inaction (e.g., refusal to disclose a source to a grand jury) is protected by the First Amendment, ask yourself whether **you** would have a First Amendment right in the same situation. If not, chances are that the member of the press doesn't have a First Amendment right under the circumstances either.

2. No "News Reporter's Privilege" [§887]

Freedom of the press does not afford reporters a privilege to refuse to answer relevant and material questions asked during a *good faith* grand jury investigation. In such proceedings, the reporters may be forced to disclose their sources and other information within their possession. However, "official harassment of the press undertaken not for purpose of law enforcement but to disrupt a reporter's relationship with news sources would have no justification." [**Branzburg v. Hayes**, 408 U.S. 665 (1972)]

3. Access to Government Information [§888]

There is no First Amendment right to obtain information in the government's possession. [**Los Angeles Police Department v. United Reporting Publishing Corp.**, 528 U.S. 32 (2000)—no right to obtain addresses of recently arrested persons]

a. Access to prisoners and prisons [§889]

Similarly, the First Amendment guarantees neither the public nor the press access to prisoners or prisons (or to other information controlled by government). [**Houchins v. KQED**, 438 U.S. 1 (1978)—no majority opinion] Thus, prison rules that forbid interviews with inmates designated by media members do not violate freedom of the press. [**Pell v. Procunier**, *supra*, §824] However, if the government voluntarily grants such access, then the public and the press must be treated equally. And where limitations that might be reasonable as to individual members of the public would impede effective reporting (*e.g.*, prohibition on cameras), such limitations may not—consistent with reasonable prison rules—be used to hamper effective media presentation of what is seen by individual visitors. [**Houchins v. KQED**, *supra*]

b. Access to criminal proceedings [§890]

The press may be excluded from some kinds of pretrial hearings (such as a hearing to suppress illegally seized evidence) if there are no reasonable alternatives to protect the defendant's right to a fair trial (which could be jeopardized if the press were present at the pretrial hearings and reported prejudicial evidence that would be inadmissible at the subsequent criminal trial). [**Gannett Co. v. DePasquale**, 443 U.S. 368 (1979)] However, the First Amendment guarantees the public *and* press a right to attend criminal (and *probably* civil) trials. But the right may be outweighed by a compelling and narrowly tailored interest articulated in findings by the trial judge. [**Richmond Newspapers, Inc. v. Virginia**, 448 U.S. 555 (1980)— no majority opinion]

e.g. **Example:** A state may not *automatically* exclude the press and public during the testimony of a minor victim in a sex-offense prosecution. Rather, there must be particularized, case-by-case determinations of the need for exclusion. [**Globe Newspaper Co. v. Superior Court,** 457 U.S. 596 (1982)]

(1) Preliminary hearings [§891]

The First Amendment right extends to elaborate preliminary hearings (which resemble an actual criminal trial) to determine whether probable cause exists to bring the defendant to trial. Such hearings often lead to guilty pleas and may be the sole occasion for public observation of the criminal justice system. [**Press-Enterprise Co. v. Superior Court,** 478 U.S. 1 (1986)]

(2) Voir dire [§892]

The First Amendment right also extends to the voir dire examination of potential jurors. [**Press-Enterprise Co. v. Superior Court,** 464 U.S. 501 (1984)—one method for trial judge to protect privacy interests of prospective jurors is to inform them that they may request questioning in camera]

(3) Defendant's right to public trial [§893]

The Sixth Amendment right of the defendant is discussed *infra,* §§1318 *et seq.*

c. Publication of truthful information [§894]

Publication of truthful information, which has been *lawfully obtained* by the media, concerning a matter of public significance may be prohibited only by a sanction that is "narrowly tailored" to further a state interest of the highest order. [**Smith v. Daily Mail Publishing Co.,** 443 U.S. 97 (1979)—making it a crime to publish name of juvenile delinquent was held invalid; **Landmark Communications, Inc. v. Virginia,** *supra,* §785—making it a crime to publish information lawfully obtained regarding confidential state proceedings was held invalid; **Cox Broadcasting Corp. v. Cohn,** *supra,* §82—awarding damages for publishing name of rape victim obtained in official court records open to public inspection also held invalid; **Florida Star v. B.J.F.,** 491 U.S. 524 (1989)—same result when name was obtained from police report that inadvertently included full name of rape victim]

(1) Unlawfully obtained information [§895]

The same rule—that publication of a matter of public concern may be prohibited only by a sanction that is narrowly tailored to further a state interest of the highest order—applies even when the information has been unlawfully obtained in the first instance, as long as the speech (i) relates to a matter of public concern, (ii) the publisher did not obtain it unlawfully nor knew who did, and (iii) the original speaker's legitimate privacy expectations are low. [**Bartnicki v. Vopper**, 532 U.S. 514 (2001)]

---

e.g. **Example:** During heated collective bargaining negotiations between a teachers' union and a school board, an unknown person intercepted a cell phone call between a union negotiator and the union's president. The tape was forwarded to a radio commentator, who played it on the radio. The commentator was sued for damages under civil liability provisions of state and federal wiretap laws that prohibited intentional disclosure of the contents of an electronically transmitted conversation when one has reason to know that the conversation was intercepted unlawfully. The Supreme Court held that the statute violated the First Amendment as applied under these circumstances. [**Bartnicki v. Vopper**, *supra*]

---

(2) **Distinguish—publication of private performance [§896]**

The First Amendment does not immunize the media from an action for damages when a performer's entire act (for which compensation is usually paid) is published or broadcast without the performer's consent. This is the functional equivalent of broadcasting copyrighted material or a sporting event. [**Zacchini v. Scripps-Howard Broadcasting Co.**, 433 U.S. 562 (1977)—human cannonball act filmed and played on the air]

(3) **Distinguish—breach of promise of confidentiality [§897]**

Similarly, the First Amendment does not immunize the media from a generally applicable law that provides for an award of damages against persons who breach a promise of confidentiality given in exchange for information. [**Cohen v. Cowles Media Co.**, 501 U.S. 663 (1991)—any restriction placed on newspaper's ability to publish truthful information was self-imposed by newspaper's promise of confidentiality]

4. **Search of Newspaper Office [§898]**

If there is reason to believe that there is evidence of a crime on the premises of a newspaper, the First Amendment does not forbid the issuance of a search warrant. However, courts must apply the warrant requirements—reasonableness, probable cause, and specificity with respect to the place to be searched and things to be seized—with "particular exactitude" to protect First Amendment interests. [**Zurcher v. Stanford Daily**, 436 U.S. 547 (1978)]

5. **Broadcasting [§899]**

Although radio and television broadcasting fall within the ambit of the First Amendment [**Los Angeles v. Preferred Communications, Inc.**, 476 U.S. 488 (1986)], they may be more closely regulated than the press. *Rationale:* Due to the limited number of frequencies available, broadcasters have a special privilege, and consequently, a special responsibility to give suitable time to matters of public interest and to present a suitable range of programs. The paramount right is the *right of viewers and listeners* to receive information of public concern, rather than the right of broadcasters to broadcast what they please. [**Red Lion Broadcasting Co. v. FCC,** 395 U.S. 367 (1969)]

a. Right to reply [§900]

The Court has upheld FCC orders, under a statutory "fairness doctrine," requiring a radio station to offer *free* broadcasting time (i) to *opponents* of political candidates or views endorsed by the station; and (ii) to any person who has been *personally attacked* in the course of a broadcast, for reply to the attack. [**Red Lion Broadcasting Co. v. FCC,** *supra*] And under a statutory right of access, the FCC may require licensed broadcasters to sell reasonable amounts of time to legally qualified candidates for federal office. [**CBS v. FCC,** 453 U.S. 367 (1981)]

(1) Distinguish—newspapers [§901]

A statute requiring a *newspaper* to print a reply to its editorials by political candidates criticized in such editorials violates the First Amendment. The government *cannot* dictate decisions respecting the content and size of newspapers or require them to disseminate messages with which they disagree. [**Miami Herald Publishing Co. v. Tornillo,** 418 U.S. 241 (1974)]

b. Political campaign advertising [§902]

The First Amendment does *not* require broadcasters to accept political advertisements. Congress and the FCC, in seeking to assure balanced coverage of public issues, could appropriately conclude that licensed broadcasters subject to the "fairness doctrine" should generally determine what should be broadcast, rather than having affluent persons monopolize air time. [**CBS, Inc. v. Democratic National Committee,** 412 U.S. 94 (1973)]

c. Editorializing by noncommercial broadcasters [§903]

The First Amendment is violated by a congressional ban on editorials by noncommercial educational broadcasters. (And the government may not impose such a ban on those broadcasters who receive government subsidies.) The expression of editorial opinion on controversial issues of public importance lies at the heart of the First Amendment. The public's interest in receiving a "reasonably balanced and fair presentation of controversial issues" may be insured by the "fairness doctrine." [**FCC v. League of Women Voters,** 468 U.S. 364 (1984)]

d. Common ownership [§904]

Similarly, to promote the diversity of information received by the public, the FCC may forbid ownership of a radio or television station by a daily newspaper located in the same community. [**FCC v. National Citizens Committee for Broadcasting,** 436 U.S. 775 (1978)]

e. **Indecent speech [§905]**

Because a broadcast has the ability to invade the privacy of the home, the First Amendment does not forbid imposing civil sanctions on a broadcaster for airing a full monologue (in contrast to isolated use of a few words) of "patently offensive sexual and excretory speech" even though the speech is not obscene—at least during those times when children are likely to be listening. [**FCC v. Pacifica Foundation**, 438 U.S. 726 (1978)—station aired George Carlin's comedy monologue entitled "Filthy Words"; *compare supra*, §637]

(1) Cable channels [§906]

For similar reasons, the First Amendment is not violated by a law that *permits* cable operators to forbid "patently offensive" sex-related materials on channels that the law requires them to lease to third parties. [**Denver Area Educational Telecommunications Consortium Inc. v. FCC**, 518 U.S. 727 (1996)—law is "sufficiently tailored" response to "compelling" interest in protecting children]

(a) Distinguish

But a law that permits cable operators to forbid such materials on "public access" channels is invalid. Since the cable operators agree with municipalities to reserve these public, governmental, and educational channels in exchange for the award of cable franchises, the cable operator's First Amendment interest in control is very weak. Furthermore, locally accountable bodies that normally supervise these channels make it likely that children will be protected. [**Denver Area Educational Telecommunications Consortium Inc. v. FCC**, *supra*]

(b) And note

Similarly a law that requires cable operators to segregate all sex-related materials on a blocked and separate channel, which may be unblocked only on written request of subscribers, is not narrowly or reasonably tailored and thus is invalid. [**Denver Area Educational Telecommunications Consortium Inc. v. FCC**, *supra*—less restrictive alternatives include honoring subscriber's request to block *by phone*, or a "lock-box" controlled by parents]

6. **Taxation [§907]**

The First Amendment does not prohibit application to the press of regulations and taxes of general applicability. But a special tax that applies only to the press (or that targets only some types of publications) can operate to censor criticism of government and is invalid unless necessary to a compelling interest. Furthermore, in this area (*compare supra*, §§351-356), the Court will *not* examine the state's whole tax structure to determine whether the special tax is just a substitute for another tax that applies generally except to the press. [**Minneapolis Star & Tribune Co. v. Minnesota Commissioner of Revenue**, 460 U.S. 575 (1983); **Arkansas Writers' Project v. Ragland**, 481 U.S. 221 (1987)]

a. **Intermedia discrimination [§908]**

A tax of general applicability may impose different burdens on certain segments of the media as long as the discrimination (i) is not content-based, and (ii) is not structured or intended to suppress particular ideas. [**Leathers v. Medlock,** 499 U.S. 439 (1991)—general sales tax that exempted all media except cable TV upheld]

   (1) Regulation [§909]

   A similar rule governs regulations that apply to one medium (or a subset of one medium) but not to others. [**Turner Broadcasting System v. FCC,** *supra*, §582—regulation of cable television justified by "special characteristics" of that medium]

7. **Cable Television [§910]**

While generally regulations of newspapers are subject to strict scrutiny, and regulations of the broadcast media are subject to less critical review, regulations of cable television transmissions are subject to review by a standard somewhere between these two. [**Turner Broadcasting System, Inc. v. FCC,** *supra*, §583] *Rationale:* The physical connection to a viewer's television set makes the cable subscriber a more captive audience than a newspaper reader and distinguishes cable from newspapers, which cannot prevent access to competing newspapers. On the other hand, unlike broadcast media, which are limited to a small number of frequencies (*see supra*, §899), there is no practical limitation on the number of cable channels; thus, the government's interest in protecting viewers' rights is weaker with regard to cable. [**Turner Broadcasting System v. FCC,** *supra*]

a. **"Must carry" provision [§911]**

A law requiring cable operators to carry local stations is subject to "intermediate scrutiny": Content-neutral regulations are valid if they do not burden substantially *more* speech than *necessary* to advance *important* government interests unrelated to suppression of speech. [**Turner Broadcasting System, Inc. v. FCC,** *supra*—"must carry" provisions directly serve important interest of preserving economic viability of local broadcasters, thus promoting dissemination of information to noncable viewers]

   (1) Courts must respect Congress's reasonable determinations [§912]

   Similar to the Court's approach to "time, place, and manner" regulations (*supra*, §753), a court must respect Congress's conclusions regarding the harm to be avoided and the need for the remedies enacted if Congress has drawn *reasonable inferences* based on *substantial evidence*. [**Turner Broadcasting System, Inc. v. FCC,** *supra*]

b. **Distinguish—content-based regulation [§913]**

A content-based cable regulation will be upheld only if it passes muster under the strict scrutiny test. [**United States v. Playboy Entertainment Group, Inc.,** 529 U.S. 803 (2000)—a law that requires cable operators to limit "sexually oriented" programs to after 10 p.m. was held invalid because of the less restrictive alternative of enabling each household to block undesired channels]

8. **Cyberspace [§914]**

The First Amendment strict scrutiny standard applies to the Internet. *Rationale:* In contrast to broadcasting, there is (i) no history of extensive government regulation of the Internet, (ii) no scarcity of available frequencies, and (iii) no likelihood that the Internet will unexpectedly invade the privacy of the home (*see supra,* §905). [**Reno v. American Civil Liberties Union,** *supra,* §637]

Chapter Six:
Freedom of Religion

CONTENTS

251

Chapter Approach

The First Amendment forbids the federal government from making laws that establish religion or prohibit the free exercise of religion. These prohibitions likewise apply to the states through the Fourteenth Amendment. Consider freedom of religion questions in terms of both the Establishment and Free Exercise Clauses.

1. **Establishment Clause**

   To be valid under the Establishment Clause, government action must: (i) have a *secular purpose;* (ii) have a principal effect that *neither advances nor inhibits religion*; and (iii) *not foster excessive government entanglement* with religion. The Court also considers whether the challenged government action has the purpose or effect of "endorsing" religion. Review the cases to familiarize yourself with permissible government "involvement" with religion (*e.g.*, providing secular textbooks or health services to parochial school students is valid, but "voluntary" prayer in the schools is not).

2. **Free Exercise Clause**

   The Free Exercise Clause invalidates government action that singles out religion for adverse treatment or hinders a particular religion. Remember that a statute interfering with *religious beliefs will always violate* the Clause, but one dealing with religious *conduct* will *rarely* be invalidated. If the government action burdening religious conduct is *neutral* and *applies to others* who engage in the conduct for nonreligious reasons, it will be *upheld* despite the burden on religion. The only exceptions involve constitutional protections besides the Free Exercise Clause (*e.g.*, the right of the Amish to educate their children, free speech, or due process concerning unemployment compensation). Finally, keep in mind that the truth of a person's beliefs is never susceptible to judicial inquiry, but sincerity of beliefs is.

A. Introduction

1. **Constitutional Provisions [§915]**

   The principal provisions of the Constitution that deal with the subject of freedom of religion are the "religion clauses" of the First Amendment, which provide: "Congress shall make no law respecting an *establishment* of religion, or prohibiting the *free exercise* thereof." (In addition, Article VI provides that "no religious test shall ever be required as a qualification to any office or public trust under the United States.")

CONSTITUTIONAL PROTECTION OF RELIGION— A COMPARISON		**gilbert**
	ESTABLISHMENT CLAUSE	**FREE EXERCISE CLAUSE**
PURPOSE	To bar government sponsorship or endorsement of religion, government financial support of religion, and active government involvement in religious activities.	To bar government from singling out religion for adverse treatment and to bar government from hindering a particular religion.
TEST	To be valid a statute or government action must:	To be valid a statute or government action must:
	(i) Have a *secular purpose*;	(i) *Not compel* anyone to adopt a particular belief; or
	(ii) Have a principal *effect that neither advances nor inhibits* religion; and	(ii) *Not specifically target* religious conduct (action or inaction).
	(iii) *Not foster excessive government entanglement* with religion.	*Note:* Usually government action regulating *general conduct* is valid—even if it interferes with religious conduct and even if there is no exception for religious conduct.

2. **Application to States [§916]**

   Both the Establishment Clause and the Free Exercise Clause of the First Amendment protect fundamental personal liberties and apply to the states under the Fourteenth Amendment. [**Everson v. Board of Education**, *supra*, §57; **Cantwell v. Connecticut**, 310 U.S. 296 (1940)]

B. Establishment Clause

1. **Goal—Benevolent Neutrality [§917]**

   The Establishment Clause does more than forbid a state church or a state religion—but it does not forbid every action by government that results in a benefit to religion. The goal is a "benevolent neutrality" by the government in respect to religion. [**Walz v. Tax Commission**, 397 U.S. 664 (1970)]

2. **Main Concerns of Establishment Clause [§918]**

   As a general matter, the Establishment Clause bars government sponsorship of religion, government financial support of religion, and active involvement of government in religious activities. [**Walz v. Tax Commission**, *supra*]

   a. **Preference [§919]**

      The Establishment Clause also bars official preference of one religious denomination over another. Any law that grants a denominational preference is subject t scrutiny, *i.e.,* it will be held unconstitutional unless the government that it is necessary to achieve a compelling interest. [**Larson v. Valente,** .. 228 (1982)]

Example—advantage: The New York state legislature created a special, separate school district and authorized its board of education to open close schools, hire teachers, etc. The board's jurisdiction was limited to Village of Kiryas Joel, which was founded and exclusively inhabited by actitioners of a strict form of Judaism called Satmar Hasidim. The village had been within another school district, but the Satmars sought to avoid assimilation into the modern world and educated their children in private religious schools. The Satmars lobbied for and obtained their own school district so that the state would pay for education of the Satmars' handicapped children without the Satmars having to send them to other public schools where they might be exposed to the modern world. *Held:* A state law that creates a special school district for the purpose of enabling one religious group to provide state-funded education for its handicapped children violates the Establishment Clause. [**Board of Education of Kiryas Joel Village School District v. Grumet,** 512 U.S. 687 (1994)]

Example—disadvantage: A state law that imposes registration requirements only on those religious organizations that get more than half their funds from nonmembers is not "closely fitted" to a "compelling government interest." [**Larson v. Valente,** *supra*]

---

3. **Three-Pronged "Test" [§920]**

If a law (or other government action) impacts on the Establishment Clause but does not involve the preference of one religious denomination over another, the Supreme Court does not judge the validity of the law or act under strict scrutiny. Instead, to be valid the law or action must:

(i) Have a *secular purpose*;

(ii) Have a principal or primary *effect that neither advances nor inhibits* religion; and

(iii) *Not foster excessive government entanglement* with religion.

[**Lemon v. Kurtzman,** 403 U.S. 602 (1971)] In applying this test, the Court also considers whether the challenged government practice has the purpose or effect of "endorsing" religion. [**County of Allegheny v. American Civil Liberties Union Greater Pittsburgh Chapter,** 492 U.S. 573 (1989) Finally, as the difficulty of reconciling a number of the cases discussed below will reveal, "the test is inescapably one of degree." [**Walz v. Tax Commission,** *supra*]

a. Aid to parochial school students [§921]

Some government programs providing assistance to *all* elementary and secondary school students—including those attending parochial schools—have been held to satisfy the three-pronged "test," above, and thus do not violate the Establishment Clause; other seemingly similar assistance programs have been found invalid.

(1) Transportation [§922]

The government may reimburse bus fares to and from school of all students, including those attending parochial schools. The purpose and effect is secular—protecting children from traffic hazards. [**Everson v. Board of Education,** *supra*]

(a) Distinguish—field trips [§923]

But government payment of field trip transportation was held invalid, because the parochial schools control the timing of such trips and the teachers play an integral part in making such educational experiences meaningful. [**Wolman v. Walter,** 433 U.S. 229 (1977)] However, this decision *would appear no longer to be valid* in view of **Zelman v. Simmons-Harris,** 536 U.S. 639 (2002) (*see infra,* §931).

(2) Textbooks [§924]

The government may lend state-approved secular textbooks to all students, including those attending parochial schools. The purpose and effect is to improve secular education. [**Board of Education v. Allen,** 392 U.S. 236 (1968)]

(a) Other instructional materials [§925]

In **Wolman v. Walter,** *supra,* the Court ruled that government could not lend parochial students instructional materials, such as maps, films, lab equipment, etc., because it was impossible to separate their secular uses from their religious uses. However, more recently, the Supreme Court has upheld a program that lends parochial schools similar instructional aids for use by their students. [*See* **Mitchell v. Helms,** 530 U.S. 793 (2000); *and see infra,* §944] Thus, *Wolman* probably no longer is valid.

(3) Health services [§926]

Public health services are religiously neutral and may be provided by government to all students, including those attending parochial schools. [**Lemon v. Kurtzman,** *supra*—also stating that a school lunch program is valid]

(a) Diagnostic services [§927]

Similarly, nonparochial school personnel may provide diagnostic speech, hearing, and psychological services to students on the premises of the parochial school. [**Wolman v. Walter,** *supra*]

(b) Sign-language interpreter [§928]

Government may also provide all deaf students with sign-language interpreters, including those students attending parochial schools. The interpreters neither add to nor subtract from the religious environment of parochial schools. [**Zobrest v. Catalina Foothills School District,** 509 U.S. 1 (1993)]

(4) Remedial, guidance, and job counseling services [§929]

A neutral government program for "auxiliary services" (*e.g.,* remedial education services, guidance services, job counseling, etc.) to *all* disadvantaged children—*including those students attending parochial schools*—with public school personnel providing such things as remedial instruction and guidance counseling, is valid. The presence of public employees in parochial schools does not automatically mean that they will inculcate religion or constitute a symbolic union between religion and government. [**Agostini v. Felton,** 521 U.S. 203 (1997)—*overruling* **Aguilar v. Felton,** 473 U.S. 402 (1985)]

(5) Tuition grants and tax credits [§930]

The Court has upheld a state income tax deduction to *all* taxpayers for expenses of tuition, transportation, textbooks, instructional materials, and other school supplies in public *and* nonpublic schools. The purpose and primary effect of this "facially neutral" law are secular—despite the fact that the great bulk of deductions may be taken only by parents of children in parochial schools. [**Mueller v. Allen,** 463 U.S. 388 (1983)]

(6) Vouchers [§931]

A program that provides tuition aid for students, with a preference for low income families, to attend a participating public or private school of their parents' choice, which had to agree not to discriminate on the basis of race, religion, or ethnic background, or to teach hatred of any person or group on the basis of these criteria, does not violate the Establishment Clause, even though a very high percentage of students who enrolled in private schools chose religiously affiliated ones. The Court emphasized that the tuition program was undertaken to enhance school choice, and it also included opportunities for students to go to "magnet" schools (with special educational emphases) and to "community" schools (publicly funded, but run by their own school boards which were academically independent from the local school districts). The Court reasoned that the fact that the aid eventually advanced the religious mission of the parochial schools and that there might be a perceived endorsement of a religious message did not invalidate the program because *any advancement or endorsement of religion was reasonably attributable to the individual recipients, not to the government.* The program was *neutral* with respect to religion and provided assistance to a broad class of citizens. The directing of aid to religious schools was wholly a result of the recipients' own genuine and independent private choice. Furthermore, the program did not create financial incentives that skewed attendance to religious schools because private schools received only half (or less) the government assistance given to community schools and to magnet schools and to public schools in adjacent school districts that were also eligible. Moreover, families who sent their children to private schools would have to co-pay a portion of the private school tuition. Under these circumstances, no reasonable observer would think that the program carried the imprimatur of government endorsement of religion. [**Zelman v. Simmons-Harris,** *supra,* §923]

CHECKLIST OF APPROVED AID TO PAROCHIAL SCHOOL STUDENTS gilbert

MOST PROGRAMS THAT PROVIDE AID TO PAROCHIAL SCHOOL STUDENTS AS WELL AS PUBLIC SCHOOL AND OTHER SECULAR PRIVATE SCHOOL STUDENTS HAVE BEEN UPHELD, INCLUDING THE FOLLOWING:

☑ Reimbursement of *bus fares* to go to and from school

☑ Lending state-approved *secular textbooks* to students

☑ Providing *health services* to students

☑ Providing *diagnostic speech, hearing, and psychological services* to students

☑ Providing *sign language interpreters* to students

☑ Providing students with *auxiliary services,* such as remedial education, guidance, job counseling, etc.

☑ Granting an *income tax deduction* for school expenses

☑ Giving all poor students *tuition vouchers* to attend an approved public or private school of their choice

b. Direct aid to church-related institutions [§932]

In addition to ruling on programs that provide aid to parochial school students, the Supreme Court has ruled on a number of programs that provide aid directly to religious institutions along with nonreligious institutions. Some programs have been held to satisfy the three-pronged "test" and thus do not violate the Establishment Clause; others have been held to violate the "test" and thus violate the Establishment Clause.

(1) Hospitals [§933]

Federal grants to church-related hospitals for construction of new wards and care of indigent patients have been held to have a secular purpose and effect and are therefore valid. [**Bradfield v. Roberts,** 175 U.S. 291 (1899)]

(2) Colleges and universities [§934]

Government grants (or tax benefits) for construction of buildings to be used exclusively for secular education at church-related colleges have been upheld. [**Tilton v. Richardson,** 403 U.S. 672 (1971); **Roemer v. Board of Public Works,** 426 U.S. 736 (1976)] The program's "purpose" and "effect" were secular (expanding facilities for secular education). Furthermore, since the *record did not show* that the secular education provided by the recipient colleges was "permeated with religion," there was no need for intensive government surveillance, and therefore there was no "excessive government entanglement with religion."

(a) But note

There must be assurance of a secular purpose and effect. Thus, in **Tilton v. Richardson,** *supra,* the Court invalidated a provision limiting the prohibition against religious use of buildings to 20 years, reasoning that the buildings would still have value at that point and their use at that time for religious purposes would have the effect of advancing religion.

(3) Counseling agencies [§935]

Similarly, government funds to religious organizations along with other public and private agencies to counsel against adolescent sexual relations and to care for teenage pregnancies have been upheld. There was a secular purpose (dealing with problems of teenage pregnancy) and the record *did not show*: (i) that a significant percentage of the funds would be granted to "pervasively sectarian" institutions; or (ii) that the religiously affiliated grantees could not perform their functions in a secular manner without intensive government surveillance. [**Bowen v. Kendrick,** 487 U.S. 589 (1988)]

(4) Elementary and secondary schools [§936]

Many government programs providing assistance directly to parochial schools have been held *invalid*—most often because they have been found to involve "excessive government entanglement with religion."

EXAM TIP gilbert

Be sure to remember that historically, the Court has looked more carefully at government programs that provide assistance to religiously affiliated *elementary and secondary schools* than it does with programs that aid other religiously affiliated institutions. In addition to the excessive government entanglement that might result, the Court has often voiced concern that the young students who attend elementary and secondary schools might not understand that the support does not constitute a government endorsement of religion.

(a) Teacher salaries [§937]

Grants for salaries of teachers of secular subjects have been held invalid. Even though they may have a "secular legislative purpose," the state's efforts to assure a "principal or primary effect that neither advances nor inhibits religion" run afoul of the third criterion—"excessive government entanglement." [**Lemon v. Kurtzman,** *supra*, §926]

1) Rationale [§938]

Unlike church-related colleges, elementary and secondary parochial school education involves substantial religious indoctrination—thus risking government support of religion, and requiring continuing surveillance of the schools' teachers and records (to ensure that teachers paid with public funds do not teach religion, and to determine how much of the schools' expenditures are religious rather than secular). While some state contact with the church-related institution may be required to assure a secular purpose and effect, excessive state involvement will invalidate the program.

2) Political divisiveness [§939]

In addition to the excessive government entanglement that can arise from monitoring aid to religious elementary and secondary schools, the Court has considered the excessive entanglement that would arise because of political divisiveness that would result from such a program. Unlike grants to colleges where most of the recipients are not church-related institutions, the teacher salary statutes involved annual appropriations primarily benefiting religious groups—so that "political fragmentation and divisiveness on religious lines was likely to be intensified." [**Committee for Public Education v. Nyquist**, 413 U.S. 756 (1973)]

(b) Maintenance and repair [§940]

Grants for maintaining school facilities have been held invalid. Despite a secular purpose, since there was no limitation on the facilities for which the funds might be used, the aid might have a "primary effect that advanced religion." [**Committee for Public Education v. Nyquist**, *supra*]

(c) Testing [§941]

Reimbursing parochial schools for costs of administering *teacher-prepared tests* (although the testing is required by state law) has been held invalid because such testing is an integral part of the teaching process, and there is no way of assuring that such tests are kept entirely free of religious instruction. [**Levitt v. Committee for Public Education**, 413 U.S. 472 (1973)]

1) Distinguish—state prepared and scored achievement tests [§942]

But the government may supply parochial schools with achievement tests used in public schools, as long as the tests are not prepared or scored by parochial school personnel (*i.e.*, parochial school personnel do not control the content or results). And the government may reimburse the parochial school for the administration and grading of such tests even if the tests are graded by parochial school personnel—as long as objective standards are used and there are ample safeguards, easily applicable, to assure that reimbursement covers only secular services without excessive government entanglement. [**Committee for Public Education v. Regan**, 444 U.S. 646 (1980)]

(d) Recordkeeping [§943]

Reimbursing parochial schools for recordkeeping required by state law is also permissible—if there is a "straightforward" audit procedure to assure that only costs of secular services are covered without excessive government entanglement. [**Committee for Public Education v. Regan**, *supra*]

(e) Instructional material [§944]

Lending religiously neutral instructional materials (*e.g.*, library books, computers), which could not supplant other purchases, to parochial

AID TO CHURCH-RELATED INSTITUTIONS— A SUMMARY OF CASES

gilbert

VALID	INVALID
Government grants to religiously affiliated hospitals for construction of **wards to take care of indigents**	Paying salaries of teachers to teach **secular subjects** in religiously affiliated elementary and secondary schools
Government grants or tax benefits to religiously affiliated colleges and universities for construction of buildings to be used **exclusively for secular education**	Government grants to **maintain the facilities** of religiously affiliated elementary and secondary schools
Government grants to religious organizations in addition to other public and private agencies to **counsel against adolescent sexual relations and to care for pregnant teens**	Reimbursing elementary and secondary parochial schools for the costs of **preparing and administering** state-required tests
Supplying elementary and secondary parochial schools with **state-prepared achievement tests** and reimbursing the parochial schools for administering and grading the tests	
Reimbursing elementary and secondary parochial schools for the **costs of state-required record keeping**	
Lending **auxiliary instructional materials** (*e.g.,* computers, library books) to elementary and secondary parochial schools as well as other schools	

schools (along with public and other nonprofit private schools) is **valid** where the program does not define recipients by reference to religion and the **challenger has not proved** that the neutral aid was used for religious indoctrination. [**Mitchell v. Helms,** *supra,* §925—*overruling* **Meek v. Pittenger,** 421 U.S. 349 (1975)]

(f) Other general government benefits [§945]

The Court has also said that general benefits—such as police protection, fire protection, or general municipal services (*e.g.,* sewage, garbage, etc.)—may also be afforded to church-related institutions. [**Everson v. Board of Education,** *supra,* §916]

c. Tax exemption for religious property [§946]

An exemption from property taxation for "real or personal property used exclusively for *religious, educational or charitable purposes*" does not violate the Establishment Clause. Neither the purpose nor the effect is the advancement or the inhibition of religion; and it constitutes neither personal sponsorship of, nor hostility to, religion. Not to grant the exemption would *increase* church-state entanglement on such issues as valuation of the property, tax liens, etc. Moreover, the exemption "does not transfer . . . revenue to churches"; rather, government "simply abstains from demanding that the church support the state." Finally, the Court noted that there is a long history of providing such an exception and "unbroken practice of according this exemption to churches [cannot] be lightly cast aside." [**Walz v. Tax Commission,** *supra,* §§ ⁓ ⁓]

(1) Preference [§947]

However, a tax exemption that is *limited* ⁓ ⁓ ⁓ ons is too narrow and violates the Establishme⁓ **Inc. v. Bullock,** 489 U.S. 1 (1989)—invalid ⁓ ligious periodicals published or distr⁓

d. Use of public facilities [§948]

The state may permit religious gr⁓ ⁓ are generally open for public use, ev⁓ facilities for "religious worship and disc⁓ establishment Clause because: (i) there is a ⁓ public forum for the exchange of ideas; (ii) if ⁓ ⁓ the public forum, the benefit to religion would be⁓ *primary* effect of advancing religion; and (iii) there wo⁓ *glement* of government and religion if the state sought to ⁓ groups. [**Widmar v. Vincent,** *supra,* §741]

e. Public funds [§949]

If a state university p⁓ ⁓es funds for campus groups to print group newspapers, it cannot deny fur⁓ for a group merely because the group's newspaper will promote a distinctly Christian viewpoint. Providing such funds does not violate the Establishment Clause as long as the program is neutral toward religion in extending benefits to recipients whose ideologies are broad and diverse. [**Rosenberger v. Rector and Visitors of the University of Virginia,** *supra,* §815] The Court distinguished programs making money payments directly to sectarian institutions by noting that here the university made payments directly to the printing companies. One member of the majority also noted that the source of funds for this program was not taxation, but rather fees from students, any of whom might possibly opt out if they objected to funding religious activities.

f. Religion and public schools [§950]

A number of public school practices conducted on *premises* as part of the school's program, whose purpose and effect is to *aid religion*, have been held to violate the Establishment Clause.

(1) Prayers and Bible-reading [§951]

The government may not prescribe any particular form of prayer to be used in schools (or other government-sponsored activities). [**Engel v. Vitale,** 370 U.S. 421 (1962)—invalidating state rule requiring the following prayer composed by a government agency be said aloud in public school classes each day: "Almighty God, we acknowledge our dependence on Thee, and we beg Thy blessings upon us, our parents, our teachers, and our country"] Religious invocations at school graduation ceremonies and sporting events also violate the Establishment Clause. (*See infra,* §§974-975.) Similarly, reading from the Bible and recitation by students of the Lord's Prayer at the beginning of the school day were found to be "religious" practices and thus invalid. [**Abington School District v. Schempp,** 374 U.S. 203 (1963)]

(a) Coercion not necessary [§952]

The fact that such programs are "voluntary"—*i.e.,* that children not wishing to participate are excused—does not save them. "The Establishment Clause, unlike the Free Exercise Clause, does not depend upon any showing of direct governmental compulsion, and is violated by the enactment of laws which establish an official religion, whether those laws operate directly to coerce nonobserving individuals or not." [**Engel v. Vitale,** *supra*]

(2) Silent prayer [§953]

A law setting aside a time of silence in public schools for "meditation or voluntary prayer" violates the Establishment Clause when its *sole purpose* (as evidenced by its text and legislative history) is to endorse a religious exercise, and it thus has *no secular* purpose. [**Wallace v. Jaffree,** 472 U.S. 38 (1985)]

(3) Anti-evolution laws [§954]

Laws prohibiting the teaching of Darwinian evolution in public schools have been held invalid. The statute's purpose was found to be religious—to placate fundamentalist sectarian convictions concerning the origins of humanity. The statute was not religiously "neutral," since it did not forbid discussion of all theories on the origin of humanity but merely evolution. [**Epperson v. Arkansas,** 393 U.S. 97 (1968)]

(a) "Creation science" laws [§955]

Similarly, a law requiring that the scientific evidence supporting the theory of creation be taught whenever evolution is taught has been held invalid. The statute had "no clear secular purpose"; rather, its primary purpose was found to be "to provide persuasive advantage to a particular religious doctrine that rejects the factual basis of evolution." [**Edwards v. Aguillard,** 482 U.S. 578 (1987)]

(4) Released time—on premises [§956]

Programs in which regular classes end an hour early one day a week and religious instruction is given *in public school classrooms* to those students who so request (other students remaining in study halls, etc.) are invalid. They constitute a "utilization of the tax-established and tax-supported public school system to aid religious groups to spread their faith." [**McCollum v. Board of Education,** 333 U.S. 203 (1948)]

(5) Posting the Ten Commandments [§957]

Displaying the Ten Commandments on the walls of public school classrooms plainly serves a religious purpose and is invalid despite the legislature's statement that it was for a secular purpose. [**Stone v. Graham,** 449 U.S. 39 (1980)]

(a) Free Exercise Clause issues [§958]

In respect to the public school religious practices held invalid, *supra,* no Free Exercise Clause considerations call for a contrary result (*i.e.,* there is no right under the Free Exercise Clause to have religious exercise or instruction in the public schools—no religion demands it, and the Establishment Clause forbids it). [**Abington School District v. Schempp,** *supra*]

(6) Academic study of religion or the Bible [§959]

Academic study of religion or the Bible in the public schools does *not* violate the Establishment Clause—since the purpose and effect is secular (*i.e.,* to educate children about their importance, not to indoctrinate in religious tenets). [**Abington School District v. Schempp,** *supra*]

(7) History and patriotism [§960]

Recitation in public schools of religious references in historic documents (*e.g.*, Declaration of Independence), the flag salute, or the national anthem *probably* does *not* violate the Establishment Clause—the purpose and effect being secular (patriotic) rather than religious. [**Engel v. Vitale,** *supra*]

(8) Equal access to facilities [§961]

As with other public facilities (*supra,* §948), permitting student religious groups in *secondary schools,* as well as other noncurriculum-related student groups, to meet for religious purposes (including prayer) on school premises during noninstructional time does *not* violate the Establishment Clause. In granting equal access to *both* secular and religious speech, the school does not endorse religion nor will secondary school students understand it to do so. [**Board of Education v. Mergens,** 496 U.S. 226 (1990)]

(a) Elementary school facilities [§962]

The equal access rule also applies to a similar, neutral program allowing religious organizations access to *elementary school* classrooms after school hours. [**Good News Club v. Milford Central School,** 533 U.S. 98 (2001)] In *Good News Club,* the Court found that children attending an after school religious class in their public school building would not likely perceive government endorsement of religion because the religious instructors were not regular school teachers and the participating children were not all the same age as in their normal classroom setting.

RELIGIOUS PRACTICES AND PUBLIC SCHOOLS—A SUMMARY OF CASES   gilbert

VALID	INVALID
Studying religion or the Bible in public schools *for academic purposes*	Government prescribed *prayer* in public school
Reciting religious references in historic documents	*Prayers* at public school graduation and sporting events
Permitting religious groups to *use public school classrooms for religious purposes on an equal basis with other groups* when the rooms are not otherwise in use	Setting aside a time of *silence* in public school *for voluntary prayer*
	Prohibiting the teaching of Darwinian evolution in public schools
	Requiring that "creation science" be taught whenever evolution is taught
	Releasing students an hour early so they can *attend religious classes in public school classrooms*
	Posting the 10 Commandments in public schools

g. Policies of public schools to "accommodate" religion [§963]

Policies of public schools to accommodate religion need not violate the Establishment Clause—even though their purpose and effect may seem to favor religion—if: (i) they do not involve religious programs in the public schools, and (ii) they further, rather than threaten, the "free exercise" of religion.

(1) Released time—off premises [§964]

Programs in which participating children are released early from public school to go to religious classes conducted at religious centers *away from* the public school do not violate the Establishment Clause. This is regarded as merely an "accommodation" to religious needs, the question of "aid to religion" being "one of degree." [**Zorach v. Clauson,** 343 U.S. 306 (1952)]

(2) Dismissed time [§965]

"Dismissed time" is distinguished from released time in that *all* students are dismissed early one day a week to encourage attendance at religious classes held off public school premises. It follows from *Zorach* that this type of program is valid, despite its religious purpose.

(3) Absence for holidays [§966]

Excusing children from public school to attend religious services (*e.g.*, on Ash Wednesday or Yom Kippur) does not violate the Establishment Clause, despite its religious purpose. This also follows from *Zorach*.

h. General government regulation benefiting religion [§967]

Government action that benefits religion violates the Establishment Clause only if its purpose and effect is to sponsor, advance, or endorse religion. If it has a secular purpose and effect, it is valid. (*Note:* It is also valid even though it has a "religious" purpose if its effect is merely to "accommodate" religion (*see supra*, §963) or if it is helpful or necessary to religious liberty; *see* discussion of the Free Exercise Clause, below.)

(1) Religious oath requirement for public office [§968]

Requiring a religious oath for public office is invalid—its purpose and effect being to sponsor religion and burden religious liberty. [**Torcaso v. Watkins,** 367 U.S. 488 (1961)]

(2) Sunday closing laws [§969]

Laws requiring businesses or government offices to close on Sundays are valid; such laws have a secular purpose and effect (even though originally to aid religion)—to provide most people with a day off—are advocated by labor and business, and are designed to create a day of rest and relaxation. [**McGowan v. Maryland,** 366 U.S. 420 (1961)]

(3) Murder, theft, and adultery laws [§970]

Laws prohibiting and/or punishing murder, theft, or adultery are also valid; even though their effect coincides with religious tenets, the purpose and effect is secular (although religion obtains incidental benefits).

(4) Insulating churches from liquor outlets [§971]

Zoning laws that bar liquor outlets within a prescribed distance of designated institutions (including churches) are probably valid because of their secular "environmental" purpose. But a law that gives churches the power to veto applications for liquor licenses near them violates the Establishment Clause. It delegates discretionary government power to churches, thus giving them the ability to advance religion. It also entangles churches in the processes of government. [**Larkin v. Grendel's Den, Inc.,** 459 U.S. 116 (1982)]

i. Public acknowledgments of religion [§972]

American history is replete with government recognition of our religious heritage and with official expressions of religious beliefs. This does *not* violate the Establishment Clause unless, "in reality, it establishes a religion or religious faith, or tends to do so." [**Lynch v. Donnelly,** 465 U.S. 668 (1984)]

(1) Prayers at opening sessions of public bodies [§973]

A state legislature's practice of opening each legislative day with a prayer by a state-paid chaplain does *not* violate the Establishment Clause. Such practice was actually authorized by the Congress that proposed the Establishment Clause and is "deeply embedded" in our history and tradition. Since adults are not readily susceptible to religious indoctrination, the practice is "a tolerable acknowledgment" of widely held beliefs. [**Marsh v. Chambers,** 463 U.S. 783 (1983)]

(a) Distinguish—prayer at graduations [§974]

The practice of public school officials having members of the clergy give invocation and benediction prayers at graduation ceremonies *does violate* the Establishment Clause. The setting is analogous to the classroom because of subtle coercive pressures on students to participate in the religious exercise at a most significant occasion in the student's life. The atmosphere at the opening session of a legislature is different because adults are free to enter and leave with little constraint. [**Lee v. Weisman,** 505 U.S. 830 (1992)]

(b) Distinguish—prayer at football games [§975]

Similarly, a school policy titled "Prayer at Football Games," authorizing a student election on (i) whether to have a student "invocation or statement" before each varsity game "to solemnize the event," and (ii) to select the student to deliver it and to decide its content, *violates* the Establishment Clause. Unlike student speeches at an open public forum (*see supra*, §948), this policy's purpose is to encourage religious messages, and its authorization of only one student for the entire football season results in the majoritarian process silencing minority views. Although the informal pressure on students to attend is not as strong as at graduation, many high school students do feel "immense social pressure" to be involved in such events. [**Santa Fe Independent School District v. Doe**, 530 U.S. 290 (2000)]

(2) Christmas Nativity scene [§976]

A city's inclusion of a Nativity scene *in the context of a larger annual Christmas display* (*e.g.*, including Santa Claus, a Christmas tree, a "Season's Greetings" banner, and the like) does *not* violate the Establishment Clause. The purpose is not "motivated wholly by religious considerations," but is rather to take account of the "historical origins" of Christmas, and the beneficial effect for religion is only "indirect, remote, and incidental." [**Lynch v. Donnelly**, *supra*]

(a) Distinguish—limited display

However, a Nativity scene in the county courthouse, with the message "Glory to God in the Highest" (in Latin), and with *no* surrounding secular objects (such as Santa Claus, reindeer and sleigh, candy-striped poles, etc.) *does* violate the Establishment Clause because it denotes government endorsement and support of religion. [**County of Allegheny v. American Civil Liberties Union Greater Pittsburgh Chapter**, *supra*, §920]

1) Contrast

On the other hand, a display that contains a Christmas tree, Chanuka menorah, and a sign declaring the city's "salute to liberty" does *not* have the effect of endorsing or supporting religion, and does *not* violate the Establishment Clause. [**County of Allegheny v. American Civil Liberties Union Greater Pittsburgh Chapter**, *supra*]

EXAM TIP   **gilbert**

The constitutionality of Christmastime displays has often been litigated and is a fairly common Establishment Clause issue on law school exams. The rules here are not terribly complicated. Displays may include religious items (*e.g.*, a nativity scene or a menorah) because they merely *reflect the historical origins* of our national Christmas holiday. However, such religious symbols may be included only along with other, nonreligious Christmastime decorations (*e.g.*, Santa, a sleigh, a Christmas tree, reindeer, etc.). Otherwise, the display will look like a government *endorsement of religion* and will violate the Establishment Clause.

---

(3) Religious displays in public forums [§977]

Permitting the Ku Klux Klan to display a Latin cross in the plaza surrounding the statehouse does **not** violate the Establishment Clause because the plaza was a traditional public forum open to expression of all private groups on equal terms—at least when the display is accompanied by a sign disclaiming government endorsement. [**Capitol Square Review & Advisory Board v. Pinette,** 515 U.S. 753 (1995)—no majority opinion]

(4) Other examples [§978]

On similar analysis, it would appear that the following are also valid: official proclamation of a National Day of Prayer; making Thanksgiving and Christmas national holidays; public compensation of chaplains in Congress and the military; making "In God We Trust" the national motto; inclusion of "One nation under God" in the pledge of allegiance to the flag; hanging religious paintings in publicly supported galleries; and providing chapels in the Capitol for worship and meditation. [**Lynch v. Donnelly,** *supra*]

4. Standing [§979]

Persons asserting violation of the Establishment Clause need not allege infringement of particular religious freedoms to have standing. It is enough that they are *directly affected* by the action complained of.

> **Example:** Department store employees prosecuted for Sunday closing law violation could claim that the law violates the Establishment Clause. [**McGowan v. Maryland,** *supra*, §969]

> **Example:** Parents of public school children have standing to challenge public school practices (Bible reading) as violating the Establishment Clause. [**Abington School District v. Schempp,** *supra*, §959]

C. Free Exercise Clause

1. In General [§980]

If the purpose of a statute or other governmental action is to single out religion for adverse treatment, or to hinder (or discriminate against) a particular religion, it violates the Free Exercise Clause unless it is narrowly tailored to advance a compelling state interest. Such laws will survive strict scrutiny only in rare cases. [**Church of the Lukumi Babalu Aye, Inc. v. City of Hialeah,** 508 U.S. 520 (1993)]

> **Example:** Forbidding members of the clergy from holding public office has been held to violate the Free Exercise Clause. The state justification for the law—that

clergy in public office would create religious divisiveness—was not supported by American experience. [**McDaniel v. Paty,** 435 U.S. 618 (1978)]

e.g. **Example:** City ordinances that barred ritual animal sacrifice in order to suppress a religion that employed such sacrifice as a principal form of devotion violate the Free Exercise Clause. The justifications for the laws (protecting public health and preventing cruelty to animals) could be served by methods short of flatly prohibiting all religious sacrifices. [**Church of the Lukumi Babalu Aye, Inc. v. City of Hialeah,** *supra*]

2. "Beliefs" vs. "Action" or "Conduct" [§981]

A distinction must be made between a statute that "interferes" with religious beliefs and a statute that "interferes" with conduct that a person wishes to engage in (or to refrain from engaging in) because of her religion.

a. Beliefs [§982]

The freedom to hold religious beliefs is absolute. The government may not compel anyone to accept a particular creed. [**Cantwell v. Connecticut,** 310 U.S. 296 (1940)]

e.g. **Example:** Requiring all public school pupils to salute the flag and recite the pledge of allegiance is invalid as applied to children whose religious scruples forbid it—government cannot require affirmation of a belief. [**West Virginia State Board of Education v. Barnette,** 319 U.S. 624 (1943)—freedom of speech and religion provisions of the First Amendment forbid requiring flag salute by any person who has ideological objection]

(1) What constitutes religious belief [§983]

Religious beliefs need not be theistic to qualify for constitutional protection. [**Torcaso v. Watkins,** *supra,* §968—listing Buddhism, Taoism, Ethical Culture, and Secular Humanism as religions that do not teach belief in the existence of God] But the Court has said that religious beliefs must constitute more than merely a philosophic rejection of contemporary secular values. [**Wisconsin v. Yoder,** 406 U.S. 205 (1972)] Although the Court has not stated an authoritative constitutional definition of "religion," neither has it ever held any asserted religious beliefs to be not "religious" for First Amendment purposes.

(a) Statutory interpretation [§984]

In construing "religious belief" in the Selective Service Act, the Court has perhaps suggested a constitutional definition: The belief must occupy a place in the believer's life parallel to that occupied by orthodox religious beliefs. Such a belief may be internally derived, but it must be something beyond a merely political or philosophical view. [**United States v. Seeger,** 380 U.S. 163 (1965)]

(2) "Truth" of beliefs [§985]

The First Amendment forbids courts (or juries) from finding that any person's asserted religious beliefs are untrue—since many of the most traditional and accepted religious beliefs could not be proved today. [**United States v. Ballard,** 322 U.S. 78 (1944)]

(a) Note

Courts must respect sincerely held religious beliefs even though they may not appear to be logical, consistent, or comprehensible to others. [**Thomas v. Review Board of Indiana Employment Security Division,** 450 U.S. 707 (1981)]

(b) Good faith [§986]

Courts *can* determine whether a person *sincerely believes* the asserted religious tenets. [**United States v. Ballard,** *supra*—person prosecuted for mail fraud for soliciting funds for his religious movement asserted that he was divine messenger, had divine healing powers, had talked to Jesus, etc.]

b. Conduct [§987]

Action (or inaction) undertaken because of religious beliefs is *not absolutely* protected by the Free Exercise Clause.

(1) Prior approach—balancing test [§988]

Under the *prior approach*, when a government regulation, enacted for a secular purpose, either burdened conduct required by some religious belief or required conduct forbidden by some religious belief, the Court balanced the following three factors:

(a) Severity of the burden

Serious burdens can arise when government regulation makes action or inaction demanded by one's religion illegal; *i.e.,* the individual must choose between criminal prosecution or forsaking a religious duty (illustrated below). But the Court also invalidated some regulations that did not make the religious duty illegal, but rather made pursuit of religious obligations more difficult—usually financially burdensome (illustrated below).

(b) Strength of state interest

Next, the Court determined whether the state interest was "of the highest order"—using such terms as "compelling" and "important."

(c) Alternative means

Finally, the Court inquired whether the state could satisfy its interest by means that imposed a lesser burden on religion.

(2) Current rule [§989]

The Court has more recently ruled that the Free Exercise Clause affords *no right to a religious exemption* from a *neutral* law that happens to impose a substantial burden on religious practice—as long as the law is otherwise constitutionally applied to persons who engage in the action for nonreligious reasons. [**Employment Division v. Smith**, 494 U.S. 872 (1990)—no exemption from drug laws for Native American Church's sacramental use of peyote]

(a) Comment

While *Smith* was decided before most of the cases below, it fits well with their results and often provides a simpler rationale for the results than the cases themselves.

(3) Decisions denying free exercise claims

(a) Polygamy [§990]

A statute making polygamy illegal was upheld as applied to Mormons whose religion demanded polygamy. [**Reynolds v. United States,** 98 U.S. 145 (1878)]

(b) Sunday closing law [§991]

A Sunday closing law was upheld as applied to a Sabbatarian (Orthodox Jew) who as a result had to refrain from working two days each week (*i.e.,* his religious Sabbath and Sunday). [**Braunfeld v. Brown,** 366 U.S. 599 (1961)]

(c) Draft laws [§992]

The Court has stated that the Free Exercise Clause does not require draft exemption for any religious objectors to military service. And it has upheld a Selective Service Act exemption that was limited to those who are religiously opposed to "war in *any* form" as applied to religious conscientious objectors to a *particular* war. [**Gillette v. United States,** 401 U.S. 437 (1971)]

(d) Veterans' educational benefits [§993]

The Court upheld the denial of veterans' educational benefits to conscientious objectors who performed alternative civilian service. [**Johnson v. Robison,** 415 U.S. 361 (1974)]

(e) Taxes [§994]

Some early decisions invalidated a vendor's license tax (flat fee) when applied to those whose religion required them to sell religious literature, because it operated as a prior restraint on the dissemination of religious *ideas*. [**Murdock v. Pennsylvania,** 319 U.S. 105 (1943)] More recently, the Court has upheld application of general taxes to religiously motivated activity.

> **Example:** The Court upheld application of the *Social Security tax* to an Amish employer whose beliefs forbade payment and receipt of Social Security benefits. [**United States v. Lee,** 455 U.S. 252 (1982)]

> **Example:** The Court upheld application of *sales and use taxes* as applied to the sale of religious material (books and tapes) by a religious organization. [**Jimmy Swaggart Ministries v. Board of Equalization of California,** 493 U.S. 378 (1990)]

> **Example:** The Court upheld the denial of the *charitable deduction from federal income tax* for fixed price payments that members made to the Church of Scientology in exchange for sessions to increase spiritual awareness and teach the tenets of the faith. [**Hernandez v. Commissioner of Internal Revenue,** 490 U.S. 680 (1989)]

> **Example:** The Court upheld an IRS *denial of tax exempt status* to private schools whose religious beliefs required them to practice racial discrimination in admissions, etc. [**Bob Jones University v. United States,** 461 U.S. 574 (1983)]

(f) Compulsory military training [§995]

A state regulation requiring all students wishing to attend the state university to take a course in military training was upheld as applied to those whose religious beliefs forbade such training. [**Hamilton v. Regents of University of California,** 293 U.S. 245 (1934)]

(g) Military dress [§996]

An Air Force refusal to exempt from its uniform dress requirements an Orthodox Jewish psychologist who wanted to wear a yarmulke while on duty at a military hospital was upheld. [**Goldman v. Weinberger,** 475 U.S. 503 (1986)]

(h) Prisoners' rights [§997]

The standard of review is different for claims by prisoners: Courts must afford deference to prison officials; and prison regulations that impinge on free exercise rights of prisoners are valid if *"reasonably related to legitimate penological objectives."* [**O'Lone v. Estate of Shabazz,** 482 U.S. 342 (1987)]

(i) Incidental effects of government programs [§998]

The Free Exercise Clause does not require government to justify otherwise lawful programs whose incidental effect happens to interfere with the practice of certain religions. [**Lyng v. Northwest Indian Cemetery Protective Association,** 485 U.S. 439 (1988)—government's building a road on public land that is sacred to Indians' religion does not require Free Exercise Clause justification even though it would virtually destroy Indians' ability to practice their religion]

(4) Decisions upholding "free exercise" claims [§999]

In a few cases, the Court *has required an exemption* from a neutral, generally applicable law for religiously motivated action, most frequently when the Free Exercise Clause appears *in conjunction with* other constitutional protections. Because these cases are based in part on other constitutional principles, it is doubtful that their results would be affected by **Employment Division v. Smith,** *supra,* §989.

(a) Right of parents to educate their children [§1000]

A law compelling school attendance to age 16 was applied to Amish parents who sincerely believed, as a fundamental tenet of their faith (rather than from personal or philosophical conviction), that high school would endanger salvation. *Held:* The state's strong interest in universal education was outweighed by the Free Exercise Clause and the constitutional rights recognized in **Pierce v. Society of Sisters** (*supra,* §522), because the Amish prepared their children for life as adults in the Amish community, which has been productive and law-abiding. [**Wisconsin v. Yoder,** *supra,* §983]

(b) Distribution of literature, solicitation of funds, use of public streets and parks, etc. [§1001]

The doctrines that have resulted in violations of "free speech" have also led to violations of the Free Exercise Clause when the case involves religious groups. [*See, e.g.,* **Cantwell v. Connecticut,** *supra,* §982]

(c) Unemployment compensation [§1002]

A law requiring an applicant for unemployment benefits to accept "suitable work" (including work on Saturday) or lose benefits was applied to a Sabbatarian (Seventh Day Adventist). *Held:* Where the state system *provides for individual exemptions* depending on the particular circumstances of an applicant's unemployment, it may not refuse to extend that system to cases of "religious hardship" without compelling reasons. [**Sherbert v. Verner,** 374 U.S. 398 (1963); *and see* **Thomas v. Review Board of Indiana Employment Security Division,** *supra* §985; **Hobbie v. Unemployment Appeals Commission,** 480 U.S. 136 (1987)]

1) Effect of *Smith*

Employment Division v. Smith, *supra,* noted that the above unemployment cases refined and were decided under the balancing test set out *supra* (§988), but distinguished these cases based on the system of individualized assessment for special exemptions from requirements of unemployment compensation. Therefore, the results of these cases, while out of step with the analysis in *Smith*, apparently would not be different if the Court were to rule on them today.

(d) Establishment Clause issues [§1003]

Even though the exemptions for religion in the above cases may be said to have a "religious purpose," they do ***not*** violate the Establishment Clause—because "accommodating" these religious beliefs, as required by the Free Exercise Clause, is not government sponsorship of religion and neither does it result in excessive government involvement with religion.

1) Permissible accommodation [§1004]

Similarly, the government may accommodate religion by alleviating burdens on religious exercise even though it would not be required to do so by the Free Exercise Clause. [**Church of Jesus Christ of Latter-Day Saints v. Amos**, 483 U.S. 327 (1987)—exemption of religious organizations from ban on religious discrimination in employment]

2) Distinguish—"absolute" religious exemption [§1005]

However, a law that gives Sabbath observers an ***unqualified*** right not to work on whatever day they designate as their Sabbath—regardless of the burden this may impose on the employer or fellow workers—goes beyond "accommodation." It violates the Establishment Clause because it has a "*primary effect* that impermissibly advances a *particular religious* practice." [**Estate of Thornton v. Caldor, Inc.**, 472 U.S. 703 (1985)]

EXAM TIP — **gilbert**

To summarize, the Free Exercise Clause prohibits government interference with religious ***beliefs***, but it generally does ***not*** prohibit regulation of ***conduct***. If the governmental action regulates ***general conduct***—including religious conduct—it is ***valid*** (e.g., banning any use of peyote is valid even though a group's religious beliefs require its use during its ceremonies). The only exceptions to this rule so far are those pertaining to unemployment compensation, free speech, and the education of Amish children.

---

c. "Accommodations" that benefit only some religions [§1006]

Accommodations for religion may not discriminate on the basis of religious affiliation or belief. But an accommodation that happens to produce "a de facto discrimination among religions"—*i.e.*, results in benefiting some religions but not others—does *not* violate either the Establishment Clause or Free Exercise Clause if there is a "neutral, secular basis for the lines government has drawn." [**Gillette v. United States,** *supra*, §992—draft exemption only for those religious objectors to *all* wars has neutral and secular purpose of effectively raising armies in a fair and evenhanded way]

3. Standing [§1007]

In accordance with the general doctrine of standing (*see supra*, §§49-52), a person asserting violation of the Free Exercise Clause must: (i) show a *direct personal injury* due to the challenged action, and (ii) ordinarily, claim an *interference with her own religious beliefs*. [**McGowan v. Maryland,** *supra*, §969—store employees, convicted of violating Sunday closing laws, had no standing to attack law as violating Free Exercise Clause because they did not allege infringement of their own religious freedom]

4. Judicial Resolution of Disputes Involving Church Doctrine [§1008]

In disputes between a local congregation and a general church hierarchy involving the right to church property (or the right to be a church official), the First and Fourteenth Amendment guarantees of religious liberty forbid courts from determining ecclesiastical questions (*i.e.*, questions of religious doctrine and practice) to resolve the case. [**Presbyterian Church v. Hull Church,** 393 U.S. 440 (1969); **Serbian Eastern Orthodox Diocese v. Milivojevich,** 426 U.S. 696 (1976)] At least absent fraud or collusion when the church tribunal allegedly acts in bad faith for secular purposes, the *decision of the church tribunal is conclusive*—despite the claim that it has not complied with its own rules.

a. Rationale

Judicial inquiry into such matters would constitute "excessive government entanglement" with religion; also, church members *impliedly consent* to be bound by hierarchical church decisions on ecclesiastical questions.

(1) Congregational churches

This rationale may extend to church members impliedly consenting to be bound by decisions of a majority of the congregation in a local church that has no general affiliation. [**Watson v. Jones,** 80 U.S. 679 (1871)]

(2) Personal rights

And the rationale may extend to disputes where personal, rather than property, rights are involved.

b. Alternative approach [§1009]

Civil courts may use "neutral principles" of property law—not involving questions of religious doctrine or practice—to resolve church property disputes. For example, the courts may examine the deeds to the property, state statutes on implied trusts, and the church rules; or the court may adopt a presumptive rule of majority representation—and in the absence of a church rule implying a trust to the general church, the court may award the property to the entity that has legal title. [**Jones v. Wolf,** 443 U.S. 595 (1979)]

Chapter Seven: Equal Protection

CONTENTS

Chapter Approach

The Equal Protection Clause of the Fourteenth Amendment limits governmental discrimination by the states. The Fifth Amendment Due Process Clause has been held to limit most similar discrimination by the federal government. Your analysis should begin by looking at the classification.

1. If the classification is *not based on suspect or quasi-suspect criteria—i.e.,* almost *all economic or social regulations*—and does not discriminate against a *fundamental right*, it will be upheld if it is *rationally related* to a *constitutionally permissible* state interest. Keep in mind that these classifications will be presumed valid and must be "wholly arbitrary" to be invalid.

2. If the government action *intentionally discriminates against a suspect class* (*i.e.,* race or national origin), *strict scrutiny* will be applied and the law will be *invalid unless* it is *necessary* to promote a *compelling* state interest, a much more difficult test. Note too that this test will usually be used for laws that discriminate against a *fundamental right*.

3. If the classification is based on a *quasi-suspect criterion* (*i.e.,* gender and legitimacy), an intermediate level test is used: To be valid, the regulation must be *substantially* related to *important* governmental objectives.

A. Introduction

1. **Constitutional Provision [§1010]**

   The Fourteenth Amendment provides: "No *State* shall . . . deny to any person within its jurisdiction the equal protection of the laws."

   a. **Federal government [§1011]**

      As previously discussed (*see supra,* §426), although there is no comparable provision in the Constitution that expressly limits the federal government, the Court has held that, in most instances (*see infra,* §1265), the Fifth Amendment Due Process Clause applies the same prohibition to the federal government.

2. **Three Major Tests [§1012]**

   It must be recognized that almost all statutes and other forms of government regulation classify (or discriminate among) people; virtually none treats all persons in the same manner (*e.g.,* income tax laws apply different rates to persons in different income brackets; wage and hours laws do not apply to persons in certain occupations;

APPROACH TO EQUAL PROTECTION ISSUES

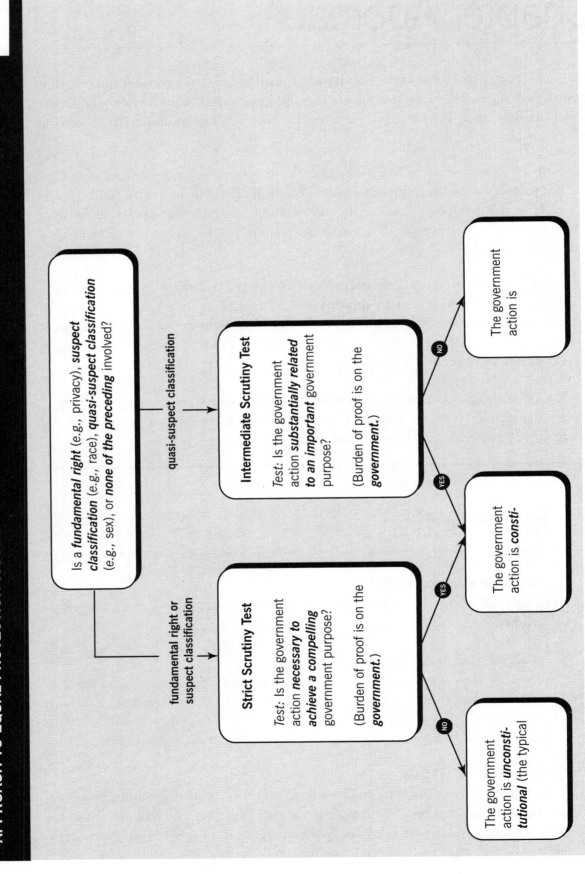

Is a *fundamental right* (e.g., privacy), *suspect classification* (e.g., race), *quasi-suspect classification* (e.g., sex), or *none of the preceding* involved?

fundamental right or suspect classification

quasi-suspect classification

Strict Scrutiny Test

Test: Is the government action *necessary to achieve a compelling* government purpose?

(Burden of proof is on the *government.*)

Intermediate Scrutiny Test

Test: Is the government action *substantially related to an important* government purpose?

(Burden of proof is on the *government.*)

NO

YES

YES

NO

The government action is *unconstitutional* (the typical

The government action is *consti-*

The government action is

etc.). Thus, the Equal Protection Clause cannot be, and is not, a guaranty that all people will be treated exactly the same under every law. In recognition of this fact, the Court has developed a number of tests for determining the validity of laws that classify. Each of these tests, including the three major ones—(i) the "traditional" (or "rational basis") test, (ii) the "strict scrutiny" (or "compelling interest") test, and (iii) the "intermediate level of scrutiny" (or "quasi-suspect class") test—is discussed below.

B. Economic and Social Regulations—Traditional Rational Basis Test

1. Extreme Judicial Deference [§1013]

When the statutory classification is not based on "suspect" or "quasi-suspect" criteria (*see infra*, §§1017 *et seq.*), the Court reviews it under the "traditional" equal protection test. This approach is used for virtually all economic and social regulations. The test is *usually* stated as follows: The classification (or discrimination) is valid if it is *rationally related* to a *proper* (or *constitutionally permissible* or *legitimate*) *state interest*. Under this test, a classification is *presumed valid* and will be upheld unless the *person challenging it* proves that it is "invidious," "wholly arbitrary," or "capricious." Moreover, the legislative body enacting the classification need not articulate its reasons for the classification—*i.e.*, the challenger must show that *no reasonable state of facts* can be conceived to justify it. [**Lindsley v. Natural Carbonic Gas Co.**, 220 U.S. 61 (1911); **McGowan v. Maryland,** 366 U.S. 420 (1961); **United States Railroad Retirement Board v. Fritz,** 449 U.S. 166 (1980)]

EXAM TIP   gilbert

The key differences among the various tests for determining whether government action is valid under the Equal Protection Clause revolve around who has the burden of proof—the challenger or the government—and what must be proved. Remember, most social and economic legislation is governed by the rational basis test. The government action will be *presumed to be constitutional* unless the *challenging party* can prove that the government classification is *not rationally related* to a *constitutionally permissible* government interest. This is a very difficult burden for the challenger, and as a result, virtually all government action that is challenged under this test is found valid.

---

a. Over- and under-inclusion [§1014]

The line drawn by the legislature may be imperfect, resulting in some over- or under-inclusiveness, and the statute may still be valid. [**Vance v. Bradley,** 440 U.S. 93 (1979)] Legislatures may proceed one step at a time and may partially eliminate a perceived evil, deferring complete regulation to the future. [**Railway Express Agency v. New York,** 336 U.S. 106 (1949)—upholding ordinance against displaying advertisements on moving vehicles, unless the ad is for the business owning the vehicle; "it is no requirement of equal protection that all evils of the genus be eradicated or none at all"; **New Orleans v. Dukes,** 427 U.S. 297 (1976)]

b. **Effect [§1015]**

By employing the rational basis test, the Court gives legislative bodies "wide latitude" in drawing classifications when enacting economic and social regulations pursuant to the police power. [**New York City Transit Authority v. Beazer,** 440 U.S. 568 (1979)—upholding a rule denying employment compensation to persons receiving methadone treatment] *Only rarely* will the Court find a violation of equal protection under this test, such as in the following examples.

Example: The federal food stamp program excluded any household containing unrelated persons. The Court found the classification "wholly without any rational basis." The legislative history indicated that the provision was aimed at excluding "hippie communes" from the program. The Court found that discrimination against this "politically unpopular group" was *not a constitutionally permissible* government interest. [**United States Department of Agriculture v. Moreno,** 413 U.S. 528 (1973)]

Example: Several municipalities passed ordinances banning discrimination in housing, employment, etc., based on sexual orientation. In response, the state voters adopted a constitutional amendment prohibiting any state or local action protecting the status of persons based on their homosexual, lesbian, or bisexual orientation. *Held:* A state constitutional provision that identifies persons by a single trait and then denies them the right to seek *any* specific protections from the law—no matter how local or widespread the injury—is so unprecedented as to imply animosity toward such persons and is thus not related to any legitimate state interest. [**Romer v. Evans,** 517 U.S. 620 (1996)]

Example: A county tax assessor valued real property at its sale price but made only minor modifications for property that had not been recently sold. As a result, some property was assessed at as much as 35 times more than comparable neighboring property. The Court held that this practice was not "rationally related" to the state policy of *assessing all property at its estimated market value.* [**Allegheny Pittsburgh Coal Co. v. County Commission,** 488 U.S. 386 (1989)]

Compare: California's Proposition 13 (which adopted an acquisition valuation system of taxation under which property is reassessed to a new value only at the time of construction or at change of ownership) produced similar disparities in property valuation. Nevertheless, the Court held that this did not violate equal protection because California had deliberately adopted a policy of assessing largely on the basis of "*acquisition value*" (rather than "market value") and Proposition 13 *rationally* furthered *legitimate* interests served by the policy. [**Nordlinger v. Hahn,** 505 U.S. 1 (1992)]

2. **Less Deferential Formulation [§1016]**

Occasionally, the Court states the "traditional" test in a way that suggests a slightly less deferential judicial standard of review: The classification "*must rest upon some ground of difference having a fair and substantial* relation to the object of the legislation." [**Royster Guano Co. v. Virginia,** 253 U.S. 412 (1920)] But even when using this formulation, the Court *almost always sustains* the classification. [*See, e.g.,* **Johnson v. Robison,** *supra,* §993—upholding federal law denying veterans' education benefits to conscientious objectors who performed alternate civilian service]

C. Suspect Classifications—"Strict Scrutiny"

1. Test [§1017]

Government action that *intentionally* (*see infra*) discriminates against racial or ethnic minorities is "suspect" and thus subject to "strict scrutiny." Under strict scrutiny, a classification will be held to violate equal protection unless found to be *necessary* to promote a *compelling state interest.*

a. "Necessary" to promote compelling state interest [§1018]

A classification is "necessary" when it is *narrowly tailored* so that *no alternative, less burdensome means* is available to accomplish the state interest. The means chosen must fit the compelling goal so closely that there is little or no possibility that the motive of the classification was illegitimate racial prejudice or stereotype.

(1) Effect [§1019]

Under this test, almost all intentional government discrimination against the following groups has been held *invalid:*

(a) *African-Americans* [*see, e.g.,* **Strauder v. West Virginia,** 100 U.S. 303 (1880)—law forbidding African-Americans from serving on grand or petit juries];

(b) *Persons of Chinese ancestry* [**Yick Wo v. Hopkins,** 118 U.S. 356 (1886)—denial of laundry licenses only to Chinese]; and

(c) *Persons of Mexican ancestry* [**Hernandez v. Texas,** 347 U.S. 475 (1954)—discrimination against Mexican-Americans in respect to jury service].

(2) Exception [§1020]

Such discrimination has sometimes been upheld. During World War II, curfew orders and forced relocation applicable only to persons of Japanese ancestry was held not to violate equal protection. [**Hirabayashi v.**

United States, 320 U.S. 81 (1943); **Korematsu v. United States,** 323 U.S. 214 (1944)—"pressing public necessity may sometimes justify racial restrictions"]

b.   Requirement of intentional discrimination [§1021]

The "strict scrutiny" test for "suspect" criteria requires that the government action have a *discriminatory purpose; i.e.,* intentional or deliberate discrimination must be shown. [**Washington v. Davis,** 426 U.S. 229 (1976)] Such "de jure" discrimination may be found in three ways:

(1)   On its face [§1022]

Government action (*e.g.,* a statute, executive or administrative order, judicial decree, etc.) that explicitly—by its written or spoken terms—discriminates is the most obvious form of de jure discrimination.

(2)   Unequal administration [§1023]

Laws or other official actions that are racially *neutral on their face* may be purposefully applied in a discriminatory manner based on suspect criteria (*e.g.,* race) and thereby become subject to the strict equal protection standard of review.

---

e.g.   **Example:** In **Yick Wo v. Hopkins,** *supra,* a statute provided that laundries could not be operated in wooden buildings without a license. The classification itself was racially neutral, but the licensing authority consistently refused licenses to Chinese applicants while granting them to others. Since the authority could offer no "racially neutral" explanation, this was held to be de jure discrimination violative of the Equal Protection Clause.

(a)   Burden of proof [§1024]

A person who alleges this form of discrimination must prove that it is intentional or purposeful. [**Snowden v. Hughes,** 321 U.S. 1 (1944)] The claimant may establish a prima facie case by showing a *substantial disproportionate racial impact* as a result of the law's administration. [*See* **Mayor of Philadelphia v. Educational Equality League,** 415 U.S. 605 (1974)—proof was "too fragmentary and speculative"] Then, the *burden shifts to the state* to show that this impact was caused by constitutionally permissible (*i.e.,* nonracial) factors. [**Castaneda v. Partida,** 430 U.S. 482 (1977)]

1)   Illustration—peremptory challenges [§1025]

If an African-American defendant claims that the prosecution used its peremptory challenges to exclude all African-Americans from the jury and shows facts or circumstances that raise an inference that the exclusions were based on race, the burden shifts to the state to come forward with a neutral explanation—*i.e.,* something other than that the prosecutor believed that African-American jurors would be partial to the defendant because of their shared race. [**Batson v. Kentucky,** 476 U.S. 79 (1986)]

a) Note
Subsequent cases have expanded *Batson* so that defendants and civil plaintiffs are also prohibited from using peremptory challenges to exclude jurors on the basis of race or sex. (*See infra,* §§1096, 1233.)

2) Illustration—capital sentencing [§1026]
Note that statistics showing that the death sentence is most frequently imposed on black defendants who kill white victims do **not** produce an inference of intentional discrimination because: (i) each death sentence is made by a unique jury and is based on innumerable special facts, and (ii) it is contrary to public policy to require jurors and prosecutors to defend their necessarily discretionary decisions. [**McCleskey v. Kemp,** 481 U.S. 279 (1987)]

3) Deference to fact finder [§1027]
The trial court's decision on the ultimate question of discriminatory intent represents a finding of fact of the sort accorded great deference on appeal, particularly on issues of credibility. [**Hernandez v. New York,** 500 U.S. 1 (1991)]

(b) Invalid on face [§1028]
In certain special areas, state action that is racially neutral by its terms may be held invalid on its face; *i.e.,* the Court may enjoin future operation of the statute at the behest of one who ***cannot show that it has been applied to him in an intentionally or purposefully discriminatory fashion.*** This has been done in the case of statutes (i) that by their terms give the administrator an "***uncontrolled discretion***" to engage in intentional racial discrimination, (ii) that have in the past been used to discriminate on the basis of race, and (iii) as to which the courts are not fully capable of remedying further discriminatory applications. [**Louisiana v. United States,** 380 U.S. 145 (1965)—literacy test for voting]

(3) Impermissible motive [§1029]
Finally, laws that are racially neutral by their terms may constitute de jure discrimination violative of equal protection if the challenger proves that the ***legislative "motive" was to discriminate*** against racial or ethnic minorities. [**Washington v. Davis,** *supra,* §1021]

It is important to remember that *only intentional discrimination* is prohibited by the Equal Protection Clause for most statutory classifications. On your exam be sure to remember the three ways in which intentional discrimination can be shown:

- *On the face* of the government action in question (*e.g.,* all people of Japanese descent must report to a detention camp);

- *By application* (*e.g.,* a prosecutor uses his peremptory challenges only against African-Americans); or

- *By its discriminatory motive* (*e.g.,* changing city boundaries to exclude nearly all African-American voters).

(a) Effect as establishing motive [§1030]

Establishing an impermissible motive is relatively easy if the effect of a law (or administrative action) bears heavily on a racial or ethnic minority and cannot be explained on permissible grounds.

Example: In **Gomillion v. Lightfoot,** 364 U.S. 339 (1960), city boundaries were changed with the effect of removing nearly all African-American voters from the city. Since there was no constitutionally permissible explanation, this was held to violate the Fifteenth Amendment.

(b) Judicial inquiry [§1031]

If the impermissible motive is not obvious from the effect of the law, the Court conducts a "sensitive inquiry" into such other factors as:

(i)   *The historic background* of the state action (*e.g.,* whether it was preceded by other racially discriminatory laws);

(ii)   The *sequence of events* leading up to the action (*e.g.,* abrupt departures from normal substantive or procedural rules); and

(iii) *Statements by members of the decisionmaking body.* (In some instances, such members may be required to testify as to their motives—unless the testimony is barred by legislative or executive privilege.)

[**Village of Arlington Heights v. Metropolitan Housing Development Corp.,** 429 U.S. 252 (1977)]

(c) Effect of showing of impermissible motive [§1032]

If the state action is shown to be motivated *in part* by a forbidden purpose, the burden of proof shifts to the state. However, the state can prevail if it shows that the same decision would have resulted despite the impermissible purpose. [**Village of Arlington Heights v. Metropolitan Housing Development Corp.,** *supra*]

---

e.g. **Example:** The motive of a provision adopted by the Alabama Constitutional Convention in 1901 that disenfranchised persons convicted of crimes involving "moral turpitude" was found to discriminate against African-Americans. The Court examined the convention's proceedings and historical studies and testimony. An *additional* purpose to discriminate against poor whites did *not* save the provision because it would not have been enacted *"but for"* the purpose of discriminating against African-Americans. [**Hunter v. Underwood,** 471 U.S. 222 (1985)]

(d) Standard of review [§1033]
The United States Supreme Court will not ordinarily disturb a federal district court's factual finding of discriminatory motive that is upheld by the court of appeals as being not "clearly erroneous." [**Rogers v. Lodge,** 458 U.S. 613 (1982)]

c. Distinguish—"de facto" discrimination [§1034]
Laws or other official actions that are racially neutral on their face, in their administration, and in their motivation may, nonetheless, be discriminatory in effect; *i.e.,* they may have a *racially disproportionate impact* (affect racial or ethnic minorities more adversely than whites). Such "de facto" discrimination is judged by the "traditional" test; it will be upheld if it is *rationally related* to a *constitutionally* permissible state interest. [**Washington v. Davis,** *supra,* §1029]

---

e.g. **Example:** A police department used results from a test on verbal and reading skills as a criterion for hiring police officers. Members of identifiable racial minorities consistently got low scores on the test, although there was no proof that the test was written or otherwise employed for the purpose of disadvantaging minority applicants. Because of the absence of any nonstatistical proof of discriminatory purpose, there was no equal protection violation. [**Washington v. Davis,** *supra*]

---

(1) De facto school segregation [§1035]
On the above theory, the fact that many schools in a district are either predominantly white or predominantly black has been found *not* to be a violation of equal protection, absent a showing of intentional acts of segregation by the school board. [**Dayton Board of Education v. Brinkman,** 433 U.S. 406 (1977)]

(2) Thirteenth Amendment [§1036]
The Thirteenth Amendment prohibits slavery and gives Congress power

to outlaw any "badge or incident" of slavery. (*See infra*, §§1249-1250.) The Court has not decided whether a racially "discriminatory purpose" is required for a violation of the Thirteenth Amendment's bar against imposing "a badge or incident of slavery" on blacks. [**Memphis v. Greene,** 451 U.S. 100 (1981)]

(3) Fifteenth Amendment [§1037]

The Fifteenth Amendment gives Congress broad power to prevent discrimination in voting. (*See infra*, §§1267-1271.) The Supreme Court has not specifically decided whether a "discriminatory purpose" is required for a violation of the Fifteenth Amendment. [**City of Mobile v. Bolden,** 446 U.S. 55 (1980)]

2. What Is a "Suspect" Classification?

CHECKLIST OF SUSPECT CLASSIFICATIONS	gilbert

LAWS OR GOVERNMENT ACTIONS THAT TREAT PEOPLE DIFFERENTLY BASED ON THE FOLLOWING CRITERIA ARE UNCONSTITUTIONAL UNLESS THE LAWS/ACTIONS ARE NECESSARY (OR NARROWLY TAILORED) TO SERVE A COMPELLING INTEREST:

☑ *Race*

☑ *National origin*

☑ *Alienage* (with some limited exceptions, if the law or action is attributable to a state agency rather than to Congress)

a. Racial (or ethnic) "classifications" [§1038]

Some government action merely "classifies" on the basis of race (or national origin); *i.e.*, it draws lines on the basis of a racial criterion but does not necessarily treat one race differently from another. For example, the prohibition of interracial cohabitation [**McLaughlin v. Florida,** 379 U.S. 184 (1964)—invalid] or of racial intermarriage [**Loving v. Virginia,** 388 U.S. 1 (1967)—invalid] ostensibly does not discriminate against members of one race; it appears to treat both races equally.

(1) Historical perspective

(a) *Strauder v. West Virginia*—broad protection [§1039]

In the first relevant case to reach the Supreme Court after adoption of the Thirteenth, Fourteenth, and Fifteenth Amendments [**Strauder v. West Virginia,** 100 U.S. 303 (1880)], the Court invalidated the state murder conviction of an African-American man because the state prohibited African-Americans from serving on juries. The Court held that the Fourteenth Amendment prohibited any law that implied inferiority of African-Americans or that constituted "steps towards reducing them to the condition of a subject race."

(b) *Plessy v. Ferguson*—separate but equal [§1040]

Less than 20 years after *Strauder, supra,* the Supreme Court modified the goals it espoused there. In **Plessy v. Ferguson,** 163 U.S. 537 (1896), the Supreme Court upheld a Louisiana law that required railway cars to have "equal but separate accommodations for the white and colored races." The Court reasoned that while the Civil War Amendments require equality, the races did not have to be mixed to guarantee equality.

(c) *Brown v. Board of Education*—invalidated separate but equal [§1041]

The "separate but equal" rule was abandoned in **Brown v. Board of Education,** 347 U.S. 483 (1954). In *Brown,* Brown and other black children were denied admission to schools attended by white children under laws requiring or permitting segregation based on race. There was proof that the schools involved had been equalized in terms of buildings, curricula, qualifications, salaries of teachers, etc. Nevertheless, the Supreme Court held that segregation on the basis of race violated the Equal Protection Clause.

(2) **Modern standard—strict scrutiny [§1042]**

Since 1954, the Supreme Court has *generally* treated racial "classifications" the same as "discriminations"; *i.e.,* they are prohibited unless *necessary* to a *compelling* state interest. [**McLaughlin v. Florida,** *supra*; **Loving v. Virginia,** *supra*]

Example: In **Anderson v. Martin,** 375 U.S. 399 (1964), the Court invalidated a state law requiring that a candidate's race be designated on the election ballot on the ground that this "induces racial prejudice at the polls." [*Compare* **Tancil v. Woolls,** 379 U.S. 19 (1964)—a state *may,* for statistical purposes, require designation of parties' race on divorce decrees]

Example: Upon her divorce from Sidoti, Palmore, who was white, was awarded custody of the couple's three-year-old daughter. Palmore then began co-habiting with a black man. Sidoti petitioned for custody based on changed circumstances. Palmore then married her co-habitant, but the trial court nevertheless modified its decree to award custody to Sidoti, finding that the modification was in the best interests of the child because she would suffer social stigmatization if she were raised in a racially mixed household. The Supreme Court invalidated the modification, holding that the racial prejudice of others cannot justify a governmental racial classification. [**Palmore v. Sidoti,** 466 U.S. 429 (1984)]

(3) **Racial segregation [§1043]**

Segregation by race is a "classification" that appears to treat both races equally. However, as discussed above, deliberate ("de jure") racial segregation in public schools violates equal protection. [**Brown v. Board of Education,** *supra*—separate facilities are "inherently unequal"; *and see* **Bolling v. Sharpe,** *supra*, §426—racial segregation in District of Columbia public schools violates Fifth Amendment due process]

(a) Scope of application [§1044]

This principle has been applied to public facilities of all types—*e.g.*, public beaches and bathhouses, municipal golf courses, public transportation, stadiums and theaters, courtrooms, and public office buildings.

(b) Proving school segregation [§1045]

Although the existence of schools segregated in fact, without more, will not establish a constitutional violation (*supra*, §1035), evidence for the necessary finding of *segregative intent* may be drawn from actions having foreseeable and anticipated disparate impact. [**Columbus Board of Education v. Penick,** 443 U.S. 449 (1979)]

1) "Segregated" [§1046]

In determining whether a school is "segregated," courts must consider the number of all minority groups in the schools (not just blacks) who have suffered unequal treatment in education. [**Keyes v. School District No. 1,** 413 U.S. 189 (1973)—segregation of Hispanics]

2) Presumptions [§1047]

The Court uses several presumptions in the school segregation area [**Keyes v. School District No. 1,** *supra*]:

a) Dual system in entire district [§1048]

A finding that school authorities intentionally segregated a *significant portion* of the school district creates a presumption that the *entire school district*—i.e., even schools with mixed racial composition—is being operated on a segregated basis. This is because of the "substantial reciprocal effect" that segregation of some schools may have on others.

b) Uniracial schools [§1049]

A finding that school authorities have intentionally segregated a *meaningful portion* of the school district creates a presumption of intentional segregation for all other schools in the district that are in fact segregated. This is because a showing of segregative intent as to some schools suggests that all other schools in the system that are in fact segregated were also intentionally segregated.

3) Rebuttal [§1050]

If a presumption of segregative intent exists, the burden shifts to the school authorities to prove that (i) irrespective of any racially neutral explanations for their policies (such as maintenance of neighborhood schools), segregative intent was not among their motivations, or (ii) if they were motivated at all by segregative intent, past intentional segregative actions did not create or contribute to the current condition of segregation, or (iii) because of natural geographic boundaries, the school district is in fact divided into separate and unrelated units. [**Keyes v. School District No. 1,** *supra*]

(c) Remedying segregation [§1051]

School boards have an affirmative duty to eliminate intentional racial segregation of schools. The burden is on the school authorities to produce a plan that promises "immediate progress," and to explain why seemingly more effective methods have not been employed. [**Green v. New Kent County School Board,** 391 U.S. 430 (1968)]

1) Scope of remedy [§1052]

The remedy in any given case must be determined by the nature and scope of the constitutional violation. It may not extend beyond the conditions produced by that violation. A system-wide remedy may be imposed only if a system-wide violation has been found. [**Dayton Board of Education v. Brinkman,** *supra*, §1035]

a) Interdistrict remedies [§1053]

A remedy for segregation may not extend beyond the boundaries of the school district that has engaged in segregation, unless it is shown that district lines were discriminatorily drawn, or that the discrimination has produced a "significant segregative effect" in the other districts included in the desegregation plan. [**Milliken v. Bradley,** 418 U.S. 717 (1974)]

Example: It is impermissible for a court to impose a remedy whose purpose is to attract nonminority students from outside the school district. This remedy seeks indirectly to accomplish the interdistrict transfer of students that cannot be accomplished directly. [**Missouri v. Jenkins,** 515 U.S. 70 (1995)]

Compare: A metropolitan-area remedy for public housing segregation may be imposed even though the segregation took place only within the city—*if* (i) the government agency that engaged in the segregation can act outside city boundaries, *and* (ii) the remedy does not "impermissibly interfere" with innocent suburban governmental units. [**Hills v. Gautreaux**, 425 U.S. 284 (1976)]

2) **Scope of duty [§1054]**

If a school system is found to have been intentionally segregated at the time of the *Brown* decision in 1954 (or thereafter), the school board may not take any action (irrespective of its purpose) that has the *effect* of continuing the dual school system—unless the school board satisfies its "heavy burden" that such action serves "important and legitimate ends." [**Dayton Board of Education v. Brinkman**, 443 U.S. 526 (1979); **Columbus Board of Education v. Penick**, *supra*, §1045]

3) **Guidelines for school authorities and courts [§1055]**

The Supreme Court has held that conditions in different localities vary so widely that *no rigid rules* can be laid down for all situations. The first obligation is that of the school authorities. Their interest in managing their own affairs must be taken into account, but if they default, a court's *equitable powers* to remedy past wrongs are broad. "The task is to correct, by a *balancing* of the individual and collective interests, the condition that offends the Constitution." [**Swann v. Charlotte-Mecklenburg Board of Education**, 402 U.S. 1 (1971)]

a) *Ordering some busing, and assigning students on a racial basis* irrespective of compactness or contiguousness of school zones may be used by school boards and the courts. Also, they may *use mathematical ratios* of black and white students in the district as a starting point in fashioning a remedy. Furthermore, they need not be "color-blind" in *assigning teachers* in order to achieve faculty desegregation.

b) *If a plan leaves some schools containing all or predominantly one race,* the school board has the burden of showing that assignments are genuinely nondiscriminatory.

c) *New school construction and abandonment of old schools* may *not* be used to perpetuate or restore segregation.

d) *Optional "majority-to-minority" transfer provisions* are valid—and they must provide free transportation to, and space available in, the school to which transfer is sought.

e) *State laws that forbid such remedial measures* violate the Fourteenth Amendment. [**Swann v. Charlotte-Mecklenburg Board of Education**, *supra*]

f) *Remedial programs* may be ordered if necessary to restore the victims of discrimination to the educational position they would otherwise have enjoyed. [**Milliken v. Bradley**, 433 U.S. 267 (1977)]

4) New school districts [§1056]

Courts have discretion to enjoin carving out new school districts from existing districts if the *effect*—irrespective of a permissible purpose—would be to hinder the dismantling of a dual school system. Although disparity in the racial composition of the two systems is not enough per se to enjoin the creation of a separate district, it is significant. [**Wright v. Council of Emporia**, 407 U.S. 451 (1972)]

5) Higher education [§1057]

The affirmative duty to eliminate intentional racial segregation *applies* to public colleges and universities as well as elementary and secondary schools. Any policy (*e.g.*, admissions) that is traceable to the prior dual system and that continues to have segregative effects is invalid unless the state proves that it has "sound educational justification" and that it is "impractical to eliminate." [**United States v. Fordice**, 505 U.S. 717 (1992)]

6) Termination of duty [§1058]

Once a racially neutral attendance pattern has been established by student assignment, the federal court *cannot* require a school district to rearrange its attendance zones annually in order to insure the desired racial mix (absent further segregative actions by the district). [**Pasadena Board of Education v. Spangler**, 427 U.S. 424 (1976)]

a) Partial withdrawal of judicial supervision [§1059]

If a district has achieved unitary status with respect to one aspect of school administration (*e.g.*, student assignments), the court *may* withdraw supervision over this category even though the vestiges of segregation may exist in respect to another category (*e.g.*, faculty assignments). Judicial discretion should particularly be informed by whether the school district has shown its good faith commitment to desegregate all aspects of the dual system and whether continued *full* judicial control is needed to achieve compliance in *all* categories. [**Freeman v. Pitts**, 503 U.S. 467 (1992)]

7)   Aid to segregated private schools [§1060]

The Supreme Court has held that the Equal Protection Clause prohibits the states from lending textbooks (or giving tuition credits) to students of private schools that "practice racial or other invidious discrimination," even though the *state's* purpose is not to discriminate. These are "basic educational tools" that significantly aid the schools themselves—and are distinguishable from generalized services (electricity, water, police and fire protection), which the government might provide to schools in common with other users. [**Norwood v. Harrison,** 413 U.S. 455 (1973)]

a)   And note

Neither may the states provide private segregated schools with periodic exclusive access to recreational facilities. Where such schools were formed in response to a court desegregation order the access violates the Equal Protection Clause. [**Gilmore v. City of Montgomery,** 417 U.S. 556 (1974)]

8)   Distinguish—nonschool situations [§1061]

The *affirmative duty* to eliminate intentional racial segregation does not extend beyond schools to such *voluntary* associations as 4-H Clubs or Homemaker Clubs operated by a state agricultural agency. [**Bazemore v. Friday,** 478 U.S. 385 (1986)]

9)   Distinguish—closing of facilities [§1062]

The Court found no equal protection violation where a city closed its public swimming pools after a court order to desegregate, "to preserve peace and order and because the pools could not be operated economically on an integrated basis." [**Palmer v. Thompson,** 403 U.S. 217 (1971)]

a)   Rationale

The Court in *Palmer* concluded that the city's purposes were legitimate, and that there was no showing of "state action affecting blacks differently from whites." **Griffin v. County School Board,** *supra,* §116, which ordered the reopening of public schools closed to avoid a desegregation order, was distinguished. There, the state was covertly aiding and maintaining "private" segregated schools that were private in name only.

(4)   "Benign" discrimination [§1063]

Because all classifications based on race carry a danger of stigmatic harm, government action that *favors* racial or ethnic minorities is subject to the same standard of "strict scrutiny" review as is government action that discriminates *against* racial or ethnic minorities. Thus, it will be upheld only if it is *necessary* (or *narrowly tailored*) to achieve a *compelling* government interest. [**City of Richmond v. J.A. Croson Co.**, 488 U.S. 469 (1989)]

(a) Remedying past discrimination against minorities [§1064]

The government has a "compelling" interest in remedying past discrimination against racial or ethnic minority groups and, under some circumstances, it may give preference to members of such groups (even if the persons benefited are not themselves the actual victims of the discrimination). However, the past discrimination must be identified by a properly authorized government body as a constitutional or statutory violation. A race-based plan cannot be used to remedy *general* past "*societal* discrimination." [**City of Richmond v. J.A. Croson Co.**, *supra*]

EXAM TIP   gilbert

Unless you've been living in a cave for the past 10 years, you probably know that the Court's recent focus in remedying past discrimination has not been on school busing and related issues (*supra*, §§1051-1059), but rather on affirmative action programs. Be sure to understand the issues involved. Affirmative action programs favor a minority race or ethnic group over the majority and so constitute discrimination against the majority. Because of this discrimination, like other government action that discriminates, an affirmative action program will be upheld only if it is *necessary* (or *narrowly tailored*) to achieve a *compelling* government interest. The Court has found that remedying past discrimination *is* a compelling government interest. But remember, if a government agency adopts an affirmative action program on this ground, it must actually be able to *show past discrimination* against the group in question and that the affirmative action *program is narrowly tailored* to remedy that discrimination; otherwise, the program will be held to violate the Equal Protection Clause.

---

1) Findings required [§1065]

An affirmative action plan need not be preceded by a *formal finding* that there has been past discrimination by the government body instituting the plan or by other private parties. But when non-minorities challenge the plan, the court must make a *factual determination* that there was a *strong basis* for the government body's conclusion that remedial action was necessary. [**Wygant v. Jackson Board of Education**, 476 U.S. 267 (1986)]

2) Numerical goals [§1066]

Flexible numerical goals may be used to remedy past discrimination. However, they must be "narrowly tailored," *e.g.*: (i) of limited duration, (ii) based on pertinent racial percentages in the relevant population, (iii) impose relatively light burdens on non-minorities, and (iv) there can be no alternative "race neutral" remedies that would be effective. [**Sheet Metal Workers' International Association v. Equal Employment Opportunity Commission**, 478 U.S. 421 (1986)—no majority opinion]

3) Deference to trial judge [§1067]

Although a judicial order to remedy past discrimination should be "narrowly tailored," substantial respect should be accorded a district judge's choice of remedies. The least restrictive means is *not* always required. [**United States v. Paradise**, 480 U.S. 149 (1987)]

4) School desegregation [§1068]

As noted previously, the Court has held that racial criteria may be used in assigning students and teachers to remedy prior *de jure* school segregation. [**Swann v. Charlotte-Mecklenburg Board of Education**, *supra*, §1055]

(b) Student diversity in higher education

1) Justice Powell in *Bakke*—race as a plus [§1069]

In 1978, Justice Powell cast the deciding vote in a case involving preferences for minority students in the medical school admissions process. [**Regents of University of California v. Bakke**, 438 U.S. 265 (1978)] In that case, the University of California had an admissions policy that set aside 16 of 100 seats in each entering medical school class for minority students. Bakke, a white student who was denied a seat in the medical school while less qualified minority students were admitted, sued, claiming that the quota system violated the Equal Protection Clause. Although a majority of the Supreme Court could not agree on a rationale, the quota system was struck down. In his opinion, Justice Powell stated that although quota systems violate the Equal Protection Clause, institutions of higher education do have a compelling interest in having a diverse class, and so such schools may consider race *as a plus* among the factors they consider when making admissions decisions.

2) Adoption of Powell's position [§1070]

While Justice Powell's opinion in *Bakke* was not joined by a majority of the Court, it has been a guidepost for most state-school admissions policies since 1978. The Court did not revisit the issue again until 2003, when a majority of the Court adopted much of Justice Powell's position. [**Grutter v. Bollinger**, 123 S. Ct. 2325 (2003); **Gratz v. Bollinger**, 123 S. Ct. 2411 (2003)]

a) Diversity as a compelling interest [§1071]

In *Grutter* and *Gratz, supra,* the schools involved argued that they had a compelling interest in having a diverse student body—not to remedy past discrimination, but rather in its own right—because students with diverse backgrounds enhance classroom discussions and the educational experience both in and outside the classroom, promote cross-racial understanding, and break down racial stereotypes for societal workforces. Much expert evidence was offered to support this claim. The Court held that it will defer to a state college or university's good faith judgment that it has such a compelling interest.

b) Race as a plus [§1072]

In his opinion in *Bakke,* Justice Powell wrote that colleges and universities should consider each applicant as an individual; while membership in a disadvantaged race may be considered as a plus, no single characteristic, including race, should automatically ensure admission. The Court adopted this position in both *Grutter* and *Gratz, supra,* holding that although race or ethnicity may be deemed a *plus,* as one of a range of factors, each applicant's qualities must be independently evaluated; if race or ethnicity is the defining criterion for admission, the admission policy will not be narrowly tailored to achieving the compelling interest of ensuring a diverse student body.

---

e.g. **Example:** In its admission process, the University of Michigan's law school required admissions officers to assess an applicant's academic ability and *all other factors* about the applicant relevant to whether the student will be an asset to the entering class. The school's policies specifically allowed officers to consider whether an applicant was from a group that has historically been discriminated against, such as African-Americans, Hispanics, and Native Americans. The officers were not told to prescribe any particular weight to this factor, although they were told to include enough applicants from historically underrepresented groups to ensure a "critical mass" of such students—*i.e.,* enough minority students so that they do not feel isolated or become spokespersons for their race. At trial, admissions officers testified that the extent that race factored into an admissions decision varied from applicant to applicant, and statistics showed that while race was a strong factor in admissions decisions, it was not the predominant factor.

Moreover, the number of minority students who enrolled each year varied significantly from year-to-year. The Court held that such a program does not violate the Equal Protection Clause. [**Grutter v. Bollinger**, *supra*]

Compare: To obtain a critical mass of minority students in its undergraduate class, the University of Michigan allowed admissions officers to give students points for being a member of a historically underrepresented minority group and for a variety of other factors (*e.g.,* academic ability, leadership ability, a good admissions essay, etc.). Being a member of an underrepresented minority group (as well as athletic ability and socioeconomic disadvantage) was worth 20 points, while high school leadership ability, a good admissions essay, etc., were worth less than five points each. Applicants with 100 points or more were guaranteed admission into the school. Under these admissions policies, virtually every academically qualified applicant who was from a group defined as a historically underrepresented minority group was admitted to the school. Such a program violates the Equal Protection Clause because it makes race the predominant factor in making admissions decisions and so the policy was not sufficiently narrowly tailored. [**Gratz v. Bollinger**, *supra*]

---

c) **Time limitation [§1073]**

Finally, in *Grutter*, the Court held that race considerations may not permanently be enshrined in admissions policies, but that periodic review of race-conscious admissions policies to determine whether racial preferences are still necessary to achieve student body diversity are sufficient to satisfy this limitation.

EXAM TIP   gilbert

Be sure to note that in *Bakke, Grutter,* and *Gratz,* the compelling interest asserted to justify granting minorities a preference in the college admissions process was **not** to remedy past discrimination; rather, the compelling interest asserted by the schools and approved by the Court was the **need to have a diverse student body** in order to achieve the goals of higher education (exposing students to different viewpoints; promoting cross-racial understanding, etc.). Also remember the lesson from *Gratz*, in order to be narrowly tailored to achieve the goal of diversity, a program **must be flexible**. Ethnicity may be considered as a plus, but may **not be the predominant criteria** for deciding whether a particular applicant is accepted.

1) De facto school segregation [§1074]

It is an open question whether school boards may use racial criteria for assignment in a voluntary effort to remedy de facto school segregation—but lower courts have upheld it.

(c) Congressional power [§1075]

The standard for judging all racial classifications drawn by the federal government is the same as for state and local action: strict scrutiny. These classifications violate the equal protection component of the Fifth Amendment Due Process Clause unless they are *narrowly tailored* measures that further *compelling* government interests. [**Adarand Constructors, Inc. v. Pena,** 515 U.S. 200 (1995)—overruling **Metro Broadcasting, Inc. v. Federal Communications Commission,** 497 U.S. 547 (1990)]

---

e.g. **Example:** Adarand Constructors, Inc., submitted the low bid for a guardrail subcontract on a federal road project. The terms of the prime contractor's contract called for additional compensation if subcontractors were hired who were certified as small businesses controlled by "socially and economically disadvantaged individuals." Thus, the subcontract for the guardrail was awarded to Gonzales Construction, which was certified as a small business controlled by socially and economically disadvantaged individuals. Adarand sued the secretary of transportation for an equal protection violation under the Fifth Amendment, and applying strict scrutiny, the Supreme Court found this race-based classification to be unconstitutional. [**Adarand Constructors, Inc. v. Pena,** *supra*]

---

1) Comment

Congress has special power under Section 5 of the Fourteenth Amendment to enforce equal protection (*see infra*, §§1251-1266). In applying strict scrutiny, the Court *may* give deference to congressional judgment in light of this power [**Fullilove v. Klutznick,** 448 U.S. 448 (1980)—upholding set aside for minority businesses of 10% federal grants for public works projects], but this is *unclear*.

2) Hiring preference for Native Americans [§1076]

A federal statute granting employment preference in the Bureau of Indian Affairs to qualified American Indians has been upheld on grounds that it was not a "racial" preference because it applied only to members of "federally recognized" tribes. [**Morton v. Mancari,** 417 U.S. 535 (1974)]

3) Distinguish—voting preference for "native Hawaiians" [§1077]

But granting descendants of native Hawaiians a voting preference for state officials that administer programs for the benefit of such persons violates the Fifteenth Amendment. Even if native Hawaiians have a status like that of Indians in organized tribes, this does not justify a racially based voting scheme for decisionmakers of critical state issues. [**Rice v. Cayetano,** 528 U.S. 495 (2000)]

(d) Legislative apportionment [§1078]

Race and ethnicity may be considered in drawing up new voting districts—without subjecting the districting scheme to strict scrutiny—as long as (i) no racial group has its overall voting strength minimized [**United Jewish Organizations v. Carey,** 430 U.S. 144 (1977)] and (ii) the district's shape and demographics (as well as more direct evidence of legislative purpose) show that race was *not* the dominant and controlling factor, *i.e.*, that other districting principles (such as respecting municipal borders) were not *subordinated* to race [**Miller v. Johnson,** 515 U.S. 900 (1995)].

1) Burden of proof [§1079]

The challenger bears the burden of proving the race-based motive. [**Shaw v. Hunt,** 517 U.S. 899 (1996)]

(5) Repeal of remedies for discrimination or segregation [§1080]

A state's simple repeal (or modification) of antidiscrimination laws (or remedies for de facto segregation) that are not required by the Constitution in the first place is *not* racial discrimination in violation of equal protection. [**Crawford v. Los Angeles Board of Education,** 458 U.S. 527 (1982)—state law providing that state courts may no longer order busing to remedy *de facto* school segregation upheld] But a state *does* violate equal protection if it reallocates decisionmaking authority in respect to *racial issues* between levels of government so as to make it more difficult for racial minorities to get favorable laws passed.

Example: A city charter that required the electorate to approve (by referendum) any city council ordinance aimed at racial or ancestral discrimination in housing, while voter approval was not required as to other kinds of ordinances, was held to violate equal protection. (The effect was to "freeze" the power of the city council to legislate in this field—to the obvious disadvantage of racial and ancestral minorities.) [**Hunter v. Erickson,** 393 U.S. 385 (1969)]

Example: A state law forbidding school boards, which had general authority over school matters (including busing), to order busing to remedy *de facto* school segregation was held to violate equal protection. (The effect was to make it harder for those seeking to end de facto segregation than for persons seeking comparable legislation.) [**Washington v. Seattle School District,** 458 U.S. 457 (1982)]

b.   State discrimination against aliens [§1081]

Most state discrimination against lawfully admitted aliens is "suspect" since aliens are precisely the kind of "discrete and insular" minority—with no direct vote in the political process—for whom judicial solicitude is appropriate. [**Graham v. Richardson,** 403 U.S. 365 (1971)] Thus, such discrimination will be upheld only if the state can prove that its action is narrowly tailored (or necessary) to achieve a compelling interest.

(1)   Distinguish—federal discrimination against aliens [§1082]

Because Congress has plenary power over the admission or exclusion of aliens (*see supra*, §169), *federal* classifications based on alienage are *not* subject to strict equal protection scrutiny. [**Mathews v. Diaz,** 426 U.S. 67 (1976)—upholding congressional denial of Medicare to certain classes of aliens, using "traditional" rational basis equal protection test]

(2)   Illustrations of invalid state laws

(a)   Welfare [§1083]

Because aliens as well as citizens pay taxes from which welfare benefits are derived, there is no compelling state interest justifying denial of welfare to resident aliens. [**Graham v. Richardson,** *supra*]

(b)   Bar admission, other professional licenses, etc. [§1084]

Because the fact that a person is an alien does not mean that he would be unqualified to practice law, such discrimination is not necessary to a compelling state interest. [*In re* **Griffiths,** 413 U.S. 717 (1973); *and see* **Examining Board of Engineers v. de Otero,** 426 U.S. 572 (1976)—law denying civil engineer's license to aliens held invalid; **Bernal v. Fainter,** 467 U.S. 216 (1984)—law precluding aliens from being notaries public held invalid]

(c)   Civil service [§1085]

Similarly, there is no compelling state interest in excluding aliens from *all* civil service employment; such a law "sweeps indiscriminately." [**Sugarman v. Dougall,** 413 U.S. 634 (1973)] However, the rule is different for civil service jobs related to the process of self-government (*see infra*).

(d)   Land ownership [§1086]

Some earlier cases upheld state laws barring aliens from land ownership [*see, e.g.,* **Terrace v. Thompson,** 263 U.S. 297 (1923)], or from exploiting natural resources [*see, e.g.,* **Patsone v. Pennsylvania,** 232 U.S. 138 (1914)]. However, these decisions are questionable in light of the more recent cases discussed above. [*See also* **Takahashi v. Fish & Game Commission,** 334 U.S. 410 (1948)—state law denying commercial fishing licenses to persons ineligible for citizenship held invalid]

(3) Effect of eligibility for citizenship [§1087]

The fact that the state discriminates only against aliens who are eligible for U.S. citizenship but choose not to become citizens is irrelevant; the discrimination is still "suspect." [**Nyquist v. Mauclet,** 432 U.S. 1 (1977)—denial to such aliens of state financial assistance for higher education held invalid]

(4) Participation in process of self-government—"traditional" test [§1088]

A state has "historical power to exclude aliens from participation in its democratic political institutions." Thus, as long as the state acts "rationally," aliens *may* be excluded from voting, jury service, elective office, and nonelective offices that formulate, execute, or review important public policy—*e.g.*, police officers [**Foley v. Connelie,** 435 U.S. 291 (1978)] or probation officers [**Cabell v. Chavez-Salido,** 454 U.S. 432 (1982)]. Furthermore, aliens may be denied positions as public elementary and secondary school teachers (because they influence the attitudes of students toward government, the political process and citizenship, as well as promote and provide an example for civic virtues). [**Ambach v. Norwick,** 441 U.S. 68 (1979)]

(5) Illegal aliens—special rules [§1089]

State discrimination against illegal aliens is *not* "suspect." However, denial of free public education to the children of illegal aliens imposes an enormous and lasting burden based on a status over which the children have no control. Thus, absent a congressional policy favoring the state rule, the discrimination violates equal protection unless it furthers a "substantial" state goal. [**Plyler v. Doe,** 457 U.S. 202 (1982)]

EXAM TIP   gilbert

There are a number of rules that you must remember regarding discrimination against aliens. First and foremost, remember that the test of constitutionality is different for *state discrimination* as opposed to federal discrimination. Congress has plenary power over alienage and may adopt laws that *rationally* discriminate against aliens. State laws that discriminate against aliens must generally past muster under the *strict scrutiny* test, which is a very difficult hurdle to overcome. Secondly, states have much greater leeway to discriminate against aliens in jobs relating to the *process of self-government* (e.g., voting, holding elective office, serving as a police officer or teacher, etc.). State discrimination against aliens concerning these jobs will be upheld as long as they are *rational*. Finally, states may discriminate against *illegal* aliens (except that they may *not* deny public education to the children of illegal aliens).

---

(6) Supremacy Clause [§1090]

Apart from the Equal Protection Clause, state laws that discriminate against lawfully admitted aliens, by imposing burdens not contemplated or authorized by Congress, conflict with Congress's plenary power over the admission of aliens. [**Toll v. Moreno,** 458 U.S. 1 (1982)—state university denial of in-state tuition to nonimmigrant aliens who are children of employees working for international organizations held invalid]

D. Quasi-Suspect Classifications— Intermediate Level of Scrutiny

1. Test—Intermediate Scrutiny [§1091]

Classifications based on gender or legitimacy are not "suspect," but neither are they judged by the "traditional" (or "rational basis") test. Intentional discriminations against members of a *"quasi-suspect"* class violate equal protection unless they are *substantially related* to *important* government objectives. [**Craig v. Boren,** 429 U.S. 190 (1976)—law that authorized serving of beer to females over 18 years old but to males only over 21 held invalid]

a. "De facto" discrimination [§1092]

As is true in respect to race and national origin (*see supra*, §1034), laws or other official actions that do not *intentionally* discriminate on the basis of gender but nonetheless have a sexually disproportionate impact are judged by the *"traditional"* test; they will be upheld if *rationally* related to a constitutionally permissible state interest. [**Personnel Administrator of Massachusetts v. Feeney,** 442 U.S. 256 (1979)—law giving hiring preference for public jobs to veterans upheld even though it severely restricted public employment opportunities for women]

2. Gender Discrimination

a. Discrimination against women [§1093]

All recent decisions have held that laws discriminating against women are *not* substantially related to an important government objective and thus violate equal protection. [*See, e.g.,* **Reed v. Reed,** 404 U.S. 71 (1972)—preferring men over women as between persons equally qualified under state law to administer estates; **Frontiero v. Richardson,** 411 U.S. 677 (1973)—federal statute limiting servicewoman's right to dependency benefit for her husband by requiring proof of actual dependency upon her for support, whereas a serviceman could obtain similar benefits for his wife without such proof]

(1) Distinguish—insurance exclusions for pregnancy [§1094]

A law excluding pregnancies from state disability insurance benefits has been upheld as "rational." The provision was held *not* to discriminate against women, but merely to exclude certain physical conditions from coverage so as to make the program (which covered both sexes) self-supporting. [**Geduldig v. Aiello,** 417 U.S. 484 (1974)]

(2) Nature of heightened scrutiny [§1095]

The "important government objective" advanced to justify categorization on the basis of gender must be *genuine*—not hypothesized for the purpose of litigation defense. Neither may the government's justification rely on *overbroad generalizations* about males and females that will create or perpetuate the legal, social, and economic inferiority of women. [**United States v. Virginia,** 518 U.S. 515 (1996)]

Example: When a state military school's policy of admitting only men was challenged, the state justified the policy by claiming that: (i) offering a diversity of educational approaches within the state (*e.g.*, some schools having men only, some schools having women only, and some schools having both) yields important educational benefits, and (ii) females *generally* would not be able to meet the school's physical requirements and would not do well under the school's adversative approach to education. The Supreme Court found these arguments unavailing. There was no evidence that the single-sex school in question was established or had been maintained with a view toward fostering a diversity of educational opportunities, and there was some evidence that *some* women could meet the school's physical requirements and thrive under the school's adversative approach. [**United States v. Virginia,** *supra*]

b. Discrimination against men [§1096]

Several decisions have held that laws that discriminate against men violate equal protection. [*See, e.g.*, **Craig v. Boren,** *supra*]

Example: The Court invalidated a law providing that a husband, but not a wife, may be required to pay alimony because the law did not serve the important state objective of assisting needy spouses; rather, this could be accomplished by treating men and women equally. [**Orr v. Orr,** 440 U.S. 268 (1979)]

Example: The Court struck down a law permitting an unwed mother, but not an unwed father, to block the adoption of their child by withholding consent. [**Caban v. Mohammed,** 441 U.S. 380 (1979)]

Example: The Court also found the exclusion of males from a state nursing school was invalid, because it perpetuated the stereotype of nursing as an exclusively women's job. [**Mississippi University for Women v. Hogan,** 458 U.S. 718 (1982)]

Example: Most recently, the Court found that using peremptory challenges to exclude males from a jury violates equal protection. [**J.E.B. v. Alabama** *ex rel.* **T.B.,** 511 U.S. 127 (1994)]

(1) Distinguish—valid discrimination against men [§1097]
Laws that discriminate against men have been upheld when found to be substantially related to an important government objective.

> **Example:** The Court has upheld statutory rape laws, which punish the male but not the female partner to the intercourse, because of the important state interest in preventing teenage pregnancy. [**Michael M. v. Sonoma County Superior Court**, 450 U.S. 464 (1981)]

> **Example:** The Court has also upheld draft registration of males only because of Congress's considered conclusion, pursuant to its military powers, that this was needed to further the important government interest of preparing for a draft of combat troops. [**Rostker v. Goldberg**, 453 U.S. 57 (1981)]

> **Example:** A state law precluding an unwed father, but not an unwed mother, from suing for the child's wrongful death unless the father has legitimated the child has been upheld because this promotes the important state objective of avoiding proof of paternity problems, which are more difficult to resolve for fathers. [**Parham v. Hughes**, 441 U.S. 347 (1979)] On similar analysis, the Court has upheld a federal statute that grants automatic United States citizenship to nonmarital children born abroad to American mothers, but requires that American fathers take specific steps to establish paternity in order to make such children United States citizens. [**Nguyen v. Immigration and Naturalization Service**, 533 U.S. 53 (2001)]

c. **Compensating women for past discrimination [§1098]**
Laws that purport to compensate for past discrimination against women have been upheld as being substantially related to an important government objective.

> **Example:** A state law granting a property tax exemption to widows, but not to widowers, has been held to further the state policy of cushioning the financial impact of spousal loss upon the sex for whom that loss usually imposes a heavier burden. [**Kahn v. Shevin**, 416 U.S. 351 (1974)]

> **Example:** A Social Security Act formula entitling female wage earners to a preference over males has been held to reduce the disparity in economic condition between men and women, caused by the long history of discrimination against women. [**Califano v. Webster**, 430 U.S. 313 (1977)]

> **Example:** The Navy's mandatory discharge procedure, which accords different treatment for male and female line officers (*i.e.,* male officers are automatically discharged if twice denied promotion, whereas female officers are not), was upheld because the promotional opportunities offered by the

GENDER CLASSIFICATIONS—A SUMMARY OF CASES gilbert

VALID DISCRIMINATION

- Law precluding an unwed father from suing for his child's **wrongful death**

- **Male only military draft**

- Naval procedure **automatically discharging men** who are passed over for promotion twice but not women

- Punishing teenage males but not teenage females for **statutory rape**

- Law **excluding pregnancy** from state disability benefits

- **Social Security preference** for women

- Giving widows but not widowers a **property tax exemption**

- Law granting **automatic citizenship** to nonmarital children born abroad to American women but requiring American fathers to take specific steps to establish paternity in order to make such children U.S. citizens

INVALID DISCRIMINATION

- Law providing that an unwed mother could block her child's **adoption** but not an unwed father

- Law requiring a servicewoman to prove that her husband is dependent on her in order to receive **dependency** benefits for him while a serviceman was not required to make a similar showing to obtain benefits for his wife

- Law preferring men over women in serving as the **administrator of an estate**

- Law providing that only ex-husbands can be required to pay **alimony**

- Excluding men from a **state nursing school**

- Excluding women from a **state military school**

- Using **peremptory challenges** to systematically exclude men or women from a jury

Navy for men had been greater than for women. [**Schlesinger v. Ballard,** 419 U.S. 498 (1975)]

d. Single-sex education [§1099]

The Court has not resolved the validity of a system of single-sex education. But if such diverse educational opportunities are not evenhanded—*i.e.,* are not "separate but equal"—they violate equal protection. [**United States v. Virginia,** *supra,* §1095— separate college for women who were excluded from Virginia Military Institute was a "pale shadow" in terms of curricular choice, faculty status, funding, prestige, and alumni]

3. Discrimination Against Nonmarital Children [§1100]

Discrimination against nonmarital children is not "suspect," but neither is it subject to the "toothless" traditional rational basis standard. [**Mathews v. Lucas,** 427 U.S. 495 (1976)] It is judged by a *"quasi-suspect"* standard, the same as that used for gender discrimination (supra, §1091). [**Clark v. Jeter,** 486 U.S. 456 (1988)—*"substantially* related to an *important* state interest"]

a. Prohibition against "punishing" innocent children [§1101]

Most state laws that discriminate against nonmarital children have been invalidated in order to assure that a state's concern over illicit relationships is not the basis for punitive measures against the product of such a relationship.

> **e.g.** **Example:** The Court found state laws excluding nonmarital children from sharing equally with marital children in workers' compensation death benefits payable on their father's death to be invalid. [**Weber v. Aetna Casualty & Surety Co.,** 406 U.S. 164 (1972)]

> **e.g.** **Example:** State laws permitting marital children (but not nonmaritial children) to maintain wrongful death actions on account of their parents' death were also struck down by the Court. [**Levy v. Louisiana,** 391 U.S. 68 (1968)]

> **e.g.** **Example:** The Court has also struck down state laws creating a support right in favor of marital children, but not nonmarital children. [**Gomez v. Perez,** 409 U.S. 535 (1973)]

b. Distinguish—some discrimination valid [§1102]

However, some discrimination against nonmarital children has been upheld as a "reasonable effort to serve administrative convenience."

> **e.g.** **Example:** Lucas filed an application for Social Security benefits for her two children following the death of their father, whom Lucas had never

married and from whom Lucas had been separated for two years prior to his death. Under Social Security regulations, children had to show dependency on the decedent in order to obtain benefits unless they fell into an excepted category, one of which was that they were marital children. Lucas's application was denied, and she appealed, claiming that the classification extending a presumption of dependency to marital children while excluding Lucas's nonmarital children violated the equal protection guarantees implicit in the Fifth Amendment Due Process Clause. The Supreme Court upheld the classification. The presumptions of dependency of marital children (and others under the regulations) are administrative aids that approximate what case-by-case adjudication would show and are reasonable to serve administrative convenience. Failure to extend the presumption of dependency to Lucas's children does not impermissibly discriminate them; they are free to prove dependency. [**Mathews v. Lucas,** *supra*]

Example: Similarly, a state may promote the just and expeditious disposition of property at death by denying intestate succession to a nonmarital child unless the paternity of the father is formally proved sometime before the death of the father. [**Lalli v. Lalli,** 439 U.S. 259 (1978)]

Example: And immigration provisions excluding a nonmarital child and the natural father from receiving preferences accorded to the "child" or "parent" of U.S. citizens have been upheld because of the broad plenary power of Congress over immigration legislation (*see supra*, §169). [**Fiallo v. Bell,** 430 U.S. 787 (1977)]

E. Classifications That Are Not Suspect or Quasi-Suspect

1. **Discrimination Against the Poor [§1103]**
   The Court has *said* that "poverty standing alone is not a suspect classification" [**Harris v. McRae,** *supra*, §520], and has *upheld* an explicit state classification adversely affecting poor people [**James v. Valtierra,** 402 U.S. 137 (1971)—state constitutional provision requiring a local referendum as a prerequisite to construction of low-rent public housing projects in the community upheld].

   a. **Distinguish—discrimination invalid [§1104]**
      In **Turner v. Fouche,** 396 U.S. 346 (1970), although the Court employed the "traditional" rational basis test, it held that a law making only freeholders eligible to be school board members violated equal protection. The classification was found to be "wholly irrelevant" to achievement of the state's asserted objectives.

b. **De facto discrimination [§1105]**

The major developments concerning discrimination against the poor have involved state laws or other official practices that have a disproportionate impact on poor people. Several decisions have held that a state's refusal to (i) waive a fee, or (ii) provide certain services free of charge for poor people in the course of criminal or civil litigation violates the Equal Protection Clause (or the Due Process Clause). Although the decisions do not readily fit into the normal equal protection framework, the holdings of unconstitutionality appear to be heavily influenced by (i) the "fundamental importance" of the right involved, and (ii) whether the state has "monopoly power" over the way the right is affected.

(1) Criminal appeals [§1106]

To assure "adequate and effective appellate review" of a criminal conviction, the state must provide indigents with a free trial transcript [**Griffin v. Illinois,** 351 U.S. 12 (1956)] and appointed counsel for the first appeal granted as a matter of right under state law [**Douglas v. California,** 372 U.S. 353 (1963)].

(a) Distinguish—discretionary appeals [§1107]

The right to appointed counsel does *not* extend to discretionary appeals from criminal convictions. [**Ross v. Moffit,** 417 U.S. 600 (1974)]

(2) Fine or imprisonment [§1108]

State laws imposing imprisonment for nonpayment of fines have the effect of discriminating against indigents. Thus, equal protection prohibits the state from imposing a fine as a sentence and then *automatically* converting it into a jail term solely because the defendant cannot immediately pay the fine in full. [**Tate v. Short,** 401 U.S. 395 (1971)]

(a) Probation revocation [§1109]

If the defendant is given probation on condition that he pay a fine (or make restitution), the "fundamental fairness" required by equal protection and due process forbids revocation of probation for failure to pay absent evidence and findings that the defendant was somehow responsible for the failure or that alternative forms of punishment (*e.g.,* public service work) were inadequate. [**Bearden v. Georgia,** 461 U.S. 660 (1983)]

(3) Divorce [§1110]

Under the Due Process Clause, states may not require the payment of court fees as a condition for judicial dissolution of marriage as to indigents who in good faith seek a divorce. The Court has limited the potential scope of this decision by noting (i) the "basic position of the marriage relationship" in society, and (ii) "state monopolization of the means for legally dissolving this relationship." [**Boddie v. Connecticut,** 401 U.S. 371 (1971)]

(4) Parental rights [§1111]

Both the Due Process Clause and the Equal Protection Clause prohibit a state from requiring indigents to pay the cost of a transcript in order to appeal from a termination of their parental rights. The Court emphasized that such cases are "quasi-criminal in nature"—a state initiated destruction of parents' fundamental interest in their relationship with their children. [**M.L.B. v. S.L.J.**, 519 U.S. 102 (1996)]

(5) Paternity actions [§1112]

Similarly, under the Due Process Clause, a state must pay for blood tests that may exculpate indigent defendants in paternity actions—at least where the state is itself requiring the mother to bring the paternity suit. [**Little v. Streater**, 452 U.S. 1 (1981)]

(6) Distinguish—bankruptcy [§1113]

However, the state *may* require payment of a fee (or a promise to pay in installments) as a condition for discharge in a voluntary bankruptcy proceeding. The *Boddie* case (*supra*) was distinguished because the "marital relationship" is of "fundamental importance"; also, a state judicial proceeding is *not the only method available* for adjustment of a debtor's legal relationship—since a debtor may also settle with creditors by negotiated agreement. [**United States v. Kras**, 409 U.S. 434 (1973)]

(7) Distinguish—welfare appeal [§1114]

On somewhat similar reasoning—particularly the fact that, unlike the marital relationship, which has "constitutional significance," welfare falls "in the area of economics and social welfare"—the Court has held that a state filing fee applied to an indigent seeking judicial review of an adverse welfare decision does not violate due process or equal protection. [**Ortwein v. Schwab**, 410 U.S. 656 (1973)]

(8) Distinguish—abortion [§1115]

Furthermore, states may deny indigents Medicaid for nontherapeutic abortions. Again (unlike *Boddie*), the state has not monopolized the means to terminate pregnancies. [**Maher v. Roe**, 432 U.S. 464 (1977)] Similarly, the state may deny Medicaid for abortions even if "medically necessary"—at least where the mother's life is not threatened. [**Harris v. McRae**, *supra*, §1103]

(9) Voting [§1116]

Cases invalidating payment requirements for the right to vote, as discriminating against poor people, are discussed *infra*, §§1146 *et seq.* [**Harper v. Virginia Board of Elections**, 383 U.S. 663 (1966)—poll tax; **Bullock v. Carter**, 405 U.S. 134 (1972)—high filing fees to get on primary election ballot]

DISCRIMINATION AGAINST THE POOR—A SUMMARY OF CASES · gilbert

VALID DISCRIMINATION	INVALID DISCRIMINATION
Failure to provide an indigent with a free trial transcript for a *discretionary appeal*	Failure to provide an indigent with a *free trial transcript* needed for an *appeal of right*
Requiring indigents to pay a filing fee in order to *appeal an adverse welfare benefits decision*	Failure to provide indigent parents with a free transcript to appeal a *termination of parental rights*
Requiring indigents to pay a filing fee in order to file for *bankruptcy*	Failure to pay for a *blood test* that might exculpate an indigent defendant in a paternity action
Denying Medicaid benefits to pay for an *abortion* except where the mother's life is threatened	*Refusing to grant a divorce* to a person who cannot pay court fees
State constitutional provision requiring a local referendum to approve local *public housing projects*	Law limiting *school board membership* to landowners
	Law automatically imposing imprisonment for *failure to pay a fine* (must exempt persons who are financially unable to pay)
	Requiring persons to pay a fee in order to *vote*

2. **Discrimination Against the Elderly [§1117]**

Laws or other official actions that discriminate against the elderly are neither "suspect" nor "quasi-suspect." They are judged by the *"traditional"* ("rational basis") test. *Rationale:* Although the Court has not authoritatively defined the criteria that make a classification "suspect" (or "quasi-suspect"), it has noted that important indicia are (i) a *class determined by characteristics that are unalterable;* and (ii) a class subjected to such a *history of purposefully unequal treatment,* or relegated to a position of such *political powerlessness,* as to command extraordinary protection from majority rule. [*See* **Johnson v. Robison,** 415 U.S. 361 (1974)] It has been held that the aged do not satisfy the second criterion. [**Massachusetts Board of Retirement v. Murgia,** 427 U.S. 307 (1976)—police officer can be compelled to retire at age 50]

3. **Discrimination Against Nonresidents [§1118]**

A bona fide residence requirement—living in the place with an intention to remain—creates no "suspect" classification. It is judged by the "traditional" ("rational basis") test. [**Martinez v. Bynum,** 461 U.S. 321 (1983)—free public education may be denied children who, apart from their parents and guardians, come to a school district solely to attend public schools]

4. **Discrimination Against the Mentally Retarded [§1119]**

Laws that discriminate against mentally retarded persons are neither "suspect" nor "quasi-suspect." *Rationale*: Government may legitimately take mental retardation into account for a wide range of decisions. And recent laws that benefit the mentally retarded demonstrate that there is *no history of prejudice* against them and that they are *not politically powerless*. [**Cleburne v. Cleburne Living Center, Inc.**, 470 U.S. 1002 (1985)]

a. **"Invidious" discrimination [§1120]**

But discriminatory government action that is not rationally related to a legitimate purpose is "invidious" and thus violates equal protection. [**Cleburne v. Cleburne Living Center, Inc.**, *supra*—ordinance requiring special permit for mentally retarded group home, but not for most other kinds of multiple dwellings (including hospitals, nursing homes, and dormitories) rests on irrational prejudice against the mentally retarded and violates equal protection]

F. Fundamental Rights—Strict Scrutiny

1. **Test [§1121]**

Government action that discriminates against (or "penalizes," or "unduly burdens") a "fundamental right"—*i.e.*, a right *explicitly or implicitly guaranteed by the Constitution*—is subject to "strict scrutiny" and violates equal protection unless found to be *necessary* to a *compelling* state interest. [*See* **San Antonio Independent School District v. Rodriguez**, 411 U.S. 1 (1973)]

2. **Freedom of Association [§1122]**

A state law that imposed *burdensome* requirements for new political parties to get their candidates on the election ballot (while exempting established political parties from such requirements) was held to violate the Equal Protection Clause because it impaired the freedom of association of the members of the new parties, and no "compelling state interest" was shown to justify the discrimination. [**Williams v. Rhodes**, 393 U.S. 23 (1968)]

a. **Nonburdensome classification [§1123]**

However, state laws imposing different, but not burdensome, requirements for small or new political parties to get their candidates' names printed on the ballot—such as using a convention process rather than a primary election—do *not* violate equal protection. [**American Party of Texas v. White**, 415 U.S. 767 (1974)]

b. **"Compelling" state interest [§1124]**

State requirements that candidates of new political parties demonstrate public support to get on the ballot have been upheld. Such requirements further a "compelling" state interest—*i.e.*, preserving the integrity of the electoral process by preventing the ballot from becoming unmanageable and confusing. [**American Party of Texas v. White**, *supra*]

(1) How much support [§1125]

Persons or parties seeking to get on the ballot may be required to demonstrate a "significant, measurable quantum of community support." [**Jenness v. Fortson,** 403 U.S. 431 (1971)—upholding requirement of nominating petitions signed by at least 5% of registered voters; groups unable to muster the 5% could still conduct "write-in" campaign]

(2) "Disaffiliation" requirement [§1126]

A law barring independent candidates in general elections if they were registered with a political party within one year prior to the immediately preceding primary has been upheld. The law did not discriminate against independents, because other provisions imposed similar disqualifications on regular political party candidates. The state's interest in "the stability of its political system" was held to be "compelling"—and the Court found "no reason for concluding that the [law] was not an essential part of [the state's] overall mechanism to achieve its acceptable goals." [**Storer v. Brown,** 415 U.S. 724 (1974)]

(3) Early filing deadlines [§1127]

A law requiring an independent candidate for President to file more than seven months before the November general election, was held to violate the fundamental rights of voters and candidates. The state's interest in regulating *presidential* elections is less important than for state and local elections because the former will be largely determined by voters in other states. The state's interests here (*e.g.,* having an informed electorate, promoting political stability) are "minimal" when compared to the significant restriction imposed by the seven-month rule on the ability of independent candidates and their supporters to take advantage of campaign developments occurring closer to the general election. [**Anderson v. Celebrezze,** 460 U.S. 780 (1983)]

c. Funding presidential campaigns [§1128]

The provision by Congress of more public funds to the two "major" political parties than to "minor" or "new" parties for presidential campaigns (*i.e.,* based on the ratio of the vote the latter receive to that of the major parties) does not violate equal protection. The general interest of Congress in "eliminating the proper influence of large contributions" is vital, and the interest in "not funding hopeless campaigns" with substantial public monies justifies withholding assistance from candidates without significant public support. Finally, those who accept public funds suffer a countervailing restriction—in that they must agree to limit their total expenditures. [**Buckley v. Valeo,** 424 U.S. 1 (1976)]

3. Right to Travel Interstate [§1129]

State *durational* residence requirements, that impose *waiting periods* before new residents may receive *vital* government benefits or services, have been held to "penalize" those who have recently exercised their constitutional right to travel interstate (*see infra*, §1243), and thus violate equal protection unless found to be "necessary to promote a compelling state interest."

a. Welfare [§1130]

A one-year residency requirement to qualify for public welfare has been held invalid because (i) budgetary and recordkeeping considerations are *not* "compelling," and (ii) deterring indigents from entering the state or limiting welfare to those who have paid taxes are constitutionally impermissible objectives. [**Shapiro v. Thompson**, 394 U.S. 618 (1969)]

(1) Varied benefits

Similarly, a law providing that persons residing in the state for less than a year may receive welfare benefits no greater than those paid in the state of prior residence is also invalid. [**Saenz v. Roe**, *supra*, §527]

b. Medical care [§1131]

A one-year residency requirement in order to qualify for free nonemergency medical care has been held invalid. Like welfare, it is a "basic necessity of life." [**Memorial Hospital v. Maricopa County**, 415 U.S. 250 (1974)]

c. Voting [§1132]

State durational residency requirements of one year in the state and three months in the county in order to vote have failed to survive "strict scrutiny." [**Dunn v. Blumstein**, 405 U.S. 330 (1972)]

(1) Permissible limits [§1133]

Voting *registration* requirements of some sort are permissible. The Court has observed that a 30-day residency and registration requirement should be sufficient to prepare voters lists, etc.; it has upheld even longer requirements (*e.g.*, 50 days) where there was a positive showing that the longer period was actually necessary. [**Marston v. Lewis**, 410 U.S. 679 (1973)— "approaches outer constitutional limits"]

d. Other rights and benefits [§1134]

Not all state durational residency requirements are invalid. Where neither "necessities of life" nor "constitutional rights" (such as voting, *infra*, §§1146 *et seq.*) are denied, the right to travel from state to state is held not to be "penalized."

(1) Reduced tuition [§1135]

The Court has upheld durational residency requirements for students to qualify for reduced tuition rates at state colleges and universities. [**Starns v. Malkerson**, 401 U.S. 985 (1971)]

(2) Divorce [§1136]

A one-year residency requirement in order to obtain a divorce has also been upheld. Obtaining a divorce is not a "necessity of life" in the same sense as welfare or medical care. Moreover, the residency requirement served "momentous" government purposes: (i) it assured a "modicum of attachment" to the state where important interests such as alimony and child custody are litigated; and (ii) it avoided collateral attack on the state's divorce decrees for lack of domicile. [**Sosna v. Iowa**, 419 U.S. 393 (1975)]

e. **"Length of residence" requirements [§1137]**

It is "impermissible" for states to apportion benefits and services according to length of residency.

Example: Alaska has an abundance of state-owned natural resources and a large income derived from selling rights to these resources. The state legislature enacted a statute by which dividends from the state's oil leases would be distributed to the state's adult residents. The amount of the dividend depended on a resident's length of residency (each resident would receive $50 for each year they resided in Alaska since it had achieved statehood). Zobel, a relatively new Alaska resident, challenged the statute on equal protection grounds. To justify its length of residency discrimination, the state asserted, among other reasons, that the discrimination merely recognized the difference in contributions that long-time vs. short-time residents had made to the state. The Court found this rationale constitutionally illegitimate—a state cannot apportion state benefits based on past taxes paid or other contributions made by citizens. [**Zobel v. Williams**, 457 U.S. 55 (1982)]

---

(1) **"Date of residence" requirements [§1138]**

Nor may a state prefer those who are residents as of a certain date over new residents in the allocation of economic benefits. [**Hooper v. Bernalillo County Assessor**, 472 U.S. 612 (1985)—property tax exemption only for those Vietnam veterans who were state residents as of a certain date not "rationally related" to the state's goals and thus violates equal protection; *and see* **Attorney General v. Soto-Lopez**, 476 U.S. 898 (1986)—state employment preference only for those veterans who were state residents when they entered military service violates equal protection]

f. **Distinguish—continuing residency requirement [§1139]**

An appropriately defined and uniformly applied requirement of residency at the time of (and during) receipt of governmental benefits, services, etc., has been held *not* to impair the right to travel interstate. *Rationale:* The person is free to move to the state and establish residence there. [**McCarthy v. Philadelphia Civil Service Commission**, 424 U.S. 645 (1976)—requiring personal residence at place of governmental employment; **Martinez v. Bynum**, *supra*, §1118]

(1) **Note**

Under this approach, a state need not continue to afford benefits to persons who are no longer residents. [**Califano v. Torres**, 435 U.S. 1 (1978)—

Social Security benefits available in United States, but not Puerto Rico, may be lost when person moves from the United States to Puerto Rico]

DURATIONAL RESIDENCY REQUIREMENTS—A SUMMARY **gilbert**

RESIDENCY REQUIREMENT	STATUS
One-year residency to receive welfare	Invalid
One-year residency to receive state subsidized medical care	Invalid
One-year residency to vote in state	Invalid
Thirty-day residency to vote in state	Valid
One-year residency to get divorced	Valid

---

4. **Right of Privacy [§1140]**

A right of personal privacy has been recognized as implicit in the "liberty" protected by the Due Process Clause. (*See supra*, §§502 *et seq.*) Hence, statutory classifications that "penalize" or unduly burden this right are subject to "strict scrutiny" under the Equal Protection Clause.

a. **Right to marry [§1141]**

Laws that "interfere *directly and substantially*" with the right to marry violate equal protection unless they can withstand "rigorous scrutiny." [**Zablocki v. Redhail,** 434 U.S. 374 (1978)—a law forbidding marriage by a person not complying with a court order to support his minor children is invalid]

(1) **Some regulation of marriage valid [§1142]**

The strict scrutiny standard does not apply to all laws regulating marriage, as where the law does not "significantly interfere" with the decision to marry. Such laws are valid if they are "rational." [**Califano v. Jobst,** 429 U.S. 1089 (1977)—terminating Social Security to person who marries is valid because it places "no direct obstacle" to marriage]

(2) **Right to procreate [§1143]**

The Court has invalidated a statute providing for the sterilization of "habitual criminals." The right to procreate is "one of the basic civil rights of man" and classifications affecting it are judged by the strict equal protection test. The statute in issue was written so as to provide for sterilization of persons convicted of larceny but not embezzlement even though these crimes are, intrinsically, similar. Thus, the statute was not narrowly tailored to achieve its purpose. [**Skinner v. Oklahoma**, *supra*, §504]

(3) Right to abortion [§1144]

Government refusal to give Medicaid for abortions, while providing it for childbirth, does *not* penalize or unduly burden the constitutional right of a woman to terminate a pregnancy; the state does not thereby create any obstacles to an indigent's obtaining an abortion that were not already present. Thus, such regulations are subject to the traditional equal protection test. [**Maher v. Roe**, *supra*, §1115; **Harris v. McRae**, *supra*, §1115] Likewise, providing public hospital services for childbirth but not for abortions does not violate equal protection. [**Poelker v. Doe**, 432 U.S. 519 (1977)]

5. Freedom of Speech [§1145]

When government restricts speech or speech-related activities, the legislation must be *finely tailored* to serve *substantial* state interests and the justification offered for any distinctions it draws must be carefully scrutinized. [**Carey v. Brown**, 447 U.S. 455 (1980)—holding unconstitutional a statute that prohibited picketing of dwellings, but exempted from its prohibition peaceful picketing of a residence that was a place of employment involved in a labor dispute; **Chicago Police Department v. Mosley**, 408 U.S. 92 (1972)—holding unconstitutional an ordinance barring all picketing near schools, but exempting such picketing of a school involved in a labor dispute]

6. Right to Vote [§1146]

Several amendments to the Constitution forbid government (state and federal) denial of the right to vote on specified grounds: "race, color, or previous condition of servitude" [Fifteenth Amendment]; "sex" [Nineteenth Amendment]; "failure to pay any poll tax or other tax" to vote in federal elections [Twenty-Fourth Amendment]; and "age" if more than 18 years old [Twenty-Sixth Amendment]. Apart from these specific prohibitions, however, there is no general right to vote mentioned in the Constitution. Nonetheless, the Court has held that government discriminations with respect to voting are subject to strict scrutiny under the Equal Protection Clause; unless they are *necessary* to a *compelling* interest, such discriminations violate the "constitutionally protected right to participate in elections on an equal basis with other citizens in the jurisdiction." [**Dunn v. Blumstein**, *supra*, §1132]

a. Denial of the vote [§1147]

A number of cases have considered state laws granting the right to vote to some *bona fide residents* of requisite *age* and *citizenship* while denying it to others. Most such laws have been held to deny equal protection—either because the discrimination could not be justified by a "compelling" state interest, or because the classification was "overbroad" (in that it was not "necessary" to promote a compelling state interest).

(1) Armed forces [§1148]

A state law that required bona fide residence as a qualification to vote, but which prohibited military service personnel stationed within the state from ever acquiring such residence, was held to violate equal protection. [**Carrington v. Rash,** 380 U.S. 89 (1965)]

(2) Poll tax [§1149]

A law conditioning the right to vote on payment of a poll tax was held to violate the Equal Protection Clause—because wealth bears no relation to voter qualification. [**Harper v. Virginia Board of Elections,** *supra*, §1116]

(3) School board elections [§1150]

A law limiting the vote in school district elections to those who have children in local public schools, or who own or lease real property, was held to violate equal protection. Even if voters could be limited to those "primarily interested in school affairs," the classification was *not narrowly tailored*—because it excluded some types of people who were interested (such as the plaintiff, Kramer, who was a 31-year-old bachelor living with his parents who was very interested in the election) and included others who were not (such as a young, unemployed bachelor who rented an apartment within the district). [**Kramer v. Union Free School District,** 395 U.S. 622 (1969)]

(4) Federal enclaves [§1151]

Persons who live on a federal enclave (*e.g.*, National Institutes of Health) located within a state cannot be denied the right to vote in state elections—because these persons are subject to important aspects of state power and are as interested in electoral decisions as those outside the enclave. [**Evans v. Cornman,** 398 U.S. 419 (1970)]

(5) Bond elections [§1152]

The right to vote on the issuance of municipal bonds cannot be limited to local property taxpayers—because nonproperty owners also have a substantial interest in the improvements to be financed by such bonds. And even if the bonds are to be paid from property taxes alone, the costs of the improvements inevitably will be passed on to nonproperty owners (as tenants or purchasers of goods and services from property owners). [**City of Phoenix v. Kolodziejski,** 399 U.S. 204 (1970); **Hill v. Stone,** 421 U.S. 289 (1975)]

(6) Waiting periods for existing residents [§1153]

Waiting periods have been held to discriminate against the right to vote as well as the right to interstate travel. (*See supra*, §§1132-1133.)

(7) Exceptions [§1154]

In several situations, the Court has upheld laws denying certain persons the vote.

(a) Felons [§1155]

State laws denying the vote to persons convicted of a felony do *not* violate equal protection. Such laws are not subject to strict scrutiny.

Rationale: Disenfranchising felons is "affirmatively sanctioned" by Section 2 of the Fourteenth Amendment (which mentions that those convicted of crimes may be excluded in computing who is eligible to vote); therefore, the Equal Protection Clause of Section 1 "could not have been intended" as applicable thereto. [**Richardson v. Ramirez,** 418 U.S. 24 (1974)]

(b) "Special purpose" elections [§1156]

Laws denying persons the right to vote in elections for officials who do not exercise "normal government authority," but rather deal with matters of "special" interest to a limited group within the community, are not subject to strict scrutiny; they are judged by the "traditional" rational basis equal protection test.

1) Water storage districts [§1157]

Thus, a law restricting the vote in elections for a "water storage district" (dealing with conservation and distribution of water and flood control) to landowners does not violate equal protection. The district's powers disproportionately affect landowners. Thus, the restriction on the franchise was "rational." [**Salyer Land Co. v. Tulare Water Storage District,** 410 U.S. 719 (1973)] Nor is this result changed by the fact that the water district is a major supplier of electricity in the state and that almost all its income comes from such sales. [**Ball v. James,** 451 U.S. 355 (1981)]

(c) Nonresidents [§1158]

Laws denying the right to vote in a governmental entity's election to nonresidents do not violate equal protection—even when those outside the entity's boundaries are subject to that entity's limited extraterritorial powers, such as its police, sanitary, and business-licensing regulations. Such laws are subject only to the traditional rational basis standard. [**Holt Civic Club v. City of Tuscaloosa,** 439 U.S. 60 (1978)]

(8) Counting and recounting votes [§1159]

Procedures for counting and recounting votes must have adequate safeguards to assure that different standards within and among different polling areas meet the rudimentary requirements of equal treatment and fundamental fairness. [**Bush v. Gore,** 531 U.S. 98 (2000)—suggesting that the decision may be limited to the situation of a state court ordering a statewide recount]

(9) Registration for primary elections [§1160]

State laws requiring a voter to register as a member of a particular party at least 30 days before a general election in order to be eligible to vote in that party's next primary election (the following year) have been upheld. Such laws serve an *important* purpose (preventing "raiding"—whereby one party's members vote in the other party's primary to distort the results). [**Rosario v. Rockefeller,** 410 U.S. 752 (1973)]

(a) Distinguish—reasonable time period [§1161]

But this time period may not be so long as to effectively prevent a person who wants to change registration from voting in the next primary—*e.g.*, a state law that prevented voting in the primary election if the voter had changed his party registration within the preceding 23 months was held invalid, because a voter would have to forgo voting in at least one primary in order to change his party registration. [**Kusper v. Pontikes,** 414 U.S. 51 (1974)—state interest in preventing "raiding" could be "attained by less drastic means"]

(10) Absentee ballots [§1162]

A law granting only certain classes of persons the right to vote by absentee ballot has been upheld using the "traditional" rational basis test. *Rationale:* The right to vote was *not* involved, since the record did not show that the state precluded appellants from voting. [**McDonald v. Board of Elections,** 394 U.S. 802 (1969)]

(a) Distinguish

However, a law denying absentee ballots to persons being held for trial and to convicted misdemeanants violated equal protection because it was "wholly arbitrary"; it discriminated between those held in their home county and those held outside their county of residence. This law effectively *denied* the right to vote. [**O'Brien v. Skinner,** 414 U.S. 524 (1974)]

(11) Ballot qualification restrictions [§1163]

State laws that impose burdensome requirements on small or new political parties attempting to get their candidates on the election ballot have been held to discriminate against the "right of qualified voters, regardless of their political persuasion, to cast their votes effectively"—as well as to discriminate against the freedom of association (*see supra*, §§1122, 1128). Such laws are thus subject to strict scrutiny under the Equal Protection Clause.

b. "Dilution" of the vote—apportionment [§1164]

For many years, the Court refused jurisdiction of cases challenging the fairness of the representation in state legislatures, on the ground that the issue was a "political question." [*See, e.g.,* **Colegrove v. Green,** 328 U.S. 549 (1946)] However, the Court abandoned this position in **Baker v. Carr,** 369 U.S. 186 (1962), which held that the courts have jurisdiction to determine the validity of state legislative apportionment plans, in order to assure to each voter the equal protection guaranteed by the Fourteenth Amendment.

(1) Congressional districts [§1165]

The provision in Article 1, Section 2—that members of Congress be chosen "by the People of the several States"—requires that congressional districts contain *equal population* "as nearly as is practicable." [**Wesberry v. Sanders,** 376 U.S. 1 (1964)] *"Precise mathematical equality"* is the goal. Departures are permissible only if "unavoidable despite a good faith effort," or if proper "justification is shown."

(a) Justifications [§1166]

If challengers show that population deviations were not "unavoidable despite a good faith effort," the state then has the burden to prove with *specificity* that each significant deviation was necessary to achieve a "legitimate goal—such as "making districts compact, respecting municipal boundaries, preserving the cores of prior districts, or avoiding contests between incumbents." [**Karcher v. Daggett,** 462 U.S. 725 (1983)]

(b) Projected population shifts [§1167]

Because districting plans are usually based on census figures, which are taken only every 10 years, projected population shifts among the districts may be considered if adequately documented. [**White v. Weiser,** 412 U.S. 783 (1973)—inadequate documentation]

(c) Preserving seats of incumbents [§1168]

The Court has left open the question of whether deviation can be justified so as to maintain existing relationships between incumbents and their constituents and to preserve seniority rights in Congress—interests that *may perhaps* be considered in the context of *state* districting (*see* below). [**White v. Weiser,** *supra*]

(d) Apportionment of districts among states [§1169]

Article I, Section 2 requires that Congress apportion representatives among the states "according to their respective numbers." Congress's good faith choice of method commands "far more deference" than state districting decisions and is *not* subject to the same precise mathematical standard. [**United States Department of Commerce v. Montana,** 503 U.S. 442 (1992)]

1) Census [§1170]

Nor does a strict mathematical standard apply to the federal government's choice of methods when it conducts the decennial census. [**Wisconsin v. City of New York,** 517 U.S. 1 (1996)—decision by Secretary of Commerce, to whom Congress delegated its authority over the census, not to statistically adjust census figures need have only a reasonable relation to accomplishing "actual Enumeration" of the population as required by Article I, Section 2, Clause 3]

(2) State legislative districts [§1171]

In **Reynolds v. Sims,** 377 U.S. 533 (1964), the Court held that equal protection requires representation in both houses of a state legislature to be based on population as nearly as practicable. Each voter is entitled to have an equally weighted vote. The fact that malapportionment is the result of a popular referendum is irrelevant because the majority cannot deny the minority the right to an undiluted vote. [**Lucas v. 44th General Assembly,** 377 U.S. 713 (1964)]

(a) Permissible deviations [§1172]

Mathematical exactness is not required, since small deviations may be unavoidable. A maximum deviation between any two districts *under 10%* requires no state explanation and is valid even though there may be other plans with even lower deviations. [**Gaffney v. Cummings,** 412 U.S. 735 (1973); **White v. Regester,** 412 U.S. 755 (1973)] However, larger deviations *cannot* be upheld unless *explained* by some acceptable state policy. [**Swann v. Adams,** 385 U.S. 440 (1967)]

EXAM TIP   **gilbert**

Be sure to remember that the rules under which the Court reviews reapportionment differ depending on whether the reapportionment involves a congressional voting district or a state office voting district. The Court requires *near mathematical equality* when it comes to *congressional district* reapportionment. But the Court is not as strict when state voting districts are in question (*e.g.*, it upheld a deviation of more than 16% among state voting districts in order to preserve political boundaries).

---

1) Preserving city or county boundaries [§1173]

Existing boundaries of political subdivisions may be taken into account by the state as long as it is done in a consistent and nondiscriminatory fashion and the final apportionment is substantially based on population. *Rationale:* Preserving the integrity of local subdivisions facilitates the enactment of legislation on matters of purely local concern, and it gives local voters a more effective voice on such matters in the state legislature. [**Mahan v. Howell,** 410 U.S. 315 (1973)—16.4% deviation justified by state to maintain political subdivision lines; *and see* **Brown v. Thomson,** 462 U.S. 835 (1983)—larger deviation justified under special circumstances]

a) Local government districts [§1174]

Because flexibility is needed for viable local government, *slightly greater* percentage deviations are allowed for local government apportionment than for state and congressional apportionment—as long as justifying factors exist. [**Abate v. Mundt,** 403 U.S. 182 (1971)]

2) Balance between two houses [§1175]

Both houses of the state legislature may be considered together, so that a slight population disparity in one may be balanced by an offsetting disparity in the other.

3) Preserving seats of incumbents [§1176]

Although considerations based on history, area size, group interests, or preservation of an incumbent's seat are *not* generally legitimate [**Reynolds v. Sims**, *supra*], the Court has held that a plan "acceptable populationwise" is not rendered invalid because its purpose was to "achieve a rough approximation of the statewide political strengths of the . . . two parties in the state large enough to elect legislators from discernible geographic areas" [**Gaffney v. Cummings**, *supra*].

(b) Multi-member districts [§1177]

Multi-member districts have been held to be *not* per se violative of the "one person-one vote" rule. But they *do* violate equal protection if, "designedly or otherwise," it is shown that they operate to minimize the voting strength of a particular racial or political group. [*Compare* **Whitcomb v. Chavis**, 403 U.S. 124 (1971)—valid, *with* **White v. Regester**, *supra*—invalid]

1) Residency requirements [§1178]

A multi-member district's representatives may be required to live in particular subdistricts irrespective of their population. *Rationale:* The representative's residence does not mean that he will not effectively represent the voters of the entire district. [**Dusch v. Davis**, 387 U.S. 112 (1967)]

(c) Gerrymandering [§1179]

State districting plans that disadvantage an identifiable racial or political group on a statewide basis *may* violate equal protection. For *political* gerrymanders, the challengers must prove (i) an intent to discriminate *and* (ii) a discriminatory *effect* of a kind that, either in actual fact or by projection, *consistently* degrades the political group's influence on the political process as a whole (*i.e.,* more than the loss of a single election). [**Davis v. Bandemer**, 478 U.S. 109 (1986)—plurality opinion] As for *racial* gerrymanders, it is unclear whether a showing of an intent to discriminate is enough (*see supra*, §1078).

(d) Relevant population [§1180]

Districting need not be based on *total* population—*e.g.*, aliens, transients, and convicts may be excluded. But distributing representation on the basis of registered or actual voters is suspect because these are not criteria for state citizenship and lend themselves to improper political influences; this will be upheld *only* if the result is not substantially different from that obtained by the use of a permissible basis. [**Burns v. Richardson,** 384 U.S. 73 (1966)]

(e) Relevant officials [§1181]

The "one person-one vote" rule applies to the *election of all* officials who perform "normal governmental functions." Thus, it applies not only to legislators, but also to administrative and executive officials who are elected by popular vote. [**Hadley v. Junior College District,** 397 U.S. 50 (1970)—trustees of junior college district]

1) "Special purpose" officials [§1182]

The duties of some officials are so far removed from "normal governmental activities" and so disproportionately affect different groups that their election can be on some basis other than population. [**Salyer Land Co. v. Tulare Water Storage District,** *supra*, §1157—upholding apportionment of votes on basis of *assessed value of land* owned for election of directors of water storage district which had limited governmental powers, all relating to water servicing activities, and its costs and charges were assessed solely against the land in proportion to benefits received]

2) Nomination of officials [§1183]

The "one person-one vote" rule applies to nomination procedures. Thus, the Court has invalidated a state law that required independent candidates for statewide office to be nominated by petitions signed by at least 200 voters from each of at least 50 of the 102 counties in the state. This procedure in effect discriminated against the residents of the more populous counties, because even if all the people in these counties wished to nominate, they would be unable to do so. [**Moore v. Ogilvie,** 394 U.S. 814 (1969)]

3) Appointed officials [§1184]

But the "one person-one vote" rule does *not* apply where a state provides for *appointment* of administrative or other nonlegislative state or local officers. [**Sailors v. Board of Education,** 387 U.S. 105 (1967)—upholding appointment of county school board members by local school boards serving unequal populations]

a) Appointment vs. election [§1185]

The Court has found "no constitutional reason" why government officials—at least *nonlegislative* officials—may not be appointed rather than elected. [**Sailors v. Board of Education,** *supra*] Thus, a state's *governor* may be chosen by the state legislature when no candidate received a majority vote in the election. [**Fortson v. Morris,** 385 U.S. 231 (1966)] And the Court has upheld *temporary* appointments of *legislators* to fill vacancies caused by death, resignation, etc.— even when the appointment is made by the political party with which the previous incumbent was affiliated. [**Rodriguez v. Popular Democratic Party,** 457 U.S. 1 (1982)]

(3) Supermajority requirements [§1186]

Provisions requiring enactments—either by the legislature or by referendum—to be approved by more than majority vote have been held *not* to violate equal protection as long as they do not discriminate against (or authorize discrimination against) any identifiable class. (*Rationale:* The Constitution does not require "that a majority always prevail on every issue.") The Court *did not pass* on (i) a requirement of "unanimity or giving a veto power to a very small group," or (ii) a requirement of "extraordinary" majorities for the election of public officers. [**Gordon v. Lance,** 403 U.S. 1 (1970)—upholding 60% requirement in state referendum for bond issue; **Town of Lockport v. Citizens for Community Action,** 430 U.S. 259 (1977)—upholding requirement that new county charter be approved by separate majorities of city and noncity voters]

(4) Remedies for malapportionment [§1187]

The federal courts have been instructed to remedy malapportionment according to general *equitable* principles. If the problem is being dealt with in the state judicial system, the federal court should usually defer. Likewise, the federal court should give the state legislature an adequate opportunity to remedy the situation. [**Scott v. Germano,** 381 U.S. 407 (1965)]

(a) Limited flexibility [§1188]

If the state or local body fails to act, the federal court will draw up a plan. However, federal courts do not have as much flexibility as these bodies; also, the plans so fashioned are held to stricter standards on appellate review, both in respect to deviation from the goal of population equality [**Chapman v. Meier,** 420 U.S. 1 (1975)], and in the use of multi-member districts [**Connor v. Finch,** 431 U.S. 407 (1977)].

7. Right to Be a Candidate [§1189]

The Court has *not* recognized a "fundamental right" to be a candidate for public office. But state laws that impose burdensome requirements on candidates are subject to *fairly* strict scrutiny under the Equal Protection Clause because of their impact on the right to vote. (*See supra,* §§1122-1128.)

a. Filing fees [§1190]

The requirement of a fee to get on the election ballot is not per se invalid. As applied to indigent candidates, however, such fees do not survive "close scrutiny" and thus violate equal protection. *Rationale:* Selection of candidates solely on the basis of ability to pay a fixed fee, "without providing any alternative means of ballot access," is not "reasonably necessary" to accomplish the state's "legitimate" election interests. [**Lubin v. Panish,** 415 U.S. 709 (1974); **Bullock v. Carter,** *supra,* §1116]

b. Existing officials [§1191]

Laws placing various limits on the ability of certain public officeholders to run for *other* elective office during their terms as incumbents are *not* subject to "strict" scrutiny and do not violate equal protection. [**Clements v. Fashing,** 457 U.S. 957 (1982)—no majority opinion]

G. "Nonfundamental" Rights

1. Introduction [§1192]

To be deemed a "fundamental right"—and thereby subject to "strict scrutiny"—the right must be "explicitly or implicitly guaranteed by the Constitution." [**San Antonio Independent School District v. Rodriguez,** *supra,* §1121] Pursuant to this doctrine, the Court has held that many important interests are *not* "fundamental" and thus discriminations affecting them are reviewable under the *traditional "rational basis" test.*

EXAM TIP   **gilbert**

For your exam you must memorize the *suspect classifications* (race, national origin, and sometimes alienage), *quasi-suspect classifications* (gender and legitimacy), and the *fundamental rights* (e.g., First Amendment rights, right to interstate travel, right of privacy, and voting rights). *Any other classification or any other right* is *not* entitled to more than the rational basis test, and thus the government regulation will usually be valid. Do not let your personal feelings lead you to apply the wrong standard (and pick the wrong answer) because you think the right is important or the group is worthy.

---

2. Welfare [§1193]

There is no constitutional right to receive public welfare. Classifications respecting welfare benefits are therefore subject only to the traditional rational basis equal protection test. [**Dandridge v. Williams,** 397 U.S. 471 (1970)—state "maximum grant" law, imposing an upper limit on the total amount of welfare assistance any one family could receive and thereby discriminating against large families, was upheld as "rational"; the law dealt only with "economics and social welfare"]

a. Disability benefits [§1194]

Similarly, a provision of the Social Security Act reducing disability benefits for those receiving state workers' compensation, but not for those who received compensation from private insurance or tort claim awards, was upheld under the "traditional" rational basis test. [**Richardson v. Belcher,** 404 U.S. 78 (1971)]

3. **Housing [§1195]**

   There is *no* constitutional right to "decent, safe and sanitary" housing. Thus, a state law giving landlords a special cause of action to evict tenants was upheld as drawing a "rational" classification. [**Lindsey v. Normet,** 405 U.S. 56 (1972)]

   a. **Unrelated persons living together [§1196]**

   Similarly, a zoning law restricting land use to "one family dwellings"—and defining "family" to mean one or more persons related by blood, adoption, or marriage but not more than two unrelated persons living together—was upheld under the "traditional" rational basis test. [**Village of Belle Terre v. Boraas,** 416 U.S. 1 (1974)]

4. **Education [§1197]**

   There is no constitutional right to a particular quality of education. Thus, a state system of public school financing that relied on property values was upheld as "rational." [**San Antonio Independent School District v. Rodriguez,** *supra*, §1121]

   a. **Bus transportation [§1198]**

   Nor is there any constitutional right to free bus service to public schools. [**Kadrmas v. Dickinson Public Schools,** 484 U.S. 1000 (1988)]

5. **Bankruptcy [§1199]**

   There is no constitutional right to discharge one's debts through bankruptcy proceedings. [**United States v. Kras,** *supra*, §1113—filing fee requirement upheld as serving a "rational" basis to make bankruptcy proceedings self-supporting, and thus not a denial of equal protection to indigents]

6. **Assisted Suicide [§1200]**

   Because there is no constitutional right to assisted suicide (*supra*, §541), it is not "irrational" for a state to permit competent persons to refuse life-sustaining medical treatment, but to forbid persons from having a physician assist them in committing suicide. *Rationale:* A physician who allows a person to refuse life-sustaining treatment simply permits him to die a natural death, but a physician who complies with a person's request for lethal medication intentionally ends the person's life. [**Vacco v. Quill,** 521 U.S. 793 (1997)]

7. **Distinguish—Important Rights [§1201]**

   In a few cases involving important—but *not* "fundamental"—rights, the Court has found equal protection violations under the "traditional" rational basis test.

   a. **Housing [§1202]**

   A law requiring a special "double bond" only for evicted tenants who wished to appeal has been held "arbitrary and irrational." [**Lindsey v. Normet,** *supra*]

   b. **Welfare [§1203]**

   A law denying food stamps to "any household containing an individual who is unrelated to any other member of the household was held to be "wholly with-out rational basis." [**United States Department of Agriculture v. Moreno,** *supra,* §1015]

H. "Irrebuttable Presumptions" and the Right to a Hearing

1. Introduction [§1204]

During the early 1970s, in several cases involving "important" interests, the Court—although declining to find a "fundamental" right—nonetheless invalidated *over-inclusive* state classifications (*see supra,* §1014) on the ground that they created improper "irrebuttable" (or "conclusive") presumptions. The Court, usually relying on the Due Process Clause rather than the Equal Protection Clause, reasoned that because all persons within the statutory classification did not satisfy the criteria on which the classification were based, *procedural due process* required that individuals be given some opportunity to show that they should be treated differently.

2. Parental Custody [§1205]

A state law provided that a father automatically lost his nonmarital children upon the death of their mother. The effect was to create an irrebuttable presumption that unwed fathers are unfit parents, which is neither "necessarily nor universally true." The Court noted that a father's interest in retaining custody of his children warranted protection, "absent a powerful countervailing interest," and held that procedural due process requires that the father be given a hearing as to his fitness as a parent. [**Stanley v. Illinois,** 405 U.S. 645 (1972)]

3. Residency Status [§1206]

A state law required that nonresidents pay higher fees to attend the state university and created an irrebuttable presumption of nonresidency for the entire period of education if the applicant filed from outside the state. The Court held that because the state had reasonable alternative means of determining residency, procedural due process required that applicants be afforded a hearing to present evidence of their bona fide residency. [**Vlandis v. Kline,** 412 U.S. 441 (1973)]

4. Pregnancy and Employee Fitness [§1207]

Where school board rules required pregnant teachers to leave work at least four or five months before the date of anticipated childbirth, the effect was to create an irrebuttable presumption that every teacher five months pregnant is physically incapable of continuing her duties. The Court noted that because this is neither "necessarily nor universally true," due process requires a case-by-case determination (*e.g.,* through medical exams). [**Cleveland Board of Education v. LaFleur,** 414 U.S. 632 (1974)] (A similar rule making a teacher ineligible to return to work until her child was three months old was also held invalid.)

5. **Food Stamps [§1208]**

   A federal statute excluded (as "not needy") any household containing a person over 18 who was claimed as a tax dependent by a taxpayer who was not himself eligible for food stamps. In effect, this operated as an irrebuttable presumption that the household was not needy. Due process was held to require that the household be given the opportunity to present evidence as to whether it was needy. [**United States Department of Agriculture v. Murry,** 413 U.S. 508 (1973)]

6. **Disability Benefits for Nonmarital Children [§1209]**

   A Social Security Act provision denied benefits to some (but not all) nonmarital children born after their parent's disability, irrespective of their dependency. The Court held that this denied *equal protection* (rather than due process), because it "conclusively excludes some nonmarital children who are, in fact, dependent upon their disabled parent" without giving them "an opportunity to establish their dependency." [**Jiminez v. Weinberger,** 417 U.S. 628 (1974)]

7. **Decline of the Doctrine [§1210]**

   In **Weinberger v. Salfi,** 422 U.S. 749 (1975), a provision of the Social Security Act denied benefits to wives and stepchildren who were such for less than nine months prior to the wage earner's death, thus creating a conclusive presumption that marriages within this time were undertaken simply to secure benefits. The Court recognized that the presumption might prove "over-inclusive" or "under-inclusive" in particular cases, but upheld it since "Congress could rationally have concluded that any imprecision . . . was justified by its ease and certainty of operation." The Court has not since used the irrebuttable presumption approach to invalidate any government regulations.

Chapter Eight:
The "State Action" Requirement

CONTENTS

Chapter Approach

As discussed in previous chapters of this book, a number of constitutional provisions prohibit the government from infringing on constitutional rights. However, as will be discussed in this chapter, one constitutional provision—the Thirteenth Amendment—extends to *private action* as well as government action. The Thirteenth Amendment prohibits the institution of slavery whether by the government or a private party.

If a question does not involve a "badge of slavery" (and so is outside the scope of the Thirteenth Amendment), to find some action unconstitutional, it is generally necessary to attribute the action *to the government*, including its agencies and officials acting under color of law. However, this does not mean that the act must be done directly by a government actor. Remember that state action may include action by individuals in some circumstances (*e.g.*, when a private individual performs a function that is traditionally the *exclusive* prerogative of the state or where the government has *required* or *significantly encouraged* private acts of discrimination). Thus, you may have to take a close look at the facts to determine whether state action is present.

A. Thirteenth Amendment

1. Constitutional Text [§1211]

The Bill of Rights and the Fourteenth and Fifteenth Amendments generally protect a number of rights against infringement *by the government*. The Thirteenth Amendment, on the other hand, is a rather rare constitutional provision in that it is not limited to government (or "state" action); rather, it proscribes private action as well: The Thirteenth Amendment provides: "Neither slavery nor involuntary servitude, except as a punishment for crime whereof the party shall have been duly convicted, shall exist within the United States, or any place subject to their jurisdiction." Thus, the Thirteenth Amendment prevents slavery or involuntary servitude from being practiced anywhere in the United States, whether by a state, the federal government, or a private individual. It is a complete prohibition.

2. What Is Involuntary Servitude?

a. Peonage [§1212]

The Thirteenth Amendment prohibits peonage—*i.e.*, impressing one into the personal service of a creditor in order to liquidate a debt. Although the amendment excepts punishment of crime, the state may not make the nonpayment of debt, or the refusal to perform personal services to liquidate a debt, a crime itself.

> **e.g.** **Example:** The Court held void a state criminal statute making failure to render services, for which an advance was received and for which no repayment had been made, prima facie evidence of an intent to defraud. [**Pollock v. Williams**, 322 U.S. 4 (1944)]

> **e.g.** **Example:** The Court also invalidated a federal statute that permitted release of convicts to employers who, pursuant to agreement with the convicts, paid their fine in exchange for agreed services, where the statute made breach of the agreement by the convict a crime. [**United States v. Reynolds**, 235 U.S. 133 (1914)]

b.   Exceptional circumstances [§1213]
There are exceptional situations where performance of a personal obligation has always been enforced.

> **e.g.** **Example:** In **Robertson v. Baldwin**, 165 U.S. 275 (1897), the Court upheld a statute that provided that seamen who desert their vessel in violation of their contracts may be arrested and forcibly returned to the vessel for service and may be criminally prosecuted for desertion. Similarly, military conscription was upheld in the **Selective Draft Law Cases**, 245 U.S. 366 (1918).

B. Fourteenth and Fifteenth Amendments

1.   Introduction [§1214]
The language of the Fourteenth and Fifteenth Amendments (including those provisions of the Bill of Rights applicable to the states) restricts only *governmental* action. The acts of mere private individuals were early held *not* to fall within their prohibition; only "state action" is restricted. [**Civil Rights Cases**, 109 U.S. 3 (1883)] However, "state action" includes *more* than action taken by the legislative, executive, judicial, and administrative branches of the federal and state governments and their subdivisions; it also includes certain actions taken by ostensibly private individuals or organizations (*see* below).

2.   Acts of Government "Agents" [§1215]
State action includes conduct of government officials acting in their official capacity—*i.e.*, "under color of law"—even though the specific action they take may be forbidden by law.

> **e.g.** **Example:** When a state *jury commissioner discriminates* against blacks in selecting jury panels, this is "state action" even though state and federal law may bar such discrimination. [*Ex parte* **Virginia,** 100 U.S. 339 (1879)]

> **e.g.** **Example:** When a state *police officer beats a prisoner to death* in an effort to obtain a confession, or stands aside while someone else beats a prisoner to death, this is "state action" because the officer, acting in his official capacity, has deprived the prisoner of life without due process of law. [**Screws v. United States,** 325 U.S. 91 (1945)]

a. Definition of government "agency" [§1216]

A corporation created by a special federal statute "for the furtherance of governmental objectives," with the President having permanent authority to appoint a majority of the directors, is "part of the government for purposes of the First Amendment," even though the authorizing statute disclaims this fact. [**Lebron v. National Railroad Passenger Corp.,** 513 U.S. 374 (1995)—Amtrak]

3. "Public" or "Government" Functions [§1217]

In a few instances, the Court has found that activities undertaken by private individuals or organizations are ones that are "*traditionally* the *exclusive* prerogative of the State*.*" The Court has characterized such an activity as a "public" or "government" function, and therefore treated it as "state action" subject to the Fourteenth and Fifteenth Amendments.

a. Elections [§1218]

The Court has held that conducting elections is traditionally an exclusively state function, and thus has invalidated racial discrimination by groups with effective control over the selection of candidates.

(1) Primaries [§1219]

A political party cannot exclude African-Americans from voting in primary elections from which the party nominee for the general election is chosen. [**Smith v. Allwright,** 321 U.S. 649 (1944)]

(2) Pre-primaries [§1220]

County political groups cannot exclude African-Americans from a pre-primary election when the winner almost always runs unopposed in the party primary and general election. [**Terry v. Adams,** 345 U.S. 461 (1953)]

b. Company towns [§1221]

A private corporation owned a town that had "all the characteristics of any other American town." The corporation caused the trespass conviction of a distributor of religious literature who refused to leave the town's business district sidewalk. The Court held this to be "state action" violating the First and Fourteenth Amendments because the town's streets, although privately owned, were the *functional equivalent* of city streets and the residents of the company town had as great an interest in receiving information as did those of an "ordinary" town. [**Marsh v. Alabama,** 326 U.S. 501 (1946)]

c. Limits of doctrine [§1222]

In most instances, however, the Court has *not* found the privately conducted activity to be a "public" or "government" function.

(1) Shopping centers [§1223]

Although a large, self-contained shopping center is in many ways similar to the business district of an ordinary town, it is *not* the "functional equivalent" of a municipality because it does not possess *all* the attributes of a town. [**Hudgens v. NRLB,** 424 U.S. 507 (1976)—*overruling* **Amalgamated Food Employees Union v. Logan Valley Plaza, Inc.,** 391 U.S. 308 (1968)]

(2) Monopoly businesses [§1224]

A heavily regulated electric company that had been granted a monopoly by the state was held *not* to have engaged in "state action" when it terminated a user's service without notice or hearing. The Court reasoned that "the supplying of utility service is not traditionally the exclusive province of the state." [**Jackson v. Metropolitan Edison Co.,** 419 U.S. 345 (1974)]

(3) Regulated businesses [§1225]

Similarly, the fact that nursing homes or specialized private schools are almost wholly funded and extensively regulated by the state does not make their conduct state action. Again, the Court reasoned that these enterprises are not "the exclusive province of the state." [**Blum v. Yaretsky,** 457 U.S. 991 (1982); **Rendell-Baker v. Kohn,** 457 U.S. 830 (1982)]

(4) Creditors' remedies [§1226]

A warehouseman authorized by state statute to sell goods stored with him for unpaid charges is *not* engaged in state action. Although resolution of private disputes *is* a traditional "state function," the bailor had state law remedies to check abuse by the warehouseman and thus the state had not delegated an "exclusive public function" to the warehouseman. [**Flagg Bros., Inc. v. Brooks,** 436 U.S. 149 (1978)]

4. Significant State "Involvement" [§1227]

A larger number of cases have found state action by private individuals (usually racial discrimination in violation of the Equal Protection Clause) because the government has *required* or *significantly encouraged* the acts of discrimination. Note that government is not constitutionally required to outlaw private discrimination—merely permitting private conduct to occur is not enough for "state action"; the state must *compel* or *significantly participate* in the private conduct. Whether such state involvement exists requires a case-by-case determination, based on the particular facts before the Court. [**Burton v. Wilmington Parking Authority,** 365 U.S. 715 (1961)]

a. **Government compulsion of private discrimination [§1228]**

When a city ordinance (or an official policy announced by the police) required racial segregation in restaurants, the action of a private restaurateur who caused African-Americans to be prosecuted for trespass when they refused to leave was held to be state action. Even though the private restaurateur would have wished to discriminate wholly apart from the ordinance, by enacting the ordinance, the state had made the choice for private persons. [**Peterson v. City of Greenville**, 373 U.S. 244 (1963); **Lombard v. Louisiana**, 373 U.S. 267 (1963)]

b. **Government administration of private discrimination [§1229]**

Where the government administers a trust which, by its terms, requires discrimination, state action will be found.

> **e.g.** **Example:** State officials acted as trustees under a private will that devised property for use as a school (or a park) and required racial discrimination. This was held to be state action. [**Pennsylvania v. Board of Trusts**, 353 U.S. 230 (1957)] Furthermore, a state court's appointment of private trustees, replacing the state officials, who had resigned as trustees to facilitate the appointment, constituted state action where the obvious purpose was to perpetuate racial discrimination which the state officials themselves could no longer implement. [**Evans v. Newton**, 382 U.S. 296 (1966)]

> **cf.** **Compare:** In litigation subsequent to **Evans v. Newton**, *supra*, the state court held that because the settlor of the trust was absolutely opposed to integration, the trust failed because its purpose had become illegal; the property therefore reverted to the settlor's heirs (the state court refusing to apply the cy pres doctrine to save the trust). The Supreme Court found no discriminatory state action; the state law as to interpretation of the will and application of the cy pres doctrine was "neutral with regard to race," and there was no evidence that the state judges were "motivated by racial animus" in construing the will. [**Evans v. Abney**, 396 U.S. 435 (1970)]

c. **Joint action by government officials and private persons—creditors' remedies [§1230]**

When creditors act pursuant to statutes that authorize the property of their debtors to be attached or sequestered with the aid of a state official (such as the sheriff), the private person's "joint participation with state officials is sufficient to characterize that person as a 'state actor' for purposes of the Fourteenth Amendment." [**Lugar v. Edmondson Oil Co.**, 457 U.S. 922 (1982)]

d. **Judicial enforcement of private discrimination—restrictive covenants [§1231]**

If state courts enforce racial restrictive covenants by all homeowners in an area by (i) enjoining a black person who purchased from a white owner from taking possession, and (ii) awarding damages against the white seller to other signatories of the restrictive covenants, there is "state action." While *voluntary* adherence to the covenants does *not* involve state action, *judicial enforcement* does. [**Shelley v. Kraemer**, 334 U.S. 1 (1948); **Barrows v. Jackson**, *supra*, §69]

(1) Comment

The implications of this doctrine (*i.e.*, that judicial enforcement of private discrimination makes it subject to the Fourteenth Amendment) are **very broad**, and logically extend to converting all private action into state action if the private discriminator seeks aid from the courts to carry out his purpose. However, the Court has made *almost* no use of this doctrine beyond racial restrictive covenants.

(2) Possible limitation—forcing otherwise unwilling discrimination [§1232]

The "restrictive covenant" cases involved judicial enforcement of private discrimination that had the effect of forcing a white homeowner (the seller) to discriminate against his wishes. This is distinguishable from the usual situation in which the discriminator seeks judicial assistance to carry out his discriminatory desires without forcing anyone else to discriminate, *e.g.*, restaurateur who refuses to serve blacks and brings a trespass action against those who refuse to leave. [*See* **Bell v. Maryland**, 378 U.S. 226 (1964)— several Justices so limiting the doctrine of the "restrictive covenant" cases]

Example: A state liquor regulation required private clubs holding liquor licenses to adhere to the clubs' constitutions and bylaws. The Court, relying on the doctrine of the "restrictive covenant" cases, held that if a court were to enforce a club's bylaw that denied membership to blacks (*e.g.*, in a suit filed by some members against the club for admitting a black person), this would "invoke the sanctions of the state to enforce discrimination." The effect would be forcing the club to engage in racial discrimination against its wishes. [**Moose Lodge v. Irvis**, 407 U.S. 163 (1972)]

e. Peremptory challenges [§1233]

Use of peremptory challenges by a private litigant in a civil trial significantly involves the state and places the court's power and prestige behind the resulting racial discrimination. Thus, state action will be found in the private party's discrimination. [**Edmonson v. Leesville Concrete Co.**, 500 U.S. 614 (1991)] The same rule applies to the use of peremptory challenges by a criminal defendant. [**Georgia v. McCollum**, 505 U.S. 42 (1992)] Thus, neither civil litigants nor criminal defendants may base peremptory challenges on race.

f. Government approval of private conduct [§1234]

When a state regulatory agency affirmatively approves a practice of a regulated business (*e.g.*, after a full investigation), the practice has been held to be state action. [**Public Utilities Commission v. Pollak**, 343 U.S. 451 (1952)—involving a challenge to a licensed bus company's practice of broadcasting radio programs in its buses]

(1) Distinguish—mere filing [§1235]

But the mere fact that the practice has been filed with and accepted by the regulatory agency does *not* make the practice state action. [**Jackson v. Metropolitan Edison Co.**, *supra*] And it follows that the mere fact an extensively regulated business engages in certain practices does *not* make these practices state action, as long as the state does not *require* or *significantly encourage* the practices. [**Blum v. Yaretsky**, *supra*, §1225; **Rendell-Baker v. Kohn**, *supra*, §1225] Similarly, the fact that a regulated business is licensed by the state (or receives state services such as electricity and water, and police and fire protection) does *not* make its conduct state action. [**Moose Lodge v. Irvis**, *supra*—liquor license; *and see* **CBS v. Democratic National Committee**, 412 U.S. 94 (1973)—opinion of three Justices regarding broadcast licenses]

(2) State policy of approval [§1236]

Where a state constitutional amendment repealed existing antidiscrimination-in-housing statutes and prevented the legislature from regulating the sale or rental of residential property in the future, and when an apartment owner then refused to rent to an African-American tenant, the Court held this to be state action. The Court reasoned that the state constitutional amendment did more than merely repeal antidiscrimination laws; its purpose was seen as *encouraging* racial discrimination, since discriminators were freed from any official censure as a matter of basic state policy. [**Reitman v. Mulkey**, 387 U.S. 369 (1967)]

g. "Symbiotic" relationship [§1237]

State action has also been found where the private discriminator was a *lessee of public property* (restaurant operated as "integral part" of a public parking structure in which it was located). The private restaurant benefited from cars parking in the public building and vice versa. [**Burton v. Wilmington Parking Authority**, *supra*, §1227]

h. Entwinement of state and private entities [§1238]

The fact that a state entity helps formulate and adopts the rules of a private entity and chooses to follow the order of the private entity pursuant to those rules, does not convert the private entity's action into state action. However, a state may be so entwined with a private organization that the organization's actions will be considered state action.

---

e.g. **Example:** The National Collegiate Athletic Association ("NCAA") is a voluntary association of public and private universities that establishes rules for its members regarding collegiate sports. Pursuant to its rules, the NCAA urged a member college to suspend its coach for recruiting violations. The coach cannot successfully sue the NCAA for violating his constitutional rights (*e.g.*, suspending him without a hearing sufficient to satisfy due process requirements)

STATE ACTION VS. NO STATE ACTION—A COMPARISON OF CASES

gilbert

STATE ACTION	NO STATE ACTION
PUBLIC FUNCTION	
Running a company town with all of the attributes of a regular town	Running a shopping mall (does not have all the attributes of a town)
Conducting an election, including party primaries	Holding a warehouseman's lien sale
SIGNIFICANT STATE INVOLVEMENT	
Enforcing restrictive covenants prohibiting sale or lease of property through use of state courts or requiring private party to follow its own bylaws that provide for discrimination	Granting a license and providing essential services to a private club
Leasing premises to a discriminatory lessee where state derives extra benefit from the discrimination (*i.e.,* symbiotic relationship exists)	Granting a monopoly to a utility
	Heavily regulating an industry
Administering a private discriminatory trust by public officials	Granting a corporation its charter and exclusive name
	Terminating a discriminatory trust rather than applying the doctrine of cy pres to convert the trust to a nondiscriminatory purpose
High school following private athletic association's rules where most public high schools belong to the association, its governing body is made up mostly of public employees, its meetings are held during school hours, etc.	NCAA's urging that public college suspend its coach for violation of NCAA rules
Using peremptory challenges in a discriminatory manner	
Allowing state official to act in a discriminatory manner under "color of state law"	
Sheriff's accompanying private person to attach a lien on a debtor's property	

because there is no state action. [**National Collegiate Athletic Association v. Tarkanian,** 488 U.S. 179 (1988)]

cf. **Compare:** An association that regulates high school sports within a single state: (i) to which most public high schools belong; (ii) whose governing body is made up mostly of public school officials; (iii) whose meetings are held during regular school hours; (iv) whose employees may join the state retirement system; and (v) which is funded by gate receipts from the regulated sports is so entwined with the state that its action can be considered state action. [**Brentwood Academy v. Tennessee Secondary School Athletic Association,** 531 U.S. 288 (2001)]

EXAM TIP   **gilbert**

Note that while many of the cases above involve discrimination, a state action issue can arise in other contexts as well. The *Tarkanian* case above is a good example (Coach Tarkanian argued that the NCAA deprived him of his *due process rights* by urging the University of Nevada Las Vegas to suspend him without a sufficient hearing). You must therefore always be on the lookout for suits arguing that *nongovernmental defendants* have deprived a person of his constitutional rights under the Fourteenth or Fifteenth Amendments. When confronted with such a situation, consider whether the private entity has undertaken a function that is *traditionally and exclusively* the prerogative of the state or whether the *state is so involved or entwined* with the private defendant that the private defendant's action can be attributed to the state. If so, there is state action and the underlying merits of the case can be heard. If not, there is no state action and the plaintiff cannot go forward with his constitutional claim against the private party.

Chapter Nine: Congressional Power to Enforce Constitutional Rights

CONTENTS

Chapter Approach

Congress's power to enforce constitutional rights probably has not been a heavily tested topic. If you do see an exam question pertaining to this topic, remember the following basic rules. The Necessary and Proper Clause gives Congress the power to adopt legislation that is necessary and proper to pass laws protecting rights of national citizenship from infringement by anyone. Similarly, the Enabling Clause of the Thirteenth Amendment gives Congress the power to outlaw "badges" or "incidents" of slavery, whether by government entities or by private persons. And under the Enabling Clause of the Fifteenth Amendment, Congress can outlaw governmental discrimination in voting.

If you were to see an examination question regarding Congress's power to enforce constitutional rights, it would most likely involve Congress's power under Section 5 of the Fourteenth Amendment. Under this Enabling Clause, Congress can adopt legislation that provides remedies for and prevents future violations of the Due Process and Equal Protection Clauses. However, Section 5 does not give Congress the power to expand substantive constitutional rights.

A. Bases of Power

1. In General [§1239]

Pursuant to the *Necessary and Proper Clause* (*see supra*, §139) and the *Enabling Clauses* of the Thirteenth, Fourteenth, and Fifteenth Amendments (which empower Congress to enforce those amendments by "appropriate legislation"), Congress is authorized to protect the exercise of (and remedy interference with) constitutional rights. To some extent, Congress has the power to legislate against policies and practices that the Court itself would not find unconstitutional (*see* below).

2. Government Action [§1240]

If the constitutional right operates only against government action (as most do; *see supra*, §1214), Congress may impose criminal or civil remedies against one who interferes when "acting *under color of law*"—generally a synonym for *"government action."*

3. Private Action [§1241]

If the constitutional right operates against private individuals as well as government action (*see infra*, §§1249 *et seq*.), Congress may legislate remedies against *anyone* who interferes.

B. Necessary and Proper Clause

1. **In General [§1242]**

   The Court has held that there are several *constitutional rights of national citizenship* which, although not enumerated in the Constitution, "arise from the relationship of the individual and the federal government." These rights are secured against *private* as well as *government* action. Thus, under the Necessary and Proper Clause, Congress has power to pass laws protecting these rights from interference by *anyone*. [**United States v. Williams,** 341 U.S. 70 (1951)]

2. **Right to Travel Interstate [§1243]**

   The right to travel among the states is a right of national citizenship. Thus, a federal statute making it a crime to interfere with another person's use of interstate highways was upheld as a valid exercise of Congress's power to protect a citizen's right to travel freely from state to state. [**United States v. Guest,** *supra*, §527]

   a. **Federal provision for civil damages [§1244]**

      Similarly, a federal statute authorizing *civil damages* for interference with constitutional rights of others, as applied in a suit for harassment on interstate highways, was upheld as a proper exercise of federal power to protect the right to travel interstate. [**Griffin v. Breckenridge,** 403 U.S. 88 (1971)]

   b. **Federal limitation on state statutes [§1245]**

      And a federal statute *banning* state *residency requirements* in presidential elections was upheld as a proper exercise of federal power to protect the right to travel freely from state to state—because Congress could find that the residency requirements unreasonably burdened the right. [**Oregon v. Mitchell,** 400 U.S. 112 (1970)]

3. **Right to Vote in Federal Elections [§1246]**

   Because the right to vote in federal elections is a right of national citizenship, Congress has been held to have power to regulate age requirements for voting in federal elections. [**Oregon v. Mitchell,** *supra*—some Justices relying on Section 5 of the Fourteenth Amendment, discussed below]

   a. **Federal primary elections [§1247]**

      The federal power over federal elections also applies to congressional regulation of *primary elections* for federal officials. [**United States v. Classic,** 313 U.S. 299 (1941)]

4. **Right to Petition National Government [§1248]**

   The final important right of national citizenship is the right "peaceably to assemble for the purpose of petitioning Congress for redress of grievances." [**United States v. Cruikshank,** 92 U.S. 542 (1876)]

C. Thirteenth Amendment

1. **Congressional Power Over Badges or Incidents of Slavery [§1249]**

The Thirteenth Amendment's prohibition of slavery applies to private as well as government action. Therefore, under the Enabling Clause in Section 2 of the Amendment, Congress has power to remedy interference by *anyone*. This power has been broadly construed. The test is whether Congress could *rationally* determine that the conduct it is making criminal (or providing civil remedies against) imposes on the victim a *"badge or incident" of slavery*. [**Jones v. Alfred H. Mayer Co.,** 392 U.S. 409 (1968)]

> **e.g. Examples:** Congress has been held to have the power to create a statutory cause of action against private persons who deprive African-Americans of "basic rights that the law secures to all free men"—*e.g.*, freedom from racial discrimination in the sale or rental of real and personal property [**Jones v. Alfred H. Mayer Co.,** *supra*]; in the making of contracts for admission to private schools [**Runyon v. McCrary,** *supra*, §526]; and in respect to "rights such as free speech, assembly, association and movement" [**Griffin v. Breckenridge,** *supra*].

a. **Scope [§1250]**

It would seem that, under the Thirteenth Amendment's Enabling Clause, Congress may prohibit *virtually* all racial discrimination *against blacks*. Moreover, Congress may also prohibit racial discrimination *against whites*. [**McDonald v. Santa Fe Trail Transportation Co.,** 427 U.S. 273 (1976)] It is an *open question* whether Congress may forbid other forms of discrimination pursuant to this power.

D. Fourteenth Amendment

1. **Power Over Equal Protection and Due Process Violations [§1251]**

Under the Enabling Clause in Section 5 of the Fourteenth Amendment, Congress has power to remedy violations of equal protection and due process. [**Katzenbach v. Morgan,** 384 U.S. 641 (1966)]

2. **Scope of Power [§1252]**

The power under the Enabling Clause to *remedy* Fourteenth Amendment violations includes prohibiting conduct that is *not itself* unconstitutional.

a. **Preventing future violations [§1253]**

In **Katzenbach v. Morgan,** *supra*, Congress was held to have the power to forbid states from requiring people to pass English literacy tests in order to vote—even though the Court would not find such tests to be unconstitutional—because the Court was able to "perceive a basis" for Congress's judgment that the racial minorities thereby enfranchised would prevent the state from unconstitutionally discriminating against them in the allocation of public services.

b. **Remedying prior violations [§1254]**

Even though state action that has only a racially disproportionate impact (but is not intentionally discriminatory) does not violate the Equal Protection Clause (*see supra*, §§1034-1037), Congress has been held to have the power under the Enabling Clause to prohibit such state action if it reasonably concludes that this is "an appropriate method of attacking the perpetuation of prior purposeful discrimination." [**Fullilove v. Klutznick,** *supra*, §1075]

c. **Limitations [§1255]**

Congress's power under the Enabling Clause of Section 5 of the Fourteenth Amendment is extensive but not unlimited. Under Section 5, Congress may not: (i) adopt legislation that expands substantive constitutional rights beyond those defined by the Supreme Court; (ii) adopt legislation that conflicts with other constitutional provisions; or (iii) dilute Fourteenth Amendment rights.

(1) **Prohibition against expanding substantive constitutional rights [§1256]**

Section 5 gives Congress the power to adopt appropriate legislation *to enforce* the Fourteenth Amendment. It does not give Congress the power to define constitutional rights or to create new constitutional rights. That is the function of the Court. Congress may only enact laws to prevent or remedy violations of rights already recognized by the courts.

Example: The Supreme Court has held that there is no violation of the First Amendment, applicable to the states through the Fourteenth Amendment, when a state incidentally burdens religious practices. [**Employment Division v. Smith,** *supra,* §989] In response, Congress adopted a statute—the Religious Freedom Restoration Act—purportedly pursuant to the Enabling Clause of the Fourteenth Amendment, providing that a state may not burden religious practices absent a compelling interest. The statute was held unconstitutional because it sought to expand substantive First Amendment rights beyond those recognized by the Supreme Court. [**City of Boerne v. Flores,** 521 U.S. 507 (1997)]

Example: The Supreme Court has held that Congress has no power under the Enabling Clause of the Fourteenth Amendment to broadly restrict age discrimination by state employers. *Rationale:* The federal law would forbid many employment decisions based on age that have a "rational basis," which the Court has held (*see supra*, §1117) is the standard for judgment under the Equal Protection Clause for age-based discrimination. [**Kimel v. Florida Board of Regents,** 528 U.S. 62 (2000)]

Example: Congress has no power under the Enabling Clause of the Fourteenth Amendment to provide a civil remedy for victims of gender-motivated violence. *Rationale:* A violation of the Equal Protection Clause requires "state action" (*see supra*, §1214) and the federal statute was not directed at states or state officials, but rather at individuals who commit the prohibited acts. [**United States v. Morrison,** *supra*, §297]

e.g. **Example:** Congress has no power to authorize the admission of confessions in state or federal courts that violate the "*Miranda* rule" (*see infra*, §1276), which is a *constitutional* decision under the Fifth Amendment privilege against self-incrimination. [**Dickerson v. United States,** 530 U.S. 428 (2000)]

(a) Scope of appropriate remedial power [§1257]

Although Congress has "wide latitude" in remedying violations of the Fourteenth Amendment, "there must be a *congruence and proportionality* between the injury to be prevented or remedied and the means adopted to that end"; *i.e.*, the remedy must be narrowly tailored to remedy the violations. Otherwise, "legislation may become substantive in operation and effect." [**City of Boerne v. Flores,** *supra*]

e.g. **Example:** The Americans With Disabilities Act ("ADA") includes provisions that, among other things, prohibit states from discriminating against disabled persons in hiring practices and require states to make reasonable accommodations for disabled employees. Under the Fourteenth Amendment Equal Protection Clause, the Court has recognized a right of disabled people to be free only from irrational state discrimination. The provisions of the ADA are not congruent and proportional to remedying only irrational discrimination; they are overinclusive because they prohibit states from making employment decisions that are constitutional under the rational basis test. [**Board of Trustees v. Garrett,** 531 U.S. 356 (2001)]

(b) Findings required [§1258]

When adopting legislation to remedy violations of the Fourteenth Amendment, Congress must identify the conduct that it found to transgress the substantive provisions of the Fourteenth Amendment. Broad, prophylactic remedies require a "history of widespread and persisting deprivation of constitutional rights."

e.g. **Example:** Congress *has* power under Section 5 to require states to provide their employees with unpaid leave to deal with serious health conditions of spouses, children, or parents. *Rationale:* The record before Congress showed that, in granting leave benefits, states had relied on gender stereotypes (caring for family members is "women's work"), which the Court has held are subject to "heightened scrutiny" (*see supra*, §1095) and this makes it *easier* for Congress to show a "pattern of unconstitutional discrimination" as to justify "prophylactic" legislation. [**Nevada Department of Human Resources v. Hibbs,** 123 S. Ct. 1972 (2003)]

---

cf. **Compare:** In 1992, Congress adopted the Patent Remedy Act. Among other things, the Act provided that states could be made defendants in private federal court suits for patent infringement violations. The record showed that some members of Congress felt that the Act could be based on Congress's power under Section 5 because it sought to protect patent rights, and patents are a form of property protected by the Fourteenth Amendment Due Process Clause. However, the Court found that Section 5 did not give Congress power to adopt the provision subjecting states to federal court suits. The congressional record did not show a widespread history of states infringing on patents and using their sovereign immunity to deny patent owners compensation. [**Florida Prepaid Postsecondary Education Expense Board v. College Savings Bank,** *supra,* §18]

---

1) **Remedying past discrimination [§1259]**

When reviewing a congressional remedy for prior discrimination, the Court will *carefully* review the congressional record to determine whether the remedy is based on a "pattern of unconstitutional discrimination." The court will favor (and *perhaps require*) "findings" rather than "anecdotal accounts." [**Board of Trustees v. Garrett,** *supra*]

---

e.g. **Example:** In **Board of Trustees v. Garrett** (discussed *supra,* §1257), the Court found that in adopting the ADA, Congress did not identify a history or pattern of irrational employment practices by the states. Therefore, Section 5 could not be the basis for the ADA provisions prohibiting the states from discriminating against disabled persons in hiring practices and requiring the states to make reasonable accommodations for disabled employees.

EXAM TIP	**gilbert**

Be wary of exam questions in which Congress adopts sweeping legislation to remedy past discrimination or other constitutional violations by the states. While such legislation could be based on Section 5 of the Fourteenth Amendment, be sure to remember that Congress *cannot use Section 5 to create new substantive rights*, and the Court may consider a law to be creating new substantive rights unless Congress makes findings that an *existing* substantive constitutional right has been transgressed regularly and the law adopted is *congruent and proportional* (*i.e.,* narrowly tailored) to remedy the transgressions (or prevent future ones). Otherwise, the legislation will be held invalid.

(2) Conflict with other constitutional provisions [§1260]

Another limitation exists when a federal statute enacted to enforce the Fourteenth Amendment comes into conflict with another provision of the Constitution. For example, Congress has no power under Section 5 to lower the voting age in *state and local* elections as a means of enforcing equal protection, because Article I, Section 2 reserves to the states the power to prescribe qualifications of voters in state and local elections and no constitutional provision has narrowed this state power. [**Oregon v. Mitchell,** *supra,* §1245—no majority opinion]

(3) Dilution [§1261]

"Congress's power under Section 5 is limited to adopting measures to *enforce* the guarantees of the amendment; Section 5 grants Congress *no power to restrict, abrogate, or dilute* these guarantees. Thus, for example, an enactment authorizing the states to establish racially segregated systems of education would not be—as required by Section 5—a measure 'to enforce' the Equal Protection Clause since that clause of its own force prohibits such state laws." [**Katzenbach v. Morgan,** *supra,* §1253]

(4) Expansion vs. dilution [§1262]

The Court has not clearly indicated the extent to which it will defer to congressional judgment when Congress passes a law that expands one constitutional right apparently at the expense of another—*e.g.,* if Congress were to restrict First Amendment freedom of the press to protect the Fifth Amendment right of a criminal defendant to a fair trial.

3. Government vs. Private Action [§1263]

As noted previously (*see supra,* §§1214, 1256), violation of Fourteenth Amendment rights requires some element of state action. Nonetheless, the conduct of private individuals *may* sometimes interfere with the exercise of such rights—and Congress has broad powers to remedy this situation.

a. State officials [§1264]

In a number of decisions, the Court has relied on the Section 5 Enabling Clause to sustain federal statutes authorizing civil damage judgments or criminal convictions against state or local officials who misuse their authority so as to violate the rights protected by the Fourteenth Amendment.

> **Examples:** Federal legislation punishing persons who, under color of state law, deprive another of any right, privilege, or immunity secured or protected by the Constitution has been upheld as applied to law enforcement officers who knowingly deprived a prisoner of his life without due process of law. [**Screws v. United States,** *supra,* §1215—police beat prisoner to death in effort to obtain a confession] Also, it has been applied to city council members. [**Owen v. City of Independence,** 445 U.S. 622 (1980)]

b. Distinguish—federal officials [§1265]

No comparable federal statute provides redress against federal officials who violate the constitutional rights of individuals. But the Court has held that the *Constitution itself* empowers federal courts to recognize a cause of action against federal agents who violate the constitutional rights of others. [**Bivens v. Six Unknown Named Agents**, 403 U.S. 388 (1971)—violation of Fourth Amendment; **Davis v. Passman**, 442 U.S. 228 (1979)—violation of Fifth Amendment based on sexual bias which denied equal protection]

c. Private individuals [§1266]

Where private individuals engage in a "joint activity" with government officials to infringe the constitutional rights of others over whom state power has been exerted, the private individuals, as well as the government officers, are subject to sanctions under federal law. Having gained the benefit of official state power, the private individuals are also subject to the responsibilities of the state. [**United States v. Price**, 383 U.S. 787 (1966)—private citizens killed civil rights workers pursuant to plan joined in by local police]

Example: In **United States v. Guest**, *supra*, §1243, private individuals prevented African-American persons from using *state-owned facilities* because of their race. Six Justices (in two separate opinions) expressed the view that "the right to use state facilities without discrimination on the basis of race" is a right secured by the Equal Protection Clause. Thus, Congress could penalize private interference with that right.

E. Fifteenth Amendment

1. Power Over Voting Discrimination [§1267]

Under the Enabling Clause in Section 2 of the Fifteenth Amendment, Congress has broad power to prevent government racial discrimination in voting. The test is whether Congress could *rationally* find that the conduct or practice it seeks to prohibit or regulate has been or may be used to deny voting rights to blacks. [**South Carolina v. Katzenbach**, *supra*, §74—Congress has power to provide a range of remedies (including suspension of literacy tests and appointment of federal voting examiners) in states where Congress has found government racial discrimination in voting]

2. Discriminatory Effect [§1268]

Even though voting regulations that have only a disproportionate racial impact (but are not intentionally discriminatory) *might* not violate the Fifteenth Amendment (*see supra*, §1037), Congress may prohibit such regulations in areas "with a demonstrable history of racial discrimination" in voting—because Congress could find that they create the "risk of purposeful discrimination." [**City of Rome v. United States**, 446 U.S. 156 (1980)]

F. Other Sources of Power

1. Introduction [§1269]
In addition to its power under the Necessary and Proper Clause and the Enabling Clauses, Congress has other sources of power that may be used to protect constitutional rights against both private and government conduct.

2. Commerce Power [§1270]
Provisions of the Civil Rights Act of 1964 (prohibiting racial discrimination in interstate transportation or in restaurants, hotels, and other places of public accommodation) have been upheld as a valid exercise of Congress's power under the Commerce Clause. [**Heart of Atlanta Motel, Inc. v. United States**, *supra*, §295]

3. Taxing and Spending Powers [§1271]
The federal government may indirectly, through its taxing or spending powers, compel persons to recognize the constitutional rights of others (*e.g.*, governmental contracts may be conditioned on the supplier's not discriminating in hiring, etc.). [**Fullilove v. Klutznick**, *supra*, §1254]

Chapter Ten: Safeguards in the Administration of Criminal Justice

CONTENTS

Chapter Approach

The following discussion covers the few aspects of "constitutional criminal procedure" that may be contained in Constitutional Law courses. You will probably not spend much time on these topics in your Constitutional Law class and are unlikely to see these issues on a Constitutional Law exam. This overview is included mostly for the sake of completeness. A thorough discussion of these topics, and many other topics not touched upon here, is contained in the Criminal Procedure Summary.

A. Evidentiary Matters

1. Use of Involuntary Confessions

a. In federal courts

(1) Constitutional provision [§1272]
The Fifth Amendment provides: "No person . . . shall be compelled in any criminal case to be a witness against himself . . . ."

(2) Effect [§1273]
An involuntary or coerced confession is deemed *inadmissible* in federal courts. [**Bram v. United States,** 168 U.S. 532 (1897)]

b. In state courts [§1274]
The Fifth Amendment provision prohibiting the use of involuntary or coerced confessions is incorporated into the Due Process Clause of the Fourteenth Amendment, and thus is binding in state, as well as federal, criminal prosecutions. [**Brown v. Mississippi,** 297 U.S. 278 (1936)]

c. Certain confessions inadmissible even though voluntary [§1275]
Under certain circumstances, even a *voluntary* confession may be inadmissible.

(1) *Miranda* [§1276]
In **Miranda v. Arizona,** 384 U.S. 436 (1966), the Court held that a confession obtained from an accused during *custodial interrogation*—before or after formal charges are filed, and regardless of voluntariness—would not be admissible unless it first appeared that the police had clearly informed the accused (i) of his right to *remain silent*; (ii) that *anything he said might be used against him*; and (iii) that he had the *right to consult with counsel* (and, if indigent, that he had the right to appointed counsel) at the time of the interrogation.

(a) Rationale

"In custody" interrogations are *inherently compulsive*, and hence there is a greater need to protect an accused's constitutional rights. This greater need justifies the requirement that the prosecution make an affirmative showing that these rights were protected where it seeks to use *any* statements (inculpatory or exculpatory) obtained from the accused during such interrogations.

EXAM TIP   **gilbert**

If a *Miranda* issue shows up on your exam, if you remember the basics, you will likely do well. In *Miranda,* the Supreme Court held that to offset the coercive nature of *custodial police interrogation*, and to assure that confessions are *voluntary*, detainees must be (i) *informed* of their rights to remain silent and to an attorney and (ii) *warned* that any statements they make can be used against them in court (*i.e.*, the *Miranda* warnings known to everyone who regularly watches a TV cop show).

---

2. Privilege Against Self-Incrimination

a. In federal courts

(1) Constitutional provision [§1277]

The privilege against self-incrimination springs from the same Fifth Amendment provision barring the use of involuntary confessions: "No person . . . shall be compelled in any criminal case to be a witness against himself . . . ."

(2) Effect [§1278]

In any federal proceeding, *civil or criminal*, a witness (whether or not a party to the action) cannot be compelled to give evidence of a *testimonial* or communicative nature that might subject him to any criminal prosecution.

EXAM TIP   **gilbert**

If an exam question presents a person pleading "the Fifth," keep in mind that *only testimonial evidence* is protected by the Fifth Amendment proscription against compelled self-incrimination. Nontestimonial evidence, such as pictures, blood samples, voice samples, handwriting samples, and the like are not protected.

---

b. In state courts [§1279]

The Fourteenth Amendment Due Process Clause incorporates the Fifth Amendment privilege against self-incrimination, so that an accused cannot be forced to give such evidence against himself in state courts either. [**Malloy v. Hogan,** *supra*, §423]

c. No comment on failure to testify in own defense [§1280]

In both federal and state courts, a defendant's failure to take the witness stand in his own defense is treated as tantamount to a claim of the privilege. Hence, no adverse inference of guilt can be drawn from not taking the stand, and neither the judge nor the prosecutor is permitted to make any adverse comment to the jury about the defendant's failure to testify. [**Griffin v. California,** 380 U.S. 609 (1965)]

3. Exclusion of Evidence Obtained by Illegal Searches and Seizures

a. In federal courts

(1) Fourth Amendment [§1281]
"The right of the people to be secure in their persons, houses, papers, and effects, against unreasonable searches and seizures, shall not be violated, and no Warrants shall issue, but upon probable cause, supported by Oath or affirmation, and particularly describing the place to be searched, and the persons or things to be seized."

(2) Effect [§1282]
Evidence obtained in violation of this provision is *inadmissible* in the prosecution's case-in-chief in federal courts. [**Elkins v. United States,** 364 U.S. 206 (1960)]

(a) "Good faith exception" [§1283]
But this exclusionary rule does not bar the admission of evidence obtained within the scope of a search warrant, even though the warrant is invalid (*e.g., not* supported by probable cause), if: (i) the warrant was issued by a *detached and neutral magistrate*, and (ii) the officer was *neither dishonest nor reckless* in preparing the affidavit and had an *objectively reasonable belief* that the warrant was valid. [**United States v. Leon,** 468 U.S. 897 (1984); **Massachusetts v. Sheppard,** 468 U.S. 981 (1984)]

b. In state courts [§1284]
The Due Process Clause of the Fourteenth Amendment incorporates the protection afforded by the Fourth Amendment, and has the same effect upon state criminal prosecutions that the Fourth Amendment has upon federal prosecutions; *i.e.,* illegally seized evidence and the fruits of illegally seized evidence must usually be excluded. [**Mapp v. Ohio,** 367 U.S. 643 (1961)]

c. What constitutes unreasonable search or seizure [§1285]
The Fourth Amendment protection extends to the unauthorized obtainment of physical evidence (documents, guns, drugs, etc.), to the interception of verbal communications (eavesdropping, wiretapping), and even to the observation of matters through an unauthorized invasion of privacy. (*See* detailed discussion in Criminal Procedure Summary.)

(1) Fourth Amendment protects people, not places [§1286]

The Fourth Amendment has been held to protect people, not places. Hence, the constitutional guarantee applies whether or not the evidence is obtained by any physical intrusion or trespass. [**Katz v. United States**, 389 U.S. 347 (1967)—excluding evidence obtained by electronic eavesdropping accomplished without any wiretap or physical trespass]

d. Enforcement of constitutional prohibitions—exclusion of evidence [§1287]

The Fourth Amendment, implemented by the Self-Incrimination Clause of the Fifth Amendment, forbids the federal government from convicting a person of a crime by using testimony or papers obtained by unreasonable searches and seizures as defined in the Fourth Amendment. [**Boyd v. United States**, 116 U.S. 616 (1886)] Such evidence is therefore *inadmissible* in federal courts *whether seized by state or federal officers*. [**Weeks v. United States**, 232 U.S. 383 (1914); **Elkins v. United States**, *supra*] The same rule applies in state courts. [**Mapp v. Ohio**, *supra*]

B. Trial Issues

1. Right to Trial by Jury

a. Petit jury

(1) Constitutional provision [§1288]

The Sixth Amendment provides: "In all criminal prosecutions, the accused shall enjoy the right to speedy and public trial, by an impartial jury of the State and district wherein the crime shall have been committed . . . ."

(2) Effective in state and federal courts [§1289]

Under the above provision, a defendant in a federal court charged with any *serious offense* (as distinguished from a petty offense) is entitled to trial by a jury. [**Patton v. United States**, 281 U.S. 276 (1930)] And the right is deemed so "fundamental" that it is fully incorporated by due process in state proceedings as well. [**Duncan v. Louisiana**, *supra*, §423]

(3) What constitutes "trial by jury"

(a) Number of jurors [§1290]

The number of jurors in federal criminal trials is 12, but this is pursuant to statute [Fed. R. Crim. P. 23] and is *not constitutionally required* [**Williams v. Florida**, 399 U.S. 78 (1970)]. The Constitution requires a sufficient number of jurors to provide *adequate group deliberation* and a *fair cross-section* of the community. [**Ballew v. Georgia**, 435 U.S. 223 (1978)]

1) Fewer than twelve jurors [§1291]

Thus, state rules have been upheld allowing the use of six jurors [**Williams v. Florida,** *supra*]; but five jurors have been deemed too few to meet constitutional requirements [**Ballew v. Georgia,** *supra*].

(b) Unanimous verdict

1) Federal courts [§1292]

The Sixth Amendment right to jury trial is deemed to give a defendant in *federal* court the right to a unanimous jury verdict. [*See* **Apodaca v. Oregon,** *supra*, §422]

2) State courts [§1293]

However, the Court has upheld *state* convictions based on a verdict by only a "substantial majority" of the jurors—as low as 75% (nine to three verdict). [**Johnson v. Louisiana,** 406 U.S. 356 (1972)]

a) Comment

This is one of the unusual situations in which *not all aspects* of one of the Bill of Rights is incorporated by the Fourteenth Amendment—so that the right receives greater protection in federal than in state courts. (*See supra*, §423.)

b) Note

The Court has *rejected* the argument that allowing less than unanimity in the verdict undermines the *reasonable doubt* standard required by due process (*see infra*, §1324); the fact that three jurors disagree does *not* in itself establish a reasonable doubt.

c) But note

When a jury is as small as six persons, the verdict must be *unanimous*. [**Burch v. Louisiana,** 441 U.S. 130 (1979)]

EXAM TIP **gilbert**

Remember, a jury of 12 is *not constitutionally required*; juries can be as small as six members. If the jury has 12 members, verdicts need not be unanimous (9-3 verdicts have been upheld), but verdicts of *six-member juries must be unanimous*.

---

(4) "Serious" vs. "petty" offenses [§1294]

Because a jury trial is guaranteed only if a "serious" offense is charged, it becomes necessary to distinguish between "serious" and "petty" (nonserious) offenses. The Court looks to the maximum potential sentence. [**Duncan v. Louisiana,** *supra*]

(a) **Potential sentence [§1295]**

Any offense that carries a potential sentence of *more than six months* is a "serious" offense, so that a jury trial *must* be afforded on demand, and this is true even in cases where the actual sentence imposed is less than six months. [**Baldwin v. New York,** 399 U.S. 66 (1970)]

b. **Selection of jurors**

(1) **Constitutional source [§1296]**

The Sixth Amendment guarantees an accused the right to *trial* before "an *impartial* jury *of the state and district* wherein the crime shall have been committed." This guarantee is incorporated in the Fourteenth Amendment Due Process Clause and is therefore binding on the states. [**Duncan v. Louisiana,** *supra*]

(a) **Note**

The guarantee is construed to require that *trial and grand juries* in both federal and state courts be both *"impartial" and* drawn from a *fair cross-section* of the community. [**Taylor v. Louisiana,** 419 U.S. 522 (1975)]

(2) **Requirement that jurors be drawn from "fair cross-section of community" [§1297]**

The right to a "jury trial" presupposes that the jury venire will be drawn from a pool *broadly representative* of the community at large. If there is systematic disproportion from a fair community cross-section either mandated by statute or resulting from consistent practice, the only remaining issue is whether there is significant justification of this infringement, irrespective of whether there was discriminatory purpose.

(a) **Application**

1) **Systematic exclusions invalidated [§1298]**

A defendant is deprived of the constitutional right to a jury trial if any identifiable segment playing a major role in the community is systematically excluded or underrepresented by a particular selection process for the grand or petit jury panel. However, the requirement of a fair cross-section may be overcome by a significant governmental interest that is incompatible with that process. [**Duren v. Missouri,** 439 U.S. 357 (1979)] *Illustrations:*

a) *Systematic exclusion of African-Americans* from petit jury panels has been held to be a denial of equal protection of law. [**Patton v. Mississippi,** 332 U.S. 463 (1947)]

b) *Systematic exclusion of Mexican-American* citizens from petit jury panels has been held to be a denial of equal protection. [**Hernandez v. Texas,** 347 U.S. 475 (1954)]

c) *Exclusion of women* from petit jury panels unless they volunteered for jury service has been held to be a denial of Sixth and Fourteenth Amendment rights to a "representative" jury. [**Taylor v. Louisiana,** *supra*] So is the *underrepresentation* of women resulting from the automatic exemption from jury service for any woman requesting not to serve. [**Duren v. Missouri,** *supra*]

d) *Substantial underrepresentation of Mexican-Americans from grand jury selection* has been held to be a prima facie denial of equal protection. [**Castaneda v. Partida,** 430 U.S. 482 (1977)—prima facie case not rebutted by showing that Mexican-Americans constituted "governing majority" in county]

2) **Distinguish—"considerable leeway" granted where no systematic exclusion shown [§1299]**

Where there is no claim that the jury panel was chosen in a manner that systematically excluded or discriminated against any identifiable segment of the community, "considerable leeway" is granted in selection of trial jurors. States are free to prescribe "relevant qualifications" and to provide "reasonable exemptions" from jury service. [**Taylor v. Louisiana,** *supra*]

a) **Proportionate representation not required [§1300]**

The right to a "jury trial" does *not* require proportionate representation of all the component groups in the community. [**Akins v. Texas,** 325 U.S. 398 (1945)] Indeed, state rules *requiring* proportional *racial* representation on jury panels have been held to *violate* equal protection—*i.e.,* race may not be considered as a factor either in inclusion or exclusion from jury service. [**Cassell v. Texas,** 339 U.S. 282 (1950)]

b) **"Blue ribbon" panels permitted [§1301]**

The Court has upheld a state's system of choosing "blue ribbon" jury panels (requiring special experience, etc.) to try certain kinds of cases. [**Fay v. New York,** 332 U.S. 261 (1947)]

3) **Peremptory challenges of jurors from particular groups permitted [§1302]**

The fair cross-section required at the venire stage may be disrupted during the jury selection process to serve a legitimate state interest. Thus, peremptory challenges to eliminate prospective jurors from groups that might unduly favor one side are permitted to assure "an *impartial* jury." [**Holland v. Illinois**, 493 U.S. 474 (1990)]

(b) Standing to challenge [§1303]

A defendant convicted by a jury panel that is not fairly chosen may challenge the verdict on this ground alone. The defendant *need not* prove that the verdict was *affected* by the exclusion, or that any different outcome was likely had the jury been properly chosen. The verdict will be reversed simply because an improperly selected jury *deprives* the accused of the constitutional right to a "jury trial"; no other prejudice need be shown. [**Taylor v. Louisiana**, *supra*]

1) Defendant need not be member of excluded group [§1304]

Thus, a defendant may raise the constitutional challenge even where he is *not* a member of the group allegedly excluded. [**Taylor v. Louisiana**, *supra*—male rape defendant had standing to challenge systematic exclusion of women from jury panel that convicted him]

2) Excluded persons may file civil suit [§1305]

The persons *excluded* from juries solely because of their race, etc., *also* have standing to challenge the jury selection process. Of course, their attack will not be on the conviction. Rather, they are entitled to file a civil suit for injunctive or declaratory relief to establish their right to serve on such juries. [**Carter v. Jury Commission**, 396 U.S. 320 (1970)]

(3) Impartial jury [§1306]

Both the accused and the accuser have a constitutional right to an impartial jury. Although a juror may have a preconceived notion as to the guilt or innocence of the accused, she must be able to lay aside her impression or opinion and render a verdict based on the evidence presented to her. [**Irvin v. Dowd**, 366 U.S. 717 (1961)]

(a) Effect of pretrial publicity [§1307]

Where a community has been repeatedly exposed to inflammatory publicity regarding an accused, due process may require a change of venue to obtain an impartial jury. [**Rideau v. Louisiana**, 373 U.S. 723 (1963)—reversing conviction where state court refused change of venue notwithstanding fact that an interview between accused and sheriff, containing admissions of capital crimes charged, was telecast three times in the community]

(b) Protection against prejudice during trial [§1308]

A jury cannot be subjected to possible influence or prejudicial associations during a criminal trial. [**Turner v. Louisiana,** 379 U.S. 466 (1965)—reversing conviction where jury deliberated in custody of two deputy sheriffs who had given key testimony against defendant during trial]

(c) Death penalty cases [§1309]

A state may not automatically exclude for cause all prospective jurors who express a doubt or scruple about the death penalty. [**Witherspoon v. Illinois,** 391 U.S. 510 (1968)] The standard for determining when a prospective juror should be excluded for cause is whether the juror's views would prevent or substantially impair the performance of his duties in accordance with his instructions and oath. [**Wainwright v. Witt,** 469 U.S. 412 (1985)] Thus, if a juror's doubts or scruples about the death penalty prevent or substantially impair the performance of his duties, he may be excluded from the jury, and the fact that this may result in a "death qualified" jury does not infringe a defendant's constitutional rights. [**Lockhart v. McCree,** 476 U.S. 162 (1986)]

2. Right to Public Trial

a. In federal courts [§1310]

In federal courts, a public trial is expressly guaranteed by the Sixth Amendment.

b. In state courts [§1311]

This right is also guaranteed in state courts. A secret trial violates the Due Process Clause of the Fourteenth Amendment. [*In re* **Oliver,** 333 U.S. 257 (1948)]

c. Suppression hearing [§1312]

The right extends to a hearing to suppress wrongfully seized evidence that is conducted prior to the presentation of evidence of guilt. It may be outweighed only by a ***compelling and narrowly tailored*** interest articulated in findings by the trial judge. [**Waller v. Georgia,** 467 U.S. 39 (1984)]

d. Scope of the right [§1313]

The right to a public trial belongs only to the ***accused,*** so that members of the public (*e.g.,* the press) do not have standing under the Sixth Amendment to complain of any exclusion. [**Gannett Co. v. DePasquale,** 443 U.S. 368 (1979)—holding that the press can be excluded under the Sixth Amendment from hearings on pretrial motions; *but see supra,* §890]

3. Right to Fair Trial [§1314]

In addition to the foregoing rights specifically mentioned in the Constitution, the

Court has deemed certain types of conduct so unfair in either state or federal court as to violate due process under the Fifth and Fourteenth Amendments. Such unfairness is usually coupled with a showing that the conduct complained of resulted in identifiable prejudice to the accused. On occasion, however, the Court has held that the conduct involves such a probability of prejudice that it is inherently lacking in due process—*i.e.,* actual prejudice need *not* be shown.

a. Trial publicity [§1315]
The Court has held in several cases that inflammatory publicity given to a crime or to the trial may have so prejudiced the minds of potential jurors as to prevent the accused from receiving a fair trial (*see supra*, §1307).

(1) Media coverage of trial [§1316]
Radio, television, or photographic coverage of a criminal trial for public broadcast does not—when properly controlled—violate due process unless the defendant shows: (i) prejudicial effect on the trial participants; or (ii) jury inability to fairly adjudicate the case. [**Chandler v. Florida,** 449 U.S. 560 (1981)]

(2) Protection of jury impartiality [§1317]
A conviction must be reversed where the trial court fails to take such steps as are reasonably necessary to protect the impartiality of the jury. [**Sheppard v. Maxwell,** 384 U.S. 333 (1966)—trial judge failed to control coverage by news media so that "bedlam reigned" and inflammatory stories were held to have so aroused public opinion as to deny accused a fair trial]

4. Right to Counsel

a. In federal courts

(1) Constitutional provision—Sixth Amendment [§1318]
"In all criminal prosecutions, the accused shall enjoy the right . . . to have the Assistance of Counsel for his defense."

(2) Effect [§1319]
The Sixth Amendment entitles an accused in federal courts to the assistance of counsel unless this right has been knowingly and intelligently waived. If an accused desires counsel but cannot afford to hire his own, defense counsel must be appointed by the trial court. [**Johnson v. Zerbst,** 304 U.S. 458 (1938); **Walker v. Johnston,** 312 U.S. 275 (1941)]

b. In state courts [§1320]
The Sixth Amendment is incorporated by the Due Process Clause of the Fourteenth Amendment, and thus the same right to counsel must be afforded in state courts. [**Gideon v. Wainwright,** *supra,* §423]

c. Scope of right

(1) Nature of charge—felony vs. misdemeanor [§1321]

The right to counsel is constitutionally required in all prosecutions that *result* in actual *imprisonment*—whether the offense is classified as a felony or misdemeanor. [**Argersinger v. Hamlin,** 407 U.S. 25 (1972)]

(a) Effect [§1322]

If the trial judge concludes that the offense is punishable by imprisonment, she must afford counsel to the accused; *otherwise, no jail sentence* may be imposed.

(b) Indigents [§1323]

Counsel need not be appointed for indigent defendants where the crime is punishable by imprisonment, but upon conviction no imprisonment occurs. [**Scott v. Illinois,** 440 U.S. 367 (1979)]

EXAM TIP   **gilbert**

Remember that the right to appointed counsel is available *only if imprisonment is actually imposed*. Thus, if an exam question involves a misdemeanor and the defendant asks for counsel, is denied, and is convicted, whether the right to counsel has been violated depends on the defendant's sentence: If he receives no imprisonment, his right has not been violated; if he receives jail/prison time, his right has been violated.

---

5. Burden of Proof [§1324]

The Due Process Clause requires proof *beyond a reasonable doubt* of every fact necessary to constitute the crime with which the defendant is charged. [*In re* **Winship,** *supra,* §425]

a. Proceedings to which applicable [§1325]

This requirement applies in every proceeding in which violation of a criminal law is charged, or as to which criminal sanctions may be imposed.

(1) Juvenile proceedings [§1326]

It applies in juvenile proceedings, at least where the juvenile is charged with violation of a criminal law. [*In re* **Winship,** *supra*—whether juvenile is "delinquent" must be proved beyond reasonable doubt]

(2) Appellate review [§1327]

Because a defendant's guilt must be proved beyond a reasonable doubt, the question of whether, after viewing the evidence in the light most favorable to the prosecution, any rational trier of fact could have found the essential elements of the crime beyond a reasonable doubt is a question of law cognizable in an appeal or a habeas corpus proceeding. [**Jackson v. Virginia,** 443 U.S. 307 (1979)]

6. **Requirement of Certainty in Criminal Statutes [§1328]**

Although all statutes must be definite and certain to be enforceable, this is a fundamental requirement regarding criminal statutes. The statute must give "fair warning" of the conduct that it makes a crime; *i.e.*, it must be sufficiently explicit to inform those who are subject to it exactly what conduct on their part will render them liable to its penalties. Moreover, the requirement of certainty *prevents arbitrary and discriminatory enforcement* of criminal statutes (*i.e.*, it assures explicit standards to guide the police as well as the public). [**Grayned v. City of Rockford,** 408 U.S. 104 (1972)]

a. **Application—vagueness [§1329]**

Statutes may be held invalid because of vagueness in defining *what conduct constitutes* the crime. *Examples:*

(1) *To be a member of a "gang."* [**Lanzetta v. New Jersey,** 306 U.S. 451 (1939)]

(2) *To engage in conduct* on city sidewalks in a manner *"annoying" to passers-by.* [**Coates v. Cincinnati,** 402 U.S. 611 (1971)]

(3) *To wander city streets late at night* "without lawful business and . . . [without giving a] satisfactory account of himself." [**Palmer v. City of Euclid,** 402 U.S. 544 (1971)]

b. **Effect of mens rea requirement [§1330]**

Vagueness in language may sometimes be cured by a requirement that the defendant have a specific intent to do that which is forbidden in vague language. [*See* **Screws v. United States,** *supra*, §1264—statute made it a crime to *willfully* violate the "constitutional rights" of others]

C. Rights Regarding Punishment

1. **Cruel and Unusual Punishment**

a. **Constitutional provision [§1331]**

The Eighth Amendment provides ". . . nor [may] cruel and unusual punishments [be] inflicted."

(1) **State courts [§1332]**

The Eighth Amendment is incorporated in the Due Process Clause of the Fourteenth Amendment and thus applies to the states, as well as to the federal government.

b. **Scope [§1333]**

The scope of the constitutional prohibition is two-fold.

(1) Punishment disproportionate to crime [§1334]

One approach is to determine whether the punishment is *"excessive"—i.e.,* whether it is grossly disproportionate to the severity of the crime, or whether it is the purposeless imposition of severe punishment. The Court itself ultimately makes this judgment, informed most importantly by the consistency and direction of legislative enactments, and also by history, precedent, and responses of sentencing juries. [**Atkins v. Virginia,** 536 U.S. 304 (2002)]

e.g. Example: Twelve years in irons at hard labor, together with accessory penalties (loss of parental and property rights and surveillance for life after release), for a relatively minor offense (falsifying public records) is "grossly disproportionate" and thus invalid. [**Weems v. United States,** 217 U.S. 349 (1910)]

(a) Punishment for illness [§1335]

Conviction under a state statute that made it a crime to be *addicted to the use of narcotics* is invalid. Imprisonment for having a certain status (addict) that the individual is powerless to overcome is analogous to criminally prosecuting a person for being mentally ill or afflicted with a cold or venereal disease. [**Robinson v. California,** 370 U.S. 660 (1962)]

(b) Capital punishment [§1336]

The death penalty is "grossly disproportionate" for the offenses of (i) rape of an adult woman [**Coker v. Georgia,** 433 U.S. 584 (1977)]; and (ii) murder committed during a felony when the defendant does not kill, attempt to kill, or intend that a killing occur, and does not play a major role in the felony which shows reckless indifference to human life. [**Enmund v. Florida,** 456 U.S. 904 (1982)—*as clarified by* **Tison v. Arizona,** 481 U.S. 137 (1987)]

(c) Length of sentence [§1337]

The length of a prison sentence cannot be grossly disproportionate to the severity of the crime. [**Solem v. Helm,** 463 U.S. 277 (1983)—life sentence without possibility of parole for seventh nonviolent felony is "grossly disproportionate"] But substantial deference must be given to sentence decisions of legislatures and sentencing courts, and successful challenges to the length of a sentence alone are rare. [**Rummell v. Estelle,** 445 U.S. 263 (1980)—upholding life sentence, *with* parole possibility, for multiple nonviolent offender; **Ewing v. California,** 123 S. Ct. 1179 (2003)—upholding a life sentence *with* parole possibility after 25 years for prior multiple serious or violent crimes]

(2) Punishment "barbaric" regardless of crime [§1338]

A second approach is to determine whether the punishment itself is disapproved by a national consensus of our society, irrespective of the crime.

(a) Stripping citizenship [§1339]

Congress may not strip an army deserter of citizenship—because making an accused a "stateless person, deprived of the right to have rights" is considered too cruel a punishment for any crime. [**Trop v. Dulles,** 356 U.S. 86 (1958)]

(b) Imposing death on insane person [§1340]

A state may not impose the death penalty on a prisoner who is insane at the *time of the punishment.* [**Ford v. Wainwright,** 477 U.S. 399 (1986)]

(c) Imposing death on mentally retarded person [§1341]

Executions of mentally retarded criminals violate the Eighth Amendment. *Rationale:* The large number of states recently barring execution of mentally retarded persons (and the complete absence of legislation reinstating such executions) provides powerful evidence that today society views mentally retarded offenders as categorically less culpable than the average criminal. Consequently, there is a serious question whether justifications for the death penalty—retribution and deterrence—apply to mentally retarded offenders. In recent years legislatures addressing the issue have voted overwhelmingly in favor of prohibition, and even in states allowing execution of the mentally retarded, the practice has become truly unusual. [**Atkins v. Virginia,** *supra,* §1334]

(d) Imposing death on juveniles [§1342]

It is not cruel and unusual to impose the death penalty on murderers who were 16 years or older at the time they committed the murder, because there is no national consensus forbidding such executions. [**Stanford v. Kentucky,** 492 U.S. 361 (1989)] However, execution of murderers who were younger than 16 at the time of their crime might be forbidden. [**Thompson v. Oklahoma,** 487 U.S. 815 (1988)—four Justices finding it cruel and unusual, one Justice finding it necessary to have a statute specifically authorizing such executions]

c. Capital punishment [§1343]

The death penalty is not, under all circumstances, cruel and unusual punishment. If the sentencing body (judge or jury) is given adequate guidance as to both *aggravating and mitigating* factors about the crime and the defendant relevant to sentencing, *and* if there is a review procedure to ensure against imposition of the death sentence for discriminatory reasons, capital punishment is permissible. [**Gregg v. Georgia,** 428 U.S. 153 (1976)]

(1) Undue discretion [§1344]

However, death penalties imposed pursuant to statutory standards that permit **unbridled** discretion, and under which the penalty may be *selectively* *and capriciously applied*, violate the Eighth and Fourteenth Amendments. [**Furman v. Georgia,** 408 U.S. 238 (1972)]

(a) Limited discretion [§1345]

It is enough, however, if the sentencer is required to find at least one *adequately defined* aggravating factor; the sentencer is *not* required to weigh the aggravating and mitigating factors pursuant to any specific standards. [**Zant v. Stephens,** 462 U.S. 862 (1983)]

(b) Racially disproportionate statistics [§1346]

Some degree of discretion in the criminal justice system is fundamental and provides substantial benefits to defendants. As long as the capital sentencer's discretion is properly confined, the fact that statistics show that the death sentence is most frequently imposed on black defendants who kill white victims does not present such an unacceptable risk of racial prejudice in the capital sentencing system as to violate the Eighth and Fourteenth Amendments. [**McCleskey v. Kemp,** 481 U.S. 279 (1987)]

(2) Mandatory death penalty [§1347]

Mandatory capital punishment for a broad category of homicides, with no meaningful opportunity for consideration of mitigating factors regarding the crime or defendant, is cruel and unusual. [**Woodson v. North Carolina,** 428 U.S. 280 (1976)—killing of a police officer; **Sumner v. Shuman,** 483 U.S. 66 (1987)—murder by inmate serving life sentence without possibility of parole]

(a) Distinguish

But the death sentencing procedure may have some "mandatory aspects"—*e.g.,* death penalty required if the sentencing jury finds an aggravating factor and *no* mitigating factors. [**Blystone v. Pennsylvania,** 494 U.S. 299 (1990)]

(3) Mitigating factors [§1348]

The capital sentencing procedures must *not explicitly* or *implicitly restrict* the sentencer from considering such mitigating factors as any aspect of a defendant's background (*e.g.,* mental retardation or an abused childhood), character, or record and any of the circumstances of the offense that the defendant proffers as relating to his "personal moral culpability" for a sentence less than death. [**Lockett v. Ohio,** 438 U.S. 586 (1978); **Penry v. Lynaugh,** 492 U.S. 302 (1989)]

(a) Unanimity [§1349]

Nor may the capital sentencing procedures require the jury to unanimously find a mitigating factor before considering it. Such a requirement could lead to a death sentence even though almost all of the jurors thought it to be inappropriate. [**McKoy v. North Carolina,** 494 U.S. 433 (1990)]

(b) Burden of proof [§1350]

However, as long as the state has the burden of proving aggravating factors, the burden of proving mitigating factors may be placed on the defendant. [**Walton v. Arizona**, 497 U.S. 639 (1990)]

(4) Permissible factors [§1351]

The sentencing jury *may* consider evidence of the defendant's probable future dangerousness (including psychiatric testimony which need not be based on personal examination). [**Barefoot v. Estelle**, 463 U.S. 880 (1983)] To this end, the jury *may* be told that the governor has power to commute a sentence of "life imprisonment without possibility of parole." Such an instruction may be given even if state law forbids the jury to be told that the governor also has power to commute a death sentence—because the omission will not tend to skew the jury to favor the death sentence. [**California v. Ramos**, 463 U.S. 992 (1983)]

(a) Victim impact statement [§1352]

The sentencing jury may also consider evidence (and argument by the prosecutor) that describes the personal characteristics of the victim and the effect of the crime on the victim's family. States may legitimately permit the jury to assess the harm caused as a result of the crime as well as the defendant's moral culpability. [**Payne v. Tennessee**, 501 U.S. 808 (1991)—*overruling* **Booth v. Maryland**, 482 U.S. 496 (1987)]

(b) Jury deadlock [§1353]

The sentencing jury may (but *need not*) be told about the consequences of jury deadlock—such as the fact that the judge will impose a sentence if the jury fails to reach a unanimous verdict. [**Jones v. United States**, 526 U.S. 227 (1999)]

2. Excessive Fines

a. Constitutional provision [§1354]

The Eighth Amendment provides ". . . nor [may] excessive fines [be] imposed . . . ."

b. Forfeitures—application of Excessive Fines Clause

(1) Punitive forfeitures [§1355]

A forfeiture that is *punitive* (in whole or in part) violates the Excessive Fines Clause if it is *grossly disproportionate* to the *gravity* of the offense. [**United States v. Bajakajian**, 524 U.S. 321 (1998)—adopting standard of Cruel and Unusual Punishments Clause, *supra,* §1334]

 Example: The Court held that forfeiture of $357,144 for the crime of merely failing to report that the cash was being transported out of the country was grossly disproportionate because the crime caused little harm (it would have been legal to take the money out of the country; the only harm was that the government was deprived of a piece of information). [**United States v. Bajakajian,** *supra*]

(2) Nonpunitive forfeiture

(a) Civil in rem forfeitures [§1356]

Civil in rem forfeitures treat the property forfeited as a "wrongdoer" under a legal fiction; the action is against the property and not against an individual, and therefore this type of forfeiture is *not* subject to the Excessive Fines Clause. The forfeiture is often said to be remedial in nature (*e.g.,* because it reimburses the government for lost revenues, as in the case of forfeitures of illegally imported property), rather than punitive.

1) Illustration—instrumentalities [§1357]

One of the traditional types of civil in rem forfeitures involves forfeiture of "instrumentalities." An instrumentality is the property that is actually used to facilitate or commit an offense, such as an automobile used to transport stolen goods.

(b) Monetary forfeitures [§1358]

Monetary forfeitures (*e.g.,* forfeiture of twice the value of illegally imported goods) have also been found to be remedial in nature where they are brought in civil actions. They are seen as a form of liquidated damages to reimburse the government for losses resulting from the offense. [*See* **United States v. Bajakajian,** *supra*]

D. Post-Trial Issues

1. Rights on Appeal

a. Appeal of state conviction

(1) In state courts [§1359]

A state is *not required* by the federal Constitution *to provide appellate review* of alleged errors in the trial. [**National Union of Marine Cooks v. Arnold,** 348 U.S. 37 (1954)] However, if it does provide such review, it cannot do so in a way that unfairly discriminates against some convicted defendants on account of their poverty. Such discrimination violates the Due Process and Equal Protection Clauses of the Fourteenth Amendment. *Examples:*

(a) **Right to transcript [§1360]**
A state must furnish an indigent defendant with a free transcript of the trial court proceedings, to the extent necessary to enable him to perfect his right to appeal. [**Griffin v. Illinois,** *supra,* §1106]

1) *Whether the entire transcript must be provided* depends on the nature of the arguments that the defendant wishes to raise on appeal and the availability of alternative devices that could serve the same function. [**Britt v. North Carolina,** 404 U.S. 226 (1971)—same rule applies where defendant seeks a transcript of prior mistrial in preparation for retrial]

2) *If the defendant makes out a "colorable" need for a complete transcript,* the burden is *on the prosecution* to show that only a portion of the transcript is required for an effective appeal, or that some "alternative device" would serve the same function—*e.g.,* a statement of facts agreed to by both sides, or a full narrative statement based on the trial judge's notes or the court reporter's untranscribed notes. [**Mayer v. City of Chicago,** 404 U.S. 189 (1971)]

(b) **Right to counsel [§1361]**
A state's failure to appoint counsel to represent an indigent defendant on a direct appeal from a criminal conviction constitutes a denial of the Fourteenth Amendment, if nonindigents can have the benefit of counsel on their appeals. [**Douglas v. California,** *supra,* §1106—state appellate court's procedure of going through appellate record to ascertain if any good would be served by appointment of counsel was held not sufficient protection, so that failure to appoint counsel violated the Fourteenth Amendment]

1) **Right extends to appeal of right [§1362]**
The right to counsel extends only to proceedings in which the accused has a *right* to appellate review—normally, to an intermediary appellate court. If the indigent's conviction has been affirmed by the appellate court, the state is *not* required to furnish him with counsel to assist in seeking a *discretionary* review by the state supreme court, or to seek certiorari from the United States Supreme Court. [**Ross v. Moffitt,** *supra,* §1107]

a) **Rationale**
The fact that an indigent defendant at this stage has had a trial transcript, a brief by appointed counsel on the first appeal as a matter of right, and often a judicial opinion on that appeal is deemed to assure him an "adequate opportunity to present his claims" when seeking discretionary review.

2. Habeas Corpus Review in Federal Courts [§1363]

By special statutory provision [28 U.S.C. §2254], a state prisoner may bring an action ("habeas corpus") in federal court to review his conviction claiming that he is being held in violation of his federal constitutional rights.

a. Exhaustion requirement [§1364]

Before a person's habeas petition may be heard, he must show that he has exhausted all state remedies. In **Fay v. Noia**, 372 U.S. 391 (1963), the Court held that the exhaustion requirement was limited only to failure to exhaust state remedies that were available to the petitioner. However, the Court seems to have narrowed this rule. In **O'Sullivan v. Boerckel**, 526 U.S. 838 (1999), the Court held that a state prisoner's failure to seek discretionary review from the state supreme court constitutes a failure of the exhaustion requirement, even if the time for appeal has passed.

b. Exception [§1365]

If the constitutional claim was not developed in the state court because the petitioner failed to comply with a state procedural rule requiring such claims to be made, the claim may be heard for the first time in the federal court only if: (i) there is a showing of *cause* for noncompliance with the state rule, and (ii) there is some showing of *actual prejudice, or* (iii) failure to consider the claim will result in a *fundamental miscarriage of justice* (*e.g.*, petitioner shows actual innocence). [**Keeney v. Tamayo-Reyes**, 504 U.S. 1 (1992)]

(1) "Cause" [§1366]

Ignorance or inadvertent error by the petitioner's lawyer does *not* constitute "cause." The petitioner must bear the risk of attorney error. [**Coleman v. Thompson**, 501 U.S. 722 (1991)]

c. Limitation [§1367]

Where the prisoner had a full and fair opportunity in the state court to litigate certain claims not directly related to the issue of guilt (*e.g.*, a search and seizure claim), such claims are not a proper basis for a grant of federal habeas corpus relief. [**Stone v. Powell**, 428 U.S. 465 (1976)]

FEDERAL HABEAS CORPUS FOR STATE PRISONERS **gilbert**

THE FOLLOWING REQUIREMENTS MUST BE MET FOR FEDERAL COURTS TO GRANT HABEAS CORPUS PETITIONS FROM STATE PRISONERS:

☑ Detention must violate *federal constitutional rights*.

☑ Petitioner must have *exhausted all state remedies.*

☑ If petitioner failed to comply with a state procedural rule, petitioner must show a *factual or legal cause* for the failure and that the failure *prejudiced* petitioner's case.

3. **Retroactive Application of Determinations Regarding Constitutional Rights of Accused [§1368]**

In recent years, the Court has had to consider repeatedly whether its decisions, recognizing some right of an accused in the criminal process, are to be applied retroactively—*i.e.*, whether the decision is merely a guidepost for future criminal prosecutions, or can be invoked by persons previously convicted (without benefit of the constitutional protection involved) to gain their freedom or, at the very least, a new trial. (For general discussion of retroactivity concept, *see supra*, §§130-131.)

a. **Factors governing [§1369]**

The Court usually determines whether its opinion is to be given retroactive effect on the basis of the following factors:

(1) **Purpose to be served [§1370]**

If the major purpose of the new constitutional doctrine is to overcome some aspect of criminal trial procedure that substantially impedes its *truth-finding function*, and therefore raises serious questions about the accuracy of guilty verdicts in the past, the new doctrine will be given retroactive effect. However, if the integrity of the truth-finding function is not challenged by the new doctrine, the Court will go on to consider these other factors:

(2) **Reliance by police [§1371]**

The extent of reliance by law enforcement officials on the old standards is considered.

(3) **Effect [§1372]**

Also, the effect on the administration of justice of a retroactive application of the new standard is considered by the Court.

b. **Rules applied retroactively [§1373]**

Under this approach, the Court has given retroactive effect to those decisions that affect "the *very integrity of the fact-finding process*"—so that the previous standard posed a "clear danger of convicting the innocent." [**Johnson v. New Jersey**, 384 U.S. 719 (1966)]

---

e.g. **Example:** The decisions establishing a criminal defendant's *right to counsel* at trial [**Gideon v. Wainwright**, *supra*, §1320] and on appeal [**Douglas v. California**, *supra*, §1361] were given retroactive effect because the assistance of counsel is fundamental to the truth-determining process at each of these stages.

---

e.g. **Example:** Likewise, the decision in **Griffin v. Illinois** (*supra*, §1360), establishing an indigent defendant's right to a free transcript on appeal of his conviction, has a retroactive effect. [**Eskridge v. Washington Prison Board**, 357 U.S. 214 (1958)]

---

c. Rules not applied retroactively [§1374]

However, where the Court concludes that *other safeguards* were available to protect the integrity of the truth-determining process at trial, and the interests of justice would be *adversely affected* by reversing convictions obtained in reliance on the previous standards, the new rule will *not* be applied retroactively. [**Johnson v. New Jersey**, *supra*]

Example: The decision in **Mapp v. Ohio** (*supra*, §1287), barring use in state courts of evidence obtained by illegal search or seizure, does not apply retroactively. *Rationale:* The rule's purpose is to *deter unlawful searches*; and this has no bearing on the guilt or innocence of the accused. Hence, the ends of justice do not require retroactive application. [**Linkletter v. Walker**, 381 U.S. 618 (1965)] A similar result and reasoning applies to the decision in **Katz v. United States** (*supra*, §1286), prohibiting use of evidence obtained by electronic eavesdropping. [**Desist v. United States**, 394 U.S. 244 (1969)]

Example: The decision in **Miranda v. Arizona** (*supra*, §1276), limiting police right to interrogate criminal suspects, has no retroactive effect. *Rationale:* Deprivation of counsel during the investigative stage does not necessarily impair the integrity of the *truth-determining* process at *trial*. [**Johnson v. New Jersey**, *supra*] The same result (and rationale) applies to the decision in **United States v. Wade**, 388 U.S. 218 (1967), dealing with an accused's right to counsel at a police lineup. But if the accused can show that the lineup was so unfairly constructed that *due process* was violated through admission of eyewitness identification, retroactive relief may be available. [**Stovall v. Denno**, 388 U.S. 293 (1967)]

Example: The decision in **Griffin v. California** (*supra*, §1280), prohibiting adverse comment on an accused's failure to testify in his own defense, also has no retroactive application. *Rationale:* The purpose of the rule (to preserve the accusatorial system) would not be advanced by retroactive application. [**Tehan v. United States** *ex rel.* **Shott**, 382 U.S. 406 (1966)]

Example: And the decision in **Duncan v. Louisiana** (*supra*, §1294), requiring states to afford jury trials in all cases involving serious criminal offenses, does not apply retroactively. *Rationale:* A nonjury trial is not necessarily unfair. [**DeStefano v. Woods**, 392 U.S. 631 (1968)]

---

d. Cases on appeal [§1375]

Even if the new rule is not given retroactive effect to all persons previously convicted, it will still be applied to cases *pending* on direct appeal at the time the new rule is announced—even if the new rule constitutes a "clear break with the past." [**Griffith v. Kentucky**, 479 U.S. 314 (1987)—*overruling* **United States v. Johnson**, 457 U.S. 1139 (1982)]

Review Questions
and Answers

Review Questions

FILL IN
ANSWER

1. Suarro Jones, a resident of Arizona who is employed by the state, sues the state of Arizona in federal court for amounts owed under the federal minimum wage law. The state moves to dismiss on the ground that federal jurisdiction is barred by the Eleventh Amendment. What ruling?

    _____

2. Suarro Jones, a resident of Arizona, sues the city of New Orleans in a federal court for amounts owed under the federal minimum wage law. The city moves to dismiss on the ground that federal courts have no jurisdiction because of the Eleventh Amendment. How should the court rule?

    _____

3. Suarro Jones, a resident of Arizona, files suit in federal court to enjoin the governor of Arizona from enforcing a state law that allegedly violates Jones's constitutional rights. The governor moves to dismiss on the ground that federal jurisdiction is barred by the Eleventh Amendment. What ruling?

    _____

4. Congress enacts a statute providing that the Supreme Court may no longer hear appeals in cases arising under the National Labor Relations Act. Is the statute valid?

    _____

5. Does the Supreme Court have mandatory appellate jurisdiction where a state court has held a federal statute invalid?

    _____

6. Bobby Brown files a class action in federal court on behalf of himself and all other state citizens under age 21 challenging the validity of a state law restricting the sale of liquor to those over age 21. By the time the case reaches the Supreme Court, Bobby Brown is 23 years of age. Should the action be dismissed as "moot"?

    _____

7. Alan Activist files suit as a federal taxpayer challenging money appropriations made by Congress to the F.B.I. because of allegedly improper activities by the F.B.I. The Government moves to dismiss on the ground that Alan lacks standing. How should the court rule?

    _____

8. Which, if any, of the following have standing to sue in federal court?

    _____

    (A) Ivanna Home files suit to challenge exclusionary zoning practices by City, alleging that the challenged zoning made it too expensive for her to purchase a home in City.

    (B) Society files suit challenging a state law requiring disclosure of Society's membership, alleging that the law infringes its members' freedom of association.

CONSTITUTIONAL LAW | 373

(C)   Environmental Protection Group files suit to block further oil drilling on the ground that it is contrary to the public interest.

(D)   State files suit on behalf of its citizens (as *"parens patriae"*) to contest federal spending measures.

9.   The Supreme Court of Idaho has affirmed a judgment in a case involving a substantial federal question. However, state common law issues were also involved in the case. Is the state court judgment reviewable in the United States Supreme Court?   _____

10.   A state statute has recently been enacted making certain business practices criminal. Sheila Jones is in fear of being prosecuted by the state under this new law because she regularly engages in the practices now prohibited. Sheila claims that the statute violates her constitutional rights. Is any relief available to Sheila in federal court?   _____

11.   Ima Voter files suit challenging a state election law that provides that an incumbent office holder shall be listed first on the ballot. Ima claims that this gives the incumbents a big advantage in any election. Should the action be dismissed as involving a "political question"?   _____

12.   Assume that the Supreme Court has just held a state statute unconstitutional. Will this decision ever be given **retroactive** effect?   _____

13.   Congress enacts legislation imposing an excise tax of $50,000 per annum on all sellers of firearms that have come from outside the state. The monies thus collected fund a government project to reimburse victims of violent crimes. The tax is invalid since its principal effect is to discourage the sale of firearms. True or false?   _____

14.   Congress passes a statute authorizing exclusion of all alien terrorists. John Kendrick has arranged with Sinead Rourke to give a series of lectures on the Irish dilemma. The Attorney General has confidential information concerning Rourke's membership in a terrorist organization. Can Kendrick successfully challenge Rourke's exclusion because it interferes with Kendrick's right of association and therefore violates his First Amendment rights?   _____

15.   Hector Gonzalez, a Mexican citizen, enters the United States illegally, but obtains a job and establishes permanent residence here. Twenty years later, his illegal entry is discovered and he is seized for deportation. Is he entitled to a hearing before being expelled?   _____

16.   Suppose New York enacts a law prohibiting naturalized citizens from holding state office during the first five years following their naturalization. Is the law valid?   _____

17.   Congress enacts a law that provides that a naturalized citizen will lose her citizenship by enlisting in the armed services of a hostile foreign government. Is the law constitutional?   _____

18. Is it permissible for either House of Congress to issue subpoenas to witnesses and to take their testimony on matters not currently the subject of pending legislation? _____

19. The President appoints Avary Richman to the Federal Resources Board, and obtains the "advice and consent" of the Senate, which is required for the appointment. Can the President later remove Richman from the Federal Resources Board *without* the approval of the Senate? _____

20. Due to an extreme shortage of natural gas, and without waiting for Congress to act, the President declares an emergency and orders federal officers to take possession of all available gas storage tanks and to supervise a program of allocations drawn up by the President. The owners of the gas challenge the seizure on the ground that the President has no such power. In whose favor should the Court rule? _____

21. A congressional committee investigating foreign policy asks the Secretary of State for certain information. The Secretary refuses on the ground that the information relates to high-level secret talks, and the President has directed him to assert executive privilege. Will the Secretary's claim of privilege be upheld? _____

22. Suppose California enacts a law that provides that resident aliens may receive welfare benefits only if they are citizens of countries that provide similar benefits for United States citizens. Is the law valid? _____

23. If a state statute conflicts with a treaty obligation, which prevails? _____

24. If an act of Congress conflicts with a treaty obligation of the United States, which prevails? _____

25. The city of Old York is on the verge of bankruptcy. To save it from bankruptcy, the state legislature passes emergency legislation authorizing the city to issue "scrip," which shall be legal tender for payment of all obligations owing by the city, and that persons receiving such scrip from the city may use it as legal tender for paying their private obligations within the state. Is the statute valid? _____

26. Is freedom of association and expression a "privilege and immunity" of national citizenship within the meaning of the Fourteenth Amendment? _____

27. Is the right of interstate travel a "privilege and immunity" of national citizenship within the meaning of the Fourteenth Amendment? _____

28. Suppose Illinois enacts a law providing that foreign corporations must pay a fee of $50,000 for a permit to sell certain types of securities within the state, whereas domestic corporations have to pay only $500 for the same permit. Acme, Inc., a foreign corporation, attacks this as violating Article IV, Section 2 (Interstate Privileges and Immunities Clause). Is Acme correct? _____

29. Congress enacts a law imposing a permit fee of $10 per annum for vehicles entering national parks. Is this law valid as applied to cars and trucks owned by Wyoming that are required to enter the park lands for state purposes? _____

30. Suppose Texas requires "all motor vehicles operated on state highways" to have a license plate issued by state authorities upon payment of a specified fee. Can this statute be applied constitutionally to federal cars and trucks using state roads? _____

31. Is a state income tax on the salaries of federal employees valid? _____

32. Suppose Alabama enacts a sales tax that requires a seller to collect from a purchaser 5% of the amount of the sale, and to remit it to the state. Is this tax valid as applied to sales made by a seller to a private contractor who is working for the United States Government on a "cost plus" basis (so that the *cost* of the tax is ultimately passed on to the federal government)? _____

33. Is the regulation of interstate commerce an "exclusive" power of Congress? _____

34. Does Congress have the power to regulate interstate commerce solely for the purpose of furthering *state* laws or policies? _____

35. Can Congress, under its commerce power, regulate an activity that is purely intrastate? _____

36. Congress enacts a law expressly authorizing the states to require out-of-state milk producers to conform to local testing and inspection standards as a condition for selling their milk within the state. The effect is that each state sets its own standards, and this makes it very difficult and expensive for out-of-state producers to compete with local producers. Is the law valid? _____

37. Congress enacts a law requiring all hospitals to maintain certain minimum emergency room facilities. Suppose Massachusetts has a law requiring hospitals in its state to contain much more complete emergency room facilities. Is the Massachusetts law valid? _____

38. Suppose Georgia enacts a law requiring national airlines servicing local airports to comply with safety standards substantially the same as the safety standards established by the Federal Aviation Administration pursuant to its comprehensive regulatory authority. Is the Georgia law valid? _____

39. Suppose Maine enacts a law prohibiting the shipment outside the state of any lobsters taken from state waters. The purpose of the law is to protect the state's lobster beds from being depleted by the heavy demands of out-of-state consumers. Its effect is to cause consumers throughout the country to pay considerably higher prices because of the nonavailability of Maine lobsters. Is the law valid? _____

40. In the absence of federal regulation, state regulation of interstate commerce is permissible as long as it is nondiscriminatory and does not regulate a subject matter that requires uniform national regulation. True or false? _____

41. Suppose Kansas enacts a law that requires any vehicle using Kansas highways to be equipped with special mufflers and emission control devices not required in most other states. The purpose is to limit the noise and smoke emissions along Kansas highways. Is the law valid as applied to out-of-state vehicles using Kansas roads? _____

42. Suppose Kentucky enacts a law providing that all bourbon whisky sold in the state be sold at the lowest price available anywhere in the nation. Is the law valid? _____

43. Suppose that the Missouri Tax Commissioner seeks to impose a property tax on trucks belonging to Ace Cattle Co. Ace resists on the ground that it is a Texas corporation and none of its trucks were actually in Missouri on tax assessment day (although Ace admits that it regularly sends its trucks in and out of Missouri as part of its cattle-raising operations). Who wins? _____

   a. Should the amount of tax be apportioned on the basis of the average physical presence of the trucks within the taxing state? _____

44. Suppose that the Kansas Tax Commissioner seeks to impose a property tax on cattle that were located on a feed lot in Kansas on tax assessment day. The owner of the cattle resists on the ground that the cattle had been raised in Texas and were being trucked to a slaughterhouse in Illinois, and were merely being fattened up for a few days in Kansas while en route. Who wins? _____

   a. Should the amount of tax be apportioned based on the number of days the cattle were in Kansas? _____

45. Interstate Railway has its headquarters in Alabama, with scheduled trips to and from Texas. May Texas validly levy a privilege tax on Railway's gross revenues derived from Texas, if properly apportioned? _____

46. General Encyclopedia Co. has a sales office in Illinois. Salespeople from this office solicit orders from customers in Illinois and Iowa. All orders are forwarded to the company's home office in Nebraska, where they are formally "accepted," and from which the books are shipped directly to the customer.

   a. May Illinois impose a sales tax on sales made to Illinois customers? _____

   b. May Iowa impose a sales tax on the sales made in Iowa? _____

47. Suppose that an Iowa law requires that all sales solicitors pay a $100 annual fee for a license to solicit sales in Iowa. Can this law be constitutionally applied to the salespeople working out of General Encyclopedia's Illinois office? _____

48. Suppose that an Iowa law requires that any foreign corporation seeking to do business in Iowa must pay $10,000 annually for the right to do business in the state,

whereas local corporations pay no more than $100 annually for the same permission. Is the law valid?
_____

49. Suppose Maine imposes a tax of $1 per pound on all lobsters exported from Maine to foreign nations. The tax is designed to conserve Maine lobsters from excessive foreign demand. Is the tax valid?
_____

50. "Any right enumerated in the Bill of Rights will receive the same protection against state action as against federal." True or false?
_____

51. Suppose New Jersey welfare authorities adopt a regulation that provides for the immediate cutoff of welfare payments to any welfare recipient who fails to report for work on county work projects when told to do so. Pursuant to this regulation, and without any sort of hearing, Paul's welfare benefits are cut off because he failed to report for work on a county road project to which he had been assigned. Is the termination of Paul's benefits proper?
_____

52. Requiring the owner of a shopping center to provide access to persons desiring to distribute handbills constitutes a taking. True or false?
_____

53. Suppose Pennsylvania enacts a law prohibiting drugstores from selling contraceptives to any person under age 16. The law is challenged on the ground that the law serves "no compelling state interest." The state seeks to uphold the law on the ground that it is valid as long as it serves a "rational purpose" (deterring younger persons from sexual relations). Which test should the court apply?
_____

54. Maxwell Smart, a former agent of the Central Intelligence Agency, makes a speaking tour of several Latin American countries during which he denounces the actions of the United States government. Maxwell also reveals the identities of several undercover CIA agents. As a result, the State Department revokes Maxwell's passport. Is this action valid?
_____

55. Does the Constitution expressly limit the federal government's power to impair contractual obligations?
_____

56. Congress enacts a law providing that resident aliens are subject to deportation if they have "ever" been convicted of a narcotics offense. A resident alien challenges this law on the ground that it would operate to impose additional punishment for conduct that took place prior to enactment of the statute. Is the law valid?
_____

57. Suppose Utah has a statute that bans exhibition of films containing any form of nudity. In reviewing the constitutionality of this statute, the court will presume it is constitutional until its invalidity is shown beyond a reasonable doubt. True or false?
_____

58. Suppose Idaho enacts a law making it a crime "to advocate or join with others to advocate the practice of peaceful civil disobedience." Is the statute valid?
_____

59. In determining whether a law that restricts freedom of speech is constitutional, it must be shown that the expression was directed to inciting, and likely to incite, *imminent* lawless action. True or false?

60. The *Daily Bugle* publishes an article by a sportswriter accusing Coach of "throwing" a football game. Coach sues *Daily Bugle* for defamation. The evidence shows that the reporter who wrote the story had no reasonable ground for believing the story was true when she wrote it. The *Daily Bugle* cannot claim any constitutional privilege for this publication because Coach is not a public official or candidate for public office. True or false?

61. "*Gay Way*" is a magazine published by homosexuals and designed to reach the homosexual community. Its pages often contain pictures of nude males and females embracing members of their own sex.

   a. In determining whether the magazine is "obscene," it may be shown to appeal to the prurient interest only of homosexuals. The fact that it would *not* appeal to the prurient interest of the rest of the community is to be disregarded. True or false?

   b. In determining whether this magazine is "obscene," the fact that it is being published for a profit is to be disregarded. True or false?

   c. The determination of whether this magazine is "obscene" must be made in light of the contemporary moral standards of the nationwide "community" and not just statewide standards. True or false?

   d. If the magazine is found to be "obscene," then any magazine dealer or distributor who sells "*Gay Way*" can be punished along with the publisher of the magazine. True or false?

62. To protect minors, City adopts an ordinance providing that billboards may not carry advertisements that display bare female breasts or buttocks. Is the ordinance valid?

63. City enacts an ordinance making it a crime for persons to use designated four-letter words in public speeches or debates. Is the ordinance valid?

64. To preserve neighborhood stability, City passes an ordinance prohibiting the posting of "for sale" signs on real estate. Is this ordinance valid?

65. Congress enacts a law banning the importation of any "obscene" materials into this country and authorizing customs officials to seize and destroy such materials without any hearing or other proceedings. Is the law valid?

66. Is symbolic conduct (conduct such as display of objects or mode of dress) always protected to the same extent as "pure" speech?

67. Suppose Indianapolis accepts advertisements for commercial products in its buses. However, it refuses to permit its buses to carry political advertisements. Candidate Juanita Jones claims this impairs her freedom of expression in public places. Is she right?

    _____

68. Suppose Philadelphia adopts an ordinance that requires all persons seeking to hold a parade or demonstration on Philadelphia streets to obtain a license or permit at least three days in advance from the police commissioner. Is this ordinance valid?

    _____

69. Suppose Colorado enacts an ordinance that homeowners are entitled to a special exemption from the property tax provided they file a sworn oath "that they have never been a member of any group dedicated to the violent overthrow of the state or federal government." Is the oath requirement valid?

    _____

70. Suppose the New Mexico State School Board requires all employees to take an oath "to support the federal and state constitutions and to oppose the overthrow of the federal and state governments by illegal means." Employees who refuse are subject to summary discharge (without a hearing). Is the Board's requirement constitutional?

    _____

71. Suppose the New Mexico State School Board requires all prospective employees to take an oath "that they have never been a member of any group dedicated to the violent overthrow of the state or federal government." Persons who once belonged to such groups are barred from employment by the Board. Is the Board's requirement constitutional?

    _____

72. Suppose the University of Iowa adopts a rule that all personnel abstain from participation in political campaigns or controversies involving the administration of the University. Professor Wallbanger writes a letter to the editor of the *Daily Bugle* highly critical of the manner in which the president of the University is allocating research funds. Wallbanger is fired for violating the University rule. Is he entitled to reinstatement?

    _____

73. Suppose Arizona requires all persons seeking to be licensed as teachers to list all organizations in which they have been members for the past 10 years. Is this requirement valid?

    _____

74. Does a news reporter have a constitutional right to withhold the sources of her news stories when disclosure is sought in a *civil* action?

    _____

75. Suppose Mississippi enacts a state law designed to further vocational guidance for high school students. All high school students are to receive aptitude tests and individual career counseling based on the test results. Public school personnel are assigned to perform these functions at all schools, public and private. Maude challenges this law as constituting financial aid to parochial schools in violation of the Establishment Clause. Is Maude's challenge valid?

    _____

76. Suppose North Carolina exempts from local property taxation any real estate used exclusively for purposes of charitable, educational, and religious worship. Angela attacks this law as violating the Establishment Clause. Is Angela's challenge valid? _____

77. Suppose New York enacts a law providing that all students attending public schools shall be let out early on the Jewish High Holy Days to enable Jewish students to attend religious services. Mark attacks this law as violating the Establishment Clause. Will Mark's challenge be successful? _____

78. Suppose Wisconsin enacts a law that requires that all children within the state attend public or private schools through the eighth grade. Jeremiah attacks this law as infringing his right to educate his children at home, which he claims is a basic tenet of a new religious group he leads. Will Jeremiah's challenge be successful? _____

79. Because of limitations in staff and facilities, public school students in Arkansas are required to attend classes four hours a day, six days a week. Paul, a Seventh-Day Adventist, challenges the requirement that his children attend school on Saturdays as interfering with the "free exercise" of their religion (which prohibits such activities on Saturday). Is Paul's challenge valid? _____

80. Suppose California enacts a law requiring all students at State University to take basic military training. Peace Anlove, a student at State University, claims this law infringes her freedom of conscience and belief because she is a pacifist. Will her challenge be successful? _____

81. Suppose New Hampshire enacts a law requiring employers to allow employees time off with pay to attend religious services on Good Friday. Murray O'Hare, an avowed atheist, challenges the law on the ground that it violates both the Establishment and Free Exercise Clauses of the Constitution. New Hampshire moves to dismiss O'Hare's suit on the ground that he has no standing to challenge the law because, being an atheist, it cannot be said to interfere with his personal rights or beliefs. How should the Court rule on the state's motion to dismiss? _____

82. A state law that grants widows, but not widowers, a property tax exemption necessarily violates equal protection. True or false? _____

83. Poverty is considered a suspect classification for purposes of equal protection analysis. True or false? _____

84. Suppose Florida enacts a law requiring new political parties to submit nominating petitions bearing the signatures of at least 5% of all registered voters. Is this law valid? _____

85. Suppose Oklahoma enacts a law that denies persons convicted of a felony the right to vote in state elections. Does this violate the Equal Protection Clause? _____

86. The right to vote cannot be restricted on grounds other than residence, age, or citizenship in any election, unless some compelling state interest is served by the restriction. True or false? _____

87. "Local boundary lines are entitled to *no* consideration in producing equal population in apportioning congressional voting districts." True or false? _____

88. The same standard of representation is required for both federal and state elections. No deviation from the one person-one vote formula is permitted without substantial justification—regardless of whether the election is to Congress or to the city council." True or false? _____

89. The "one person-one vote" principle does not apply in the election of an official who performs only administrative functions—*e.g.,* the state treasurer. True or false? _____

90. In an effort to conserve available funds, School Board adopts a program limiting the number of classes in which students may enroll. Student challenges this program on the ground that it impairs the "constitutional right to a quality education," and that the limit on the number of classes serves no "compelling state interest" and is not the "least burdensome alternative" available. Who wins? _____

91. Is a filing fee required for bankruptcy proceedings violative of equal protection to indigents? _____

92. Suppose Kentucky grants to Meadowbrook Race Track, Inc. (a private company) the exclusive right to operate horse races in the state. Meadowbrook enforces a policy whereby persons under age 21 are excluded from the track. Bobby, a minor, challenges this policy as discriminatory "state action" by Kentucky. Is he correct? _____

93. Do any of the constitutional amendments *expressly* prohibit private (as opposed to governmental) actions affecting the rights of other citizens? _____

94. The Fourteenth Amendment is a limitation on state action, and is not a source of power to the federal government. True or false? _____

95. All federal civil rights legislation is based on the Thirteenth, Fourteenth, or Fifteenth Amendment. True or false? _____

96. Is a *unanimous* verdict constitutionally required in both federal and state prosecutions? _____

97. Mei-Ling is charged with speeding; the maximum sentence for this offense is a $50 fine. Does Mei-Ling have a constitutional right to trial by jury? _____

98. Darius is a black man. He is tried and convicted by a jury consisting of both whites and blacks. He appeals his conviction solely on the ground that Asian-Americans

had been systematically excluded from the jury and therefore the jury is not representative of the community. Does Darius (not being Asian himself) have standing to raise the exclusion of Asian-Americans?

99. Helen Haventapenny has been subpoenaed to give testimony before a grand jury investigating organized crime. Helen is indigent and demands that the court appoint an attorney to advise her and appear with her before the grand jury. Is she entitled to such assistance?

100. Is a person entitled to counsel in a state criminal trial even where the crime charged carries no prison sentence?

101. Dawn Onnerluck is on trial for murder. State law provides that if Dawn claims the killing was accidental or justified, she must bear the burden of proof on this issue; failing this, the killing will be deemed to have been with malice aforethought. Is this law valid?

102. Magda, who is indigent, is convicted of murder. After affirmance of her conviction by the state supreme court, Magda seeks appointment of counsel to assist her in seeking certiorari from the United States Supreme Court. Is she constitutionally entitled to such assistance?

103. Which of the following factors is entitled to the greatest weight in determining whether a new decision by the Supreme Court affecting the administration of criminal justice will be given retroactive effect?

   (A) Police officers have acted in reasonable reliance on former decisions of the Court.

   (B) The primary purpose and effect of the new standard is to deter police misconduct and disregard for constitutional rights of defendants.

   (C) The new decision was formulated for the purpose of ending some aspect of criminal procedure that raised questions as to the accuracy of guilty verdicts in the past.

Answers to Review Questions

1. **MOTION GRANTED** The Eleventh Amendment bars suits by a private citizen against any state (including the state in which the citizen resides). [§6]

2. **MOTION DENIED** The Eleventh Amendment prohibits suits by a private citizen against a *state*, but this does not apply to subdivisions of a state. [§13]

3. **MOTION DENIED** Because the governor is enforcing an allegedly unconstitutional law, under **Ex parte Young** he is stripped of his official character so that suit is not barred under the Eleventh Amendment. [§§14-15]

4. **YES** Article III, Section 2 expressly gives Congress the power to regulate the *appellate* (but not original) jurisdiction of the Supreme Court. [§§2, 21-32]

5. **NO** Nearly all the Supreme Court's appellate jurisdiction is by discretionary writs of certiorari. [§§27-28]

6. **NO** Although the class representative's individual controversy may have become moot, he may continue to pursue a class action as long as the claims of other class members survive. [§47]

7. **MOTION GRANTED** There is not sufficient "nexus" between his status as taxpayer and the allegedly illegal activities of the F.B.I. [§58]

8. **ONLY (B)** (A) No standing because general financial inability by itself is not sufficient "direct and immediate injury" resulting from challenged practice. [§§50, 52]

    (B) Standing because disclosure of membership would also affect the ability of the group to obtain members; thus, the infringement of members' constitutional rights also causes injury to the group itself. [§70]

    (C) No standing because standing cannot be predicated on claim of injury to the public at large. [§§50, 53]

    (D) No standing because the state may not assert the claims of its citizens against the federal government with respect to a federal spending program. [§74]

9. **DEPENDS** If the state court judgment can be supported entirely by a state ground and clearly indicates that it is based on state law, the Supreme Court will not review. [§§86-89]

10. **YES** As long as no criminal prosecution is yet pending, federal declaratory relief is available. (Declaratory relief is deemed to produce much less tension with state interests than enjoining a pending state prosecution.) [§§97-101]

11.	**NO**	The mere fact that the suit seeks protection of a political *right* does not mean it presents a political question. [§127]
12.	**YES**	The Court's declaration of unconstitutionality has full retroactive effect in all cases still open on appeal and as to all events regardless of when they occur. [§130]
13.	**FALSE**	A tax that also has the effect of regulating will be upheld if Congress has the power to regulate the subject of the taxed activity or if the dominant intent of the tax is to raise revenue (which can be shown by the fact that the tax in fact raises revenue). Congress can regulate sales of firearms that travel in interstate commerce. [§§152-156]
14.	**NO**	If Congress has a bona fide reason for excluding an alien, citizens may not complain that such exclusion interferes with their First Amendment rights. [§§169-170]
15.	**YES**	Due process procedural protections are available to an alien resident in the United States (whether here legally or *illegally*). [§171]
16.	**NO**	The rights of native-born and naturalized citizens are equal; hence, this limitation would be a violation of the Fourteenth Amendment Equal Protection Clause. [§176]
17.	**MAYBE**	Congress can take away citizenship if the citizen, through words or conduct, manifests an intent to relinquish citizenship. Enlisting in the armed services of a hostile foreign government *may* manifest such intent. [§177]
18.	**YES**	It is the *power* to legislate, which implies the power to investigate; pendency of legislation is not essential. [§§180-181]
19.	**MAYBE**	It depends on the status of the Federal Resources Board. If it is strictly an arm of the executive branch, appointees are removable by the President at will. However, if this is an administrative agency created by Congress, removal may be limited to the causes specified in the statute creating the agency. [§§196, 198]
20.	**OWNERS**	The President has no inherent law-making power in internal affairs. [**Youngstown Sheet & Tube v. Sawyer**] (Note, however, that parts of *Youngstown* indicate that the President has inherent power to act in cases of great national emergency as long as Congress has not expressly denied such power.) [§§202, 210-211]
21.	**PROBABLY**	Presidential claims of privilege for communications that relate to diplomatic and security matters are given utmost deference by the courts. [§215]
22.	**NO**	No state regulation (direct or indirect) is permitted in the field of external affairs. The statute here would be viewed as an attempt to influence welfare policies of other countries. [§227]

23.	**TREATY**	A state statute that conflicts with a treaty provision is invalid. [§§230-231]
24.	**LAST IN TIME**	Acts of Congress are of equal weight with treaties and thus, the last expression of the sovereign will control where there is a conflict. [§232]
25.	**NO**	"Coinage of money" is an exclusive *federal* power, and the issuance of scrip as legal tender for private debts would probably be so regarded. [§246]
26.	**NO**	The Bill of Rights is *not* included in the Privileges and Immunities Clause. [**Slaughterhouse Cases**] [§255]
27.	**PROBABLY**	Source of this right is unclear, but *it is* constitutionally protected. [*See* **Saenz v. Roe**] [§§254, 527-528]
28.	**NO**	The Interstate Privileges and Immunities Clause protects only "citizens" of each state, and a corporation is not a "citizen." [§260] (*Note:* Acme may be able to attack this statute on Commerce Clause or equal protection grounds. [§§315, 303])
29.	**YES**	Generally, the federal government may tax state government property or activities, as long as the federal tax does not discriminate by taxing them and not other property or activities similarly situated. Furthermore, operation of these vehicles is not an activity that is unique to state sovereignty. In addition, the tax may be upheld as a user fee. [§270]
30.	**NO**	State laws may not tax or burden federal activities. [§§272-273]
31.	**YES**	No unreasonable burden on the federal government is deemed imposed thereby. [§275]
32.	**YES**	See **Alabama v. King & Boozer.** [§§276-277]
33.	**NO**	Although the Commerce Clause grants to Congress the power to regulate interstate commerce, it is deemed *concurrent* with state power over transactions occurring within the state. [§284]
34.	**YES**	This is deemed a valid exercise of congressional power; there need be no national goal served thereby. [§289]
35.	**YES**	As long as it has a *national economic effect, i.e., substantially affects* more than one state. [§295]
36.	**YES**	Congress's broad power over interstate commerce includes the power to *authorize the states* to regulate where they otherwise would not have power to do so—even where the effect is to *discriminate* against interstate commerce. [§§300-302]

37. **YES**   There is no apparent intent to supersede state regulation of hospitals, and the field is not one that apparently requires uniform national regulation. There is no direct conflict with the federal law because compliance with the state law would also constitute compliance with the federal. (Result would be contra, of course, if the state law made *compliance* with federal law more difficult or expensive.) [§§306-313]

38. **NO**   Where Congress has provided complete regulation of a particular field (interstate airlines), *any* state regulation is preempted; it need not conflict. [§§306-313]

39. **NO**   Regulations for protection of local natural resources are usually not upheld. [§§319-320]

40. **FALSE**   The nature and extent of the burden on interstate commerce must also be *outweighed* by the interests served by the state regulation. [§§331-341]

41. **NO**   The burden on interstate carriers in complying with the stricter Kansas standards would outweigh whatever interests Kansas has. [§337]

42. **NO**   This may force sellers to lower prices elsewhere. The Twenty-First Amendment does not allow state regulation on the local sale of liquor if the practical effect is to regulate liquor prices in other states. [§348]

43. **TAX COM-MISSIONER**   Property tax may properly be imposed if there is a "nexus" between the taxing state and instrumentalities used to convey commodities interstate. [§§361-362]

     a. **YES**   Some "fair apportionment" is required when instrumentalities have more than one taxable situs. [§§363-369]

44. **OWNER**   Commodities in the course of interstate shipment are exempt from local tax. Here, the "break" in transit was *not* intended to end the interstate movement, and hence the goods remained exempt. (Result would be different if they were on feed lot pending owner's disposition.) [§§370-372]

     a. **NO**   Either the goods are taxable or they are not; there is no apportionment where goods are in the course of interstate shipment. [§370]

45. **YES**   Privilege taxes may be imposed if the activity taxed has a substantial nexus to the taxing state, the tax is fairly apportioned, the tax does not discriminate against interstate commerce, and the tax fairly relates to services provided by the taxing state. [§§373-374]

46.a. **YES**   Maintenance of a local sales office is a sufficient taxable incident even though the sale was technically made in Nebraska (order "accepted" there). [§398]

b.	**NO**	Sales solicitors ("drummers") representing an out-of-state manufacturer are not a sufficient taxable incident where the sale was consummated outside the state (order accepted in Nebraska). [§§382, 400]
47.	**NO**	Flat license fees may not be levied on interstate sales solicitors even if local sales people are subject to the same tax. [§382]
48.	**NO**	Under the Equal Protection Clause, a state may not impose more onerous taxes or other burdens on foreign corporations than on domestic corporations unless the discrimination is rationally related to a legitimate state purpose. Here, there is no showing of a legitimate state purpose. [§406] Moreover, the statute discriminates against interstate commerce.
49.	**NO**	The Import-Export Clause prohibits states from taxing goods after they have begun their physical entry into the stream of exportation. Thus, assuming the lobsters have entered this "stream," they are not subject to the tax. [§412]
50.	**FALSE**	Not all rights have been incorporated by the Fourteenth Amendment, and *certain* aspects of an incorporated right may be treated differently in state courts. [**Apodaca v. Oregon**] [§§419-424]
51.	**NO**	A welfare recipient has a protectable interest in continued receipt of welfare payments, and due process requires some sort of hearing prior to termination. [§442]
52.	**FALSE**	This does not unreasonably impair the value or use of the property as a shopping center. [§483]
53.	**COMPELLING STATE INTEREST**	State regulation of contraceptives invades the constitutional right of privacy, and is subject to the strict standard of scrutiny. [§§501, 505]
54.	**YES**	It is reasonable to revoke the passport of a person whose conduct in foreign countries presents a serious danger to national security and foreign policy. [§531]
55.	**NO**	Article I, Section 10 imposes such a limitation on the power of the *states*. Federal legislation adjusting economic interests retroactively is permissible if done for a rational purpose. [§§543, 556]
56.	**YES**	Deportation is not considered "punishment" for ex post facto purposes. [**Harisiades v. Shaughnessy**] [§560]
57.	**FALSE**	When government restricts freedom of expression, the Court weighs the importance of First Amendment rights with the nature and scope of the restraint, the type and strength of the government interest, and whether the restriction is narrowly tailored to achieve that interest. [§579]

58. **NO**   A state may not penalize advocacy of the use of force except when the advocacy is directed to inciting or producing imminent lawless action and is likely to incite or produce such action. [§606]

59. **TRUE**   At least, this is the most recent formulation of the "clear and present danger" test. [**Brandenburg v. Ohio**] [§606]

60. **FALSE**   Coach could fall in the category of a "public figure," which is covered by the constitutional privilege. [§§621-622]

61.a. **TRUE**   **Mishkin v. New York**. [§638]

   b. **TRUE**   Commercial activity does not narrow the protections of the First Amendment. (*Compare:* "Pandering" in advertising may be considered.) [§§643-644]

   c. **FALSE**   The Court has rejected the contention that community standards be determined on a "national" basis. [§640]

   d. **FALSE**   Dealers must be shown to have *knowledge of contents*. [§§647-648]

62. **NO**   Not all nudity is obscene, even as to minors. [§§633, 635, 637, 649]

63. **NO**   Profanity or offensiveness alone is not enough (no direct tendency to cause immediate acts of violence). [§§660-661]

64. **NO**   **Linmark Associates, Inc. v. Township of Willingboro**. [§679]

65. **NO**   Although the government has the power to exclude "obscene" materials from import into this country, adequate procedural safeguards must be afforded. [§724]

66. **NO**   If there is an important state interest independent of the speech aspects of the conduct, it may be regulated despite the incidental limitation on speech. [§726]

67. **NO**   A city transit system is not a "public forum." [§§761-763]

68. **DEPENDS**   On whether the ordinance sets forth clearly defined standards to govern the issuance of the permits. [§§767-774]

69. **NO**   Due process requires that the burden be on the state to prove that a person is not qualified for the exemption. Placing upon the taxpayer the affirmative burden of proving by loyalty oath that she was not engaged in the forbidden activity is unconstitutional. The statute is also substantively invalid under the First Amendment. [§§854-855, 858-861]

70. **YES**   **Connell v. Higginbotham; Cole v. Richardson**. [§§859-860]

71.	**NO**	"Mere membership" is not enough (must have been "knowing" and with "specific intent to further unlawful aims"). [§862]
72.	**YES**	Wallbanger's exercise of First Amendment rights cannot serve as a basis for dismissal from public employment. [§867]
73.	**NO**	This law is too broad. It would force prospective teachers to reveal their association with many organizations that have no bearing on their loyalty or professional competence. [§§880-881]
74.	**PROBABLY**	Although the Court has not ruled on this (since **Branzburg v. Hayes** applies to *criminal* proceedings [§887]), as a general rule the press's First Amendment rights are no greater than the general public's. [§886]
75.	**NO**	**Agostini v. Felton**. [§929]
76.	**NO**	Neither the purpose nor the effect of the exemption is the advancement or inhibition of religion. [**Walz v. Tax Commissioner**] [§946]
77.	**NO**	**Zorach v. Clauson**. [§§964-966]
78.	**UNCLEAR**	There is no right to a religious exemption from a neutral law that happens to impose a substantial burden on religious practice, notwithstanding **Wisconsin v. Yoder,** which struck down compulsory attendance in *high school* for the Amish based on *long history* of preparing children for life. [§§989, 1000] However, the law may be challenged as violating the right of parents to educate their children. [§522]
79.	**PROBABLY NOT**	There is no right to a religious exemption from a neutral law that happens to impose a substantial burden on religious practice. [§989]
80.	**NO**	**Hamilton v. Regents of University of California**. [§995]
81.	**MOTION DENIED**	A person claiming violation of the Free Exercise Clause must show some infringement of his personal beliefs, but *all persons who are directly affected by the action complained of have standing* to attack state action in violation of the Establishment Clause. [§§979, 1009]
82.	**FALSE**	It has been found substantially related to the achievement of an important governmental objective. [§1098]
83.	**FALSE**	The Supreme Court has said that poverty standing alone is not a suspect classification. [§1103]
84.	**PROBABLY**	State requirements that new political parties demonstrate public support to get on the ballot have been upheld where the requirements were not unduly burdensome because they further a "compelling" state interest. [§§1124-1125]

85.	**NO**	Disenfranchising felons is expressly authorized in the Fourteenth Amendment. [§1155]
86.	**FALSE**	In "special interest" elections, different standards apply. [§§1156-1157]
87.	**TRUE**	Avoiding fragmentation of political subdivisions does not justify deviations from population for congressional districts. [§§1165-1166]
88.	**FALSE**	Some greater percentage of deviation is allowed for state as opposed to congressional elections and for local government apportionment than for state apportionment, as long as justifying factors exist. [§1174]
89.	**FALSE**	Equal protection is applicable to the election of all officials who perform normal *governmental* functions. [§1181]
90.	**SCHOOL BOARD**	A student's right to a particular quality of education is *not* a right guaranteed by the Constitution. Consequently, statutes regulating education are reviewable under the traditional rational basis test. [§1197]
91.	**NO**	There is no constitutional right to discharge one's debts through bankruptcy proceedings. The filing fee helps make bankruptcy proceedings self-supporting. [§1199]
92.	**NO**	State action will not be found merely because the state has granted a monopoly to a private business. To constitute "state action," there must be either a delegation of a traditional state function performed exclusively by the state or *significant* state involvement with the *challenged action* of the private party. (No showing that state authorized or encouraged Meadowbrook to exclude Bobby.) [**Jackson v. Metropolitan Edison Co.**] [§§1224, 1227]
93.	**YES**	The Thirteenth Amendment ban on slavery. [§§1249-1250]
94.	**FALSE**	The Enabling Clause of the Fourteenth Amendment authorizes Congress to enforce the amendment by "appropriate legislation," and this is a major source of power in the civil rights area. [§§1251-1266]
95.	**FALSE**	One example is that provisions of the Civil Rights Act of 1964 have been upheld as a valid exercise of Congress's power under the Commerce Clause. [§1270]
96.	**NO**	Unanimity is required in federal, but not state, prosecutions. [§§1292-1293]
97.	**NO**	A jury trial is guaranteed only where a "serious" offense is charged. An offense is "serious" if it carries a potential sentence of more than six months. Thus, this is not a "serious" offense. [§§1294-1295]
98.	**YES**	A defendant may raise this challenge even when he is not a member of the group allegedly excluded. [§1304]

99. **NO**   The right to counsel is limited to criminal *prosecutions*. [§§1318-1323]

100. **NO**   The right to counsel is constitutionally required only in prosecutions that result in actual imprisonment. [§§1321-1323]

101. **NO**   Prosecution must prove *every element* of the crime charged beyond a reasonable doubt. Malice aforethought is an essential element of murder and must be *proved by the prosecution*. [§1324]

102. **NO**   The right of counsel on appeal extends only to proceedings in which the accused has the *right* of appellate review. [§1362]

103. **(C)**   New standards will always be given retroactive effect so as to protect the integrity of the truth-finding process. [§§1369-1373]

Exam Questions
and Answers

QUESTION I

A State X statute makes it a misdemeanor to "distribute any leaflet within 20 feet of an election booth while such booth is open for election purposes." Jones knowingly violates this statute by distributing handbills supporting his candidacy for mayor. He does so on the advice of his counsel, who tells him that the statute is unconstitutional. A criminal prosecution for violation of the statute is subsequently commenced against Jones.

Another state statute makes it a misdemeanor to "distribute in a public place any leaflet that does not have printed thereon the name of a person responsible for printing said leaflet, except that this requirement shall not apply to the distribution of political leaflets." Smith desires to print and distribute an anonymous leaflet urging citizens to keep their children in integrated public schools. He consults the prosecuting attorney, who tells him that he is not certain whether such a leaflet would fall within the "political leaflet" exception. Smith distributes the leaflet. The day prior to the distribution, the State X Supreme Court rules in another case that the "political leaflet" exception applies only to leaflets concerning candidates for public office or issues on the ballot. When the prosecutor learns of this ruling, he initiates criminal proceedings against Smith.

What defenses should Jones and Smith raise against their respective prosecutions, and what rulings should result? Discuss.

QUESTION II

Assume that the United States has recently adopted the following statute:

> Whoever travels in interstate or foreign commerce or uses any facility in interstate or foreign commerce, including the mail, with intent to: (a) incite a riot, or to organize, promote, encourage, or carry on a riot, or to commit any act of violence in furtherance of a riot, or to aid and abet any person in inciting a riot or committing any act of violence in furtherance of a riot, and (b) thereafter performs or attempts to perform any overt act specified in paragraph (a), shall be fined not more than $10,000 or imprisoned not more than five years, or both.

> For purposes of this chapter: A riot is a public disturbance, involving acts of violence by assemblages of three or more persons, which poses an immediate danger of damage or injury to property or persons.

Adolf, a militant racist, comes to your office. He tells you that immediately after he made an impassioned speech in another state, members of his audience engaged in rioting, burning, looting, and killing. Nevertheless, he wishes to continue advocating his philosophy through speeches and correspondence of similar content in other states.

Can Adolf immediately challenge the constitutionality of the Act by a suit in a federal court? Assuming suit is possible, what constitutional grounds might Adolf urge and with what likely result? Discuss.

QUESTION III

DM, a Michigan corporation, maintains a vessel which transports cargo among several states on the Great Lakes. The vessel, equipped with hand-fired coal boilers, emits smoke of a density and duration that exceeds the limits imposed by the Smoke Abatement Code of Lakeport, a city in Michigan. Violations are punishable by a $100 fine, 30 days' imprisonment, or both. No such code exists in other ports visited by the vessel. Pursuant to a comprehensive federal statute governing seagoing safety, the Coast Guard has inspected, approved, and licensed DM's vessel (including boilers and fuel).

DM's vessel puts into Michigan's ports for occasional refueling and repairs. Loading and unloading is done at main terminals located in other states. Michigan has levied its personal property tax on the full value of DM's vessel, and no such tax is imposed by the other states visited.

After trials in Michigan's courts, DM is convicted of violating Lakeport's Smoke Abatement Code **and** is found liable for the Michigan property tax. Michigan's highest court has affirmed both decisions, and the United States Supreme Court has granted review. What should be the decision of the Supreme Court, and for what reason? Discuss.

QUESTION IV

A state statute provides scholarship grants of $2,000 per year for any military veteran enrolled in college. This statute is, in turn, limited by the state's so-called Jones Act, which prohibits distribution of monetary grants to "any person who presently supports, is a member of, or in the past year has been a member or supporter of, any organization known by him to advocate the violent overthrow of the state government."

The Jones Act requires that each applicant for a grant submit a sworn statement declaring that he meets the conditions imposed by that Act. The State Welfare Department is then directed to investigate each application, and in case of any doubt, to hold a hearing at which the applicant has the burden of showing that he is not barred by the Act from receiving the scholarship grant.

Zadora brings suit in state court to have the Jones Act declared invalid insofar as it limits scholarship grants. He alleges that he is a veteran; that, although not presently attending college, he has been accepted for enrollment at the start of the next term; and that he would be deprived of a state scholarship because, as a matter of conscience, he cannot submit the sworn statement required by the Jones Act.

Accepting his allegations as true, the state courts decide against Zadora on the ground that the state may condition scholarship grants on whatever grounds it chooses, since such grants are strictly a matter of legislative grace.

On review by the United States Supreme Court, what federal constitutional issues are presented and how should they be resolved? Discuss.

QUESTION V

Suppose that an Illinois statute provides that "an employee entitled to vote in a general election may absent himself from his employment for four hours between the opening and closing of the polls without penalty, and any employer who deducts wages for that absence is guilty of a misdemeanor." Durlington, a railroad corporation doing business in Illinois and engaged in interstate commerce, has company regulations providing that "employees may absent themselves for the purpose of voting on election day for any number of hours, provided that advance notice is given designating the particular hours of absence, and provided further that wages shall not be paid for any absences in excess of two hours." Federal legislation regulates the work hours of railroad employees, but does not deal with the voting situation. After trial in an Illinois court, Durlington is convicted of violating the Illinois statute on proof that wages for two hours were deducted for many of its employees who absented themselves, after giving notice, for four hours on election day.

(1)   On appeal to the highest court of Illinois, what federal constitutional questions may be raised by Durlington, and how should they be resolved? Discuss.

(2)   Assume that on appeal the highest court of Illinois holds the statute invalid on the sole ground that it infringes a particular provision of the Illinois Constitution. What federal remedy, if any, would be available to the Illinois prosecutor? Discuss.

QUESTION VI

Suppose that a statute of Alabama concerning adoption states that only agencies licensed by the state may place children for adoption, and that the primary duty of such agencies shall be to promote the best interests of the child, including his or her moral and spiritual well-being.

Another section of the statute provides: "The race and religious affiliation of the adoptive parents shall be the same as that of the natural parents, or in the case of nonmarital children, that of the mother."

Husband ("H") and Wife ("W") apply to Agency, a duly licensed nonprofit corporation, to adopt the next available nonmarital black child. H is black; W is white; and both are professed agnostics. Their application is rejected after an Agency investigation. In a letter to H and W, Agency states, "Although our investigator found you highly qualified to be adoptive parents in other respects, we must reject your application because the social problems created by the difference in your ethnic backgrounds and your lack of religious affiliation combine to indicate that the requested adoption would not be in the best interests of the child."

H and W file suit in the appropriate Alabama court seeking a declaratory judgment that the quoted requirements of the statute are unconstitutional, and an order compelling Agency to process and approve their application. The trial court denies relief, and the Alabama Supreme Court affirms.

Assuming all questions are properly preserved, discuss the issues that are likely to arise on review by the United States Supreme Court and how they should be resolved.

QUESTION VII

Dave contracts with the General Housing Administration, a federal agency, to carry bulk building materials to be used in the construction of a postal building between highway points within Texas. After entering into the contract, he performs services only for the government.

Suppose Texas laws require any commercial carrier to obtain a permit from the state's Public Utility Commission, which is granted on proof of financial responsibility and the safety of the carrier's equipment. Dave never obtains a permit.

On several occasions while engaged in the performance of his government contract, Dave is arrested by state highway patrolmen, in each case for violating a state statute prohibiting any speed "greater than is reasonable or prudent having due regard for the traffic on, and the surface and width of, the highway." On the last such occasion, after Dave had ignored the prior citations, his driver's license is suspended by the Texas Director of Motor Vehicles pursuant to statute, pending an administrative hearing which Dave has the right to request. Concurrently, Dave is ordered by the Texas Public Utility Commission to cease transportation of all goods until he obtains a state permit.

Dave continues to perform his contract without regard to suspension of his driver's license or the required carrier's permit. He is subsequently arrested and charged with violating Texas statutes making it a crime for any person to drive on state highways while his driver's license is suspended, or to carry goods for hire on the highways without a permit.

What constitutional defenses may be raised by Dave to the charges of (1) transporting goods for hire without a permit, (2) driving while his license was suspended, and (3) speeding? Discuss.

QUESTION VIII

Suppose that a Massachusetts statute requires submission of all motion picture films, books, magazines, and newspapers to the State Obscenity Commission for examination prior to issuance by the Commission of a permit allowing their public exhibition, sale, or distribution. The Commission is directed to refuse a permit if the item submitted contains obscene matter, which is defined as "matter dealing with sex in a manner appealing to prurient interest, that is, matter having a tendency to excite lustful thoughts."

Dexter distributes films for public exhibition and magazines for sale to the public throughout Massachusetts. He applies to the Commission for a permit to distribute a film entitled *The Decameron*, and a picture magazine called *Love*, but refuses to submit either the film or the magazine for examination.

(1)   Is the Commission constitutionally authorized, by reason of Dexter's refusal, to deny him a permit to distribute: (a) The film? (b) The magazine? Discuss.

(2)   Assume that Dexter is constitutionally required to submit the film so that the Commission may examine it for obscenity. Does the statutory test for "obscene matter" satisfy constitutional requirements? Discuss.

ANSWER TO QUESTION I

As to Jones

Freedom of Speech: Jones might argue that the State X statute violates his First Amendment rights (made applicable to the states by the Fourteenth Amendment). In **Mills v. Alabama**, 384 U.S. 214 (1966), the Supreme Court held that a state statute prohibiting any campaigning on election day was invalid as applied to a newspaper editorial encouraging voters to vote in a certain way. However, the present case is distinguishable from *Mills*, because the statute prohibits only campaigning within 20 feet of election booths and forbids only one type of activity (leafletting). Thus, *Mills* is of little help to Jones.

It has been held that *certain types of public property may be shut off entirely* to the exercise of First Amendment activities. [**Adderly v. Florida**, 385 U.S. 39 (1966); **Cox v. Louisiana**, 377 U.S. 288 (1965)] To come within this rule, the property must be either not open to the general public or such that exercise of First Amendment activities would interfere with its normal use. In the present case, some, but not all, election booths may meet this requirement. An election booth may be set up in a city hall, firehouse, courthouse, college dormitory, fraternal lodge, or private home. Some such locations are either not open to the general public or are property on which leafletting would interfere with the property's normal use (*e.g.*, courthouse while trial is being held). Other locations (*e.g.*, city hall) *are* generally open to the public, and the legislature could not prohibit all First Amendment activities thereon.

Even if a location cannot be absolutely closed to First Amendment activities, many such activities are subject to reasonable regulation as to time, place, and manner. In deciding whether a regulation is constitutional, the Court *weighs the substantiality of the state interest against the First Amendment interest*. Specifically with regard to election laws, the Court has stated that the greater the restriction the regulation imposes on the right to vote, the more substantial the state interest must be. [*See* **Burdick v. Takushi**, 504 U.S. 428 (1992)] Here, the regulation imposes little on voting rights. Requiring a leafletter to stand 20 feet away from an election booth does little to prevent the leafletter from disseminating his message; he is still well within the visual and aural range of voters. Moreover, the regulation probably serves a compelling interest—the smooth operation of elections. Leafletting within 20 feet of an election booth might confuse those waiting in line to use the booth and might make it more difficult to process voters. It also could intimidate voters. For these reasons, the Court has upheld a regulation forbidding campaigning activity within 100 feet of a polling place. [**Burson v. Freeman**, 504 U.S. 191 (1992)] Thus, the regulation here likely will be upheld.

Scienter: Jones cannot successfully argue that he inadvertently violated the law. It has been held that a statute making it unlawful to possess an obscene writing or book was invalid because it did not require knowledge of the contents of the book. [**Smith v. California**, 361 U.S. 147 (1959)] But that case was based on the chilling effect the statute would have if book sellers could be prosecuted for possessing obscene books without knowledge of their contents—*i.e.,* sellers would probably stock only books that, after a cursory examination, appeared totally "pure." In the present case, the statute has no such chilling effects: Leafletters know when they are within 20 feet of an election booth and are thereby violating the law. Moreover, Jones knowingly violated the statute and even consulted an attorney for advice. Hence, any contention that he had no such knowledge or that the statute chilled his First Amendment rights would not be accepted.

As to Smith

Freedom of Speech; Vagueness: Smith's obvious defense is that the statute is void for vagueness. Whenever a statute touches First Amendment freedoms, it must be drawn with special precision. Otherwise the statute will have a chilling effect—*i.e.,* a person who fears violating the statute will restrict his speech to avoid even constitutionally protected expression.

In the present case the statute prohibits distribution of leaflets without the sponsor's name printed on the leaflet, unless the leaflet is a "political leaflet." The term "political leaflet" is vague, as attested by the fact that the prosecuting attorney did not know whether Smith's leaflet was "political." Because of this uncertainty, all leafletters (except perhaps those leafletting for candidates for public office) would identify the person responsible for printing the leaflets. But in so identifying the sponsor, the leafletters may be forgoing their First Amendment rights. Hence the statute's vagueness and concomitant chilling effect render it unconstitutional.

Overbreadth: The prosecutor might argue that any statutory vagueness was cured by the State Supreme Court's ruling before Smith distributed the leaflet. But because the court interpreted "political leaflet" to mean only a leaflet concerning candidates for public office or issues on the ballot, the interpretation itself probably violates the First Amendment. Any state interest in knowing the sponsors of leaflets does not justify demanding disclosure of the sponsors of *all* nonelection leaflets. The statute, as construed by the court, would require disclosure of many leaflets that carry messages of great public interest and are clearly within the First Amendment. The state has no pressing interest in disclosure of sponsors, and anonymity may be important. Even as construed, therefore, the statute has a "chilling effect"—*i.e.,* sponsors, if identified, might alter the content of their leaflets so as to avoid any public, private, or governmental reprisals. This in turn renders the statute as interpreted unconstitutional.

Content Discrimination: The state court's interpretation is likewise unconstitutional for the related reason that it discriminates between types of leaflets on the basis of their contents. Rather than regulating the time, place, or manner of leafletting (as in the Jones problem above), the statute regulates only leaflets which are not of a special type. The Supreme Court has held that, absent substantial justification, a state statute permitting only some kinds of speech on certain property violates equal protection as well as the First Amendment. [**Chicago Police Department v. Mosely,** 408 U.S. 92 (1972)] Similarly, permitting distribution of only certain types of leaflets without disclosure of sponsors probably violates equal protection, because the state apparently could not offer a substantial justification for such discrimination.

ANSWER TO QUESTION II

Enjoining the Federal Statute ("Ripeness"): For Adolf to immediately challenge the constitutionality of the statute, the issue must be "ripe" for decision. Article III limits the jurisdiction of the federal courts to "cases" or "controversies." Furthermore, the Federal Declaratory Judgment Act permits a final judgment declaring rights and liabilities of parties only in cases of "actual controversy." To satisfy these requirements, Adolf must show that he wants to engage in specific activities and that there is a real likelihood that the statute will be enforced against him. The facts do not indicate that prosecution against Adolf has been threatened or that the statute has been enforced against anyone in the past (although this may be relatively unimportant due to the statute's recent enactment).

The greatest ripeness problem is that Adolf has apparently not expressed a desire to engage in specific activities proscribed by the statute. Adolf has not expressed an intent to incite a riot, organize a riot, aid a riot, etc. Rather, he wishes to continue advocating his philosophy through speech and correspondence with content "similar" to the earlier speech. Because the composition of his speech and audience is not specific, it is possible that none of the speeches would "incite, organize, promote, or encourage a riot" (and therefore fall within the statute's proscription). Unless Adolf can show that his speechmaking and correspondence, given their content and audience, regularly or inevitably incite or promote riots and that it is his intent to incite, organize, promote, etc., a riot, the issue may not be "ripe"; and Adolf may have to await criminal prosecution before challenging the constitutionality of the statute.

Congressional Power: *Assuming* Adolf can maintain his action for declaratory relief, he might argue that the statute is unconstitutional because Congress had no power to enact it. However, the statute is clearly supported by the ***Commerce Clause***. Under that Clause, Congress has plenary power over the channels and facilities of interstate commerce and can properly prohibit certain persons or pieces of correspondence from entering into interstate commerce. The fact that the proscribed overt act takes place in only one state is irrelevant, because the act is only necessary to prove that the defendant had a certain intent when he traveled in interstate commerce or used interstate communication facilities.

Right to Travel: Adolf might also argue that the statute violates his constitutional right to travel. The right to travel freely between states is a privilege of national citizenship and is strongly protected against state interference. However, the right is not absolute and can be overriden by a substantial or compelling governmental interest. The government's interest is afforded substantially greater weight if federal rather than state interests are involved.

In the present case, the federal government's interest is in preventing persons from causing riots. If militants are permitted to travel from state to state, inciting riots in each, local authorities would be hindered in taking effective action, and the federal government might be forced to combat this serious evil. Against this strong federal interest, the statute in question impinges on the right to travel in only a minor way. Militants are not barred from interstate travel and can avoid the terms of the statute simply by refraining from inciting or encouraging riots in the destination states. Since the impingement on Adolf's right to travel is minor and the federal government's interest in preventing interstate travel of riot-provokers is substantial, there is probably no constitutional violation on this ground.

Freedom of Speech: Adolf could also attack the statute on the ground that it violates his First Amendment right to freedom of speech. Again, however, this right is not absolute, even though it occupies a preferred position among all constitutional rights. The test for determining when government may punish advocacy of illegal action is not clear. In **Dennis v. United States** and **Yates v. United States,** the Court said the test involved the imminence of the evil occurring *and* the gravity or seriousness of the evil advocated. The more serious the evil, the less imminent it need be. The **Brandenburg v. Ohio** test, however, makes imminence an *independent* requirement and says nothing about the seriousness of the evil. Furthermore, *Brandenburg* appears to require an evil intent by the speaker. To complicate matters even more, the Court in *Brandenburg* approvingly cited the *Dennis* and *Yates* decisions. Possibly *Brandenburg* meant that imminence is only an independent factor when the evil being advocated is not extremely serious, in which case *Brandenburg* would be consistent with *Dennis* except insofar as it also seems to require an evil intent by the advocate.

The statute in question appears to punish only advocacy that will produce an imminent evil. It expressly prohibits speech that incites or promotes a riot, and "riot" is defined to mean a public disturbance that poses an immediate danger of damage or injury. But because a riot exists whenever violence is perpetrated against people or property by three or more persons, the statute does *not* require the danger to be serious. For example, a person would violate the act if he incited three persons to violently kick out the window of an abandoned warehouse. Similarly, the statute only requires that the advocate intend to incite others to commit an immediate evil; it does not require that the evil intended be serious.

Applying the *Brandenburg* test, the statute may be constitutional, because it requires the evil advocated to be imminent. However, *Brandenburg* also appears to require an evil intent. The statute in question requires only an intent to incite or promote an immediate evil, no matter how minor the evil may be; and this may not satisfy the evil intent test. The statute, however, apparently would be constitutional under the *Dennis-Yates* test, because that test requires no independent showing of evil intent. Hence, the validity of the statute may depend on which test is applied.

Overbreadth and Vagueness: Even if the statute is valid under the *Dennis-Yates* or *Brandenburg* tests for advocacy, it is still probably unconstitutional on its face under the First Amendment. The statute—which is clearly addressed to speech as such—not only proscribes advocacy of criminal acts, but also penalizes encouragement and the aiding and abetting of such acts. This may include speech that would, by itself, be quite harmless, and because speech falling short of advocacy is proscribed, the statute is overbroad. Moreover, the statute is unconstitutionally vague: An individual who wishes to make a speech could not determine beforehand whether his proposed speech could be considered as "encouraging" a riot, and thus might severely censor his speech or not make the speech at all. Such "chilling effects" are not permitted under the First Amendment.

The statute in question is also overbroad for a second reason. It penalizes not only advocacy of criminal conduct, but also mere *attempts* to advocate illegal conduct. Because an attempt violation could be based on nonadvocating speech, expression could be punished even though it did not satisfy the *Dennis-Yates* or *Brandenburg* standards—clearly an unconstitutional proscription.

In sum, because the statute is vague, punishes speech short of advocacy, and may punish advocacy that does not satisfy the *Dennis-Yates* or *Brandenburg* standards, it is unconstitutional.

ANSWER TO QUESTION III

Decision on Smoke Abatement

Preemption: DM might argue that the Lakeport Smoke Abatement Code is preempted by the federal statute and hence is invalid under the Supremacy Clause. Although there may be no direct conflict between the two statutes, the Lakeport act cannot be upheld if Congress intended the federal statute to constitute complete and exclusive regulation of the area.

The federal statute is a comprehensive act governing safety of seagoing vessels. If Lakeport's act required additional safety features on vessels, it would probably be found preempted by the federal act. But the Lakeport act is an air pollution measure, which presumably does not deal with safety requirements at all. It is unlikely that Congress, when passing the safety act, intended to prevent states or their subdivisions from regulating smoke output or other nonsafety aspects of shipping vessels.

If the legislative history were examined, however, one might find statements indicating that the federal bill was passed to alleviate problems created by varying state specifications for vessels. Any such indication would support DM's argument that states or their subdivisions, unable to demand different boiler specifications under a safety act, should not be able to destroy the uniformity of the federal act under the guise of pollution, health, or other nonsafety measures. A comparison of the federal statute and the Lakeport act might also reveal that boilers meeting the pollution standards set by the Lakeport act could not satisfy the federal safety requirements—in which case the Lakeport act would clearly be invalid. Assuming this is not the case, however, and assuming the legislative history does not indicate that Congress intended to displace local pollution measures, the Lakeport act would not be preempted by the federal safety statute.

Commerce Clause: DM might also contend that the Lakeport act violates the Commerce Clause. However, absent conflicting federal legislation and subject to certain limitations, states may regulate local activities even though the regulation affects interstate commerce. One limitation is that states may never discriminate against interstate commerce; but this does not invalidate the Lakeport act, because local smoke emitters are also apparently subject to the act.

Whether nondiscriminatory state legislation violates the Commerce Clause must be determined by the "undue burden" test. Under this test, the Court weighs the detriment to the national interest imposed by the legislation against the strength and merit of the state's interest in the regulation. Here, the Lakeport act seems to impose only a minor burden on interstate commerce. Because no other ports visited by DM's vessel have a similar act, there is no indication that compliance with the act would prevent the vessel from docking at other ports. However, the cost of bringing vessels up to the Lakeport standards *would* be relevant to the Court's determination, as would information on how many ships would satisfy Lakeport's act without alteration of boilers. This information is, of course, not provided.

On the other hand, Lakeport's interest in clean air, since it is one involving health, safety, or social welfare, is afforded much greater deference than an act designed merely to protect economic interests. Lakeport's interest in safeguarding the health of its residents could well be affected if vessels docking there were allowed to pollute the air with dense clouds of smoke. Because the burden on interstate commerce is probably minor and the benefit of the act substantial, and because there is no indication that Lakeport's interest could be effectively served by less burdensome legislation, the act would be valid under the Commerce Clause.

Decision on Property Tax

Situs: As a general proposition, a state may levy an ad valorem property tax on an instrumentality of interstate commerce if the instrumentality has acquired a "taxable situs" within the state, thereby satisfying the *Due Process Clause*. A taxable situs always exists in the state of domicile, although if the instrumentality receives benefits or protection from other states, it may be taxable by them as well. In the present case, the vessel is owned by a Michigan corporation, so Michigan is the *domiciliary state* and may levy an ad valorem tax on the vessel.

Apportionment: The domiciliary state need *not* apportion the value of interstate instrumentalities unless the taxpayer can prove that a certain part of the instrumentalities have acquired a taxable situs elsewhere. To do this, the taxpayer must show either that the instrumentalities are permanently located elsewhere, or that they were habitually employed in interstate commerce in other states and thereby acquired a taxable situs there. DM's vessel probably meets the second criterion. Although not located permanently in some other state, it does all of its cargo hauling between other states, and docks in Michigan only for occasional refueling and repairs. The vessel probably acquired a taxable situs in one or more of the other states in which it docks and, whether or not other states are in fact taxing the vessel, Michigan must apportion its tax to satisfy objections under the *Commerce Clause*.

A method of apportionment will be upheld if it roughly reflects the instrumentality's average physical presence within the state. For example, if DM's vessel spends 5% of its dock time in Michigan ports, Michigan should be allowed to levy its tax on 5% of the vessel's value. But the Michigan tax was levied on the full value of DM's vessel. If DM can show that the vessel has acquired a taxable situs in some other state or states (*see* discussion above), the Court should find that this lack of apportionment is an unconstitutional burden on interstate commerce—in the absence of authorizing federal legislation.

ANSWER TO QUESTION IV

Freedom of Association: The state court decision failed to consider whether the Jones Act benefits are unconstitutionally conditioned in that they violate the First Amendment prohibition of abridgments on freedom of association. This prohibition applies to the states through the Due Process Clause of the Fourteenth Amendment.

Vagueness: The Jones Act prohibits distribution of scholarship aid to any person who is a member of or supports a group known to him to advocate the violent overthrow of the state government. This standard is vague because of the term "supports," which could encompass not only membership and active participation, but also attendance at meetings and even mere sympathy for the organization. An individual who considered applying for Jones Act benefits in the future might well be chilled by this vague standard: *e.g.,* he might avoid any conduct or speech that could possibly be construed as support for a group advocating overthrow of the state government (even though constitutionally protected). Hence, the standard violates the First Amendment.

Overbreadth: The Jones Act standard is also overbroad. The state may deny governmental benefits for associating with certain groups only when the group engages in activities not constitutionally protected *and* the individual is an active member of the group, has knowledge of the group's illegal advocacy, and has the specific intent that the group's aims be accomplished. Under the Jones Act, benefits would be denied even where the applicant is only a passive member or supporter. Moreover, the prohibition against distribution of benefits applies even though the applicant has no specific intent to further the group's unlawful aims. A denial based on such conduct is likewise unconstitutional under the First Amendment.

Burden of Proof: Even if the substantive standard found in the Jones Act was not vague and overbroad (*see* discussion above), the Act would be unconstitutional on the ground that the applicant has the burden of proof at the hearing provided under the Act. Where the state imposes a civil "penalty" by conditioning benefits on the applicant's speech or associations (in contrast to imposing a civil disability in order to serve a legitimate state regulatory end), the First Amendment requires that the *state* bear the burden of showing that the applicant engaged in unprotected speech or association.

Right to a Hearing: Placing the burden of proof on the wrong party may be particularly objectionable in the present case, because due process usually requires some form of notice and hearing before an individual may be deprived of liberty or property interests by the state. The interest in obtaining scholarship aid under the Jones Act may be such a "property interest" that requires a hearing before deprivation. An applicant who appears to satisfy all of the legitimate conditions to aid under the Act seemingly has a legitimate claim to the grant; and before the state withholds benefits, the applicant should be given a hearing at which the state has the burden of proving the applicant engaged in speech or association that is not constitutionally protected.

Standing and Ripeness: Although the Jones Act is constitutionally deficient in a number of respects, Zadora may not challenge the Act unless he has standing—which requires a direct and immediate personal injury due to the Act's unconstitutional requirements. Zadora has alleged that he is a veteran, that he has been accepted for enrollment at the start of the next term, and that, as a matter of conscience, he could not submit the sworn statement required by the Jones Act. These allegations establish standing, because Zadora's unwillingness to satisfy the allegedly unconstitutional requirement will have the immediate injurious effect of depriving him of scholarship aid.

The constitutionality of the sworn statement requirement is also "ripe," because Zadora has been accepted for college and it appears clear that the allegedly unconstitutional requirement will be enforced against him.

However, Zadora may not have standing to attack the constitutionality of the burden of proof requirement at the hearing. Because he has refused to submit a sworn statement and will not receive a hearing, he may not be injured by the requirement that he carry the burden of proof. Furthermore, the burden of proof issue may not be ripe, because the burden of proof requirement may never be applied to him. However, if the Court believes that Zadora has a substantial chance of succeeding in his contention, there is little reason to prohibit him from challenging the second stage of the proceedings. The "real likelihood of harm" requirement would be satisfied, and a comprehensive attack on the statutory scheme is consistent with notions of judicial economy.

Conclusion: Zadora will clearly prevail in his challenge. The requirement of a sworn statement is both unconstitutionally vague and overbroad, and placing the burden of proof on the applicants at the hearing violates the First Amendment and due process. Zadora has standing to challenge the sworn statement requirement and the issue is ripe. He should also have standing to attack the burden of proof requirement, and this issue should also be found ripe—because Zadora's challenge to the statement requirement is so substantial that he will likely be faced in the near future with the burden of proving that he is not barred from receiving scholarship aid. Even if Zadora does not yet have standing to attack this requirement and the issue is not yet ripe, he will certainly be able to do so once he prevails in his attack against the statement requirement.

ANSWER TO QUESTION V

(1) **Preemption:** The first constitutional issue is whether the federal legislation preempts the state statute, making the state statute invalid under the Supremacy Clause. Although

there is no direct conflict between the state and federal legislation, there may be a conflict in policy or a congressional intent to occupy the field. For example, the federal act may have been enacted to achieve national uniformity in working hours of railroad employees. Such an objective would be frustrated by the Illinois act since railroad service in Illinois on election day might be inferior to service in other states. Also, Durlington, a railroad doing interstate business, would be required by the state act to make special arrangements on election day for employees in only one state. Any congressional interest in uniformity should be given considerable weight in resolving the preemption question, because operation of the railroads is of substantial national interest.

Of course, a review of the legislative history may instead reveal that Congress wished to leave this problem to the states. Even so, however, such legislative history must be considered in light of the countervailing factors discussed above. The national interest in railroad operations, the desirability of uniformity in such operations, and the fact that railroad operations are extensively regulated by Congress would probably outweigh anything less than overwhelming evidence that state rules on election leaves of absence are permissible. If the Illinois Supreme Court agrees that the state act is in conflict with the policy of the federal legislation, the state act is invalid.

Commerce Clause: A second possible constitutional objection to the Illinois statute is that it constitutes improper regulation of interstate commerce and is therefore invalid under the Commerce Clause. The act is clearly not invalid on the ground that it discriminates against interstate commerce because it applies to all employers in the state. Hence the Illinois court should apply the "undue burden" test used to determine if nondiscriminatory legislation is an unreasonable burden on interstate commerce—*i.e.*, weighing the extent of the burden on interstate commerce against the strength and merit of the state interest in regulation. Although few facts are given, it is probable that a required four-hour leave of absence will severely hamper the operations of a number of interstate enterprises. For example, goods traveling from Illinois to another state may be delayed a full day because of the railroad's decreased work force in Illinois, and passenger service could become unsafe. In the present case, Durlington already gives a leave of absence, but only with advance notice. Presumably the advance notice requirement exists so that the employer can, despite leaves of absence, schedule the day's operations in the way that will have the least effect on its passenger and cargo service. By not requiring advance notice from employees, the Illinois statute makes it exceedingly difficult for the employer to do this.

Balanced against this burden on interstate commerce is the state's interest in having its residents take an active role in the democratic process. Statutes furthering such an interest involving the social welfare are generally accorded more weight than statutes protecting local economic interests. However, the state's interest could probably be achieved in a manner that would be less burdensome on interstate commerce; *e.g.*, leaves of absence only for the first or last hours of the shift. Such a provision would enable all workers to vote en route to work or while returning home, and would not disrupt the middle of companies' shifts.

Furthermore, the act could have provided for advance notice of absence so that the employer could make necessary arrangements for adequate service. Because the act does place a substantial burden on interstate commerce, and because the state's interest could be protected by less burdensome legislation, the act could be found invalid under the Commerce Clause.

Due Process and Equal Protection: The state act is not vulnerable on either due process or equal protection grounds, because it falls within the category of economic and social legislation. Such legislation is upheld under the Due Process Clause unless no reasonable state of facts can be conceived to support it, or unless it bears no rational relationship to the end sought. Illinois could reasonably have concluded that the statute in question would lead to a larger voter turnout. As for equal protection, any rational classification or discrimination is valid. Thus the statute could not be invalidated on the ground that only employees entitled to vote are eligible for the paid leave of absence.

Contracts Clause: Similarly, the state act does not impair the obligation of contracts (as prohibited by Article I, Section 10). The proscription of the Contracts Clause is not absolute: The reasonableness of the state legislation is the test when the law regulates only private contracts, and legislative judgment is usually afforded substantial deference. In the present case, the state has a strong interest in increasing voter turnout, while the employment contracts allegedly impaired will be affected only one day each year. Balanced against the state's interest, this impairment is not substantial enough to constitute a Contracts Clause violation.

Just Compensation Clause: Finally, the Illinois statute is not an unconstitutional taking of property without just compensation. Such takings are prohibited by the Fifth Amendment, and this prohibition applies to the states under the Fourteenth Amendment Due Process Clause. But any legislation involving the state's police power places some burden on the use of the property, so that the line between permissible regulation and a taking is a matter of degree. In deciding whether an act constitutes a taking, the court generally balances the public need against the private cost. As discussed above, there is a substantial state interest here in increasing participation in the electoral process, and the cost to the employers is minimal because of the infrequency of general elections. Thus, the act should be held a valid exercise of the state's police power rather than an unconstitutional taking.

(2) Adequate State Ground: If the highest court of Illinois holds the statute invalid on the sole ground that it infringes a provision of the Illinois Constitution, the Illinois prosecutor would be confronted by the doctrine of adequate state grounds. Despite the presence of a federal question in the case, the Supreme Court will not review state court judgments if the state court judgment can be supported entirely on a state ground. The doctrine does not apply when the state ground is not "adequate" (*e.g.*, when it does not dispose of the entire issue). The facts do not disclose what the state constitutional provision is, so it cannot be determined whether the state ground is really adequate. However, if the state court relied on a Due Process Clause or impairment of contracts provision in the state constitution, the prosecutor may be foreclosed from further action.

ANSWER TO QUESTION VI

State Action: As will be discussed below, the adoption agency's decision probably violates the First Amendment freedoms of religion as applicable to the states through the Fourteenth Amendment, the Fourteenth Amendment Equal Protection Clause, and the right to marry, which is part of the constitutional right of privacy. Because these constitutional provisions apply only to state action and the adoption agency here is a private corporation, a preliminary issue arises as to whether the adoption agency's action constitutes state action.

State action includes not only action by the state, but also certain actions undertaken by ostensibly private individuals where the individuals are performing exclusive government functions or there is significant government involvement. Here, it is uncertain whether adoption services will be considered to be an exclusive government function because, historically, the government has not been the only entity running adoption agencies. Moreover, the mere fact that the adoption agency has been licensed by the state or indeed that it has been given a monopoly will not be enough to make the agency's action state action. [**Jackson v. Metropolitan Edison Co.**, 419 U.S. 345 (1974)] However, where a private individual's action is compelled by state law, there is sufficient government involvement for the individual's action to constitute state action. [**Peterson v. City of Greenville**, 373 U.S. 244 (1963)] Because the adoption agency here was compelled by the state statute to discriminate on the basis of race and religion, the agency's action constitutes state action.

Race and Equal Protection: The Alabama statute contains an explicit racial classification. Such classifications are "suspect" and will not be upheld unless they are necessary to accomplish some substantial or compelling state objective. In the present case, the state's interest is in promoting the best interests of the child. Under certain circumstances, a racially mixed family may affect the child's well-being, and this interest may satisfy the substantial state interest test. But the statute would not permit adoption even where a thorough investigation indicated that, because of the community's racial mix or other factors, an interracial adoption would have no adverse effect on the child. Because a statute that takes account of such special cases would protect the state's interest just as well as the existing statute, the statute could be held to violate equal protection.

Right to Marry: The statute may also be an impermissible burden on the constitutional right to marry. As exemplified by the present case, the statute effectively prohibits racially mixed couples from adopting children of any race, thereby imposing a direct and substantial disability on anyone who marries a person of a different race. Unless the Court concludes that the state has a substantial compelling interest in so acting (*see* discussion above), imposition of this disability could be unconstitutional.

Freedom of Religion: The letter from the adoption agency states a second ground for rejection, namely, the parents' lack of religious affiliation. The Alabama statute provides that adoptive parents shall have the same religious affiliation as the child's natural parents. This requirement may be unconstitutional, under both the Establishment and

Free Exercise Clauses of the First Amendment (applicable to the states by the Fourteenth Amendment).

Free Exercise: The "same religion" requirement imposes an indirect burden on the exercise of religion because a couple not affiliated with a major religious group may have to wait years before an agency can provide a child. Likewise, members of very small religious denominations may never be able to adopt a child. Because the statute actually focuses on religion rather than being a neutral law, it is doubtful that the court would apply the relaxed standard of **Employment Division v. Smith**. Rather, the statutory burden could be unconstitutional unless the state can show that the law is narrowly tailored to serve a compelling interest. [*See* **Church of the Lukumi Babalu Aye, Inc. v. City of Hialeah,** 508 U.S. 520 (1993)] Because a statute requiring consideration of the effect of religious differences on a case-by-case basis would probably serve the state's interest equally well, the indirect burden is probably impermissible.

Definition of "Religion": The Free Exercise Clause prohibits the imposition of burdens only on religious beliefs or conduct. H and W are professed agnostics, and it is questionable whether agnosticism is a religious belief. However, the Supreme Court has never held any asserted religious beliefs not to be religious for First Amendment purposes; and if H and W possess beliefs that occupy a place in their lives parallel to that occupied by orthodox religious beliefs, the Free Exercise Clause would likely prevent the imposition of burdens on their beliefs not necessary to achieve a compelling state interest.

Establishment: The "same religion" requirement may also violate the Establishment of Religion Clause of the First Amendment. The statute has a purpose to aid religion—*i.e.,* it is specifically designed to promote the child's spiritual well-being. The statute also aids religion generally, and certain religious denominations in particular. Where either the purpose or effect of a statute is to aid religion, the statute will usually violate the Establishment Clause. Because both tests are satisfied here, the Court would likely hold the statute unconstitutional on this basis.

ANSWER TO QUESTION VII

Federal Immunity from State Regulation

Transporting goods for hire without a permit: The Supremacy Clause has been held impliedly to require that activities of the federal government be free from burdensome state regulation. This means that the states may neither *unduly interfere* with the functioning of federal agencies, nor directly control work that a contractor is performing for the United States. The states may, however, regulate government contractors as long as the regulation does not prescribe the manner in which they are to perform their contracts.

In the present case, Dave is a contractor performing services *only* for the federal government. If he must comply with the Texas requirement that commercial carriers obtain permits from the Public Utility Commission, granted only to financially responsible carriers that use safe equipment, the federal government's operations could be severely hindered: Not only might the processing procedure delay construction, but also the state standards restrict the federal government's initial choice of carriers. Thus, because Dave is probably immune from the permit requirement, he cannot constitutionally be prosecuted for failure to satisfy the requirement.

Driving while license suspended: Because Dave is a carrier, a state requirement that all persons driving motor vehicles have a valid operator's license would clearly interfere with his work for the federal government. As noted earlier, such a requirement could unduly limit the government's choice of contractors and interfere with operations after the contract is entered into. In a case involving a federal employee, rather than a contractor, it was held the state could not require the employee to obtain a driver's license to operate a mail truck. [**Johnson v. Maryland,** 254 U.S. 51 (1920)] This same immunity would presumably extend at least to exclusive federal contractors while they are operating vehicles pursuant to their contract.

In the present case, however, Dave did not simply refuse to obtain a driver's license—he had a license when he began performing his contract, and lost it only after ignoring a number of speeding citations. Whether Dave should be immune from prosecution under these circumstances is not clear.

The state could take the position that if Dave is not immune from the speeding charges (*see* discussion below), he cannot be immune from charges arising from his failure to honor the license suspension—which is the penalty for ignoring the citations. This argument is not persuasive, however, and is inconsistent with the principle of governmental immunity. If the speeding charges are valid, the state does have an interest in punishing Dave, but where there is a conflict, this interest must yield to the federal interest in carrying on its operations free from undue state interference.

Moreover, the state's interest in punishing Dave was probably achieved for the most part by suspending his license, because he may not legally operate a motor vehicle except in the course of his work for the federal government. If the state does not think this limitation is an adequate punishment, it can take legal action to enforce the traffic fines, something the state has apparently not yet done. In any event, the fact that the state may lawfully cite Dave for speeding should not permit it to interfere with federal operations. Thus, because Dave was engaged in the performance of his contract at the time he was arrested for driving while his license was suspended, he cannot be prosecuted constitutionally for this offense.

Speeding: Dave's immunity should not extend to speeding violations, because the federal interest is not unduly interfered with or impaired by enforcing the speed law against Dave. When the federal government entered into its contract with Dave, it presumably did not contemplate that Dave would exceed the speed limit when delivering supplies. The facts do not indicate any interest of the federal government that would be served by allowing Dave to freely violate the speed law, and because governmental immunity should arise only when a conflict exists between the state interest (in protecting against the harms of speeding) and federal interests, immunity should not shield Dave from the speeding charges.

Vagueness: However, Dave may avoid conviction on the speeding charges on the ground that the state speeding law is vague. The statute will not be held void "on its face," because neither the statute nor Dave's conduct concerns freedom of speech or any other constitutional right. If it is void for vagueness at all, it must therefore be because it is vague as applied. A less strict standard is employed as to this type of statute than as to statutes that concern a constitutional right and are allegedly void on their face because of a potential chilling effect on the exercise of constitutional rights.

The speeding statute requires that drivers not drive at speeds "greater than what is reasonable under the circumstances." Persons of common intelligence would probably differ as to application of the statute, so that there could be significant disparities in enforcement; *i.e.,* on any given stretch of highway at any given time, one law enforcement officer might believe 40 m.p.h. to be a reasonable speed, while a second officer might consider 70 m.p.h. reasonable. A motorist in turn might feel 50 m.p.h. is reasonable. Whether the motorist is cited, therefore, depends on which officer observes him.

Because of this vagueness and probable discrepancies in application, Dave should be able to avoid prosecution under the statute unless, perhaps, he was driving at a speed that no person of common intelligence would believe reasonable (*e.g.,* 80 m.p.h. in a school zone). Unless Dave is such a "hardcore" violator, however, the state should not be allowed to prosecute him on the speeding charges.

ANSWER TO QUESTION VIII

(1) **Censorship Systems**

(a) **Movies:** Although governments generally may not censor speech before it is uttered or published, some forms of prior restraint and censorship are permitted. But to be upheld, censorship plans must contain adequate procedural and judicial safeguards. In the area of movie censorship, such a system must contain at least the following procedural safeguards:

(i) The standards for imposing censorship (or denying a license) must be narrowly drawn, reasonable, and definite. That is, only "obscene" films or films otherwise not protected under the Constitution may be covered by the censorship program.

(ii) The censor must promptly seek a judicial injunction if a permit is not issued.

(iii) In the judicial proceeding, the censor must bear the burden of proving that the film is not protected.

(iv) The judicial determination must be rendered promptly.

[**Freedman v. Maryland,** 380 U.S. 51 (1965)]

Censorship programs that satisfy these procedural safeguards are permitted on the ground that movies differ from other forms of expression, and that the time delays inherent in the programs are relatively less burdensome.

The statute in question fails to satisfy these safeguards. First, the statute allows denial of a permit even in cases where the film is not "obscene" according to constitutional standards (*see* discussion in (2), below). Second, the statute says absolutely nothing about judicial proceedings; and as indicated, for the statute to be valid it must require the censorship board promptly to seek a judicial injunction, the censor must have the burden of proving the film is unprotected, and there must be a prompt judicial determination. The Massachusetts statute allows the State Obscenity Commission to refuse permits without any judicial determination on whether the film is unprotected.

If the Massachusetts statute were not invalidated, there would be an undue burden on First Amendment freedoms. After the Commission refused to issue a permit, the applicant would be forced to seek judicial relief before his film could be exhibited (or run the risk of criminal prosecution by exhibiting it). Without a statutory provision for expedited judicial determination, the applicant might face lengthy delays before a decision was reached. Absent a statutory allocation of the burden of proof, the judge might give the Commission's ruling a presumption of validity. Because of these failings, the Massachusetts statute is invalid, and the Commission may not constitutionally deny Dexter a permit even though he refused to submit his film.

(b) **Magazines:** Although some licensing systems are permissible for films, government may not establish any form of licensing board to which publications must be submitted for advance approval of content. The rationale for this distinction is that the time delays inherent in censorship systems impose an undue burden on publications, while such delays do not overly burden the distribution of films.

Thus, a state wishing to control the content of publications may proceed against distribution of an item only after it has had some distribution. If a court then determines that the item is obscene, it may enjoin further distribution. The Massachusetts statute requires neither prior distribution nor a judicial hearing, but permits the state to censor books, magazines, and newspapers whenever the Commission determines they are obscene. The statute is therefore void on its face; and the Commission may not deny Dexter's application for a permit to distribute his magazine.

(2) **Obscenity:** Not every depiction of sex is obscene. The Supreme Court has held that several separate elements must be present before an item can be deemed obscene.

[**Miller v. California**, 413 U.S. 15 (1973)] First, the dominant theme of the material when considered as a whole must appeal to a prurient interest in sex. In determining this, the Court considers whether the material appeals to an average person's prurient interest in sex. Second, the material must affront contemporary community standards relating to sexual matters in such a way as to be patently offensive. The "standards" examined need not be "national"; a statewide standard has been upheld. Third, as a whole the material must lack political, literary, scientific, or artistic value. There must be separate proof of each of these three elements before material can be deemed obscene.

The Massachusetts statute defines obscene matter as "matter dealing with sex in a manner appealing to prurient interest, that is, matter having a tendency to excite lustful thoughts." This definition clearly fails to satisfy the standard set forth above. For example, although the statute speaks of "appealing to prurient interest," it is not at all clear *whose* prurient interest must be appealed to before material can be determined obscene. Under the Massachusetts standard, a children's magazine presumably could be labeled obscene (and therefore banned from display or distribution) if it had a tendency to excite lustful thoughts in child molesters. But, as noted above, material may generally not constitutionally be considered obscene unless it appeals to the average person's prurient interest in sex. Thus, the Massachusetts statute is unconstitutional.

Moreover, even if the statutory language satisfied the "prurient interest" requirement, the statute fails to require that material affront contemporary community standards before it can be deemed obscene. Under the statute, a book that has a tendency to excite lustful thoughts in some readers could be determined obscene by the Commission even though the great majority of the public might consider the book unobjectionable. Because a state may not treat material as obscene unless it is patently offensive, this is another basis for holding the Massachusetts provision invalid. The statute is likewise unconstitutional in that it would permit a finding of obscenity even as to material that has serious political, artistic, scientific, or literary value; *e.g.*, medical books containing pictures of naked persons could be banned despite the obvious value of such books to the scientific community.

Although states have occasionally been permitted to define obscenity in terms varying somewhat from the *Miller* standard, the Massachusetts statute is so broad and general that it almost certainly is invalid. In effect, the act gives the Commission power to declare obscene anything that might merely "excite lustful thoughts," or might appeal to any person's prurient interest, regardless whether the material has any redeeming virtues. Any definition permitting such results clearly fails to satisfy constitutional standards.

Table of Cases

International Harvester Co. v. Department of Treasury - **§395**

International Society for Krishna Consciousness, Inc. v. Lee - **§762**

Irvin v. Dowd - **§1306**

Itel Containers International Corp. v. Huddleston - **§415**

J

J.E.B. v. Alabama *ex rel.* T.B. - **§1096**

Jackson v. Metropolitan Edison Co. - **§§1224, 1235**

Jackson v. Virginia - **§1327**

James v. Valtierra - **§1103**

James Daniel Good Real Property, United States v. - **§441**

Japan Line, Ltd. v. County of Los Angeles - **§415**

Jenkins v. Georgia - **§§640, 645**

Jenness v. Fortson - **§1125**

Jimenez v. Weinberger - **§1209**

Jimmy Swaggart Ministries v. Board of Equalization of California - **§994**

Johnson v. Louisiana - **§1293**

Johnson v. Maryland - **§281**

Johnson v. New Jersey - **§§1373, 1374**

Johnson v. Robison - **§§993, 1016, 1117**

Johnson v. Zerbst - **§1319**

Johnson Oil Refining Co. v. Oklahoma - **§365**

Johnson, United States v. (1982) - **§1375**

Johnson, United States v. (1966) - **§184**

Jones v. Alfred H. Mayer Co. - **§1249**

Jones v. Helms - **§529**

Jones v. North Carolina Prisoners' Labor Union - **§825**

Jones v. Wolf - **§1009**

Jones, United States v. - **§1353**

Joseph v. Carter & Weekes Stevedoring Co. - **§374**

Joseph Burstyn, Inc. v. Wilson - **§716**

Joseph E. Seagram & Sons, Inc. v. Hostetter - **§348**

Juidice v. Vail - **§104**

K

Kadrmas v. Dickinson Public Schools - **§1198**

Kahn v. Shevin - **§1098**

Kahriger, United States v. - **§§156, 157**

Kaiser Aetna v. United States - **§489**

Kansas v. Colorado - **§137**

Kansas v. Hendricks - **§536**

Karcher v. Daggett - **§1166**

Kassel v. Consolidated Freightways Corp. - **§§328, 337**

Katz v. United States - **§§1286, 1374**

Katzenbach v. McClung - **§295**

Katzenbach v. Morgan - **§§1251, 1253, 1261**

Keeney v. Tamayo-Reyes - **§1365**

Keller v. State Bar of California - **§873**

Kelley v. Johnson - **§526**

Kendall v. United States *ex rel.* Stokes - **§212**

Kent v. Dulles - **§530**

Kentucky Whip & Collar Co. v. Illinois Central Railroad - **§289**

Ker v. California - **§423**

Kern-Limerick, Inc. v. Scurlock - **§277**

Keyes v. School District No. 1 - **§§1046, 1047, 1050**

Keyishian v. Board of Regents - **§§860, 862**

Keystone Bituminous Coal Association v. Benedictis - **§495**

Kilbourn v. Thompson - **§181**

Kimel v. Florida Board of Regents - **§1256**

Kingsley Books, Inc. v. Brown - **§708**

Kingsley International Pictures Corp. v. Regents - **§717**

Kleindienst v. Mandel - **§169**

Kleppe v. New Mexico - **§179**

Klopfer v. North Carolina - **§423**

Kokinda, United States v. - **§763**

Kolender v. Lawson - **§542**

Konigsberg v. State Bar - **§§882, 883**

Korematsu v. United States - **§1020**

Kosydar v. National Cash Register Co. - **§412**

Kovacs v. Cooper - **§§749, 758**

Kramer v. Union Free School District - **§1150**

Kras, United States v. - **§§1113, 1199**

Kunz v. New York - **§769**

Kusper v. Pontikes - **§1161**

Kwong Hai Chew v. Colding - **§171**

L

Ladue, City of v. Gilleo - **§760**

Laird v. Tatum - **§42**

Lakewood v. Plain Dealer Publishing Co. - **§772**

Lalli v. Lalli - **§1102**

Lambert v. Wicklund - **§518**

Lamb's Chapel v. Center Moriches Union Free School District - **§§582, 735, 762**

Lamont v. Postmaster General - **§569**

Landmark Communications, Inc. v. Virginia - **§§785, 894**

Lanzetta v. New Jersey - **§1329**

Lapides v. Board of Regents - **§9**

Larkin v. Grendel's Den, Inc. - **§971**

Larson v. Domestic & Foreign Commerce Corp. - **§5**

Larson v. Valente - **§919**

Lassiter v. Department of Social Services - **§457**

Law Students Civil Rights Research Council v. Wadmond - **§§859, 884**

Lawrence v. Texas - **§525**

Leathers v. Medlock - **§908**

Lebron v. National Railroad Passenger Corp. - **§1216**

Lee v. International Society for Krishna Consciousness - **§762**

Lee v. Weisman - **§974**

Lee, United States v. - **§994**

Legal Services Corp. v. Velazquez - **§815**

Nixon, United States v. (1974) - §§214, 215, 216

Nollan v. California Coastal Commission - §486

Nordlinger v. Hahn - §1015

Norfolk & Western Railway v. Missouri Tax Commission -
§§366, 367

North Dakota Board of Pharmacy v. Snyder's Drug Stores
- §464

North Georgia Finishing, Inc. v. Di-Chem, Inc. - §452

Northeast Bancorp, Inc. v. Board of Governors - §304

Northwestern States Portland Cement Co. v. Minnesota -
§376

Norwood v. Harrison - §1060

Nyquist v. Mauclet - §1087

O

O'Bannon v. Town Court Nursing Center - §437

O'Brien v. Brown - §126

O'Brien v. Skinner - §1162

O'Brien, United States v. - §§726, 727

O'Connor v. Donaldson - §534

O'Hare Truck Service, Inc. v. City of Northlake - §869

Ohio v. Akron Center for Reproductive Health - §518

Ohio Civil Rights Commission v. Dayton Christian
Schools, Inc. - §108

Ohralik v. Ohio State Bar Association - §§673, 693

Oklahoma Publishing Co. v. District Court - §702

Oklahoma Tax Commission v. Jefferson Lines, Inc. -
§397

Oliver, In re - §§423, 1311

O'Lone v. Estate of Shabazz - §997

Oregon v. Mitchell - §§1245, 1246, 1260

Organization For a Better Austin v. Keefe - §751

Orito, United States v. - §654

Orr v. Orr - §1096

Ortwein v. Schwab - §1114

Osborne v. Ohio - §§593, 652

O'Shea v. Littleton - §§41, 111

O'Sullivan v. Boerckel - §1364

Ott v. Mississippi Valley Barge Line Co. - §365

Owen v. City of Independence - §1264

P

Pacific Gas & Electric Co. v. Public Utilities Commission -
§563

Pacific States Telegraph & Telephone Co. v. Oregon -
§125

Palazzolo v. Rhode Island - §496

Palko v. Connecticut - §421

Palmer v. City of Euclid - §1329

Palmer v. Thompson - §1062

Palmore v. Sidoti - §1042

Panama Refining Co. v. Ryan - §144

Papish v. Board of Curators - §875

Paradise, United States v. - §1067

Parden v. Terminal Railway - §9

Parham v. Hughes - §1097

Parham v. J. R. - §455

Paris Adult Theatre I v. Slaton - §§632, 653

Parker v. Brown - §340

Parker v. Levy - §830

Pasadena Board of Education v. Spangler - §1058

Patsone v. Pennsylvania - §1086

Patton v. Mississippi - §1298

Patton v. United States - §1289

Paul v. Davis - §§430, 526

Payne v. Tennessee - §1352

Peel v. Illinois Attorney Registration & Disciplinary
Commission - §691

Pell v. Procunier - §§824, 888

Penn Central Transportation Co. v. New York City -
§§482, 495

Pennekamp v. Florida - §778

Pennhurst State School & Hospital v. Halderman - §15

Pennsylvania v. Board of Trusts - §1229

Pennsylvania v. Nelson - §§308, 312

Pennsylvania v. Union Gas Co. - §18

Pennsylvania Coal Co. v. Mahon - §§491, 495

Pennzoil Co. v. Texaco, Inc. - §105

Penry v. Lynaugh - §1348

Perez v. Campbell - §250

Perez v. United States - §296

Perry Education Association v. Perry Local Educators'
Association - §§737, 762

Personnel Administrator of Massachusetts v. Feeney -
§1092

Peterson v. City of Greenville - §1228

Philadelphia v. New Jersey - §317

Philadelphia Newspapers, Inc. v. Hepps - §628

Phillips v. Washington Legal Foundation - §478

Phoenix, City of v. Kolodziejski - §1152

Pickering v. Board of Education - §§867, 869

Pierce v. Society of Sisters - §§522, 1000

Pike v. Bruce Church, Inc. - §§321, 338

Pink, United States v. - §242

Pinkus v. United States - §637

Pittsburgh, City of v. Alco Parking Corp. - §497

Pittsburgh Press Co. v. Pittsburgh Human Relations
Committee - §§672, 674

Planned Parenthood v. Ashcroft - §517

Planned Parenthood v. Danforth - §§510, 513, 515,
516

Planned Parenthood of Southeastern Pennsylvania v.
Casey - §§507, 509, 510, 511, 520

Playboy Entertainment Group, Inc. v. United States -
§913

Plessy v. Ferguson - §1040

Plyler v. Doe - §1089

Poe v. Ullman - §40

Poelker v. Doe - §1144

Pointer v. Texas - §423
Pollock v. Farmers' Loan & Trust Co. - §134
Pollock v. Williams - §1212
Pope v. Illinois - §§640, 641
Poulos v. New Hampshire - §773
Powell v. McCormack - §128
Presbyterian Church v. Hull Church - §1008
Press-Enterprise Co. v. Superior Court (1986) - §891
Press-Enterprise Co. v. Superior Court (1984) - §892
Price, United States v. - §1266
Primus, In re - §832
Printz v. United States - §269
Prize Cases - §209
Procunier v. Martinez - §829
Prudential Insurance Co. v. Benjamin - §§302, 350
Pruneyard Shopping Center v. Robins - §§489, 564, 764
Public Utilities Commission v. Pollak - §1234

Q

Quill Corp. v. North Dakota - §§401, 405
Quilloin v. Walcott - §526

R

R.A.V. v. City of St. Paul - §662
R.M.J., In re - §691
Radio Station WOW, Inc. v. Johnson - §80
Railroad Commission v. Pullman Co. - §113
Railway Express Agency v. New York - §1014
Raines v. Byrd - §66
Raymond Motor Transportation, Inc. v. Rice - §337
Red Lion Broadcasting Co. v. FCC - §§899, 900
Redrup v. New York - §658
Reed v. Reed - §1093
Reeves, Inc. v. Stake - §323
Regan v. Taxation with Representation of Washington - §811
Regan v. Wald - §531
Regents of University of California v. Bakke - §§1069, 1072
Reid v. Covert - §236
Reidel, United States v. - §653
Reitman v. Mulkey - §1236
Rendell-Baker v. Kohn - §§1225, 1235
Reno v. American Civil Liberties Union - §§637, 914
Reno v. Condon - §267
Renton, City of v. Playtime Theatres, Inc. - §§655, 752
Republican Party of Minnesota v. White - §810
Rescue Army v. Municipal Court - §§38, 90
Reynolds v. Sims - §§1171, 1176
Reynolds v. United States - §990
Reynolds, United States v. - §1212
Rice v. Cayetano - §1077
Rice v. Santa Fe Elevator Co. - §311
Richardson v. Belcher - §1194

Richardson v. Ramirez - §1155
Richardson, United States v. - §64
Richmond, City of v. J. A. Croson Co. - §§1063, 1064
Richmond Newspapers, Inc. v. Virginia - §890
Rideau v. Louisiana - §1307
Riley v. National Federation of the Blind of North Carolina - §§565, 720, 756
Rivera v. Minnich - §459
Rizzo v. Goode - §111
Robel, United States v. - §862
Roberts v. United States Jaycees - §§526, 568, 578, 581
Robertson v. Baldwin - §1213
Robinson v. California - §1335
Rodriguez v. Popular Democratic Party - §1185
Roe v. Wade - §§502, 506
Roemer v. Board of Public Works - §934
Rogers v. Bellei - §177
Rogers v. Lodge - §1030
Rome, City of v. United States - §1268
Romer v. Evans - §1015
Rosario v. Rockefeller - §1160
Rosenberger v. Rector and Visitors of the University of Virginia - §§815, 949
Rosenblatt v. Baer - §§614, 619
Ross v. Moffitt - §§1107, 1362
Rostker v. Goldberg - §1097
Roth v. United States - §§632, 633, 634
Roudebush v. Hartke - §128
Rowan v. United States Post Office - §750
Royster Guano Co. v. Virginia - §1016
Rubin v. Coors Brewing Co. - §681
Ruckelshaus v. Monsanto Co. - §476
Rummel v. Estelle - §1337
Runyon v. McCrary - §§526, 1249
Rust v. Sullivan - §§812, 815
Rutan v. Republican Party of Illinois - §866

S

Sable Communications of California, Inc. v. FCC - §§637, 641
Sacramento, County of v. Lewis - §§471, 472
Saenz v. Roe - §§254, 527, 528, 1130
Saia v. New York - §749
Sailors v. Board of Education - §§1184, 1185
Salyer Land Co. v. Tulare Water Storage District - §§1157, 1182
San Antonio Independent School District v. Rodriguez - §§1121, 1192, 1197
San Francisco Arts & Athletics, Inc. v. United States Olympic Committee - §840
Sandin v. Conner - §432
Santa Fe Independent School District v. Doe - §975
Santosky v. Kramer - §458
Scales v. United States - §844

Takahashi v. Fish and Game Commission - **§1086**

Talley v. California - **§742**

Tancil v. Woolls - **§1042**

Tashjian v. Republican Party of Connecticut - **§794**

Tate v. Short - **§1108**

Taylor v. Louisiana - **§§1296, 1298, 1299, 1303, 1304**

Tehan v. United States *ex rel.* Shott - **§1374**

Terrace v. Thompson - **§1086**

Terry v. Adams - **§1220**

Testa v. Katt - **§269**

Texas v. Johnson - **§729**

Texas Monthly, Inc. v. Bullock - **§947**

Texas, United States v. - **§11**

Thirty-Seven Photographs, United States v. - **§724**

Thomas v. Review Board of Indiana Employment Security
    Division - **§§985, 1002**

Thompson v. Oklahoma - **§1342**

Thompson v. Western States Medical Center - **§686**

Thornburgh v. Abbott - **§828**

Thornhill v. Alabama - **§833**

Thornton, Estate of v. Caldor, Inc. - **§1005**

Tidal Oil Co. v. Flanagan - **§544**

Tileston v. Ullman - **§67**

Tilton v. Richardson - **§934**

Time, Inc. v. Firestone - **§622**

Time, Inc. v. Hill - **§631**

Times Film Corp. v. City of Chicago - **§714**

Timmons v. Twin Cities Area New Party - **§795**

Tinker v. Des Moines Independent School District -
    §§728, 816

Tison v. Arizona - **§1336**

Toll v. Moreno - **§1090**

Toomer v. Witsell - **§261**

Torcaso v. Watkins - **§§968, 983**

Town of—*see* name of party

Trafficante v. Metropolitan Life Insurance Co. - **§53**

Train v. New York - **§212**

Trainor v. Hernandez - **§106**

Trop v. Dulles - **§1339**

Troxel v. Granville - **§521**

Turner v. Fouche - **§1104**

Turner v. Louisiana - **§1308**

Turner v. Safley - **§823**

Turner Broadcasting System, Inc. v. FCC (1997) -
    §§583, 910, 911

Turner Broadcasting System, Inc. v. FCC (1994) -
    §§582, 909

12-200 Ft. Reels, United States v. - **§654**

Twining v. New Jersey - **§254**

U

Union Tank Line Co. v. Wright - **§364**

United Building & Construction Trades Council v. Mayor
    & Council of Camden - **§§259, 325**

United Foods, Inc., United States v. - **§874**

United Jewish Organizations v. Carey - **§1078**

United Mine Workers v. Illinois Bar Association - **§832**

United Public Workers v. Mitchell - **§37**

United States v. - *see* name of defendant

United States Civil Service Commission v. National
    Association of Letter Carriers - **§587**

United States Department of Agriculture v. Moreno -
    §§1015, 1203

United States Department of Agriculture v. Murry - **§1208**

United States Department of Commerce v. Montana -
    §1169

United States *ex rel*. Knauff v. Shaughnessy - **§170**

United States *ex rel*. Mezei - **§170**

United States Parole Commission v. Geraghty - **§47**

United States Postal Service v. Council of Greenburgh
    Civic Associations - **§763**

United States Railroad Retirement Board v. Fritz - **§1013**

United States Term Limits, Inc. v. Thornton - **§252**

United States Trust Co. v. New Jersey - **§§546, 554**

University of Pennsylvania v. Equal Employment
    Opportunity Commission - **§822**

Usery v. Turner Elkhorn Mining Co. - **§556**

V

Vacco v. Quill - **§1200**

Valley Forge Christian College v. Americans United - **§62**

Vance v. Bradley - **§1014**

Vance v. Terrazas - **§177**

Veazie Bank v. Fenno - **§153**

Vermont Agency of Natural Resources v. United States *ex
    rel*. Stevens - **§50**

Village of—*see* name of village

Virginia v. Black - **§§577, 662**

Virginia, *Ex parte* - **§1215**

Virginia State Board v. Virginia Citizens Consumer
    Council - **§674**

Virginia, United States v. - **§§1095, 1099**

Vitek v. Jones - **§429**

Vlandis v. Kline - **§1206**

Von Hoffman v. City of Quincy - **§551**

WX

WHYY, Inc. v. Borough of Glassboro - **§353**

W. T. Grant Co., United States v. - **§46**

Wade, United States v. - **§1374**

Wainwright v. Witt - **§1309**

Walker v. City of Birmingham - **§725**

Walker v. Johnston - **§1319**

Walker v. Sauvinet - **§424**

Wallace v. Jaffree - **§953**

Waller v. Georgia - **§1312**

Walters v. National Association of Radiation Survivors -
    §444

Index

enjoining. *See* Enjoining state action

mootness, **§44**

CRUEL AND UNUSUAL PUNISHMENT, §§1331-1353

See also Criminal justice safeguards

D

DEATH PENALTY

See Criminal justice safeguards

DECLARATORY RELIEF

advisory opinions and, **§§36-42**

civil, **§§102-110**

criminal, **§§98-99**

DEFAMATION, §§607-631

criminal libel, **§620**

fact vs. opinion, **§629**

group libel, **§608**

intentional infliction of emotional distress, **§630**

invasion of privacy, **§631**

malice, **§§612-617**

not protected, **§607**

opinions, **§629**

political candidates, **§619**

presumed or punitive damages, **§§625-628**

private individuals, **§§623-628**

public figures, **§§621-622**

public issues, **§609**

public officials, **§§610-620**

   malice, **§§612-617**

   official conduct, **§618**

DELEGATION OF POWER

foreign affairs, **§228**

legislative powers, **§§144-148**

standards requirement, **§145**

to judicial branch, **§148**

DESEGREGATION

See Equal protection

DILUTION OF RIGHTS

See also Enforcement of constitutional rights

Congress's remedial power, **§§1261-1262**

voting rights, **§§1164-1188**

DISABILITY BENEFITS

due process, **§§443-444**

nonmarital children, **§1209**

DIVORCE

See Due process; Fundamental rights

"DOING BUSINESS" TAXES, §§373-380

DRAFT CARD BURNING, §727

DRIVER'S LICENSE, §§450-451

DRUMMERS

See State taxation of interstate commerce

DUE PROCESS

Commerce Clause and, **§359**

constitutional provisions, **§427**

interests not enumerated, **§425**. *See also* Fundamental
   rights

persons protected, **§426**

procedural due process, **§§427-459, 500**

   antipsychotic drugs for prisoners, **§456**

   attachment, **§453**

   causes of action, **§435**

   civil forfeiture, **§441**

   commitment to mental institution, **§§454-455**

      children, **§455**

   creditors' remedies, **§452**

   "deprivation," **§§436-439**

   disability benefits, **§§443-444**

   driver's license, **§§450-451**

   eminent domain, **§500**

   government employment, **§§434, 445-446**

   hearing, **§440**

   irrebuttable presumptions, **§§1204-1210**. *See also*
      Irrebuttable presumptions

   "liberty," **§§429-432**

      defamation by government, **§430**

      loss of employment, **§430**

      parental interests, **§431**

      prison discipline, **§432**

   license suspensions, **§§450-451**

   parental rights, **§§457-458**

   paternity, **§459**

   prisoners, **§456**

   public education—suspension, **§§447-449**

      academic dismissal, **§449**

      corporal punishment, **§448**

      temporary suspension, **§447**

   timing and scope of hearing, **§440**

   unbiased tribunal, **§427**

   utility services, **§433**

   welfare benefits, **§442**

   "property," **§§433-435**

      public employment, **§434**

state taxation of commerce, **§§357-359**

substantive due process, **§§460-542**

   deprivation of life, liberty, or property by government
      officer, **§§471-472**

   economic and social regulations, **§§461-470**

      "arbitrary or irrational" test, **§463**

      business regulation, **§§463-464**

      public health and safety, **§§463-464**

      punitive damages, **§§465-470**

      rational relationship, **§463**

   fundamental personal rights, **§§501-541**. *See also*
      Fundamental rights

      compelling government interest, **§501**

      medical treatment, right to reject, **§§539-541**

         no right to assisted suicide, **§541**

         standard of proof, **§540**

I

Free Exercise Clause, §§980-1009
    exemptions, §§999-1005
        test, §989
funding campus group newspapers, §949
hospitals, §933
incidental effects, §998
judicial resolution of church disputes, §§1008-1009
Lemon test, §920
military dress and training, §§995-996
polygamy, §990
prisoners' rights, §997
protectable beliefs, §§982-986
public acknowledgments of religion, §§972-978
    Christmas displays, §§976-977
    prayers, §§973-975
racial discrimination, §994
religion defined, §§983-984
religious displays, §§976-977
religious groups and free speech, §1001
standing
    Establishment Clause, §979
    Free Exercise Clause, §1007
state regulations
    oath of office, §968
    public solicitation and canvassing, §1001
    Sunday closing laws, §§969, 991
    unemployment compensation, §§1002-1005
    when invalid, §967
    zoning, §971
tax exemptions, §§946-947
taxes, §994
three-pronged test, §920
unemployment compensation, §§1002-1005
use of public facilities, §§948, 961-962
veterans' benefits, §993

**RETROACTIVITY OF CONSTITUTIONAL
                 DECISIONS, §§130-131, 1368-
                 1375**

RIPENESS, §38

S

SALES TAXES
See State taxation of interstate commerce

SEARCHES AND SEIZURES, §§898, 1281-1287
constitutional provisions, §§1281-1284
    federal courts, §§1281-1283
    state courts, §1284
defined, §§1285-1286
exclusionary rule, §§1282-1283
    "good faith exception," §1283
newspaper office, §898
unreasonable search or seizure, §§1285-1286

SEGREGATION
See Equal protection

SELECTIVE INCORPORATION, §§419-424

SELF-INCRIMINATION, §§845, 847, 1272-1280, 1287
disclosures, §§847, 875
exclusionary rule and, §1287
involuntary confessions, §§1272-1274
    constitutional provisions, §§1772-1774
        federal courts, §1273
        state courts, §1274
    inadmissible voluntary confessions, §§1275-1276
        Miranda rule, §1276
    privilege against, §1227
        civil and criminal proceedings, §1278
        constitutional provisions, §1277
        failure to testify, comment on, §1280
        federal courts, §1278
        state courts, §1279

"SEVERABILITY CLAUSE," §135

SEX DISCRIMINATION, §§586-592
See Gender discrimination; *see also* Equal protection

SHOPPING CENTERS, §§564, 764, 1223

SIGNIFICANT STATE INVOLVEMENT
See Individual rights as limitations

SIXTH AMENDMENT
See Counsel, right to; Criminal justice safeguards; Jury
           selection; Jury trial

SMITH ACT, §§600-601

SOUND TRUCKS, §749

SOVEREIGN IMMUNITY, §4

SPECIAL PURPOSE ELECTIONS, §§1156-1157

SPEECH, §§561-914
See also Association, freedom of; Defamation;
           Obscenity
boycotts, §§838-839
Brandenburg test, §606
broadcasting, §§899-913
    cable television, §§906, 910-913
    content-based regulation, §913
    editorializing, §903
    "fairness doctrine," §§900-901
    indecent speech, §§905-906
    ownership limitations, §904
    political advertising, §902
    taxation, §§907-909
censorship. *See* Speech, prior restraint
"clear and present danger" test, §§597, 599
commercial speech, §§665-695
    content regulation, §§670-671
    definition, §§666-669
    false or misleading prohibition, §671
    greater regulation, §665
    illegal matters, §672
    overbreadth doctrine inapplicable, §673
    prior restraint, §674

as nonfundamental right, **§1193, 1203**

procedural due process, **§442**

Z

ZONING

Notes

Notes

Notes

Notes

Notes

Notes

Notes

Notes